The Bible in History

The Bible in History

How the Texts Have Shaped the Times

DAVID W. KLING

OXFORD
UNIVERSITY PRESS

2004

OXFORD
UNIVERSITY PRESS

Oxford   New York
Auckland   Bangkok   Buenos Aires   Cape Town   Chennai
Dar es Salaam   Delhi   Hong Kong   Istanbul   Karachi   Kolkata
Kuala Lumpur   Madrid   Melbourne   Mexico City   Mumbai
Nairobi   São Paulo   Shanghai   Taipei   Tokyo   Toronto

Copyright © 2004 by David W. Kling

Published by Oxford University Press, Inc.
198 Madison Avenue, New York, New York 10016

www.oup.com

Oxford is a registered trademark of Oxford University Press

Library of Congress Cataloging-in-Publication Data
Kling, David William, 1950–
The Bible in history : how the texts have shaped the times / David W. Kling.
    p.   cm.
Includes bibliographical references and index.
ISBN 0-19-513008-1
1. Bible—Influence.   2. Church history.   I. Title
BS538.7.K55 2004
220'.09—dc21   2003012106

9 8 7 6 5 4 3 2 1

Printed in the United States of America
on acid-free paper

To Gordon S. Kling Sr.
&
To the memory of E. Regina Kling

Acknowledgments

As the reader will observe from textual references and endnotes, this work is greatly indebted to the scholarship of others. It is also indebted to the suggestions, insights, and assistance of numerous other people. Apart from my own earlier ruminations on this project (discussed in the introduction), an impetus for this book came in 1994 from John Corrigan, whose manuscript draft of the "Christianity" section in the subsequently published *Jew, Christians, Muslims: A Comparative Introduction to Monotheistic Religions* (Prentice-Hall, 1998) I was asked to review. Corrigan's attention to the role of Scripture in the history of Christianity, though not extensive, meshed with my own embryonic thoughts about the role of Scripture in Christian history. I wondered, could a more comprehensive story of the Bible's influence in Christian history be told in a way that would at once blend history and hermeneutics? Could I offer some insight into why a particular biblical text came to the fore, was given a particular interpretation, and subsequently influenced the course of Christian history? What follows, of course, is an answer to these and many other questions raised by the readers and listeners of presentations of this book in its various stages of development.

I first tried out the general shape of this book in two settings—an ecclesiastical and an academic. For listening patiently to underdeveloped ideas and prodding greater clarity of expression, I thank the participants in a 1996 adult education class at Immanuel Presbyterian Church (Miami) and students in a 1998 fall seminar at the University of Miami. Among the latter, I gratefully acknowledge the indulgence of Glaister Brown, Scott Chadda, Jessica Gilbride, Kateri

Hilton, Nathan Novak, Kristen Oostdyk, Jenny Reider, and Renata Schwedhelm. Another student, Sarah Thompson Chule, rendered helpful bibliographic assistance and commented on several chapters. Thanks also to Alex Cuenca, my student assistant, for reconfiguring the manuscript to conform to the guidelines of Oxford University Press.

A number of colleagues, known and unknown to me personally, took time away from their own work to lend assistance. For adding conceptual clarity to this project, I thank Mark Noll and several anonymous readers for Oxford University Press. Henry Green, Dexter Callender, Nancy Hardesty, Daniel Pals, Willard Swartley, and Michael Westmoreland-White offered bibliographic suggestions and/or clarifications on portions of chapters. Bernard McGinn, Mickey Mattox, Douglas Sweeney, Martin Marty, J. Denny Weaver, Stuart Murray, Arnold Snyder, Will Coleman, and Douglas Jacobsen read and commented upon individual chapters. I have also benefitted from conversations with longtime friends Bruce Hultgren and David and Margo Miller.

To three scholars and friends who read the entire manuscript, I express my heartfelt thanks. In his usual timely and efficient manner, Craig Blomberg offered balanced judgments and bibliographic suggestions. I am especially grateful to two colleagues in the Department of Religious Studies at the University of Miami. With the eye of an assiduous editor, Stephen Sapp combed through the entire manuscript and saved me from infelicities in grammar and diction. John Fitzgerald plunged me deeper into the complex world of biblical scholarship, offered extensive, thought-provoking comments, saved me from embarrassing blunders, and heightened my respect for his own field of biblical studies.

The staffs of several libraries answered queries and offered much-needed assistance. Thanks to the library personnel and specialists at St. John Vianney College Seminary (Miami), Western Michigan University, Associated Mennonite Biblical Seminary, and especially the University of Miami, whose staff processed hundreds of interlibrary loan requests.

Several other people and institutions deserve special thanks for their encouragement and largesse. I probably would not have written this book if it were not for Cynthia Read of Oxford University Press, whose enthusiastic endorsement of this project in its prospectus stage enabled me to work with the confidence that what I was doing would eventually appear in print. I could have not sustained this project without the financial assistance of several granting agencies. The University of Miami supported this work through a summer Max Orovitz Research Grant and a General Research Grant for travel. I am especially grateful to the Lilly Endowment–funded Louisville Institute for its generous Christian Faith and Life Sabbatical Grant that enabled me to devote the 1999–2000 academic year to this project.

Family members did not contribute anything directly to this work, but I have been sustained by their love in the realization that the meaning of human relationships far exceeds the meaning of texts. Parents-in-law Gordon and Phyllis Bacon deserve special recognition for their care and support through the years. Thanks to my children—Elizabeth Corson and son-in-law Jack Corson, Justin Kling, Phillip Kyrk, and Hannah Kling—for enriching life in so many ways and offering a welcomed respite from "another day at the office." A thank-you hardly expresses appreciation to my wife, Barbara, who has graced my life and on numerous occasions adjusted her busy schedule to accommodate my scholarship.

This book is dedicated to parents whose call to serve and minister in the Christian church inspired me in the pursuit of another, though not unrelated, calling. It is to them that I owe my first exposure to the Bible.

Contents

The Bible in History

Introduction

The basic idea for this book originated in the classroom. Over the past two decades I have taught in two kinds of educational environments: one a private, nonsectarian university, the other a variety of Christian settings, including a Protestant college, a Catholic seminary, and a number of Protestant churches. In my experience, students in both groups labor under misapprehensions that, although quite different, are related. On the one hand, university students may learn something from a course in the history of Christianity, but when the last assignment is completed and the final exam taken, they have little knowledge of the Bible's relationship to developments in the history of Christianity. Ironically, it is as if the Christian faith, often labeled a "religion of the book," were bereft of a guiding sacred text throughout its history. By contrast, although students in Christian educational settings have a working knowledge of the Bible, they have little understanding of how various biblical texts have been interpreted and applied throughout history. For them there is a different irony: it is as if the Christian faith, often called a "historical religion," were devoid of twenty centuries of history. And so the idea occurred to me, now expressed in the pages that follow, to make some attempt to bridge the gap between Scripture and its place in the history of Christianity.

Given the specialties and subspecialties of the field, historians of Christianity seldom venture into the discipline of biblical scholarship. In fact, a perusal of general works on the history of Christianity turns up limited references to the impact of the Bible as a formative influence in Christian history. Apart from a discussion of the formation and role of sacred texts as they relate to the early Christian community and a comment on Luther's "evangelical breakthrough" in his reading of Romans 1:17, few narratives on the history of Christianity consider specific biblical texts in any depth. Biblical scholars, although they are attuned to historical developments, typically focus on the original *Sitz im Leben*—the life setting in which the text was produced and used—rather than on the appropriation and application of a text in subsequent history.

Several consequences arise from detaching biblical texts from their application in diverse historical contexts. For one, such neglect creates a false impression that sacred texts are static, stable entities, that they function independently of time and place. But this has never been so. First, the Bible itself is embedded in a variety of cultural contexts and reflects the influences of its social settings. Second, because of the changing nature of life itself, nearly every generation of Christians has reinterpreted Scripture (with varying degrees of self-awareness) in order to make the Bible relevant to their concerns. This interpretive task is precisely what the hermeneutical enterprise endeavors: to understand how a biblical text is to be interpreted and applied in the present-day situation.[1] In the words of Paul Ricouer, "Hermeneutics is the very deciphering of life in the mirror of the text."[2] We decipher life by carrying on a dialogue with the text about our world and its world.

Consider the example of Anthony, the subject of the first chapter. After hearing the words of Jesus, "If you wish to be perfect, go, sell your possessions, and give the money to the poor, and you will have treasure in heaven," this obscure Egyptian Christian in the late third century took this advice with a literal-minded passion. He gave away his possessions, left the civilized world, headed to the desert, and became the putative founder of the monastic movement. Throughout the centuries, however, other Christians have understood Jesus' words to the rich young man quite differently, and, in fact, some see in Anthony a perversion of Jesus' intent. No, they argue, Anthony was more influenced by his surroundings (e.g., a general ascetic environment) than he was by a correct reading of the text. What, then, was the rise of monasticism? A continuation of themes adumbrated in the New Testament, an unwitting concession to the ascetic milieu of the ancient world, or some combination? Such questions prompt other questions engaged throughout this book. Why do particular texts become the focus of attention? What factors give rise to a new understanding of a text? What traditions or pre-understandings does an interpreter bring to the text? How do we understand the interaction between text—be it in oral form as in Anthony's case or in written form as in Luther's—and the interpreter? Who discerns the correct meaning of a text—the learned, the pious, the ecclesiastical authorities, the poor, the marginalized? Is there a single meaning, or are their multiple meanings to the text?[3]

As a work of both history and biblical studies, this book addresses the history of eight texts—in some cases a single text, in others clusters of related texts, and in still others, whole chapters or large portions of a particular book in the Bible. Although I discuss my criteria for choosing particular texts later, the necessary limitation of texts indicates that this study is intentionally episodic, illustrative, and selective rather than exhaustive or comprehensive in scope. Dozens, even hundreds, of texts have exerted influence in the history of Christianity (though exactly how one measures influence is not easy to define). In tracing the history of only eight texts, I offer not so much an introduction to the history of biblical interpretation as "the operation of taking soundings"[4] or identifying certain texts at certain moments in history that resonate ("sound") in the lives of individuals and extend to a larger Christian community. Each chapter is shaped roughly like an hourglass. That is, I trace the history of a text on either side of a particular episode in which the text undergoes an innovative interpretation. This critical juncture—the neck of the hourglass—becomes the primary focus of attention in each chapter.

As noted, the concerns of this book address a wide audience of nonprofessionals (students, informed laypeople) and scholars. For the uninitiated in the academic guild, as well as for instructors who may wish to use this book as a supplement to other reading or to assign only selected chapters, I have sought to provide sufficient historical background so that each chapter stands alone as a discrete unit. Where possible, I have also sought to avoid the technical language and apparatus that characterize contemporary biblical studies.

At the same time, by undertaking an interdisciplinary study of history, theology, and biblical studies, I hope to offer scholars new ways of thinking about the function of sacred texts within the cultural communities that engage and appropriate them. Historians, biblical scholars, theologians, and ethicists will obviously find some things that are familiar to them, but this work of synthesis is intended to broaden their interdisciplinary horizons. For example, this project extends the previous work of Gerhard Ebeling, Karlfried Froelich, Ulrich Luz, Roland Murphy, and recent scholars (primarily biblical) who have expressed a renewed appreciation for the *Wirkungsgeschichte*, or history of the effects that Scripture has produced in many contexts throughout the history of Christianity.[5] My work differs from theirs, however, in its focus on the role of a biblical text in a particular historical episode; that is, a historical event or development is the framework for the understanding and application of a biblical text.

Ebeling envisioned the history of Christianity as the complex interplay of self-understanding and biblical interpretation, but as Froelich has remarked, "There seems to be no comprehensive attempt anywhere to write church history from the angle of the history of the exposition of Scripture. Ebeling himself . . . never tackled the task."[6] After working on this project for nearly a decade I think I know why. The task is simply too daunting. The influence of hundreds of texts upon thousands of individuals and groups over the course of two thousand years is a challenge too big for any one individual to comprehend.

In its attention to "hourglass episodes," this book proceeds chronologically. I have applied three criteria in selecting such episodes.

1. *Significance*. The primary criterion of selection is the extent to which an interpretation or application of a biblical text significantly shaped or was invoked as a critical text in the subsequent history of Christianity. I am not suggesting that great shifts in the Christian church necessarily turn on important biblical texts, for great shifts tend to be attitudinal and general in scope. As the historian Edmund Morgan observes, "Change in Christian thought, even so radical a change as in the Reformation, has usually been a matter of emphasis, of giving certain ideas a greater weight than was previously accorded them or of carrying one idea to its logical conclusion at the expense of another."[7] During such upheavals, a specific scriptural text is cited (e.g., Luther's use of Rom. 1:17), brought to bear on the situation, and accorded a special status, often thereby assuming a paradigmatic quality. Reasonable people will disagree about what events I deem significant—perhaps more about what I have left out than what I have included—but my list generally accords with the consensus of other historians of Christianity and biblical scholars concerned with the history of texts. Space limitations required eliminating a number of texts and episodes of comparable significance to those that are included.[8]

2. *Diversity of traditions and texts*. I have taken into account the major Christian traditions, though with different degrees of emphasis roughly proportionate to my assessment of each tradition's historical impact. I have also selected a variety of settings among diverse peoples, although emphasis is given to American developments for reasons of my own academic expertise and the intended reading audience. In addition, I have chosen a variety of scriptural genres such as narrative, poetry, and didactic literature.

3. *Interpretive strategy and varied themes*. I have selected incidents that demonstrate a cross section of exegetical and hermeneutical approaches, be they simplistic or sophisticated. Moreover, I have chosen episodes that illustrate the varied application of scriptural texts in matters related to church polity (chapter 2), theology (chapter 4), ethics (chapters 1, 5, 6, 8), and religious experience (chapters 3, 7). Some texts have been a source of comfort; others have been a source of social transformation; still others have been the basis of revolutionary behavior.

As I have intimated, this book is less concerned with the most accurate or latest critical understanding of a sacred text than with the way a text was appropriated by an individual or a community. Along the way I consult biblical scholars and literary critics and apply their insights to establish a modern critical reading of the text. However, this approach is of secondary importance to discerning the impact of a text within a particular historical setting. From the perspective of some biblical scholars, this approach may appear to be an irrelevance, especially if a text was grossly misunderstood in light of modern historical-critical scholarship.[9] Why should anyone care about the influence of a flawed interpretation of Scripture? But raising this question gets to the very heart of what this project is about, namely, describing the assumptions, pre-suppositions, or *mentalité* by which Christians apprehend a sacred text and live out its teachings. Experience accompanies and even informs these assumptions to create a dynamic interplay among belief, experience, and Scripture. Put another way, on some occasions Scripture confirms one's predispositions; on others, it challenges or alters them. The dynamics of scriptural interpretation point to the fact that a sacred text, as with all literature, is contested territory. And truth be faced, it is no less hotly contested among contemporary scholars.

For readers unfamiliar with the history of biblical interpretation, it may be helpful to note briefly its broad contours.[10] Perhaps the simplest way of viewing this complex history is to demarcate the traditional period from the modern period or, to be more precise, to distinguish between the pre-historical-critical (more commonly but less accurately known as "precritical") and the historical-critical period. The latter emerged during the Renaissance and came into its own in the eighteenth and nineteenth centuries. This distinction, it should be noted, locates the interpretive enterprise among the learned and privileges their understanding of the Bible. Such is a conventional perspective, for the very existence of a text implies a literate reader, one who is able to discern meaning in the written word. Yet other ways have been proposed. On occasion, especially since the Reformation, there has been the recognition that the Spirit of God enables the unlearned, even the illiterate, to grasp the basic teachings of Scripture. The cross-cultural missionary enterprise has proceeded on this assumption. Throughout Christian history, not only have the learned *read* the Word, but also perhaps more often the ignorant have *heard* it. The theme of exodus in the African American experience discussed in chapter 6 highlights the latter perspective. At the same time, in the precritical period, both black slaves and literate Euro-Americans shared the traditional interpretation of Scripture, for both groups affirmed that the words and sentences (as heard or read) accurately described real events and real truths. This assumption underlay the traditional view of the Bible.

Hans Frei has noted three basic elements of the "traditional realistic interpretation of biblical stories."[11] First, the Bible describes actual historical people and events. Thus Moses actually existed, and the exodus event actually occurred as described. Second, a single narrative, what has been called a "grand narrative" or "metanarrative," holds the Bible together. For Christians, this narrative is the story of redemption, foreshadowed and anticipated in the Old Testament and fulfilled in the New with the coming of Christ. Thus Moses, in leading the people of Israel to the Promised Land, foreshadows or prefigures Christ, who led his followers to the heavenly Promised Land of the celestial city. The story of Moses was indeed true, but it also prefigured the larger narrative of Christ's redemptive work. Third, if the world as described in the biblical narrative is "the one and only real world," then its message transcends time and space. The reader sees her own life, attitudes and actions, motivations and behavior, in the biblical narrative. All of life is filtered or understood through this real biblical world.[12]

We see this view of Scripture embedded in the New Testament itself. Through a typological (or figurative) and christological interpretation of the Old Testament, the authors of the New Testament believed that the Hebrew Scriptures anticipated or foreshadowed the coming of Christ. For example, in Luke 4:16–19, Jesus quotes from the Book of Isaiah (61:1–2; 58:6) to announce that "today this scripture has been fulfilled in your hearing" (Luke 4:21). The author of Hebrews envisions the prophecies and promises of the Old Testament fulfilled in the "new covenant" that now through the unique priesthood of Christ superseded the old Jewish system. Paul draws a correlation between Adam and Christ (the new Adam) and between Israel and the church (the new Israel). Thus even as the New Testament emerged, its writers were conscious that all of Scripture bore the imprint of God's salvation history that culminated in Christ.

In the early church, two understandings of Scripture predominated. Both reflected continuities with the early hermeneutical approaches of Jewish rabbis, ancient philosophers, and the writers of the New Testament. The literal approach, which often bordered on extreme literalism, referred to what the divinely inspired author intended to convey by what he wrote. It involved the meaning of the smallest of units (words, phrases, sentences) and extended to paragraphs, chapters and whole books. This textual meaning or contextual meaning communicated belief in the divine origin, authority, and trustworthiness of Scripture. The other way of interpreting Scripture, one that reached its greatest expression during the medieval period, was the spiritual or allegorical meaning of the text. In this reading, the text pointed to Christ or some higher, deeper, or hidden spiritual truth than was contained in the literal sense. Whether a reader approached Scripture in a literal or spiritual way, both patristic and medieval interpreters assumed that the normative sense of Scripture must accord with the rule of faith, that is, with what Christians believe and the church teaches.

Under the influence of John Cassian (ca. 360–435) these two modes of interpretation expanded into what became known as the medieval fourfold sense of Scripture: the letter (facts), allegory (what is to be believed), the moral (what one is to do), and the anagogical (what is hoped for). As we will see with Bernard of Clairvaux in chapter 3, the literal sense was not abandoned but often was obscured or neglected because of what the other senses offered the interpreter: an elasticity of interpretation that fed the imaginative and creative spiritual juices of the commentator. A text had not one but multiple meanings, and together these conveyed a variety of truths, though all pointed to the one Truth. To be sure, commentators who followed this fourfold interpretive scheme engaged in flights of fancy, but their fidelity to Catholic dogma reined in the possibility of heterodox interpretations.

In varying degrees, the application of modern critical methods to understanding the Bible—"critical" because these methods applied literary, grammatical, scientific, and technical methods to the ancient text and made judgments about it ("critical" comes from Greek, *krisis* = judgment)—challenged the traditional ways of viewing the Bible. With the Renaissance cry of *ad fontes* ("to the sources") came a renewed interest in the meaning of original ancient texts and other sources. Scholars, notably Desiderius Erasmus (1466–1536) and John Colet (1466–1519), began to read Hebrew and Greek, the original languages of the Bible that had been largely ignored (or were unavailable) in the West since Jerome's Latin translations in the fourth century. This attention to the ancient languages resulted in a greater interest in the original meaning of the text (i.e., the author's intention) and in the minimization (though not the abandonment) of the allegorical interpretation. The contributions of the Protestant Reformers Martin Luther and especially John Calvin proved decisive in establishing the grammatical-historical method. Calvin wrote commentaries on nearly every book of the New Testament wherein he stressed the necessity of historical and literary context, as well as the analogy of faith (i.e., Scripture is interpreted by other like passages of Scripture).

Reacting to the Protestant stress on the literal sense of Scripture, Catholics continued to emphasize the value of the allegorical as the traditional time-honored interpretation. Still, the literal (plain) sense gained currency, abetted by the eighteenth-century Enlightenment and the subsequent historical and archaeological discoveries that enlarged the contextual understanding of the biblical Near East and uncovered genres of literature (legal, historical, poetic, and wisdom texts) similar to that of the Bible. With these finds, the allegorical method all but disappeared.

The modern critical perspective assumes that the events described in the Bible reflect a particular historical background. The Bible did not magically appear or drop down from heaven; rather, its style and content disclosed the cultural settings of the writers. Scripture's literary forms or genres confirmed its place within the larger context of Near Eastern culture (Old Testament) and the Greco-Roman world (New Testament). Increasingly, the Bible was subjected to the same rigorous critical scrutiny as other ancient literature. At the same time, its study was increasingly disconnected from church doctrine as academics (with varying degrees of religious commitment) investigated its contents free from the constraints of ecclesiastical boundaries.

In the last two centuries, scholars have raised questions about the Bible's authorship, date of composition, sources used by the authors, purpose in writing, audience, and genre (style, form, content, function). Some concluded that the diversity and irreconcilable differences of Scripture were so vast as to rule out any kind of unity—the very unity that informed the traditional view and that Calvin and other Reformers affirmed as the analogy of faith. In some cases, critical methods were joined with naturalist assumptions to yield skepticism regarding biblical miracles and the divine nature of Jesus. John Goldingay observes how this approach differed from the traditional view of the Bible: "In the precritical period interpreters would have taken for granted that there was no distinction between the story told by a biblical narrative and the events that actually took place in biblical times, or between the figure traditionally associated with a particular book and its actual author. During the critical age it is these distinctions that have been taken for granted, and the major concern in interpretation of the stories has been to establish and defend views of their historical background and reference."[13] In the traditional view, the exodus was a real event as described; the critical view assumed no such similitude. One might of course reach the conclusion that the exodus was a real event (either in every detail or in a general way)—but only after subjecting the narrative to critical scrutiny.

It is beyond the scope of this introduction (and the intention of the book) to discuss the complex twists and turns in contemporary biblical scholarship, but several summary observations are in order. First, increasing dissatisfaction with the limits of the historical-critical method combined with the exposure of biblical scholars to the interpretive methods of the social sciences and literary theory have resulted in the proliferation of new interpretive approaches. Literary methods, for example, tend to focus on the text itself in its final form (not on the pre-text as is the focus of historical methods), the relationships among texts, and the interplay between the text and the reader. In the past thirty years, structuralist criticism, narrative criticism, and reader-response criticism, to name several literary methods, have assumed their place alongside conventional historical-critical inquiry. Not just two or four levels of understanding Scripture govern the life of the church or rule the academy; rather, multiple and often competing approaches characterize the interpretive enterprise. To be sure, there is general agreement that the historical-critical method is a useful tool and that the primary task of interpreting biblical texts is to determine (or approximate) what the writers were conveying to people in their own time. But an emphasis on the pre-text (e.g., sources and traditions) has been viewed by some scholars as of limited value in establishing the meaning of the existing text. Some have objected that the historical-critical method so brackets the transcendent intention of the text that it skews the very nature of the text itself. Others contend that the narrow focus on the original meaning of the text limits or eliminates the relevance of the text for people today. Others complain that the method is so rooted in European Enlightenment assumptions that it cannot address the concerns of the Third World. Still others wonder whether it is possible to discern the original meaning of the text unless they recognize biases of such things as culture, gender, and economic situation in the interpretive process.

These objections point to a second observation: hermeneutics has increasingly preoccupied the contemporary study of Scripture.[14] Hermeneutics (derived from Hermes, the messenger god of the Greeks) defines the rules, guidelines, or methods by which one determines the meaning of Scripture—not only the meaning in its original context but its meaning for today. Although most Christians consider Scripture the rule of faith and practice, an appeal to "What does the Bible say?" is, by itself, inadequate. Why is it that Christians differ in their views of creation, war, or roles of women in the church? The Bible, written under diverse circumstances and cultural settings and addressed to diverse audiences, contains diverse points of view. Moreover, diverse interpretive methods can yield and—as this book demonstrates—*have* yielded diverse understandings of a particular text. One can exegete a text, that is, determine the meaning of the text as the author of the text intended his original audience to understand it, but once established, how does the meaning of *that* text correlate with other related texts? Moreover, what principles or axioms are brought to bear in making those texts applicable for the contemporary Christian community? How does one bridge the cultural chasm between the ancient writers and the twenty-first-century reader? Or, more germane for our purposes, how was that cultural gap bridged throughout and at particular moments in two millennia of Christian history? These are the questions of hermeneutics that I engage in what follows.

"To a large extent," writes Wesley Kort, "either by acts of dependence or by acts of rejection, Western culture can be understood as a long and complex commentary on and reapplication of biblical texts."[15] Similarly, Northrop Frye has described Scripture's profoundly shaping influence as a kind of "great code" for comprehending Western culture.[16] I offer this study as a way of describing and explaining how the Western Christian tradition—or, better yet, selected individuals, groups, and institutions within that tradition—encountered, grappled with, and were shaped by the sacred text. Most of us (despite our visually saturated culture) continue to be inspired by texts of one sort or another, be they stories, lyrics, or poems. Such texts may not be accorded a sacred status, but they nonetheless alter our ways of thinking and behaving. So this book makes explicit what is implicit. It seeks to highlight those texts that have transformed people's lives and that have a significant bearing no less pertinent today than in the past. At the same time, the biblical texts I have chosen influenced ordinary people in extraordinary ways that not only transformed individuals but also inspired a movement or a collective response that would eventually take on a life of its own and reshape the contours of history.

I

"Follow Me"

Anthony and the Rise of Monasticism

Then someone came to him and said, "Teacher, what good deed must I do to have eternal life?" And he said to him, "Why do you ask me about what is good? There is only one who is good. If you wish to enter into life, keep the commandments." He said to him, "Which ones?" And Jesus said, "You shall not murder; You shall not commit adultery; You shall not steal; You shall not bear false witness; Honor your father and mother; also, You shall love your neighbor as yourself." The young man said to him, "I have kept all these; what do I still lack?" Jesus said to him, "If you wish to be perfect, go, sell your possessions, and give the money to the poor, and you will have treasure in heaven; then come, follow me." When the young man heard this word, he went away grieving, for he had many possessions.

—Matthew 19:16–22

The Bible is full of stories—and for good reason. Storytelling was one of the fundamental aspects of ancient culture. Stories functioned in ancient times much like books, television, movies, videos, and computers function in our modern world: to instruct, inform, and entertain. Although storytelling is something of a lost art in contemporary culture, Christians everywhere and literate people in the Western world have some familiarity with ancient biblical narratives. I grew up on a steady diet of biblical stories, all presented as real and literal. The Old Testament contained unforgettable action stories and heroes: the ten plagues upon Egypt, Moses and the parting of the Red Sea, Joshua and the battle of Jericho, the boy David slaying the giant Goliath, Jonah and the whale, to name only a few. The New Testament, though containing fewer spectacular stories, had its share of riveting tales, whether conveyed as real events or instructive parables: the resurrection of Lazarus, the feeding of the five thousand, the Good Samaritan, Zacchaeus the tax collector, the Prodigal Son, and the day of Pentecost, when "tongues of fire" descended upon the first Christians. The life of Jesus was, of course, "the greatest story ever told," as Fulton Oursler titled his best-selling book of 1950.[1]

During my childhood, I learned biblical stories through the medium of the flannel-graph board. Today, church schoolteachers often rely on overhead projectors or videos, even Christian "comics," but in the 1950s and 1960s, "flannel-graph stories" were the standard visual teaching aid. A board, about the size of a painting easel, was covered with flannel cloth; on the board were placed flannel cutout figures and props. As the teacher told the story, she (and the teacher was always a she) would visually re-create the story on the board by adding and removing figures and scenes as the story progressed. Over time, these lessons shaped both my imagination and my perception of the biblical world.

It is one thing to be regaled, even smitten, by stories as a child, quite another thing to internalize and act on them as an adult. One of the distinguishing features of the stories that Jesus told was their purposive nature. Typically, they called for a response from the listener: emulate the wise, not the foolish builder; choose the straight and narrow path over the winding and broad one; change your ways, change your attitudes; come and follow me. Through stories or parables, Jesus constantly challenged his listeners to make a decision. And in his personal contact with others, he was even more direct. The gospel writers not only record stories Jesus told but also present us with stories about Jesus' encounters with a variety of people: the rich and the poor, the wise and the ignorant, the religious seeker and the spiritually indifferent, the upright and the degenerate.

One of the best known stories in the Gospels, though one that I cannot recall seeing in a flannel-graph lesson, is that of the "rich young ruler." The title itself represents a composite picture drawn from the three synoptic Gospels (see Matt. 19:16–22; Mark 10:17–22; Luke 18:18–23), for only Matthew notes that the man is young, and only Luke that he is a ruler. Although there are subtle shifts in emphasis among the synoptic narratives, all three focus on the issue of true and false discipleship.[2] What does it mean to be a follower of Jesus? All three iterations emphasize that obedience consists in more than following the Jewish law (for the interlocutor informs Jesus that he has done so), but in following a "higher righteousness," Jesus himself. In the Matthew passage, if the man were to be "perfect"—the Greek is *teleios*, meaning in the biblical Jewish sense, "mature," or complete in one's discipleship—if he were "to have eternal life," then, Jesus informed him, he must forsake those things that meant the most to him: "Sell your possessions, and give the money to the poor." Upon hearing this, the rich young ruler hesitated and eventually "went away grieving," for he was unwilling to give up those things that meant the most to him—his possessions. What Jesus asked of the man—what ultimately mattered, what would make him "perfect"—was not even love of neighbor or complete obedience (though these are important) but, above all, the setting aside of all distractions and all loves to follow Jesus himself.[3]

That is the crux of the story. But what exactly did Jesus mean in his counsel? How is discipleship specifically manifested? Anyone engaged in a discussion of literature quickly discovers that conversations about the content of a short story or a novel produce several interpretations or layers of meaning. In the story of the rich young ruler, we can readily grasp the principle of discipleship, but the specific form that discipleship should take is somewhat elusive. Is the literal application to be made universal? Was Jesus calling his followers to sell their possessions and give to the poor? Anthony (ca. 251–356), the subject of this chapter and the putative founder of monasticism, thought so. Immediately after hearing this passage read in church, Anthony acted. He divested himself of his inherited wealth, became an anchorite (from the Greek word *anachorein*, "to withdraw, to leave"), and retreated from society to the vast and uninhabited Egyptian desert. Did this act of "holy madness" represent the true meaning of discipleship or a perversion of Jesus' intent? The biblical text makes no mention of withdrawing as Anthony did. Being a nomad or wandering disciple—a characteristic of the first followers of Jesus—is not the same as becoming a hermit. Is the life of a monk a necessary precondition of attaining perfection? To what extent is the divestiture of wealth to be universalized and Anthony's monastic life embraced?

The text that so moved Anthony, "arguably the central monastic scriptural text," eventually became the source of what Catholic and Orthodox interpreters refer to as "the evangelical counsels"—the ideals of poverty, chastity, and obedience—given by Jesus to those who seek perfection.[4] In traditional Catholic thought, this text, with its appeal to "perfection," confirmed a higher form of Christian life, distinct from the common obligations of all Christians.

In the latter part of the fourth century, Ambrose (ca. 339–97), bishop of Milan and one of the five "fathers" of the Western church, was the first to use the story of the rich man and Jesus to differentiate between "precepts" and "counsels." As the number of Christians from a variety of social backgrounds increased, perhaps it was inevitable that Jesus' words to the rich man, understood by earlier interpreters as applicable to all, would be tempered in applicability. Ambrose observed that despite the rich man's affirmation of following the commandments, Jesus counseled him to go one step farther: sell all that he had. "There are two ways of commanding things," the bishop noted, "one by way of precept, the other by way of counsel." Or as Paulinus (353/4–431), bishop of Nola (Spain), put it, Jesus gave counsel, not a command: "The freedom of the will . . . is not coerced but persuaded." Similarly, John Cassian (ca. 360–435), a monk and student of early Egyptian monasticism, observed that "Christ . . . forces no one to the highest reaches of virtue by the obligation of a precept, but he moves by the power of a free will and inflames by salutary persuasion [counsel] and by the desire for perfection." Augustine (354–430) judged precepts as "lesser things" and counsels as "greater things," making a qualitative spiritual distinction between those who followed one or both instructions.[5]

By traditional Catholic and Orthodox reasoning, then, all Christians are expected to follow the commands of Christ as introduced in the Old Testament (e.g., "You shall not commit adultery") and expanded on in the New ("But I say to you, any man who lusts after a woman has committed adultery in his heart"). But Jesus' words to the rich man are not words of command but of counsel or advice. They thus require the free choice on the part of the hearer as to whether they are obeyed. God equips people with different abilities and gifts. A few will advance beyond the norm to dedicate themselves to deeper understanding and more thorough observation of the commands and counsels of Christ. Some Christians will follow Anthony's literal application of the story of the rich young ruler, though most will not. Saintly, heroic behavior is universally admired but seldom imitated.

There are other, less radical ways of interpreting the story of the rich young ruler than as the biblical basis for the monastic and religious life. Perhaps Jesus was telling the young man that he had made possessions his consuming passion, that he simply needed to reorder his priorities and not necessarily divest himself of his wealth. Perhaps Jesus was speaking hyperbolically when he said "all," meaning only a large amount. Or, again, the text might be interpreted allegorically. According to Hilary of Poitiers (ca. 315–67), Venerable Bede (ca. 673–735), Paschasius Radbertus (ca. 790–865), and a handful of other exegetes throughout the history of interpretation, the rich man represented the Jews who remained tied to the law, whereas the poor represented the Gentiles open to the truths of the gospel.[6] From all these interpretations, the principle is clear: following Jesus requires the man's allegiance. Still, because the specific application remains ambiguous, widely varying applications have been proposed throughout history.

An examination of other New Testament passages complicates the issue. Attitudes regarding wealth and possessions vary, contends Martin Hengel, to the extent that "we cannot extract a well-defined 'Christian doctrine of poverty.'" For example, in other passages in Matthew, notably the Sermon on the Mount, "a nuanced attitude towards wealth" is evident.[7] Among other gospel writers, the evangelist Luke expresses sensitivity to the poor and outcast (through the words and actions of Jesus), and he emphasizes the willingness of Christians to share goods and practice hospitality, but even he does not make wholesale condemnations of possessions. According to Luke T. Johnson, Luke employs the language of possessions not so much literally but "as a symbol of the state of a man's heart before God."[8] In Luke's gospel, Jesus pronounces blessings on the physically poor (compare Matthew, where this beatitude is for the poor in *spirit*), the hungry, the rejected, and the persecuted and inveighs against the rich with imprecatory "woes." Yet when Zacchaeus, the despised tax collector for the Romans, informs Jesus that he will give half (not all) of his possessions to the poor, Jesus responds by saying, "Today salvation has come to this house" (Luke 19:8–9). In the Book of Acts, Luke relies on his Greek rhetorical training to describe an idealized version of the Jerusalem church practicing a kind of communalism, where they "had all things in common," so that "there was not a needy person among them" (Acts 2:44–45; 4: 32–37). At the same time, he dedicates his work to Theophilus (Luke 1:3), probably his patron and therefore likely a man of material means.

Taken together, however, the message of Matthew, Mark, and Luke is unmistakably clear. According to Jesus, how one uses one's money indicates the true state of the heart: "For where your treasure is, there your heart will be also. . . . No one can serve two masters; . . . You cannot serve God and wealth" (Matt. 6:21, 24). Wealth and material possessions make it particularly difficult to hear the message of the kingdom of God, for they becloud judgment and create a false sense of security in opposition to complete dependence on God. As Ulrich Luz observes in his discussion of the rich man, "The surrendering of possessions of which Jesus now speaks is no more optional than discipleship or the love of one's enemies."[9] At the very least, the rich are challenged to give to others as God's mercy and human need require.

Turning to Paul's writings, we find no mention of Luke's communalism but a stress on self-sufficiency and giving to others. Paul himself received from others, for he acknowledged Phoebe as his patron (Rom. 16:2). The apostle instructs one group of followers to labor and toil so as not to be a burden (2 Thess. 3:6–10) and another to be generous givers (2 Cor. 9:6–11). The wealthy are enjoined not to abandon the making of wealth but to use their wealth on behalf of the poor. Paul did not make his own poverty and homelessness— self-imposed, voluntary conditions for the sake of the gospel—a universal norm, yet he repeatedly called all believers to use their possessions for others, to give where needed in an absentminded way with no thought of material reward in this life. "Paul as much as Jesus," writes Craig Blomberg, "recognizes the danger of mammon as an idol and its potentially damning effects. Christ must be served rather than money."[10]

Attitudes toward wealth (and poverty) are related to a broader category of ascetic behaviors discussed (with varying degrees of emphasis) in the New Testament. In Western antiquity, asceticism (from the Greek *askesis*, "to exercise") referred initially to physical training for athletic contests and then was extended to include philosophical, ethical, and spiritual training. Applied to the Christian context, definitions of asceticism vary. According to William

Countryman, it is "a relatively demanding bodily praxis, voluntarily under-taken, that sets those who adopt it apart from and, in the view of some, above the ordinary run of people in the world." Although asceticism is often viewed in negative terms in the sense of denying the body of food or sex, Marilyn Dunn suggests that it "might more productively be seen as a collectivity of disciplines which aim at the transformation of the self and the construction of a new one." Such ascetic transformation challenges and critiques the prevailing culture and may be viewed as a countercultural or a culturally subversive move-ment.[11]

The extent to which asceticism is featured in the New Testament has been a topic of recent interest among biblical scholars.[12] After surveying New Tes-tament views on the three traditional aspects of asceticism in the ancient world—voluntary poverty, abstinence from food, and celibacy—Hans von Campenhausen concludes that "there is no one abstract principle that can settle it all. . . . It is clear that the New Testament can give no such answer to the question whether asceticism is right or wrong itself." Consider the Gospel of Matthew. Jesus sometimes challenges those who would become his disciples to leave the familiar home setting—the very center of economic life and society in the ancient world—and follow him into a life of voluntary poverty. At the same time, though single himself, Jesus upholds the marriage covenant and neither encourages nor praises celibacy (see Matt. 19:10–12). As well, though he practiced fasting, Jesus did not require it of his disciples or followers, though he clearly assumed that they would fast (see Matt. 6:16–18), just as he assumed they would give alms (i.e., share their wealth) and pray (see Matt. 6:2–15). According to Anthony Saldarini, ascetic "laws and practices promulgated in the Gospel of Matthew are often undetermined and suggestive rather than explicitly worked out into a disciplinary or ascetical program with practices fully explained and related to one another."[13] In addition, ascetic extremes are tempered by the Old Testament doctrine of creation, with its pronouncement of "good" on the natural order, and by the New Testament doctrine of the incarnation, with its proclamation of God appearing in the flesh. In both cases, a positive, not negative, value is placed on the material and physical aspects of life.

We may conclude from the biblical record that doing God's will in obedi-ence to Christ may involve ascetic renunciations, but only when such practices are freely embraced. Discipleship, a higher spiritual state, or greater consecra-tion to God's service is the end, and renunciation but one of the means. As we will see, later Christians would draw upon Matthew and the other Gospels as guides for a more systematic and zealous ascetic life, and in fact they would claim that they had the Gospels on their side. At the same time, because the New Testament contains various perspectives on wealth, it is not surprising, even expected, that believers could come to diverse conclusions depending on which texts they emphasized.

These perspectives on wealth in Scripture pale in comparison to the range of responses found in the history of Christianity. In his discussion of the history of interpretation of the story of the rich man, Richard Haskin finds eight different types of explanations. They range from unlimited applicability (including literal, nonliteral, and mixed) to limited applicability (a religious vocation or the period of Jesus' ministry only) to a limited application to the rich man yet applicable to all in a nonliteral sense. Moreover, Haskin concludes that three distinct trends characterize this history of interpretation. First, the interpretation of the story of the rich man has known two periods of creativity, the patristic era and the sixteenth-century Protestant Reformation period. Second, throughout history, there has been a general movement away from a literal interpretation of the story to some kind of nonliteral or spiritual interpretation. Several broad influences account for this, the primary one being Christianity's accommodation to the culture of the West. Christians saw little tension between the values of the society and their own religious faith, and especially as the West became more economically affluent, Jesus' words to the rich man taken in the literal sense appeared quaint and irrelevant. "It is quite possible," contends Haskin, "that it is these conditions in the Western world which predispose an exegete not to discover within a pericope such as ours anything fundamentally concerned with wealth, poverty, and the Christian life." Third, except for the text's profound impact on the rise of monasticism, it has had little influence upon the course of history.[14]

Among the varied understandings of the story of the rich man, I cite but a few examples in the history of interpretation. The earlier patristic interpreters, including the influential biblical exegete Origen (ca. 185–ca. 254) and Cyprian (d. 258), the bishop of Carthage, emphasized the necessity of abandoning wealth and possessions if one wished to be perfect. For neither was the act of dispossession a good in itself (for it could heighten fears and cravings), but taking Jesus' words literally was a prerequisite for following the Lord in complete obedience.[15]

A well-known exception to this literal interpretation was advanced by Clement of Alexandria at the end of the second century. Though given to ascetic tendencies himself, this famous Christian teacher defended the wealth of his rich parishioners in his treatise "Salvation of the Rich Man." Over against Anthony's "ascetic" interpretation of the rich young ruler, Clement offered a "liberal" interpretation. He interpreted Mark's rendition of the rich young ruler in a spiritual fashion, concluding that the story did not require a literal reading. To keep his wealthy parishioners from despairing of their status vis-à-vis New Testament pronouncements about the dangers of riches, Clement argued that riches were neutral, even useful, and that Jesus' words really referred to the desire for, not the possession of, riches. Indeed, "it is no great thing or desirable to be destitute of wealth."[16] What truly matters is poverty of spirit, not poverty of possessions. At the same time, Clement assumed with Origen and Cyprian that "the words of Jesus to the rich man, while not explicitly addressed to everyman, have relevance for every man who is rich in the things of the world."[17]

In the sixteenth century, the Anabaptist Hutterites embraced a position closer to Anthony's than Clement's, but they eschewed the individual's renunciation of wealth for a communal ownership of goods. Peter Walpot, a Moravian Hutterite leader, defended the "Bruderhof" system of economic community on the basis of the story of the rich young ruler: "It is clear that those who hold onto their wealth—unable to renounce their possessions and place them before the spiritually poor for the common use—are not able to become disciples and followers of Christ." Responding to the Catholic distinction between precept and counsel, Walpot observed that "to sell all is a general commandment and not a new counsel. So the person who keeps his property and possessions does not obey Christ. Christ also has no place among his elect for those who keep their wealth." Indeed, "private property does not belong to the Christian Church," for it "is a thing of the world, of the heathen, of those without divine love, of those who would have their own way."[18] To this day in rural communities in Canada, Montana, and the Dakotas, the Hutterites continue to practice what Walpot preached.

In the eighteenth century, John Wesley, the founder of Methodism, offered a more Pauline response to wealth. The words of Jesus to the rich man were "never designed for a general rule." They applied to him because wealth had become his preoccupation, but for others, to sell all "would be an absolute sin." At the same time, Wesley ministered to the economically depressed social classes during the early stage of England's industrial revolution and was exceedingly concerned for the poor. The itinerant evangelist urged his followers to "gain all you can; save all you can; give all you can"—with an emphasis on the third imperative. A century later, during America's era of the so-called robber barons, the Reverend Henry Ward Beecher defended the wealth of his upper-middle-class Protestant parishioners (not to mention his sizable salary) by quipping, "God has intended the great to be great and the little to be little."[19]

This much can be said: history offers no consensus on what it means practically to "follow me." Responses range from the "rags" of Anthony to the "riches" of Frederick Price, the popular "gospel of wealth" televangelist in Anaheim, California, who preaches that it is God's will for Christians to become rich. Quoting as his proof-text Jesus' words in John 14:13–14 ("And whatsoever you ask in my name, that will I do. . . . If you shall ask any thing in my name, I will do it"), Price correlates robust faith with material prosperity.

Modern biblical commentators, self-consciously limited in their quest to discern the original meaning of the text, considerably mitigate the widely varying responses in history. They generally agree that when Jesus instructed the young man to sell his possessions, he was not issuing a universal rule. Rather, it was an "ad hoc" command, limited to a particular situation (notwithstanding

Matthew's earlier demand that "perfection" is incumbent upon all [5:48] and his contrast of the rich man's refusal to dispense with his possessions with the action of the disciples who left everything [19:23–27]).[20] Nor, according to contemporary scholars (Catholics included) was Jesus advocating a two-tier morality—one for masses of ordinary Christians and another for an elite of superior Christians.[21] Many agree with the conclusions of John Calvin, the sixteenth-century Protestant Reformer, who declared, "Our Lord is not proclaiming a general statement that is applicable to everyone, but only to the person with whom He is speaking." In his *Institutes of the Christian Religion*, Calvin concluded his discussion of Matthew 19:21 (and his argument against monasticism) by observing, "When Christ commands the covetous rich man to give up all that he has, it is like commanding an ambitious man to give up all his honors, a voluptuary all his pleasures, or a shameless man all means of lust." Jesus insisted that *anyone* who followed him must renounce all impediments to discipleship, whether wealth, personal ambition, or family. Obeying the commandments, even the greatest commandment, was secondary to following Jesus. Dietrich Bonhoeffer, in *The Cost of Discipleship*, wrote of the confrontation between Jesus and the rich young man, "Here is the sum of the commandments—to live in fellowship with Christic.... The call to follow means here what it meant before—adherence to the person of Jesus Christ and fellowship with him. The life of discipleship is not the hero-worship we would pay to a good master, but obedience to the Son of God."[22]

Although biblical commentators concur that Jesus demanded the surrender of anything that hinders one from commitment to God, they offer differing assessments of wealth. Some point out that scribal legislation prohibited the giving away of all of one's possessions precisely because it would reduce a man to poverty and dependence upon others. The real issue was not selling all, but following Jesus, to be introduced to a new way of life based on fellowship with him. And yet Jesus did not stand in the scribal tradition or advocate the covenantal model that assumed material reward for devotion ("godly materialism"); rather, he took a prophetic stance, closer to the sectarian Qumran community than the Pharisees. Jews typically regarded natural possessions—and marriage and family—as signs of divine favor, but Jesus' "theology of reversal" inverted these values, even to the point of confusing his own disciples.[23] After Jesus informed his disciples that "it is easier for a camel to go through the eye of a needle than for someone who is rich to enter the kingdom of God," they asked in amazement, "Then who can be saved?" (Matt. 19:24, 25).

One commentator challenges the ready dismissal of wealth as a hindrance to true discipleship:

In ancient times and on into the present, the opinion has been popular that riches in themselves are no problem, and that only when the wealthy man engages in evil practices is he in spiritual danger.

But the force of this passage is precisely to the effect that riches in themselves *are* a hindrance to a person's participation in the Kingdom of God and that the mere accumulation of wealth and consequent attachment to it can prevent a person from following Christ.[24]

Ulrich Luz, directing his remarks to Protestants, observes, "We must learn again that a central issue of faith is how one deals with money. . . . The obedience of discipleship must fundamentally change the way we deal with our own money, because money governs the world, and following Jesus is love's protest against this 'government.' "[25]

Perhaps the most balanced judgment comes from Eduard Schweizer. He notes that Jesus' counsel to the young man was neither a blanket endorsement of poverty nor the creation of two classes of Christians. "All one can say," he concludes, "is that a special form of service is required of some and to them it is granted, giving them great responsibility and richer ministry."[26] Hundreds of years earlier, in a far different context from our own, Anthony well understood the dangers of riches. To follow Christ entailed freeing himself of wealth, embracing an ascetic existence, and retreating to the desert. His act of obedience forever altered the life of the church.

The Life of Anthony

The story of Anthony provides an instructive example of how a particular historical context shaped the understanding of Scripture and, conversely, how Scripture shaped what became one of the most important movements in the history of Christianity. Anthony was not the first monk (nor was Egypt the original home of monasticism), but his biography, believed to be written by Athanasius (ca. 295–373), the controversial and often exiled bishop of Alexandria, became one of the most influential works in Christian history. Depending on one's judgment of the monastic movement, that influence was for good or for ill. Adolf von Harnack, the nineteenth-century German Protestant scholar, referred to Athanasius's *Life of Anthony* as "probably the most disastrous book that has ever been written," whereas a recent, more sympathetic observer considers the work "next to the Gospel of St. Mark the most important biography of early Christianity."[27] *The Life of Anthony*, our primary source of knowledge of Anthony, is not the kind of critical work that we expect from modern biographers.[28] Written shortly after Anthony died and at the request of monks in the West, *The Life of Anthony* represents a genre of writing called hagiography—the story of a holy one or a saint. Intended to heighten devotion and to inspire acts of piety, the *Life* shaped and transformed its readers. Indeed, others sought to imitate Anthony's heroics, whether in the desert of Egypt, the mountain cliffs of Greece, or the rural environs of Europe.

Athanasius writes for two reasons. He offers an apologia for the monastic life, but he also writes to defend Christian orthodoxy against the Arians, his theological archenemies. Anthony is thus presented as an exemplar of holy living and orthodox thinking. Despite Athanasius's idealized portrait of Anthony, the *Life* is not fantasy. It may border on historical fiction, but in other ways Athanasius's writings comport with what is known about the Egyptian church in the fourth century. For example, Athanasius's descriptions of Anthony's exposure to Scripture in Coptic translation and of Egyptian monasticism in general agree with other contemporary accounts of Egyptian Christianity. However polished or refined, *The Life of Anthony* is, according to Douglas Burton-Christie, "based on fact."[29]

Anthony, though an educational dropout, was every pious parent's dream. Born to wealthy Coptic Christians in the village of Coma in Lower Egypt, Anthony feared the worldly influences of other children attending the Greek academies. He never received a formal education and, consequently, never learned to read or write.[30] He was, however, an obedient child who dutifully attended church services with his parents and listened to the teachings and readings of the priest. Despite the wealth surrounding him, Anthony did not crave the good life. When he was eighteen or twenty, his parents died, leaving him responsible for his younger sister and the family's two-hundred-acre estate. In our own day, and no doubt in Anthony's, most twenty-year-olds, after a requisite period of grief, would enjoy the benefits of a large inheritance. But Anthony was different, for he was troubled by the responsibilities of wealth.

Six months after his parents' deaths, while on his way to church, he pondered how the apostles gave up everything to follow Christ (Matt. 4:20) and how, in the Book of Acts (4:35), some Christians sold all their possessions, gave the proceeds to the disciples to be used for the poor, and stored up treasures in heaven. Upon entering the church, Anthony heard the priest read the words of Jesus from the Gospel of Matthew: "If you wish to be perfect, go, sell your possessions, and give the money to the poor, and you will have treasure in heaven." The verse haunted Anthony. He too was young, rich, and pious; he too lacked spiritual maturity. Jesus' counsel, Anthony concluded, was plainly meant for him. And so, after returning home, he gave away his possessions to the townspeople, sold the remainder and gave the proceeds to the poor, but kept aside a few things for his sister. Soon after, Anthony attended church and heard the priest read again from Matthew: "Do not be anxious about tomorrow, for tomorrow will take care of itself" (6:34). Here was the clincher. Anthony promptly gave away the rest of his possessions and placed his sister in the care of a Christian community of virgins.

He now made a complete break with his past. He left home, encamped in a hut near the edge of town, and sought spiritual advice from a neighboring hermit who had lived in solitude since his youth. Athanasius informs us that Anthony "prayed constantly, since he learned [from Scripture] that it is necessary to pray unceasingly in private." His inability to read was no handicap, because "he paid such close attention to what was read that nothing from Scripture did he fail to take in—rather he grasped everything, and in him the memory took the place of books." A life of spiritual and physical discipline ensued. Anthony learned the Christian virtues of prayer, study, watchfulness, patience, fasting, gentleness, and love of Christ. He resisted the devil's blandishments, including the temptation to return to his old life. He continued to discipline his body by fasting for three or four days at a time, restricting his diet to bread and water, and sleeping on a rush mat. "The soul's intensity is strong," he reasoned, "when the pleasures of the body are weakened."[31]

After years of building up his soul's stamina, Anthony was now prepared to confront the demons of the desert. He left his hut and moved into the mortuary chamber of an Egyptian tomb, supplied periodically with bread and water from a friend. Living among the bones of the dead, he battled with demons, rebuked them with the words of Scripture, and reminded them that "nothing shall separate me from the love of Christ" (Rom. 8:35). When Anthony emerged from the tomb some fifteen years later, he was hailed as a spiritual warrior who had fought and conquered the powers of darkness. He then withdrew farther into the desert to an abandoned fortress on Mount Pispir, across the Nile River, where he lived for nearly twenty years in almost total seclusion, praying, fasting, and weaving mats from palm leaves that he sold or exchanged for bread.[32]

As word circulated of Anthony's exploits, a train of visitors and disciples followed. Some sought out his spiritual counsel; others desired to emulate his example. The hermit who wanted only to be alone had attracted a crowd, and around the year 305, he gathered some disciples into a quasi community. Anthony was soon recognized as an authoritative holy man whose powers, teaching, and pastoral advice were much in demand.[33] He healed the sick and performed other miracles, offered guidance to fellow monks, argued with philosophers, and counseled emperors (Constantine and his sons), judges, and military officers seeking his advice. On several occasions Anthony traveled to Alexandria, first to comfort Christians being persecuted by the emperor Maximin (308–13), and later publicly to renounce the heretical Arians.

After 313 he withdrew to the eastern desert, near the Red Sea, about one hundred miles southeast of Cairo. For the next forty years, Anthony resided in his "Inner Mountain," Mount Colzim (now St. Anthony's Mount), and occasionally visited the "Outer Mountain," where other monks lived and people visited. To the end, Anthony remained ever the holy man. Athanasius informs us that Anthony "kept his fervent commitment to the discipline from his youth to such an advanced age. He never succumbed, due to old age to extravagance in food, nor did he change his mode of dress because of frailty of the body, nor even bathe his feet with water, and yet in every way he remained free of injury."[34] According to tradition, Anthony died on January 17, 356, at the age of 105, ostensible proof that what is good for the soul is good for the body.

The Rise of Monasticism

Within several decades of its writing, *The Life of Anthony* circulated among Greek-speaking Christians in the eastern Mediterranean, and by 375, Evagrius, bishop of Antioch, translated the *Life* for Latin-speaking Christians in Gaul and Italy. Thanks to Athanasius's biography, Anthony attained star status throughout the Roman Christian world by the year 400. Hundreds and eventually thousands followed his flight into Lower Egypt. Toward the end of the fourth century, a traveler through Egypt and Palestine reported that the inhabitants of the desert equaled the population living in towns. In the words of Athanasius, "There were monasteries in the mountains and the desert was made a city by monks." There are reports of more than five thousand monks living in the Nitrian Valley alone. By the year 500, perhaps as many as twenty thousand men and women had made the desert their refuge. A whole new, alternative society was brought into being.[35]

But why the desert, and why such deprivation? Every major religion has an ascetic tradition, but each tradition assumes its own distinct character, shaped by a variety of influences, be they the sacred texts of the tradition, current philosophical ideas, or geographic, economic, and political factors. And each tradition produces its own heroes whose physical, mental, and spiritual discipline sets them apart from others. In considering Christian monasticism, students of the ancient world and early Christianity agree that the roots of monasticism are complex, but they disagree as to the importance given to the individual influences that contributed to the phenomenon. For purposes of clarity and economy, I will limit this discussion to four factors, and then turn to the often overlooked but formative role of Scripture in shaping the monastic ideal.

1. A General Mood of Asceticism

Monasticism may be viewed as a specific response—and by far the most popular—to a general climate of asceticism in the ancient world. According to Anthony Meredith, Christians and Greeks shared a religious milieu that included "asceticism in food, a belief in the need of some form of divine aid, the need for physical and psychological withdrawal in order to further the process of reflection, and finally some, admittedly attenuated, belief in the value of prayer." I have already noted ascetic tendencies present in early Christianity, and clearly, monasticism's origins are closely related to earlier forms of Christian *askesi*. The New Testament writers reflect the demand for self-discipline, but as Campenhausen cautions, "The prevalence of ascetic tendencies in the early Christian period should not be overestimated." Nonetheless, owing in large part to Hellenistic influences on Christianity, such tendencies persisted. By the second century, for example, an "order" of widows lived off the charity of Christians in exchange for intercessory prayer and service, and there appeared in Syria a band of wandering ascetics who had no possessions.[36] Toward the end of the third century, "Sons and Daughters of the Covenant" lived as celibates in small, segregated households and offered spiritual advice to the Christian community in Syria. That monasticism became a geographically widespread movement throughout the Roman world attests to the pervasive mood of asceticism, for parallel movements to the one in Egypt developed, as just noted, in Syria, and also in Mesopotamia, in Cappadocia, and, by the sixth century, in the western regions of the empire.

In addition, influences from pre- and post-Christian religious traditions and philosophies contributed to the ascetic milieu and undoubtedly reinforced existing Christian practices. All in some way sought mastery over the body. As early as the fourth century, Eusebius of Caesarea cited the influence of earlier Jewish ascetic groups such as the Theraputae of Lower Egypt and the Essenes of the Qumran community. Outside of the Judeo-"orthodox" Christian matrix, the religious philosophies of Manicheanism and Gnosticism embraced the ascetic, world-denying ideal. Both stressed the evils of matter and the goodness of the spiritual realm. Both stressed a heavenly rather than a physical and earthy citizenship, sharing a view of humanity infused by a Platonic dualism. According to Plato, the body is a prison of the soul, or a "weight" that ties down humanity; therefore, the body must be disciplined so that it can be refined and transformed, ultimately making it less material and more spiritual. We hear of Plotinus, the Neoplatonic philosopher of the third century, who "lived as one ashamed to have been born into a human body."[37] Philosophers affirmed that the "good life" (or virtuous life) required various ascetic behaviors ranging from bodily disciplines and physical withdrawal from society (Epicureans, Cynics, and radical Stoics) to spiritual and psychological withdrawal (aristocratic Stoics, Peripatetics, and Neoplatonists).

Clearly, the Christian monastic movement tapped into this broad stream of ascetic thought and practice. Origen, the brilliant Christian thinker who proposed a theology of monasticism, adopted the ascetic lifestyle of the philosophers of his day—and then some. The church historian Eusebius viewed Origen as emulating the ideal philosopher but within a Christian context.

> For many years he persisted in this philosophic way of life, putting away from him all inducements to youthful lusts, and at all times of the day disciplining himself by performing strenuous tasks, while he devoted most of the night to the study of the Holy Scriptures. He

went to the limit in practising a life given up to philosophy; sometimes he trained himself by periods of fasting, sometimes by restricting the hours of sleep, which he insisted on never taking in
bed, always on the floor. Above all, he felt that he must keep the
gospel sayings of the Saviour urging us not to carry two coats or
wear shoes and never to be worried by anxiety about the future. . . .
About the same time, while responsible for the instruction at Alexandria, Origen did a thing that provided the fullest proof of a mind
youthful and immature, but at the same time of faith and self-
mastery. The saying "there are eunuchs who made themselves eunuchs for the kingdom of heaven's sake" he took in an absurdly literal sense [by the act of self-castration].[38]

Despite structural similarities to the *askesis* of philosophers, there were
differences. The means to the end of godliness for Manicheans, Gnostics, and
Neoplatonists were hidden knowledge or a classical education; for Christian
ascetics such as Origen, it was obeying Christ's commands. In contrasting
Christian with pagan *askesis*, Anthony Meredith observes that "whereas the
pursuit of poverty in obedience to Scripture and a strong sense of dependence
on God marks the effort of Antony, neither of these features appears in the
lives of either Pythagoras or Apollonius."[39]

2. A New Ideal

Ideas alone did not make monasticism popular. Monasticism arose amid one
of the most decisive shifts in Christian (and Western) history. This shift, beginning with the conversion of the emperor Constantine (312–37) to Christianity, forever altered the status of Christianity in the empire and indirectly
accelerated the growth of the monastic movement. Before Constantine came
to power, Christians lived in an inhospitable environment where they faced the
threat of social harassment, physical persecution, and even death. New Testament writers captured this sense of the impermanence of life and threat of
persecution in referring to Christians as "aliens and exiles" (1 Pet. 2:11), whose
"citizenship is in heaven" (Phil. 3:20). Other early Christians expressed similar
thoughts as both the prospect and the reality of persecution continued to be a
fact of life for many Christians. The author of 1 Clement (usually dated ca. 96)
employed the verb *paroikousa*, meaning "sojourns" or "has temporary residence," to describe the churches residing in Rome and Corinth. The anonymous author of a letter to Diognetus depicted Christians as those who "dwell
in their own fatherlands, but as if sojourners in them; they share all things as
citizens, and suffer all things as strangers. Every foreign country is their fatherland, and every fatherland is a foreign country."[40]
The Roman political authorities generally tolerated other religions—their

policy was one of absorption rather than exclusion—but they took exception to cases of suspected treason and sedition. Christianity was eventually labeled an illicit religion because its followers refused to recognize both the gods upon whom the empire was founded and the divinity or "genius" of ruling emperors. Christians were deemed unpatriotic at best, traitors as worst.

They were also viewed as social misfits. Accusations against Christians ranged from the warranted to unwarranted, from the legitimate to the bizarre. They were considered intolerant and called "atheists" and "haters of the human race" for their refusal to worship other gods. Such undivided loyalty could threaten the basic structures of society by setting pagan parent against Christian child or by endangering the livelihood of craftsmen who built pagan shrines and likenesses of the gods. One of the more bizarre accusations (familiar to the readers of weekly tabloids) involved accusations of cannibalism and sexual promiscuity. Why did Christians practice their faith in secret? critics asked. What of the common meal where blood and flesh are consumed? And what about the Christian invocation of "brothers and sisters"—an all too obvious reference to incestuous relationships. Finally, Christians were blamed for natural disasters. Tertullian, the second-century Latin Christian, graphically portrayed the dilemma: "If the Tiber floods the City, or the Nile refuses to rise, or the sky withholds its rain, if there is an earthquake, famine, or pestilence, at once the cry is raised: Christians to the lions."[41]

Indeed, Christians were thrown to lions—and branded and maimed and starved. But the persecuted represented a small minority. Although pre-Constantinian Christians were always liable to persecution and even death, the vast majority never faced martyrdom. Up until the middle of the third century, persecution depended on local circumstances of popular feeling and the disposition of local authorities. Then, beginning with the emperor Decius (249–51) and extending into the reign of Diocletian (303–11), under whom the "Great Persecution" raged, the state tried (unsuccessfully) to quash Christianity.

It is within this context of harassment and suppression that the martyr ideal arose. Those facing death had to look no farther than Jesus himself for an example to follow. He suffered and died as a witness (the literal meaning of martyr) to the kingdom; so, too, Christians followed him in a "baptism of blood" or "second baptism." For enduring (or in some cases embracing) bodily persecution and death, martyrs were accorded a special place in the church and recognized as having special spiritual authority. Those who confessed their faith in the face of persecution were seen as receiving the gift of prophecy and visions, much like Old Testament prophets. As models of spiritual purity, linked closely to God, they became recognized as intercessors, both in this life and in the life to come. The martyr, then, was known in his or her own day as the ultimate Christian, the heroic one who stood firm, successfully fought the powers of darkness, and triumphed in the Spirit.

The end of persecution brought an end to martyrdom. Constantine's coming to power introduced an altogether new situation for Christians. Eusebius was astonished by the sight of a Christian emperor fraternizing with Christian bishops at the Council of Nicaea in 325: "One might easily have thought it a picture of the kingdom of Christ, the whole a dream rather than a reality."[42] But reality it was. The Christian community was no longer an enemy of the empire but its ally, no longer a sect but a church prepared to absorb all of society. Previously the state built pagan temples, supported pagan priests, and suppressed Christianity; now under Constantine and succeeding Christian emperors, the state built Christian basilicas and churches, supported Christian bishops, and, by the end of the fourth century, suppressed pagan religions. In this altogether novel situation and into the vacuum created by the disappearance of the martyr stepped a new holy man—the monk. Whereas martyrs died a physical death for their Christian beliefs, now monks died within to the pleasures of the world. Whereas tales of the martyrs were often couched in the language of gladiatorial combat, so now the monk emerged as another kind of heroic Christian athlete.

3. A Form of Protest

The end of persecution and the increasingly favored status of Christians portended an inevitable decline in Christian standards. As congregations swelled, the standards of discipleship inevitably lowered. As Christians began to feel at home in this world, the otherworldly desert beckoned. The rise of monasticism, then, may be seen as a form of protest against lax requirements, growing wealth in the church, and the pressures of church organization. In the epigrammatic phrase of Roland Bainton, "When the masses entered the church, the monks went to the desert." Even before the end of persecution, there is evidence of growing numbers and increasing wealth in the church, but with the end of persecution, the wealth and power of the church increased rapidly as the Christian faith became a source of prestige. To adopt the emperor's faith could enhance one's opportunities in the world. As one notable pagan Roman senator said in jest to Pope Damasus (366–84), "Make me a bishop of Rome and I will became a Christian tomorrow."[43]

In this new context, bishops assumed greater responsibilities for the administration of revenue and the social, political, and economic duties of the church. Their position was further enhanced when Constantine introduced state contributions to church funds (for poor relief) and the bishops were exempted from taxation. The position of the bishop became a coveted prize, with the possibility of enrichment. In such a favorable environment, more and more people entered the church, including the rich and wellborn. The contrast between ascetics and ordinary Christians became more pronounced, so that the first monks who retreated to the desert served as mirrors, reflecting the realities and the ideals of the early Christian community. According to Wilfred

Griggs, "The appearance and growth of monasticism in third century Egypt is another expression of the perceived inadequacies of the ecclesiastical organization spreading from Alexandria into the rest of the country."[44] Monks sought freedom from a growing church establishment.

4. A Form of Escape

If we focus on Anthony's Egypt, the cradle of monasticism, we may view the rise of monasticism as a form of escape from the demands of the empire. Beginning in the third century, the Romans increasingly integrated Egypt into the orbit of the Greco-Roman world and, in so doing, ushered the country into a period of transition and crisis. They introduced greater efficiency in governing Egypt, especially in the collection of taxes and military requisitions, but on the heels of taxation came economic distress. In our own day, financially strapped businesspeople seek relief from distress through the assistance of shrewd accountants and lawyers who help restructure their debt, or they may take extreme measures and file for bankruptcy. In cases where laws have been violated, they may flee the country both to avoid prison and to retain their ill-gotten gain. In the third century, Egypt's upper crust—those in a position similar to Anthony's—abandoned the *polis* and fled from the tax collector to outlying desert regions. As the elite fled, greater burdens were placed upon peasants, who, in turn, followed suit. By the end of the third century, increasing numbers of people opted out of civilization and abandoned their villages in a conscious act of *anachoresis*. Some fled to neighboring towns or villages; others escaped to the fringes of the desert. Over time, whole villages, notably those contiguous to the desert, were abandoned. The problem became so acute that Roman authorities paid bounties for returnees. Questions addressed to an oracle by despairing farmers reveal the level of anxiety: "Am I to become a beggar?" "Shall I be sold up?" "Should I take flight?" "Shall I get my salary?"[45] Although there is little evidence of tax evaders turning into Christian monks, the possibility of flight became a reality of Egyptian life in the third and fourth centuries.

Following this chronicle of the conditions favorable to the rise of Christian monasticism—a general climate of asceticism, the need for a new ideal following the age of the martyrs, a form of protest against a growing spiritual laxity, and a way of escape from the harsh conditions imposed on Egypt by Rome—several caveats are in order. First, although the monastic movement flourished in the fourth and fifth centuries, monasticism existed *before* Constantine came to power. The Constantinian era provided a suitable environment for the development of monasticism, but it did not in any sense "cause" Christian monasticism. Prior to Constantine, the threats and realities of persecution had scattered Christians into the desert and hills of Egypt, where some took up a hermitlike existence. Anthony's first master, for example, is said to have been an elderly hermit surviving from the Decian persecution of the mid-third century. And yet what began as a trickle in the second and third centuries reached flood stage in the fourth and fifth centuries as thousands headed to the desert of Egypt and the caves of Syria. Second, although socioeconomic conditions in Egypt resulted in flight from towns and villages, we have no statements from monks that such circumstances led them to the desert. Rather, as Peter Brown has observed, the decision to flee to the desert "sprang quite as much from the disruptive effects of new wealth and new opportunities as from the immemorial depredations of the tax collector." Witness Anthony's flight. Third, we should not exaggerate the tension between monks and the institutional church. There were repeated contacts between desert monks and lay Christians, and instances where monks were ordained as bishops—sometimes grudgingly but more often accepting the vocational legitimacy of the priesthood and episcopate.[46]

These qualifications make clear that certain conditions favored the development of monasticism, but they hardly created the phenomenon itself. There were other factors of a genuinely religious nature that must be emphasized. I have already noted the influence of the martyrs and alluded to protomonastic practices in early Christian communities. I now turn to the specific ways in which Scripture shaped the monastic ideal.

Scripture in the Desert

As we have seen, the words of Jesus in Matthew 19:21 became the immediate cause of Anthony's pilgrimage to the desert. Such an incident, where a passage of Scripture, even this very same passage, has a life-changing outcome, is not uncommon. In his *Confessions*, St. Augustine related how, in agony over the condition of his soul, he heard the voice of a child "coming from a neighboring house, chanting over and over again, 'Pick it up, read it; pick it up, read it.'" Believing the voice was a divine command to open the Bible and read whatever passage appeared before his eyes, he obeyed, for he had recently heard how Anthony had been converted "after accidentally coming into church while the gospel was being read." Augustine's eyes lit upon Romans 13:13: "Not in rioting and drunkenness, not in chambering and wantonness, not in strife and envying, but put on the Lord Jesus Christ, and make no provision for the flesh to fulfill the lusts thereof." "I wanted to read no further," he wrote, "nor did I need to. For instantly, as the sentence ended, there was infused in my heart something like the light of full certainty and all the gloom of doubt vanished away."[47] More than eight centuries later, after hearing the very passage that transformed Anthony's life, Francis of Assisi (ca. 1180–1226) forsook a life of wealth and revelry, embraced "lady poverty" as his chivalrous ideal, and created a new religious order dedicated to the apostolic ideals of obedience, poverty, chastity, and service.

Clearly, an individual must be primed for the kind of spiritual transformations that we see in an Anthony, Augustine, or Francis. A number of circumstances—social, political, economic, or psychological—occasion receptivity to personal transformation. A text of Scripture, an individual's state of being, and other social influences converge in such a way as to bring about a new understanding, commitment, or way of behaving. For Anthony, a peculiar state of mind, the conditions of his personal life, and his contemplation of the disciplines of the primitive church prepared him for radical action after hearing the reading of Matthew 19:21.

Often overlooked in the details of Anthony's life and in the desert monks in general is the extent to which Scripture—and not just the Matthew 19:21 passage—permeated their experience. Several recent studies correct this neglect, and in so doing challenge the (Protestant) critique of monasticism as antibiblical. Anthony Meredith observes five salient themes in *The Life of Anthony*: Scripture, physical withdrawal, *askesis*, prayer, and demonic activity. He concludes that Scripture stands apart from the other four because it is "normative for the rest and influences the existence and forms the others take."[48] In addition to the Matthew 19:21 text, other biblical passages are crucial to Anthony's spiritual life, particularly Ephesians 6:12 ("For our struggle is not against enemies of blood and flesh, but against . . . the cosmic powers of this present darkness, against the spiritual forces of evil in heavenly places") and 1 Thessalonians 5:17 ("Pray without ceasing").

In a recent revisionist work, Samuel Rubenson challenges Athanasius's idealistic portrayal of the unlettered, saintly Anthony, and yet he affirms that Anthony remained biblically grounded. By reconstructing Anthony's mental world from what he argues are genuine letters of St. Anthony, Rubenson juxtaposes the simple illiterate monk in Athanasius's *Life* with a philosopher who was perhaps "the first real Coptic author." According to Rubenson, Anthony was indebted to the Platonic tradition, mediated by the Christian philosopher Origen. Still, however much Anthony developed a Christian *gnosis* (i.e., the presence of a secret, hidden truth behind the plain words of a text), "it is the Biblical message that is his message."[49]

Douglas Burton-Christie sounds a similar refrain in *The Word in the Desert*, a work that examines not just Anthony but the larger movement of desert spirituality in the fourth and fifth centuries. He claims that

> any attempt to understand the history of early monasticism must
> take into account the central role that Scripture played in the life of
> the monks. Whether it was *the* primary force behind the rise and
> development of early monasticism is uncertain; but it was surely

among the key influences shaping the early monks' life and spirituality. . . . The texts were proclaimed, recited (in solitude and in community), memorized, ruminated upon, and discussed. They served
as a basic frame of reference and primary source of sustenance to
the early monastics. . . . Certain key texts . . . especially those having
to do with renunciation and detachment, stood at the beginning of
desert monasticism, serving as primary sources of inspiration for
the whole movement.[50]

Although Scripture shaped the spirituality of the desert, so too the desert
setting shaped the spirituality derived from Scripture. Used within the context
of Christian spirituality, "desert" is not only a geographic space (a barren, inhospitable wilderness—not necessarily a barren, sandy region), but it symbol-
izes a temporary site or condition of religious testing. We must recognize that
all spiritual quests require a degree of isolation, for the very nature of spirituality is the soul's solitary quest after God. In both the Bible and the monastic
movement, the desert provided the transformative setting for the soul's encounter with God. Scripture characterizes the desert as a place of journey to
God, "a place," in Andrew Louth's words, "where the human is refined and
God revealed."[51] The Israelites escaped from Egypt into the desert for a period
of testing and preparation. Elijah fled evil Queen Jezebel to Mount Horeb in
the Sinai Desert, where he spent forty days and nights (1 Kings 19:1–9). John
the Baptist appeared in the desert region proclaiming a baptism of forgiveness
and the coming Messiah (Mark 1:4–8). Jesus "was led up by the Spirit into the
wilderness to be tempted by the devil" (Matt. 4:1). There he fasted "forty days
and nights."

So, too, monks, in their journey to God, retreated to the desert and self-
consciously patterned their lives after Elijah and John the Baptist. Anthony
deemed Elijah a monastic model, and Jerome, who lived in Rome and later in
monastic retreat in Bethlehem, claimed that Elijah founded the eremetical life.
We speak today of giving people their "space," that is, allowing them a sense
of freedom and independence. The monks' pursuit of God entailed creating
their own psychological space of isolation that could be attained only by physical separation from society. By this radical act monks renounced those things
that stood in the way of spiritual perfection. Stripped of a dependence on psychological and material props, the monk in solitude and silence uncovered the
hidden motivations of the heart. "The desert fathers and mothers," writes Belden Lane, "opted to thrive on the boundary where life and death meet, living
as simply as possible, with as few words as necessary, separated from the fragile
anxieties of the world they had left behind."[52] The formidable, terrible desert
provided an ideal setting for the search for God.

But where God is, there is Satan as well. The desert—hot, stark, dry, and
uninhabited—was known as the abode of demons. And burial tombs, situated

in outlying areas and often bordering the desert, were also believed haunted with demons. The desert, then, became the setting for the most intense earthly encounter between good and evil, God and Satan. The desert was a combat zone and the ascetic Anthony became what Richard Valantasis calls "the combative subject" who "withdraws from the demands of the exterior society to wage a war on the interior society of demons, distractions, thoughts, and impulses."[53]

As we have seen, *The Life of Anthony* records many tales of battles with demonic forces, first in the Egyptian burial tombs, then in the remote recesses of the desert. This work, along with other writings of desert spirituality (e.g., *The Sayings of the Desert Fathers*, Palladius's *Lausaic History;* John Cassian's *Institutes* and *Conferences*), describes the devil's intrigue as a dual assault upon mind and body. First, demons or demonic ideas "got in the heads" of monks by presenting thoughts of sex, food, and wealth. Such evil thoughts invaded the heart, the place where *logosmoi*, or conscious trains of thought, resided, and "occluded it, divided it, and destroyed any chance of a single-hearted devotion to, and search for, God." By their temptations the demons sought not merely to break down the monks' resistance but to compromise their focused fidelity to God. Second, the devil committed physical assault, typically described (and graphically depicted in Grunewald's paintings) as physical contests between the monk and a demon who came disguised in a variety of life-forms: a scorpion, bull, hyena, lizard, serpent, wolf, and a woman. These battles were won only by wielding the weapon of Scripture. When demons attacked him, Anthony "prayed and lay chanting psalms," and "they immediately began to wail and cry out" and soon were repelled.[54]

The battle against the demons was as much a battle against the self as a battle against the external forces of evil. And battle against the self invariably involved a war against the desires of the body. Was the early monastic movement an irrational hatred of the body, as many have concluded? Was the monk, in the words of W.E.H. Lecky, the nineteenth-century Irish historian and lover of civilized values, "a hideous, distorted, and emaciated maniac, without knowledge, without patriotism, without natural affection, passing his life in a long routine of useless and atrocious self-torture, and quailing before the ghastly phantoms of his delirious brain"? Or was the monastic movement, according to the classicist E. R. Dodds, indicative of a larger "disease endemic to the entire culture of the period"?[55] To be sure, there were extreme cases, particularly in Syria, "the Wild and Wooly West," where the likes of the popular Simeon Stylites (ca. 396–459) lived perched atop a fifty-foot column (it was believed he was closer to the demons of the upper air) and dispensed wisdom to locals and travelers for more than thirty years. Yet the mainstream ascetic tradition expressed by Anthony and the desert monks in Egypt derived less from hatred of the body than from their singular focus on God. Kallistos Ware observes that "natural asceticism"—the reduction of one's bodily conditions to a minimum but not a hatred of the body whereby one subjects it to torment and pain—"is warfare not against the body but for the body." It "has a positive objective: it seeks not to undermine but to transform the body, rendering it a willing instrument of the spirit, a partner instead of an opponent."[56]

Unlike the modern view of the body, monks tended to view it as a closed or self-contained system of energy whose intake required strict monitoring. Theoretically, or in the original state of nature prior to the fall, the body was capable of running on its own "heat," requiring only enough nourishment to maintain that heat. But when sin entered the world, the body stuffed itself with excess food, resulting in a surplus of energy that expressed itself not only in overeating but also in outbursts of anger and in heightened sexual appetite. Monks practiced what has been confirmed by modern medical research: a reduction in diet to a state of semistarvation suppresses sexual appetites. In particular, monastic diets eliminated meat, a food thought to make the body "moist" and to produce semen (a derivative of the four humors of the body: blood, black bile, yellow bile, and phlegm). The "drier" the diet—roasted chickpeas, dried fruit, and coarse bread made with bran were monastic staples—the drier the body and hence the less chance for lustful thoughts, nocturnal emissions, erections, and so forth.[57]

By restricting the body's intake of food, the monk pursued the goal of returning to the paradisiacal state, to the unsullied image of God before the fall. In The Life of Anthony, Athanasius described this perfected condition on several occasions. He reports that after Anthony spent twenty years in an abandoned fortress pursuing an ascetic life, he emerged fully preserved. When his friends saw him, "they were amazed to see that his body had maintained its former condition, neither fat from lack of exercise, nor emaciated from fasting and combat with demons, but was just as they had known him prior to his withdrawal." A half century later, near death, Anthony "remained free of injury . . . and generally he seemed brighter and of more energetic strength than those who make use of baths and a variety of foods and clothing."[58]

As much as asceticism was practiced—and I should add to its routines the disciplines of sleep deprivation, exposure to hot and cold temperatures, and days of fasting—it was not the summum bonum of monastic piety. Rather, asceticism was a necessary precondition to the goal of purity of heart. As remarkable as Anthony's physical appearance was to others, even more suggestive of his return to an uncorrupted state was the condition of his heart. Anthony evidenced what Peter Brown calls "the quintessentially fourth-century gift of sociability." That Anthony stood out in a crowd and displayed an irresistible attractiveness was indicative of a saint whose will was bent toward God. Anthony's life illustrates a pattern characteristic of many monks: his flight in order to escape was followed by return.[59] That is, Anthony's solitary withdrawal to the desert for the purpose of encountering God eventuated in a world-affirming engagement with others. Geographically, Anthony remained in the desert setting; but spiritually, he ministered to others, offering pastoral advice, leading others, or becoming a spiritual mentor and friend. His years of solitude in prayer and meditation prepared him (though this was not Anthony's intent in withdrawing to the desert) to become a spiritual guide.

It was in the physical and conceptual setting of the desert that Scripture informed and shaped the lives of monks. Several underlying assumptions guided the monks (and the Christian community at large) in their understanding of Scripture.[60] First, they viewed the Bible as a special revelation. God not only inspired Scripture, but each word was the bearer of divine reality communicated to the reader or hearer by the Holy Spirit. Thus only the believer such as a monk whose Christian disciplines facilitated inner illumination could truly understand the text. Unbelievers and heretics could never quite "get it." Second, Jesus' view of Scripture was the hermeneutical norm. His reinterpretation of the Mosaic law, his recognition that all parts of Scripture were not to be given equal weight (e.g., his stress of love over the demands of the law), and the example of his own life provided the standards by which to understand Scripture.

In all likelihood, the Bible was available to monks in a highly portable codex form (small book) and written in Coptic, the native language of the early Egyptian monks.[61] Given the low literacy rates, most monks learned Scripture through oral transmission, typically by way of the liturgy or through the master-apprentice relationship in which "desert fathers"—wise old sages who had mastered Scripture, vanquished the demons, and perfected their hearts—communicated to novice monks.

Our primary source of knowledge for the monastic use of Scripture is *The Sayings of the Desert Fathers*, a collection of moral and proverbial sayings (*apophthegmata*) from the hermits of the Egyptian desert that began to be circulated perhaps as early as the late fourth century.[62] Within this work, references to Scripture abound. The Gospels are the most frequently quoted texts, constituting about half of all New Testament references. Matthew, the most popular Gospel in the early church and also the most frequently cited Gospel in the *Sayings*, accounts for about a third of all New Testament texts.[63]

As important as the written text was for spiritual instruction, desert monks placed less emphasis on the written than the spoken word. "Words were *heard* in the desert much more than they were read." There was, in fact, ambivalence among desert monks about possessing and reading books. Not only were Bibles and other books expensive (they were painstakingly copied, handwritten manuscripts), but on a more basic level there existed the apprehension that once words became "frozen" or objectified in a sacred book, they could possibly become a "dead letter" rather than the "living word." Recall that for Anthony, "memory took the place of books."[64] The "sayings" of the desert fathers were exactly that—stories circulated orally from memory whose content was informed by Scripture. When committed to memory, Scripture took on a deeply personal and potentially expansive and subjective meaning. Once a text was memorized, once lodged deeply within the mind and heart, there was the possibility of its detachment from the immediate biblical context. The question of what the text meant in its original context had less importance than its applicability to the life situation of the monk. In short, Scripture functioned on a practical or personal level for the desert monks, so that its "words" transcended the restricted meaning of the event as originally encountered or intended in the text.

As we have seen, to the desert monks, passages of renunciation, such as Jesus' words to the rich young ruler, were taken as moral counsel.[65] To follow Jesus meant renouncing possessions and making a complete break with all social and familial ties. The monastic goal, expressed either as holiness or as love for God, meant divesting oneself of all worldly cares and living as Jesus taught in the Sermon on the Mount. Only by clearing away all distractions, especially the grip of possessions, could one encounter God with purity of heart and clarity of purpose.

In this search for holiness, Matthew 19:21 became a paradigmatic text not only in Anthony's spiritual formation but also in the burgeoning monastic movement and the church at large. Depending on the audience—monks or all Christians—the text had a dual application. For Basil the Great (ca. 330–79), bishop and monastic founder in the Eastern church, Jesus' instructions to the young man will lead some to separate from the world by living a monastic existence of poverty. Others, especially the rich, should limit their wealth to that which was necessary for their maintenance and give away the remainder to those in need. Even the care of children was no excuse for the accumulation of wealth, for Jesus' words to the rich man are "a commandment that is obligatory for all Christians." Similarly, John Chrysostom (349–407), the "goldenmouthed" priest in Antioch, archbishop of Constantinople, and shaper of Orthodox liturgy, linked Matthew 19:21 to almsgiving. He warned his parishioners in Antioch of the dangers of wealth and implored them to spend riches on the needy and to live on no more than was necessary. Other church leaders in the third and fourth centuries, including the bishops Cyprian of Carthage, Maximus of Turin, Paulinus of Nola, and Augustine of Hippo, invoked the text as an exhortation to share with the needy.[66]

More often, Matthew 19:21 found special favor as a monastic text to be literally followed in abandoning wealth and possessions. In addressing monks, Jerome (ca. 342–420), Augustine, and Basil appealed to the text, as did John Cassian, who recounted the call of the "blessed Anthony" and repeatedly cited Matthew 19:21 in *The Institutes* and *The Conferences*, two works that profoundly influenced Western monasticism.[67]

As this text and others became part of the life and soul of monastic existence, as monks were spiritually nourished from the words of Scripture, their lives were renewed and eventually transformed. They became not only hearers

but also doers of the word. According to Douglas Burton-Christie, their interpretation of Scripture "meant allowing the text to strip away the accumulated
layers of self-deception, self-hatred, fear, and insecurity that were exposed in
the desert solitude and in the tension of human interaction." The path that led
to purity of heart was defined by how deeply the monk allowed himself (or
herself) to be transformed by the living words of Scripture, particularly the
commandment to love. Indeed, "It would not be an exaggeration to say that
the biblical commandment to love, more than any other, defined and gave
shape to the world in which the desert fathers lived."[68] And so it was that the
exacting material conditions of the monk's life and his constant rumination
upon Scripture transformed his very consciousness. In such an alien, unfor-
giving environment, monks learned to love. "As strange as it sounds," writes
Belden Lane,

> given the austere, threatening quality of the monks' life in the wil-
> derness, what the desert finally taught them was love. There in the
> wilds, they could be ignored enough, invited outside of themselves
> enough, to love and to be loved in a way that met the deepest social
> needs of the tension-filled world of late antiquity. Loving God, loving
> other people, loving the created world in which they were placed—
> this was the grand and hoped-for conclusion of *apatheia*, that sub-
> lime indifference which ever ended in love.[69]

After Anthony

The eremetical form of monasticism practiced by Anthony and the first monks
of the desert soon gave way to a communal or "cenobitic" (in Greek, *koinos
bios* = common life) form. Groups of monks lived together in obedience to a
"master" or abbot and followed a "rule" that defined the monastic life in a
highly organized and centralized way. We have, in fact, already seen this transition in Anthony himself, who in his later years attracted visitors and gathered
disciples. No less than in Anthony and the desert fathers, Scripture informed
and structured life and learning in these communities.

Around 315–320 at Tabennesis in the Thebaid region, Pachomius (286–
346), a near contemporary of Anthony and a genius at organization and administration, was the first to initiate hundreds of desert recruits into some
form of communal life. "Holy Scripture," notes Armand Veillux, "was for the
Pachomian monk, the first—and in some measure the only—rule of his monastic life. It was, at the same time, the guiding inspiration of his spirituality."
Just as Scripture worked its transforming power among eremetical monks, so
instruction in the Pachomian monastery "was intended to allow the scriptural

message to penetrate into the soul of each monk, and there work conversion, *metanoia*."⁷⁰ In Greece, Basil the Great wrote no monastic rule proper and founded no order comparable to that of Pachomius, but he supported the communal life, and by his spiritual advice and ascetical teachings (generally referred to as the Rule of St. Basil), he profoundly influenced monasticism in the East.

In the West, the Rule of St. Benedict, a short rule attributed to Benedict of Nursia (ca. 480–547) in Italy, eventually prevailed throughout all of Europe. Influenced by Pachomius, Benedict's Rule begins with "the Scriptures stirring us" and ends with, "For what page or word of the Bible is not a perfect rule for temporal life?" The Rule is filled with 130 biblical quotations (especially the Psalms); and prayer, work, social relations, the role of the abbot, and the reception of guests are understood within a biblical framework. In short, "the Rule is Biblical in its inspiration, in its demands, in the opportunities it offers."⁷¹

In the ensuing centuries monastic communities and orders multiplied, guided by yet other rules written for circumstances far different from the desert. Yet the model of Anthony, especially his willingness to become "perfect" by ridding himself of all possessions and other hindrances in the soul's quest for God, remained the defining moment for monasticism and the measure of true spirituality. As Jean Leclercq observed in his evocative work on medieval spirituality, "St. Anthony remained truly the Father of all monks. . . . He represents for all, an ideal whose essential characteristic is its potential for realization in different ways. St. Anthony's life . . . is not simply an historical text, a source of information about a definitely dead past. It is a living text, a means of formation of monastic life."⁷² Moreover, Matthew 19:21 remained a paradigmatic text. Two twelfth-century reformers—one declared a heretic by the church (Peter Waldo), the other made a saint (Francis of Assisi)—invoked the text in abandoning wealth and embracing a life of voluntary poverty. In his rule for fellow mendicants, Francis reiterated the text, stressing its literal application as a guide for the newly formed Franciscan order. Paradoxically, as a begging order, the Franciscans depended upon the largesse of those with jobs—those considered spiritually inferior yet guarantors of the Franciscan way of life by their almsgiving and hospitality.

But note, the literal application of Matthew 19:21 remained restricted to a select group, first to monks, and then to clergy (often drawn from monastic communities). Laypeople, however, while instructed to be good stewards of their resources, were exempt from the divestiture of wealth and possessions. In the sixteenth century, Protestant Reformers challenged this distinction between counsels and precepts, rejected any literal understanding of the text, and thus represented a new departure in the history of interpretation. Their primary criticism was leveled against monasticism, but since the story of the rich man figured foundational to the monastic movement, the reformers necessarily engaged Matthew 19:21 and parallel passages. The Reformers dismissed monastic spirituality, with its enforced celibacy and rejection of possessions, arguing that it lacked a clear basis in the Bible, manifestly contradicted human nature, and embodied an attempt to earn God's favor through one's effort. From their perspective, monasticism was neither of God nor of nature.

Martin Luther, himself a onetime monk, declared, "Marriage is good, virginity is better, but liberty is best."[73] He rejected the two-tiered morality of medieval Catholicism, claiming that the distinction between counsels and precepts was an invention, made up by Catholics "out of their own heads without any support of Scripture." There was no spiritually qualitative difference between a maid and a monk. On the one hand, the life of a monk may be chosen, for "lifelong poverty, obedience, and chastity may be observed"; on the other hand, it "cannot be vowed, taught, or imposed." Whereas Anthony "willingly chose to live as a hermit and of his own will chose to live unmarried, after the pattern of the gospel," his followers "made this way of life into a vow, into a matter of obligation and compulsion. . . . The rule of Anthony, which is the rule of Christ," was perverted into law.[74]

In his specific engagement with Matthew 19:21, Luther interpreted Christ's words to the rich man as a universal precept or commandment, meaning that people are to love God above all things. For Luther, Jesus' words were another way of stating the first commandment ("You shall have no other gods before me"). Jesus' instructions indicated that the man had not perfectly and rightly followed the Ten Commandments, for had the man done so, he would be willing to sell everything and give the proceeds to the poor. The response of the rich man revealed that he placed his love of possessions over his love of God. "Therefore the meaning of this commandment," summarized Luther, "is to be understood spiritually and to mean, first, that the heart ought to be separated from possessions, that you esteem God higher and set him above them; also, when necessity requires that you not only sell all but also follow Christ, giving up body and life for his will." This spiritual understanding, of course, had a long history. Luther sounded like Clement of Alexandria when he observed that possessions per se are not wrong, for Christ himself "did not sell all, but ate and drank, and had clothes"; it is the attachment to possessions that must be avoided.[75] Nevertheless, there is in Luther's interpretation a new emphasis, one that joins Christ's call to sell all with the Ten Commandments, which for Luther expresses the complete Christian ethical ideal.

Other Reformers offered varying interpretations of Matthew 19:21, yet they all rejected the precepts-counsels distinction, and none held that the call to sell all had universal intent. For example, the Lutheran David Chytraeus and the Reformed leaders Calvin and Heinrich Bullinger argued that the words had specific application to the rich man, not general relevance, and thus downplayed the passage's critique of possessions. Jesus was not calling his followers to abandon their possessions, nor was he overly concerned with the danger of wealth. Rather, the passage dealt with spiritual issues such as placing God first in all things, covetousness, and keeping the commandments.

Moreover, assessments of the social order were inserted into their discussion. Calvin and Philipp Melancthon in particular urged the prudent use of possessions and the frugal and sober management of one's money. They also advised the poor to be content with their lot. Clearly, writes Richard Haskin, "it is difficult to avoid the suspicion that at points in [their] discussions what is termed the Protestant ethic, or certain attitudes of early Protestantism toward human society, did play in influential role."[76] Indeed, the Lutheran and the Reformed faiths would find their greatest support among the upper and growing middle classes—those having the greatest stake in wealth and possessions. In contrast, we have seen earlier that simple, rural Anabaptists—those repeatedly denounced by mainline Reformers—interpreted Jesus' words to the rich man as a command to share all goods in a communal setting.

Since the sixteenth century, neither Catholic nor Protestant interpreters have proposed much that is new or unique in the history of the interpretation of Matthew 19:21 and parallel passages. To be sure, some interpreters propose that Jesus' expectation of the imminent end of the present age influenced his negative view of wealth, and some suggest that Jesus' words about perfection were not his but a Matthean editorial insertion signaling a transition to the ethic of a developing Catholicism. But in both cases—and there is scholarly dispute about these proposals—no novel application of Jesus' words had been advanced—perhaps because all of the interpretive possibilities have been exhausted. The overall trend has been to place primary stress on a religious or spiritual meaning (the rich man = any idol that keeps one from trust in God alone), but also to recognize that the deceit of riches is a critical impediment to unconditional obedience to Jesus.

Conclusion

And what of desert spirituality—the call not only to a life of poverty but also to other ascetic behaviors, including withdrawal from society? However much Protestant Reformers and subsequent Protestants recoiled against the monastery, we must recognize that the first monks of the Egyptian desert read and understood the Bible within their own distinct cultural framework, through the lenses of their own knowledge and experience. To be sure, ascetic behaviors led not only to the subordination of the body to the spirit but also to an antibody proclivity. Perhaps these first monks misunderstood and misapplied the "letter" of what Jesus was saying to the rich young ruler, but they carried out the "spirit" of his message with a fervor and devotion unrivaled in their day.

That spirit later proved to be the source of periodic renewal not only in

Catholicism—indeed, it is impossible to think about the Christian tradition apart from the monastic tradition—but also within a number of seventeenth- and eighteenth-century Protestant movements, including German evangelicals, Pennsylvania Pietists, and English Methodists. In word and deed, Protestants have tempered their traditional antimonastic prejudice. As François Biot points out, Protestant monasticism is no oxymoron: various Protestant monasteries and religious communities have existed in Europe since the seventeenth century, including the more recently formed Taizé community in France. Even Karl Barth, perhaps the greatest Protestant theologian of the twentieth century, recognized an inner integrity to monastic solitude and distance from the world that Protestants had largely abandoned and needed to recover.[77]

In our own day there is a growing recognition that the desert fathers can fill, or at least speak to, the spiritual void in modern life—albeit in a comfortable, middle-class kind of way. One need not retreat permanently to the desert to address this spiritual vacuum. A weekend retreat will do, or at least will serve as a point of departure for reflection and meditation. Among the better known contemporary authors whose writings invite the reader to consider the virtues of the contemplative life are Thomas Merton, Henri Nouwen, and Kathleen Norris. In *The Seven Storey Mountain* (1948), hailed as a modern classic of spiritual autobiography, Merton chronicles a pilgrimage that culminated in his entry into a Trappist monastery in Gethsemani, Kentucky. His many other writings, including *The Wisdom of the Desert* (1960), recommend monastic values as a counterbalance to the violence, materialism, and clamor of modern life. In *The Way of the Heart* (1981), Nouwen, another prolific and popular author, describes how the disciplines of desert spirituality speak poignantly to the challenges of contemporary ministry. Taking the voice of the Lord heard by a desert sage—"flee, be silent, pray always"—as a fitting summary of desert spirituality, Nouwen suggests that this triadic formula will "allow us to save ourselves and others from the shipwreck of our destructive society."[78]

Norris, a poet who left New York City with her husband to take over a family farm in North Dakota, was first introduced to monastic ways during a Lutheran retreat in 1983. She has since become a Benedictine oblate—an associate who lives in the world but follows some of the Rule and attends some of the services of the community. In her best-selling *Dakota: A Spiritual Geography* (1993), Norris draws from the wisdom of the desert fathers and contemporary Benedictine monks to describe how the soul is nourished in the windswept North Dakota landscape of silence and deprivation. "Asceticism," she remarks, "is a way of surrendering to reduced circumstances in a manner that enhances the whole person. It is a radical way of knowing exactly who, what, and where you are, in defiance of those powerful forces in society—alcohol, drugs, television, shopping malls, motels—that aim to make us forget."[79] In her equally popular *Cloister Walk* (1996), a record of her nine-month stay at St. John's Abbey in Minnesota, Norris even discovered a "mysterious, pleasing and gracious way" of those who practice celibacy. "I've seen too many wise old monks and nuns whose lengthy formation in celibate practice has allowed them to incarnate hospitality in the deepest sense," she writes. "In them, the constraints of celibacy have somehow been transformed into an openness that attracts people of all ages, all social classes. They exude a freedom."[80]

In another era and in such a fundamentally different context that it requires a leap of historical imagination to fathom, Anthony essentially said and did the same thing. His example remains both a source of inspiration and a model for those who answer Jesus' invitation, "Come, follow me."

2

"Upon This Rock"

Peter and the Papacy

And I tell you, you are Peter, and on this rock I will build my church, and the gates of Hades will not prevail against it. I will give you the keys of the kingdom of heaven, and whatever you bind on earth will be bound in heaven, and whatever you loose on earth will be loosed in heaven.

—Matthew 16:18–19

Casual conversation about the papacy often revolves around either a place (Rome) or a person (St. Peter). I have never met anyone who was not impressed by a visit to the Vatican, especially to St. Peter's Basilica, where high in the cupola the Latin words of Matthew 16:18 are engraved in six-foot-tall gold letters. To observe such magnificent architecture, to visit the site of the oldest and greatest institution in Western civilization, and to see the leader of more than a billion Christians is truly an awe-inspiring experience. When conversation turns to St. Peter, however, it often transgresses boundaries, moving from the "sacred" to the "profane." I have in mind the hundreds—probably thousands—of "St. Peter at the gates" jokes that circulate through every known medium. As holder of the "keys" to eternal life, St. Peter determines—by whim, fancy, or calculus—what persons will enter the pearly gates of heaven.

More thoughtful conversation about the pope frequently turns to whether one is for or against a certain papal pronouncement or position, or if one is for or against the very institution of the papacy. I recall a discussion I had in high school with a good friend, basketball teammate, and devout Irish Catholic over the validity of the papacy. In worthy Protestant fashion I argued that nowhere did the Bible teach or endorse one leader over all Christians with power to determine doctrine, faith, morals, and especially who would (or would not) go to heaven. A St. Peter-at-the-gates joke was no joke to me. I cannot remember my friend's response—not because he did not have one, but as is the case in most heated discussions, I did not hear what he was saying. So much for an attempt by a couple of high school friends to bridge the ecumenical gap. We should not have been surprised. In 1967, around the same time as our conversation, Pope Paul VI was making his own ecumenical overtures, while admitting that "the pope—as we all know—is undoubtedly the gravest obstacle in the path of ecumenism."[1]

Today, nearly four decades later, despite scores of interreligious dialogues that have reached agreement on many issues (Scripture, baptism, worship, confession, creeds), the pope still remains the gravest obstacle to Christian unity. To put the matter in bold relief: Catholics recognize the spiritual primacy of one leader (the pope or the bishop of Rome) and understand his office as divinely ordained. Protestants view the papacy as an institution not of divine but of human origins. And Eastern Orthodox adherents are willing to accept the pope as primus inter pares (first among equals) but not as the sole head of the Christian community. In light of New Testament teaching on the unity of believers (John 17:21; Gal. 3:28; Eph. 4:4–5), Christians have fallen woefully short of this ideal—if not confessionally, certainly ecclesiologically.

Is there any way out of this stalemate, or must Christians be content to recognize that serious historical and theological divisions will never be overcome? A number of New Testament scholars recognize that for any real ecumenical advance to be made, attention must be given to those biblical texts traditionally cited in support of the papacy. If some consensus can be reached regarding these texts, they argue, then substantive dialogue can proceed from this terra firma. But the results of their efforts, though encouraging, have not resulted in any major breakthrough. The weight of history, tradition, and Catholic Church teaching and dogma has offset the insights gained and the consensus reached among Catholic and Protestant exegetes. In 1979, in the first speech of his pontificate, Pope John Paul II reiterated the traditional Petrine texts (Matt. 16:18–19; Luke 22:31–32; John 21:15–17) as the basis of a Catholic understanding of the papacy. "We are completely convinced," he noted, "that all modern inquiry into the 'Petrine ministry' must be based on these three hinges of the Gospel." And the latest Catechism of the Catholic Church (1994) reaffirms the importance of these texts as the basis of authority for those who succeeded Peter in his ministry.[2]

Such official pronouncements reveal the wide chasm separating traditional Catholic teaching from recent biblical scholarship. Nearly forty years ago, F. C. Grant, the Anglican biblical scholar, observed that the real problem in making ecumenical progress was not papal primacy (or even papal infallibility), for he believed these could be defended on historical or pragmatic grounds. "The real obstacle," he noted in 1965, "was the violence done to the New Testament in every attempt to defend the papacy as an institution dating from the first century and founded by Christ himself." Writing twenty-five years later, Ulrich Luz, the German Lutheran scholar, observed that "the exegetical consensus of today corresponds exactly to those positions that were put under solemn anathema by the first Vatican Council in 1870." And by the reckoning of Hans Küng, the longtime disaffected Catholic theologian, "the Papacy as it is today depends in many respects not upon the original commission [the Petrine text], but upon a very problematical historical development."[3]

What specifically does the Catholic Church teach about Peter and those popes who stand in an unbroken succession of power and authority? First, there is a particular form of apostolic ministry conferred by Jesus himself on Peter (a "Petrine function"). Second, the pastoral authority of Peter is passed on through the office of the bishop of Rome. Third, this office is of divine origin, based on divine law (iure divino), and willed by Christ himself. And fourth, the pope has a jurisdictional authority, expressed at the First Vatican Council (1869–70) as supreme (subject to no human power); full (supreme in faith, morals, discipline, and government); ordinary (a power that inheres in the office); immediate (acts directly without an intermediary); and episcopal (acts with the same authority of a bishop in his diocese). There is, then, a historical, theological, and canonical (legal) basis to the papacy. In support of these claims, Catholics appeal to the so-called Petrine passages in Scripture—proof-texts of Peter's special authority. These texts have traditionally been the foundation upon which a theological and historical case is made for Peter's presence in Rome, Rome as the center of Christianity, and the bishop of Rome as the head of the church. The doctrine of papal primacy—"a claim on the part of the Bishop of Rome to a responsibility and an authority in guiding the Church universal that is beyond that of any other church or bishop"—is based upon this reasoning.[4]

The one biblical text carrying the most weight in defense of papal primacy is, of course, Matthew 16:18–19. No other passage in the Bible has been the focus of so much controversy. Jesus' words to Peter, following Peter's confession that Jesus was "the Messiah, the Son of the living God" (v. 16), have been the source of scholarly debate, dogmatic pronouncements, and enduring and acrimonious divisions among Christians for centuries. Before the middle of the sixteenth century, Catholic exegetes interpreted this text in a variety of ways. Identifying the person of Peter as "this rock" was one of several interpretations in currency. The polemics of the Protestant Reformation, however, hardened the interpretive categories, and consequently, by the mid-sixteenth century, Catholic exegetes defended the divine office of the papacy against Protestant critics by appealing to Matthew 16:18–19 as a proof-text. Jesus' reference to "this rock," they uniformly agreed, was an unambiguous reference to Peter, upon whom the new church was to be established. Moreover, Peter was given a spiritual authority to forgive sins, discipline, and if necessary, to excommunicate those who persisted in sin. Come what may—even the threat of death—the Roman church with Peter and his successors at its head would not be destroyed.

At the First Vatican Council, prior to its statement on papal infallibility, the dogmatic constitution *Pastor Aeternus* reiterated the Petrine texts as the basis of the primacy of the Roman pontiffs over the universal church. Appealing to the writings of the church fathers and previous councils, *Pastor Aeternus* confidently asserted that these texts "had *always* been understood by the Catholic Church" to support papal primacy.[5] Short of interpreting "always" in the most restrictive sense (i.e., to mean that Catholic exegetes did not deny to Peter an office and powers peculiar to him), *Pastor Aeternus* was historically inaccurate. As noted, earlier biblical commentators assigned a variety of meanings to "rock." Jesus' reference to "rock" could mean Peter, exegetes concluded, but it could also mean Peter's confession of faith, the faith of the church, and Christ himself. No single, consistent interpretation prevailed in the Catholic Church until the papacy was subjected to hostile criticism by Protestant Reformers.

Even if we assume that the post-sixteenth-century Catholic exegesis of this text is correct—and most scholars today believe it is insofar as "rock" refers to Peter—other difficulties arise. First, non-Catholics and even many Catholics observe that there is little if any scriptural support for the notion of a succession of Peter's special authority and function to the bishops of Rome. To be sure, most Catholic scholars still find scriptural support for at least a general form of apostolic succession by an appeal to Acts 1:12–26, where Judas is replaced by Matthias. (Protestant scholars counter by citing Acts 12:2, where there is no indication that the disciple James was replaced after being killed.) Second, the idea of a pope's juridical authority is viewed as a benevolent dictatorship at best, tyranny at worst, and one that, again, has no biblical basis. Third, the first known appeal to the Petrine text in support of the authority of the bishop of Rome was not made until the middle of the third century. How can a case for papal primacy be built on a passage of Scripture that no one bothered to cite as a supporting text until, presumably, several hundred years after the fact? Do we have a case of special pleading (as non-Catholics argue) or simply an explicit recognition of what had been implicitly affirmed and developing (as Catholics argue)? Here we are faced with the complex relationship between historical development—in this case, the emergence of the bishop of Rome as the leader of the Christian church—and the role that biblical texts and their interpretation play in such a development.

Viewed *historically*, the Petrine text is what one scholar suggests may be a "hermeneutical secondary legitimation" to justify those already in power or what another calls a "retreat from exegesis to later history." From this perspective, developments in history (i.e., the rise of the papacy) prove that the text must refer to Peter and his successors in Rome. Viewed *exegetically* by the standards of modern biblical scholarship, the text has limited use in establishing the primacy of Roman bishops. Some Catholic biblical scholars, though not the Catholic magisterium (the teaching office of the church), have taken the position that although the New Testament does not unequivocally prove the office of the papacy based on Peter himself, neither does it categorically rule out the gradual development of such an office. The ministerial primacy of one person is not necessarily contrary to Scripture, as even Protestant Reformers such as Martin Luther (in his early years), Philipp Melancthon, and John Calvin conceded. Through the confluence of a "Petrine trajectory" in the New Testament and historical circumstances (not to mention the guidance of the Holy Spirit, Catholics aver), there emerged Roman primacy.[6]

Apart from theological or biblical considerations, some claim that "if Christianity did not have a pope it would have to invent one." Viewed from a perspective of human organization, the Jesuit sociologist Andrew Greeley notes that "even if the papacy was not part of a divine institution of the Church, it still would have developed out of organizational necessity."[7] But the fact remains: whether divinely instituted, historically conditioned, or necessitated by growth, the papacy eventually based its claims to rule upon the Petrine text. Despite the alleged secondary status of the text, the papacy and its supporters eventually invoked the text as primary proof for the existence of the Petrine office. For this reason, then, the text merits examination. Not only did it become the locus classicus in defense of papal primacy; it also vividly illustrates the impact of historical circumstances on biblical interpretation.

I begin, then, with the present "state of the Petrine text," noting some of the key interpretive issues. No exhaustive or definitive treatment of the text is intended, but rather, in summary fashion and in a selective way, I seek to point out how modern biblical scholars have approached and interpreted the text. Although exegetes differ over the meaning of various words and phrases, the vast majority affirm that Peter was indeed "the rock" upon whom Christ built his church. From a somewhat extended exegesis of this passage I turn to the "Petrine ministry" in the New Testament, viewing Peter in the wider context of the early church.

In the postapostolic environment, how was Peter linked to Rome and eventually to the concept of papal primacy? This simple yet crucial question requires a rather complex answer. I trace formative developments in the rise of the papacy up through the fifth century by attending to the historical and theoretical underpinnings of the office, including references to the Petrine text. Finally, I survey various interpretations of the Petrine text from the medieval period through the Reformation era. Between roughly 1550 and 1950, the interpretive categories ossified along confessional lines. Not until Oscar Cullmann's landmark historical study on Peter (1952) and the opening of ecumenical dialogue following the Second Vatican Council (1962–65) was the text revisited in a context of mutual understanding and improved relations among Christian bodies.

The Petrine Text in Modern Biblical Studies

Biblical scholars view the Petrine text as part of a larger pericope beginning with verse 13 and ending with verse 20. To be sure, the focus of this text is on Jesus, not Peter. More specifically, it is about Jesus as Messiah, as builder of his church and giver of the keys. Only within that emphasis does the question of Peter's role emerge.

> [13]Now when Jesus came into the district of Caesarea Philippi, he asked his disciples, "Who do people say that the Son of Man is?" [14]And they said, "Some say John the Baptist, but others Elijah, and still others Jeremiah or one of the prophets." [15]He said to them, "But who do you say that I am?" [16]Simon Peter answered, "You are the Messiah, the Son of the living God." [17]And Jesus answered him, "Blessed are you, Simon son of Jonah! For flesh and blood has not revealed this to you, but my Father in heaven. [18]And I tell you, you are Peter, and on this rock I will build my church, and the gates of Hades will not prevail against it. [19]I will give you the keys of the kingdom of heaven, and whatever you bind on earth will be bound in heaven, and whatever you loose on earth will be loosed in heaven." [20]Then he sternly ordered the disciples not to tell anyone that he was the Messiah.

Summary

In this scene Jesus retreats with his disciples to Caesarea Philippi, twenty-five miles north of the Sea of Galilee. Now free from his enemies (the Herodians, Pharisees, Sadducees, and scribes), Jesus poses two questions to his disciples: Who do people think he is, and who do the disciples think he is? To the first, the disciples respond that people identify Jesus with those who played various prophetic (but not messianic) roles. To the second question, Simon Peter answers that he is the Christ, the Son of the living God. Peter's confession marks a turning point in the disciples' understanding of Jesus. He is more than a prophet, more than the harbinger of a new age; rather, he embodies the new age and will bring about a new order. "Matthew's point is clear," writes Daniel Patte. "People who observe Jesus and his ministry *from a distance* can recognize him as a man sent by God, but they can only conceive his relationship with God as a somewhat *distant* relationship. By contrast, the disciples who are in an *intimate relationship with Jesus* by sharing his ministry can recognize his *intimate relationship with God*, as expressed by the phrase 'Son of the living God.' "⁸

Jesus then pronounces a blessing on Peter because God, not a human being ("flesh and blood"), has revealed to Peter the true nature of Jesus. Peter is not merely a spokesman or representative of the disciples: he is called the rock, and upon him a new community will be built that death cannot destroy. Moreover, Peter is given authority to determine who is in a proper relationship with God, and thus who will be admitted to the coming kingdom. The text closes with Jesus telling his disciples to inform no one that he is the Christ. In sum, this is a crucial passage in Matthew, characterized as a pronouncement story with two key parts: Peter's confession and Jesus' response. Earlier in the Gospel, Jesus was rejected by his own people (see 13:54–58); now he promises to establish a new community—the church.

Critical Perspectives

Before the rise of modern critical scholarship, it was assumed that the sayings of Jesus were authentic in every way. What was recorded as Jesus' very words were indeed his words, and what was described as the occasion and place of his sayings were as the gospel writers described them. Beginning in the late eighteenth century, however, scholars raised doubts about the genuineness of Jesus' sayings and the settings in which they were uttered. Among the more skeptical critics in the nineteenth century were Christian Wilke and H. J. Holtzmann. Working from a hypothesis that the early church embellished parts of the Gospels for its own purposes, Wilke around midcentury and Holtzmann later in the century concluded that verses 16b–19 were not originally a part of Matthew's gospel. They observed (as had others before them) that this passage was unique in Matthew. Peter's confession of Jesus as the Christ at Caesarea Philippi was common to the other synoptics—with minor variations (cf. Mark 8:27–30; Luke 9:18–21)—but verses 16b through 19 (beginning with "the Son of the living God") were recorded only in Matthew. Not only was the text not found in the synoptics, noted Wilke, but its placement was jarring and conflicted with Jesus' subsequent words to Peter in verse 23 ("Get behind me, Satan!"). Moreover, the anachronistic reference to "church" (a later organizational development, foreign to a mind-set of Jesus who expected the world to come to an end very soon) made the text all the more dubious. Wilke and Holtzmann concluded that this passage was a pious invention, added to the Gospel of Matthew sometime in the latter half of the second century. Armed with such conclusions, they demolished the Catholic contention of prima facie biblical support for the papacy.⁹

In the twentieth century, the pendulum has swung back and forth from scholars who defend the genuineness of the text to critics who deny it. At midcentury, Oscar Cullmann noted that the issue was "in flux" and cited a 1950 study of thirty-four scholars who were about evenly divided on the issue. Writing about these contested verses in 1973, a national commission of Catholic and Protestant (Lutheran) scholars asserted: "We can reach virtual unanimity that there are no significant textual problems in them and that they are not later interpolations." Still, there is no consensus regarding the historical sources and traditions of the Petrine text. The same commission affirmed the authenticity of Jesus' words but disputed the original setting and suggested a postresurrection tradition. Arriving at these conclusions requires dealing with degrees of probability or authenticity, and by the admission of scholars themselves, determining the historical strands behind this passage is a highly speculative enterprise.[10]

Scholarly opinion on Matthew 16:17–19 ranges from those who assert that Jesus himself spoke these words (or something close to them) at Caesara Philippi, to those who conclude that these words were put in Jesus' mouth by Matthew in Antioch, Syria—the likely setting of the book's composition. Thus while scholars agree that the Petrine text was not inserted after the evangelist completed writing the Gospel, they continue to disagree over its historicity from several perspectives: first, whether in fact Jesus spoke the words that are recorded; second, if he did speak them, when and where they were spoken; and, third, if he did not speak them, when and where they were composed and who composed them. By Ben Meyer's reckoning, "Few gospel texts have been branded unhistorical more emphatically than Matt. 16:17–19."[11]

Among those skeptics who confirm Meyer's observation are Rudoph Bultmann, Eduard Schweizer, Günther Bornkamm, and Ulrich Luz. They contend, in the words of Schweizer, that "these sayings do not derive from Jesus, neither did Matthew compose them." In their estimation (though Luz admits, "Sometimes the basis of my argument is rather fragile"), these verses first circulated in a Greek-speaking church in Syria (Antioch) where Peter was the founding apostle of the church.[12] Of course, if Jesus did not speak these words to Peter, then the historical basis of the biblical (though perhaps not the theological) claims of the Roman Catholic Church to Peter's primacy are considerably diminished, if not unfounded. Consider Luz's comment cited earlier regarding contemporary exegetical views that challenge the views of the Catholic hierarchy. At Vatican I, *Pastor Aeternus* declared the following:

> If anyone then says that the Blessed Apostle Peter was not established by the Lord Jesus Christ as the chief of all the apostles, and the visible head of the whole militant Church, or, that the same received great honor but did not receive from the same our Lord Jesus Christ directly and immediately the primacy in true and proper jurisdiction: let him be anathema.
>
> If anyone then says that it is not from the institution of Christ

the Lord Himself, or by divine right that the blessed Peter has perpetual successors in the primacy over the universal Church, or that
the Roman Pontiff is not the successor of blessed Peter in the same
primacy, let him be anathema.[13]

By the canons of Vatican I, Luz and company stand condemned.

Among those supporting the integrity of the text are Ben Meyer, Robert
Gundry, and coauthors W. D. Davies and Dale Allison. Like Luz, Davies and
Allison concede "there is no certainty in the sea of scholarly doubt," but nevertheless they make a strong case in favor of the traditional view as a genuine
saying of Jesus spoken at Caesarea Philippi.[14] Somewhere in the middle (probably the majority view) are those such as Oscar Cullmann and the national
commission of scholars noted previously who affirm that the sayings are authentic but place the setting either at the Last Supper (Cullmann) or in a postresurrection context (the commission).

Exegesis

Because of the complex character of the Petrine text and the variety of interpretations proposed throughout the history of Christianity, I proceed in the
manner of biblical exegetes who explicate units (words and phrases) of the text.
Again, no effort is made to offer a detailed or definitive analysis but to suggest
where interpretations converge and diverge.[15]

"You are Peter" Following Peter's declaration about Jesus as the Messiah
and Son of the living God, Jesus makes a declaration about Peter. He begins
by giving him a new name or, as some contend, a new title—Peter (Greek =
Petros). Like Abram and Jacob in the Old Testament, who were given new
names (Abraham and Israel) when they were given new responsibilities, so
Simon receives the name of Peter at the assumption of his new responsibilities.
According to some exegetes, the rhetorical parallel with Genesis 17 is unmistakable: in both accounts a new people is brought into being. In the first, a
covenant is established with Abraham, and the Jewish people are established
as a nation; in the second, a covenant is established with Peter, and the Christian church is established as a new covenant community. Moreover, just as
Abraham is identified as "the rock" from which Israel was hewn (Isa. 51:1–2),
so too Simon is referred to as "rock."

"and on this rock I will build" Here we encounter the phrase that has resulted in so much spilled ink—and blood. To what does "rock" (in Greek =
petra) refer? Most modern scholars, be they liberal or conservative, Protestant
or Catholic or Orthodox, now conclude that "the most natural interpretation is
that of the Roman Catholic tradition: the rock is Peter."[16] Joseph Burgess, writing in 1976, observed that it was possible to speak of "an ecumenical breakthrough" in the understanding of this passage. What we have, exegetes say, is

Jesus engaging in wordplay or making a pun. He gives Simon the name Peter (rock or "Rocky") and tells him that he is the rock upon whom he will build his new community. But if Peter is the rock, then why in the Greek language is "Peter" in the masculine and "rock" in the feminine? In Aramaic, the spoken language of Jesus (and thus the language behind the Greek), there is identity: the common noun *kêpa* is used in both places. When translated into Greek, the masculine *Petros* is a more appropriate designation of person (Peter), whereas *petra* is used as a literary variant. Donald Hagner is convinced that "the Aramaic word play on the same word remains the most convincing explanation" for Peter is the rock upon whom the church is built.[17]

"my church" This noun (in Greek, *ekklēsia*) is used only twice in the canonical Gospels, both times in Matthew (here in a universal sense and in 18: 17 in a restrictive sense as a reference to a local group). As noted earlier, some contemporary scholars view the use of this word as strong evidence that the passage derives from the later church, not from Jesus himself. Those who defend the basic integrity of the text argue that the use of "church" reflects editorial changes made by the evangelist Matthew. In an earlier version (or as an oral saying of Jesus), the word may have been "temple" (in Hebrew, *qāhāl* = the assembly of Israel; in Aramaic, *gehala* = a people set apart for God's special purpose). At least behind the term *ekklēsia* lies the idea of the temple as community—from Jesus' perspective a new temple with an indestructible rock foundation. In any case, the use of the word "church" is entirely consistent with Jesus' aims. He thought that his death would not bring an end to the movement that he had begun, that the apostles would constitute the core of that continuing community, and that he would drink again of the fruit of the vine with his disciples in the kingdom of God. He announces that a new community of Israel—now a messianic community—will be brought into being and built by him. Christ's promise to Peter, "I will build my church," was given expression at the first gathering of the messianic community in Jerusalem with Peter as its leader.

"and the gates of Hades will not prevail against it" Because a rock foundation assures permanence (see Matt. 7:24–25), the church (assuming "it" refers to church) will not be destroyed. In Hebrew Scriptures, Hades or *sheol* was the place of the dead. The idea of an underworld realm of the dead with gates (the point of entry into the realm or "city" of the dead and the strongest part of the city's fortification) was a common belief in the ancient Near East. Used as a metaphor, "gates of Hades" has been variously interpreted to mean the powers of evil, the powers of death, the rulers of Hades, the power of Satan, and the underworld's demonic forces. Whatever specific meaning one assigns, the meaning is clear: not even the gates of Hades are stronger than Jesus the Messiah and the community he has brought into being. The powers of death or of the underworld cannot contain or hold in check the new community.[18]

"I will give you the keys of the kingdom of heaven" With Peter's commission-

ing as rock comes the ability and/or power (symbolized by keys) to grant access to enter the kingdom. Whereas scribes, Pharisees, and teachers of the law lock people out of the kingdom (see Matt. 23:13 and Luke 11:52), Peter will grant them access. The one who has the key of David (Isa. 22:22) has messianic power (Rev. 3:7), and Jesus as the messianic son of David gives that power to Peter. Accompanying this authority comes the right, exercised as a steward entrusted with keys, to admit or deny entrance into the kingdom. Peter's use of the keys is almost certainly related to his subsequent preaching, by which he (and others) through evangelization "opened the door" to God's kingdom (see Acts 14:27; 1 Cor. 16:9; 2 Cor. 2:12).

Scholars disagree on the extent of Peter's power. Is the power of the keys related to "binding and loosing" (v. 19b, c)? The ecumenical contributors to *Peter in the New Testament* conclude that it is difficult to determine whether the power of the keys is equivalent to the same power of binding and loosing. If the power is the same, then Peter has no more power than the other disciples who in Matthew 18:18 are given the same power to bind and loose. If, on the other hand, binding and loosing are but a manifestation of Peter's broader powers of the keys, then one can argue—as does the Catholic Church—that Peter's powers are unique. In the "Dogmatic Constitution on the Church" (*Lumen Gentium*), the Second Vatican Council reiterated the traditional Catholic view: "Our Lord made Simon Peter alone the rock and key bearer of the Church."[19]

"and whatever you bind on earth will be bound in heaven, and whatever you loose on earth will be loosed in heaven" The terms "bind" and "loose" are Jewish idioms and technically refer to a rabbi's power to lay down a law (bind) and to make exceptions to it (loose). Again, there is disagreement regarding the precise meaning of these terms. A significant minority of scholars thinks that Peter's role as initiating and following up on evangelical breakthroughs is what Jesus had in mind (as is more clearly indicated in John 20:23, with its similar structure and language). Most contemporary scholars attribute binding and loosing to a teaching or preaching function. Peter is thus the "chief rabbi" or *"the* scribe" (cf. Matt. 13:52). As a teacher, he passes on the instructions and ethics of Jesus. His responsibilities also include discipline as it pertains to permitting or forbidding certain conduct. Thus Peter (and the other disciples as well) declares the terms of admission to the kingdom of heaven. He has the power to determine who becomes a part of the new community based on their response to the good news of the kingdom.[20]

To summarize this discussion of the Petrine text. First, like Abraham of old, who was given a new name, became the head of a new people, and was called a rock, so Peter follows in parallel fashion. The text attributes to Peter a certain preeminence among the disciples in the early Christian community. Second, Jesus assures Peter that he is the rock upon whom a new community will be built, and in that community Peter's authority to "bind and loose" will be ratified in heaven. Over against traditional Protestant exegesis, Peter is more than just a model and spokesman for the disciples. "He plays a unique role as firm basis and authoritative teacher in the church." To deny as much is simply "a denial of the evidence." Yet in Matthew's account, Peter's authority is local, not universal. Third, over against traditional Roman Catholic exegesis, Peter is not the first officeholder from whom successive leaders will draw their authority. "Rather, he is a man with a unique role in salvation-history. . . . His significance is the significance of Abraham, which is to say: his faith is the means by which God brings a new people into being."[21]

Peter Elsewhere in the New Testament

Although the Petrine text is central to the Catholic Church's affirmation of papal primacy, it is but one of many New Testament texts that mention Peter. By moving beyond the particular passage of Matthew 16:18–19, we enlarge our understanding of Peter in the life of Jesus and the early Christian community. When the image or images of Peter are assembled from the New Testament record, Peter emerges as both a unique and a typical disciple. Later New Testament writings tend to accord greater prominence to Peter in view of the historically important role he played in the early church. In this composite portrait[22] Peter appears as

1. A *preeminent disciple*. He is mentioned first in lists of the apostles (Matt. 10:2; Mark 3:16; Luke 6:14), the receiver of a special blessing from Jesus (Matt. 16:17), the one outsiders consult when seeking knowledge about Jesus (Matt.17:24–27), the first to whom the risen Lord appears (1 Cor. 15:5; Luke 24:34; Mark 16:7), and the most important of the twelve disciples in the Jerusalem community (Acts 2:14–36; 4:8–12; 5:3–16; 10:9–48; 12:3–17).

2. A *great "fisherman,"* or missionary, of the early Christian community to Jews and also to Gentiles (Luke 5:1–11; John 21; Acts 10; 1 Cor. 1:12, 9:5; Gal. 2:7; 1 Peter 1:1).

3. A *shepherd* (pastor) instructed by Jesus to feed and tend the sheep (John 21:15–17), and the principal *presbyter* (1 Pet. 5:1).

4. A *recipient of special revelation* or visions (Acts 5:1–11; 10:9–16; 12:7–9; 2 Pet. 1:16–18).

5. A *confessor* (Matt. 16:16) and *guardian of the true faith* (2 Peter 1:20–21; 3:15–16).

6. A *typical disciple*, called along with the others (Matt. 4:18–22): he is not the only one to confess Jesus to be the Son of God (Matt. 14:33); he is not the only disciple to whom a blessing is given (Matt. 13:16–17); he is not the only disciple to receive a special revelation (Matt. 13:11, 16–17); he is not the only disciple who has the power to bind and

loose (Matt. 18:18); he is accountable to leaders in Jerusalem, particularly when James emerges as the prominent new leader of the church (Acts 3:1–11; 4:13); and he teams up with John in ministry (Acts 8:14). In the Gospel of John, John "the beloved disciple" is portrayed as a model for all Christian disciples, whereas Peter becomes an alternative, if not competitive, model.

7. A *writer of letters* or a person in whose name letters were written (1 and 2 Pet.).

8. A *weak, impetuous, sinful* man. Peter's faith in Jesus fails and he sinks in water (Matt. 14:28–31). Soon after Jesus calls Peter a "rock" he calls him a "stumbling block" and "Satan" (Matt. 16:23) because of Peter's inadequate understanding that the Messiah must suffer. Peter affirms that he will never deny Jesus but he does (Matt. 26:35).

With this cursory examination of Peter in the New Testament, we may conclude the following regarding the Petrine office. On the negative side, both Catholic and non-Catholic scholars agree that there is no biblical evidence to support the creation of a perpetual office of supreme church authority based on Peter. In his recent and important study on papal primacy, the Jesuit Klaus Schatz addressed the issue in this way: "If we ask whether the historical Jesus, in commissioning Peter, expected him to have successors, or whether the author of the Gospel of Matthew, writing after Peter's death, was aware that Peter and his commission survived in the leaders of the Roman community who succeeded him, the answer in both cases is probably 'no.' "[23]

On the positive side, several comments are in order. First, when the trajectory of images of the apostles is traced to the end of the apostolic era, Peter and Paul emerge as the most influential and enduring. Moreover, in the post–New Testament period, and notably in the Western church, the Petrine trajectory eventually outdistances all others. Obviously Peter remained an important, if not the most important, figure in the postapostolic period. Second, although the New Testament is silent about a successive office based on Peter, it does not rule out its gradual development. Viewed from the Catholic Church's perspective, "the later development of the Petrine trajectory represents that Spirit-guided development of a direction already given in the New Testament. In part that development was determined by the accidents of history. And in part it was due to the eventual joining of the Petrine trajectory to a related but separate tradition which was also developing, that of the Roman church."[24]

Indeed, a number of factors—the loss of Jerusalem as the "mother church" in the war of 66–70 and the subsequent destruction of the Temple and large portions of the city, Peter and Paul's presence in Rome, the stature of Rome as the capital city, Rome as the only apostolic see in the West, the strong leadership and significant wealth in the Roman church, and the fate of the empire itself—all of these enabled the bishop of Rome to exercise authority over other churches. By the end of the fifth century the church at Rome was viewed as a supreme court of appeals and the focus of ecclesiastical unity. Through all of this, it is clear that claims to papal primacy were related more to unanticipated consequences than to a preexistent blueprint. To the development of Roman primacy and the fate of the Petrine text we now turn.[25]

Early Forms of Church Leadership and the Rise of the Papacy

Peter, Paul, and Rome

The New Testament makes no explicit reference to Peter's presence in Rome,[26] yet the emergence of Rome as a center of Christianity was related to the dual apostleships of Peter and Paul. There is general agreement that both apostles died in Rome, possibly as martyrs during Nero's persecution in 64–68 c.e., but there is no evidence that they were there at the same time (when Paul writes to the church in Rome [ca. 57], Peter is not mentioned). Some of the earliest postapostolic writings confirm their presence in the city. Around 96 c.e., the writer of 1 Clement, a presbyter in the Roman church, observed that Peter and Paul died in Rome (5.3–7)[27]—according to later tradition, Peter by upside-down crucifixion, for he did not want to be compared to Jesus—and Paul by beheading. Several decades later, Ignatius, a leader of the church in Antioch, referred to Peter and Paul as giving instructions to the Romans (Rom 4.3). In addition, archaeological evidence points to these leaders' presence in the city. In the second century, Christians built basilicas for Peter on Vatican Hill and for Paul on the road to Ostia outside the city walls. The construction of these churches, intended to honor the remains of Christian saints and martyrs, suggests that Christians presumed the two apostles were buried at those sites.

Although it can be established that Peter and Paul had something to do with the Christians of Rome, it cannot be confirmed that they were the original founders of the church there. From the scant extant evidence about Peter in Rome, few definitive statements, other than negative ones, are possible. He was not the first missionary who brought Christianity to Rome; moreover, we do not know when he came to Rome, how long he was there, and what leadership, if any, he exercised in the Roman church.

When or how Christianity made its way to Rome is unknown. It could have occurred as early as the middle to late 30s with the return of Pentecostal pilgrims from Jerusalem. Many connect the arrival of Christianity in Rome with Claudius's expulsion of the Jews (ca. 49), for Suetonius says he did so at the instigation of "Chrestos" (Christus?). Raymond Brown proposes that the new faith came from Jerusalem to Rome in the 40s, and that by the 50s a Christian community was in existence. Paul's letter to the Romans, written around the year 57, offers some clues as to the age and vitality of the Christian movement in Rome. He reports that the Romans' faith "is proclaimed throughout the world" (1:8b) and that "for many years" he desired to visit them (15: 23b). His greetings in chapter 16 to twenty-five friends and former associates attest to a committed group of Christians. A sizable Christian group—or, more accurately, a number of household assemblies or cells (see 16:5)—may be inferred from the non-Christian, Roman historian Tacitus. In his account of Nero's persecution, he notes that "an immense multitude was convicted"— presumably not a number recently evangelized.[28]

These reports of a concentrated number of Christians in Rome illustrate a pattern in the geographic spread of Christianity: cities on major highways were the most important centers of the new faith. The beginnings of the church as described in the Acts of the Apostles occurred in the most important city of the Jews (Jerusalem) and ended in the most important city of the empire (Rome). The apostle Paul carried out most of his work in urban areas, initially into the Jewish communities of Greco-Roman cities such as Antioch. This urban emphasis continued, as indicated by the fact that late in the first century, while on his way to martyrdom, Bishop Ignatius directed his letters to churches in cities. To be sure, Christian work extended into rural areas (e.g., the "many villages of the Samaritans" [Acts 8:25]), but the bulk of the church's witness was carried out in urban areas.

Given this urban focus, by the end of the first century the Christian movement expanded into four general regions, each with its main ecclesiastical city. In the west there was Rome; in the east, Ephesus and Antioch; in Egypt, Alexandria; and in North Africa, Carthage. By the second and third centuries, Antioch faded from the picture as the other churches grew in size and reputation under the strong leadership of gifted bishops. Each city had its own distinctive character that was reflected in its church. For example, in many respects the leaders of the Roman church mirrored their civil counterparts insofar as both groups displayed certain qualities of character identified with the Roman mind-set: discipline, organizational ability, respect for authority, and an emphasis on law. The leaders of the church at Rome tended to be practical, no-nonsense types, rarely given to theological speculation (Rome produced no great theologians) but skilled in organizational and legal matters. In the same way, the church in Alexandria reflected the Hellenistic, cosmopolitan, intellectually oriented nature of that city, and hence it became one of the primary centers of theological inquiry and speculation.

By the third and fourth centuries, after the emperor Constantine transferred the capital from Rome to the east (ca. 330), Constantinople overshadowed Ephesus, Alexandria, and Carthage. Jerusalem was recognized as an important city of Christian beginnings, but due to conflict with the Jews and the eventual destruction of the city by Titus's forces in the rebellion of 66–70, the church never developed the power and prestige of the other centers of Christianity.

The kind of leadership exercised in these major cities reflected the variety of leadership patterns found in the New Testament, which does not prescribe a single form of church polity, and what is mentioned is local in reference.[29] For example, in the first church in Jerusalem, leaders who are full of faith and the Holy Spirit are chosen to handle a specific problem of discrimination against a group of widows, not appointed to an office wherein such charismatic authority inhered (Acts 6:1–8). Elders also played an important role in the Jerusalem church (Acts 15:2), with James eventually emerging as the primary leader in the church. Elsewhere, prophets and teachers are active in the church of Antioch (Acts 13:1–3).

The apostle Paul's concept of ministry is guided by the view of the church as the "body of Christ" where each member exercises spiritual gifts (Rom. 12; 1 Cor. 12; Eph. 4). To be sure, some members had more regular ministries and specific leadership responsibilities within the body. Paul himself, personally commissioned by Christ (not appointed by other leaders), had a unique role and authority, and prophets and teachers communicated a new revelation or gave instruction, respectively. Paul also speaks of bishops (or overseers) and deacons as leaders in the Philippian church (Phil. 1:1), though exactly what these terms mean is not clear.

Some scholars embrace a classic, evolutionary model in their understanding of developing church leadership patterns. They detect a movement from Paul's view of a highly fluid, Spirit-filled designated ministry where the gift (*charism*) enables ministry, to an increasingly static, institutional ministry where the gift is conferred and comes with the office after the laying on of hands (1 Tim. 4:14; 2 Tim. 1:6). Found in the pastoral letters, this latter development, contend many scholars, is post-Pauline; that is, these epistles were written not by Paul but by a pseudonymous Pauline author in the late century. The author of the pastorals lists the qualifications of bishops or overseers (*episkopoi*) and elders (*presbuteroi*), but he sometimes conflates the two offices and offers no directives in terms of a specific polity (see Titus 1:5–9; 1 Tim. 3; 5:17; Acts 20). What is clear, however, is a structured and authoritative view of church ministry. Countering this trend toward institutionalization are the writings of the Gospel of John, the Johannine Epistles, Hebrews, and Revelation, which point toward an individual's direct and personal relationship to God (John), a pastoral function of ministry (Hebrews), and a prophetic function (Revelation). In sum, fluid forms of leadership and ministry characterized first- and second-generation Christian communities.

By the early second century, multiple forms of ministry continued, though with greater emphasis on official leadership roles. In some churches, elders ruled; in others, bishops; in some instances, leaders were appointed; in yet others, they were elected. What is known of continued ecclesiastical leadership throughout the Christian community in the first three centuries is sketchy, but the evidence points to the emerging importance of a mono-episcopate (a single overseer of a church), the idea of apostolic succession, and the prominence of the bishop of Rome. As Christian communities faced external and internal threats in the form of persecution and heresy (e.g., Gnosticism and Montanism), greater uniformity in ecclesiastical organization prevailed. Such uniformity was characterized by a single bishop in some way connected to apostolic leadership and leading a local or regional community. Obviously, the church at Rome, given the dual presence of the apostles Peter and Paul, claimed a special authority. In the first three centuries, church leaders and thinkers throughout the empire increasingly recognized Rome as a center of Christianity. At the same time, the literary evidence yields no clear-cut claims to, or recognition of, papal primacy. An examination of several key documents traditionally cited to support primatial claims bears this out.

Clement's First Letter to the Corinthians

One of the most controversial documents of the postapostolic period—and the earliest Christian document outside the New Testament—is the anonymous letter of 1 Clement. Like the Petrine text, this document is colored by centuries of conflict between Catholic, Orthodox, and Protestant partisans. Defenders of the Catholic hierarchy viewed it as a categorical affirmation of papal primacy. Detractors denied that it supported Roman primacy yet in the same breath bemoaned its appeal to structure and authority. For nineteenth-century German scholars such as Rudolph Sohm and Adolf von Harnack, the letter demonstrated the loss of a genuine New Testament charismatic leadership. In their judgment, before the end of the first century a movement of the Spirit had been displaced by concerns for order and succession. Institutionalization, with its structure and predictability, destroyed antistructure and spontaneity. More recent judgments of 1 Clement by Catholic and non-Catholic scholars alike defend neither the primacy of the papacy nor the betrayal of the primitive faith.[30] Rather, they view the letter as making a compelling case for Rome's stature as a mature church with a desire to maintain peace and religious purity among Christian churches.

The author of 1 Clement, traditionally viewed as a presbyter in the church at Rome writing in the name of the Roman church, wrote to the church at Corinth at the end of the first century in an effort to resolve a festering conflict. Some young members of the Corinthian church, dissatisfied with the older leaders' neglect of their spiritual gifts, sought to displace them. The author of 1 Clement believed that it was right and necessary for the church in Rome to intervene. Foreshadowing later developments, 1 Clement set forth a hierarchical view of the ministry and stressed the need for obedience to duly elected authorities. The letter advised the Corinthians (without a hint of juridical authority) to follow the appointed leaders; that is, to follow those presbyter-bishops who assumed the pastoral care of the church founded by the apostles (42.1–5).

What the letter of *Clement* did not mention was as important as what it did mention. The letter makes no appeal to Roman juridical authority—yet implies that because of Rome's apostolic authority, it is justified in admonishing Corinth. Nor is there any mention of a chain of succession to sacramental power in the Roman church alone. Nor does the author appeal to the rule of a single bishop over the church. In short, the letter reflects the concern of the leadership in a respected church who is seeking to resolve a divisive situation. The authority of *1 Clement* is a matter of intrachurch order. The *church* of Rome—not the presbyters and clearly not the bishop of Rome—sees it as her duty to intervene. At the same time, the very fact of Roman intervention discloses the importance of Rome. As Cyril Richardson observes, "Something of her unique place as the church of the imperial city, and the church of Peter and Paul (ch. 5), must surely have been in the writer's mind."[31]

Ignatius's Letter to the Romans

Another literary source that points to the prominence of Peter, Rome, and, for the first time, the clearly defined role of the bishop is the letters of Ignatius. The bishop of a small but growing group of Christians in Antioch, Ignatius was arrested for an offense against the Roman authorities (probably his refusal to participate in the cult of the emperor Trajan) and then sent to Rome to die as a martyr for the faith.

His *Seven Letters* (ca. 98–117) express several concerns. One was his impending martyrdom, which he anticipated with great enthusiasm ("Let me imitate the Passion of my God," *Rom.* 6.3), even with a macabre delight ("I am God's wheat and I am being ground by the teeth of wild beasts," *Rom.* 4.1). Another concern was the incipient heretical movements of the Judaizers (who downplayed Jesus' divinity) and the docetists (who downplayed Jesus' humanity), who threatened to divide the church. To combat these heresies, Ignatius counseled obedience to church authorities. Like Clement, Ignatius stressed a hierarchy of leadership but conceived it differently. He emphasized the need for one leader (a bishop or mono-episcopate), but he ignored an apostolic or historical succession. Ignatius conceived of church authority as a Platonic correspondence between heavenly types and human antitypes. Thus, "Let the bishop preside in God's place, and the presbyters take the place of the apostolic council, and let the deacons . . . be entrusted with the ministry of Jesus Christ" (*Mag.* 6.1; see also *Eph.* 6.1).

Ignatius also accorded Rome a place of special importance. As noted earlier, he mentioned the presence of Peter and Paul in Rome, and he also implored the Romans not to intervene on his behalf, implying that the Roman church had the political connections possibly to prevent his martyrdom. Additionally, in his greeting he ascribed to the church a district or regional authority and hailed its widely known reputation for extensive acts of charity. Indeed, this tradition of practical aid, dating back to the apostle Paul, enhanced the prestige of the church and contributed to the growing authority of the bishop of Rome. Paul, for example, expected the Roman church to contribute to his support (Rom. 15:24). In Clement's *Letter to the Corinthians* there is mention of Romans going to prison in place of others, with some even becoming slaves in order to free others (55.2). Justin, the Christian apologist and martyr, wrote in approximately 150 of Rome's aid to orphans, widows, the sick, the poor, prisoners, and visitors (*First Apology* 67). By the mid-third century, the impressive size and outreach of the church at Rome were apparent. The bishop (or "president," as Justin calls him) of Rome was directing a staff of forty-six presbyters, seven deacons, seven subdeacons, forty-two acolytes, and fifty-two exorcists, readers, and doorkeepers, and he cared for more than fifteen hundred widows and orphans—all of whom were supported by the common funds of the church in a city of thirty to fifty thousand Christians.[32]

Irenaeus's Against Heresies

A third and crucial source for our knowledge of the authority of the bishop in general and the importance of the bishop of Rome in particular is Irenaeus's *Against Heretics*. In challenging the Gnostics' "mad ideas" to a secret tradition, Irenaeus, the bishop of Lyons, connects the present authority of the bishops to the original apostles, arguing that the true faith was passed on successively and publicly from the apostles to bishops and their successors (Book III.3.1).

He singles out Rome as an example because it is "that very great, oldest, and well-known Church, founded and established at Rome by those two most glorious apostles Peter and Paul" (III.3.2). Then, in a sentence that became a flash point of controversy among Christian traditions, Irenaeus asserts that "every church must be in harmony with the Church because of its outstanding pre-eminence, that is, the faithful from everywhere, since the apostolic tradition is preserved in it by those from everywhere" (III.3.2). Is Irenaeus supporting a full-blown doctrine of papal primacy, as some Catholic partisans argued? Not likely. The key term "be in harmony with" (Latin = *convenire ad*) literally means "assemble at," or metaphorically "be in agreement with," the church of Rome. Rome is important and is an exemplar, for "the apostolic tradition in the Church and the preaching of the truth has come down even to us" (III.3.3). Even now (the end of the second century), notes Irenaeus, Eleutherius, the twelfth bishop of Rome, serves in the place of the apostles.

At the same time, allusions to the Roman church do not support the claim of primacy, though they do support the traditions of Rome's double apostolic foundation. Irenaeus makes no mention of Peter's episcopate in Rome. He advocates a plurality of ecclesiastical centers based on their tie to an apostolic foundation. He does, however, single out Rome for special consideration because of its apostolic credentials, because of its recognized stature and theological orthodoxy, and because in the western portion of the empire it was the only clearly recognizable church of apostolic origin.

By the end of the second century, what conclusions can be reached regarding Rome's ecclesiastical authority? From the sources discussed here, Rome is considered a significant, if not in some way the unique, center of the Christian faith—and yet without a claim to primacy. To guard against heresy, a connection to the apostolic tradition becomes increasingly critical. In the tradition of Jewish priestly succession lists, Christians such as Irenaeus begin to trace their apostolic roots as a means to ensure fidelity to the original deposit of faith.[33] Deviation is also combated by a mono-episcopate that emerges throughout key ecclesiastical centers in the empire.

What about the Petrine text? "In all this development," writes Hans Küng, "it is a remarkable fact that Matthew 16:18 f. in its complete wording is not quoted on a single occasion in all the Christian literature in the first few centuries." The first known use of the text was by Tertullian, the Latin Christian apologist-turned-Montanist, who in the early third century attacked a bishop (probably Agrippinus of Carthage) for exaggerating his authority based on an appeal to Matthew 16:18. The particularly striking aspect about this incident is that an appeal is made to Peter's authority but not to Rome. Christ gave Peter the keys of the kingdom and the power to bind and loose, but "this power is Peter's personally and, after that, it belongs to those who have the Spirit," not to those who lead a hierarchical church—whether at Rome or another prominent eccesiastical city (*On Purity* 21).[34]

The Petrine Text in the Third Century: Origen and Cyprian

In the middle of the third century, Origen wrote the first extant commentary on the Gospel of Matthew, in which he addressed the Petrine text. The most significant member of the Alexandrian school of exegesis, Origen was influenced by Platonism as mediated in Judaism by Philo and in Christianity by Clement of Alexandria. Just as in Plato's allegory of the cave the material world was a mere shadow of an ideal spiritual world, so Origen, in his approach to Scripture, considered the literal-historical meaning of the text as inferior to the truer spiritual meaning. For Origen, the allegorical method was not only an aid to faith but also a means to reconcile crudities (e.g., anthropomorphisms about God) and discrepancies in the Bible. He thus developed a scheme for interpreting biblical texts according to Paul's (and Plato's) threefold analysis of human personality: body, soul, and spirit (1 Thess. 5:23). Origen designated the bodily as the literal and inferior sense in Scripture, the soul as the moral sense, and the spiritual as the deepest, superior sense. This latter allegorical-mystical sense revealed the "unspeakable mysteries" of the truth, for all of Scripture had an underlying spiritual meaning, but not all of Scripture was to be understood in its historical-literal sense.[35]

When Origen turned to the Petrine text, Peter emerged not as a historical person but as an exemplar or a character type representing all Christians who should be rock solid in the faith. "For a rock," Origen wrote, "is every disciple of Christ of whom those drank who drank of the spiritual rock which followed them, and upon every such rock is built every word of the church." He noted that some people believed that the church was built on Peter, but then he asked, "What would you say about John the son of thunder or each one of the Apostles?" Not only are these early apostles rocklike, but "all bear the surname of 'rock' who are the imitators of Christ."[36] The word "rock," then, was interpreted both typologically and christologically.

Origen's exegesis of the Petrine text made a profound and lasting impact. His interpretation was adopted by Jerome and became the standard interpretation by Catholic exegetes through the medieval period and an accepted interpretation by Protestant exegetes into our own day. As we will observe, those who defended the interests of the papacy offered alternative interpretations of the Petrine text, but biblical commentators consistently reiterated Origen's allegorical or spiritual understanding of Scripture.

The first known appeal to the Petrine text as a buttress for papal primacy dates from the middle of the third century. In this citation, the claim to primacy was known only through those opposing it, namely, Cyprian of Carthage in North Africa and Firmilian of Caesarea in Cappadocia. Some introductory comments about Cyprian's appeal to Matthew 16:18 are in order. Cyprian (d. 258), the bishop of Carthage, championed the unity of the church and the role of the local bishop as a guarantor of that unity. In his letters he commented upon the Petrine text, offering varied meanings of "rock." Generally, he interpreted "rock" to mean Peter upon whom the church was founded, but on occasion he also interpreted it to mean bishops. In one letter, after citing Matthew 16:18, he wrote, "From this source [rock] flows the appointment of bishops and the organization of the Church, with bishop succeeding bishop down through the course of time, so that the Church is founded upon the bishops and every act of the Church is governed through these same appointed leaders" (*Ep.* 33.1.1). On another occasion he coined the phrase "chair of Peter" (*cathedra Petri*), but he applied it to the local situation and not Rome. In a well-known passage he noted that "God is one and Christ is one: there is one Church and one chair founded, by the Lord's authority, upon Peter" (*Ep.* 43.5.2).[37] For Cyprian, Peter symbolized the oneness of church organization, but he was not *the* special authority.

Cyprian's view was made even more forcefully in the *Unity of the Church*. Here he defended his own position as lawful bishop of Carthage as well as that of Cornelius, the bishop of Rome, who was pitted against the pretender bishop, Novatian. Ignoring the dispute about which of two extant versions of chapter 4 is truly Cyprian's (the wording of one has Protestant sympathizers, the other Catholic),[38] we might reduce Cyprian's thinking to the following: Rome's authority is special but not superior. Rome functions as a kind of primordial church, and the bishop of Rome stands in historical succession to Peter, but only in an honorific sense can the bishop of Rome claim primacy. If Peter is the rock, notes Cyprian, Paul's letter to the Ephesians (2:20) makes clear that all the apostles and prophets are the foundation of the church.

We encounter the Petrine text as proof for the prominence of the bishop of Rome used for the first time in the context of a bitter exchange between Cyprian and Pope Stephen. The issue that provoked these animosities involved rebaptizing heretics or schismatics. Should those who had followed Novatian and were subsequently baptized into his communion but regretted their decision and now sought entry into the orthodox Roman church be rebaptized? Cyprian, following the path of strict discipline and exclusivity, said yes; Stephen, preferring the path of flexibility and inclusiveness, said no. Firmilian, the Greek bishop from Caesarea, sided with Cyprian and attacked Stephen for his "appalling discourtesy" and "insulting arrogance," calling him one "who vaunts that he has succeeded to the occupancy of the chair of Peter" (Ep. 75.2.3, 75.3.1). No letter from Stephen survives, but Firmilian referred to Stephen as "a man who finds the location of his bishopric such a source of pride, who keeps insisting that he occupies the succession to Peter, upon whom the foundations of the Church were laid" (Ep. 75.17.1).[39] Ironically, the context of this first appeal of a Roman bishop to Peter's authority is one where the claim is denied. Cyprian and Firmilian defended the rule of the mono-episcopate but rejected the extension of that rule beyond a local or regional setting. Stephen's claims fell on deaf ears.

The Fourth Century: Conciliar Claims and Roman Counterclaims

A similar view of Rome's limited regional authority was expressed at the first ecumenical council held at Nicaea (325). Called by the emperor Constantine, whose actions would both benefit and challenge the church at Rome, the council went only so far as to recognize the authority of the bishop of Rome over churches in his area (Canon 6). The boundaries of that authority were not specified as they were for the bishops of Antioch and Alexandria. Obviously, a regional system of ecclesiastical leadership was affirmed, devoid of clear central authority. At the time of Constantine, then, when the fortunes of the church underwent a seismic shift, the bishop of Rome remained a regional leader. He—or, perhaps more accurately, the church in Rome—was accorded a special prestige, but in the words of the historian Geoffrey Barraclough, the bishop of Rome "was in no sense a pope and laid no claim to the position of pope."[40]

Throughout the empire, the Christian church remained an organization of episcopal churches, each characterized by its own special diverse customs and practices, comprising a loose network of churches, though increasingly modeled in its structures after the imperial government.

Not until the latter part of the fourth century is it possible to document clear theological claims to Roman primacy based on Peter. In fact, until this time what we know of the papacy in general is piecemeal and shrouded in legend. Beginning with Pope Damasus (366–84), however, and extending through Leo I (440–61), the doctrinal basis of papal primacy was established. Not unlike a few popes who succeeded him, Damasus attained the bishopric of Rome through intimidation, violence, and the murder of his rivals. Intrigue aside, Damasus was an able pope who advanced the papal claims. Throughout his tenure, he repressed heresy, referred to Rome as the "apostolic see" (or seat), and argued that the true test of a theological orthodoxy was the endorsement by the bishop of Rome.

Damasus reacted quickly against two decisions at the Council of Constantinople (381) that compromised Rome's prestige and limited her rule. The council (1) propounded that the patriarch of Constantinople was of first rank with the bishop of Rome "because Constantinople is New Rome" (Canon 3) and (2) also upheld the discipline of the Council of Nicaea that forbade a bishop to interfere in the affairs of another diocese (Canon 2). Pope Damasus responded by calling his own countercouncil in Rome the following year. There he announced that Rome was "the first see of the Apostle Peter" and staked his claim by citing the Petrine text as a theological justification for a universal Roman primacy. The council ruled that the authority of the church of Rome was based not on past councils (as was Constantinople's claim to authority) or past decrees. Rather, it was based on the words of Jesus, "Thou art Peter."[41] Moreover, the second and third ecclesiastical centers were Alexandria and Antioch because they also were founded by Peter. The church at Constantinople could make no such claim. In brief, Damasus became the first Roman bishop to articulate the doctrine of Petrine supremacy

The Fifth Century: From Spiritual Primacy to Jurisdictional Primacy

The popes who succeeded Damasus continued to reiterate the theme of the bishop of Rome as the successor to Peter. Innocent I (402–17) is often called the "first pope" because of his assertions of the primacy of the bishop of Rome. He contended that every Western church had its origins in Rome, beginning with Peter, and that if a church could not establish its Petrine origins, "it is necessary for them to follow what the Roman church observes." Robert Eno summarizes the consensus of thought from Damasus to Sixtus (432–40):

"Unity must be uniformity with Roman ways since Rome alone has always without deviation observed and preserved the apostolic tradition. There is no room for differences."[42]

In what context did the church of Rome flex its ecclesiastical muscle? At the very time when the bishops of Rome enlarged their claims, the Roman Empire was crumbling. By the mid–fifth century, Rome was troubled. Barbarians entered the empire, and imperial rule was practically nonexistent. Earlier in 410, Alaric the Goth sacked Rome—an incident symbolic of the "decline and fall" of the empire. In these tumultuous times, the bishops of Rome began to take on the role of civic organizer and defender, and by default they became sovereigns over not only the city of Rome but also outlying areas. In the process, they advanced claims to primacy over the whole church.

Leo the Great (440–61) epitomized these developments, for in a situation of imperial decline he articulated a theory of papal primacy that has remained in place to the present. As I have noted, with the capital transferred from Rome to Constantinople, the bishop of Rome increasingly competed for authority with leaders in the East, be they patriarchs or emperors. Closer to home in Italy, as government headquarters were moved first to Milan (286), then to Ravenna (402), the city of Rome sank to the level of a provincial outpost. Imperial decline was accompanied by ecclesiastical decline. Against these pressures, beginning with Leo, the popes of the fifth and sixth centuries reacted and in the process defined and asserted the doctrine of papal primacy. Their claims to primacy were not novel, but beginning with Leo I, we witness a stridency hitherto unknown in the bishops of Rome. Leo introduced ideas of juridical authority based on the Roman legal concept of succession and inheritance. "Skillfully building upon the foundations laid by his predecessors," writes Donald Grimes, "Leo sought to blend together into a cohesive ideology the Scriptural, legal, and theological themes they had proposed in support of the Roman primatial claims."[43]

Whenever Leo discussed the authority of the bishop of Rome, he cited the Petrine text, emphasizing that with Peter's confession and Christ's blessing, the Christian faith was built upon the solid rock of Peter, "chief of all the Apostles" (*Letter* 10.1). Leo stressed the idea that the apostles received their authority not from Christ but from Peter. So, too, popes received their power through Peter. Peter continued to "live" in the bishop of Rome in a mystical way, for he "more fully and effectually performs what is entrusted to him and carries out every part of his duty and charge in Him and with Him" (*Sermon* 3.3). Historically, all other bishops derived their authority—just like the apostles—from Christ through Peter: "And as that remains which Peter believed in Christ, so that remains which Christ instituted in Peter" (*Sermon* 3.2).[44]

Legally or judicially, the pope stood as a "vicar" (Leo was the first to use this title) or substitute for Peter, dependent on Peter with all of Peter's unique powers. Leo took for himself the old heathen title of the emperors, *pontifex maximus* (chief priest), emphasized the "rule" and "principality" of the bishop of Rome, and conceived of the church as a monarchy ruled by the pope acting on Peter's behalf. Peter was "the rock" on whom the Lord built his church. His successor had full power (*plentitudo potestasis*) over the church—its rule, its teaching, its judgments, and its laws. Thus the pope was Peter's successor in a mystical, historical, and legal sense. Accordingly, if the fullness of power in the church was accorded the bishop of Rome, then it followed that Rome was the head of all the churches.

How could Leo make such claims? Would Constantine have permitted such inflated expressions by a Roman bishop? Undoubtedly not. Pope Leo's assertions were tolerated because of the rapid decline of the empire. In the East, where doctrinal controversies raged over Nestorianism (the teaching that Jesus was two separate persons, one divine and one human) and Monophysitism (the teaching that Jesus had a divine nature but not a human one), there was at least one party willing to recognize Rome's hegemony, if only to gain an ally. Moreover, Emperor Valentinian III, in an edict issued in 445, recognized papal primacy in the West (though not binding on the East). Leo continued the Roman tradition as a defender of the orthodox faith when, in his famous "Tome," he condemned Eutyches and defined the permanent distinction of Christ's two natures in his one person. After his letter was rejected at the Council of Ephesus (449), he declared the meeting a sham (a "robber synod") and supported the calling of another council.

Two years later, at the Council of Chalcedon, "Leo's Tome" was approved with the acclamation "Peter has spoken thus through Leo." However, with papal representation absent, the council ratified Canon 28, which recognized Constantinople as a see equal to Rome in that both were imperial cities. The pope's claim to fullness of power was just that—a claim without teeth in the East. In response to the council's decision, Leo rescinded the canon. In his mind the council had rejected the divine right of Rome (though the council's intention is debatable) and based the authority of Rome on historical and political grounds alone. This incident, which Francis Dvornik calls "the first misunderstanding between the Church of the East and the Church of the West," turned on two different views of church organization.[45] On the one hand, the church in the East adopted the principle of adaptation or accommodation to the political divisions of the empire; hence, the recognition of Constantinople. On the other hand, the church in the West adopted the principle of apostolic and Petrine origin; hence the defense of Roman primacy.

In the West, not doctrinal but organizational chaos begged for the exertion of strong leadership. The confusion caused by encroaching Germanic tribes resulted in synodal collapse. Bishops who only twenty years earlier had resisted papal interference now turned to Rome for help and support, and indeed, the papacy came to the rescue. In 452, Leo saved Rome from immediate plunder when he dissuaded Attila the Hun from attacking the eternal city. Three years later he met Gaiseric the Vandal outside the walls of Rome, and though he could not keep him from looting the city, he at least persuaded him not to torch it and massacre its citizens.

At the end of the fifth century, Pope Gelasius (492–96), operating under similar circumstances as Leo but with even greater conviction, left no doubt as to who ultimately ruled the church. He declared that "the see of blessed Peter the Apostle has the right to unbind what has been bound by sentences of any pontiffs whatsoever, in that it has the right of judging the whole Church. Neither is it lawful for anyone to judge its judgment, seeing that the canons have willed that it may be appealed to from any part of the world, but that no one may be allowed to appeal from it." Capitalizing on the weakened condition of the Byzantine Empire and drawing support from Theodoric, king of the Ostrogoths and master of Italy, Gelasius denied to emperor Anastasius the right to intervene in religious affairs at his discretion. In his famous twelfth letter to Anastasius, Gelasius boldly announced the "two swords" or "two powers" theory. The theory recognized two divinely ordained powers in the world— "the sacred authority of the Popes and the royal power."[46] Of the two, however, the spiritual power—that is, the bishop of Rome—was ultimately supreme, for he had to give an account to God for the actions of civil rulers. Against the Eastern empire's backdrop of "caesaropapism," where the emperor assumed ecclesiastical authority, Gelasius argued "that bishops, not the secular power, should be responsible for the administration of the church." In formulating church dogma, discipline, and law, the church acted independently. Gelasius's theory was cited repeatedly in the future by popes and canonists not only to clarify the relationship between church and state but also to support the supremacy of the papacy.

Summary

By the end of the fifth century, the bishops of Rome envisioned themselves as heirs of St. Peter, endowed with his authority and charged with ruling over the church. In the West, this view was generally, though not uniformly, accepted, whereas in the East, it was generally, though not uniformly, rejected. The appeal to Matthew 16:18–19 as a proof-text supporting the preeminence of the bishop of Rome was a post facto assertion. Possibly, Pope Stephen cited it in the mid–third century, but the earliest confirmed use of the text by a pope was Damasus at the end of the fourth century. In addition, throughout the patristic era, no single, dominant exegetical interpretation of the Petrine text(s) prevailed. One nineteenth-century study calculated that forty-four church fathers interpreted "rock" as Peter's confession and only seventeen identified "rock" with Peter himself. Increasingly, however, the bishops of Rome claimed that the text applied specifically, if not uniquely, to their rule.

By the fifth century, the Petrine text was associated with two overlapping lines of ecclesiastical development. Innocent I asserted primacy in spiritual matters, and then Leo asserted jurisdictional primacy. The bishop of Rome was not merely a spiritual guide to be consulted for advice. He was also viewed as commissioned by Peter to rule over the church with jurisdictional power. The power to bind and loose was envisioned as the exclusive prerogative of the bishop of Rome. At the same time, however, the pope rarely interfered directly in the affairs of local dioceses. According to William La Due, "There is practically no evidence to indicate that he attempted as a matter of policy to control episcopal appointments or the selection of the clergy for other significant positions in the dioceses."[47] Rather, the pope functioned more or less as the final court of appeal, asserting his prerogative to rule in disputes of canon law and church practice.

The Petrine Text in the Medieval Period (500–1500)

The Latin West

I now take leave of specific developments in the papacy, not because they are irrelevant but because by the end of the fifth century, the theoretical foundations of papal primacy had been firmly established. The history of the papacy during the medieval period may be seen as an increasingly successful attempt (though at times flawed) by the papacy to extend its authority into northern Europe and to make good on its claims to spiritual and juridical primacy. Such claims were supported by forgeries (e.g., the Pseudo Isidorian Decretals, the Donation of Constantine), continued papal pronouncements and decretals, forceful popes, and, later in the period, a spate of canonical writings. However, only beginning in the eleventh century did the papacy truly become head of the Catholic Church. Whereas in the first millennium the actual exercise (not just assertions) of primacy appears in conjunction with ecumenical councils, the second millennium witnessed the exercise of primacy apart from ecumenical councils that had included both the East and the West.

Indeed, there occurred nothing less than a fundamental shift in paradigms. Throughout the first millennium, writes Harmann Pottmeyer, "popes understood themselves to be, first and foremost, witnesses to the apostolic and universal tradition of the church. Their universal pastoral function consisted in preserving this tradition and in restoring the inherited order of the church when it was violated." In the second millennium, however, the paradigm shifted from one of witness to actions taken to redefine the tradition. The "church discovered itself as an active subject shaping itself, its tradition, and its life."[48]

Where does Matthew 16:18 fit into this profound shift? Ironically, just as today scholarly and pontifical interpretations of the Petrine text diverge, so in the medieval period a similar divergence occurred. For a time, these interpretive approaches passed each other as two ships passing in the night. Until the mid–twelfth century, biblical commentators exegeted the text without reference to papal theory and generally seemed unaffected by the ideology of Leo the Great. In fact, most commentators seemed to have no idea that the Petrine text could refer to the pope. Working as expositors of the text rather than apologists for the papacy, medieval exegetes felt perfectly justified in interpreting *petra* as Christ, not as a literal reference to Peter. Not until under the influence of Pope Innocent III's fresh reading of the text in the thirteenth century did commentators begin to cite this text as an endorsement of papal primacy.

During the early period (ca. 650–950), commentators essentially reproduced the views of the fathers of the church. As Theodore Tahaney observes, "All biblical interpretation was characterized by universal and complete submission to the authority of the patristic past and a faithful reproduction of its ideas, conclusions, and even language." The preservation of knowledge, not its advancement, remained the priority. Jerome, indebted to Origen's exegetical approach, was the most influential commentator of the early medieval period. As we have seen, Origen emphasized the spiritual understanding of Scripture from which he extracted several meanings from the text. At times he interpreted Peter as a type—a representative figure of the true, spiritual Christian—whose confession extended to all Christians who affirmed the same. In this sense, all confessing Christians were "the rock." At other times, Origen interpreted "rock" christologically: Christ himself was the rock of the church. Bolstered by 1 Corinthians 3:11 ("Another foundation no man can lay except the one that is laid, which is Christ Jesus") and Jesus' parable in Matthew 7:24 (about building a firm house on the rock), Origen presented Christ as the rock upon whom the church is built.[49]

Just as Jerome followed in Origen's interpretive footsteps, so medieval commentators reproduced Jerome's views. Their spiritual reading of Scripture suggested multiple ways of reading the text (allegorically, typologically, anagogically), with little attention paid to the literal-historical interpretation. At the same time, as reform-minded popes, theologians (e.g., Thomas Aquinas), and especially canonists redefined the church, they offered an alternative exegesis of the text by reiterating and refining Leo's views. Pope Gregory VII (1073–95), for example, the bold champion of the "reform papacy" initiated earlier by Leo IX (1049–54), advanced a monarchical ("one body, one head") model of Petrine primacy. In his efforts to reform the papacy, end clerical corruption, and abolish the practice of lay investiture (laypeople making ecclesiastical appointments), Gregory proposed a new conception of the church, one where Christ gave to Peter and his successors royal power of universal jurisdiction over the church. "The pope as shepherd and witness to tradition . . . now became the pope . . . as supreme lawgiver and judge."[50] To bolster his claims, Gregory appealed to the Petrine texts and the fullness of power accorded the successor of St. Peter.

In similar fashion but with increasing zest, Innocent III (1198–1216), whose pontificate represents the zenith of the medieval papacy insofar as papal ideals matched reality, invoked the Petrine texts as referring to Peter and his successors, the bishops of Rome. He observed that Christ affirmed Peter's unique role as head over the church before his passion (Matt. 16:18–19), during his passion (Luke 21: 31–32), and following his resurrection (John 21:15–17). Continuing the theme of *plentitudo potestasis*, Innocent argued that Peter alone received the "fullness of power," and thus Peter alone and his successors—not only vicars of Peter but now, decisively, vicars of Christ—can forgive the sins of everyone. Since Peter received the keys first, it is through him, even from him, that all other clergy exercise the keys of the kingdom. The pope is no longer the first among equals but stands over the college of bishops and the church, representing Christ himself. In a rhetorical gambit—what Ernest Kantorowicz calls "monopolizing by exclusion"—Innocent claimed for the papal office what had earlier been extended to others. In Innocent, "the essentially-papal understanding of the role and power committed to Peter had finally been framed in categories which where dramatically defined centuries later in the constitution *Pastor Aeternus* of the First Vatican Council."[51] Indeed, Innocent and successive popes wed their vision of papal authority to the Petrine texts, and in turn the interpretation of these texts increasingly conformed to their vision.

Meanwhile, biblical exegetes, even those who supported the centralizing tendencies of the papacy, felt no compulsion to follow papalist interpretations. They reiterated the ancient view that the foundation of the church is Christ alone and that Peter's commissioning by Christ applied to the other apostles with him and, by extension, to their episcopal successors. The exclusive appeal to Peter's primacy continued to be mitigated by reference to Matthew 18:18. Some commentators, like Paschasius Radbertus in the ninth century, better known in history for supporting the "real presence" view of communion, equated *petra* with Christ. Others, such as Bruno of Segni (d. 1123), interpreted "rock" to mean the faith that Peter confessed. "Surprisingly," writes Christopher Ocker, "a papalist interpretation of this passage was new to biblical exegetes as late as the thirteenth century, even though popes had tirelessly used it to support their claims to power since late antiquity."[52]

In the fourteenth century, the Spanish Franciscan canonist Alvaro Pelayo (1280–1352), continued the tradition of multiple interpretations. He hewed to the pontifical line in suggesting that *petra* meant Peter but conceded that a truer, more spiritual meaning was Christ. So, too, Giles of Rome (d. 1316), general of the order of Augustinians and a supporter of papal supremacy, invoked the traditionalist reading of Matthew 16:18 ("rock" = Christ, not Peter), though he argued that among the apostles, Peter was closest to the rock. Another papalist of the fourteenth century, Hervaeus Natalis, in his effort to limit a pro-episcopal interpretation of the text (i.e., bishops, not the bishop of Rome, are the loci of authority), contended Christ's commission lacked authority because of its preresurrection utterance. The power of conferral occurred after the resurrection when Christ reinstated Peter (following his denial) with the instruction to feed his sheep (John 21:15–17).[53] Interestingly, Natalis's case would have been bolstered had he been aware of the conclusions of those modern scholars who place Christ's commission to Peter in Matthew 16 *after* the resurrection.

One way, and an increasingly standard way, to resolve multiple interpretations of a text such as Matthew 16:18 was to appeal to canonical authorities. To that end, a Bible concordance attributed to Jean of Nivelles, abbot of Joucels, provided a long list of canons following Matthew 16:18. He cited the history of the papacy from the Aaronic priesthood to Peter, the presence and martyrdoms of Peter and Paul in Rome as conferring primacy upon that see, Peter as the dispenser of sacramental authority, the sovereignty of papal jurisdiction over all other ecclesiastical courts, and so forth—the very claims made by committed papalists.[54]

Among the few known fourteenth-century papalist exegetes, John Baconthorpe's *Postilla* on Matthew proposed the standard allegorical reading of the Petrine text but then advanced a papalist alternative similar to Giles's interpretation: Christ is the rock but Peter the chief beneficiary of his authority. Moreover, the purity of the church resided in Peter, for Christ bestowed upon him the power of the keys that are exercised in three ways: the penitential key, the juridical key, and the key of discipline (excommunication and absolution). Baconthorpe's interpretation of Matthew 16:18 illustrates that, in the words of Christopher Ocker, "the biblical foundations of papalist theory would remain complex, because fourteenth-century commentators who were committed to the papal party were prone to adapt traditional (non-papalist) interpretations to their own ends. . . . They did not simply grab the old interpretation of the popes, that the 'rock' is Peter."[55]

The Greek East

In the Eastern church, even after the schism in 1054, Orthodox writers continued to reiterate the views of ancient writers, in part because some were unaware of the centralizing tendencies of Rome. That is, they affirmed the special authority of Rome in ecclesiastical affairs and reiterated their agreement with the Council of Chalcedon (451) that acclaimed Leo as the successor of Peter. Although these affirmations seemed to play into the hands of papalists, Orthodox commentators never understood this power as absolute. After all, in the East there were other "apostolic sees" (Jerusalem, Antioch) whose bishops could claim to be successors to Peter as well, though admittedly, the prestige of Rome, thanks to its status as capital and the presence of Paul and Peter, gave it a rank above the others.

According to John Meyendorff, up until the eleventh century Byzantine ecclesiastics and exegetes were unaware that the West was giving this claim a sharper, more focused direction toward papal primacy. When they finally grasped the magnitude of Rome's claims, they responded in a variety of ways, though they always made the distinction between the personal ministry of Peter and his succession. Meyendorff identifies two types of Byzantine documents that addressed the issue of Roman primacy: those that restated ancient views in recognition of Peter's faith and episcopal primacy, and those of a polemical bent that responded to Rome's papalist claims.[56] Both types of documents shared the position that the centralizing and interventionist policies of papacy signaled a departure from previous history.

A somewhat analogous development among exegetes and preachers took place in the East as among exegetes in the West. Whereas in the West, exegetes went their own interpretive way, either unaware of or reluctant to embrace a papalist reading of Matthew 16, so too in the East some exegetes ignored both the schism of 1054 and the increasingly strident claims of popes to primacy over the whole of Christendom and reaffirmed well-worn views. On the one hand, these commentators reiterated the popular patristic interpretation of "rock" as "faith." Simon became the rock (Peter) because of his rocklike faith in the divinity of Christ. Origen, the Cappadocians, Chrysostom, and Augustine affirmed that it was Peter's faith that made it possible for him to become the rock on which the church was founded. So, too, observed Theophanes Kerameus, a twelfth-century preacher, and Callistus I, patriarch of Constantinople in the fourteenth century, the keys were given not to one single person but to the faithful.[57]

At the same time, not just his faith alone but Peter himself was accorded a special place by Eastern exegetes. Photius, the ninth-century patriarch of Constantinople, basically restated the views of Cyprian in the West (whom he never read) and Gregory of Nyssa that "on Peter repose the foundations of the faith." "He is the coryphaeus of the Apostles," "the chief of the apostolic chair," "the rock of the church," and the "keybearer of the Kingdom of heaven." Throughout the fourteenth century, patriarchs and commentators echoed a similar refrain: "The great Church of Christ is built on Peter" (Peter, patriarch of Antioch); "He is indeed, blessed, Peter, the Rock on which Christ has established his Church" (Arsensius, thirteenth-century patriarch of Constantinople); and Peter is the "first of the Apostles" (Gregory of Palamas, the fourteenth-century theologian).[58] Despite these favorable views of Peter, no commentator endorsed a strict Roman ecclesiology. Peter is undeniably special, and there is a succession of Peter in the episcopal ministry; however, that succession is not limited to Rome but extends to all bishops.

As papalist interpretations (and actions) filtered into the East, they were increasingly countered by polemical retorts from Byzantine theologians and prelates in the twelfth and thirteenth centuries. Several polemicists resurrected Canon 28 of the Council of Chalcedon, and in a tit-for-tat logic followed the

"imperial" criterion of primacy. Now that the capital has moved to Constantinople, the privilege of primacy belongs to it. So asserted the metropolitan of
Ephesus, George Tornikes, in an 1155 letter to Pope Hadrian IV. Other Byzantine polemicists made a very un-Orthodox move (i.e., departing from tradition) by rejecting ancient assertions of Peter's primacy among the apostles and
emphasized that the same powers given to Peter were extended to the other
disciples. Still others accepted the personal role of Peter among the apostles
but denied his succession in Rome alone; Peter's and the other apostles' mission was worldwide, not restricted to a single geographic locale.

This latter view gained wider acceptance after Latin crusading armies captured Constantinople in 1204 and Pope Innocent III followed with the appointment of bishops to sees in the East and eventually installed a Latin patriarch
in Constantinople. Increasingly, Byzantine theologians made the distinction
between the apostles (of whom Peter is "first," "coryphaeus," and "rock") and
the episcopal ministry. The apostles ministered to the whole world, whereas
bishops minister in a local setting. Peter was not the bishop of Rome but a
teacher—in Rome, to be sure, but also elsewhere. When Jesus said to Peter,
"You are Peter and upon this rock I will build my church," he was not restricting "church" to Rome but to churches throughout the world. Roman primacy
came not from Peter but only from Rome's imperial status.[59]

Similar antipolemical arguments continued from theologians of the fourteenth and fifteenth centuries. Barlaam the Calabrian and Nilus Cabasilas emphasized that the primacy of Peter was not limited to Rome (though Rome has
primacy of honor, and thus the bishop of Rome is first among equals) but
extended to all those churches built on Peter's confession. The succession of
Peter, observed Symeon of Thessalonika, the fifteenth-century theologian and
liturgiologist, is the succession of the true faith, not the bishop of Rome. In
sum, Greek theologians from the eleventh through the fifteenth centuries reaffirmed the patristic view that the succession of Peter is dependent on the
confession of true faith. Rome erred in identifying the primacy of Peter with
a universal primate situated in Rome. Yes, Peter was "first," "coryphaeus," and
a "rock," but the bishop of every local church succeeds him, not the bishop of
Rome alone.[60]

The Petrine Text in the Sixteenth Century

Catholic Interpretations

One might think that in response to the Protestant Reformation, with its blistering attack on the papacy, Catholic commentators and theologians would
immediately come to the defense of the hierarchy by embracing the pontifical
reading of the Petrine text. Such was not the case. Given the tardy response

on the part of the Catholic hierarchy to answer the Protestant movement—the Council of Trent (1545–63) was not called until a generation of Protestant reform had passed—it should come as no surprise that the inherited practice of multiple readings of *petra* persisted. John Bigane suggests four readings of *petra* by Catholic exegetes during the sixteenth century: faith, Christ, Peter, and a plurality of interpretations. All reiterated previous views. Because the diversity of interpretations represents a combination of the other views, I will leave it aside and turn to the other three interpretations.

A number of commentators maintained the Origenist interpretation of rock as faith. Erasmus, for example, concluded that rock referred to the faith of Peter. An inveterate critic of a corrupt papacy, Erasmus rejected the equation of rock with Peter and the papacy. "I marvel," he noted, "that there are those who twist this passage to refer to the Roman pontiff."[61] Others ascribed alternative meanings to rock as faith. Rock could mean Peter's profession of faith, but it could also mean the faith of the entire church or any Christian who confessed that Jesus was the Son of God.

A second interpretation identified rock with Christ. Origen had proposed this view as well, although among the church fathers of the West, Augustine was its notable proponent. In the sixteenth century, John Major and Jacques Lefevre argued that the demonstrative pronoun "this" pointed to Christ the rock. Lefevre rejected any identification of Peter with rock because in the next breath Jesus called him Satan (Matt. 16:23).[62] How could one so unstable and undiscerning be the rock upon whom Christ would build his church? Moreover, the "keys" belonged not to Peter only but to all Christians. There was some overlap with the "rock as faith" interpretation inasmuch as Peter, in his confession, was speaking on behalf of all disciples.

The third interpretation, *petra* as Peter, was what Bigane calls "an exegetical novelty." Actually, this interpretation was not altogether new among biblical commentators, for in the tenth century, Odo of Cluny cited the three Petrine texts in recognition of Peter's superior status. But in the sixteenth century it was carried one step farther in the direction of Innocent III's interpretation and identified with the successors of Peter, the Roman pontiffs. As we have seen, it is one thing to identify *petra* as Peter but quite another to connect the bishops of Rome with Peter and a Petrine office. The learned Cardinal Cajetan, a loyal papist and interrogator of Luther, appealed to "the plain context of the literal sense" of the text and concluded that the rock was Peter *and* the continuing office and foundation within the church, namely, the papacy.[63]

Other Catholic partisans engaged the text in a more intellectually rigorous manner. As pressure mounted from Protestant opposition, exegetes such as Mathias Bredenbach in 1560 examined the philological origins of the Petrine text. Anticipating the findings of modern scholars, Bredenbach appealed to the text's Syrian origins and thus argued for an Aramaic substratum preceding

Matthew's Greek translation. He reasoned that the Greek variations of *kêpa* (the masculine *Petros*, and feminine *petra*) reflected grammatical suitability, not lack of identity.[64] Thus *petra* referred to the person of Peter.

By 1560 *petra* identified as Peter emerged as the near-unanimous Catholic interpretation. "From that date onwards," concludes Bigane, "almost all Roman Catholic exegetes understand the 'petra' of Mt. 16:18 to be Peter and sometimes also his successors the popes. . . . Anti-Luther feelings and a concern to protect Peter's governance of the church were operative in this shift."[65] In the next four centuries *petra*—understood to mean Peter and his successors, the Roman pontiffs—became the official teaching of the Catholic Church.

Protestant Interpretations: Martin Luther

If we set aside Luther's rhetorical bombast, his views may be seen as representative of the Protestant Reformers and, indeed, of those interpretations that prevailed among many Protestants until the 1950s. Throughout his career and increasingly so in later life, Luther excoriated the papacy as "a figment of human imagination and invention," "a blasphemous, accursed office," and so far removed from Christ that it was "anti-Christ." In characteristic polemic, Luther called the church "the papal hellish scum" and the pontiff the "ass-pope." "Moreover," he vented, "we may with a good conscience take his [the pope's] coat-of-arms, which features the keys and crown, to the privy, use it for wiping, and then throw it into the fire."[66] Not surprisingly, Luther desired to be remembered for his hatred of the papacy. His strong scatological antipapal invective was motivated largely by the conviction that the papacy had abandoned its pastoral duty of shepherding the people and feeding them with the word of God.[67] The papacy was not simply an a-biblical tradition but an unbiblical, postapostolic invention that led people away from Christ. A false tradition had besmirched the authority of the Bible, for in both word and action, the papacy contravened the plain teaching of Scripture.

Luther not only grounded his judgments upon *sola scriptura* but also developed a hermeneutic by which to understand the holy book. His approach, which I will take up more fully in chapter 4, was based on three principles. First, Scripture was above all a written revelation of God in Christ. Anything that detracted from Christ as the source of faith—for example, the accretions of tradition or the misinterpretation of the Petrine text—was anti-Christ. Second, as an exegete, Luther rejected the allure of allegory, that "beautiful harlot who fondles men in such a way that it is impossible not to be loved."[68] He urged the historical and literal meaning of Scripture, and along with other Reformers generally eschewed medieval allegorical and spiritual readings of the text. Third, he interpreted Scripture in light of other passages of Scripture.

Thus, Matthew 16:18–19 should not be viewed in isolation from other texts that referred to Peter (and the apostles) as "binding and loosing" or "the rock."

Throughout his many references to the papacy and the Petrine text—from the Leipzig debate (1519) to his treatise, "Against the Roman Papacy, An Institution of the Devil" (1545)—Luther followed this general hermeneutic. Indeed, the crucial exegetical text at the Leipzig debate with John Eck was the Petrine text, especially the interpretation of "rock." To support the papal reading of the text, Eck appealed to the weight of tradition, especially to the church fathers and other medieval authorities. How, he queried, could Luther challenge the wisdom of the past? By what right did Luther claim to understand Scripture better than the popes, councils, doctors, and universities? Luther responded by appealing to Scripture: "I should withstand them all alone by the authority of the apostle [Paul], that is, by divine right, as he writes (1 Cor. 3:11): 'No other foundation can anyone lay than that which is laid, which is Jesus Christ.'" Later in the debate Luther appealed to tradition by noting (as also noted here) that church authorities offered not one but multiple interpretations of "this rock." "Rock" referred not to the person of Peter (and his successors) but to faith. Upon the faith of his followers (the disciples, not Peter alone), Jesus Christ would build his church. Clearly, as Scott Hendrix suggests, Luther's exegesis conformed to his understanding of the nature of the church: "The church was not tied to any one person or place but extended as far as the circle of all believing Christians extended and was knit together by their faith in the word."[69]

By the same token, in "To the Christian Nobility of the German Nation" (1520), Luther argued that the "keys" were given not to Peter alone but to the whole community. Nor were they divinely ordained for juridical purposes but, as the natural meaning of the text implied, to the binding and loosing of sin. That same year, in "On the Papacy in Rome," he offered an extended commentary on Matthew 16:18, interpreting it in light of other Scripture. What was given to Peter in 16:18 was given to all the disciples in 18:18. Moreover, Peter's confession ("You are the Christ, the son of the living God") was not his alone; he was speaking for all the disciples. "Therefore, it is as clear as day here that all the apostles are equal in all power to Peter. . . . For St. Peter never selected, made, confirmed, sent, or ruled over an apostle."[70]

Given Luther's christological reading of the Bible it was natural for him to point beyond *petra* as faith to the source of that faith, Christ himself. This interpretation, as we have noted, and as Luther himself readily pointed out, was advocated by the church fathers, including Augustine, Cyprian, and John Chrysostom. The rock, wrote Luther, "is solely the Son of God, Jesus Christ, of whom the Scripture is full, and no one else." Did not Peter himself attest to the same in 1 Peter 2:4, where he referred to Christ as "the living stone" and (quoting Isaiah 28:16) as "the chief cornerstone" (v. 5)?[71]

Conclusion: "Nevertheless"

With Luther our discussion has come full circle. His reading of Matthew 16: 18–19 was not significantly challenged by Protestants until the rise of modern biblical scholarship in the nineteenth century, and even then most Protestant exegetes continued to affirm his interpretation. Only recently, as I have noted, has a scholarly consensus been reached regarding the text in general, and near unanimity (with some significant voices of dissent) has been reached in interpreting "this rock," namely, that it refers to Peter. Perhaps, then, the most appropriate way to conclude this discussion is to offer a summary, acknowledging that the Petrine text is bound up in a complex of related issues.

First, viewed historically, the Petrine text has been one of the most disputed and variously interpreted texts in biblical exegesis—among both biblical scholars and confessional traditions. Nevertheless, many Catholic, Orthodox, and Protestant biblical scholars now agree that the text neither proves nor disproves the doctrine of papal primacy. The text says nothing about Peter as the bishop of Rome, the idea of apostolic succession, or primatial power. Yet throughout the New Testament, Peter is depicted not only as a representative disciple but also as a unique disciple in his special relationship to Jesus and his special role in the Christian community. It should be noted, however, that some Protestant scholars, such as Oscar Cullmann, are convinced that the New Testament record is not neutral but excludes a Petrine office insofar as it applies to apostolic succession.[72]

Second, in a related way, Catholic scholars seek to make a distinction between dogmatic theology and biblical exegesis. One may construct a theological argument for papal primacy and still recognize that the Petrine texts do not unambiguously endorse apostolic succession or a Petrine office. Nevertheless, the hierarchy continues to appeal to the Petrine text(s) as warrant for papal primacy. The First Vatican Council, "relying upon the clear testimonies of Sacred Scripture," prior popes, and councils, invoked the Petrine texts to make the boldest statement ever about papal primacy. Nearly one hundred years later, under considerably different circumstances, the Second Vatican Council appealed to the Petrine texts, though with less emphasis on hierarchy and more on collegiality as it pertained to the pope and his relationship to other bishops.

Third, the historical record yields no appeal to Matthew 16:18–19 as a biblical proof-text for papal primacy until the mid–third century, and even then, it comes to us secondhand from Firmilian as a report of what Pope Stephen said. Nevertheless, this belated recognition of the text confirmed what already was in place: the church in Rome had emerged as the most important church in the West, and the bishop of Rome as its most important leader. At first regionally, then throughout the western portion of the Roman Empire and even occasionally from the East, churches looked to Rome to provide leadership in matters of spiritual guidance, jurisdictional authority, and doctrinal orthodoxy.

Fourth, beginning in the fifth century with the explicit statements of Pope Leo I, the bishops of Rome consistently invoked the Petrine text as proof positive that the bishop of Rome was the successor to Peter. And as his successor, he was given spiritual and jurisdictional power over Christians—even, in the words of the Council of Florence (1439) that were directed against Eastern claims and then reiterated at Vatican I—a "primacy over the whole world."[73] Such proof-texting, to be sure abetted by other arguments, has guided the papacy into the present. Nevertheless, throughout most of the history of the Christian church, Catholic biblical commentators interpreted the text (especially "this rock") in a variety of ways, the most popular being the Origen-Jerome interpretation. According to this typical or spiritual interpretation, "this rock" referred not to the person of Peter but to the faith of every disciple. Catholic exegetes, while loyal to the hierarchy, felt under no obligation to interpret "this rock" as a reference to the person of Peter or to extract from the text the establishment of the office of St. Peter and his successors. Not until the last half of the sixteenth century, after Protestants attacked both the institution of the papacy and the pontifical interpretation of the Petrine text, did the Catholic position solidify. Two centuries later, in an act of historical amnesia, the First Vatican Council argued that the pontifical interpretation "has always been understood by the Catholic Church" in this way.

Finally, while the debate over the "correct" interpretation of the Petrine text has considerably abated, the issue of papal primacy remains a sticking point in Catholic-Orthodox-Protestant dialogue. However muted or finessed, there is simply no way around the issue of authority. The chief obstacle to full communion between Orthodox and Catholics believers remains "the particular form of primacy among the churches exercised by the bishops of Rome." And this authoritative chasm remains just as (if not more) problematic between Protestants and Catholics. Nevertheless, such disagreements over the Petrine office must be viewed as an intramural debate *among Christians*. Protestants and Catholics *disagree*, but they disagree *in the faith*. At the same time, history demonstrates that these kinds of "family feuds" are often more hostile, bitter, and intractable than feuds where parties have little in common. As several observers noted in the early 1990s, short of charting a new theological terminology or a new theological direction for ecumenical discussion, there is probably no way to resolve the differences.[74]

Interestingly, however, a recent proposal aimed at addressing this impasse has come from the pope himself. Pope John Paul II's 1995 Encyclical Letter on Commitment to Ecumenism, *Ut unum sint* (That they may be one), calls for a papacy conceived more as a "service of love recognized by all concerned" than of domination. Bishop John Quinn places the document on a par with

Vatican II in its revolutionary implications insofar as "for the first time it is the Pope himself who raises and legitimizes the question of reform and change in the papal office in the Church." The issue thus turns back upon the Roman Catholic Church and the papacy itself. Indeed, the burr under the ecumenical saddle in Orthodox, Anglican, and Protestant dialogues with Catholics has not been the papacy per se but a certain kind of papacy. By Quinn's reckoning, any ecumenical breakthrough requires addressing two major problems: the papacy's centralization—how can Christian unity be reconciled with the continued expansion of centralization?—and fundamental reform of the large bureaucratic arm of the church, the Curia. Without addressing these internal issues, ecumenical dialogue remains hollow. To be sure, the successor of Peter has taken the initiative and proposed a new direction for ecumenical discussion.[75] But where it will lead—whether Catholic bishops will seize the moment and engage the issue of primacy and whether other Christian communions, after several decades of dialogue, will not abandon their efforts—remains to be seen.

3

"Let Him Kiss Me with the Kisses of His Mouth!"

Bernard and the Song of Songs

Let him kiss me with the kisses of
    his mouth!
For your love is better than wine,
your anointing oils are fragrant,
your name is perfume
    poured out;. . . .
Draw me after you, let us make
    haste.

—Song of Songs 1:2–4

The book is largely ignored today. In the distant past, Jewish sages warned that only those men above the age of thirty who had previously studied other books of the biblical canon should read it. Origen, the great patristic thinker of the third century, counseled those with carnal urges not to read it: "I advise and counsel everyone who is not rid of the vexations of flesh and blood and has not ceased to feel the passion of his bodily nature, to refrain completely from reading this little book." Gregory of Nyssa, the fourth-century theologian who inherited Origen's allegorical approach toward the book, threatened with hell anyone who interpreted this love poem literally. Bernard of Clairvaux, the twelfth-century abbot, insisted that his sermons on the book were appropriate only for spiritually mature monks, those with "well prepared ears and minds" who were "disciplined by persevering study."[1]

There is no other book in the Bible quite like the Song of Songs (also known as Canticles and the Song of Solomon). It lacks all major religious terms in the Old Testament vocabulary: divine names (the book makes no mention of Israel's God), words associated with worship, and basic theological terms such as evil, sin, grace, righteousness, justice, and covenant. It has little, if any, legal, ethical, or didactic content, and it tells nothing of Israel's sacred history. Unlike other love themes in biblical poetry—in the Psalms between humans and God, in the prophets between God and Israel—as the passage in the epigraph suggests, the Song is a secular love poem pulsating with erotic content.[2]

Open to the pages of this short book of 117 verses (in the Old Testament, only Ruth is shorter) traditionally ascribed to Solomon, and you will find frank expressions of heterosexual love. In this beautiful paean to love between man and woman, the young woman falls in love: "My beloved is mine and I am his" (2:16). "His desire is for me" (7:10). He lies nestled between her breasts: "My beloved is to me a bag of myrrh that lies between my breasts" (1:13). She expresses sexual longing and desire: "Draw me after you" (1:4). "Upon my bed at night I sought him whom my soul loves; I sought him, but found him not" (3:1). The young man extols the beauty of his betrothed's eyes, hair, teeth, lips, cheeks, neck, and breasts, concluding, "You are altogether beautiful, my love; there is no flaw in you. . . . You have ravished my heart. . . . How sweet is your love" (4:7, 9, 10). The lover cannot be found: "I opened to my beloved, but my beloved had turned and was gone. . . . I sought him, but did not find him; I called him, but he gave no answer" (5:6).

A wedding procession is described (3:6–11). The lovers give themselves to each other in sexual ecstasy (5:1) and lovemaking (7:12). The Song describes the full range of the emotions between lovers: possession and elusiveness, tears and ecstasy, presence and absence, wounding and forgiveness, dissolution and absorption. In the final chapter the maiden declares, "For love is strong as death, passion fierce as the grave" (8:6). The Song's dialogue and controlling images characterize ancient Egyptian love poetry: the garden, the banquet, the chamber, and the bed. Even in the twenty-first century, the Song's description of lovers' emotions and the setting for expressing love continue to resonate in modern ears. As one commentator observes, this erotic poem "has the power to transform lovers into people who are in tune with the mystery of the natural world, with the unique dignity of the human person, and with the distinctive features of mutual passion and commitment."[3]

In spite of its uniqueness as a biblical genre (or, as we shall see, because of it) and the misgivings of Origen, Gregory, and Bernard, the Song of Songs was the most frequently read and expounded book in the medieval monastery. Nearly one hundred extant commentaries survive from the sixth to fifteenth centuries, and the records of catalogs of biblical commentaries indicate far more. With the advent of print in the fifteenth century and the Protestant Reformation in the sixteenth, preoccupation with the Song of Songs showed no sign of abating. By one estimate more than five hundred commentaries on the Song of Songs had been written by 1700, a "prodigious" and "astounding" output.[4]

In the history of interpretation, writes Marvin Pope, "no composition of comparable size has provoked and inspired such a volume and variety of comment and interpretation as the biblical Song of Songs." Although one German scholar referred to its interpretive history as a theological *Raritätenkabinnet*— a "collection of curiosities"—two general approaches, allegorical and literal, have prevailed through the centuries. The allegorical is the older and predominant tradition in both Judaism and Christianity. According to this view, the Song depicts the deep love between God and his people, whether in Judaism as the mutual love between God and Israel or in Christianity as the love between Christ and the church or the individual soul.[5]

In word and hymn the allegorical view has persisted into our own time. In my King James Version of the Bible, the following chapter headings to the Song assume an allegorical method of interpretation: "The church's love unto Christ," "Christ awaketh the church," "Christ's love for the church," and "Calling of the Gentiles." Hymnody also sustained the allegorical view. As a youngster I learned the lyrics of "The Lily of the Valley," a popular gospel tune found in many an evangelical hymnal. The song clearly identifies the "lily of the valley" with Jesus, not the woman who describes herself in Song 2:1 as "a rose of Sharon, a lily of the valleys." Modern commentators conclude that the woman is not boasting of her stunning beauty; rather, she is modestly understating her attraction: she is one among many.[6] Yet in the gospel hymn the phrase "lily of the valley" refers to Jesus and to his unique attraction—"the fairest of ten thousand to my soul."[7]

Countering this popular sentiment in song, scholars since the nineteenth century affirmed a literal interpretation of the Song, and marriage counselors in recent times have endorsed the book as a guide to marriage (though it is by no means clear that the lovers are married) and sexual relations. When I informed a friend I was working on this chapter, he immediately lent me a book titled *Solomon on Sex: A Biblical Guide to Married Love.*[8]

So what is one to make of the Song of Songs? There is no certainty of authorship. The most commonly accepted view is the alleged authorship of Solomon, the presumed author of Proverbs and Ecclesiastes. It is not clear, however, that the Hebrew superscription in 1:1 ("The song of songs, which is Solomon's") attributes authorship to Solomon. It could also mean that the book is written to Solomon, concerns Solomon, or fits within the Solomonic/wisdom literary tradition. A number of recent scholars attribute authorship to a woman (after all, a woman's voice predominates in the story). In addition, although the book's acceptance into the canon of Scriptures is firmly supported in ancient Jewish and Christian traditions, the criteria for its inclusion are unclear. Some are convinced that without its allegorical reading, this love poem would have never been admitted into the canon. Precisely when it was canonized in Jewish and Christian Scriptures is uncertain, though by around 100 C.E. both traditions recognized its canonical value. Rabbi Akiba ben Joseph (d. 135 C.E.) defended its inclusion in the Hebrew canon by asserting, "The whole world is not worthy of the day the Song of Songs was given to Israel, for all of Scripture is holy, but the Song of Songs is the Holy of Holies."[9]

How and why did the Song reach such an exalted state in medieval Western Christianity, only for all practical purposes to disappear from the canon by modern times? How is it that medieval male monks, dedicated to lives of chastity and celibacy, found in the erotic poetry of the Song of Songs a natural outlet for their spiritual aspirations? Why did Bernard of Clairvaux and before him a long train of commentators propose that of all the great canticles in Hebrew and Christian Scriptures, this song "stands at a point where all the others culminate"—as the superlative in its title suggests Song *of Songs*? The briefest, single-word answer to be explored throughout this chapter is "allegory." To cite the argument of one scholar, "I submit that the Song of Songs was so popular partly because it provided an extraordinarily rich ground for the elaboration of allegory, and therefore provided an unparalleled opportunity for finding the truth hidden beneath the figures of the text." When tilled and cultivated, the "rich ground" of the Song yielded a variety of spiritual interpretations whose harvest was unmatched by any other song in Scripture.[10]

The history of the interpretation of the Song of Songs provides an instructive lesson in the theological presuppositions and cultural assumptions that all interpreters bring to their task. Rather than focus on a single verse or passage (though 1:2 is given significant attention), as in previous chapters, this chapter examines the varied interpretive approaches taken toward an entire book. It is not exhaustive but is limited to representative and/or influential commentaries.[11] The specific focus is on Bernard of Clairvaux, the twelfth-century Cistercian abbot whose "sensuously personal engagement" in his *Sermons on the Song of Songs* ranks among the great masterpieces of Christian mysticism and Latin literary expression.[12] Working within an inherited allegorical interpretive tradition but in a highly personal manner, Bernard associated the Song of Songs with the love between God and the individual soul. His *Sermons* and other works (e.g., *The Steps of Humility and Pride, On the Necessity of Loving God,* and *Five Books on Consideration*) not only exerted a profound influence in his own time but also wielded a continuing influence in subsequent centuries.

I begin with the literary influences on Bernard, returning to the ancient church fathers, particularly Origen, whose *Commentary on the Song of Songs* was not the first but was the most influential Christian commentary from late antiquity to the twelfth century. Championed by Origen, the allegorical approach shaped the medieval commentary tradition and reigned as the interpretive paradigm in Western Christianity for fifteen hundred years, though to be sure, the very nature of allegory permitted radically different interpretations. In the medieval period, the quintessential expression of an allegorical reading of the Song is found in Bernard, who had direct access to Origen's *Commentary* and, like many medieval exegetes, "unwittingly depended upon Origen's vision of the Song of Songs."[13] I thus examine Bernard's *Sermons on the Song of Songs*, placing this work within the particulars of Bernard's life, his view of Scripture, and the monastic milieu in which it was written. Finally, I consider briefly the history of interpretation of the Songs from the Reformation to the beginning of modern historical-critical study in the late eighteenth century and into our own time. Although the range of modern interpretations is less speculative and fanciful than previous allegorical interpretations, multiple theories have been advanced to explain the Song's origins and content.

Literary Antecedents of Bernard's *Sermons on the Song of Songs*

How is it that a book filled with erotic imagery could express profound spiritual mysteries? Influenced by Platonic allegorizing, the necessity of interpreting the Old Testament in light of Christ's coming, and New Testament imagery of the church as the bride of Christ (see esp. Eph. 5:23–32), Christian exegetes of late antiquity expunged the sensual from the Song of Songs in favor of a spiritual, christological interpretation. The same cultural forces that we saw in chapter 1 contributing to the rise of monasticism figured into the application of a particular allegorical interpretation to the Song of Songs: an ascetic milieu that devalued the body and uplifted the spirit.

Modern interpreters of the Song find in Freudian psychoanalytic theory or in avant-garde "queer theory" compelling explanations for the popularity of allegory. In his 1977 commentary, Marvin Pope proposed that allegorizing the Song provided the means for repressing sexual appetites within an increasingly ascetically driven culture. He maintained that

> from the early days of the Church, Solomon's salacious Song, which at first blush tended to appeal to the pernicious pruriency of men, women, and children, had to be interpreted in a way that would eliminate the evil impulse and transform and spiritualize carnal desire into praise of virginity and celibacy and sexless passion of the human soul and/or the Church for God, and of God's response in kind. This was accomplished by means of the allegorical interpretation. . . . Celibate Christian theologians were thus able by allegory to unsex the Sublime Song and make it a hymn of spiritual and mystical love without carnal taint.[14]

In a recent article, Stephen Moore employs the categories of queer theory to analyze the Song's attraction to medieval monks. Among other things, queer theory insists that all sexual behaviors are social constructs, not something determined by biology or judged by eternally fixed standards of truth and morality. Moore suggests that allegorical readings of the Song are not only expressions of sexual repression but also "discourses of sexual *expression*—and of deviant sexual expression, at that." Allegorizing the Song not only spiritualized an erotic heterosexual relationship but also "had the effect of turning it into something still more unthinkable ... the expression of an erotically charged relationship between two male parties instead." After all, it is the male monk (who viewed himself as the bride in the Song) who is possessed (embraced, kissed, ravished, and so forth) by the bridegroom (Christ or God). The allegorical interpretation—no longer merely spiritual but subversive—thus becomes the ecclesiastically approved arena for a normally forbidden homoeroticism. Though unconscious of this tendency, commentators could not mask what they so valiantly tried to repress in their repudiation of the flesh. "Allegorical exposition of the Song thereby replicates the deadly struggle of male celibacy itself. What must be overcome in either instance is the sexual, the sensual, the fleshly, the female." No wonder the Song received so much attention from monks. "It is the book of professional celibates, past masters of repression and sublimation."[15]

In response to such claims of monastic sexual repression or displacement of sexual energies, Denys Turner observes that most monks seemed happy and well adjusted. The monk was fully aware, not ignorant (a precondition of the Freudian notion of "repression") of his sublimation of sexual desire: "He *knows* what he is doing, he *intentionally* denies to himself a genital outlet for his sexuality and *deliberately* transfers his sexual energies upon a spiritual object." Turner and more recently Tod Linafelt argue that other forces were at work among monks. An inherited language of Neoplatonic eroticism combined with their own preoccupation with a biblical and eschatological theology resulted in a particular allegorical reading of the Song. Similarly, Carey Ellen Walsh views allegorical interpretation (particularly in the case of Bernard) as "a heuristic and adroit appropriation of the Song's sexual imagery for understanding the devotional life." In a culture that pitted spirit against flesh, the allegorical sense "simply proposed that the spirit was a more likely site for biblical meaning than was the body."[16]

In his 1990 commentary, Roland Murphy contends that well over a millennium of allegorical interpretation "cannot be adequately explained as an exercise in pathological rejection of human sexuality." He avers that "allegory served a much broader purpose. . . . It facilitated the construction of a Christian worldview, providing the intellectual mechanism to effect a synthesis between Old Testament witnesses to God's providential love for humankind and what was confessed to be the preeminent display of that love in the Christ event." Indeed, commentators in the patristic and medieval eras interpreted the Old Testament not as the history of Israel but as the history of the church that began with Israel. The Old and New Testaments were not two distinct books but two epochs or times, the Old anticipating in an imperfect and incomplete way the perfect and complete salvation realized in the New. As Augustine noted, "The New Testament is hidden in the Old. The Old Testament is manifested in the New." Allegory and other figurative meanings supplied the interpretive bridge linking the Old Testament to the New.[17]

Origen

In earlier chapters, we observed Origen's profound influence on the history of biblical interpretation through his exploitation of the allegorical method. At once a brilliant scholar, Christian philosopher and apologist, popular and powerful preacher, ascetic and martyr, Origen established a catechetical and then a more advanced school of learning in Alexandria (c. 204–30) before continuing similar activities in Caesarea (230–50). Origen was the first to expound a theory of biblical interpretation, and his *Commentary on the Song of Songs*, written from 240 to 245, displays his exegetical virtuosity. He was not the first commentator on the Song of Songs (there are extant fragments of what are probably Easter homilies by Hippolytus [d. 235] of Rome), but it was Origen who exercised the greatest influence on subsequent interpreters. R. P. Lawson notes that Origen's *Commentary*, with its emphasis on a God-given power to ascend to God and join him in a union of love, is "the first great work of Christian mysticism."[18] Although Origen's ten-volume Greek text is lost and we have only three books of his *Commentary* (ending with 2:15) and two homilies on the Song of Songs, these writings exerted a pervasive influence in medieval Europe through Latin translations preserved by Rufinus and Jerome.

Origen's overarching exegetical principle is guided by his doctrine of the soul and its striving toward perfection. Working within the Platonic framework of correspondences and yet grounding such speculation in Scripture and the traditional rule of faith that clarified their basic meaning, Origen affirmed that earthly things are copies of divine realities. "All things visible have some invisible likeness and pattern."[19] Spiritual realities lie behind temporary or corruptible material realities. Human love finds its true analogue in divine love, the source of love. A God who is love created humans who are made in the likeness and *after* the image of God and who seek to share that love. However, Adam's fall into sin tarnished that image, necessitating redemption—the process of restoration whereby the soul returns to its divine source. This process, thwarted by temptation and sin, requires resistance and renunciation of the world, penance and good works, and healing and training of the spiritual faculties. The end result is perfection—a return of the soul's original form of existence to participation in its divine source.

Origen applied these underlying theological and philosophical principles to his *Commentary on the Song of Songs*. As Rowan Greer remarks, "His hermeneutical principle is really nothing more than his theological view." In the prologue of his commentary, Origen states that each human consists of two persons: an inner (the invisible, spiritual soul) and an outer (the visible, corporeal, material, earthly body). In earthly existence these two are conjoined, though their essential characters remain distinct. Scripture observes this distinction by using homonyms or identical terms to describe either person, as when, for example, the term "child" or "babe" is used to describe the spiritually immature. People of the "simpler sort" or those who live by the flesh are incapable of distinguishing between the inner and outer person and so misunderstand the Song of Songs. That is why the Song poses such a severe problem for immature believers: they cannot get beyond the carnal and mistakenly focus on human rather than spiritual love. Just as the material body retards the growth of the soul, so eros (carnal love) veils the meaning of the text. The mature, those whose lives are purified of the lust of the flesh and who depend upon the presence of the Holy Spirit in illuminating the deeper meaning of Scripture, understand that the Song contains hidden meaning that refers to "the love of the Bride for her celestial Bridegroom—that is, of the perfect soul for the Word of God."[20]

Origen's goal, then, was to demonstrate the progress of the soul's enlightenment to the divine mysteries in conformity to the perfect church. One of the standard modern criticisms of Origen has been that his allegorizing led to highly imaginative and arbitrary reading of the text—to the point that he extracted anything from the text that struck his fancy. To be sure, Origen chafed at those passages of Scripture that seemed inconsistent with the nature of God or that apparently advocated immoral behavior. For example, Genesis 20 relates the story of Abraham's lying to Abimelech, informing him that Sarah his wife was his sister, so as to protect himself. According to Origen, the Holy Spirit purposed to "envelop and hide secret mysteries in ordinary words under the pretext of a narrative of some kind and an account of visible things."[21] When properly discerned and allegorized under the guidance of the Spirit, the account indicated the following: Sarah symbolized the virtue of the soul, and Abraham called her his sister because he wanted to share her, not keep her to himself as he would his wife.

However much Origin was given to occasional capricious interpretations of Scripture, Karen Torjesen and others have shown that his commentary and homilies on the Song of Songs follow a clear pattern, attentive to the text, and in conformity with church teaching.[22] Arbitrary or subjective interpretations were held in check by both the text's literary character and Origen's fidelity to church doctrine. According to Origen, notes Torjesen, "The allegorical meaning is itself to be found within the historical sense of the text." In his prologue to the commentary, Origen announces, "It seems to me that this little book is an epithalamium, that is to say, a marriage-song, which Solomon wrote in the form of a drama and sang under the figure of the Bride, about to wed and burning with heavenly love toward her Bridegroom, who is the Word of God."[23] Origen understands the genre of the Song as a drama with various scenes and featuring the characters of bride, bridegroom, maidens, and friends of the bridegroom.

But one must pursue the story's inner, hidden meaning. Torjesen contends that Origen follows an integrated five-step exegetical scheme.[24] Consider the opening verse. Origen begins by reproducing the words of Scripture, "Let him kiss me with the kisses of his mouth" (1:2). Second, he reminds the reader that the Song is a drama or "simple story." The bride appears onstage; her bridegroom has sent gifts for a dowry, but he is not with her. She longs for his love and kisses, and so prays to God, "Let him kiss me." With the plain meaning at hand, one must now pursue a twofold allegorical or "inner meaning"— the ecclesiastical and psychological.

Thus in the third step Origen views the text in the context of the church or "the whole assembly of saints." The bride is the church, accompanied with the dowry of the law and the prophets, who longs for the direct kisses of the coming Christ (Logos). "The kisses are Christ's, which He bestowed on His Church when at His coming, being present in the flesh, He in His own person spoke to her the words of faith and love and peace." Fourth, the words and setting are reinterpreted psychologically, to apply to the soul "whose only desire is to be united to the Word of God and to be in fellowship with Him, and to enter into the mysteries of His wisdom and knowledge as into the chambers of the heavenly Bridegroom." Christ has already bestowed the gifts of the dowry: natural law, reason, and free will. But since these gifts do not satisfy the soul's desire and love, "let her pray that her pure and virginal mind may be enlightened by the illumination and the visitation of the [direct kisses of the] Word of God Himself." Fifth, what was applied to the individual soul is now urged upon all.[25]

Throughout his commentary Origen follows this systematic interpretation, moving from the story of human lovers to the deeper, hidden meaning of the text. Concludes Torjesen, "The dramatic situation is extrapolated from the words of the text, the teachings on the church are drawn from the details of the dramatic situation, the church is the model for the soul, and the soul is the model for the reader. . . . It is the soul that is moved and incited by participating in the marriage song of the church and Christ." For Origen, the allegorical conveys the true meaning of Scripture, whereas the literal is the most basic and inferior interpretation, intended for simple believers who cannot apprehend the meaning of metaphors, parables, and allegories. His exegesis is motivated by pastoral concerns, theological relevance, and as Elizabeth Clark proposes, a contextual relevance aimed at uniting Jews and Gentiles in the church at Caesarea. At the same time, his loftier goal, communicated in both an affective and an intellectual tone, is to inspire in his readers the sublime vision of the Song, namely, the soul's journey into communion with God. Indeed, later interpreters such as Bernard were more interested in the "transportable" theme of the individual soul's relation to Christ than in immediate ecclesiastical or theological concerns, though to be sure such concerns surfaced in a recontextualized form.[26]

The Latin Fathers

In the fourth and fifth centuries, theological giants such as Ambrose, Jerome, and Augustine as well as lesser-known church authorities worked within the Origenist framework. They continued to apply the Song in both a personal and an ecclesiastical sense and yet interpreted it to meet the preoccupations and challenges of their own day. Although none in this trio of church fathers wrote commentaries on the Canticle, each relied on this source—Ambrose profusely. In his interpretation of the Old Testament, the bishop of Milan "took the Song of Songs as the center of his hermeneutics."[27]

Latin writers expanded on Origen's contribution in four major ways.[28] First, Ambrose and Jerome relied upon the Song in support of the emerging ideal of virginity. "Ambrose," notes Bernard McGinn, "is the first in the West to apply the language of the Song directly to the life of female virgins."[29] The bishop's ascetic treatises (*On Virgins, On Virginity*) are filled with references to the Song of Songs. He is especially fond of 4:12 and advises the virgin to remain "enclosed" and "sealed" so that she "preserves her fruit."[30] In Jerome's famous Letter 22 to the young virgin Eustochium, he cites the Song more than twenty-five times as he offers incentives and instructions for a life of chastity and seclusion.[31]

Second, with this emphasis on virginity, perhaps it was only a matter of time before the Song was applied to Mary. Ambrose became the first in a long line of interpreters extending through the Middle Ages to give the Song a mariological interpretation, though his references are more allusive than expansive, more a continuation of praise for virginity than developed mariological motifs. For Ambrose, Mary becomes the virgin of 4:12, whose womb remained "enclosed and sealed" during the birth of Jesus (*in partu*), thus ensuring Jesus' sinless state.

Third, Jean Danielou has shown how the church fathers, Ambrose in the West and Cyril of Jerusalem in the East, invoked the Song in baptismal rites of initiation. Ambrose was particularly fond of 4:2: "Thy teeth are as flocks of sheep, that are shorn, that come up from the washing." So the church (the flock) through baptism contains those who have "put off their sins and been joined to her." Similarly, in his *Procatechesis*, Cyril repeatedly quoted 5:3 ("I have put off my garment; how shall I put it on again?") in reference to the stripping off of old garments by baptismal initiates.[32]

Fourth, later patristic writers invoked the Song to defend church doctrine promulgated in the years between the great Councils of Nicaea (325) and Chalcedon (451). In particular, two heretical movements, Arianism and Donatism, motivated new ecclesiastical interpretations of the Song. One of the most popular texts (and one of the most problematic from a modern critical perspective) cited against heretics was 2:15, "Catch us the foxes, the little foxes, that ruin our vineyards."[33] To Gregory (d. after 392), the orthodox bishop of Elvira near Granada in southern Spain, those "little foxes" were Arians (those who denied the divinity of Jesus) who destroyed the theological purity of the church.[34]

Appeals to the Song cut both ways. Schismatic Donatists and their vigorous opponent, Augustine, invoked the text to defend their respective views. A fourth-century North African resistance group that challenged church authority and defined the church as a separated body of pure and holy saints, the Donatists envisioned the church as an "enclosed garden and a sealed fountain" (Song 4:12). No gross sinner, especially those who collaborated with pagan government authorities during persecution and handed over the Scriptures to be burned, could be a part of the church. Augustine countered this view of the church with a more realistic one and cited Song 2:2 ("lily among brambles") to support his case. The church is a mix of good and bad, saints and sinners. And yet the true identity of the church exists independently of the spiritual state of its members, for its survival depends on the objective promises of God and the objective efficacy of the sacraments. Indeed, the "enclosed garden and sealed fountain" excluded sinners, but such terms referred to the church known only to God (the invisible church) and not to humans (the visible church).[35]

By the end of the fifth century, Origen's spiritual reading of the Song had become the established tradition in the West, though as we have just seen, depending on the circumstances, this spiritual reading could inspire a variety of interpretations. A singular exception to the triumph of allegory was the literal interpretation advanced by Theodore of Mopsuestia, bishop of Cilicia (392–428) and a member of the so-called Antiochene school of historical-literal exegesis. He considered the Song useless—not because he believed the literal sense was its true meaning but because it was never read publicly among Jews or Christians.[36] And yet because Theodore concluded the Song was nothing more than a love poem, his legacy suffered the ignominious fate of posthumous condemnation at the Second Council of Constantinople in 553.

Variations and Innovations on an Allegorical Theme

Apart from Theodore's view, the history of interpretation from the fifth to the eleventh century amounts to little more than a reiteration of themes already mentioned. To be sure, there are shifts and new accents. The widespread acceptance of John Cassian's fourfold sense of Scripture expanded Origen's threefold sense to provide one more allegorical lens by which to illumine the meaning of Scripture. And as the ecclesiastical context changed, so interpretation of the Song was accommodated to fit a new context of heightened ecclesiastical politics. For example, the eleventh-century investiture controversy

that pitted reform-minded popes against rulers who insisted on making ecclesiastical appointments (i.e., investing ecclesiastics with the ring and staff of the
church) prompted revision of the notion of the church as the bride of Christ.
Commentaries on the Song by advocates of reform such as Bruno of Segni,
John of Mantua, and Robert of Tombelaine depicted the bride not in general
ecclesiastical terms as belonging to Christ but as married to reform-minded
popes. Ann Astell points out that the bride of the Song became "the contemporary church embroiled in the investiture controversy, the faithful Virgin-
Bride whose loyalty to Christ and his vicar, Gregory VII, exposes her to the
persecution of Henry IV." In his commentary, Bruno (d. 1123) imitated the
dialogic and lyrical structure of the Song to depict the bride's courageous,
virginal resistance to the false bridegroom, whether in the form of philosophers, heretics, or tyrants such as Henry IV, who imprisoned Bruno in 1082
for his stubborn resistance to lay investiture practices.[37]

Another zealous advocate of reform, the Benedictine Rupert of Deutz (d.
1129), a near contemporary of Bernard, personified the bride to refer to the
Virgin Mary. The most prolific author of the twelfth century and one of the
most creative in his interpretation of the Song, Rupert intended, as he put it,
"to add a little something" to the contributions of previous exegetes.[38] That
"little something" was the first Marian interpretation of the entire Song. As we
have seen, previous commentators extracted notions of virginity and referred
to Mary in a handful of texts, but no one until Rupert made Mary the central
figure of the whole Song, who throughout the book dialogues with her Son,
the "bridegroom."

Developments in liturgy prepared the way for Rupert's mariological exposition, as they did for a general heightened exegetical interest in the Song.
"In the history of western Christian interpretation," observes Ann Matter, "use
of the Song of Songs in praise of the Virgin is a precursor, and to some extent
a determinant, of a tradition of exegesis in the mariological mode."[39] As early
as the seventh century, liturgies for the feast of the Nativity of the Virgin, the
Assumption of Mary, and the Purification of the Virgin Mary included portions
from the Song. During the month of August, monks read the book during the
night office. In the ninth century, the Carolingian church expanded these liturgies, especially the liturgy of Assumption. From these liturgical settings, the
Song received increased exegetical attention, though not until the twelfth century was the liturgical use of Mary in the Song integrated into the formal
commentary tradition.

According to Rachel Fulton, a half dozen commentators in the twelfth
century, including Rupert, identified the bride of the Song with Mary and the
beloved with her son, Jesus. These Marian commentators—all monks who
espoused themselves to Mary as spiritual husbands—offered an innovative
reading of the Song. No mere recyclers of allegory and tropology, they argued

that the Song literally, or "historically," recorded the life of Mary and Jesus. Recall that previous interpretations from Origen on had designated the Song's bride as either the church (an allegorical reading) or the soul (a tropological reading), and the bridegroom (in both readings) as Christ. Moderns, of course, would classify the Marian understanding of the Song as another level of allegory, but to these twelfth-century commentators, the Marian reading is "historical" because it "really" tells the story of the relationship between Christ and his mother. Although the Gospels tell us little about Mary and her relationship to Jesus, the Song reveals that relationship in intimacy and depth. "By reading the Song 'historically,'" notes Fulton, "the exegetes were able to hear the voices they so longed to hear, the voices of Mary and Christ." They "appropriated the Song's verbal sensuality as the ideal vehicle for the mimetic re-creation of the events of evangelical history."[40]

For example, according to Rupert the "historical" sense of the Song meant the events in the Gospels that referred to Mary as the mother of God. "This he justified," writes John Van Engen, "on the grounds that just as all Scripture tends toward Christ the Word, so also all prophecy converges upon Mary, the bearer of that Word."[41] Thus Rupert found in nearly every verse in the Song a corresponding verse in the New Testament (primarily the Gospel of Luke). So "Let him kiss me with the kisses of his mouth" (1:2) prophesied and corresponded to the Annunciation in Luke 1:26–38, where the angel Gabriel "kisses" Mary with the words "Greetings, favored one! The Lord is with you" (v. 28). The "historical" exemplary Mary fulfilled the prophecy of the Song in her own life and encouraged others to do the same. With this Marian reading of the entire Song, Rupert supplied "the form classic to the commentary genre." Indeed, with Rupert and other Marian commentators, "the categories of the 'real' shifted in the twelfth century from the 'allegorical' to the 'historical,' from devotion to the Virgin as the Throne of Wisdom to devotion to Mary as the loving and suffering, quintessentially *human* and *historical* mother of Jesus."[42]

I note one other emphasis in the history of the Song's interpretation between the sixth and eleventh centuries, one that remained secondary to the ecclesiastical interpretation but that anticipated and informed Bernard's approach to the Song. In addition to equating the young female lover in the Song with the bride of Christ (i.e., the church) and the Virgin Mary, monastic commentators during these six centuries continued the Origenist tradition of identifying the bride-bridegroom relationship as the individual soul's relationship to God. At first glance, the identification of the female bride with a male monk seems incongruous, if not a total wrenching of the Song's context. Allegory, of course, lifted contextual restraints, but gendered language also eased this transition. Greek, Latin, and Spanish render the word for soul as a feminine noun (*psyche, anima, alma*) and hence posed no linguistic barrier to equating the bride with soul—or, more naturally, as we have just seen, with an idealized version of the Virgin Mary. The same holds true for the relationship between the bride and church, for in Greek, Latin, and Spanish "church" is a feminine noun as well.

Whereas Origen emphasized the soul's perfection as a form of knowledge (Grk., *gnosis*) of God, the Western monastic tradition, with a greater awareness of the intractability of human corruption, depicted the soul's perfection as an issue of the heart. Love and desire (*affectus*) took precedence over intellectual enlightenment (*ratio*). Ascent to God was possible, but not without first understanding the descent of God in the flesh and his death on a cross in order to repair the damage of human sin. Whereas the Greek Origen interpreted the Christian life as "an unequivocal 'ascent,'" the Latin monastic tradition emphasized the sin-strewn, moral barriers to the path of perfection.[43] Perfection remained the goal with the admission that one lived in the "now but not yet": a degree of perfection could be attained in this life, but only fully consummated in the next. The Song of Songs, with its erotic imagery of yearning and desire, provided a vivid picture of the soul's "now but not yet" condition, its contemplative state of desire and anticipated rest in the love of God.

One of the first Western monks to interpret the Song as the soul's yearning for God was the Benedictine pope Gregory I (590–604), "father of the medieval papacy." All that survived of his commentary in medieval Europe were two homilies exegeting 1:1–8, and yet his work exerted a profound influence. Gregory's brief commentary became the primary reference of later exegetes, due in part to his stature as model pope, but more so because of the originality of his work.[44]

Unlike Origen, who considered the literal (historical or narrative) significance of the Song, Gregory directly engages its spiritual meaning, which is "hidden under the cover of the letter." One must seek the interior or allegorical meaning of the Song through the exterior word: though it speaks of the body and its physical delights, one must "be taken, as it were, out of the body." God condescends to use "the language of our shameful loves in order to set our hearts on fire with a holy love." This sublime Song, then, "is the song of union with God which is sung by the Bridegroom and Bride at their wedding."[45]

Moreover, the Song speaks not only to the church but also directly and personally to Gregory the monk. The kiss of 1:2, for example, refers not only to the church's desire for the coming of Jesus but also to the individual's desire for and recognition of unworthiness before God. The kiss upon the soul reflects the monastic virtue of compunction—a pain of the spirit whose cause is both the awareness of sin and the desire for God.[46]

In the centuries to follow, other commentators followed Gregory's lead of monastic idealism as the hermeneutical key to interpreting the Song of Songs. Of special note is Haimo of Auxerre, the ninth-century abbot who wrote "the most popular Song of Song commentary of the Middle Ages." Distinguished by its immediacy and personal tone, his commentary prepared the soil for the growth of a genre that expressed the meaning of the Song as a marriage of the soul to Christ.[47] This primary mode of interpretation fully blossomed among twelfth-century commentators, and Bernard's *Sermons on the Song of Songs* stood above all others.

Bernard of Clairvaux (1090–1153)

Bernard's *Sermons on the Song of Songs* is a product of both time-honored tradition and innovative change in twelfth-century Europe. It evidences the long shadow of the monastic *lectio divina*, an inherited spiritual interpretation of the Song, profound social and religious changes in his day, and his own personal genius. Scholars of Bernard have referred to his *Sermons* as "among the supreme masterpieces of Christian mysticism" and as "one of the greatest masterpieces of universal literature."[48]

The man behind these masterful sermons was, observes Jean Leclercq, "one of those great men of whom it is difficult to write without either animosity or admiration—in other words, without passion. . . . Nothing he does is ordinary."[49] Bernard has variously been called "the last of the fathers," "the theologian of love," "the honey-tongued doctor," "the uncrowned ruler of Europe," "a man for all seasons," "the conscience of Europe," and "a difficult saint." His later image and influence outdistanced that of his lifetime. In *Paradiso* of the *Divine Comedy*, Dante chose Bernard to replace Beatrice as the guide to the final stage of mystical contemplation. Renaissance humanists such as Petrarch praised the abbot's teachings and style of writing. John Wycliffe appealed to Bernard's *On Consideration* in his critique of the curia's and papacy's abuses and extravagance. With the print revolution of the fifteenth century, Bernard's works surpassed those of all other church fathers in the number of editions. The Protestant Reformers Luther and Calvin made him into one of their own: a reformer of church misconduct and champion of true spirituality (Luther: "I love Bernard as the one who . . . preached Christ most charmingly"). In France, Louis XIII in 1652 named him "Protector of the Crown." Pascal's famous aphorism, "You would not seek me if you had not already found me," was drawn verbatim from Bernard's treatise *On the Love of God*.

In Protestant England, the Puritans quoted Bernard nearly as much as Augustine. The nineteenth-century church historian Adolf von Harnack called Bernard "the religious genius of the twelfth century." The medieval philosopher Etienne Gilson inaugurated a new era of Bernardine studies by taking him seriously as a theologian. In 1953, the eighth centenary of his death, Pope Pius XII named Bernard as the Doctor Mellifluous, a true doctor of the church. An 1891 bibliography of works on Bernard cited 2,761 references, and a second bibliography published in 1957 listed more than one thousand publications. Down through the centuries popes such as Eugenius IV (1431–47), John XXIII (1958–63), and Paul VI (1963–78) pondered and appealed to Bernard's *On Consideration* as a model of papal and curial reform. In our own day, Bernard continues to be cited and read by Catholics and Protestants as a model of spirituality.[50]

Who was this active and contemplative, mystic and preacher, ascetic and politician, gentle and violent person? Given the conflicting early biographies of Bernard, it is difficult to sift through the real and the fictional and establish his true persona. Enemies condemned him and dismissed his legacy; friends praised him and promoted his canonization. Recent biographers observe that the conflictive, paradoxical, aggressive tendencies in Bernard are related to his overall desire to expand Cistercian ideals. Dom Jean Leclercq, the most prolific scholar of Bernardine studies (his thirty books and seven hundred articles deal mostly with Bernard), remarked that "Bernard fought to defend his ideal and sought to put into key positions churchmen who he knew would favor its expansion." More recently, Adrian Bredero argued that Bernard integrated two contradictory elements—his life and actions on one hand and his writings on the other—in a single effort to promote the monastic life (the active side) and to pursue the monastic life (the mystical path).[51]

Born in 1090 just outside of Dijon, France, Bernard was the middle child of a pious Burgundian knight and his wife. According to Brian McGuire, Bernard lived a safe, secure life, free of trauma or great crises—the very opposite of what presumably constituted a twelfth-century saint in the eyes of modern skeptical historians.[52] Certainly, they speculate, some kind of personality dysfunction or trauma led men to become clerics or enter the monastery, for no one in his right mind would repress his natural sexual appetites. But in the estimation of Leclercq, Bernard was "a unified personality," with a strong if not domineering temperament, who "possessed that quality of joyousness which is recognized as the hallmark of an integrated person."[53] Bernard does not fit the typical model (often based on Augustine's *Confessions*) of a medieval saint's developmental history: "a painful childhood, a growing awareness of sin, especially of the sexual kind, and then a process of conversion culminating in some religious awakening that changes one's life completely."[54] One can certainly find such examples (e.g., St. Anselm), but the pattern does not seem to fit Bernard.

The earliest biography of Bernard, the twelfth-century so-called *Vita Prima* by William of St. Thierry, describes Bernard fleeing sexual temptations from women attracted to him. In his discussion of the history of interpretation of the Song of Songs, Marvin Pope lifted up this incident, claiming it "throws light on the saint's zeal for asceticism and his contempt for the flesh, especially female flesh." He offered this summary of the incident, linking it to Bernard's approach toward the Song:

Young Bernard once exchanged admiring glances with a girl and experienced an erection which so perturbed him that he dunked himself in an icy pond till the tumescence subsided and then and there he resolved to become a monk. This experience helps one understand Bernard's obsessive elaboration of allegorical interpretations of the Canticle in order to purge it of any suggestion of carnal lust and make it show forth the life of the spiritual unstained by sex and sin.[55]

McGuire counters Pope's conclusions by noting that the *Vita Prima* "contains hagiographical cliches about how he [Bernard] avoided sexual temptations, . . . tales one can dismiss either as literary imitation of similar anecdotes about earlier saints or as confirmation that Bernard was attracted to women." The narration of such incidents reveals more about William and his interest in passing on monastic ideals than about Bernard. An obvious but sometimes neglected axiom of historical understanding is the recognition that the assumptions and concerns of one era are not shared by cultures of another era. Leclercq wisely cautions that we must be careful not to allow "the artificially stimulated and commercially exploited eroticism of our own sex-ridden age" to distort the life of one who lived in a "less erotically preoccupied society." Nothing in Bernard's life—his actions (e.g., his dealings with Abelard) or his writings (e.g., his *Sermons on the Song of Songs*)—suggests that his life was the outcome of sexual repression. "Perhaps an industrious scholar," concludes McGuire, "will one day find sizeable skeletons in Bernard's closet, but I see none, only the tale of a boy who grew up in family surroundings where he was loved and could love in return."[56]

Around the age of seven Bernard entered the local monastic school at Saint-Vorles, in the same region as the founding monastery of Citeaux. Though he was steeped in a noble military tradition, a life of warfare and conquest held no personal attraction for him. To be sure, he never condemned military life and later became the chief propagandist of the Second Crusade (1145–49), a fiasco that attempted to take back the Holy Land from the Arab Muslims. Bernard and the many monks who were recruited from the military elite, however, exchanged a career of physical battle for spiritual warfare. Bernard's was a spiritual crusade for the hearts and minds of young men in service to God within the community of monks. With his mastery and love of Latin, he chose to wield words, not the sword.

Bernard and the Cistercians

Bernard not only shaped but was shaped by the world in which he lived. He came on the scene of European growth and expansion after a previous century of recovery from the "dark ages." He thus grew up in a period of economic expansion, population growth (with the attendant rise of towns and urban centers), crusading ideals, cultural revival, and ecclesiastical ferment instigated largely by the reforms of Pope Gregory VII (1073–85). In many respects, monastic orders, especially newer ones such as the Cistercians, were influenced by these developments.

At the age of twenty-one Bernard entered the new and struggling monastery of Cîteaux (Lat., *Cistercium*), located a few miles south of his family's estate. He brought with him his family (uncles, brothers, and cousins) and friends—thirty recruits in all, who had already lived at the family estate for a period of trial and preparation. The entrance of this sizable contingent revealed two abiding character traits in Bernard: an ability to lead and persuade—indeed, he had an irresistible charm—and, like Augustine, a desire to be with friends.

Cîteaux was founded in 1098 when Robert, abbot of the Benedictine abbey of Molesmes in Burgundy, left with twenty-one monks to follow strictly the letter of St. Benedict's Rule and model their lives on the desert fathers. Rejecting centuries of accretions to the rule, the Cistercians created a "school of charity" that harked back to the primitive fundamentals: solitude and community, prayer and manual labor (*ora et labora*), rigor and austerity. Simplicity regulated the Cistercians' way of life, from their undyed grayish woolen habits (they were called "white monks," distinguishing them from the traditional black habits of the Benedictines) to their plain diet, unadorned liturgy, and stark architecture.

In 1115 Bernard was appointed abbot of a new monastery at Clairvaux, the third daughter house founded by Cîteaux. He enforced an extreme ascetic regimen that soon had monks rebelling and his stomach ailing. The new abbot relented in his demands but not before inflicting permanent damage to his own health: for the remainder of his life he suffered from gastric illnesses. He remained an energetic monastic reformer and aggressive expansionist, criticizing the extravagance of Cluniac monasteries and recruiting new members into the Cistercian order. Over time, Bernard founded some seventy monasteries, and if one includes the branch houses from these monasteries, a total of 167 houses were directly linked to him. That Clairvaux founded fewer than a dozen houses in the century following the abbot's death testifies to the singular influence exerted by Bernard during his lifetime.[57]

Another reason for the astounding expansion of the Cistercian order is related to the composition of its community. In an important departure from the norm, newer orders such as the Cistercians admitted adults only. Older orders typically recruited oblates, that is, children from noble families offered by their parents to the monastery. These oblates grew up in the monastic milieu: they were educated in monastic schools and admitted into monastic orders and thus knew no life other than that within the cloister. Whether they liked it or not, the monastic life had been forced upon them. The Cistercians

adopted a different recruitment strategy, primarily to ensure dedicated observance of monastic life. Those who entered the order as adults (both males and
females) knew what they were getting into; they had made a voluntary choice;
many were educated; all had experienced life; and many had read about or
experienced secular love. Jean Leclercq suggests that with these adult recruits
a new psychological and spiritual dynamic permeated the monastery, one that
made the teaching of filial and divine love more explicit.[58]

Bernard emerged as the master of this distinct spirituality, and he soon
gathered around him a circle of faithful disciples, including William of St.
Thierry, Aulread of Riveaux, and Guerric of Igny. The implications of this new
spirituality for a renewed understanding of the Song of Songs should not be
missed. Cistercian spirituality wrought a "fundamental transformation" of the
commentary genre in the twelfth century.[59] In an environment where many
members of the community had experienced adult love and even marriage, the
most natural image to express the bond between the soul and God was that
between adult lovers. And of course the book of the Bible that best expressed
that love was the Song of Songs. No wonder the Song resonated so deeply first
within the walls of the monastery (the Cistercians made extensive use of the
Song in their liturgy) and then beyond into the larger culture, where it became
the subject of devotional and secular literature, music and painting. Fascination
with the Song in past centuries gave way to preoccupation in the twelfth and
thirteenth centuries.

Bernard dedicated himself to the life of a contemplative, but he could not
contain himself within the cloister or remain silent. His involvement in the
affairs of Europe is perhaps best seen as an extension of his fervent convictions
joined with a temptation to power. In the second quarter of the century he
became one of the most dominant leaders in the Western church, and for
nearly two decades (from the early 1130s through the late 1140s), about one-
third of his time was spent away from his monastery. Briefly, these activities
ranged from healing the papal schism of 1130–37 and influencing the choice
of the new pope, Innocent II; corresponding with nearly 550 people all over
Europe; preaching the Second Crusade (and later, after its failure, regretting
it) at the behest of Pope Eugene III, one of his former monks; and denouncing Abelard, the brilliant scholastic, for heresy. I alluded earlier to scholars'
attempts to explain the contradictory elements in Bernard's life—to reconcile Bernard's private life with his public life, his monastic vows with his public
presence. Perhaps a clue is found from Bernard himself in his *Sermons on
the Song*: "In spite of her longing for the repose of contemplation she is burdened with the task of preaching; and despite her desire to bask in the Bridegroom's presence she is entrusted with the cares of begetting and rearing
children."[60]

Bernard's Sermons: Method and Context

Bernard's eighty-six *Sermons on the Song of Songs* are traditional in approach and theological content but original in their passion and personal disclosure. The allegorical reading of the Song was assumed. With previous interpreters, Bernard begins at the simple, literal level: the Song is a wedding song written by Solomon. But to remain at this "superficial" or "uncouth" level, writes the abbot, "would be nonsense." The Song "is preeminently a marriage song telling of chaste souls in loving embrace, of their wills in sweet accord, of the mutual exchange of the heart's affections." It is a book about the marriage of the soul to God, the bond of love between God and the individual. As we have seen, nine centuries earlier Origen approached the Song from this perspective and inaugurated a venerated tradition of allegorical interpretation. Bernard's spiritual exegesis followed Origen's lead (he replicates Origen's interpretation of 1:2), and he knows the work of other commentators, including Gregory the Great. However, the overall tenor of his *Sermons* is uniquely his own, though he often invokes his "absolute need of the help of the Holy Spirit" in interpreting the Song.[61]

In addition, Bernard's work is informed by a deep knowledge of not only Scripture and the church fathers but also the Greek Neoplatonic mystical tradition and by reflecting on his own personal experience in the monastery. In an era described by Colin Morris as "the discovery of the individual," we see in Bernard (and pursued more systematically among his disciples) the combination of traditional spirituality with a new humanism. To know God, we must know ourselves. For Bernard, "knowledge of God and self . . . are essential for salvation," and the Song serves as the guide to this inner quest.[62]

Bernard composed his *Sermons* over an eighteen-year period, beginning in 1135 until his death in August 1153. Like many other monastic commentators, he did not complete his project; his last sermon comments on the beginning of chapter 3 of the Song. However, as is attested by the four-volume, 850-page English edition, if he did not completely exhaust the Song's contents, he probably said all that needed to be said about love. "Bernard of Clairvaux," notes Marvin Pope, "takes the prize in his own century and in any century for devout and prolific prolixity on the Canticles." His *Sermons* are not so much formal exegetical commentary as an occasion for exploring what Bernard describes as "the ecstatic ascent of the purified mind to God, and the loving descent of God into the soul."[63]

One of the most striking characteristics of the abbot's *Sermons* is his encyclopedic knowledge of Scripture. The Bible was the most studied book of the Middle Ages and of course, all monks were known for their knowledge and memorization of Scripture, but among the Cistericans a dynamic biblical revival developed with Bernard at the lead.[64] According to G. R. Evans, "All Bernard's theological reflections, his sense of the divine, his vision of God, his heightened perception of the beauty of holiness, arises like distillation from his study of the Bible."[65] However, as scholars have recently pointed out, Bernard's exposure to Scripture took place not through direct study of the Vulgate—the first concordance to the Latin Vulgate was not produced until the thirteenth century—but through the liturgy and the church fathers.[66]

Bernard's vast and profound study of Scripture—received secondhand—shaped his psyche and produced a literary vocabulary saturated in Scripture, as his *Sermons on the Songs* bear out. A recent edition of the *Sermons* identified 5,526 biblical quotations, ranging from Genesis to Revelation.[67] Although the marriage metaphor and the erotic language in the Song aptly describe the love between God and the soul, Bernard draws from hundreds of other passages in Scripture, including the Psalms, the Gospels of Matthew and John, and Paul's epistles, to expound the spiritual dimensions of human experience. Despite his focus on the Song of Songs, the primary biblical text (and motif) running throughout the Sermons and an essential feature of his mystical theology is 1 John 4:8, "God is love."

Not only a mind saturated in biblical texts but also a distinct form of monastic spirituality shaped Bernard's *Sermons on the Song*. His interpretive method reflects the ancient art of sacred reading (Lat., *lectio divina*). Developed in the earliest communal monasteries and institutionalized in the monastic rules of Benedict, Pachomius, and others, *lectio divina* is, in the words of Michael Casey, "a technique of prayer and a guide to living. It is a means of descending to the level of the heart and finding God."[68] All monasteries gave attention to sacred reading, but the practice waxed and waned throughout the Middle Ages. With its stress on knowledge of Scripture and union with God, the Cistercian community accorded *lectio divina* special prominence.

Sacred reading entailed a four-step spiritual process, one that roughly correlates with Origen's threefold understanding of Scripture and more exactly with John Cassian's fourfold understanding. The following diagram, borrowed from Casey, charts the fourfold sequential levels of reading Scripture.[69]

The Four Moments of *Lectio Divina*

SENSE	FACULTY	FUNCTION	PRAYER
1. Literal	Intellect	Understanding the text	*Lectio*
2. Christological	Memory	Contextualizing the meaning	*Meditatio*
3. Behavioral	Conscience	Living the meaning	*Oratio*
4. Mystical	Spirit	Meeting God in the text	*Contemplatio*

The monk began with the literal sense and proceeded to the "true" or "inner" meaning of the text. Numbers two through four correspond to the allegorical reading of Scripture in the broadest sense, though as we have seen, allegory was most typically applied in the christological sense. The "behavioral" sense corresponds to the tropological or moral meaning of the text, and the "mystical" reflects the anagogical or eschatological meaning. The earlier discussion here observed the various "sense" levels as applied to the Song of Songs, though not in such a tidy manner. Interpretation of the Song defied such simplification. Commentators went beyond a private reading of the Bible that characterized *lectio divina* and applied, for example, an ecclesiastical or Marian interpretation to the Song. Or they might blend the levels, as Bernard did, into a kind of "mystical tropology." On the tropological level, Bernard applied the Song's message of love to his monastic brethren; on the mystical and ultimate level, he appropriated its message in order to experience the love of God.

Lectio divina, then, encouraged and reinforced a variety of spiritual approaches and interpretations of biblical texts. As Beryl Smalley observes, "The spiritual exposition [of Scripture] . . . drew its sap through the roots of lectio divina from the soil of the old monastic tradition." Standing firmly in this tradition, Bernard "was truly the last of the Fathers"—so-called because he was the last to write on major theological topics without recourse to scholastic methods.[70] Indeed, Bernard stands on the cusp of a transformation in the church's approach toward Scripture. From Gregory the Great to Bernard and beyond, monastic communities pursued the traditional *lectio divina*.

Toward the end of the twelfth century, however, an alternative approach emerged within newly created cathedral schools and then universities. In these exhilarating scholastic settings, clerics studied Scripture primarily to gain knowledge, to shed light on intellectual and moral issues. Texts were examined and questions proposed and resolved through logical disputation. In contrast to divine reading, with its emphasis on savoring the Word and gaining personal benefit by prayerful submission to the Spirit, the scholastic approach stressed the text itself, the sacred page (Lat., *sacra pagina*), and the new knowledge derived by applying the Aristotelian method to its contents.

On several occasions in his *Sermons* Bernard alluded to these distinctive approaches toward Scripture. At one point he observed, "My purpose is not so much to explain words as to move hearts. I must both draw the water and offer it as drink, a work that I shall not accomplish by a spate of rapid comments but by careful examination and frequent exhortation." Elsewhere he contrasted feigned with proper humility, concluding, "We attain to this voluntary humility, not by truthful reasoning but by an infusion of love, since it springs from the heart, from the affections, from the will."[71]

Bernard's Sermons: The Mystical Ascent

Bernard's *Sermons*, written over the course of nearly two decades, contrasts sharply with emerging scholastic methods. Lacking in systematic exposition, this work is punctuated by "unexpected turns, repetitions, and above all, retardation, and digressions."[72] In part, these idiosyncrasies reflect the nature of monastic theology, characterized by its suggestive, intuitive, and poetic approach. In addition, they can be explained by the long period of composition. Changes in Bernard's circumstances and attitudes and in issues facing the monastic community are reflected throughout. Indeed, it is as if the *Sermons* are used intermittently for journaling or diary-keeping purposes. There are entries not only about scholasticism but also jabs at opponents, be they doctrinal deviants, heretics, or the "ingrate Jew." More often he criticizes the failings of his community: monks sleep during divine office, boast of their former wayward lives without a hint of remorse or humility, offend each other, and disrupt the peace.[73] Throughout his *Sermons*, self-expression and personal disclosure abound. Sermon 26 begins with a two-page explication of Song 1:4 ("I am black but beautiful"), then turns into a fourteen-page, highly personal lament over the death of his brother Gerard, the bursar of the abbey.[74]

Such self-awareness is emblematic of Bernard's more focused expositions of the Song and represents a significant turn in the Song's interpretative history. Under "the artistry of the Spirit," the Song becomes a source of spiritual illumination, an entrée into a mystical encounter with God. Bernard McGinn defines this mystical element as "that part of . . . belief and practices that concerns the preparation for, the consciousness of, and the reaction to what can be described as the immediate or direct presence of God."[75] Through the guidance of Bernard and other twelfth-century interpreters, the Song of Songs offers steps toward, an awareness of, and a response to the direct presence of God. Unlike Origen's and Augustine's noetic mysticism, Bernard's is an affective mysticism rooted in feeling and "taste."

The Song, then, should be interpreted in a personal, intimate, mystical way. Bernard begins Sermon 3 by challenging the monks to search their hearts:

> Today the text we are to study is the book of our experience. You
> must therefore turn your attention inwards, each one must take
> note of his own particular awareness of things I am about to dis-
> cuss. I am attempting to discover if any of you has been privileged
> to say from his heart, "Let him kiss me with the kiss of his mouth."
> Those to whom it is given to utter these words sincerely are compar-
> atively few, but any one who has received this mystical kiss from the
> mouth of Christ at least once, seeks again that intimate experience,
> and eagerly looks for its frequent renewal.[76]

And so Bernard advises the monks, "When you consider the lovers themselves, think not of a man and a woman but of the Word and the soul." Spiritual truths are accommodated to human understanding through the veil of the letter and communicated through analogy. Descriptions of human love provide a fitting analogy, what McGinn calls a "privileged symbol," for expressing this ineffable spiritual union of the divine and human. "If a love relationship is the special and outstanding characteristic of the bride and groom," writes Bernard, "it is not unfitting to call the soul that loves God a bride."[77]

With Origen, Bernard believes that the Song may be applied to Christ and the church, but ultimately, he distills the various levels of understanding the Song to an individual engagement with its contents: "Only personal experience can unfold its meaning."[78] A notable passage from Sermon 79 captures the intent of this marriage song:

> Who is it whom your soul loves, for whom you inquire? Has he no name? Who are you and who is he? I speak like this because of the strange manner of speech and extraordinary disregard for names, quite different from the rest of Scriptures. But in this marriage song it is not the words which are to be pondered, but the affections be- hind them. . . . The language of love will be meaningless jangle to one who does not love, like sounding brass or tinkling cymbal.[79]

Or as Bernard puts it elsewhere, "It is desire that drives me on, not rea- son."[80] It is the quenching of the soul's thirst for God that is the subject of the Song. But why this desire for God, and what steps can be taken to fulfill it? Desire begins with Bernard's anthropology (view of the human nature) and culminates in his mystical theology (the systematic discourse on the union of the soul and God). The ladder of ascension to God begins at the bottom rung with the human condition. Bernard's first sermons discussing Song 1:2 ("Let him kiss me with the kisses of his mouth") ingeniously instruct in this spiritual ascent to God. But it is in his later sermons (especially 80–83) that he provides a searching analysis of the human condition.

Bernard delineates the intention and plight of human existence in con- ventional Christian categories. In love, God created humanity; humans were made to love God and praise their creator. Bernard quotes repeatedly from 1 John 4: "In this is love, not that we loved God but that he loved us" (v. 10); "God is love, and those who abide in love abide in God, and God abides in them" (v. 16b); "We love him because he first loved us" (v. 19). Before humans can fully love God, however, they must examine their own hearts. When they begin to see themselves "in the clear light of truth," they discover that they exist "in a region where likeness to God has been forfeited."[81]

When we scrutinize our fallen state, we discover the truth about ourselves: we are mortal, weak, blind, corrupt, fearful, worldly, and separated from God. To know oneself is to understand that humility is the necessary "foundation" for building the spiritual life. And as we know ourselves, we discover truths about God: God is immortal, omnipotent, omniscient, and incorruptible. We also discover truths about God's view of and intention for humanity: God made us with dignity, in his image and likeness so we can commune with him. Every soul, no matter how infected with sin, may aspire to communion with God.

"Love is a great reality," writes Bernard in a summary of his spiritual doctrine, "and if it returns to its beginning and gets back to its origin . . . it will always draw afresh from it, and thereby flow freely."[82] An examination of human experience uncovers its existential plight: though fallen, miserable creatures, humans are made for communion with God.

In Sermons 80–83 Bernard articulates a view of humanity taken up previously by the church fathers and based on the Genesis account of humanity's creation in the image and likeness of God (Gen. 1:26).[83] Elsewhere, in *Grace and Free Choice*, Bernard provides a more lengthy and different assessment of the matter, but here the discussion is restricted to his *Sermons*. In Sermon 80 Bernard begins by discussing the affinity of the soul to the Incarnate Word (Christ). On the one hand, Christ is the true and perfect image of God, for he is of the same substance as God; by his very existence as God he is at once great and upright. Humans, on the other hand, are made in or after that image. Whereas the Word is the Father's image as righteousness, wisdom, and truth, the human soul is none of these, and yet "it is capable of them and yearns for them." On account of sin the soul lost its uprightness (or rectitude), though it retains something of its greatness (or dignity). "Man passes as an image, but he limps, as it were, on one foot, and has become an estranged son."[84]

Bernard shifts the word emphasis from image to likeness in Sermons 81 and 82. He attributes to the soul a threefold likeness to the Word: "natural simplicity of substance" insofar as it is living (though not in a state of blessedness), immortality (though not in an absolute and complete sense like God, for humans die), and free will (though crippled by sin). All three are constituent elements of the soul's likeness to the Word and can never be lost. In language reminiscent of Paul, Augustine, and as we will see, Luther, Bernard expounds at length upon the bondage of the will. Although the will is weak, powerless, and controlled by sin, it remains free because "what is done willingly is done freely. It is by sin that the corruptible body oppresses the soul, but it is the result of [misordered] love, not of force." The soul fell of its own accord but now, given its inherent depravity, lacks the wherewithal to rise above its fallen condition. "So, in some strange and twisted way the will deteriorates and brings about a state of compulsion where the bondage cannot excuse the will, because the action was voluntary, nor can the will, being fettered, free itself from bondage."[85]

The result is an "unlikeness" to the Word. The soul has not lost its original form—"the primal likeness remains"—but it is "concealed" by something added to it, "covered by the disguise of human deception, pretense, and hypocrisy." Our true nature is deformed by original sin, and yet "the soul has not in fact put off its original form but has put on one foreign to it." This condition "increases the soul's distress at the unlikeness." Bernard appeals to the Platonic idea of correspondence (like seeks like, only like can know like) and the words in 1 John 3:2 ("We know that when he will appear we shall be like him, for we shall see him as he is") to describe the soul's ability and desire to be reunited with its source. He closes his sermon by observing that "a oneness of spirit, a reciprocal vision, and reciprocal love" occur when sin is finally removed in the beatific vision. "When what is perfect comes, what is partial will be done away with; and the love between them will be chaste and consummated, full recognition, open vision, strong unity, indivisible fellowship and perfect likeness. Then the soul will know as it is known and love as it is loved, and the Bridegroom will rejoice over the Bride."[86]

What are the steps, what is the process of the soul's unification with God? How does one recover or return to one's true self, to what one was truly meant to be? In an earlier sermon, Bernard remarked that "what nature cannot do, grace can." The one "on whom the merciful unction of the Holy Spirit deigns to pour out the grace of its gentleness, will be immediately restored to a truly human condition." The bride is drawn by the bridegroom ("for without me you can do nothing" [John 15:5]), who through the Spirit infuses his loved one with grace.[87]

Moreover, one relies on God's grace offered in Christ the Word, who is the perfect realization of what humankind should be. In Sermon 83 Bernard observes that "the soul returns and is converted to the Word to be reformed by him and conformed to him." Elsewhere he discusses the accommodation of God to humankind by coming in the flesh. "He became incarnate for the sake of carnal men, that he might induce them to relish the life of the Spirit."[88] Because humans in their fallen condition know only carnal love, Christ became incarnate. Christ condescended in bodily form as the first step in the return of the soul to him. In short, God in Christ met humanity on humanity's terms: "I think this is the principal reason why the invisible God willed to be seen in the flesh and to converse with men as a man. He wanted to recapture the affections of carnal men who were unable to love in any other way, by first drawing them to the salutary love of his own humanity, and then gradually raise them to a spiritual love."[89] This attachment of sense-bound humanity to the bodily form of Christ (Bernard emphasizes Christ's passion in particular) is the first step in a reorientation of love that leads eventually to spiritual love. There is, however, no instant panacea. The cure is long. Despite Bernard's suggestion that all may attain union with God, the only place where this could be successfully accomplished was in the monastery. Within the cloistered walls of Citeaux, "the world's glamour and entanglements have been firmly repudiated," the monastic virtues are exercised, and the discipline of *lectio divina* is practiced.[90] Here the monk may be freed from carnal love in surrender to divine love.

In his first sermons on the Song (3–8) Bernard outlines the process of mystical ascent, expositing the spiritual meaning of "Let him kiss me with the kisses of his mouth." He notes that the Song begins with the last of three kisses and that he must discuss the first two so that the last will be understood more fully. Through a series of ascending spiritual kisses ("the kiss of the feet" and "the kiss of the hand") culminating in the "kiss of the mouth of Christ," mystical union is realized.[91] These kisses approximate the threefold division of spiritual ascent familiar in both Eastern and Western Christianity since Origen's day, then given classic shape by Pseudo-Dionysius in the sixth century, and later canonized as the *via purgativa* (ascetical purification), *via illuminativa* (progressive sanctification), and *via unitiva* (mystical union with Christ).[92] In Sermon 4, Bernard depicts this triple kiss in two other ways:

> There is first the forgiveness of sins, then the grace that follows on good deeds, and finally that contemplative gift by which a kind and beneficent Lord shows himself to the soul with as much clarity as bodily frailty can endure. The heartfelt desire to admit one's guilt brings a man down in lowliness before God, as it were to his feet; the heartfelt devotion of a worshiper finds in God renewal and refreshment, the touch as it were, of his hand; and the delights of contemplation lead on to that ecstatic repose that is the fruit of the kiss of his mouth.[93]

The first "kiss of the feet" is penance, the "sign of genuine conversion of life." God offers the grace of forgiveness to the sinner who turns toward God. Bernard enjoins his readers to follow the humble posture of the sinful woman in the Gospel (Luke 7:36–50): "Prostrate yourself on the ground, take hold of his feet, soothe them with kisses, sprinkle them with your tears and so wash not them but yourself." Not until you hear Christ's pronouncement, "Your sins are forgiven," can you "dare to lift up a face suffused with shame and grief." Penance excites a keen awareness not only of divine judgment but also of divine mercy. "If you temper that fear and sorrow with the thought of God's goodness and the hope of obtaining his pardon, you will realize that you have also embraced the foot of his mercy. It is clearly inexpedient to kiss one without the other."[94]

The "kiss of the hand" is the stage dedicated to holy living. Though sins are forgiven, they do not cease immediately. The potential for spiritual renovation now exists, but the image and likeness of God are not immediately restored. "It is a long and formidable leap from the foot to the mouth, a manner of approach that is not commendable. Consider for a moment: still tarnished as you are with the dust of sin, would you dare touch those sacred lips? Yesterday you were lifted from the mud, today you wish to encounter the glory of his face? No, his hand must be your guide to that end."[95] So it is that a life of heartfelt devotion to God and good deeds to others occupies most of a Christian's life, and for monks and nuns this occurred in the daily structure of prayer and reading.

Finally, "through many prayers and tears, we humbly dare to raise our eyes to his mouth." "Only a few of the more perfect" experience the kiss of the mouth, which bestows a foretaste of things to come in the glory of heaven. A fleeting, transitory state, "this kiss of participation . . . enables us not only to know God but to love the Father, who is never fully known until he is perfectly loved." Because knowledge and love together are necessary preconditions for this kiss, "two kinds of people . . . may not consider themselves to have been gifted with the kiss, those who know the truth without loving it, and those who love it without understanding it." Therefore, "this kiss leaves room neither for ignorance nor for lukewarmness."[96]

In Sermon 8 Bernard declares that the bride receives the kiss not by the mouth but by the kiss of his mouth. That is, the bride receives the kiss not directly from Jesus the bridegroom but through the interposition of the Holy Spirit. In one of Bernard's rare references to the Trinity, he observes, "If, as is properly understood, the Father is he who kisses, the Son he who is kissed, then it cannot be wrong to see in the kiss the Holy Spirit, for he is the imperturbable peace of the Father and the Son, their unshakable bond, their undivided love, their indivisible unity."[97]

Bernard provides another variation of the threefold pattern of spiritual healing in Sermons 10–12. Centered on the phrase "your anointing oils are fragrant" (1: 3), he uses three perfumes of the bride—"the ointment of contrition, that of devotion and that of piety"—to describe the first two steps in the ladder of ascent (scents?). "The first is pungent, causing some pain; the second mitigates and soothes pain; the third heals the wound and rids the patient of the illness." The first oil is applied to the feet, the second to the head, the third directly to the wound (the second and third being roughly analogous to the "kiss of the hand"). The third ointment of "merciful love" ranks far superior to contrition and devotion, for is manifested in outward acts of kindness toward one's neighbor. However, this ointment is the penultimate test of God's abiding love in one's heart, for Bernard was more interested in the individual's appropriation of love than in its social expression.[98]

Perhaps the most organized presentation of the path to mystical love is found in Sermon 23. The Song's text, "The king has brought me into his rooms" (1:3 [v. 4 in modern translations]), is used as a metaphor to explore the dynamic process of *lectio divina* culminating in the contemplative experience. The "rooms" are several and include the garden (5:1) and the bedroom (3:4) found in latter passages. As a mnemonic device and for literary purposes, Bernard once again invokes the triple pattern. "Let the garden . . . represent the plain, unadorned historical sense of Scripture, the storeroom its moral sense, and the bedroom the mystery of divine contemplation."[99] Each of these rooms is further subdivided into threes.

In the garden, Scripture is read as an account of the history of creation, reconciliation, and restoration of a new heaven and a new earth. In the storeroom, Scripture becomes the instructor of those who are saved. One not only obtains knowledge but also commences the work of personal transformation aided by the grace of God and making use of the spiritual senses of smell, taste, and touch. The bride begins in the spice room of discipline, "where the stubborn will, worn down by the hard and prolonged schooling of experienced mentors, is humbled and healed." Next she moves to the ointment room, where, by "a sweet refinement," she becomes "pleasant and temperate" in her relations with others. She then occupies the wine cellar, where "an earnest zeal for the works of love" transforms her soul "to forgetfulness of self and indifference to self-interest. This is the unique and exquisite lesson of the Holy Spirit infused in the wine room."[100]

Finally, in the bedroom, the bride experiences the mystery of divine contemplation in a threefold manner. She ascends through contemplating God as judge, teacher, and bridegroom. Bernard's knowledge of the bedroom is incomplete—he is "more concerned to know myself, as the Greek motto advises"—but "if I knew nothing at all there is nothing I could say." As he does throughout his *Sermons*, Bernard appeals to his own experience in order to help his fellow monks: "I shall tell you how far I have advanced, or imagine I have advanced." To know God is one thing, to fear God is another. In knowledge "you are prepared," in wisdom "you are initiated." "Instruction makes us learned, experience makes us wise." And yet you will not find peace in a "teacher's auditorium" or at "a bar of justice." No, the "place where God is seen in tranquil rest" is the bedroom of the bridegroom. "To me," Bernard writes, "this is truly the bedroom to which I have sometimes gained happy entrance. Alas! how rare the time, and how short the stay!" In the sanctuary of the bedroom "one may indeed be at rest. The God of peace pacifies all things, and to gaze on this stillness is to find repose."[101]

Elsewhere in his *Sermons* the abbot variously describes the contemplative state as "an ecstasy of spirit," "going outside of oneself, . . . transcending the self," a drunkenness of the Spirit, where love is the wine; a "sleep . . . which is vital and watchful, which enlightens the heart" and transports the mind; a "death . . . since the ecstatic soul is cut off from awareness of life though not from life itself." As is often observed by those who attain an ecstatic state, words fail: "The mind is enraptured by the unutterable sweetness of the Word." Ecstatic love transcends the ordinary boundaries of order, decorum, and rhetoric. "The *affectus* have their own language." Just as words fail two lovers in the act of consummation, so in the higher reality of spiritual marriage (from which human marriage derives its full meaning), love has its own "cries of delight." Bernard calls it a "belch"—an eructation that cannot be anticipated or controlled. The language of ecstasy surpasses "reasoned discourse, a deliberate utterance, a premeditated speech" and is expressed as "spontaneous impulse." The contemplative state "does not stop to consider the order, the grammar, the flow, or the number of words it employs, when it cannot contain itself."[102]

Such is the divine state of the soul's mystical contemplation. Ascending the ladder of loves, from carnal to intellectual and finally to its state of true repose in its source, the soul finds rest in union with God. The individual self is neither lost in nor merged with the divine ("their substances are not inter-mingled"); rather "their wills are in agreement." In this life, the soul's search for God is filled with "a desire that is intense, a thirst ever burning, an appli-cation that never flags."[103] Not until the next life, with the complete transfor-mation of human desire to its source, when "we shall be like him because we shall see him as he is" (1 John 3:2), will this search be consummated.

Bernard introduced a whole new genre of exegesis (if we may even call it that) that became immensely popular in the twelfth and thirteenth centuries and persisted through the sixteenth century. Monks continued the Bernardine mys-tical tradition of love and the soul in the Song of Songs, though the form tended to be that of the treatise, not biblical commentary. The love language of the Song also extended beyond the walls of the monasteries into other settings of vernacular and/or secular literature. As Ann Matter and others have shown, the Song's popular versatility may be seen in vernacular commentaries on the Song, vernacular devotional writings, and a broad range of poetry, in both Latin and vernacular literature.[104] Writers drew from previous well-established modes of interpretation to plunder the Song's content in support of reform, mariological piety, and other forms of spiritual devotion. Whatever the inter-pretive method, an underlying assumption persisted: the Song's literal descrip-tions of physical love mirrored a deeper, spiritual love between God and the human person or the church.

The Song's Interpretive History in the Reformation and Modern Eras

For all the attention given by sixteenth-century Protestant Reformers to the plain, literal sense of Scripture, their approach to the Song of Songs illustrates the continued influence of allegory and a reticence to interpret the Song as a human love poem.[105] Protests against Catholic allegorizing notwithstanding, Protestants interpreted the Song of Songs spiritually. To them, there was no carnal meaning whatsoever; the spiritual sense, that is, the sense intended by the Spirit, *was* the literal sense. Nearly all Protestant commentators worked within the time-honored tradition of viewing the poem as a dialogue between Christ and the church or the faithful soul, replacing references to the Catholic Church, Mary, and the monastic milieu with Protestant doctrine and vocabu-lary.

Martin Luther, the only prominent Protestant to write a complete com-mentary on the Song, offered an alternative to the traditional range of allegor-ical interpretations, yet for all intents and purposes he remained within the broad non-literal tradition. His approach toward the Song belied his stinging critique of allegorical exegesis. "When I was a monk," he noted, "I allegorized everything. Afterward through the Epistle to the Romans I came to some knowledge of Christ. I recognized then that allegories are nothing; that it's not what Christ signifies but what Christ is that counts." He blamed Origen and Jerome for more than a thousand years of wayward interpretation. "God forgive them. In all of Origen there is not one word about Christ."[106]

In spite of this general condemnation of allegory and his particular criticism of earlier interpretations of the Song as "immature and strange," Luther could not bring himself to view the Song's plain language for what it was: a love poem. "The poem," he concluded, "is entirely figurative." He dismissed the minority view of those who supported a literal reading of the Song. He rejected the Jewish interpretation of it as a poem describing "the union of God and the synagogue." And he abandoned the prevailing tropological Christian interpretation of the Song as a description of the union between God and the soul, proposing a creative substitute.[107] According to Endel Kallas, Luther modeled his novel interpretation after a poem by the emperor Maximilian. That is, the ancient King Solomon wrote about his own political exploits just as Maximilian recounted his own successes in figurative language.[108] "I think," wrote Luther, "it is a song in which Solomon honors God with his praises; he give Him thanks for his divinely established and confirmed kingdom and government. . . . It deals with . . . the divinely ordained governments, or with the people of God."[109]

Unlike the allegorical approach, which often detached the historical context from the loftier spiritual effort to know the mind of God, Luther's figurative interpretation exhibits sensitivity toward Solomon so as to know the mind of the author. As Kallas observes, "Not only does Luther reject allegory, but his method of exposition centers on the historical and the need to interpret the Song of Solomon with particular concern for authorship and historical context."[110] Luther went on to link this figurative reading of the Song with present-day application: "Any state in which there is a church and a godly prince can use this song of Solomon's just as if it had been composed about its own government and state." Luther read the Song as a hymn of praise by Solomon for God's blessing upon his kingdom. The bride is thus the kingdom who in 1:2 is "kissed" or shown favor by God. Luther concluded his commentary by admitting the provisional nature of his work: "If I am wrong about this, a first effort deserves lenience. The musings of others have a much larger share of absurdity!"[111]

Although sharing continuities with the past, in a fundamental way Protestants departed from the medieval mystical tradition. As we have seen, Bernard expressed the relationship of the Word and soul as an ecstatic union, expressed most appropriately in the explicit language of the marriage bed. Erotic human love provided the closest and best analogy to divine love. Protestants, however, demystified and desacralized this Catholic reading in favor of a more figurative, rationalistic, or moralistic interpretation. In a sense, celibate monks were safe in imagining the relationship between God and the soul in sexual language, whereas married Protestant commentators, having experienced human sexual union in a nonidealized way, rejected all references to carnal love as appropriate for describing the relationship of the Word to the soul. According to George Scheper, early Protestants tended to see the Song's nuptial metaphor in contractual terms: marriage constituted a mutual pledge of faithfulness, tenderness, affection, and consent. They continued to interpret the Song spiritually, but they generally eschewed a mystical application whose interpretation depended on the sexual (not domestic) emphasis of the nuptial metaphor. Moral teaching derived from didacticism replaced the passions of mysticism. A related development occurred in the realm of religious literature, where the differences are manifest in the passionate poetry of the Spanish Catholic mystic John of the Cross (1542–91) and the didactic prose of the English Independent Protestant John Bunyan (1628–88) in *The Pilgrim's Progress*.[112]

Throughout the seventeenth and much of the eighteenth century, both within Catholicism and Protestantism, some form of allegory remained the primary method of interpreting the Song. Several dissenters such as Hugo Grotius, the Dutch jurist and theologian, and J. B. Bousset, the great French preacher and bishop, espoused a literal reading of the Song as love poetry, but their views found few adherents until the twentieth century. In England, annotations in the Puritan Geneva Bible read much like those noted at the outset of this chapter in the King James Bible. According to the marginal comments, "Let him kiss me with the kisses of his mouth" referred to the "faithful soul inflamed with the desire of Christ." Some Puritans recognized the Song as a prophetic allegory about the history of the church, beginning with either Abel or David and extending to the Last Judgment or the return of Christ, respectively. In one of the more innovative interpretations of the day (though clearly linked to earlier ecclesiastical interpretations), John Donne (1572–1631) used the Song as an apology for the authority and universality of the Church of England. John Wesley, the leader of the evangelical movement in eighteenth-century England, promoted the traditional allegorical view of the Song as a poem of spiritual love and marriage between Christ and the Church.[113]

Little changed in the traditional approach toward the Song until the end of the eighteenth century, when issues that have occupied the modern historical-critical agenda began to emerge in Germany. The biblical scholar Johann Friedrich Jacobi and Romantic poet and philosopher Johann Gottfried von Herder led the way, viewing the Song as a dramatic poem. Jacobi suggested it told the story of King Solomon's competing with a humble shepherd boy for the hand of a "Shulammite" (i.e., a girl from Shunem = Sulam) maiden, whereas Herder argued more convincingly that it was a collection of erotic love poems assembled in dramatic form.[114] In addition, the interpretation of the Song as a text for wedding ceremonies—broached initially by Origen—received renewed attention by J. G. Wetzstein.

More novel interpretations came on the scene in the nineteenth century. A Roman Catholic priest suggested that the Song was a dream, basing his conclusion on 5:2, "I sleep, but my heart wakes." Christian Ginsburg offered the first feminist interpretation of the Song, contending its message defended the equality of women.[115] Generally, however, scholars either persisted in upholding a traditional allegorical view or veered in the direction of modern literary theory in viewing the Song as a drama or wedding poem.

In the first half of the twentieth century, all three of these interpretations fell out of favor, though they bequeathed their central insights to an emerging cultic interpretation that continues to have its supporters. Scholars gave increasing attention to the Song's place in the context of Near Eastern religions whose cultic practices involved the ritual representation of sacred marriage between a fertility god and goddess as part of a larger cycle of the birth, death, and rebirth of the fertility god. In the early part of the century T. J. Meek concluded that the Song was patterned after Canaanite fertility cults: worship of foreign gods was exchanged for Yahweh and his consort. In his 1977 commentary, Marvin Pope connected the Canticle not to marriage but to ancient cultic funeral feasts, citing the phrase in 8:6 ("For love is strong as death, passion fierce as the grave") as the Song's denouement.[116]

Two recent nonliteral interpretations may be cited. In his 1988 study, Raymond Tournay argues that the Song is a double entendre: on one level, it is an erotic love poem, but on another, it is "a love poem oriented ultimately toward what was the supreme and invincible hope of the chosen people of the Second Temple period: the coming of the Messiah, at the same time a new David and a new Solomon awaited so anxiously by the daughter of Zion." Similarly, a 1992 work by Luis Stadelmann, reminiscent of Luther's approach and suggestive of the novel historical allegorical interpretation proposed by a fellow Jesuit earlier in the century, argued that the Song is a coded text whose content is "the restoration of the Davidic monarchy in Judah after the exile." Thus, in 1: 2–4, the bride represents aboriginal Jews who yearn for the return of the king to the Davidic throne in Jerusalem.[117]

The reigning consensus among contemporary scholars is that the Song is a collection of poems about human love. Dietrich Bonhoeffer maintained the Song was "included in the Bible as a protest against those who believe that Christianity stands for a restraint of passion."[118] To be sure, divergent views regarding its literary structure, the number of poems that it comprises, the weight given to the Song's prominent characters, the meaning of specific words or phrases, and the intention of the Song's author/compiler mute any univocal agreement. Feminists, for example, sympathetic to the role of women in the literary framework of the Song, emphasize the Song's nonsexist content and suggest that it bears the imprint of women's poetry.[119] In her landmark study *God and the Rhetoric of Sexuality* (1978), Phyllis Trible proposed that the Song of Songs "redeems a love story" that has "gone awry" in the Genesis 2–3 account of creation and fall:

> In Eden, the yearning of the woman for harmony and her man continued after disobedience. Yet the man did not reciprocate; instead, he ruled over her to destroy unity and pervert sexuality. Her desire became his dominion. But in the Song, male power vanishes. His desire becomes her delight. Another consequence of disobedience is thus redeemed through the recovery of mutuality in the garden of eroticism. Appropriately, the woman sings the lyrics of this grace: "I am my lover's and for me is his desire." . . . Throughout the Song she is independent, fully the equal of man. Although at times he approaches her, more often she initiates their meetings.[120]

As one perspective within the broad spectrum of literal interpretations, the feminist view affirms the natural meaning of the Song. The Song celebrates human love, shared in an environment of harmony and delight. Males are neither aggressors nor abusers, and females are neither passive objects nor victims. Together they savor God-given love.

Conclusion

The Song of Song is undeniably for lovers, but between whom—humans and God or humans only? From the third through the nineteenth century, commentators favored the former, in the twentieth century the latter. I have suggested a number of factors that contributed to these divergent interpretations: views of sexuality and the self, hermeneutic assumptions in approaching the biblical text, theological emphases and conditions in the church, and socio-economic circumstances.

Broadly speaking, the rise of historical-critical methodology created the wedge between traditional and modern interpretations of the Song. In so doing, it raised a number of questions that scholars only recently (in the last thirty years) have begun to pursue in a systematic fashion. Does one hermeneutical approach necessarily preclude another? Is there only one meaning of a text (an "original" meaning), or may there be multiple meanings, some primary, others secondary? More specifically, should Bernard's traditional, mystical interpretation of the Song be dismissed out of hand as the product of an uninformed era? Must one give up erotica for allegory, a natural meaning for a mystical one?

Roland Murphy, who gave most of his scholarly life to a critical understanding of the Song of Songs, once remarked that "it is paradoxical that Bernard, for all his allegorical flights, often captured the literal meaning of a passage *on the level of experience.*[121] In the form of homily, not commentary; interpretation, not analysis; open-ended conjecture, not tightly argued conclusions, Bernard's expression of the universal experience of love was unsurpassed. Though he purposed to describe the mutual love of God and humans, he had to "go through" human love to illustrate the union of human and divine love. On this level—what Bernard called the "carnal"—he captured the human experience of love. For Bernard, notes Carey Walsh, employing a different metaphor, "Eroticism is not disarmed, just extended in his mystical reading."[122]

But can his spiritual understanding of the Song be defended in the text itself? Murphy thought it could, observing that, among other things, Bernard's consistent use of sexual imagery to depict the mutual love of God and humans, though not found in the literal historical sense of the Song, has intertextual affinities with other biblical passages (e.g., Hosea 1–3; Jeremiah 2) that describe God's covenantal relationship with his people. Although the author of the Song did not have in mind the divine-human relationship, the meaning Bernard derived from the text was nevertheless a biblically valid inference. As Francis Landy observes, the Song "has implications beyond itself."[123] Indeed, the Song of Songs speaks not only of a paradise of human love regained in this world but also of a paradise of human and divine love consummated in the world to come.

4

"The Righteous Will Live by Faith"

Luther's Search for a Gracious God

For I am not ashamed of the gospel; it is the power of God for salvation to everyone who has faith, to the Jew first and also to the Greek. For in it the righteousness of God is revealed through faith for faith; as it is written, "The one who is righteous will live by faith."
—Romans 1:16–17

Among the major figures discussed in this book, no one has written more, and no one has more been written about than Martin Luther. Over the course of his career, Luther wrote hundreds of pamphlets, sermons, and treatises (averaging a publication every two weeks for twenty-five years), becoming the foremost publicist of the sixteenth century. According to Mark Edwards, Luther "dominated to a degree that no other person . . . has ever dominated a major propaganda campaign and mass movement since." The German Weimar edition of his works now totals over one hundred volumes, averaging seven hundred pages each, and includes sixty-four volumes of theological and devotional treatises. Works about Luther—then and now—run into the thousands, perhaps making him the most written about figure except for Jesus. In the mid-1960s, Gordon Rupp noted that Luther publications averaged six hundred per year, and in 1983, the five-hundred-year anniversary of Luther's birth, this output showed no signs of abating.[1] Given Luther's prominence as an amazingly prolific writer and as a controversial figure of the sixteenth century, it should not surprise us that he has been examined from nearly every conceivable angle. He wrote on myriad topics. In addition to biblical and theological subjects, he commented on food and drink, sex and marriage, child nurture and education, social conditions and politics, Catholics, Jews, and Muslims—to name but a few.

Of all the words that Luther penned and all the thoughts that engaged him most, none was more important than "justification by faith"—the subject of this chapter and one of the great themes of the Reformation that remains at the heart of Protestantism to this day.[2] Luther's rejection of what he perceived as a corrupt "works righteousness" in the church and his liberating insight into the graciousness of God resulted in what Anders Nygren, the Swedish Lutheran theologian, called a "Copernican revolution" in theology. Luther shifted the late medieval focus of attention away from what humans could do to gain favor in God's sight (e.g., by engaging in pious acts of prayer, making pilgrimages, or purchasing indulgences) to what God did in Jesus Christ for humankind. Defenders of Luther, though not without some exaggeration, have described this as a shift from a human-centered (anthropocentric) to a God-centered (theocentric) understanding of the Christian faith, from what Luther called a "theology of glory" to a "theology of the cross." Religion is not about doing something. You do not have to justify yourself before God (i.e., make yourself right) by depending on your own human effort to be loved by God. There are no conditions ("If you do this, then . . ."). God-given faith alone (*sola fide*) recognizes that for Christ's sake, God "justifies the ungodly" (Rom. 4:5) through the death and resurrection of Jesus Christ. And this faith alone justifies the sinner before God. This is the unconditional promise of salvation.[3]

Stating that the church "stands or falls" on the doctrine of justification by faith, Luther and his fellow Reformers challenged the Roman hierarchy and its dogma.[4] Basing his conclusions on the sole final authority of Scripture (*sola scriptura*), Luther declared that the institution of the papacy was a human invention, monasticism largely a fraud, and the sacramental system of the church (though certainly not all sacraments) a medieval accretion. His fundamental insight not only decisively transformed European Christianity but also had political and cultural repercussions.

As with all great historical figures, the problems in coming to terms with Luther are several. First, there is the image problem. Who was Luther? To the Catholics of his day, he was a heretic, a "wild boar in the vineyard," as Pope Leo X called the rebel whom he excommunicated in 1521. To his followers, especially after his death, Luther was elevated to the status of "prophet," the "Dr. Luther, of blessed memory," the man called by God to lead the Reformation of the church. Since 1700 Luther's image has varied widely, depending on the use to which Luther is put. For example, during the Enlightenment, he was cast as the hero of individual conscience, the man who liberated Europe from the superstitions of the Middle Ages. Beginning in the nineteenth century, Marxist historians condemned him as a peasant killer who aligned himself with the interests of the state. In more recent times, as Heiko Oberman notes, an ecumenical consensus has taken the bite out of Luther and dressed him up in the garb of the one, holy, Catholic Church. Every generation has interpreted Luther afresh according to its own presuppositions and pressing issues.[5]

A second problem in coming to terms with Luther lies in the perceived inevitability of his contributions. One hears, "He was destined to become a great reformer." Or "He came upon an era in history crying out for reform." Or a typically naïve Protestant view has Luther sitting alone, Bible in hand, pointing to what is apparently self-evident in the words of Romans 1:17, "The righteous shall live by faith." Yet nothing in Luther's upbringing predicted his later radical turn of thought, challenge to ecclesiastical authority, and eventual role as a reformer—a title he never claimed for himself.[6] Moreover, Luther's hostility toward Catholicism is often read through the lens of subsequent history. The eventual polarization of Catholics and Protestants, beginning with the Council of Trent (1545–63) and culminating in the Wars of Religion (1618–48) created such diametrical faiths that Luther's own indebtedness to his Catholic past is overlooked.

Another popular misconception is the notion that the Reformation originated in and radiated from Luther's doctrine of justification by faith. But as scholars have observed repeatedly, there were many different kinds of Reformations—intellectual, ethical, social, cultural, political, and ecclesiastical—with many different kinds of Reformers: magisterial and popular, humanist and Reformed, radical and Catholic. Luther's Wittenberg and his doctrine represent one place and one trajectory of thought (to sure, critical) in a complex and multifaceted movement.

Luther's discovery or, more aptly, his rediscovery of a gracious God was not merely an exercise of intellect. As is the case in most religious breakthroughs, his insight came after a passionate internal struggle. His crisis was at once theological and existential, a crisis born of doubt, anxiety, and bouts of depression. Luther's fundamental question was not posed in the abstract, such as "How does humanity find fellowship with God?" Rather, like the Philippian jailer before Paul and Silas, Luther personalized the issue: "What must I do to be saved?" (Acts 16:30).

Because Luther's dilemma and eventual breakthrough were tied intimately to his family circumstances, education, and spiritual and theological training as a monk, I begin this chapter with special attention to that period of his life designated as "the young Luther"—Luther's biography up to the indulgence controversy and his break with Rome (1517–18).[7] By this time, writes Bernard Lohse, "the basic concepts, although not all the details," of Luther's Reformation theology "were firmly established."[8] Thematically, I focus on Luther the professor of biblical studies and his engagement with the Bible in the context of his lectures on the Psalms (1513–15), Romans (1515–16), and Galatians (1516–17). During the course of Luther's lectures (never intended for publication)—perhaps by the beginning of his Romans lectures—a critical shift occurred in his understanding of God. His lectures evolved from an engagement with late medieval scholastic theology to a new biblical theology, from an emphasis on God's justice understood in a punitive sense (the God who punishes) to a declarative sense (the God who acquits the sinner). Put differently, the content of Luther's lectures shifted from an emphasis on the necessity to love God and achieve a right standing before him in humility to a faith in Christ alone who offers grace as the ground of salvation. Although Luther had yet to work out the full implications of this new insight (reached probably by 1519), his *Lectures on Romans* displayed the fundamental strands of his Reformation theology. In his subsequent *Lectures on Galatians* and other writings he grounded his insight in a new biblical hermeneutic, notably the distinction between law and gospel.

Given the importance Luther attached to Romans 1:17 as crucial for his new insight, I conclude the chapter with a discussion of this text as a locus classicus for the Protestant doctrine of justification. First, I view it within the context of the history of doctrine and biblical interpretation in the Western church and raise the question of whether Luther discovered a new thing or reappropriated a neglected doctrine. Second, I discuss recent developments within the Lutheran-Catholic ecumenical dialogue on the doctrine of justification and note how recent insights of modern biblical commentators relate to that dialogue.

Luther's Early Years

Martin Luther was born on November 10, 1483, to Hans and Margarethe (Hannah) Luther in the town of Eisleben, Germany, about 120 miles southwest of modern Berlin.[9] Within a year of his birth the family moved to nearby Mansfeld, a small but important mining center in Germany. Hans, of peasant stock, took up copper mining and leased a pit belonging to the counts of Mansfeld. Though this was a financially risky, often marginal, business, Hans obtained the necessary credit to open a mine shaft. In Martin's early years, the family lived on the edge of poverty, but his father, in an environment reminiscent of California's gold rush years, eventually prospered, paid off his loans, joined the city council, and became one of Mansfeld's leading citizens.

Martin attended Latin school from about age six until age thirteen or fourteen, and then he spent a year (1497–98) at Magdeburg on the Elbe River, perhaps under the guidance of the Brethren of the Common Life. Soon after, Luther moved to Eisenach, the town of his mother, where his education continued for the next four years (1498–1501). Recent discoveries about Luther's mother and her family provide a portrait of Martin surrounded and encouraged by Hannah's relatives and family friends during his years in Eisenach.[10] But the classroom was another matter. In an environment where rote learning and memorization were motivated by fear and cruelty, it was not always a happy experience for Martin. Teachers were strict, even brutal, as is attested by Luther's account that he was struck fifteen times in one morning for failing to decline a Latin noun that he had never been told to learn. But learn he did. At Mansfeld, Martin completed the first part of the medieval curriculum, the trivium, consisting of Latin grammar, logic, and rhetoric. He also received a rudimentary religious education and committed to memory the Apostles' Creed, entire psalms, and various prayers of the Catholic Church, including the Lord's Prayer.

Luther's upbringing might be characterized as within a frugal, middle-class family—some might say a "modern" environment insofar as the family rose above peasant status. As much as is known, his parents followed the religious and superstitious conventions of the day. Luther's mother was convinced that a "witch" lived nearby, casting spells, causing illness and injury, and threatening the lives of her children. Hans followed the popular devotional activity of his day by purchasing a special indulgence for the local parish church. No doubt Martin absorbed much of the piety and superstition of his day. Supernatural forces engaged in life-and-death struggles, inhabiting the landscape of his childhood, and they remained ever present throughout his adult life. As he observed in his now classic Reformation hymn, "A Mighty Fortress Is Our God" (1529),

> And though this world, with devils filled,
>   Should threaten to undo us,
> We will not fear, for God has willed
>   His truth to triumph through us.
> The prince of darkness grim,
> We tremble not for him;
> His rage we can endure,
> For lo! his doom is sure,
>   One little Word shall fell him.

But I am anticipating later developments. Luther was far from being able to assert confidently the triumph of God and the defeat of Satan by "one little Word." Continuing education, a life-changing decision, increasing spiritual despair, and immersion in biblical studies preceded such a bold proclamation.

University of Erfurt (1501–5)

In April 1501 Luther enrolled at the University of Erfurt, one of Germany's oldest and most prestigious universities. He more than compensated for his modest Latin education with his extraordinary mind and ambition, earning his B.A. (1502) and M.A. (1505) within the minimum amount of time stipulated by the statutes of the university. Luther received a traditional medieval education in the liberal arts, one that adhered to scholastic method with its emphasis on the rational explanation of religious belief. Drawing upon the rediscovery of many long-forgotten writings of Aristotle, scholastics such as Peter Abelard (1079–1142) and Thomas Aquinas (ca. 1225–74) brilliantly applied the categories of Aristotelian philosophy to prove the intellectual coherence of the Christian faith.

The scholastic edifice was constructed on the foundation of logic. In Luther's day, the fundamental texts remained the works of Aristotle: *Prior* and *Posterior Analysis*, and for advanced students, *Metaphysics* and *Ethics*. Students were drilled in dialectical reasoning, testing theses against countertheses, seeking resolution through syllogistic logic and ordered reasoning. One of the models of scholastic reasoning that Luther later imbibed was Peter Lombard's four-volume *Sentences* (1157–58), a standard textbook containing a wealth of quotations from the church fathers and offering a comprehensive and systematic overview of Christian doctrine. The method, format, questions, and distinctions of *Sentences* shaped theological discussion for centuries, as this compendium became required reading of theological students from the early thirteenth to the middle of the seventeenth century.

Despite the important role of scholasticism in Luther's education, the popularity of this method of learning had peaked well before 1500 and was coming under increasing criticism, particularly from humanist scholars such as Erasmus of Rotterdam. In 1503, Erasmus published *Handbook of the Christian Soldier*, an eventual runaway best-seller that went through twenty-three editions from 1515 to 1521. The humanist proposed reforming the Catholic Church by returning to Scripture and the works of the church fathers. Moreover, he emphasized "inner religion" or personal piety, not rational apprehension, as the key to understanding God. Eventually Luther, while rejecting the overall humanist agenda, became equally convinced that scholasticism, however valuable as an intellectual tool, not only failed to discover new truths but also failed to encompass the mystery and inscrutability of God.

Following completion of requirements for the M.A. degree, Luther prepared to continue his education in one of the professional faculties. Acceding to his father's wishes, he entered the faculty of law. Within three months of beginning the study of law, however, and much to the dismay of friends and family, Luther changed his plans and entered the monastery. The immediate circumstance prompting this abrupt move was an event often likened to the apostle Paul's dramatic conversion on the road to Damascus. But in Luther's case no conversion experience accompanied the high drama. In late June 1505, after a visit at home, Luther was returning to Erfurt when a fierce thunderstorm struck. The terrified young man prayed that if he were delivered he would enter the monastery. "St. Anne," he cried to the patron saint of miners, "help me! I will become a monk!" Despite pleas from his friends to reconsider, Luther held up his end of the bargain, and on July 17 he entered the cloistered Augustinian Observant order in Erfurt. His father was not pleased. In a fit of rage, he wrote his son an angry letter and temporarily disowned him. To Hans, Martin had made an impulsive, wrongheaded decision, mistaking the deceit of the devil as the direction of God. Years later Martin would agree.

The Cloister

What prompted this abrupt volte-face? In retrospect, Luther declared that he joined the cloister "in order to obtain my salvation." Next to baptism, becoming a friar (or a monk) was the surest way to heaven, for taking the vow—and fulfilling it—was akin to a second baptism that cleansed the soul of sin. For those who wanted the highest degree of assurance that their sins were forgiven, the cloistered life beckoned. Luther, then, was driven to the cloister not with the intent of fleeing the evils and distractions of the world or to enrich his faith by study and meditation, but, as Heiko Oberman observes, "He was driven by his desire to find the merciful God. . . . Searching for the merciful God was a crucial part of the monastic life and was by no means a unique expression."[11] After a requisite trial year as novitiate, he made his final profession in September 1506, pledging his commitment to Christ and the community and taking the traditional vows of poverty, chastity, and obedience.

Luther had not entered just any cloister. Of the twenty-two cloisters in Erfurt, including Benedictine, Carthusian, Franciscan, and Dominican houses, Luther chose the Augustinian Observant order. He never stated why he entered this order, but given his aptitudes and inclinations it was an appropriate choice. As an "observant" order (over against the nonreformed or "conventual" orders), the Erfurt Augustinian cloister was part of a widespread reform movement, under way since the fifteenth century, dedicated to returning to the original strict rules of the order. None of the contemporary satirists' criticisms about indolent, ignorant, and incontinent friars applied to this cloister: a severe ascetic life given to prayer, meditation, and study ordered its life.

In 1503 John Staupitz, dean of theology and chair of biblical theology at the newly founded University of Wittenberg, became the leader (vicar general) of the Observants in the region of Saxony, which included Erfurt. Staupitz became the most important figure in Luther's life during his fifteen years in the cloister, especially after Luther's permanent transfer to Wittenberg in 1511. The vicar general took a special interest in this exemplary friar, advised him on spiritual matters, instructed him to seek a doctorate in theology, and appointed him in 1512 to replace himself as professor of biblical theology at the University of Wittenberg. According to Luther, "Staupitz laid all the foundations" for his later theological insights by encouraging him to read the Bible and to rely on the blood of the crucified Christ for his salvation. Luther's central theological emphasis, his "theology of the cross," was indebted to Staupitz's influence.[12]

Although the details of Luther's life in the Black Cloister (so named for the black clothes worn by the friars) from 1505 to 1511 are sketchy, we do know that he was ordained a priest in 1507 and that he culminated his training in the usual way by celebrating his first mass. Whether it was stage fright, a common occurrence in new priests, or the presence of his father, who was now reconciled to his son's decision, Luther became terrified during the service. Visibly shaking, he nearly dropped the bread and wine and bolted from the altar during the saying of the Eucharistic prayer. Here he was a mortal, sinful man, consecrating the elements of the bread and wine, speaking directly to God, reenacting the sacrifice of Christ for the living and the dead, and offering the food of divine grace and hope of salvation to those who received the sacrament. The sacred rite was indeed an awesome transaction—nearly more than Luther could handle.

Human unworthiness and God's majesty, the inability of a sinful man to satisfy the demands of a righteous and holy God—these haunted Luther, engendering *Anfechtung*, Luther's term for the dreaded spiritual anxiety and desolation that overcame him. Luther found no comfort in a loving father God or in an interceding Christ. Though familiar with Bernard of Clairvaux's preaching on the beauty of Christ and hearing Staupitz's personal entreaties to trust the forgiveness of Christ, Luther could not get beyond the notion that on the day of judgment Christ would separate his sheep from the goats. In short, Luther lacked assurance that God was merciful to him, a sinner.

Why this dreaded feeling that he never lived up to God's strict demands? Did not the church offer spiritual counsel and a theologically satisfying explanation of salvation? For many it did, but not for Luther. "The real problem," observes Martin Brecht, "lay in the fundamental structure of medieval theology and piety. A person was supposed to bring forth a certain holiness from within himself in order to be able to meet God and associate with him. But this is precisely what Luther did not consider himself able to do."[13] Others, such as Gasparo Contarini, the Catholic lay reformer, cardinal, and later mediator between Catholics and Protestants, expressed similar despair but quickly resolved his spiritual doubts by recognizing that Christ's sufferings satisfied the debt of sins. But unlike Contarini's seemingly swift resolution, a long, tortuous path lay ahead before Luther found peace. In his early years in the monastery, Luther embraced the cloister with his heart, soul, and mind. "He had gone crazy over monasticism,"[14] notes a biographer, even to the point (like Bernard of Clairvaux) of recruiting others to join him. But over time Luther became increasingly restless and despondent, convinced that a sinless condition was unattainable and that nothing he did could ever please God.

A more systematic examination of the church's traditional ways to salvation clarifies the source of Luther's doubt. First, there was the way of self-help or the ascetic way, the way of the friar and monk. When he took his vows, Luther not only threw himself at God's mercy but also recognized that good works confirmed his devotion to the God of mercy. At his induction, the prior prayed, "Oh, God, may our brother sit at Thy right hand at the Last Judgment and be glad that he fulfilled his monastic vows completely." Fulfilled *completely*. Luther was up to the challenge, later noting that "if ever a monk could get to heaven through monastic discipline, I should have entered in."[15] He disciplined his body through fasting and self-flagellation and deprived himself of sleep and warmth. He disciplined his soul, seeking to love God with all his heart and mind. But questions haunted him: Have I done enough? How can I be sure that I've done all that I can to please God, that my acts of ascetic piety sufficiently compensate for my sins and so balance the spiritual ledger?

The sacraments offered a second means of the assurance of salvation. To borrow Jerome's metaphor, baptism provided the first plank after the shipwreck of original sin, and penance provided the second and only plank by which one could safely reach the shore of salvation.[16] Penance addressed postbaptismal sins with the purpose of restoring the Christian to the body of the faithful. Within the church, penance functioned to maintain discipline and to cure and console the guilty conscience. Confession was necessary, medieval writers noted, because the New Testament commanded it (they cited Matt. 16:19; John 20:20–23; Luke 17:14; and James 5:16), although some found it difficult to prove that Jesus himself instituted the sacrament. In the ritual itself the penitent identified the sin, expressed deep sorrow (contrition), and confessed the wrong to a priest who, acting in Christ's place, pronounced satisfaction or absolution after the penitent, as a test of sincerity, made proper penance or engaged in penitential exercises.

If confession is good for the soul, then Luther should have been feeling pretty good, for he was a regular at the confessional, often daily, up to six hours at a time. Relief came, if only temporarily, and the assaults of the devil (*Anfechtungen*) abated. But more often Luther doubted his purity and repented not because of the offense against God, but, like the "gallows sorrow" expressed by a criminal, because he feared the punishment of hell.[17]

The duration of confession was compounded by its nature, for monastic confession was far more rigorous than lay confession. In the cloister the confessor sought to uncover not just the act itself but the motive behind the act, to probe hidden thoughts and repressed feelings. Such interrogations frightened Luther and left him spiritually defeated. "My conscience could never give me certainty," he observed, "but always doubted and said, 'You have not done this correctly. You were not contrite enough. You omitted this in your confession.'"[18] Luther (and he was not alone in this regard) would go to his priest and confess his shortcomings. Then after returning to his cell, he would remember a sin he had forgotten to confess. Back to the confessor he would go.

And so it went. Luther worked himself into a near neurotic state. He was, in the parlance of friars, in *cloaca*, literally in the toilet, or down in the dumps, tormented with *Anfechtungen*.

In his popular biography of Luther, Roland Bainton observed that the penitential system was directed toward particular lapses, not the universal character of sin with its inherent corrupting effects. Consequently, Luther "arrived at a valid impasse," an impasse that could not be attributed to emotional pathology. "Sins to be forgiven must be confessed. To be confessed they must be recognized and remembered. If they are not recognized and remembered, they cannot be confessed. If they are not confessed, they cannot be forgiven. The only way out is to deny the premise." Luther was caught in a vicious cycle, repeatedly cast back on his own feeble, inadequate resources, and so plagued with his unworthiness that an exasperated brother in the monastery exclaimed, "God is not angry with you, but you are angry with God." Not until 1518, after Staupitz urged Luther to see penance not so much as an effort to placate an angry God but as a spiritual exercise centered on God's love for his sinful creatures expressed in the cross of Christ, did Luther find relief in this sacrament.[19]

Mysticism provided a third way to find peace with God. The phrase "Let go and let God," however casually invoked in our own time, describes the way of the mystic as the way of surrender. There are hints that Luther read the *Revelations* of Bridget of Sweden (d. 1373) and the mystical writings of Bonaventure (d. 1274), and that he was acquainted with Dionysius the Aeropagite. Staupitz, with mystical leanings himself, counseled Luther to follow this path, and later, in 1516, Luther imbibed the writings of Johannes Tauler (d. 1361), the famous German mystic. Withdrawal, contemplation, and eventual ecstasy, not engagement and external acts, defined the mystical way. If God had created the divine soul in humans, they had the potential to become divinelike. Rather than doing acts of devotion to please God, the mystic gave in to the love of God; God-absorption displaced human self-absorption. As one climbed the ladder of contemplation, the self gave way to the Other.

As much as Luther tried, he had neither the temperament nor the theological outlook to join the ranks of the mystics. He could not reconcile his own sense of sin and alienation with a holy, majestic God. The impasse was too wide, the chasm too deep, the effort too centered on human hubris. During his early years in the cloister, he could not bring himself to love God or to think of God as love. "Love God?" he noted in retrospect, "I hated him!" Over time, however, Luther developed a mystical theology based not on love and absorption into the divine but on God-given faith and mediated by the Word of God. In the sense that God spoke to believers through his Word, Luther garnered from mysticism an emphasis on the cross and Christ's sufferings that would become a key to his understanding God's justifying grace.[20]

As much as can be reasonably conjectured, such was the condition of

Luther's soul during his years in the Erfurt monastery. A year after his ordination a request came from the arts faculty at the University of Wittenberg for a lecturer on Aristotle's *Ethics*. To his dismay—for he was growing to despise Aristotle—Staupitz assigned him to the one-year teaching post. Luther obeyed, and following his return he was chosen to accompany another friar to Rome in the winter of 1510 on business of the order. The duo was sent to protest Staupitz's plan to bring all Augustinian monasteries in Saxony, including the independent Erfurt cloister, under the Observant rule.

Although the mission failed (the general of the Observants refused to hear the case), all was not lost. The 850-mile journey to Rome—at once the Holy City and a filthy place polluted by garbage and waste, not to mention prostitutes and beggars—became a pilgrimage for Luther. To free his grandfather from purgatory he, like pilgrims to this day, ascended the *Scala Sancta* of the palace of Pontius Pilate on his knees. He made hurried stops at churches, shrines, cathedrals, and basilicas. Reflecting later in life on his trip to Rome, Luther observed that what had impressed him most was not the city's piety but its profanity. Italian priests, whom Luther never liked, flippantly rattled off ten masses before he could get through one. And they were irreverent, mocking the doctrine of transubstantiation by chanting in Latin at the altar, "Bread thou art and bread thou shalt remain." What began as a sacred journey turned into a profoundly disillusioning experience.

Luther returned to Erfurt, reported to his superiors, but now had concluded that submission to Staupitz was the appropriate path. His incensed brethren suggested that he and John Lang, Luther's close friend who agreed with him, join Staupitz in Wittenberg. And so the two friars, personae non grata at Erfurt, transferred to Wittenberg—Luther in the summer of 1511 and Lang in early fall.

Luther's Theological Studies: The *Via Moderna*

The change from one cloister to another did little to relieve Luther's spiritual anxieties. His anguished yearning for assurance of salvation through bouts of *Anfechtungen* continued to preoccupy him well into his Wittenberg period, for his continued education and theological training exacerbated his problems. There is general consensus among scholars that he imbibed the thinking of a scholastic school known as the *via moderna*, or "new way." Both at the University of Erfurt and in the cloister, where intellectually superior friars like Luther were ordered to pursue theological studies, the *via moderna* predominated. Of the various schools within the *via moderna*, Luther was most influenced by the writings of the Franciscan school of William of Ockham (ca. 1285–1347) and Gabriel Biel (1410–95).[21]

Luther thus encountered the *via moderna*'s understanding of salvation—

one that he later criticized as Pelagian (or semi-Pelagian), though in a technical sense his criticism was unwarranted.[22] The *via moderna*'s teaching on justification demonstrated analogical affinities to the medieval political context, for it was based on the idea of covenant (*pactum* or *testamentum*), especially the notion of obligation. Just as a covenant between a king and his subjects defined mutual obligations (e.g., the subjects obeyed the king in exchange for protection), so a sacred covenant between God and humankind spelled out the conditions for salvation. This divinely initiated covenant expressed God's own self-imposed limits. That is, the *via moderna* distinguished two powers in God. On the one hand, God is omnipotent; he has absolute power (*potentia absoluta*). He can do anything, including act beyond human comprehension, even in a capricious manner. On the other hand, he deigns to act in human history in a particular way (*potentia ordinata*) through covenant obligations.

This particular way sought to reconcile human depravity and human responsibility within God's economy of salvation. First, it recognized that humans have a remnant or spark (*synteresis*) of the divine within. One can perform good deeds and become better by fanning the spark. At the same time, human endeavor is not enough. Few theologians suggested that anyone could do good works sufficient for salvation. Indeed, grace came from God alone through Jesus Christ (Eph. 2:8–9). By God's gracious initiative, mediated through the sacraments (baptism infused or imparted grace; penance renewed grace after each mortal sin), salvation was made available to those who met the conditions of the covenant. What must a person do? Every university student knew the answer by heart: "God will not refuse grace to those who do what is within them." "Do what is within you!" (*facere quod in se est*). "Do the best you can. Although your best is not sufficient to merit salvation, God will honor your effort, however weak, with his saving power." Thus, according to scholastic casuistry, the granting of God's grace followed the merit of "congruity"—creaturely effort to do good, and the merit of "condignity"—the effort to do good by the grace of God. "For the *moderni*," observes Alister McGrath, "this meant that God had ordained that his gift of justifying grace was conditional upon a particular response on man's part—and once that condition was met, the bestowal of grace followed as a matter of necessity."[23] A person, then, was truly justified only to the extent to which grace was realized in works. This idea reflected the Aristotelian notion that the virtuous person "actualizes" the potential (in the Christian sense, the "habitual grace") that is within.

The *via moderna*'s understanding of salvation troubled Luther in several ways and became, in the words of Gerhard Ebeling, "the hidden atomic fission which set up a chain reaction leading to the events of the Reformation."[24] First, as was the case with medieval piety in general, the question was raised, "Have I met the preconditions? How do I know I've done my best? How do I know if I've been sufficiently contrite in the confessional? Is sorrow for my sin a mask for fear of punishment?" The uncertainty tormented Luther. At bottom,

Luther concluded his depravity was so total that he could not meet the basic precondition, that of his own doing he could not please God.

Second, Luther became increasingly disillusioned with scholastic philosophy. Despite the importance that the *via moderna* placed on Scripture as the true source of theology, its adherents revised biblical concepts according to philosophical rules and format. Luther followed the *via moderna*'s emphasis in exalting Scripture over human reason, but as he immersed himself in the Bible, he became more and more critical of scholastic philosophy. God could not be confined by the "rancid rules" of logicians, for God had his own purposes that far transcended the bounds of human reason. Aristotle's definition of righteousness as human merit skewed the Christian idea of God's righteousness, so that God as judge rewarded everyone according to his merit. "The whole of Aristole," wrote Luther, "is to theology as shadow to light."[25] The vocabulary of ancient pagan philosophers—"prime mover," "form," "infusion," "substance"— had become the vocabulary of the church, obfuscating and polluting the true Christian faith.

For Luther, there was simply no way out of the quandary posed by medieval piety and scholastic philosophy. Nor was there a way out as long as he engaged in "navel gazing." The more he tried to fan the divine spark within, the more he realized he was doing it only to ward off the fires of hell. The more he confessed, the more he incurred God's disfavor, for God knew his true motives. Luther had come to a stalemate. Some outside influence was needed to enable him to resolve what was at once a deeply personal and a theological problem. That influence would come from his superior, Staupitz, and from his study of a book, the Bible.

The Professor and the Bible

I have noted that the bad blood between Luther and his Erfurt brethren resulted in his transfer to Wittenberg in the summer of 1511. A frontier village of 2,500 beer-making and beer-imbibing inhabitants, the upstart Wittenberg was no match for the sophistication and natural beauty of Erfurt. But Elector Frederick the Wise had grand plans for his new university and Staupitz had grand plans for Luther. Overwhelmed by the business of the order, the vicar general needed relief, especially from his teaching responsibilities as professor of biblical theology at the university. And so upon Luther's arrival, Staupitz informed him that he was to begin studies for a doctorate and become his replacement.

Luther progressed rapidly and was awarded the degree on October 19, 1512. A few days later he began lecturing to monastic students, probably on the Book of Genesis. So began Luther's career as a professor that ran nearly uninterrupted, year after year, until his death in 1546. And so continued the evolution of Luther's thought in an astoundingly creative period of about five years. *An-*

fechtungen persisted, but they now became a stimulus to biblical studies. "I didn't learn my theology all at once," he observed. "I had to ponder over it ever more deeply, and my spiritual trials [*Anfechtungen*] were of help to me in this, for one does not learn anything without practice."[26]

It is uncertain when Luther began studying the Bible. As a student in Latin school, he had memorized the Lord's Prayer and selected Psalms, but he claimed—probably to suggest that the Bible was neglected before he uplifted its centrality—that he never saw a Bible until his junior year in the library at the University of Erfurt. In all likelihood, however, Luther not only was exposed to the Bible but also heard and memorized large portions of it before he entered the cloister. As a novice, Luther, along with the other friars, was given a complete Latin Vulgate Bible with the injunction: "industriously to read, thoughtfully to hear, and carefully to study."[27] Luther took this command to heart. With his prodigious memory he developed a phenomenal knowledge of the content of the Bible.

Once he fully entered the cloister, private Bible study gave way to Bible courses where readings focused more on textbooks than on the Bible itself. Scripture was revered, but its understanding was rooted in accepted church sources and tilled in the soil of scholastic methods. Luther's passion for biblical studies caught the eye of Staupitz, who, as part of his reform effort, reinstated the study of Scripture within the Observant cloisters. Thus when Luther arrived at Wittenberg, his career path had become a fait accompli. He would become professor of biblical theology. Assuming this position marked a turning point in Luther's life and, subsequently, in the history of Christianity. "It is no exaggeration to say," remarks Gerhard Ebeling, "that never in the history of the university has the work of a scholar, in the study and in the lecture-room, had so direct and extensive an influence upon the world, and changed it so much."[28]

Like every newly minted Ph.D. teaching for the first time, Luther relied on what he had learned from his own professors. But—and this is where his penetrating mind and huge appetite for learning set him apart from others—he surpassed his teachers, broadened his reading to include ancient and contemporary scholars, and formulated his own conclusions. He was a driven, possessed man, not engaged merely in an academic enterprise with the goal of transmitting knowledge or creating it, though, to be sure, he did both. Rather, he was engaged in a life-and-death search for a gracious God.

Lectures on the Psalms *(1513–15)*

Beginning in mid-August 1513 and continuing through the spring of 1515, Herr Professor Luther lectured on the Psalms. Classes were held at 6:00 A.M. in the summer semester and 7:00 A.M. in the winter semester (the times were changed several years later to noon to accommodate Luther's popularity) and met twice a week. His choice of the Psalms was appropriate. Of all the books of the Bible he knew the Psalms best (probably by heart), for they were regularly chanted in the cloister and constituted the center of friary spiritual life. In addition, the Psalms described in the most poignant language Luther's own existential dilemma. The book covers the gamut of human emotion—from despair to favor, from desolation to comfort, from sorrow to joy. Also, among Old Testament books, the Psalter had the most influence on views of the Christian doctrine of justification (the texts of Ps. 31:1 and 71:2 being most relevant). Finally, as Luther and as Christians throughout the centuries interpreted it, Psalms was a Christian book, a christological hymnal of the Bible. "It most clearly promises the death and resurrection of Christ," observed Luther, "and described his kingdom, and the nature and standing of all Christian people." For this reason, "it could well be called a 'little Bible' since it contains . . . all that is found in the whole Bible."[29]

Luther organized his lectures within the conventions of scholastic biblical commentary, though in subsequent lectures on other books of the Bible he reworked, revised, and eventually rejected the inherited interpretive schema. As we have seen in earlier chapters, medieval biblical exegesis was inspired by the dictum of Scripture (as variously interpreted by Origen and Augustine), "The letter kills but the Spirit gives life" (2 Cor. 3:6). The plain or historical sense of Scripture ("the letter"), containing facts—at times trite and objectionable—gave way to a deeper, spiritual understanding of the text. During the late patristic period, this twofold approach was further refined (or expanded, depending on how one views it) into the *quadriga* or fourfold sense of Scripture. Every student in the later Middle Ages knew the jingle "The letter lets you know what happened, and allegory what you must believe; the moral what you must do, and the anagoge what you may hope for." Scripture thus had (1) a literal or historical sense; (2) an allegorical sense that pointed to Christ and/or the church; (3) a moral or tropological sense directed toward individual Christian behavior; and (4) an anagogical or eschatological sense that pointed to the Christian's hope after death. As we have seen in earlier chapters, wild flights of speculation were held in check by the recognition that the literal sense of Scripture precedes the spiritual interpretation, and the subjection of the individual's interpretation to the church's teaching.[30]

At the onset of his *Lectures* Luther explicitly advocated the medieval hermeneutical approach: "No allegory, tropology, or anagogy is valid, unless the same truth is expressly stated historically elsewhere. Otherwise Scripture would become a mockery." At the same time, the literal sense pointed beyond itself to a deeper spiritual insight: every prophecy and all prophets (i.e., those who wrote the Bible) should be understood as speaking of Jesus Christ. Although Luther followed a tradition going back to New Testament writers and the church fathers who interpreted the Old Testament as a Christian book, a more direct and radical influence on his approach to the Psalms was the French humanist Jacobus Faber Stapulensis (Jacques Lefèvre, d. 1536). Stapulensis proposed a twofold understanding of the literal sense: the usual understanding of the plain, historical sense and a truer meaning, the christological sense. In actuality, Faber paid little attention to the historical sense. He virtually ignored Hebrew Scripture as a historical and theological body of writings with its own integrity, for the literal sense was "the intention of the prophets and of the Holy Spirit speaking in Him," namely, Christ.[31]

For Luther, as for Stapulensis and others, Scripture was about Christ—foreshadowed and promised in the Old Testament, incarnate and fulfilled in the New. Every word of Holy Writ pointed toward Christ. And yet Luther carried forward this approach in new, creative, and radical ways. As he expressed it in the preface to his *Lectures on the Psalms* (which he called the "Preface of Jesus Christ"!), "Every prophecy and every prophet must be understood as referring to Christ the Lord, except where it is clear from plain words that someone else is spoken of. For thus He Himself says: 'Search the Scriptures, . . . and it is they that bear witness to Me' (John 5:39). Otherwise it is most certain that the searchers will not find what they are searching for."[32]

Following the medieval exegetical schemata of the gloss and scholia (a method applied not only to the Bible but also to other authoritative documents of the church), Luther cast his christological exegesis within the mold of scholastic commentary. The gloss was a marginal and interlinear exposition of individual words and terms of a biblical text, and the scholia took up longer portions of the text requiring exposition. In preparation for his lectures, Luther commissioned Johann Grunenberg, the printer for the university, to produce a special edition of the Psalter in Jerome's Latin version with extrawide margins and ample space between lines. With a raven's quill in hand, Luther filled the white spaces with his own gloss. As he lectured—really, dictated—in Latin from these glosses, students recorded Luther's words in their own Psalters. Once the glosses were finished, the longer exposition (scholia) followed. Luther thus followed the conventional medieval exegetical procedures but with a profound hermeneutical difference. Gerald Bruns suggests that "Luther produced for his students something like a modern, as opposed to a medieval, text of the Bible—its modernity consisting precisely in the amount of white space around the text. In a stroke Luther wiped the Sacred Page clean as if to begin the history of interpretation over again, this time to get it right."[33]

As Luther worked his way through the Psalms, preoccupied with issues of God's judgment and righteousness, he adumbrated ideas that emerged with full clarity in his subsequent writings. Luther scholars have observed that the bulk of the *Lectures* contain traditional scholastic themes but that as they progress, a change in understanding of the relationship between God and humankind can be detected. Some commentators argue that his lectures on Psalm 31 are crucial; others point to Psalm 71 and 72; still others to Psalm 118. Here I make no attempt to resolve this debate; rather, I offer pointers in the direction of Luther's new understanding of God.

First, Luther framed his discussion of justification within the categories of the *via moderna*, but he revised the conditions of preparation for God's grace and invested the traditional vocabulary with new meaning. According to the *via moderna*, the basis of justification was viewed as a covenant involving human accomplishment (doing that which is within oneself) and God's grace. Humankind offered God humility, and God in turn offered his justifying grace, for "God gives grace to the humble" (James 4:6). Throughout his lectures Luther emphasized the virtue of humility—*the* monastic virtue—as a necessary precondition of saving grace. "But now the whole righteousness of God is this," Luther observed in his discussion of Psalm 71:19. "To humble oneself into the depth. Such a one comes to the highest, because he first went down to the lowest depth. Here he properly refers to Christ, who is the power of God and the righteousness of God through the greatest and deepest humility." Examining Luther's discussion of this psalm and others (especially Psalm 113), David Steinmetz proposes that Luther no longer considered humility a virtue that merited God's grace; rather, humility became a virtue only *after* God extended his grace to the sinner.[34] The reason: the sinner is incapable of presenting a disposition of pure moral virtue as the ground of God's grace. Luther continued to refer to *synteresis*, but in a way that suggests that humans long for the good and desire to please God but lack the moral wherewithal to realize the good.[35]

God has indeed established a covenant in which he promises to give grace to the humble, but antecedent to humankind's expressed humility is the confession of sin and recognition that God himself is justified in his word of judgment and grace. Luther appeals to "do what is in oneself," but he rejects the notion (taught by Gabriel Biel) that one has the capacity to love God by exercising natural moral abilities. All that he can do is to "ask," "seek," "knock," and cry out in faith for a virtue that he does not possess. Yes, humankind does what is within but in a very different sense from that understood within the framework of the *via moderna*. A person is justified not by love (whether a disposition or an act) but by faith alone, not by "faith active in love" but by "faith living in Christ."[36]

Second, as Luther exegeted the meaning of "thy righteousness" (Ps. 71:19) and "in thy righteousness deliver me" (Ps. 31:1; 72:2), he began to shift the emphasis from the literal-prophetic meaning, referring to Christ, to the tropological one, referring to the individual believer. For example, considered in its "literal" sense, Psalm 31:1 was a prayer of Christ to the Father. Tropologically, however, it referred to the deliverance of the individual ("me") bestowed by God's righteousness through faith in Christ. Luther thus began to relate the divine action in Christ to the work of God in the soul. He closed his discussion of Psalm 71 with the following: "Therefore, whoever wants to relish the apostle and other Scriptures must understand everything tropologically: Truth, wisdom, strength, salvation, righteousness, namely that by which He makes us strong, safe, righteous, wise, etc. So it is with the works of God and the ways of God. All of them are Christ literally, and all of them are faith in him morally."[37] Luther appealed not to the traditional tropological approach of "What must *I* do? What demands are placed upon *me* in the power of the justifying love of God?" Rather, his tropological interpretation pointed to faith (not love) that apprehends Christ. In this vein, in his lecture on Psalm 72, Luther distinguished two meanings to the righteousness of God, one as the judgment of God, the other as the justifying faith in Christ:

> God's judgment is tropological. This is the most frequent use in
> Scripture. This is the judgment by which God condemns and causes
> to condemn whatever we have of ourselves, the whole old man with
> his deeds. . . . This is properly humility, yes humiliation. For it is not
> the one who regards himself that is righteous, but the one who con
> siders himself detestable and damnable in his own eyes . . . he is
> righteous. . . . In the same way the righteousness of God is also
> threefold [i.e., understood in the three spiritual senses]. Tropologi
> cally it is faith in Christ. Rom. 1:17: "For the righteousness of God is
> revealed in the Gospel from faith to faith."[38]

To what extent do these comments reveal a turn in Luther's theology? Scholars like Gordon Rupp suggest that Luther's understanding of the righteousness of God during his lectures on the Psalms, especially Psalms 70 and 71, took a "probable" innovative turn. Clearly, a revision of the traditional conditions of justification and a tropological interpretation of the righteousness of God as faith in Christ represent a shift in Luther's thought. But if we follow another scholar's suggestion, it was essentially "a conceptual clarification," preparatory for Luther's eventual breakthrough. In his lecture on Psalm 119, Luther seems to be moving closer to the idea that the reception of grace is itself a gift of God's grace. Quoting verse 11 ("Thy words have I hidden in my heart, that I may not sin against Thee"), Luther noted that "what we propose is nothing, unless the grace of God disposes it." Perhaps we do best to heed David Steinmetz's observation that "the years 1513 to 1515 mark an intermediate period in Luther's theological development. During this time he broke with the old medieval approach to Scripture and laid the foundation for the new approach to the text which he constructed after 1516."[39]

In conclusion, several thematic strands weave their way through the *Lectures on the Psalms* and anticipate the pattern of Luther's overall theology (his *theologia crucis*, or "theology of the cross") and hermeneutic. First, Christ is the center of Scripture. Apart from the crucified and resurrected Christ, there is no true knowledge of Scripture. As the content of Scripture, Christ comes to sinners in both judgment and grace. Second, the condition of justification is not humility but faith, not obedience to the moral demands of the law but a faith rooted in trust and dependence upon Christ. Third, the interpretation of

Scripture is derived from living communion with God. For Luther, one should engage the text in an intensely personal or existential way. Truth can be understood only by experiencing it. Finally, Scripture reveals a dialectical tension of polar yet complementary and necessary opposites. Luther was forever fond of expressing biblical truths in paradoxical sets of twos. In his *Lectures on the Psalms* he stresses such themes as human sin and divine holiness, the spirit and letter of Scripture, and a God whose grace is revealed yet hidden under his judgment.[40]

Luther's Breakthrough

Clearly, Luther's *Lectures on the Psalms* anticipates themes in his doctrine of justification by faith, but it is difficult to determine how conscious he was of a novel theology. Exactly when this new theological understanding emerged clearly remains the subject of a prolonged and highly contested debate among Luther scholars. Nearly every date from 1505 to 1519 has been proposed, though modern scholars are generally divided between an early (1513–15) or a later (1518–19) discovery date.[41] Luther himself spoke often of his breakthrough and identified Romans 1:17 as the crucial text, but only once did he give a narrative account of his discovery. According to Heiko Oberman, the account represents a condensation of Luther's many insights and structurally conforms to Augustine's *Confessions*. As we have seen in earlier chapters, there is a pattern to such experiences: the obscured but "true" meaning of the text is revealed to the struggling exegete in a flash of illumination. In Luther's case, his new theological insights resulted from intensive exegetical work fueled by a determination to resolve difficult passages, no matter how long it took. When he got stuck on some passages, for example, Romans 1:17, he cast aside secondary sources and, as he put it, "sweat over the Bible."[42]

Luther's description of his "tower experience" (*Turmerlebnis*)—so-called because his breakthrough occurred in his third-floor study located in the tower of the monastery—is the most complete account of his transformation. Written some thirty years after the event in his preface to the Latin edition of his works (1545), this autobiographical fragment indicates that Luther's breakthrough came after he had lectured on Romans (1515–16), Galatians (1516–17), and Hebrews (1517–18). Some scholars take Luther at his word: sometime in 1518–19 he experienced his breakthrough. Others believe that lapses in memory muddled Luther's chronology, and so they assign an earlier date for the breakthrough. Still others observe that Luther did not state that his discovery took place in 1519, only that it was complete by that date. For some scholars the *when* of the discovery is intimately tied to the *what* of the discovery. For others, the *when* is irrelevant; the point is, *something* happened. Luther's account of his theological insight, though written long after the fact, exudes the palpable excitement of a new discovery:

I had indeed been captivated with an extraordinary ardor for understanding Paul in the Epistle to the Romans. But up till then it was not the cold blood about the heart, but a single word in Chapter 1 [:17], "In it the righteousness of God is revealed," that had stood in my way. For I hated that word "righteousness of God," which, according to the use and custom of all the teachers, I had been taught to understand philosophically regarding the formal or active righteousness, as they called it, with which God is righteous and punishes the unrighteous sinner.

Though I lived as a monk without reproach, I felt that I was a sinner before God with an extremely disturbed conscience. I could not believe that he was placated by my satisfaction. I did not love, yes, I hated the righteous God who punishes sinners, and secretly, if not blasphemously, certainly murmuring greatly, I was angry with God. . . . Thus I raged with a fierce and troubled conscience. Nevertheless, I beat importunately upon Paul at that place, most ardently desiring to know what St. Paul wanted.

At last, by the mercy of God, meditating day and night, I gave heed to the context of the words, namely, "In it the righteousness of God is revealed, as it is written, 'He who through faith is righteous shall live.'" There I began to understand that the righteousness of God is that by which the righteous live by a gift of God, namely by faith. And this is the meaning: the righteousness of God is revealed by the gospel, namely, the passive righteousness with which merciful God justifies us by faith, as it is written, "He who through faith is righteous shall live." Here I felt that I was altogether born again and had entered paradise itself through open gates. There a totally other face of the entire Scripture showed itself to me.[43]

For Luther, the righteousness of God not only condemns sinners—this was the notion he could not get past—but also frees them. Drawing from the traditional Catholic theological distinction between God's "active" and "passive" righteousness, Luther shifted the emphasis away from God's active righteousness (from God's vindictive righteousness against sinners who vainly tried to appease God through good works) to God's passive righteousness (God's righteousness revealed in mercy toward the sinner). Amid the bad news of judgment there is good news of mercy. God's righteousness demands that his laws are obeyed, and yet because human beings cannot keep the law ("For all have sinned"), they stand condemned. At the same time, this judgment is lifted by a merciful, loving judge, who pronounces a "not guilty" verdict on the condemned. Humans are not objectively righteous, that is, they are not now truly righteous within their own being (they remain prone to sin), but they are *declared* righteous.

This declaration is made possible by Christ who himself met the precondition of righteousness. By taking upon himself humankind's sin, death, and the wrath of God, Christ's atonement worked what Luther called a "sweet exchange": condemned humanity now has Christ's own righteousness, life, and grace. To use Luther's oft-cited analogy: just as a mother hen covers her chicks with her wing, so God covers humanity in his righteousness. Humans remain what they are—sinners—but God, out of his love, offers them a protective shield. The change in humans is not ontological but relational. Or to slightly alter the analogy: God clothes humans in his righteousness, although inside they remain sinners. They are thus "righteous and sinners at one and the same time" (*simul iustus et peccator*). Luther discovered that a new relationship with God was established not by following in Christ's steps—the path of humility and works righteousness—but as he heard by faith God's word to him. That word was the good news of the gospel, freely offered to those who place their faith in Jesus Christ.

As noted earlier, exactly *when* Luther's discovery came to him is uncertain. Clearly, his early *Lectures on the Psalms* (he returned to them again in 1519) provide clues into his doctrine of justification by faith, but his mature thinking on the subject required several more years of "sweating over the Bible." Indeed, there is a consensus among scholars that Luther's evangelical breakthrough came gradually through steady development and growth.[44] The one constant remained Luther's continued engagement with Scripture.

Lectures on Romans (1515–16)

In the history of biblical interpretation and in the broader context of the history of Christianity, Paul's treatise to the Romans has exerted a profound influence. "The impact that this letter has had on the Christian church," writes Joseph Fitzmyer, "is incalculable. . . . One can almost write the history of Christian theology by surveying the ways in which Romans has been interpreted." Paul's letter decisively shaped Augustine's theology, beginning with his conversion in the garden when, upon hearing the words "Take up and read, take up and read," he opened the Bible to Romans 13:13b–14. It became the pivotal, life-changing book in the life of John Wesley, whose "heart was strangely warmed" upon hearing the reading of Luther's "Preface to the Romans" at a Moravian meeting on Aldersgate Street in London in 1738. And it altered the theological perspective of Karl Barth, rousing him and European theologians from their "dogmatic slumbers" following World War I. In his preface to his commentary on Romans (1918), Barth observed, "The reader will detect for himself that it has been written with a joyful sense of discovery. The mighty voice of Paul was new to me: and if to me, no doubt to many others also." Barth's words sound strikingly similar to Luther's description of his evangelical experience—an experience that, as we have seen, grew out of his engagement with the book of Romans.[45]

In their general tone and approach, Luther's Romans lectures hardly resemble his Psalms lectures. Whereas his *Lectures on the Psalms* displayed a formality, complexity, and prolixity that challenge the most astute reader, Luther's *Lectures on Romans* are clear, engaging, almost conversational in tone. Something has happened. There is an authenticity to this work: we hear Luther's voice and convictions resounding throughout the text. Although Luther retains the medieval organizational structure of the gloss and scholia, he seldom reverts to the *quadriga* and instead uplifts the historical-grammatical-christological reading of the text. Also he has become increasingly critical of scholastic philosophy, and for the first time he attacks his teachers in the *via moderna*. "I owe to the Lord this duty of speaking out against philosophy and persuading men to heed Holy Scripture. . . . I have been worn out by these studies for many years now. . . . I have come to see that it is the study of vanity and perdition."[46]

We also observe that he has introduced a theological soul mate: "blessed Augustine." Luther was familiar with Augustine's writings—he had earlier read *The City of God* and other writings—but in the intervening period between his *Lectures on the Psalms* and *Lectures on Romans*, Luther encountered Augustine's anti-Pelagian writings and *On the Letter and the Spirit*. Throughout the Romans lectures, Luther refers to these and other writings of Augustine on nearly 120 occasions. With the help of Augustine's insights into human depravity, God's grace, and the futility of works righteousness, with recourse to his own vast knowledge of Scripture (he makes sixteen hundred direct quotations from the Bible), and with his penetrating mind, Luther apprehends the gospel, the good news of salvation. He discovers the joyful appropriation by a God-given faith of the mercy of God that is extended to humankind on account of what Christ has done on the cross. If in the past Luther's eyes focused on the word "righteous" in Romans 1:17 ("The righteous shall live by faith"), they are now directed to the word "faith." In these lectures, Luther clarifies the doctrine of justification: faith alone and Christ alone justify the sinner before God.[47]

Before expanding on the content of these lectures, I should note two rather surprising observations. The first concerns the history of the transmission of the text of Luther's *Lectures on Romans*. This work, now viewed as absolutely critical to Luther's understanding of the gospel, was virtually unknown until 1899, when Professor Johannes Ficker of Strassbourg discovered a copy of the lectures in the Vatican library. Not content with just a copy, Ficker searched for the original and found it in a display case at the Royal Library in Berlin. Ficker published a preliminary version in 1908 and then a definitive edition in 1938, as volume fifty-six of the Weimar edition of Luther's works. Needless to say, the publication of Luther's *Lectures on Romans* had a profound effect on Reformation studies and inspired a renaissance of Luther scholarship.[48]

Second, given Luther's several "Table Talk" remarks and his famous comment in the 1545 preface to his Latin works that Romans 1:17 was crucial to his evangelical breakthrough, it is surprising to discover that this passage receives relatively little attention in his *Lectures*.[49] The full verse reads, "For in it [i.e., the gospel; see v. 16] the righteousness of God is revealed through faith for faith; as it is written, 'The one who is righteous will live by faith'" (NRSV). In his comments on "the righteousness of God is revealed," Luther succinctly summarizes his views of the gospel and juxtaposes them with the "vain philosophies" of men (e.g., Aristotle and the scholastics):

> Only in the Gospel is the righteousness of God revealed (that is, who is and becomes righteous before God and how this takes place) by faith alone, by which the Word of God is believed. . . . For the righteousness of God is the cause of salvation. And here again, by the righteousness of God we must not understand the righteousness by which He is righteous Himself but the righteousness by which we are made righteous by God. This happens through faith in the Gospel.
>
> The righteousness of God is so named to distinguish it from the righteousness of man, which comes from works, as Aristotle describes it very clearly in Book III of his [*Nicomachean*] Ethics. According to him, righteousness follows upon actions and originates from them. But according to God, righteousness precedes works, and thus works are the result of righteousness.[50]

The core of Luther's evangelical breakthrough is evident: through faith in the gospel humankind is made righteous. God's righteousness is not only an attribute of God but also a divine gift to humanity. Humans are not made righteous before God by their works, for as Luther states in his scholia on Romans 14:1, "man of himself can do nothing." It is thus "most absurd" to support the Pelagian statement that "'God infallibly pours His grace into him who does what is within his power,' if we understand the expression to mean that he does something or can do something." Such thinking has almost "overturned" the whole church.[51] Works (acts of love and devotion toward God) are a consequence, not a condition, of God making humankind righteous.

The overall theme and thrust of the *Lectures on Romans* is laid out in Luther's first paragraph in the scholia. Here he observes the depth of human depravity, the consequent failure of works righteousness, God's redemption of the sinner by the application of an "outside" and "foreign" righteousness, "and the need for a God-given humility. "The chief purpose of this letter," he writes in the very first sentence, is "to break down, to pluck up, and to destroy all wisdom and righteousness of the flesh."[52] Luther reiterates the dialectic between an egocentric and theocentric fellowship with God, between the righteousness humans offer and the righteousness that comes from God. A false "theology of glory" speculated on the invisible God and his works, whereas the true "theology of the cross" focused on the crucified Christ.

Luther completely rejects the idea of humankind's inclination toward the good or of a divine spark within (*synteresis*). He criticizes scholastic theologians ("O fools, O pig-theologians!") who "have been under the delusion that original sin, like actual sin, is entirely removed" in the sacrament of baptism. "The ancient fathers Ambrose and Augustine spoke different and in the way Scripture does." But scholastics such as Peter Lombard had an inadequate view of original sin, recognizing it as merely a privation or lack of original righteousness. But as humankind's inability to keep the law so manifestly reveals, the will remains in bondage to sin. "For this reason philosophy stinks in our nostrils, as if our reason always spoke for the best thing."[53] No, "according to the apostle [Paul] and the simplicity of meaning in Christ Jesus," original sin "is a total lack of uprightness, . . . a propensity toward evil, . . . a nausea toward the good, a loathing of light and wisdom and a delight in error and darkness."[54]

If, then, even saints remain diseased within, devoid of any *synteresis*, how are they declared righteous or justified before God? Humankind cannot be freed of this "curvedness, iniquity, and crookedness except by the grace of God." Though they remain sinners by their very nature, God in his mercy imputes (or credits) to them a "foreign," "external," "outward," or "alien" righteousness. "They are sinners in fact but righteous in hope." God's "imputation is not ours by reason of anything in us or in our own power." Drawing upon the well-known analogy found in Augustine and in writers of the medieval period, Luther likens Christ to the great physician, "our Samaritan," who begins to heal the sinner, "having promised to him the most complete cure unto eternal life." A person never becomes completely righteous (or completely healed) in this life, "for he is at the same time both a sinner and a righteous man."[55]

Throughout his lectures, when Luther speaks about faith and the righteousness of God, he invariably refers to Christ, the mediator. As he rhetorically queries, "Does something other than faith in Christ with its good works seem to be required for justification?"[56] Luther's commentary on Romans 2:15 ("And among themselves in turn their thoughts accuse or defend them") captures the thrill of his new discovery and summarizes the "sweet exchange" between Christ and the sinner:

> For if the heart of a believer in Christ accuses him and reprimands him and witnesses against him that he has done evil, he will immediately turn away from evil and will take refuge in Christ and say, "Christ has done enough for me. He is just. He is my defense. He

has died for me. He has made His righteousness my righteousness, and my sin His sin. If He has made my sin to be His sin, then I do not have it, and I am free. If He has made His righteousness my righteousness, then I am righteous now with the same righteousness as He.[57]

Luther's *Lectures on Romans* proved pivotal to his theological development and, as it turned out, to his subsequent break with Rome. He articulated the great themes of Reformation theology: justification (and hence salvation) is by faith alone (*sola fide*), by grace alone (*sola gratia*), and through Christ alone (*solo Christo*). His followers later concluded that justification by faith is "the summary of all Christian doctrine," and "the article by which the church stands or falls."

His *Lectures* also anticipate the other fundamental conviction of the Protestant Reformation, namely, Scripture alone (*sola scriptura*), although he did not make public this view until the Leipzig debate with John Eck in July 1519. The debate, instigated by the indulgence controversy that had broken out over Luther's Ninety-five Theses (posted on October 31, 1517), forced his hand. The debaters initially took up the issue of the divine origin of the papal office, particularly focusing on the Petrine text. Luther granted the primacy of honor due the pope but rejected the office's divine institution. As Eck probed, questioned, and challenged, Luther admitted that both councils and popes had erred. Finally, Eck forced Luther to verbalize his growing conviction: "A simple layman armed with Scripture is to be believed above a pope or a council without it. . . . For the sake of Scripture we should reject pope and councils." This single admission had revolutionary implications. Before Luther, the principle of Scripture alone was never advocated. "No one," avers Bernard Lohse, had "ever critically reexamined [church] tradition on the basis of Scripture."[58]

Luther declared what came to be called the *formal* principle of the Reformation: all church teaching is to be measured by Scripture. He did not eschew all tradition but viewed it as a less reliable guide to the meaning of the Christian faith than Scripture. Luther and his followers affirmed the great christological and Trinitarian formulations in the traditional creeds, and, as we have seen, he found in Augustine and other church fathers valuable allies. But he rejected tradition that did not conform to his understanding of the plain teaching of Scripture. A creeping moralism, with its striving for perfection and the predominance of philosophy over biblical theology, though a part of the church's tradition, subverted the teachings of Scripture and thus required repudiation.[59]

Luther's Hermeneutic

If the Bible alone became the battle cry of Luther and Protestants, upon what interpretive principles was the Bible correctly understood? Without a teaching magisterium to ensure correct interpretation, who decided what interpretation was correct? At the Diet of Worms (1521) on the eve of his bold stand before Germany's princes, prelates, and emperor Charles V, that very question and the logic to which it led tormented Luther: "Are all the others in error? Have so many centuries walked in ignorance? What if it should be you who err, and drag so many with you in error, to be eternally damned?" Amid these *Anfechtungen*, Luther found the courage to face his accusers. When asked to retract his writings that attacked the papacy, he declared, "Unless I am proved wrong by the testimony of Scriptures or by evident reason I am bound in conscience and held fast to the Word of God . . . therefore I cannot and will not retract anything. . . . God help me. Amen."[60]

The testimony of Scripture required understanding and interpretation, and, as noted, Luther gradually developed new principles of interpretation. To assist his endeavor he learned the biblical languages, first Greek and then Hebrew (in which he felt himself more proficient), in order to exegete more accurately the meaning of the text. Here the humanist contribution of *ad fontes*—back to the (ancient) sources—abetted by the print revolution, proved invaluable. Luther fully utilized humanist scholarship, including Johann Reuchlin's *Hebrew Dictionary* (1506), the Amerbach brothers' edition of *Augustine's Works* (1490–1506), and especially Erasmus's edition of the Greek New Testament (1516). When exiled to the Wartburg Castle in 1521, Luther relied exclusively on Erasmus's Greek New Testament for his German translation. Though he rejected the humanist agenda of moral improvement without a radical theological reconstruction, Luther owed considerable debt to humanist scholarship.[61]

Scripture Interprets Scripture

What interpretive principles guided Luther's understanding of the Bible? Luther knew the familiar saying that epitomized the difficulties of a proper hermeneutic: "The Scripture has a wax nose." Distortion, manipulation, alteration—these can easily happen by arbitrary interpretation. Luther's first principle, then, was to know Scripture and to comprehend its fundamental message. He expressed this conviction in his Christmas sermon of 1522: "Go to the Bible itself, dear Christians, and let my expositions and those of all scholars be no more than a tool with which to build aright, so that we can understand, taste, and abide in the simple and pure word of God."[62] The Bible, not learned exegesis, binds the soul to God. "The simple and pure word of God" brought certainty and assurance to the conscience, as Luther made clear in his 1545 narrative of his evangelical breakthrough. Luther asserted a unique Protestant principle: the Bible is its own interpreter. No external authority (papal pronouncements, church tradition) is required to verify its message and meaning, for Scripture is perspicuous.

But who does the interpreting? As much as Luther and the Reformers stressed the plain sense of Scripture and the necessity of each Christian to learn and understand the Bible for himself or herself, they tempered these convictions by injecting the necessary role of the pastor-scholar. Conclusions reached by private interpretation should agree with those taught by properly trained church leaders. Yes, Scripture should be made available to all and personally engaged by all, but an elite core of scholars who know the ancient languages and presumably have the clearest grasp of the biblical writers' intentions guides its correct interpretation. Those parts of Scripture that are unclear should be interpreted in light of the clearer portions that witness to the central core of the faith—Christ's incarnation, his cross, and resurrection. Beginning with this baseline principle, the so-called analogy of faith, Luther formulated a distinct hermeneutic.

The Spirit and the Letter

One of Luther's key interpretive principles is the distinction between the Spirit and the letter, between that which enlivens the heart and possesses a person and that which is remote and foreign. He followed the well-known interpretive tradition, first formulated by Paul in 2 Corinthians 3:6, "The letter kills, but the Spirit gives life," though in Paul's case he was distinguishing between the law under the old covenant and the Spirit as the determinative element in the new. Paul's distinctions were given new meaning, beginning with Origen's allegorizing. As early as his Psalms lectures, however, Luther limits the allegorical reading of Scripture and uplifts the historical-literal approach—an approach that is not literal (he was no literalist) but christological. "In the whole Scripture," Luther asserts, "there is nothing else but Christ, either in plain words or involved words."[63] There may be obscure, hard to understand passages, but the content of Scripture is plain: it is the revelation of God in Christ—a fact no less true of the Old Testament than of the New. Christ is the eternal Word of God present as promise in the Old Testament and incarnated as fulfillment in the New. Earlier theologians had stressed the centrality of Scripture, so in this regard Luther was not original. His contribution lay in placing Christ, revealed by the Spirit, in the center of the Bible. As he was fond of saying, the Bible is the cradle in which the Christ child was laid. Christ enables one to understand the Bible, not vice versa. The Bible becomes the Word of God as it is inspired by the Holy Spirit and brings saving knowledge of Jesus Christ.

Some books of the Bible present the clarity of Jesus as the Savior better than others. The Gospel of John, the writings of Paul (especially Romans), and 1 Peter are a cut above the rest of the New Testament, for they plainly proclaim Christ and him crucified, and for that reason they should be perused daily. Luther preferred those books of the Bible that described Christ's mission (especially his suffering, resurrection, and grace and promise to those who responded in faith) to those that narrated his mission (as found in the synoptic Gospels). "The Epistles of St. Paul are more of a gospel than Matthew, Mark and Luke. For the latter do not describe much more than the history of the works and miracles of Christ. But no one gives a finer account of the grace which we have through Christ than St. Paul."[64]

Luther's Jesus is not primarily Jesus the ethical teacher, the teacher of the Sermon on the Mount (though Luther believed these teachings applied to all Christians), as he was for humanists such as Erasmus or, as we will see in the next chapter, for radical Reformers such as the Anabaptists. Rather, Luther's Jesus was Paul's Jesus, Christ the redeemer. Given his selective criteria, he dismissed some books of the Bible as unworthy of the canon itself, though he never rejected them. In effect, he created a "canon within the canon." The Book of James, "an epistle full of straw," and Revelation were neither apostolic nor prophetic; and both Hebrews and Jude were of dubious value.[65]

Law and Gospel

Another interpretive principle, one that eventually displaced the conceptual scheme of letter and Spirit though it remained closely allied to the theme of Christ the center of Scripture, is Luther's distinction between "law" and "gospel." Luther alludes to this distinction, discerning which he called "the greatest skill in Christendom," in his lectures on Galatians (1516–17) and then develops it more fully in subsequent lectures, particularly when he returned to lecture on Galatians in 1531.[66] Paul's letter to the Galatians is a stinging rebuke of Peter and a "Judaizing" party within the church who insist that the Galatians be circumcised and follow the law. Paul argues for "the truth of the gospel" (2:5, 14), the good news that God has acted in Jesus Christ to redeem all people (4:4–5). This redemptive activity, conveyed by the Spirit, is received by faith and not by works of the law. The way to God is by faith in Christ, not by coercing Gentiles into Jewish observances.

Luther extends Paul's discussion to clarify the dialectical yet complementary relationship between law and gospel. Law and gospel are found in the Old and New Testaments, and both are to be preached, but they are not to be confused. "For unless the Gospel be plainly discerned from the law, the true Christian doctrine cannot be kept sound and uncorrupt." The law is every command of Scripture, expressing the perfect will of God. But the law cannot justify; in fact, the law condemns, for humankind cannot fulfill the demands of perfect righteousness. It discloses a person's "sin, his blindness, his misery, his impiety, ignorance, hatred and contempt of God, death, hell, the judgment and deserved wrath of God." The law is God's "mighty hammer," which "striketh terror into the conscience."[67]

Because the law shows one how far a person falls short, it drives one to

Christ, to the gospel, to the good news of grace. The law is the demand, whereas the gospel is the promise and the gift, revealing forgiveness, grace, righteousness, and life. If "the law teaches what you owe and what you lack," then "Christ gives you what you should do and have." The moral law is not abrogated—it remains a guide for Christian ethics (here Luther answers his Catholic opponents' charge of "antinomianism," i.e., against all moral law), but humankind is saved by grace, not works. "One does not become righteous by doing righteous deeds. Rather, one does righteous deeds after becoming righteous." The believer no longer stands under the law in a legal relationship to God but under grace in a loving relationship as a new creation in Christ. "For Luther," observes Philip Watson, "both the [active] righteousness that punishes and the [passive] righteousness that justifies, both wrath and grace, both Law and Gospel, are works of one and the same God, whose inmost nature is pure love."[68]

Was Luther's "Discovery" New?

Perhaps at no other time in the history of Christianity than during the Reformation has a single book of the Bible, Paul's Epistle to the Romans, had such a profound influence.[69] Luther was not alone in expounding on this book, nor was Romans considered a "Protestant" book. During the sixteenth century, the combined output of Protestant and Catholic writers exceeded sixty commentaries. T. L. Parker inventoried fourteen separate commentaries from 1529 to 1542, noting that of those written by deliberate choice, Catholics wrote five and a Protestant one.[70] Just as interpretations of the Petrine text did not harden along ecclesiastical lines until after the Council of Trent (see chapter 2), so too commentaries on Romans lacked a polemical, defensive status until the council distanced its views on justification from the Reformers. In fact, during this period of commentary production, Catholics and Protestants made repeated efforts to reconcile their differences.

This somewhat fluid state of doctrinal clarification raises the question of innovation. Was Luther's insight into Romans 1:17 all that new? Did Luther do little more than shift the emphasis of the Christian faith and introduce (or reemphasize) a vocabulary to describe that shift? Luther himself did not think so: "Others have attacked the life [i.e., the morals]; I have attacked the doctrine of the church." His convictions challenged the very foundations of the Catholic Church—the institution of the papacy, a hierarchy of spiritual levels among Christians, the sacramental system, ascetic spirituality, the intercession of saints—to an extent that a spiritual and, consequently, cultural and social "revolution" occurred in Western Christianity.[71]

But was his view of *justification by faith alone* novel? According to Luther, once he had attained an accurate understanding of Romans 1:17, all of Scripture took on a new meaning. This text and the doctrine extracted from it became *the* guiding principle of Luther's biblical theology. And yet at the turn of the nineteenth century, the Catholic scholar Heinrich Denifle argued that sixty doctors of the Western church had exposited Romans 1:17 in the same way that Luther had in his purportedly "new" discovery. In an impressive 360-page appendix of texts culled from the church doctors, Denifle demonstrated that "not a single writer from the time of Ambrosiaster [the anonymous fourth-century and earliest known Latin commentator on Paul's epistles] to the time of Luther understood this passage . . . in the sense of the justice of God which punishes, of an angry God. All, on the contrary, have understood it of the God who justifies, the justice obtained by faith."[72] Was Luther simply ignorant of these writers? Was he a liar? Was his memory defective?

In response to Denifle's blistering attack on Luther's integrity, reviewers clarified several issues. First, Luther's intellectual world consisted of scholastic theologians, not biblical exegetes. He was reacting against theological conceptions of divine justice as expressed by the *moderni* (whom Denifle omitted from his list), not by a long train of biblical commentators on Paul's Epistle to the Romans. In all likelihood, Luther knew little of the earlier Western tradition. Second, as a young monk Luther found the concept of the justice of God to be the main source of his *Anfechtungen*. Once he arrived at a new understanding of this concept, the doctrine of justification became the foundation of his theology and soon emblematic of the Protestant movement. The magnitude of this doctrine thus distinguished Protestantism from Catholicism.[73]

Apart from this monumental shift in emphasis, a shift that has set Protestant churches on a different doctrinal course for nearly five centuries, was Luther's doctrine of justification by faith an innovation? Luther and other Reformers argued that they were returning to past teaching, particularly earlier views of justification articulated by Paul and Augustine, which had been perverted by late medieval scholastic theology. Thus only in the sense that one judged late medieval theology "orthodox" could the Reformers be accused of doctrinal innovation. As observers have noted, on the eve of the Reformation a wide range of views on the doctrine of justification existed, and not until the Council of Trent (1545–63) were limits placed on this doctrinal diversity.[74]

According to Joseph Fitzmyer, three broad understandings of "the righteousness of God" prevailed throughout the Middle Ages and into Luther's day. The first two relate to attributes of God, whereas the third refers to a status given by God. First, "the righteousness of God" referred to God himself, the upright quality of God's faithfulness, or God's fidelity to his promises. Second, in a "distributive" sense, the phrase referred to God's punitive or vindictive justice; that is, God's rule or rectitude as he rewarded humans according to their just deserts. This was the view of the *via moderna*—to be sure, a minority view among Catholics—that Luther initially adopted. Third, in a "communicative" sense, "the righteousness of God" referred to a righteousness *from* or given by God, conferred on sinners who believed. Augustine, among others, accepted this understanding.[75]

Luther's "discovery" of this third sense was thus in line with the views of the day except in two crucial respects. Luther did not so much restate old doctrine as he proposed (in the words of Gordon Rupp) "new categories of thought with new relations to one another, and with a new technical vocabulary" based on the Bible. Previous commentators may have understood the doctrine along similar lines as Luther, but they minimized its significance, and unlike Luther, they did not risk their lives to defend its proper place within the church. Indeed, there were "many other things" Jesus taught (John 21:25) and many other things that the apostles preached and Paul taught (cf. 2 Pet. 3:16), but the doctrine of justification by grace through faith made all other teachings comprehensible.[76]

In addition to making the doctrine of justification the centerpiece of his theology, Luther broke sharply with the Western theological tradition by insisting on an *extrinsic*, not *intrinsic*, righteousness in humankind. Recall the terms Luther used to describe this extrinsic righteousness—alien, foreign, external—and the phrase that summarized this view: *simul iustus et peccator*. The presence of sin does not cancel one's status as a Christian; one does not have to be perfectly righteous to be a Christian. One's outward standing before God is changed—one is now declared righteous—and an altered inward state of holiness ("sanctification" is the common theological term) complements, rather than is intrinsic to, the event of justification. Although there is continuity between Luther and the Reformers and earlier theologians regarding the *mode* of justification (a process by which humankind is made righteous), there is an unambiguous discontinuity regarding the *nature* of justification (the content of being made righteous).[77]

By the mid-1530s Luther's views were further refined and somewhat modified by Philipp Melanchthon, his close associate and colleague at the University of Wittenberg, as well as by John Calvin, the leader of the Reformed movement. In the Catholic tradition going back to Augustine, the doctrine of justification included both an event—the declaration of the sinner as righteous through faith in the work of Christ—and a process of being made righteous (becoming holy) through the work of the Holy Spirit. Melanchthon and Calvin, though fulsome in their praise of Augustine, believed the church father misunderstood this doctrine because of his deficiency in Hebrew and Greek.

According to the Reformers, since Augustine never learned Greek, he mistakenly attributed more to the doctrine of justification in its Latin rendering (*justificare* = "to make righteous") than the term in its original Greek (*dikaioun* = "to declare righteous") could bear.[78] On the basis of their own "advances" in philology, Melanchthon and Calvin distinguished between being "declared righteous" (justification) and "becoming righteous" (the process of sanctification and regeneration that describes this spiritual change in the believer's inner nature).[79] The latter came after, not so much in chronology as in sequence, and was a result of the former. Augustine described these as two sides of the same coin and used the term "imparted" to describe the inherent change (wrought by God's grace) within the believer who is "made righteous." Again, on philological grounds, Melanchthon and Calvin reasoned that Christ's righteousness is "imputed" and external (not imparted, not internal, not infused), and that the sinner is "counted" or "declared" (not made) righteous. According to this view of "forensic justification," God, the judge in the court of heaven, pronounces divine judgment: the sinner is declared righteous. With this view, notes McGrath, Protestants introduced "a fundamental discontinuity . . . into the western theological tradition where none had ever existed, or ever been contemplated, before."[80]

Why these seemingly petty semantic distinctions? Both Catholics and Protestants insisted on the primacy of faith in Christ as the root of justification. Both officially agreed that no one earns salvation by doing good works, though popular Catholic piety skewed this belief by placing an inordinate amount of emphasis on gaining and storing up merits. Both agreed that good works were not the basis but the consequence of one's relationship to Christ. At the Council of Trent, however, the church reaffirmed the teachings of Augustine on justification and condemned the Protestant view. In the words of the seventh canon, justification "is not only a remission of sins but also the sanctification and renewal of the inward man through the voluntary reception of the grace and gifts whereby an unjust man becomes just." Moreover, "faith, unless hope and charity be *added to it*, neither unites man perfectly with Christ, nor makes him a living member of His body." There must be some righteousness within individuals—a righteousness given by God—which would allow God to justify them. The sacraments, of course, play a critical role. Baptism, the first plank in the shipwreck of original sin, provided initial justification. Penance, the second plank, addressed subsequent sin and renewed "those who through sin have forfeited the received grace of justification."[81]

According to the Reformers, this intermediate gift of righteousness, from which proceeded acts of love, smacked of conditions placed on the promise of justification by faith, implied human cooperation with God's grace, and hence undermined trust in God alone for salvation. Moreover, they argued, the logic was questionable. A declaration of justification is based on a perfect righteousness. But how is it, the Reformers asked, that if one is *inherently* righteous, one needs to *grow* in righteousness? Behind this inconsistency lurked the problem of assurance. How can one be sure one is a Christian? For Protestants, all had been done by Christ, meaning that being righteous in God's eyes did not include growth in righteousness. Thus the Reformers affirmed that the internal process of sanctification or regeneration (what Catholics called growing in righteousness) was distinct, though admittedly inseparable, from justification.[82]

The Doctrine and Text (Romans 1:17) in Recent History

The history of the doctrine of justification since the Council of Trent is a tale of two traditions. On one hand, the Roman Church has not made the doctrine of justification the focus of attention. On the other, Lutherans (and other Protestants) have claimed the central importance of the doctrine, albeit not with a single voice and sometimes in highly discordant ways. Clearly, the different emphases between Catholics and Lutherans have fostered different patterns of thinking and speaking. In considering God's saving action, Catholics are more apt to speak in Augustinian transformationist language of a process by which humans, created in the image of God but now fallen, are brought to renewed life through the infusion of God's saving grace. Lutherans are more apt to speak of the sinner standing before God in a double, simultaneous, paradoxical relationship of hearing words of judgment and forgiveness, law and gospel.[83]

To illustrate these perspectives, consider the approaches of these two traditions toward the doctrine of forensic justification. Lutherans want to safeguard this doctrine to emphasize the unconditional character of God's grace.[84] Love and works are affirmed but are viewed as the inevitable consequence rather than part of justification itself. Catholics consider justification so conceived as narrowly restrictive. To be sure, Catholic theologians and biblical scholars recognize a forensic element in justification, but they widen the meaning of the term to include such biblical images as adoption, redemption, healing, sanctification, regeneration, and reconciliation.

As recent ecumenical discussions indicate, Catholics have gone so far as to admit that the image of righteousness/justification is more widespread in New Testament teaching than the church has previously recognized and that the image is of "chief" importance in expressing the gospel message.[85] For their part, Lutherans recognize that the theme is more nuanced and some would even say more limited in expressing the gospel than previously expressed in their history. A common Catholic-Lutheran statement that grew out of discussions and position papers between 1978 to 1983 affirmed the following: "*Our entire hope of justification and salvation rests on Christ Jesus and on the gospel whereby the good news of God's merciful action in Christ is made known; we do not place our ultimate trust in anything other than God's promise and saving work in Christ.*" As a follow-up, the Joint Declaration on the Doctrine of Justification (1997) summarized the fruits of these ecumenical endeavors over the past thirty years. "Together, we confess: By grace alone, in faith in Christ's saving work and not because of any merit on our part, we are accepted by God and receive the Holy Spirit, who renews our hearts while equipping and calling us to good works." Two years later, on October 31, 1999, the Lutheran World Federation and the Roman Catholic Church became official signatories to the declaration. Representatives described it as "a peace document," "a description of the road we are traveling not the end of it," and recognized that sixteenth-century mutual "anathemas" (condemnations) on the teaching of justification no longer applied.[86]

But sticking points remain. Catholics have been willing to recognize the doctrine of justification as *one* legitimate (even "chief") way of understanding the gospel but not as *the* fundamental article by which church teaching and preaching are measured.[87] Moreover, whereas the Catholic Church affirms that salvation begins with God's grace, it balks at surrendering some notion of human cooperation, be it through penance or acts of charity.

Despite these continuing differences, the divide between Catholics and Luther has been considerably narrowed, thanks in large part to the research of modern biblical scholars. When "the righteousness of God" (a phrase used by Paul in Rom. 1:17; 3:5, 21, 22, 25, 26; 10:3 [twice]; 2 Cor. 5:21) is examined from the perspective of modern biblical scholarship, further light is shed on the meaning of the term and its formulation as doctrine.[88] Differences that remain between Catholic and Protestant commentators are rooted in hermeneutical assumptions (and, for Catholics, one must add fidelity to tradition) that filter the meaning and emphasis given to the doctrine of justification. Thus while some agreement may be reached on exegetical grounds, distinct hermeneutical approaches allied with tradition and dogma prevent consensus on the substantive issue of whether the doctrine of justification is *one* way or *the* way of understanding the Christian message.

Recent biblical scholarship concludes that throughout his writings, Paul uses the term "righteousness of God" both as a gift from God and as an attribute or quality of God. A helpful guide in this regard is James Dunn, a prominent New Testament scholar. Among his many works, Dunn has written a lengthy two-volume commentary on Romans as well as coauthored a shorter, more accessible work on the doctrine of justification.[89] Agreeing with almost every commentator, Dunn considers Romans 1:16–17 Paul's thematic statement for his entire letter. Because of Luther's focus on 1:17, the crucial affirmation in verse 16b—and the key to understanding verse 17—is often overlooked. The text of these two verses reads,

> [16]For I am not ashamed of the gospel; it is the power of God for salvation to everyone who has faith, to the Jew first and also to the Greek. [17]For in it the righteousness of God is revealed through faith for faith; as it is written, "The one who is righteous will live by faith."

In verse 16 Paul boldly proclaims that the "good news" of God's transforming power in converting, sustaining, and resurrecting is available to all who believe, to both Jews and God-fearing Gentiles. To believe, a necessary and indispensable precondition for salvation, is to accept the gospel and to find in it new life in Christ.

Verse 17 is thus premised ("For") on the main theme of the saving power of the gospel ("in it"). Building on a key exegetical breakthrough in contemporary scholarship, Dunn suggests that to understand "the righteousness of God," the phrase that so tormented Luther, we must get behind Paul's use of the Greek and situate it in his Jewish background and rabbinic training. Under the influence of Greco-Roman thought patterns, the Western tradition came to understand "righteousness" as an absolute ethical norm by which various behaviors and actions are compared and contrasted. But a more accurate rendering ascribes to righteousness (in Hebrew, *sedeq*) a relational quality, denoting the action of partners in a covenant.[90] The idea is "to make right" or "to put in a right relationship" (with himself), not "to make just."

Understood in this way, people who are righteous are those who live uprightly, who rule justly, who uphold the Torah, or who are acquitted before a judge's tribunal. When attributed to God, righteousness is rooted in his covenant with his people, and thus may be better expressed as his "uprightness," "covenant faithfulness," or gracious activity to save his people. "God is righteous," notes Dunn, "when he fulfills the obligations he took upon himself to be Israel's God, that is, to rescue Israel and punish Israel's enemies." Throughout the Old Testament, particularly in the Psalms and Isaiah, the righteousness of God is depicted as nearly synonymous with God's saving action: "the righteousness of God as God's act to restore his own and sustain them within his covenant."[91]

Once we grasp the meaning of Paul's language, observes Dunn, we are in a position to untangle the two knotty issues that have divided Christians over the centuries. First, does the "righteousness of God" refer to an attribute of God, or is it a status God communicates to the sinner who believes? Dunn proposes that when the two senses are viewed within the claims of God's covenantal relationship, both views are tenable. The righteousness of God is both something that God is (loving, relational in character) and something God does (communicates that covenantal relationship). Or, as expressed by another commentator, the righteousness of God is *the act by which God brings people into a right relationship with himself.*[92]

With the second issue we return to the conflicted meaning of "to justify." Does it mean "to make righteous" or "to declare (or count) righteous"? Traditionally, Catholic and Protestant scholars have lined up in predictable ways, with Catholics affirming the former (though sometimes both) and Protestants the latter (and never both). Again, Dunn dismisses the either-or categorization for *both*, siding with the views expressed by Ernst Käsemann in his pivotal essay published in 1969. Divine righteousness is a gift, but it is also a power; it is a status as well as an activity. When justification or righteousness is used in Scripture, it bears both an action orientation ("making righteous") and a being orientation ("declaring righteous"). With Käsemann, Dunn affirms that one must view "divine righteousness as a gift which has the character of power, because God is savingly active in it. . . . It is God's righteousness which enables and in fact achieves man's righteousness."[93]

The phrase "revealed for faith through faith" (alternate translations read "from faith to faith," or "through faith for faith") is ambiguous in its meaning, though many commentators (Luther for one) suggest it is a rhetorical device, emphasizing faith and faith alone (*sola fide*) or faith all the way.[94] Luther cited analogous usage in 2 Corinthians 3:18 ("We are being changed . . . from one degree of glory to another"), Psalms 84:7 ("They go from strength to strength"), and Revelation 22:11 ("He that is righteous, let him be made righteous still") to support his claim that the righteousness of God is by faith from beginning to end.[95] One could also note similar phrases in 2 Corinthians 2:16: "from death to death," "from life to life."

Finally, Paul completes his emphasis on a faith-righteousness that comes from God by appealing to Hebrew Scripture, quoting Habakkuk 2:4.[96] The KJV reads, "The just shall live by faith," whereas other versions express it as "He that is just by faith shall live" (RSV) or "The one who is righteous will live by faith" (NRSV). The reason for the different expressions is that in the Greek, the phrase "by/through faith" is situated between "the just" ("the righteous") and "shall live," thus raising the question of what it modifies. Note the different emphases in these phrasings: in the first the stress is on *being righteous* by faith, in the second *living* by faith. I need not go into the technical discussion surrounding these different renderings (e.g., it relates not only to issues of grammatical construction but also to Paul's use of texts, his deliberate or non-deliberate omission of "*his* [faith"] from Hab. 2:4), but note that for Luther, the emphasis was placed on faith. Dunn contends that Paul is deliberately ambiguous, for the apostle wants to emphasize that faith includes "both the initial act of receiving the gospel and the continuing process toward salvation."[97]

What does this cursory view of modern perspectives on Romans 1:16–17 yield? Clearly these commentators provide a deeper and richer understanding of "the righteousness of God" than Luther proposed, though none contradicts his basic insight.[98] As I have pointed out, agreement (or disagreement) on the meaning of a single text cannot resolve more basic hermeneutical issues. The question persists: What convictions and principles decide the center of Scripture? Because the doctrine of justification deals with the reconciliation between sinful humanity and God, both Catholics and Lutherans recognize that justification by faith is the heart of the gospel. In the words of Alister McGrath, the doctrine "constitutes the real center of the theological system of the Christian church."[99] Thus in refocusing attention on this doctrine, Luther made a profound and necessary contribution to church doctrine, however unappreciated and condemned by Catholics in his own day.

Luther's existential crisis and the reorientation of his theology to the biblical text constituted what Gerhard Ebeling has called the "hermeneutical circle." The combination of Luther's "sweating over the Bible" and real-life circumstances (his *Anfechtungen*) brought about a new understanding of Scripture and, with it, a new hermeneutic; in turn, his new hermeneutic engendered new insights into individual texts such as Romans 1:17. The legacy of Luther's "hermeneutical reorganization" was the rediscovery of the gracious character of God in Jesus Christ, a God who loves, sustains, forgives, and declares righteous those who "have sinned and fall short of the glory of God" (Rom. 3:23).[100]

5

"Love Your Enemies"

Anabaptists and the Peace Tradition

Blessed are the peacemakers.

—Matthew 5:9

But I say to you, Do not resist an evildoer. But if anyone strikes you on the right cheek, turn the other also; . . . You have heard that it was said, "You shall love your neighbor and hate your enemy." But I say to you, Love your enemies and pray for those who persecute you.

—Matthew 5:39, 43–44

Let every person be subject to the governing authorities; for there is no authority except from God, and those authorities that exist have been instituted by God. Therefore whoever resists authority resists what God has appointed. . . . The authority does not bear the sword in vain! It is the servant of God to execute wrath on the wrongdoer.

—Romans 13:1–2, 4

The year was 1968. Overseas, the United States was embroiled in an escalating war in Southeast Asia. On January 31, the first day of the Vietnamese New Year (Tet), North Vietnamese Communists shocked U.S. and South Vietnamese forces by waging invasions throughout South Vietnam, even threatening the capital city of Saigon. On the domestic front, as the violence of war played itself out on the evening television news, demonstrations against the war mounted. Then came the assassinations of Martin Luther King Jr. in Memphis on April 4 and Robert Kennedy in Los Angeles on June 6. Race riots erupted in sixty cities. In August, student antiwar demonstrators disrupted the Democratic National Convention in Chicago, turning downtown Grant Park into a war zone. Seemingly within a single year, American society unraveled.

I turned eighteen in 1968 and, by law, was required to register for the military draft. In a high school English class, I wrote an article that appeared later in our local newspaper for an occasional column, "Today's Teen Says." The gist of the article, titled "High School Sports Prepares for Life," extolled the character-building nature of organized sports. To illustrate how discipline, teamwork, and the "no pain, no gain" formula learned from sports carried over into other life experiences, I suggested that these characteristics were among the necessary survival skills for those sent off to war in Vietnam. Soldiers "have to be toughened to withstand the pressure of the enemy," I wrote, and organized sports prepared young men to be tough. Taught at home, church, and school to believe in the righteous cause of my country, I assumed that America's involvement in the Vietnam "quagmire" was honorable and defensible.

Moreover, as a Christian, I assumed that after reasonable efforts at peacemaking and diplomacy failed (and here I also assumed that the United States had made such reasonable efforts), war often became a necessary choice between the lesser of two evils. Without knowing it, I stood in the "just-war" tradition first fully articulated from a Christian perspective by Augustine. Living amid the fall of the Roman Empire in the fifth century, Augustine Christianized the arguments of the Latin jurist and orator Cicero and argued that Christians have the legitimate right to take up arms and engage in war under five conditions. First, the purpose of war must be peace. Second, the object of war must be to maintain justice, that is, the defense of life and property. Third, the motive of war must be Christian love, for "love does not exclude wars of mercy waged by the good."[1] Fourth, the wager of war must be the state, as revolution against established authority is prohibited. And fifth, the conduct of war must respect noncombatants, hostages, and prisoners. In short, under some conditions, one can justify the taking of human life. Augustine's position was adopted by the Western church, refined by Aquinas, and generally accepted by Protestants, including those within my own denomination.

But did the waging of war in Vietnam meet Augustine's conditions? And beyond that, was the waging of *any* war Christian? These were the questions that so deeply divided the American populace, the majority of whom identified with the Christian faith. For the time being, I found myself unwittingly supporting America's "just" cause in Vietnam.

And then I went off to college. To be sure, it was a conservative evangelical college, but like nearly every institution of higher learning in the late 1960s and early 1970s, it was hardly immune from the social and political upheavals of the day. For many, including myself, May 4, 1970, was a turning point in "consciousness-raising." On that day, the Ohio National Guard killed four students during an antiwar rally at Kent State University. Around the country campuses erupted in protest with marches, teach-ins, sit-ins, and violence. On my campus, a small group gathered outdoors with a popular professor to grieve over the events at Kent State and denounce the war in Vietnam.

At the theological seminary contiguous to the college campus, "Kent State" galvanized a handful of seminarians to form the People's Christian Coalition (no relation to and at the opposite end of the political spectrum from Pat Robertson's Christian Coalition, founded in 1989). Dismayed by the seminary's silence on such social issues as poverty and the war in Vietnam, these young evangelicals espoused a theology of Christian radicalism through their tabloid-style magazine, the *Post-American* (renamed *Sojourners* in 1975). The cover of its first issue in the fall of 1971 pictured Jesus with a crown of thorns on his head and wrapped in an American flag. The caption read, "And they crucified him." The message was clear: American Christianity was crucifying Jesus again. To editor Jim Wallis, the U.S. version of the gospel "had become almost completely lost in a church that had become captive to its culture and trapped by a narrow vision of economic self-interest and American nationalism."[2] What was needed was a Christian radicalism found in a "new order," whose members would live "by the values and ethical priorities of Jesus Christ and His Kingdom in the midst of the indifference and injustice of the American church and state." The *Post-American* thus appeared as "an evangelical publication radically committed to social justice and peace."[3] I attended several meetings of the People's Christian Coalition held in the cafeteria shared by college and seminary students, and with increasing interest I read and collected copies of the *Post-American*. This was not mainstream evangelical Christianity, wedded to the just-war tradition of Augustine. This was a faith that challenged the existing order, embraced peace (a "nonviolent resistance" variety), and demanded economic justice.

Like thousands of other young men in the 1960s, I confronted the question, Is it moral to take the life of another human being? That question is not asked today with the same urgency as it was during the Vietnam conflict, when young men were being drafted into military service. Although I never served in the armed forces—I had educational deferments and then, by the time my deferments expired and the draft lottery was instituted, the war was winding down—I wrestled with the Christian attitude toward war. Many opposed the war in Vietnam not because they were opposed to all war on strict religious grounds ("I am commanded by God and Jesus not to kill under any circumstances") but because, they argued, this *particular* war was unjust. The classification of "conscientious objector" to war, once reserved for those from "historic peace churches" (Brethren, Mennonites, and Quakers) widened to include "selective conscientious objectors." This category embraced both Christians who opposed *this* war on religious grounds (it does not fit just-war criteria) and nonreligious dissenters who opposed the war for political reasons (e.g., the United States has no business interfering in another country, Vietnam is not of strategic interest). Did I object to this particular war or to all wars? On strictly religious grounds or for political reasons as well?

Listening to members of the People's Christian Coalition, absorbing articles in the *Post-American*, and reading other literature exposed me to the Anabaptists, a group identified with the historic peace churches, as well as to the peace tradition within the Roman Catholic Church. The *Post-American* accentuated the twentieth-century Catholic contributions of Dorothy Day and the Catholic Worker movement, Thomas Merton, and especially the social activism of the brothers Philip and Daniel Berrigan (the latter serving as a contributing editor). Although Anabaptists and Catholics joined in common peace causes, I was drawn particularly to the Anabaptist tradition.

This chapter focuses on the emergence of the Anabaptist peace tradition in the sixteenth century and its various expressions extending into our own day. Unlike in previous chapters the purpose here is not to consider the history of the interpretation of a text—in this case, "peace texts"—but to understand the circumstances surrounding this developing peace tradition and the biblical texts marshaled and hermeneutic employed to support the Anabaptist position. I begin by locating the Anabaptists in their sixteenth-century context, noting their distinctive beliefs that set them apart from other Christians. I then turn to historiographical or interpretive issues, raising the question of when and to what extent peace convictions characterized early Anabaptism. I am particularly interested in the debate surrounding whether the peace tradition developed initially from a well-articulated biblical vision or from historical expediency (or both). Was the Anabaptist embrace of peace texts articulated in the movement's embryonic form, or, as with the Petrine text, did the peace texts become a "secondary legitimation" of an already existing reality? To address this question, I consider the origins of Anabaptism and the biblical basis upon which Anabaptists made their case for pacifism. Finally, I turn to recent Anabaptist perspectives on pacifism, noting the influential work of John H. Yoder.

The Anabaptist Tradition

Apart from religious historians and Christians concerned about peace issues, few people have specific knowledge of the Anabaptist tradition. What people do know has come in condensed and often skewed form via the big screen. *Witness* (1985), a popular suspense movie starring Harrison Ford, offered a Hollywood version of a subgroup within the Anabaptist tradition. Ford plays a Philadelphia cop who ends up in an Amish community in Lancaster County, Pennsylvania, after he discovers an Amish boy has been a witness to a murder. In most people's minds (and this is the image the movie projects), the Amish are a historical curiosity, a quaint, old-world people set apart by their simple dress, peace-loving ways, rural lifestyle, horse-drawn buggies, quilt making, barn raising, and rejection of the wider world around them. But few are aware that the Amish split off from a larger Mennonite group in the late seventeenth century or that the Mennonites (named after Menno Simons, the main leader and organizer of northern European Anabaptism) are one of several groups that trace their origins to the Anabaptist movement of the sixteenth century.

Among the major groups to emerge from the Protestant Reformation, the Anabaptists are the least known and the least understood. Historians have referred to them as the "stepchildren of the Reformers" and locate the Anabaptist movement within the "left wing of the Reformation" or the "Radical Reformation." Such nomenclature is employed to distinguish the Anabaptists from "magisterial Reformers" such as Luther, Ulrich Zwingli, and John Calvin, who enlisted the authority of the state ("magistrates") to support religious reform. The Anabaptists departed radically from the three major Protestant groups (Lutherans, Calvinists, and Anglicans) over issues such as the relationship between church and state, the use of coercion in religious matters, the taking of oaths, adult baptism, and the legitimacy of warfare. In a word, Anabaptists embraced the "free church" or "believers church" tradition, rejecting the twelve-hundred-year tradition of "Constantinian Christianity" that legally bound together the faith of Christians and the force of state. They thus fashioned their own view of history, interpreting the rule of Constantine as the beginning of the "fall" of the church and their own movement as the restoration or restitution of Christianity. Unlike other Protestant groups intent on renewing the existing social-political-religious order, the Anabaptists proposed a separate Christian alternative to the existing social order. Although existing in a variety of forms in the sixteenth century, by the seventeenth century the Anabaptist movement congealed around three general groupings: the Mennonites, the Amish (a splinter from the Mennonite body), and the Hutterites. Today, each of these groups is further divided into numerous subgroups.[4]

That the name Anabaptist stuck is testimony to the fact that history is both made and written by the winners. "Anabaptist" (*Wiedertäufer* in German) was not a self-designation but a pejorative term, meaning literally "to rebaptize." For those who embraced the conviction and practice of believers baptism, infant baptism was no baptism at all, and hence baptism as an adult was not a rebaptism but a true first baptism. Anabaptists preferred to be called "evangelicals," "Christians," "believers," and particularly "brethren" (*Brüder* in German-speaking regions, *Doopsgezinde* in Dutch). They stressed *Nachfolge Christi* (following Christ) in his words and actions, which meant following the way of the cross rather than the way of the sword. Like Jesus, who refused to embrace violence, counseled love of one's enemies, and suffered the death of a common criminal on a Roman cross, so his disciples were not above their master. The true church was a suffering church; the faithful Christian must necessarily experience persecution and martyrdom. The *person* of Christ (his exemplary life of ministry to the poor and downtrodden for which he suffered a martyr's death) became just as important as the *work* of Christ (his death as a sacrifice for human sin).

Such a perspective, in the violence of the sixteenth century, made the Anabaptists a hunted and persecuted people. In an age of religious intolerance, most (though, as will be noted shortly, not all) Anabaptists refused to defend themselves or engage in warfare. They were pacifists or peacemakers who followed Jesus' beatitude, "Blessed are the peacemakers" (Matt. 5:9). The results were predictable: Anabaptism turned into an underground movement whose members endured extensive persecution and physical displacement and wandered in a constant search for refuge.

Throughout the sixteenth century, between 3,000 and 4,000 Anabaptists were burned at the stake, drowned in rivers, starved in prisons, or beheaded. *The Bloody Theater, or Martyrs Mirror of the Defenseless Christians* (1660) chronicled the testimony of these and other Anabaptist martyrs. Over the centuries, the *Martyrs Mirror* has been a fixture in Mennonite homes, at once a grim and inspiring reminder that the early history of the Anabaptists paralleled the "baptism in blood" of the Christians in the early church. The work may be likened to the better known *Foxe's Book of Martyrs* (1563), which extolled the courage and endurance of Protestant martyrs during the reign of "bloody" Queen Mary as the *Martyrs Mirror* recounts the carnage and slaughter of faithful Anabaptists.[5]

The pages of the *Martyrs Mirror* are filled with a biblical defense of Anabaptist ways. In letters from prison, exchanges with interrogators, and admonitions to fellow believers on the death stand, Anabaptists, like other Protestants, appealed to Scripture as their final source of authority. For example, when charged with acting contrary to the emperor's mandate that only the gospel and the Word of God were to be followed, Michael Sattler, a former Benedictine monk and perhaps the most significant first-generation Swiss Anabaptist leader, replied, "I am not aware that we have acted contrary to the Gospel and the Word of God; I appeal to the Words of Christ."[6] Charged with refusing to resist should the dreaded infidel (Muslim) Turks invade, Sattler responded, "It is written, 'Thou shalt not kill.'" For these and other offenses against the church and state, Sattler was sentenced to torture and death on May 20, 1527.

In their defense of adult or believers baptism, Anabaptists appealed repeatedly to the New Testament order of baptism found in the so-called Great Commission of Matthew 28:19 and Mark 16:16. After his apprehension by authorities, Hans Schlaeffer, a former Catholic priest, referred to the last instructions from Christ. Before his ascension, Christ commanded his disciples, "Go ye into all the world, and preach the gospel to every creature. He that believeth and is baptized shall be saved" (KJV, Mark 16:16; Matt. 28:19). As the New Testament plainly narrates, noted Schlaeffer, the Word of God must first be taught, accepted, understood, and believed; then and only then are converts to be baptized. Becoming a disciple comes first, baptism follows.[7]

When Catholic interrogators and Protestant theologians appealed to the authority of the church fathers, Anabaptists were not impressed. Whereas Luther found in "blessed Augustine" insights into Scripture that paved the way for his doctrine of justification, the Anabaptist Joos Kindt found no such ally. When, during Kindt's interrogation, a Catholic priest asked, "Does not Augustine say," Kindt interrupted, "Don't speak of Augustine, for I do not know him; I hold no doctrine save that of the apostles and prophets, and of the words which our Saviour brought from high heaven, . . . and sealed with his blood; for this I want to go into the fire; but Augustine, Gregory, Ambrose, these I know not."[8]

Kindt's appeal to Scripture as the only source of authority implicitly points to the social origins of the Anabaptists. Unlike the university-educated Catholic priests and magisterial "learned" Reformers, few of the early leaders of the Anabaptist movement had professional education. And the lives of those who did were often cut short by death. Anabaptism, then, was largely a reform movement "from below," rooted in local congregations and led by a wide assortment of ordinary laypersons, including (as disparagingly described by a Franciscan monk) "weavers at the loom, cobblers on their bench, bellow makers, latern-tinkers, scissors-grinders, broom makers, thatchers, and all sorts of riff-raff, and poor, filthy, and lousy beggars."[9]

What are we to make of the Anabaptist appeal to *sola scriptura*, the common cry among all Protestants? I will take up Anabaptist hermeneutics in more detail later, but at this point some general comparisons between Luther and the Anabaptists may be helpful in clarifying two quite different biblical and theological orientations—despite their shared basis of authority.

What differentiates the two is that each had different starting points; each brought different questions and issues to their understanding of Scripture. Luther's existential search for a gracious God led him to the doctrine of justification by faith and a christo*logical* reading of Scripture. The Anabaptist search for a community of faith guided by following Christ led them to their ethic of obedience and a christo*centric* reading of Scripture. Luther's hermeneutic was thus soteriological: Jesus Christ was regarded primarily as savior, the supreme and final revelation of God, the one in whom one has redemption through his death and resurrection. Luther understood the faith in primarily doctrinal terms, and the doctrine of justification by faith became the hermeneutical key by which to read Scripture.[10]

The Anabaptist hermeneutic centered on the life and message of Jesus and their implications for Christian community. Anabaptists affirmed the doctrine of justification by faith but went beyond this starting point to focus on the new life and community to which salvation leads. "If Luther and other reformers took credit that the *gospel* had been restored against its Catholic perversion," notes Hans Hillerbrand, "the Anabaptists gloried in the restoration of the *church*."[11] With Catholics, they considered Luther's theology lopsided, exaggerating what God does *for* humans and minimizing what God does *in* them with human cooperation. Moreover, they considered Luther's (and the other Reformers') hermeneutic tied to preexisting doctrinal assumptions. Hence the doctrine of justification became the grid through which one read Scripture.

Anabaptists began not with the Pauline doctrine of justification but with Jesus' life, words, and death and interpreted other relevant passages from this perspective. Just as Luther developed a canon within the canon, so Anabaptists established levels of authority in the Bible, uplifting in particular the Gospels that portrayed the life and teachings of Jesus. But by what criteria? Because the coming of the Messiah was the most important event in Israel's history and the final and complete revelation of God, Jesus' words and deeds had greater authority than anything else found in Scripture. Above all, Jesus was to be followed. "The Anabaptist genius," writes Ben Ollenburger, "lay not in exegetical technique or hermeneutical novelty or even in any theological discoveries, but rather in the simple (and expensive) commitment to do what Jesus says." This commitment of obedience to Christ became "the *sine qua non* for understanding Scripture."[12]

How did the Anabaptists reach such conclusions? To answer that question, I will trace their sixteenth-century origins, focusing in particular on the Swiss Brethren in Zurich, where the earliest form of Anabaptism emerged. I turn first, however, to definitions and interpretations of Anabaptism. The historiographical and theological debate surrounding the origins of Anabaptism reveals the assumptions and predilections by which scholars have approached the movement. On the one hand, scholars within the Anabaptist faith tradition generally engaged in the search for a usable past. That is, as an exercise in self-understanding and identity formation, they mined the tradition to validate their own current beliefs. On the other hand, those distanced from the tradition reached considerably different conclusions. More recently, in the wake of revisionist studies, these opposing perspectives no longer hold. My goal is to clarify the assumptions behind these interpretations and in so doing attend to the influences and circumstances by which Anabaptists reached their convictions about the teachings of Scripture.

Definitions and Interpretations of Anabaptism

Anabaptism is typically classified under the general rubric of what the historian George Williams labeled the "radical reformation," "radical" in the sense of returning to biblical "roots." In a monumental study of the theology and history of leaders and movements, first published in 1962, Williams identified three "loosely interrelated congeries of reformations and restitutions": Anabaptists, Spiritualists, and Evangelical Rationalists.[13] What united these groups around the "radical" banner was the conviction, reached either through the dynamics of historical circumstance or by conscious design, that religious reform must be advanced independent of the political establishment.

Anabaptism itself was a "perturbingly heterogeneous" movement.[14] Although it is fairly easy to trace the Lutheran and Reformed movements because they congealed around major leaders, Anabaptism claimed no leaders of the stature of a Luther or a Calvin, nor did it have a head of state as in England to shape religious policy. It also lacked a single confessional norm or a cohesive organizational structure. From its beginnings, Anabaptism was characterized by a diverse leadership of scholars, priests, monks, laymen, peasants, and noblemen, recruited from a variety of backgrounds and geographic locales, who advanced assorted and often divergent views.

As noted earlier, authorities regarded the Anabaptists as a disruptive force, referring to them by such epithets as *Schwärmer* (Luther's favorite term meaning enthusiasts or fanatics), heretics, and, of course, Anabaptists. In the confessional polemics of the day, Luther and especially Heinrich Bullinger, the Reformed leader and Zwingli's successor at Zurich, tarred all Anabaptists with the same brush by identifying the movement with the revolutionary teachings of Thomas Müntzer or with the millenarian, violent, polygamous Anabaptists in Münster, Germany. To be sure, Müntzer and the Münsterites cannot be divorced from the Anabaptist legacy, but they represented a thin strand (many would say a separate or deviant one), not the whole thread of early Anabaptism.

But conventional or established views have a staying power, even among professional historians, well into the twentieth century. In 1963, G. R. Elton, a leading British scholar of the Reformation, repeatedly portrayed the Anabaptists as "arrogant" and apportioned the balance of a chapter on "The Radicals" to the violent expressions of Müntzer and the Münsterites. He concluded that Anabaptism "was a violent phenomenon born out of irrational and psychologically unbalanced dreams, resting on a denial of reason and the elevation of that belief in direct inspiration which enables men to do as they please."[15]

Obviously Elton did not share the views of Harold Bender. Twenty years earlier, in his presidential address before the American Society of Church History, Bender described an "Anabaptist vision" diametrically opposed to Elton's conclusions.[16] Bender built upon the insights of the German sociologist Ernst Troeltsch, who proposed a "church-sect" typology to differentiate mainstream, inclusive, state-supported churches from marginal, exclusive, voluntary-based sects such as the Anabaptists. In his dual effort to speak to "outsiders" (the historical profession) by rehabilitating a much maligned and misunderstood group, and to "insiders" (his own Mennonite brethren) by supplying a usable past, Bender, a professor at Goshen College and Seminary (Indiana) and founder and editor of the *Mennonite Quarterly Review*, argued that the Anabaptists descended from a single source. The origins of Anabaptism (and the Mennonites who later emerged in the Low Countries) were to be found in the Swiss canton of Zurich in the years 1523 to 1525, in the circle of Conrad

Grebel. Bender distanced "Anabaptism proper," a movement that "maintained an unbroken course in Switzerland, South Germany, Austria, and Holland throughout the sixteenth century, and has continued until the present day in the Mennonite movement," from the desultory, fleeting, and aberrant "mystical, spiritualistic, revolutionary, or even antinomian related and unrelated groups."[17]

Derived from this singular source, the Anabaptist vision, really, the vision of Jesus as Bender understood it, included (1) "a new conception of the essence of Christianity as discipleship" modeled after Christ; (2) "a new conception of the church as a brotherhood" based on voluntary membership; and (3) "a new ethic of love and nonresistance" that eschewed "all warfare, strife, and violence, and the taking of human life." Anything that deviated from this model—the spiritualism of Hans Denck or the chiliasm of Hans Hut or the violence at Münster—was aberrant and, as it turned out, temporary, having no lasting effects.[18]

Bender and colleagues who defended this thesis maintained that Anabaptism was a peaceful, respectable Protestantism taken to its logical conclusion, the culmination of the original vision of Luther in Wittenberg and Ulrich Zwingli in Zurich, who then capitulated to political authorities in order to advance reform. Indeed, asked Bender, was not "the surrender of their original vision" of a church composed solely of earnest Christians "the tragic turning point of the Reformation?"[19]

While applauding Bender's efforts to rescue Anabaptism from the dustbin of neglect and the poisoned well of prejudice, not all Mennonite scholars were convinced that the "normative" Anabaptism so described by Bender was factually true or a "consistent Protestantism" (Bender's words). Walter Klaassen and Robert Friedman pointed to differentiating elements and wondered whether Bender projected an ideal view and an artificial uniformity on a multifaceted movement. Klaassen regarded Anabaptism as "neither Catholic nor Protestant but in fact a movement of different dimensions." Friedman, Bender's colleague and close friend, argued that Anabaptists were not guided primarily by Pauline ideas, as was the case with the Reformers. Rather, Anabaptism was sui generis, "the only example in church history of an 'existential Christianity' where there existed no basic split between faith and life, even though the struggle for realization or actualization of this faith into practice remained a perennial task."[20]

By the early 1970s, the Bender thesis cracked under the weight of historical revisionism. As new methods and perspectives enlivened the historical profession in general and Reformation studies in particular, revisionists (typically a younger generation of scholars) proposed a very different interpretation of Anabaptist beginnings. In his 1972 monograph, *Anabaptists and the Sword*, James M. Stayer, a non-Mennonite with no stake in the "Anabaptist vision," rejected Bender's "kind of doctrinaire historiography" as a perversion of historical principles and set out to prove that Anabaptist teachings on the sword varied from group to group.[21] Several years later, in a landmark article in Anabaptist historiography, Stayer, Werner Packull, and Klaus Depperman argued for a "polygenesis" paradigm to explain Anabaptist beginnings. They proposed three distinct Anabaptist origins: Swiss, South German/Austrian, and North German/Dutch. They readily admitted that the first adult baptisms occurred in Zurich and that an awareness of the Swiss Brethren existed in other areas. "But a number of Anabaptist movements arose that were independent of the Swiss Brethren, certainly to the same degree that Zwingli or Bucer was independent of Luther. They had basically different memberships and theologies." Moreover, the authors emphasized social-historical factors rather than ideational or theological ones as the primary driving force behind Anabaptist origins, reiterating that nonviolence was an option embraced by only some of the Anabaptist groups. Only over time (around 1565) did Anabaptism develop from its messy, complicated roots to an identifiable separatist, pacifist sect along the lines described by the Bender school and associated in our own day with the three main Anabaptist bodies of Mennonites, Hutterites, and Amish. To the surprise of the revisionists (especially Stayer), nearly all Mennonite scholars accepted this new perspective and adopted it as a working assumption.[22]

Twentieth-century Anabaptist historiography is thus characterized by a swinging pendulum of paradigms. Bender responded to earlier, simplistic characterizations linking Anabaptists with violence and proposed his own singular theory of pacifistic, biblically based beginnings. Responding to this monogenetic paradigm, revisionists proposed a multiple-source theory of origin. Like the Bender paradigm, the polygenesis paradigm has raised it own set of interpretive issues, including those of Mennonite self-identity and the role of the Bible in shaping Anabaptist origins.[23] With the latter issue I return to a basic problem and theme discussed in earlier chapters, namely, the derivation of biblically grounded convictions. The Bender school described the early Anabaptists as acting out of scriptural norms from the beginning; that is, once they had Scripture in hand and read and pondered its meaning, they reached certain self-evident theological and ethical conclusions. Working from this biblical blueprint (namely, the life and teachings of Jesus), they then put it into practice in a manner more consistent than that of other Protestants.

The polygenesis school complicated and challenged this idealistic reading of Anabaptist beginnings. Rather than working from a plan in hand, Anabaptists forged their views in an ad hoc manner as they confronted changing historical circumstances. Their thoughts, ideas, and convictions developed slowly within the context of disappointment, opposition, and persecution. Nonresistant Anabaptism was born, hypothesized Stayer in an article prior to the publication of his 1972 monograph, only after other efforts had failed. "Sects without a real possibility of revolution, and with a very real experience of the misuse of power, arrived with compelling historical and religious logic at this most radical form of apolitical thought." In another revisionist work, Hans-Jürgen Goertz concluded that "pacifism and the free-church ideas of the Swiss Brethren can be perceived historically as the result of the experience of powerlessness of the early Anabaptists—who searched the Scriptures for the justification of their misery."[24]

Among historians with Anabaptist-Mennonite commitments, the polygenesis paradigm has not mitigated the search for a usable past. In *Becoming Anabaptist* (1987), J. Denny Weaver observed that the principles that define Anabaptists did not constitute "a planned program of reform worked out in advance by individuals gathered around an open Bible. Rather, they emerged over a period of several years through trial and error in response to the results of various attempts at reform." Nevertheless, though recognizing the contingency of history and its relativizing effects, Weaver suggested that "when examined through the eyes of faith, . . . truth emerges from particular situations." This truth is discovered in several "first level" or "regulative principles . . . which structure a way of life, an alternative society." Chief among these normative principles is following Christ's way of nonviolence.[25]

Like Weaver, Arnold Snyder has argued that as a Mennonite believer, historical inquiry does matter, that present-day Mennonites can learn from their past. Snyder recognized Anabaptism's pluralist roots and yet affirmed a "theological unity" (e.g., an emphasis on the work of the Holy Spirit) within the diversity—but one that departed sharply from Weaver's "first level principles." In his *Anabaptist History and Theology* (1995), Snyder asserted that pacifism was a secondary or peripheral consideration when viewed in light of the original theological core of the Anabaptist movement. Anabaptists shared some common theological understandings with Catholics (e.g., acceptance of ecumenical creeds) and some with Protestant evangelicals (e.g., antisacramentalism, authority of the Bible alone), but they affirmed others that were unique to them, including pacifism.[26] But because pacifism was not shared by all early Anabaptists and only later came to be embraced as a core teaching, Snyder placed it on the periphery of earliest Anabaptist concerns.

Snyder's work has elicited a heated debate. In a 1998 review, Weaver accused Snyder of choosing to make nonviolence secondary to the narrative and feared that Snyder's interpretation "opens the door to the accommodation of violence rather than seeing the rejection of violence as theologically normative." If nonviolence was peripheral to the earliest of Anabaptist concerns, then why not for modern Anabaptist concerns? Weaver detected in Snyder's account a "potential to weaken the commitment to rejection of the sword as a normative Christian stance for the modern, peace church heirs of Anabaptism." Snyder retorted that Weaver was more concerned with theological correctness than historical accuracy; the contention that his work compromised the cause of nonviolence was baseless, even irresponsible. He rejected Weaver's suggestion that he interjected an artificial construct in delineating the Anabaptist core.

Rather, "Weaver's critique has simply confused the *chronologically* secondary nature of the violence question (which is a matter of record) with a supposed *choice* on the part of the narrator to tell the story that way. . . . That the story happened a particular way in the sixteenth century does not constitute a demonstration that I, as author, therefore believe that nonviolence is *theologically* secondary." Weaver and others remain unconvinced and continue to assert that certain assumptions (intended or unintended) have shaped Snyder's work to the detriment of contemporary Mennonite theology.[27]

Unlike Stayer, a self-described "profane historian with a liberal perspective," who argued that Anabaptist pacifism was derived primarily from historical expediency and secondarily from a biblical vision, Weaver and Snyder extracted from historical circumstances those theological principles that came to guide Anabaptism even if they were not consistently lived out among Anabaptists themselves. The same point that is made of the sixteenth century applies perforce to the first centuries of the church before Constantine. Both eras provide normative structures, since in both eras Christians came closest to living out the true meaning of the faith. Such principles, notes Weaver, though stated less dogmatically than by Bender, do turn out to be identical to the "Anabaptist vision": Jesus is the norm of truth; the church that follows Jesus is a new community; and this new community rejects violence and practices nonresistance. As John H. Yoder puts it, Anabaptism defines "not a century but a hermeneutic," the correct and normative way of reading and understanding Scripture. Anabaptism is thus "the recourse to Scripture (as) an authoritative guide for church renewal."[28]

Recently, Abraham Friesen has mounted a strong challenge to the prevailing polygenesis thesis. Friesen argues that the rise of Anabaptism is directly traceable to Christian humanism in general and Desiderius Erasmus in particular. Citing the influence of Erasmus's *Annotations*—translations and paraphrases of the New Testament on Anabaptists leaders such as Conrad Grebel, Balthasar Hubmaier, and Menno Simons—Friesen dismisses the thesis of multiple origins. There is evidence that Erasmus influenced Anabaptist views on oaths, pacifism, and egalitarian views of society, but the most convincing proof of the Dutch humanist's influence is found in the Anabaptists' wholesale appropriation of his interpretation of the Great Commission in Matthew 28: 18–20.[29]

Earlier interpretations of this text, going back to the church fathers, focused on the Trinitarian baptismal formula, where in verse 19 Jesus instructed his disciples to "make disciples of all nations, baptizing them in the name of the Father, and the Son, and the Holy Spirit." Christological debates in the early church centered on this text (which in some sense equated the Son and the Father) and those in Acts (2:38; 10:48; 19:5) where believers were baptized in the name of Jesus only. As a humanist devoted to *ad fontes* (back to the sources), Erasmus broke with the traditional focus of interpretation and read the text from a literal-historical perspective. The focus of his attention became the sequence described in these verses: first making disciples, then baptizing (all verses refer to believers baptism), and then teaching with a response of obedience.

Friesen points out that proto-Anabaptists read Erasmus and adopted his reading of the Great Commission. This explains the similarity in views between the Swiss Brethren and Dutch Mennonites, "in spite of the at times very different set of economic, social, and political—not to speak of intellectual and cultural—conditions prevailing in the two regions." Friesen expands his tantalizing thesis to suggest, "Not only is the Great Commission as interpreted by Erasmus the key to the problem of the *intellectual origins* of Anabaptism; it is also the key to understanding the movement as a whole."[30]

Most Anabaptist scholars concede Erasmus's influence on a few key leaders and acknowledge that the Great Commission texts as understood by Erasmus did indeed become the central texts supporting adult baptism. Yet to argue for a wholesale influence on the movement is to ignore the grassroots nature of Anabaptism. The majority of Anabaptists had no direct access to Erasmus, and yet they reached similar conclusions, not because the humanist's ideas trickled down from a few Anabaptist leaders but because they, like Erasmus, were drawn into a broader current of late medieval spirituality.

Anabaptist Beginnings: The Swiss Brethren

Whether from a singular source or many, the origins of Anabaptism lie with the Swiss Brethren movement, for it chronologically precedes other forms of Anabaptism. Because my purpose is not to provide a broad overview of the sixteenth-century Anabaptist movement but to locate the context in which a pacifist ethic first emerged, I limit this historical narrative to the genesis of the movement in the 1520s and 1530s.[31] We begin with Protestant reform in Zurich, trace the growing dissent among radicals toward Zwingli's program, and conclude with a discussion of the Schleitheim Confession (1527), a landmark document articulating the pacifist position. Admittedly, we run the risk of flattening the historical landscape and committing the blunder of the Bender school. Suffice it to say, pacifism was not immediately accepted everywhere and by all Anabaptists. However, by around 1565, as the diverse, amorphous movements congealed, pacifism had become one of the core doctrines of Anabaptist belief.

January 21, 1525, is to Swiss Anabaptism what October 31, 1517, is to Lutheranism. Just over seven years after Luther posted his Ninety-five Theses to protest indulgences in the Catholic Church, a small group of dissidents in Zurich gathered at the house of Felix Mantz, where George Blaurock had Conrad Grebel baptize him, and then Blaurock and Grebel baptized fifteen others.

By the end of January, nearly one hundred adults had been rebaptized, and a movement was born. Just as the Ninety-five Theses expressed thoughts that had been percolating in Luther's mind for years, so these baptisms signaled the culmination of earlier discussions and disputations. In their own way, both Luther and the Anabaptists protested against current religious practices. But whereas Luther circulated his theses for discussion with hopes of reforming existing church practices, the Anabaptists committed a more radical act having not only religious but also severe political repercussions. Luther committed his own act of insubordination and resistance later at the Diet of Worms, but he secured the support and protection of local authorities and then carried out reform under the auspices of the German princes. Without such legal support, Anabaptists were deemed at once religious heretics and political revolutionaries. Those practicing "rebaptism" challenged the church-in-state assumptions in place for well over a millennium and became subject to capital punishment according to the Code of Justinian (529). By a cruel irony, the Second Imperial Diet of Speyer (1529) at once gave birth to Protestantism (the term "Protestant" is first introduced) and announced death to Anabaptism by applying the Justinian Code to this new heresy.

The rise of Anabaptism was inextricably linked to the progress of Protestant reform in Zurich. Ulrich Zwingli had come to Zurich in 1519 not as a Protestant Reformer but as the people's priest at the Grossmünster (Great Minster). By 1522, however, this university-trained humanist scholar, devotee of Erasmus, electrifying preacher, and dynamic personality had moved into the Protestant camp by his own independent study of Scripture. Zwingli attracted young, university-trained humanist disciples, including Felix Mantz and Conrad Grebel, the future leaders of the Swiss Brethren, to pursue the study of Greek classics. Moreover, he initiated a program of reform calling into question the veneration of images, fasting during Lent, and the celibacy of the clergy. Growing controversy over reform eventually prompted the governing city council (perhaps at Zwingli's behest) to call public disputations between advocates and opponents of reform.

In the spring of 1522 Zwingli accompanied his supporters to the home of the printer Christoph Froschauer, where they (though not Zwingli) ate meat during the prescribed meat-less Lenten season. This so-called Affair of the Sausages marked the public inauguration of the Swiss Reformation. When disagreement between the evangelical party and Augustinian monks forced the city council to intervene, Zwingli successfully defended the actions of the fast-breakers and the cause of reform in general at the First Disputation (January 1523), where the city council issued a statement that all preaching must be based on Scripture.

Emboldened by the council's support, the radicals expressed more strident anticlericalism, touching off iconoclasm (the destruction of church images) in Zurich and in the surrounding villages under the jurisdiction of Zurich. Two groups of radicals emerged. One consisted of the radical disciples of Zwingli who urged reform in a more thorough way and at a faster pace than Zwingli was willing to countenance. This Zurich group included artisans (a weaver, baker, carpenter), Mantz, the son of a canon of the Grossmünster, and Grebel, the cultured but unpredictable son of a Zurich patrician family. The other group consisted of rural priests, such as Simon Stumpf, Wilhelm Reublin, and Johannes Brötli, who pressed for popular and iconoclastic reform. In the village of Zollikon, for example, a large wooden crucifix was destroyed and its remnants divided among the poor.

These rural reformers' support for religious reform had weighty political implications. Several village congregations (whether they were future Anabaptists or simply rebellious peasant congregations is unclear) asserted the right of local autonomy. They called for an abolishment of the tithe (a mandatory 10 percent tax on land and produce that was controlled by religious authorities in Zurich), and the right to elect their own pastors. The Zurich council opposed these moves, though criticized the abuse of tithes. Amid this increasing unrest, Zwingli sided with the council, believing the Christian council would move things in the right direction at the appropriate time. Grebel became incensed by Zwingli's gradualism, calling him a "wretched prattler" and "archscribe."[32]

At this point, as revisionist historians have made clear, the radicals had neither abandoned the use of government authority to carry out reform nor introduced the notion of a "gathered church," separate from the existing ecclesiastical community. Their concerns and the growing tension with Zwingli focused on the issue of authority. Zwingli supported a "top-down" ecclesiastical framework, where church and civil authorities in Zurich worked in concert to determine the nature and pace of reform. Radical priests in outlying areas supported a "bottom-up" church organization, where local reformed congregations took the lead. The debate was not over a territorial church per se but over who determined what the newly reformed church would look like—a central authority in Zurich or local, autonomous congregations. In a sense, Zwingli's radical Zurich disciples were peripheral to this debate insofar as they were not priests, who had the ability to institute changes in their local churches. Indeed, it became increasingly evident that these urban radicals had little power to influence the outcome of reform.

In October 1523 the Zurich magistrates held a Second Disputation to discuss worship practices, namely, the use of images and the mass. Both were rejected, but when it came to implementing the abolition of the mass and institution of the Lord's Supper, Zwingli left the matter to the magistrates. The pace of reform, though not its specific content (according to Zwingli, the council was "not to sit in judgment over God's Word"), was placed in the hands of the civil authorities, who took eighteen months to alter communion practices. Zwingli's radical supporters were incredulous and protested his acquiescence. Zwingli declared previously that he would preach and act regardless of what the council decided, but now faced with a dilemma, he stated that nothing should be done without the expressed approval of the magistrates. In so doing, he committed the reformation in Zurich to the gradual, incremental changes made by a cautious civil government and thus retained the old model of the Christian society. Thus by the end of 1523 two distinct reform parties existed in Zurich: the Zwinglian party and a somewhat differentiated group of radicals—those from Zurich and priests from rural communes, some of whom (e.g., Stumpf) suggested killing priests to bring about reform.[33]

The year 1524 marked a turning point for the Zurich radicals. The issue of baptism surfaced as the first substantive theological difference with Zwingli. Influenced by Erasmus's writings, Zwingli had earlier expressed doubts about the validity of infant baptism. In a sermon preached in December 1521, Zwingli affirmed that unbaptized infants would be spared hell, and he reiterated this idea in his Sixty-seven Articles of January 1523.[34] Now, among the radicals, doubts about infant baptism increasingly turned to conviction. They had written to Andreas Karlstadt, Luther's former colleague in Wittenberg, and he responded to their overtures with a visit to Zurich. This "father of Anabaptism" had rejected Luther's sacramentalism and by 1523 opposed infant baptism, and no doubt during his visit in Zurich he conversed with the radicals about his views.

At the same time, it was becoming clear to the Zurich radicals that options for accelerating reform had run out. Zwingli rebuffed a suggestion from the Grebel circle to replace the existing council with a "godfearing" council. Denied a base of power from which to effectuate reform, they turned to pacifism, finding in their study of Scripture (with the help of Erasmus's annotations and paraphrases) an analogous situation among the first Christians. In their famous letter to Thomas Müntzer of September 1524, Grebel described a maturing conviction: "After we took Scripture in hand, and examined all sorts of items, we gained some insight." These included the exclusion of singing in worship, a conception of the Lord's Supper as "an exhibition of unity," the renunciation of violence (Christians "employ neither worldly sword nor war"), and a denunciation of infant baptism ("a senseless, blasphemous abomination, contrary to all Scripture") in favor of adult baptism that "signifies that one should be and is dead to sin, and walking in newness of life and spirit." Here Grebel described the identifying marks of Anabaptist ecclesiology: a minority, nonviolent, suffering church, set apart from society, and defined as a free church by believers baptism. Highly critical of Luther, Grebel urged Müntzer to stand firm against "those in Wittenberg who fall from one perversion of Scripture into another," but to do so without resorting to violence.[35]

In A Declaration of Faith and Defense, Felix Mantz expressed the radicals' growing conviction in believers baptism. Mantz reiterated Erasmus's interpretation of Matthew 28:18–20, written in December, just one month before the first believers baptism. After the apostles received Christ's teachings, "they were also poured over with water externally to signify the inner cleansing and dying to sin."[36] In addition, growing unrest in the rural areas, including opposition to infant baptism, and continued discussions about adult baptism by the Zurich radicals forced the calling of a Third Disputation on January 17, 1525. At this first formal discussion over baptism, both sides remained intransigent. Zwingli defended infant baptism, the radicals adult baptism. Zwingli's erstwhile colleagues increasingly linked infant baptism with a clerically controlled church. The radicals became convinced, writes Walter Klaassen, "that clerical leaders, even the new evangelical ones, could not be trusted, because their faithfulness to sola scriptura was compromised by social and political considerations. . . . Infant baptism was the sign of the disenfranchisement of ordinary Christians. It preempted their own decision and kept them dependent on the clergy."[37] The results of the disputation were predictable: Zwingli controlled the discussion, and the city council ruled that infant baptism was biblical, ordered that all unbaptized children be baptized within eight days under penalty of expulsion, and prohibited any more meetings of the Zurich radicals.

Such were the events that precipitated the adult baptisms at the home of Mantz's mother on January 21. The baptizing movement quickly spread to the rural communes of Witikon and Zollikon; at Zollikon the first Anabaptist congregation was constituted. Soon Anabaptist conventicles spread to nearby areas, including Waldshut in the Black Forest, where Balthasar Hubmaier, the most learned and prolific among the first generation of Anabaptists (the only one to possess a doctor's degree), convinced the authorities to institute a "magisterial Anabaptist Reformation." In other villages, peasants armed themselves to defend their own brand of popular Anabaptism, and though short-lived (Catholic forces soon put down the rebellion), their attempts belie the notion that all early Anabaptists embraced pacifism and separatism.

Meanwhile, in Zurich discussions between Zwingli and the radicals degenerated into shouting matches, and eventually the force of law intervened. Anabaptists were imprisoned, fined, warned, and then released upon promise no longer to attend Anabaptist meetings. But Anabaptist persistence met increasing resistance. Grebel was arrested in October 1525 and imprisoned along with Mantz and Blaurock. In a scene repeated numerous times throughout the sixteenth century, the Anabaptist prisoners debated clerical authorities (in this case, Zwingli) over their Anabaptist convictions. After being sentenced to terms of indefinite length, the three were retried in early March 1526, at which time the Zurich council took the drastic measure of imposing the death penalty for rebaptism. Two weeks later the men escaped from jail. Before capture and certain martyrdom, Grebel died of the plague in August 1526. In January 1527, Mantz was rearrested, tried, and drowned, becoming the first Anabaptist martyr in Zurich and the first to die at the hands of Protestants. Blaurock, after being beaten and then banished from Zurich (he was not a citizen), was eventually arrested in the Catholic Austrian Tyrol region and burned at the stake for heresy on September 6, 1529.

At this juncture, with the failure of the Zurich radicals to enact reform and the pronouncement of death upon them, the Anabaptists withdrew from the larger society to create their own alternative community. Purification through separation—not reformation—became the predominant theme. Sectarianism, characterized by a church of "true believers" separate from "the world" and opposed to the state, thus emerged within the dynamics of history in conjunction with convictions drawn from Scripture. This dialectic between events (social and political) and ideas (theological convictions) moved the Anabaptists in a separatist, nonviolent direction. Clearly this stance was not derived from a preexisting blueprint (few movements begin this way) but evolved within the vicissitudes of history. The Bible functioned as *the* touchstone of authority to shape and inspire Anabaptist thought and action, just as it did for the other reformers. Anabaptists read Scripture, memorized it, studied it, discussed it, and applied it. A specific way of reading the Bible emerged, defined by an interpretive community of lay and often unlearned people who rejected the "official" or elite interpretive community, whether ecclesiastical or civil. Because the Anabaptists read the Bible through the lens of the oppressed and persecuted, they reached specific conclusions about its meaning and application.[38]

This new self-understanding attained formal expression in the Schleitheim Confession of 1527. A classic statement of the "Anabaptist vision," the confession brought form and structure to a movement heretofore varied and scattered. Tradition ascribes authorship to Michael Sattler, the same person whose martyrdom was noted at the beginning of this chapter. A former Benedictine monk at St. Peter's in the Black Forest, Sattler had only recently joined the Anabaptist cause and emerged as the leader of the Swiss Brethren in the summer of 1526. Conscious of the movement's tenuous existence, Sattler met with other Anabaptist leaders in Schleitheim (on the Swiss-German border) and drafted the "Brotherly Union of a Number of Children of God Concerning Seven Articles."

The Schleitheim Confession (or Articles) signifies the formal clarification of Swiss Anabaptist views. Published in February 1527, its seven articles clarify Anabaptist positions on (1) baptism, (2) church discipline, (3) the Lord's Supper, (4) separation from the world and all evil, (5) selection of a pastor, (6) the sword, and (7) oath-taking.[39] The first three defined the beliefs of all Anabaptist groups: adult baptism following confession of faith, the practice of the ban as discipline within the fellowship of baptized believers (according to Matt. 18:15–18), and observance of the Lord's Supper as an act of Christian unity in remembrance of Christ's broken body and shed blood. The last four articles introduced new commitments. Sattler, an ex-monk, called the church to the monastic ideal of separation from the world and its violence. Article 4 affirmed a dualistic cosmology. There are two kingdoms, "nothing else . . . than good or evil, believing and unbelieving, darkness and light, . . . Christ and Belial, and none will have part with the other." Article 5 on the choice of pastor by the local congregation reflected the demands of the peasants. The last two articles, longer than any of the previous ones, detailed the relation of the Christian to the state. Article 6 disallowed the use of violence and committed the movement to an "apolitical" and pacifistic stance. "The sword is an ordering of God outside the perfection of Christ," who "teaches us and commands us to learn from Him, for He is meek and lowly of heart." Article 7 rejected oath-taking of any kind (let your "yes" be "yes" and your "no" be "no"), including the common and widespread civil oaths of allegiance.

"The Sword" and Anabaptist Hermeneutics

Upon what biblical basis did Anabaptists make the case for pacifism? More generally, how did the Anabaptists, claiming above all to be biblicists, arrive at Article 6, a position so at odds with the mainline Reformers? Here we are faced with a hermeneutical standoff, primarily because nowhere in Scripture is war or the use of force explicitly and categorically condemned. The people of the biblical era experienced profound ambiguity about war and recorded their ambiguity in Scripture. The Old Testament appears to command the participation of God's people in warfare, and the New Testament does not directly address the ethics of war, though if one follows the plain meaning of numerous New Testament passages, war and the use of violence are ruled out for the Christian. Engaging in physical battle in the Old Testament is transposed into spiritual battles in the New, where the fight against evil is described in battle imagery (see Eph. 6:10–18; 2 Tim. 4:7). Given this tension between the testaments, clarifying their relationship became one of the key hermeneutical issues debated during the Reformation.[40]

A more immediate interpretive issue involved the Christian's role in civil government and the use of violence. The magisterial Reformers introduced profound theological changes, but they did not alter the church-state structure set in place during the age of Constantine. The pre-Constantinian Christians followed generally the path of nonresistance, rejecting the violence of the empire and service in the army (not until 170–180 is there mention of a Christian in the military) not only because they had no stake in power but also because they believed that bloodshed was morally wrong.[41] As they came to share in imperial power and united the church with the state, however, post-Constantinian Christians considered state-sanctioned violence not only morally permissible but also a positive good and a Christian duty. The radical Reformers' goals was restoration of New Testament principles, one of which they claimed was to leave the use of the sword in the hands of the pagan rulers.

I have already noted some of the primary divergences between Luther and Anabaptists, but we need to extend the discussion and investigate more systematically early Anabaptist exegesis and hermeneutical principles. Let us first return to Article 6 of the Schleitheim Confession on the use of "the sword," a term in currency among all the Reformers, referring to the temporal powers (judicial and police) of the state. As James Stayer has observed, Anabaptist discussion of the sword was situated within a larger conversation broached earlier in the Reformation.[42] Protestant Reformers, in their appeal to the historical, contextual understanding of Scripture, rejected the allegorical interpretation of Luke 22:38 ("And they said, Lord, behold, here are two swords. And he said unto them, 'It is enough'") that had prevailed since Pope Gelasius proposed the "two swords theory" in the late fifth century. According to this view, God ordained a spiritual (ecclesiastical) sword and temporal (civil) sword to govern all of society. From the church's perspective the spiritual sword was the more lethal of the two, for ultimately, the pope answered directly to God for the actions of a ruler. It was upon this conceptual basis that early medieval theorists proposed a Holy Roman Empire and later theorists provided the rationale for a papal theocracy that wielded both swords.

In place of the "two swords" of Luke 22:38 the Reformers invoked the "one sword" of Romans 13:4. Discussing the Christian's relationship to a pagan Roman government, Paul writes that the governing "authority does not bear the sword in vain! It is the servant of God to execute wrath on the wrongdoer." Discussion of the sword between magisterial Reformers and Anabaptists turned on this pivotal text. All reform groups thus shared a common premise: there was one sword that functioned in the temporal sphere. But who should wield it—Christians or non-Christians or both? Simply put, Protestants faced reconciling both the Old Testament Mosaic Law (civil codes that advocated capital punishment) and Romans 13 (which advocated the necessity of the government's use of the sword and hence, if Christians held office, their inevitable use of the sword) with the Sermon on the Mount (which advocated a nonresistant response to evil).

According to Luther's "two-kingdom" theology, the sword was an expression of law and not of gospel, a divinely willed necessity (Romans 13) but outside the rule of Christian love (Matthew 5). True Christians did not require the sword; they (ideally) lived in harmony with fellow Christians. But the fallen and violent non-Christian world necessitated it. Luther placed the sword in a kind of neutral category, neither of Christ nor of the devil. Because the Christian was not to shun the world, a Christian ruler could wield the sword as a service to God in a similar way that others served God through their various callings (e.g., as a farmer or artisan). Its use was a necessity—just as the law was necessary to expose sin and drive one to Christ—but again, not an explicit Christian expression because it was devoid of gospel.

In contrast to Luther's neutral and paradoxical views, Zwingli expressed a positive and straightforward attitude toward the sword. Indeed, if necessary, the sword should be brought to bear to transform Zurich into a Christian society, a kind of miniature *corpus christianum*. As we have seen, the government was to control the affairs of the church in determining the pace of reform and ensuring that reform was carried out. Prior to his arrival in Zurich, Zwingli had been deeply influenced by Erasmus's christocentric piety and "prudential pacifism." Though never able to eschew all war (e.g., defensive war against the threatening Turks), Erasmus made clear his views: "Whoever proclaims Christ proclaims peace. Whoever preaches war, preaches that which is most unlike Christ."[43]

Early on, Zwingli continued this Erasmian stance. In 1522, he wrote a pacifist tract in which he argued that the aggressive wars in the Old Testament should be either spiritualized (Christians are engaged in a spiritual battle) or moralized ("God punishes the wicked with the wicked"). However, by the following year, when it became clear that unifying the Protestant Swiss Confederation could not be realized by peace, Zwingli became an active supporter of war in order to realize God's purposes. He eventually took up the sword himself and died in the battle of Kappel in 1531.[44]

Rather than view the Old and the New Testaments as polar opposites, Zwingli interpreted these differences hierarchically. To be sure, Christ taught perfection (peace), but such perfection could never be realized in this life. Hence, on a lower but necessary level, the sword may and must be wielded to bring about a Christian society. Moreover, Christian subjects should be content only with a Christian ruler and thus, if they are the majority, may revolt against an unchristian despot or tyrant. Clearly, Zwingli envisioned a more positive role for the state (and its necessary use of the sword) than did Luther, one in which the state and church intimately cooperated to create a Christian society.[45]

These views of Luther and Zwingli provided the backdrop for the developing Anabaptist view of the sword that culminated in the Schleitheim Confession. Like Zwingli, the humanist Grebel's circle had been influenced by Erasmus and followed Zwingli's earlier pacifist views. Grebel himself had urged Thomas Müntzer to abandon violent apocalypticism and prophetic vengeance. "True believing Christians . . . employ neither worldly sword nor war, since with them killing is absolutely renounced: unless, indeed, we would still be under the Old Law—in which (so far as we understand) war was, after the promised land had been conquered, only a plague." Here Grebel made a crucial hermeneutical distinction (a distinction embraced publicly in the Schleitheim Confession) between the gospel, which prohibits killing, and the "Old Law," which allowed it. Pacifism was to become the norm for Anabaptists, and yet this stance appeared to have little impact on other would-be Anabaptists. I have noted Hubmaier's efforts in Waldshut to create an Anabaptist *corpus chris-tianum*, and George Blaurock, the first in the Grebel circle to be rebaptized, apparently never made known his views on nonresistance.[46]

Not until the Schleitheim conference did private conversation become public declaration. This conference and the document issued from it have stirred historical debate over their role in the development of Anabaptist pacifism and separatism. Did the document endorse quietism and apolitical withdrawal from the world, or did it introduce the idea of social and political struggle? Did the Anabaptists who framed this document endorse a quietist abandonment of the world, or did they, in spite of a climate of persecution, intend to engage the world and affirm their place in the civil realm? Did this document represent a consensus view within the emerging Anabaptist movement?

It is not necessary to resolve the historical debate over this question, but I should point out that the way one reads the confession and the context surrounding it influences one's answer to the question. In a recent article, Gerald Biesecker-Mast suggests that "the rhetorical movement of the text itself can tell us a great deal about the practical problems and possibilities that characterize the article's [i.e., Article 6] position on the sword." The confession "moves from the position of antagonism (mutual exclusivity)," as expressed in Article 4, "to one of dualism (legitimate difference)—when accounting for the sword" in Article 6, "and then back to antagonism."[47]

Article 4 enjoined separation from the world: the Lord "orders us to be and to become separated from the evil one." Because the use of the sword lay squarely within the camp of evil, its use was not non-Christian (Luther) but unchristian. "Thereby shall also fall from us the diabolical weapons of violence—such as sword, armor, and the like, and all their use to protect friends or against enemies—by virtue of the word of Christ: 'you shall not resist evil' " (Matt. 5:39). The position of antagonism is moderated in Article 6, which states that "the sword is an ordering of God outside the perfection of Christ." Luther placed the sword in a neutral state, whereas the Anabaptists placed it in the camp of Satan (Article 4), but they nevertheless recognized that the sword "punishes and kills the wicked, and guards and protects the good." The sword is a useful and legitimate ordering of God within the realm of law, though its use is outside the perfection of Christ. Government and church have two different but legitimate functions.

Article 6 is a more complex statement, one that recognizes the inherent ambiguity about the relationship of Anabaptists to the civil order over against the dualistic, separatist stance of Article 4. This back-and-forth rhetorical structure of Articles 4 and 6, notes Biesecker-Mast, suggests that the authors of the confession were not so much articulating a preexisting theological blueprint as responding to a specific situation. Human depravity required the coercion of state—Anabaptists were not anarchists but sought to be civil, law-abiding subjects—but a Christian must not participate in that world of depravity, since it lies outside the intention of Christ. Here, then, was the linkage between separatism and pacifism—two distinct but often combined postures toward the larger, adversarial society. Not all sectarian groups are pacifist (the separatist but violent Jonestown community in Guyana of the 1970s comes to mind), but as social analysts have often pointed out, "Both impulses embody a minority consciousness, a protest stance against the larger social system."[48]

To answer the question of "whether a Christian may or should use the sword against the wicked for the protection and defense of the good, or for the sake of love," the confession appealed to the actions and words of Jesus. He was "meek and lowly of heart" (Matt. 11:29). Jesus advised mercy and forgiveness, not stoning as prescribed by the law, in dealing with a woman caught in adultery (John 8:11). So the means of discipline within the Christian community is not physical force but the ban, a form of spiritual excommunication. Jesus refused to render judgment in a dispute between two brothers over an inheritance (Luke 12:13–14). So Christians should withdraw from the world and its litigious ways. Jesus refused kingship. So Christians should reject civic office and follow the model of Jesus who "suffered and left us an example, that you should follow in his steps" (1 Pet. 1:21). The world is "armed with steel and iron, but Christians are armed with the armor of God": truth, righteousness, faith, and peace (Eph. 6:13–16).[49]

As Stayer notes of these scriptural proofs, "Refusal of force and authority was not, as has often been pointed out, the primary point of any of these texts, but this interpretation of them was consistent with the general picture of Jesus that the Swiss Brethren derived from the Gospels."[50] Indeed, it is this christocentric piety that formed the basis of the Anabaptists' nonresistant ethic and set them apart from the other Reformers. Absent from Article 6 are scriptural references to Jesus' words in the Sermon on the Mount to "turn the other cheek" and "love your enemies" (Matt. 5:39, 44). Although this teaching was somewhat peripheral in the Schleitheim Confession (Article 4 cited Matt. 5: 39), it become central in the religious disputations between the Anabaptist and Reformed parties at Zoffingen in 1532 and Bern in 1538. In fact, from then on Jesus' words in the Sermon on the Mount became the locus classicus of all subsequent Anabaptist discussions regarding their pacifist convictions.

A summary of the Anabaptist arguments advanced at the Bern Disputation indicates the trajectory of Anabaptist hermeneutics among the Swiss Brethren. Both Anabaptist and Reformed leaders agreed that the debate should center on *sola scriptura*. From the perspective of the Reformed clergy (no doubt influenced by Zwingli's earlier writings) who set the agenda for the debate, the heart of the hermeneutical dispute was the relationship between the Old and New Testaments. They endowed both testaments with equal authority and validity, maintaining, for example, an analogy between circumcision in the Old and infant baptism in the New, and the continued religion-in-state from the Old to the New.

Included among their criticisms of the Anabaptists was the charge of a wooden literalism: they "hang on the letter too much." To wit: Anabaptists refused to take oaths based on Jesus' instructions in the Sermon on the Mount: "Do not swear at all. . . . Let your word be 'Yes, Yes' or 'No, No'" (Matt. 5:34, 37). To Anabaptists, the clarity and authority of Jesus' words were unmistakable in meaning. To opponents, Jesus used exaggerated language to make a general point regarding truth-telling. They could not be accused of a misguided literalism that led to all kinds of bizarre Anabaptist behaviors. In St. Gall (Switzerland) and in the Netherlands, for example, a handful of Anabaptists strictly obeyed Jesus' words to his twelve disciples in Matthew 10:9–10 and so wandered about the countryside without weapons, money, or a change of clothes. Others followed Jesus' instructions in Matthew 10:27 and preached from rooftops. Still others embraced Jesus' teaching that those who enter the kingdom must be like children and so resorted to infantile behavior. Needless to say, more learned and sober Anabaptist exegetes decried these exhibitions, but opponents had all the necessary proof to expose a problematic hermeneutic.[51]

In discussing the Bern Disputation, Walter Klaassen suggests, "The Anabaptists seem to have been the only Protestants in the sixteenth century that took a historical view of the Bible. They viewed the drama of God's redemption as a process, initiated by God in particular with Abraham, and moving forward to a climax in Jesus Christ, in whom God would conclude human history."[52] The Old Testament was viewed as preparatory, lacking finality—a shadow of things to come, whereas in the New Testament God's revelation was complete, finished—fully illuminated by Jesus Christ. Indeed, all of Scripture pointed to Christ as the center.

Thus far no Reformer would disagree. Klaassen continues: "What God did in Christ in his final word to men, and therefore what Christ, who was perfectly obedient to the will of his Father, said and did, is simply God's demand."[53] Old Testament justice was based on proportionate or equitable punishment for wrong (the *lex talionis*)—"an eye for an eye, and a tooth for a tooth." Moreover, the Old Testament contains many statements supporting warfare. But Jesus insisted on a different ethic: "Do not resist an evil-doer. . . . Love your enemies and pray for those who persecute you" (Matt. 5:38, 43).

At the onset of the debate, the Anabaptist leaders agreed with the Bern clergy that the Old Testament was authoritative, "where Christ has not suspended it."[54] Clearly, Jesus' teachings on nonresistance suspended Old Testament notions of justice. For these early Anabaptists, an ethic of radical obedience to the teachings of Jesus guided their interpretation of Scripture. As expressed by Sattler in the Schleitheim Confession and by Anabaptist Brethren in the Bern Disputation, the life and teachings of Jesus provided the norm of conduct for the church.

To be sure, the teaching and practice of the Swiss Brethren could descend into a harsh legalism, with an emphasis on the "law of Christ" over the "love

of Christ." The ban became so significant among Dutch Mennonites that according to George Williams "Anabanism" became a more appropriate label
than Anabaptism. However their nonresistant ethic was communicated, as love
or law, Anabaptists derived it from a hermeneutic that elevated the words and
teaching of Jesus above other expressions of divine revelation. In so doing, they
affirmed that the teachings of Jesus took precedence over the Old Testament
use of the sword.[55]

One of the most significant Anabaptist answers to the testamental relationship came from the pen of Pilgram Marpeck (ca. 1495–1556).[56] An engineer
in the Tyrol region who led Anabaptist communities in Strasbourg and Augsburg, Marpeck was one of the few early Anabaptist leaders to die of natural
causes. In the *Testamenterleütterung* (Explanation of the Testaments, ca. 1544–
50), a lengthy treatise of some eight hundred pages, as well as in other writings,
he clarified the relationship between the Old and New Testaments. Marpeck
recognized the use of the moral law in uncovering sin, and indeed one could
not preach the gospel without first preaching the law. But there was a fundamental difference between the Old and New, a difference Marpeck characterized as between "yesterday" and "today."[57] God's nature or moral will have not
changed, nor does a God of wrath rule the Old Testament and a God of love
the New. But the testaments fit different historical circumstances that must be
taken into account. Thus whereas God's nature does not change, humanity—
embedded as it is in history—does, and God deals with his creatures accordingly in a successive series of covenants.

This hermeneutic, of course, set Anabaptists apart from Reformers.
Zwingli, for example, in his debate with the Anabaptists, argued for a singular
covenant between humans and God, beginning with Abraham and continuing
to its fulfillment in Christ. God's revelation does not change through time, nor
does it contradict itself. Hence baptism in the New Testament is the continuation of circumcision in the Old; the covenant inaugurated by circumcision in
now sealed by baptism; and therefore baptism belongs to all children within
the covenant family. According to Zwingli's interpretation, the teachings of
baptism in the New Testament are an insufficient guide.[58]

Both Anabaptists and Reformers agreed that the Old Testament contained
the promise of what was fulfilled in the New with the incarnation. But the
Anabaptists went a step further. They affirmed that God's purposes in history
were worked out within history in such a way that the transition from the Old
to New Testament reflected a change in God's purposes. The relationship of
the Old and the New Testaments was not "flat" but historical. "At no point
could the Old Testament," writes William Klassen in his monograph on Marpeck, "be brought in to attenuate the Christian ethic or to revert the Christian
church from freedom to bondage. The provisional role of the Old Testament
was fulfilled . . . the practices and standards of the Old Testament dare not
become normative for the church."[59] Jesus' words, "you have heard it said,"

encapsulated the old covenant, whereas "but I say to you" embodied a new, stricter criterion of judgment. To be sure, Marpeck admitted a necessary co-ercive role for civil authority and even armed support from Anabaptists in defensive measures, but he denounced those who used force in matters of faith, be it physical or legal. The Christian must then fight only with the "weapons and sword of the Holy Spirit."[60]

In sum, the realm of Christ, ruled by the noncoercive Spirit, became the locus of hermeneutical authority. There was little urgency to reconcile war-making activity in the Old Testament with peacemaking in the New, for the New superseded the Old. What is in opposition to Christ is not binding on Christians, even though it is in the Bible. Jesus' teachings on nonresistance and his life of patient suffering carried the argument. The views articulated by Conrad Grebel in his letter to Müntzer, by Michael Sattler in the Schleitheim Confession, by Anabaptist leaders at the Bern Disputation, and by Pilgram Marpeck shared this common interpretive strategy. All made Jesus the ultimate source of authority and, to a greater or lesser degree, made a fundamental distinction between historical periods in the Old and New Testaments.

Recent Anabaptist-Mennonite Perspectives on Pacifism

From Isolation to Engagement

The arguments for peace and nonresistance advanced in the sixteenth century, though expanded, modified, and refined in succeeding centuries, remain the basis for contemporary American Mennonite identity. A study of twenty-seven Mennonite confessions of faith between 1527 and 1975 indicated that peace convictions were one of their central features. Within these confessions a con-sistent appeal was made to the example of Jesus and the Sermon on the Mount, with Jesus' nonresistant instructions in Matthew 5:38–48 receiving the most attention.[61]

During the last half of the twentieth century, however, the way in which peace was understood and practiced within the American Mennonite com-munity underwent a profound alteration. The old sectarian model of with-drawal from the world and passive nonresistance was severely challenged. An-swering critics such as Reinhold Niebuhr, who accused Anabaptists of irresponsibly abandoning the world, of living like "parasites on the sins of others," in the years after World War II Mennonites reformulated their views on nonresistance. Formerly characterized as *Die Stillen im Lande*, "the quiet of the land," Mennonites transformed passive nonresistance into vocal, active nonviolent resistance. Broad social changes contributed to this revision. The exodus from the farm to suburban and urban areas ("from the plow to profes-sions"), the entry of Mennonite men into (alternative) military service during World War II, and the pursuit of higher education brought Mennonites into close contact with the modern world. As Mennonites participated increasingly in public life, the sectarian stance, typically known as "nonconformity," conflicted with a more engaging posture.[62]

A theological reconstruction, "a paradigm shift of major proportions," preceded this change and in large measure reflected the Mennonite move into the mainstream of American life.[63] Unlike their Amish brethren, who maintained the historic doctrine of two kingdoms (expressed in the social order by sectarianism), Mennonites reformulated the stark dualistic tension between a non-resistant church and sword-wielding world expressed originally in the Schleitheim Confession. After Hitler had wreaked violence and death upon millions, could the church stand any longer on the sidelines? Could the church maintain its traditional quiescence as nations raced to build nuclear armaments? Could the church simply exempt itself as governments and evil social structures oppressed the powerless, maintained laws of racial discrimination, and bombed Vietnam indiscriminately?

Increasingly involved in the fabric of public life, many Mennonites responded with a resounding no. Not two moral standards (one for the church and one for the state) but one, "the lordship of Christ," defined this new theological stance. According to Leo Driedger and Donald Kraybill,

> The erection of the lordship [of Christ] canopy in Mennonite consciousness brought a dramatic change in position and perspective.
> . . . The kingdoms of this world suddenly dropped in esteem. They were now viewed sometimes as agents of rebellious principalities and powers—disobedient to the high standards of God's righteousness which God required of *all* under the lordship of Christ. No longer looking down across the moat of separation, Mennonites were now looking down to the rebellious agents of darkness, and giving a "prophetic witness." They called the rebellious powers to live *up* to the holiness and righteousness of God, to the Lord of history to whom "all men were accountable." Mennonites, in brief, had demythologized the state.[64]

Two kingdoms remained, but both—the church *and* the state—fell under the lordship of Christ, particularly in matters of peace and justice. With this revised theology in hand, Mennonites engaged in "prophetic witness" and called authorities to the righteousness of God. During the tumultuous 1960s and 1970s, Mennonites engaged in political activism and nonviolent action, including running for public office, signing petitions, participating in public demonstrations, marching with civil rights supporters, lobbying in Washington, refusing to register with the Selective Service, pouring blood on draft files, and trespassing on nuclear facilities. In their own right, these activities were acts of force insofar as they were confrontational and designed to effect change, though in a nonviolent manner. By the 1980s and 1990s, these forms of nonviolent resistance gave way to a new strategic emphasis on activist peacemaking. Mennonites participated in various initiatives aimed at confronting volatile situations, addressing injustice, mediating conflict, and bringing reconciliation in local, national, and international settings.

Jesus' Sermon on the Mount remained normative, but an emphatic shift occurred from nonresistance ("do not resist an evildoer" [Matt. 5:39]) to peacemaking ("blessed are the peacemakers" [Matt. 5:9]). Mennonites debated whether this shift was faithful to historic Anabaptist teachings. Did it represent a concession to the new realities of being enmeshed in the modern world? As Mennonites assimilated, had they domesticated Jesus? Could one remain true to the tradition and actively engaged in the world? Was this shift from passive nonresistance to nonviolent activist peacemaking a compromise? Or was this new tack merely a change in emphasis?[65]

John H. Yoder

As heirs of the Anabaptist fidelity to Scripture, Mennonites turned to the Bible to legitimate their transformation from quietism to activism. The best known scholar to articulate a biblical rationale for nonviolent resistance was John H. Yoder. A prominent scholar within the Mennonite community and undoubtedly the most influential Mennonite to a wider ecumenical audience, Yoder served in several Mennonite institutional settings before assuming a full-time teaching post in theology at the University of Notre Dame in 1977.[66] Throughout his career, beginning in the 1950s and until his sudden death in 1997, Yoder embodied the post–World War II Mennonite engagement with the wider culture.

His landmark study, *The Politics of Jesus* (1972), represents the most significant contribution to a Christian peace ethic understood within the framework of modern biblical scholarship. Stanley Hauerwas has remarked "that when Christians look back on this century of theology in America *The Politics of Jesus* will be seen as a new beginning." Many a divinity school student encountered this provocative work in the 1970s, and it continues to receive acclaim and have wide appeal within and beyond the academy. To Jim Wallis, the founding editor of *Sojourners* (noted at the beginning of this chapter), Yoder "inspired a whole generation of Christians to follow the way of Jesus into social action and peacemaking."[67]

The Politics of Jesus is not a plea for direct Christian participation in the political order. Elsewhere, Yoder contended that the Christian church should witness to the state as an alternative community and so encourage the government to choose policies that most closely resemble kingdom ethics.[68] In *The Politics of Jesus* Yoder ties this view to his argument that Jesus' ethic of nonresistance was a political act that challenged prevailing political structures, and hence, the call to discipleship has political implications. Highly critical both of mainstream ethicists who offered a variety of reasons for evading Jesus as an ethical norm and of biblical scholars who "develop vast systems of crypto-systematics" and so neglected broader ethical concerns, Yoder sought to connect New Testament studies with contemporary social ethics. Jesus' advocacy of justice and nonviolent resistance reflected Old Testament ethics and was expressed not only in the Gospels (Yoder relies primarily on Luke's account) but also consistently throughout the New Testament. "Jesus is, according to the biblical witness, a model of radical political action."[69] Jesus did not abandon politics (the path taken by sectarian pacifists) but was a political revolutionary who threatened society by creating an alternative nonviolent community of love, service, and justice—the very kind of community the church should embody today. His actions and teachings so enraged the political authorities that they crucified him. The cross of Calvary, Yoder writes in an effort to dispel modern misunderstandings of "cross-bearing," is "the inevitable suffering of those whose only goal is to be faithful to that love which puts one at the mercy of one's neighbor, which abandons claims to justice for oneself and for one's own in an overriding concern for the reconciling of adversary and the estranged."[70]

Yoder's political characterization of Jesus' life and death challenged not only mainstream ethical views but also the views of many Mennonites, including those expressed by Guy Hershberger in his classic study, *War, Peace, and Nonresistance* (1944; 3rd ed., 1969). Yoder agreed with Hershberger's contention that "God has provided one fundamental moral law which has been and is valid for all time"—the law revealed in the Ten Commandments and the life and teachings of Jesus. He and other activists built upon this insight to call for a single moral law that applied to not only the church but the state as well. But Hershberger, seeking in his own day to find a middle course for Mennonites between fundamentalist withdrawal from politics and modernist social engagement, continued a nonpolitical stance. He proposed that "the outlook of the New Testament is entirely unpolitical," and "the Christian ethic places its emphasis on the doing of justice rather than on seeking or demanding justice for one's self."[71] Yoder and others reached different conclusions. They argued that the New Testament accounts had profound political implications and that the church should urge the state to be more just.[72]

In an earlier essay and reiterated in *The Politics of Jesus*, Yoder also took issue with Hershberger's interpretation of the Old Testament accounts that advocated and even glorified bloodshed, apparently with divine approval. In considering the relationship between the testaments, Hershberger went beyond the earlier approach (as we saw in Marpeck) that strictly divided the testaments based on Jesus' words, "You have heard it said . . . but I say to you." Hershberger argued that the Mosaic civil law of the Old Testament, which permitted vengeance and retaliation, "represented a temporary concession on the part of God to the lowered moral state and spiritual immaturity of that time, a concession made necessary by the sin of man, and not by the will of God." The various Old Testament commands of God regarding killing (e.g., the command to slay the Amalekites, to hew Agag into pieces) were "permissive commands given to a sinful, lean-souled people who had chosen to live on a lower 'sub-Christian' level."[73]

Yoder offered a third alternative. He observed that in some instances, the death penalty and holy war in the Old Testament were not a concession. One could argue, as do Christians who permit warfare, that there is a division of realms between the Old and New Testaments. That is, one can reconcile the testaments if one recognizes that they are talking about two different subjects. The Old Testament concerns itself with civil order of the Hebrew people; in such a context, war is permitted. The New Testament says little about civil life (other than to "Render unto Caesar the things that are Caesar's" and "Be subject to the powers that be"), and hence its urgings to nonviolence, renunciation of rights, and a willingness to suffer apply only to the Christian individual or to the church, not to the state. But this perspective is flawed, argues Yoder, on several counts, one of which underplays the unmistakable social and political language found throughout the New Testament.[74]

Perhaps the most serious problem in viewing war as a divine concession is that it simply does not comport with Old Testament accounts. In an effort to reconcile war with the later perspective of Jesus and the New Testament, this view ignores the historical and anthropological context of killing. The question to ask, suggests Yoder, is not how Old Testament violence differs from what came later, but how it differs from what went before and how it related to other forms of violence in the Near East. Consider the command given by God to Abraham to sacrifice his only legitimate son, Isaac (Genesis 22). In our own time, we would consider this instruction morally outrageous, contravening God's own rules. We ask, What does this command say about the nature of a God who asks a father to kill his son? Wrong question, contends Yoder, for it is a *modern* question, influenced by Western fatherly sentiment and a highly personalized view of the self. We must understand the story within its own cultural context. The issue was not the morality of killing. In his day, for Abraham to sacrifice his firstborn son was not out of the ordinary. It was a common cultic custom, something all the neighbors did, "no more ethically scandalous or viscerally disturbing than the killing of the villain in a western film is to most watchers today." Abraham was put to the test not to gauge his fatherly instincts or ethics but to trust God for his survival.[75]

In the same way that God tested Abraham's trust in God's provision alone, so holy war becomes a test of Israel's obedience. Relying upon the work of Millard Lind, an erstwhile colleague at Associated Mennonite Biblical Seminaries, Yoder discusses the exodus account as *the* paradigm of God's action in Israel's history. When the Hebrews did not fight but stood still and trusted in God, they were delivered from the Egyptians. "The Lord will fight for you, and you have only to be still" (Exod. 14:13). According to Lind, "A scholarly consensus exists that the war narratives are characterized by the exclusive prerogative of Yahweh's fighting and a denial of the efficacy of human fighting. While all narratives are affected by this concept, many narratives present the case not as trust in Yahweh *and* human fighting, but trust in Yahweh which *excludes* human fighting."[76] Israel's self-understanding was rooted in supernatural interventions in its early history, beginning with the miraculous deliverance from Egypt and continuing through the conquest of Canaan.

In the mind of Jesus and his followers, Yoder maintains, the holy war in Israel's past was a matter of trust and obedience, not recourse to violence in order to ensure justice. God promised the Israelites that the occupants of the land of Canaan would be driven out by God's intervention, "little by little" (Exod. 23:30), by an angel (23:20, 23), by "my terror" (23:27), and by "pestilence" (23:28). The most impressive victories came when God alone acted, such as at Jericho (Joshua 6), or when God reduced the military force to a handful of torchbearers, such as in Gideon's defeat of the Midianites (Judges 7). From its early history through the conquest, the kingdoms, after the exile, and through the prophets vision of peace (*shalom*) and demand for justice, Israel's spiritual health and survival were premised upon a trust in God's miraculous deliverance rather than reliance upon military might or violence.[77]

Bloodshed abounds in such accounts, but holy war was a ritual event in which whole Canaanite cities were set apart (*herem*) and made the object of sacrifice to God. No spoils were to be gained from holy war that was an "*ad hoc* charismatic event" of Yahweh's doing and not the result of detailed military strategy.[78] Holy war, then, was unique, limited geographically to the Hebrew kingdom of God and politically to a theocratic state. In the message of Jesus, however, "kingdom" acquired an expanded meaning. In his life and ministry, Jesus proclaimed that a new age was of fulfillment was at hand. The kingdom of God was no longer restricted to a particular ethnic people within particular physical boundaries but included all people (foreigners and enemies) who accepted Jesus as Lord.

Once we view the history of Israel in this light, we can understand how Jesus' message of liberation and revolution without recourse to violence resonated in the ears of his hearers. Jesus was not a futuristic dreamer but one whose message recapitulated God's saving activity: "A believing people would be saved despite their weakness, on condition that they 'be still and wait to see the salvation of Jahweh.'" There were other options open to Jesus, including the crusading, revolutionary approach of the Zealots.[79] But he chose the path of Isaiah's suffering servant (Isa. 40–55) and called into being a community of voluntary commitment whose own path paralleled the hostility and rejection of their leader. Jesus was not just a moralist or a teacher or a sacrificial lamb or a God-man—to be sure, he was all of these—but above all, he was "the bearer of a new possibility of human, social, and therefore political relation-ships."[80]

Jesus' nonviolent way of the cross decisively demonstrated that God acted toward his enemies in suffering love. Beyond the Gospels, Paul's letters and other New Testament writings amply testify to this way of discipleship. On the individual level, the themes of disciple/participant and imitator of the love of God and the life of Christ pervade the New Testament. Moreover—and this is one of Yoder's most significant insights—Paul grasped the political implica-tions of Jesus' life and death. From the Pauline doctrine of "principalities and powers," Yoder derives a sociopolitical critique of existing structures of power, be they human traditions, religious institutions, or social, political, and eco-nomic structures.[81] Relying upon the New Testament research of Henrik Berk-hof and G. B. Caird, Yoder observes that the powers were created by God to serve a useful ordering purpose (Col. 1:15–17), but they are fallen in the sense that they no longer serve humans in wholly beneficial ways. They have become idols, enslaving humankind and demanding absolute loyalty. For humans to live a truly free and genuine existence, their powers must be broken. And this is what Jesus did.

> In his death the Powers—in this case the most worthy, weighty rep-resentatives of Jewish religion and Roman politics—acted in collu-sion. Like all men, he too was subject . . . to these powers. . . . But morally he broke their rules by refusing to support them in their self-glorification; and that is why they killed him. . . . But he did not fear even death. Therefore his cross is a victory, is the confirmation that he was free from the rebellious pretensions of the creaturely condi-tion.[82]

According to Paul, Jesus "disarmed the principalities and powers and made a public example of them, triumphing over them in him" (Col. 2:15). Thus while the powers continue to serve an ordering function (e.g., a tyrannical government is better than anarchy), their absolute dominion over Christians is broken. Because their claims cannot demand ultimate obedience and be-cause they are "fallen," Christians must sometimes refuse to cooperate with the powers and suffer the consequences, even to the point of death.

This understanding of "the powers" clarifies Paul's teaching on "the sword" in Romans 13. Yoder challenges mainstream "Constantinian" Catholics and Protestants who argue that because government is established by God, Christians are to obey the government in its use of the sword, be it by the death penalty or warfare. How does one reconcile Jesus' words in Matthew 5 with Paul's words in Romans 13:1–7? Yoder makes six observations, summa-rized as follows.

1. Contrary to most Protestant political thought, the Romans 13 text is not the only or necessarily the central New Testament text on the Christian's relation to the state. Other texts suggest that the state is ruled over by Satan (in the temptation story Jesus does not challenge Satan's statement to rule over earthly kingdoms) and that demonic "powers" persecute the church (Rev. 13).

2. The text is part of a single literary unit that includes chapters 12–13. Because the overarching message is one of "Christian nonconformity and suffering love" (12:14–21 gives instruction on responding to enemies, e.g., v. 21: "Do not be overcome by evil, but overcome evil with good"), any interpretation of 13:1–7 that does not include this message misreads the context.

3. The text enjoins subordination to whatever government is in power, including the existing tyrannical Roman government. It does not uphold a particular kind of divinely ordained government and hence rules out "just" rebellion against non–divinely ordained government.

4. The instruction "be subject to the governing authorities" (v. 1) was given to people who had no say in Roman government. The text cannot refer to the Roman Christians serving as police or in the military, for sword bearing was not one of the functions the government asked of its people. The Romans did not have universal conscription, and hence there was no pressure on Christians to serve in the military.

5. The "sword" to which Christians are called to be subject refers to judicial or police functions, not to capital punishment or war. "At the very most the only relevance of Romans 13 to war would be to a very precise operation carried on within the very clear limitations of all the classic criteria that define the 'justifiable war.'"

6. Government is "ordered" (a better translation than "ordained") by God in the sense that God lines it up with his purpose, but it is not self-justifying. "The text does not say that whatever the government does or asks of its citizens is good." Being subordinate or subject to a government is not the same as obeying it. A conscientious objector is subordinate in accepting the consequences of government-imposed penalties for his refusal to go to war.

In sum, Matthew 5 and Romans 13 are not contradictory. One is not forced to choose between the personal ethic of Jesus and the social ethic of Paul, between personal faithfulness and social responsibility. "They *both* instruct Christians to be nonresistant in all their relationships, including the social. They *both* call on the disciples of Jesus to renounce participation in the interplay of egoism which this world calls 'vengeance' or 'justice.'" Christian nonresistance is not an option for the heroic few; rather, it is the core of Christian faithfulness.[83]

Conclusion

Since this discussion has taken us in a number of directions—personal, historical, biblical, and ethical—I conclude with several summary statements and observations about the Anabaptist peace witness. First, in its origins, Anabaptism was a diverse, multifaceted phenomenon, at once a radical religious and social movement. Consequently, Anabaptist biblical hermeneutics was not solely the result of theological ideas that emerged directly from the pages of Scripture or from the pen of Erasmus; nor was it only the result of political, social, or economic factors. A dialectical interplay among these influences, dialogue within the Anabaptist community, and debate with opponents eventually generated a hermeneutic that uplifted the life and teaching of Jesus, including his ethic of nonviolence. The community's social context shaped the interpretive process, and the interpretation influenced the community; praxis reinforced interpretation and vice versa.[84]

Second, given the recognized authority of the whole Bible, some principles of interpretation had to be applied to reconcile discrepancies regarding war and the use of force over against other clear instructions to make peace, follow the way of nonresistance, and love one's enemies. One of the more critical hermeneutical issues involved the relationship between the Old and New Testaments. Another concerned Paul's discussion of the sword in Romans 13. As we have seen, Anabaptists developed several interpretive strategies (e.g., isolating a canon within the canon, emphasizing the in-breaking presence of the reign of God) to reconcile those portions of Scripture that condoned killing and the use of force with those that enjoined peacemaking. Historically, however, the Anabaptist genius lay not in hermeneutical novelty or exegetical insights but in the commitment to follow Jesus. The central Christian witness was Christ himself, and he became the prism through which to filter the various perspectives on war in the Bible.

Third, the Anabaptist-Mennonite nonviolent ethic has been expressed in a variety of ways, ranging from the sectarian nonresistance of the Swiss Brethren in the sixteenth century to the most recent activist peacemaking efforts of the Mennonites. Mennonites have debated among themselves the suitability of terms such as "defenseless Christians," "nonresistance," "pacifists," "nonviolent resistance," and "loving resistance." The use of these terms often implies a certain posture toward society (open, closed, prophetic, accommodating), which is then grounded in or derived from certain biblical models and hermeneutical principles. Despite a consistent pacifistic stance over the centuries, Mennonites have revised its lived-out meaning in a variety of ways.[85]

Fourth, according to Anabaptist historical analysis, Constantine's imperial policies not only recast the nature of the church but also compromised its integrity, eventuating in a "great reversal" or "fall."[86] Jesus' Sermon on the

Mount, the most frequently quoted portion of Scripture by noncanonical writers in the early church, could not be reconciled with the demands, aspirations,
and powers of a unified state and church. Thus over the centuries, the content
of Jesus' message became irrelevant or selectively applied. The demands of the
Sermon on the Mount to follow the path of nonresistance and love one's enemies became either applicable to a few (Jesus' disciples or, later, monks who
lived by the "evangelical counsels" of perfection) or restricted to individual and
not political relations (Luther) or diluted by distinguishing between an acceptable resistance but not acceptable revenge (Calvin), or an exaggerated command meant to illustrate a new disposition (Wilhelm Herrmann), or intended
for an "interim"—a very short period since Jesus thought the world would
soon come to an end (Albert Schweitzer), or postponed until the Second Coming of Christ (dispensationalism), or an "impossible possibility" (Reinhold Niebuhr), or viewed as less important than Jesus' coming to give his life for the
sins of humanity (dogma over ethics, belief over obedience, orthodoxy over
orthopraxy)—to mention but several evasive responses.[87] One could cite numerous other reservations lodged in modern biblical criticism, but the point
is that since Constantine (though, of course, not because of Constantine alone)
Jesus as a norm within the mainstream Christian ethical tradition faded from
relevance.[88]

At the same time, advances in biblical scholarship (the reservations just
cited notwithstanding) and a spirit of ecumenicity have brought together representatives from the historic peace churches and those from churches traditionally supporting a just-war approach in a unified peace witness or in "just
peacemaking."[89] The potential for mass nuclear destruction and the realities
of violence and oppression around the world have lent urgency to such coop-
erative endeavors. An active peace witness is no longer confined to a sectarian
group on the fringe of Christianity, and the message of peace is no longer
considered tangential to the biblical message. Certainly, this is the abiding
legacy of the sixteenth-century Anabaptists.

6

"Let My People Go"

Exodus in the African American Experience

The Egyptians became ruthless in imposing tasks on the Israelites, and made their lives bitter with hard service in mortar and brick and in every kind of field labor. . . . Then the LORD said, "I have observed the misery of my people who are in Egypt; I have heard their cry on account of their taskmasters. Indeed, I know their sufferings, and I have come down to deliver them from the Egyptians. . . ." Then the LORD said to Moses, "Go to Pharaoh and say to him, 'Thus says the LORD: Let my people go, so that they may worship me.'"
—Exodus 1:13–14; 3: 7–8; 8:1

For nearly ten years, until my early teens, our family would make an annual summer vacation trip from the upper Midwest to visit my grandparents and other relatives in Hope, Arkansas. This was not merely a trip to another part of the country; it was a trip to another world. People sounded different, the air smelled different, the scenery looked different. As we drove on two-lane highways deeper and deeper into the South, signs of poverty became increasingly apparent. Ramshackle homes, inhabited by poor whites and impoverished blacks, and discarded, rusted-out farm equipment frequented the rural landscape. Arriving in Hope amid suffocating heat and humidity, we entered a world of southern mores, one defined by gracious hospitality and racial segregation. My uncle called us "Yankees." I never knew exactly what *he* meant by the term, but I did know that it set us northerners apart from our southern kin, and I knew it had something to do with a bygone war.

Hope typified the rural Deep South of the 1950s and early

1960s. Signs posted in entrances to public places such as rest rooms, restaurants, and parks, announced "Colored" or "Whites Only." My relatives, law-abiding citizens and devout Christians, embraced this southern way of life as normal. The message was clear: whites ruled. They controlled the political and economic bases of power and kept blacks "in their place" by overt and covert means, ranging from denying blacks equal educational opportunities and public facilities to occasional night visitations by the Ku Klux Klan. From what I witnessed, blacks apparently accepted their lot and observed the customs of southern life without complaint. I was unaware of any dissatisfaction or civil unrest among Hope's African American community and certainly not among those with whom I had personal contact—the black women who provided daily domestic help for my apparently wealthy relatives.

I eventually learned that my childhood perceptions were skewed and tinged with racism. Hope's black population lived with little or no hope of ever escaping grinding poverty or oppressive racism. They knew firsthand what it meant to be second-class citizens in a land dedicated ostensibly to freedom for all people. Two now famous African Americans who grew up not far from Hope opened my eyes to a world of rural southern blacks far removed from my naïve childhood perceptions. Twenty miles south of Hope is Stamps, the childhood home of the prize-winning poet and novelist Maya Angelou. In her 1969 autobiography, *I Know Why the Caged Bird Sings*, Angelou described growing up in this southern town, one that just as easily could be "Chitlin' Switch, Georgia; Hang 'Em High, Alabama; Don't Let the Sun Set on You Here, Nigger, Mississippi; or any other name just as descriptive." She recalled that "segregation was so complete that most Black children didn't really, absolutely know what whites looked like. Other than that they were different, to be dreaded, and in that dread was included the hostility of the powerless against the powerful, the poor against the rich, the worker against the worked for and the ragged against the well dressed."[1]

Among the many traumatic childhood experiences that reinforced her sense of racial inferiority, Angelou recounts the time when the town's white dentist, the very man who had once borrowed money from her grandmother to keep from losing his building, refused to examine her two abscessed teeth. Maya's grandmother implored the man to help the sick child, reminding him of her own assistance years before. His response: "I'd rather stick my hand in a dog's mouth than in a nigger's."[2]

Fifty-five miles due east of Hope is Bearden, the boyhood home of James Cone, a theologian who challenged the existing white theological paradigm and has authored pathbreaking works on black liberation theology. Cone recalls Bearden as "the place where I first discovered myself—as black and Christian":

> There, the meaning of black was defined primarily by the menacing presence of whites, which no African-American could escape. I grew

up during the age of Jim Crow (1940s and early '50s). I attended segregated schools, drank water from "colored" fountains, saw movies from balconies, and when absolutely necessary greeted white adults at the back doors of their homes. I also observed the contempt and brutality that white law meted out to the blacks who transgressed their racial mores or who dared to question their authority. Bearden white people, like most Southerners of the time, could be mean and vicious, and I, along with other blacks, avoided them whenever possible as if they were poisonous snakes.[3]

As a child who took his faith seriously, Cone was baffled by segregated worship practices. "Black and White Christians had virtually no social or religious dealings with each other, even though both were Baptists and Methodists—reading the same Bible, worshiping the same God, and reciting the same confessions of faith in their congregations." One faith but two worlds—in Angelou's words, the white world of "the unknowing majority" and the black world of "the knowing minority."[4] A mere three generations earlier, social relations had been defined by the white world of masters and the black world of slaves.

Collective experiences shape the way a group—be it a nation, race, or ethnic entity—interprets and engages the world. For African Americans, the peculiar collective experience of slavery mingled with their African heritage to shape a particular way of understanding Scripture and practicing the Christian faith. Their lives of slavery, oppression, and discrimination led blacks to identify with a similar experience recorded in the Bible. The story of God's deliverance of the Israelites from Egyptian bondage as recorded primarily in the Book of Exodus—a story of redemption and liberation, freedom and hope, and the promise of God's faithfulness—became their story.

They needed no theologian to impress upon them the centrality of this theme in Israel's history; their theology grew out of identifying their own lived experiences with a God who heard the cries of the oppressed and delivered them out of bondage. To this day, observes Thomas Hoyt, "Blacks tend to share a perspective on the Bible that celebrates God's liberating action in history. . . . Perhaps because of the real effect of the brutality of slavery, segregation, and discrimination, blacks share a common ethos of salvation in which the biblical story speaks naturally to their story. This is what some call 'the hermeneutical privilege of the poor and the oppressed.' "[5]

Christian history has witnessed many exodus movements patterned and conceived after the biblical exodus. As scholars have observed, the exodus event is a paradigm, not only the central event in Israel's ancient past but, according to Michael Walzer, "a big story, one that became part of the cultural consciousness of the West." Time after time in myriad creative ways, Jews and Christians (even Muslims) envisioned themselves as the Israelites of old, subjected to oppressive conditions but delivered by God's power and rewarded a Promised Land (figuratively or literally) for maintaining their faith. Indeed, as Donald Akenson points out, "Every European nation at one time or another has had leaders or prophets who say that their country is chosen of God and is, in effect, the successor of the children of Israel, and that its citizens are living in the promised land."[6]

Historically, exodus movements have been generally expressed in two ways. Some movements, such as those of the New England Puritans, the Mormons, the Afrikaners of South Africa, and the Jews of America, were actual physical migrations, viewed as a kind of exodus to the Promised Land. In such instances, God delivered a people out of the hands of their oppressors, protected them during their "wilderness" journey, and rewarded them with new land—sometimes, for example, as Amerindians would find out, at the expense of others. Other exodus movements, such as those identified with black liberation theology in North America and liberation theology in Latin America, appropriated the exodus motif theologically, in the sense of liberating one's outlook, raising one's consciousness, and demanding justice on behalf of the poor and oppressed.

Not surprisingly, no other group has appropriated the exodus theme so often and in so many diverse ways as African American Christians. The biblical exodus is their story, for just as the Israelites encountered Yahweh in bondage, so they first encountered Christianity amid their own enslavement. Exodus themes permeated the consciousness of African American slaves, shaped the outlook of free blacks, and, in our own time, retain a powerful hold in the African American community. "Without a doubt," writes historian Albert Raboteau, "the Exodus story was the most significant myth for American black identity, whether slave or free."[7] Throughout their history, blacks have equated Pharaoh and Egypt with white slaveholders, racists, and general oppression, and identified themselves first with the Hebrew slaves, then as those freed by their "Moses" from bondage and headed toward—though often failing to reach—the Promised Land. Just as Moses never entered Canaan but viewed it from afar on Mount Pisgah, so African Americans, despite freedom from slavery, have never entered the American Promised Land of full equality and economic well-being.

The exodus motif abounds in African American songs, sermons, novels, poetry, and real-life episodes and is personified in Moses-like liberators. A brief inventory of exodus themes spanning four centuries of African American history illustrates both the pervasiveness and multiple uses of this sacred story:

- Slave spirituals, such as "Go Down Moses," "I Am Bound for the Promised Land," "Don't Cry Mary, Pharaoh's Army Got Drowned," "Turn Back Pharaoh's Army" center on the exodus theme of deliverance.

- Called "the Moses of her people," Harriet Tubman made nineteen trips to the slave South and freed more than three hundred slaves.[8]
- A conspirator in a 1822 slave rebellion confessed that the leader, Denmark Vesey, *"read to us from the Bible, how the children of Israel were delivered out of Egyptian bondage."*[9]
- Thomas Wentworth Higginson, the New England Unitarian minister, militant abolitionist, and captain of a regiment of freed Gullah slaves during the Civil War, recounted his black soldiers singing as they crossed a river, "We'll cross de mighty river, We'll cross de danger water, . . . O Pharaoh's army drowned! My army cross over."[10]
- When Lincoln issued the Emancipation Proclamation, freed blacks hailed him as their Moses.
- Following the Civil War, blacks migrating from the South to arid Kansas became known as "Exodusters," and one of their leaders, "Pap" Singleton, referred to himself as the "Moses of the Colored Exodus."[11]
- Black Christians, as a driving force in the segregation of southern churches, viewed their self-separation as an exodus of communal liberation.[12]
- From 1750 to 1925, "Moses" was one of the more popular male names in the African American community.[13]
- Black immigration and nationalist periods of the last quarter of the nineteenth century have been given the name Black Exodus.[14]
- Paul Lawrence Dunbar (1872–1906), America's first professional black literary man, captured the essence of the religious beliefs of slaves in "An Antebellum Sermon" (1896), a popular dialect poem that articulated hopes for freedom expressed in the exodus account of Moses and Pharaoh.[15]
- In his pioneering study, *The Souls of Black Folk* (1903), W. E. B. Du Bois (1868–1963) invoked the Promised Land theme in a challenge to American whites: "Is this the life you grudge us, O Knightly America? . . . Are you so afraid lest peering from this high Pisgah, between Philistines and Amalekites, we sight the Promised Land?"[16]
- When the civil rights leader and writer James Weldon Johnson (1871–1938) poeticized "the rather vague memories of sermons" he heard in his childhood, one such sermon that left its indelible mark was "Let My People Go."[17]
- The lyrics to "We'll Understand It Better By and By," by the Philadelphia Methodist minister and songwriter Charles Tindley (1865–1933), captured the hopes of blacks from the Great Depression of the 1930s through the civil rights movement of the 1950s and 1960s:

> Trials dark on every hand, and we cannot understand.
> All the ways that God would lead us to that Blessed Promised Land.

But He guides us with His eye and we'll follow till we die.
For we'll understand it better by and by.[18]

- In Ralph Ellison's literary classic, *Invisible Man*, a blind pastor from Chicago portrays the founder of an all-black college as a Moses, shouting, "LET MY PEOPLE GO."[19]
- Martin Luther King Jr. used the language of Exodus to describe the black civil rights struggle and attained the status of a black Moses leading his people to the Promised Land of American equality.
- Claude Brown entitled his 1965 autobiography *Manchild in the Promised Land*; more recently, Al Sharpton, the controversial black minister and activist from New York City, titled his *Go and Tell Pharaoh* (1996).[20]
- Black liberation theologians, such as James Cone, consider the exodus event as paradigmatic in the construction of their theology.
- Exodus themes remain popular in contemporary black preaching, providing the context for denouncing social ills and announcing God's liberating intentions.
- As their titles indicate, recent publications dealing with African American history and ethics explicitly engage exodus themes: *An African-American Exodus, The Promised Land, Xodus, Bound for the Promised Land, Exodus!* and *Canaan Land*.[21]
- Lauryn Hill, the popular hip-hop singer, invokes exodus imagery in her 1998 rap "The Final Hour":

Our survival since our arrival is documented in the Bible
Like Moses and Aaron
Things are gonna change, it's apparent.[22]

The appeal to and use of the biblical theme of exodus by African Americans is the subject of this chapter. Unlike earlier chapters, which traced the history of a biblical text (or book) through two millennia and examined its interpretation among a variety of groups, this chapter considers the way in which the exodus motif has been appropriated in the African American community. Before launching immediately into these varied appropriations, however, I consider the Book of Exodus from chapters 1 to 15:21, the story of Israel in Egypt to the final liberation. The Israelites' escape from Egypt is "*the* crucial event of the whole Hebrew tradition."[23] In a technical sense, this event defines the exodus. The term "exodus" or "exodus event," however, has a broader usage, applying to all those events within the period from Moses to Joshua, including the oppression, the struggle for freedom, the actual escape from Egypt, wandering in the wilderness, and finally, the eventual conquest of Canaan.

After examining the biblical exodus, we will explore the exodus theme within the larger backdrop of American history, especially its shaping role among the Puritans and their heirs. One of the central themes of American religious history—the encounter between black and white—can be told through the lens of contrasting perspectives of the exodus theme.[24] Finally, I will consider the pervasive and multiple uses of the exodus motif in African American history. We will observe its prevalence in slave spirituals and narratives, its appropriation in antebellum sermons and discourses, its rhetorical appeal in an age of immigration, and, finally, its varied applications in the twentieth century, including its evocative and symbolic use in the civil rights movement, liberation theology, and contemporary sermons.

The Original Exodus

Nearly all nations have foundational events that define their histories. In the West, these events have often been movements for freedom or independence, such as the American or French Revolutions or, more recently, the collapse of the Soviet Union and the reunification of Germany. In the ancient history of the people of Israel, the exodus marks one such foundational event. Before this experience of deliverance from Egyptian bondage, God dealt with individual persons or families (e.g., Abraham, Isaac, Jacob, and Joseph) and not with a people unified in covenant faithfulness to God. As the Book of Exodus unfolds, one God now deals with one nation. The exodus event defines the people of Israel and provides the focal point in subsequent Jewish history, so much so that Old Testament authors mention it more than any other event in Israel's history. According to biblical theologians, so central is the grand narrative of Exodus that the rest of the Bible is but commentary on this event. Exodus, notes Pinchas Lapide, "is the core of the entire Jewish tradition."[25]

The story of the exodus revolves around the life of Moses or, more accurately, Yahweh's relationship to Israel and Moses' leading role in that relationship. Moses' accomplishments are expressed in what is called *heroic narrative* or *heroic saga*, an Old Testament genre of literature that focuses on the life and accomplishments of a hero, particularly emphasizing displays of courage and wisdom. The Book of Judges, for example, is a collection of heroic narratives recounting the deeds of Deborah, Gideon, and Samson. One function of this genre is to instruct the reader through the hero's virtues and vices, particularly as the hero confronts internal struggles of idolatry and external conflict with foreign enemies. In the case of Moses and the exodus, external conflict with the Egyptians precedes the internal struggles of the Israelites with false gods.

The Book of Exodus defines the relationship between God and Israel, first through Yahweh's act of deliverance from Egyptian bondage, then through a covenant with his people, including the giving of the Law (Ten Commandments) at Mount Sinai and the promise of the conquest of Canaan (described in the Book of Joshua). Exodus contains the core of Israelite religion: theology, ethical commands, and priestly and ritual instructions.

Until the nineteenth century the Book of Exodus was taken at face value. That is, the places cited and the people involved, not to mention God's miraculous intervention, were accepted as factual. Around 1875, however, archaeologists and biblical scholars began questioning the historicity of the account, pointing out that there was no direct evidence from other sources to corroborate the events described therein. They observed, for example, that nonbiblical sources made no mention of Israel in Egypt, although we now know that foreigners did go to Egypt and that rulers during the Nineteenth Dynasty (ca. 1305–1224 B.C.E.)—the likely time when the Hebrews left Egypt—initiated building projects and forced people to labor. Moreover, the 1897 find of the "Israel Stela," part of a hymn of victory of the Egyptian Pharaoh Merneptah, contained the first (though exaggerated) nonbiblical reference to Israel: "Israel is laid waste, his seed it not; Hurru [the land of the biblical Horites, or Greater Palestine] is become a widow for Egypt." The stele dates to around 1230 and thus attests to the existence of "Israel."[26]

Regarding the exodus event itself, scholars pointed out that the exact place of crossing the Red Sea (or Sea of Reeds) was unknown. The location of other places mentioned in the exodus itinerary (with the exception of the oasis at Kadesh-Barnea)—even the location of Israel's critical engagement with God at Mount Sinai–Horeb—could only be conjectured. Moreover, because there was no mention of Moses outside of the Bible, a few skeptics even doubted that such a person ever existed.[27]

More recently, various scholars have argued that the lack of extrabiblical evidence is not a sufficient reason to question the basic historical veracity of the exodus event. Slaves, after all—whether Israelites in Egypt or Africans in America—leave behind few traces in the record. In addition, official records and inscriptions in the Near East recorded impressive events, not ones of disaster or defeat, such as the drowning of Pharaoh's army. Many scholars thus conclude that the exodus event is plausible; the event represents the tradition of various groups that experienced something along the lines of the narrative.[28] But caution is the rule. As one biblical commentator observes, "It is far better to speak of the narrative of Exodus *in* history rather than *as* history and to be content with the general historical context we *can* have rather than longing for some specific historical proof we *cannot* have, at least until some dramatic new evidence is presented."[29]

Complicating the issues raised by the absence of external corroboration is the composition of the book itself. The literary features of the Book of Exodus are exceptionally complex, and a discussion of them would take us far afield of our purposes. Suffice it to say that the book bears the imprint of several layers of tradition and editorial revision, beginning as early as the time of

Moses and extending into the third century B.C.E. For many years commentators dissected the Book of Exodus into its constituent parts and focused nearly exclusively on the literary sources behind its final form. The result of this source-critical approach was both positive and negative. On the one hand, it demonstrated that the biblical text had a long and interesting prehistory. On the other hand, concentration on the individual sources often resulted in a fragmentary view of the text, leaving the reader with little sense of the book's overall unity.

In the 1970s, however, a trend emerged among commentators to view the book as a whole, as it stands as canonical Scripture—as the *textus receptus* (received text) of the Old Testament. Beginning with Brevard Childs's influential commentary in 1974, a number of scholars stressed the theological unity of the book as it pertained specifically to the character of God.[30] They emphasized not so much the history of the text prior to its present form but the literary and theological characteristics of the finished product. Though containing various traditions and sources, in its completed form Exodus communicated one theology, one faith history, and one creed: God is in control of history.

To be sure, the approach of these commentators (and more recent scholars employing other methods), with their reliance on the critical tools of the trade, is far removed from the simple precritical embrace of the exodus story by African Americans. And yet both sophisticated scholars and illiterate slaves reached similar conclusions about the exit from Egypt and deliverance at the Red Sea: it is a paradigmatic event proclaiming that God is present and in control of history. For blacks, however, there has been an existential reality that far exceeds the informed conclusion of scholars.

The Book of Exodus opens with a list of the descendants of Jacob who have settled in Egypt. As told in the Book of Genesis, Joseph, one of Jacob's twelve sons, has been sold by his jealous brothers to Ishmaelite or Midianite merchants, who in turn sell him in Egypt to Potiphar, the captain of the guard in Pharaoh's court (Gen. 37:25, 28, 36; 39:1). Despite several setbacks, Joseph remains faithful to his God and rises to prominence in the government. When famine drives Joseph's brothers to Egypt in search of food, they encounter their brother, who has ascended to second-in-command and been given oversight of the country's grain supplies. Following several twists in the plot, reconciliation between Joseph and his brothers occurs, and with the Pharaoh's blessing, the descendants of Jacob settled peacefully in Egypt.

We then read in Exodus 1:8, "Now a new king arose over Egypt who did not know Joseph." Several hundred years have passed since Joseph's sojourn—enough time for his descendants to increase in size (they were "fruitful and prolific") and pose a threat to the native people. Fearing increased Hebrew might, even siding with potential invaders, the new Pharaoh launches several schemes for reducing their power. First, he presses them into forced labor to

build the supply cities of Pithom and Raamses. "But the more they were oppressed, the more they multiplied and spread" (1:12). To reduce the Hebrew
population, the king commands two midwives, Shiphrah and Puah, to kill all
the baby boys they deliver. But the women refuse to go along with the order,
for they "feared God," and in an act of civil disobedience they "let the boys
live" (1:17). When confronted by Pharaoh, they inform him that the "vigorous"
Hebrew women gave birth before they could arrive. Finally, in desperation, the
paranoid king announces that all sons born to Hebrews are to be drowned in
the Nile River.

One mother, fearing for her baby's life, places him in a small basket and
hides him by the river's edge. He is then discovered among the bull-rushes
and rescued by Pharaoh's daughter, though not without the interposition of
Miriam, the baby's sister, who offers and is given permission to find a care-
taker—her own mother—for the infant. Pharaoh's daughter rears the child in
the king's household and names him Moses, meaning "he who pulls out."

The Bible provides no information about Moses from this time on until,
as a grown man, he kills an Egyptian who enraged him by beating a fellow
Hebrew (2:11-12). We have in this incident a profile of Moses' character traits—
traits that would surface repeatedly throughout Exodus: a passionate sense of
social justice, a wholehearted identification with the plight of his people, and
a tendency to act first—often in anger—and think later.[31] When Moses' crime
is exposed, he flees to Midian, a region in west central Arabia, where he settles
down and marries. Meanwhile, the king of Egypt dies, but the Israelites are
given no relief. They "groaned in their slavery and cried out" to God who, after
a virtual absence in the narrative, "heard their groaning," "remembered his
covenant," "looked upon the Israelites," and "took notice of them" (2:24-25).
With the appearance of God, the narrative shifts to the primary focus of the
book: Yahweh's presence with and in the midst of his people Israel, particularly
in two events: God's deliverance of the Hebrews from Egyptian bondage and,
in response to this rescue, the establishment of a covenant and the subsequent
giving of the Law at Mount Sinai.

Indicative of this shift in actors is the (divine) call narrative of the deliverer-
liberator, Moses, in chapter 3. While Moses is tending the flock of his father-
in-law, Jethro, "beyond the wilderness" at Horeb or Mount Sinai (v. 1), an angel
of the Lord appears to him in a flame of fire in a bush. In this revelatory
experience of *mysterium tremendum*, God introduces himself to Moses for the
first time and calls out, "Moses, Moses!" Moses replies, "Here I am." God
instructs him, "Come no closer! Remove the sandals from your feet, for the
place on which you are standing is holy ground" (vv. 4-5). God identifies himself: "I am the God of your father, the God of Abraham, the God of Isaac, the
God of Jacob." Terrified, "Moses hid his face, for he was afraid to look at God"
(v. 6).

God reiterates that he has seen the misery of the people in Egypt, heard their cries, and knows their sufferings; he announces that he has come not only to deliver them but also "to bring them up out of that land to a good and broad land, a land flowing with milk and honey, to the country of the Canaanites" (v. 8). God then commissions Moses: "I will send you to Pharaoh to bring my people, the Israelites, out of Egypt." But in the first of repeated excuses, Moses demurs: "Who am I that I should go to Pharaoh?" God ignores Moses' objection that he lacks the necessary credentials to confront Pharaoh and assures him, "I will be with you." Moses persists: but what if I go to the people of Israel, tell them that " 'The God of their fathers has sent me to you,' and they ask me, 'What is his name?' what shall I say to them?" (vv. 10–13).

God replies, "I AM WHO I AM" (v. 14) or, perhaps more accurately, "I will be what I will be" or "I will be there with you." However the sacred Tetragrammaton* is translated, this much is grammatically clear in this key expression of Hebrew theology: God is an actor ("I cause to happen"), the creator ("I create whatever I create"), the one who is (self-sustaining and self-sufficient), and a God of personal relationships, not an abstract Being. He is the one who encounters the people and assures them of his continuing presence. God promises to act through Moses, to give him miraculous power and to deliver the Israelites (4:1–9).

But Moses offers another excuse, noting that he lacks the necessary eloquence to carry out the task, and he asks God to send someone else in his place (vv. 10, 13). Angered by Moses' temporizing, God informs this skittish prophet that he will make Aaron, Moses' brother, the mouthpiece of God to the people. On Moses' return to Egypt he meets Aaron in the wilderness and tells him of all that God has told him and of the signs given to him. The duo appear before the people, Aaron speaks the words of the LORD, performs signs in their sight, and "the people believed" (v. 31).

Making Pharaoh believe was not as easy. Moses and Aaron go to Pharaoh and announce, "Thus says the LORD, the God of Israel, 'Let my people go, so that they may celebrate a festival to me in the wilderness' " (5:1). An obdurate Pharaoh responds, "Who is the LORD, that I should heed him and let Israel go? I do not know the LORD, and I will not let Israel go" (v. 2). Not wanting their request to be entirely dismissed, Moses and Aaron lower their demands and ask for a three-day leave of absence, only to be turned down by Pharaoh. The king demands that the Israelites get back to work, increases their workload by requiring them to find the straw they need to make bricks, and refuses to lower their daily quota of bricks.

---

* The sacred Tetragrammaton, the personal name for God, is a Greek term for the four Hebrew consonants, YHWH, that make up the name of Israel's God. Israelites originally pronounced the name, but later they considered it too holy to pronounce, and wishing to avoid violating the commandment ("You shall not make wrongful use of the name of the LORD your God"), they substituted the word "Adonai" ("Lord" in Hebrew) in its place.

When Moses and Aaron are blamed for bringing more hardship on the people, Moses shifts the blame to God: "Why have you mistreated this people? . . . You have done nothing at all to deliver your people." (5:22, 23). God assures Moses that "by a mighty hand" Pharaoh will let the people go, and instructs him once again, "Go and tell Pharaoh king of Egypt to let the Israelites go out of his land" (6:1, 10). A reluctant Moses again makes the excuse that Pharaoh will not listen to him because he is a poor speaker. But God will have none of it: "See, I have made you like God to Pharaoh, and your brother Aaron shall be your prophet" (7:1; see also 4:16). The Lord assures Moses that through "signs and wonders" he will rescue the Israelites from the Egyptians (7:3, 5). And so ten plagues—exemplifying a contest between Yahweh and Egyptian deities, over whom Yahweh has total control—are inflicted upon Egypt. Not until the tenth plague, marking the institution of the first Passover, when the Lord "passes over" the Israelite children but kills the Egyptian firstborn (in a reversal of fortunes), does Pharaoh relent and expel the Israelites (chaps. 7–12).

The Israelites thus begin their trek that will eventually (later than sooner) take them to the Promised Land of Canaan. But Pharaoh, his heart "hardened" once again, has second thoughts and decides to overtake them. Alert to fears among the people, Yahweh assures Moses that he will be glorified in the defeat of Pharaoh and his army. But when the people see the advancing army they conclude they are doomed and, in a litany heard repeatedly during their wilderness sojourn, complain to Moses that they would have been better off dying in Egypt than in the wilderness.

Moses reassures them: "The LORD will fight for you, and you have only to keep still" (14:14). God then instructs Moses to lift his staff and stretch out his hand over the Red Sea; the waters divide, and the people begin crossing to other side. When the pursuing Egyptians enter the sea, Moses again stretches out his hand; the waters return to normal, and in this final act of Yahweh's mighty power against the Egyptian oppressors, Pharaoh's army drowns. To celebrate this divine act of liberation, Moses and Miriam recite victory poems rejoicing that Yahweh defends his people and acts on their behalf whenever he deigns to intervene (15:1–22). These hymns, notes one commentator, are "a kind of summary of the theological base of the whole Book of Exodus."[32]

In conclusion, the first fifteen chapters of Exodus narrate themes that form the core of Israel's identity. The remainder of the book (as well as portions of Deuteronomy and Numbers) includes the giving of the Law at Mount Sinai, forty years of wandering in the desert, and instructions for worship. Other scriptures (Joshua, Numbers 13–32) describe the eventual entry into Canaan and division of the land among the tribes. A consistent motif throughout this story of bondage, deliverance, wandering, and conquest is Yahweh's presence, guidance, activity, and covenant faithfulness among the Israelites.

Despite God's gracious provision, the people often grumble against, resist, ignore, and disobey Yahweh's instructions. Even Moses himself, because he disobeyed the Lord's instruction (see Num. 20:1–12), is denied entrance to the Promised Land and thus can only view it from Mount Pisgah (Deut. 34:1–4). The Israelites are free from Egyptian bondage, yet freedom brings new privileges and obligations, including the responsibility of love and obedience to Yahweh. The transformation of consciousness requires more time and effort than physical relocation. The Israelites eventually reach the Promised Land, but all is not paradise.

Exodus in America: The Puritan Legacy

I have argued throughout this book that no biblical text—especially a classic text like Exodus—works its way through history without multiple interpretations and applications. Nor does a text proceed through history in an autonomous fashion, unconnected to former interpretations. There is a history of effects. As a central paradigm and, indeed, by Werner Sollors's estimation, as "one of America's central themes," the exodus has been interpreted in multitudinous, even conflicting ways.[33] Perhaps no two groups better illustrate this interpretative tension than New England Puritans, expatriates from England, and African Americans, forced migrants from Africa. Each drew upon the exodus story to make sense of their own histories but in quite different ways. Consider the foundational events in their respective histories, events that, though in the distant past, shaped the future, and defined black-white relations well into the twentieth century—even in the Arkansas towns of Hope, Stamps, and Bearden.

In 1619 a Dutch frigate or warship arrived on the shores of Virginia carrying twenty "negars" from West Africa. The exact status of these Africans is uncertain. Perhaps they arrived as indentured servants, possibly as slaves. Either way, they had at some point been captured, sold, and now came unwillingly in bondage to America. By the 1660s the status of all Africans forcibly brought to America was established by law: they were slaves, bought and sold on the market, subject to the whip of the overseer, shackled and branded, separated from tribe, torn from spouse and children. To these African Americans, America became, as they discerned from the Bible stories taught to them by white missionaries or, more frequently, by black preachers, their Egypt, their land of bondage.

A year after the Dutch frigate arrived in Virginia, a group of Puritan separatists (the Pilgrims) arrived in Plymouth, Massachusetts. Given their penchant for typological biblical interpretation, the Puritans linked their own history to biblical types.[34] Drawing upon the exodus event, they viewed repressive

England as their bondage and their sojourn in Holland and then the transatlantic voyage as their wilderness. Now at last in America they had reached their Canaan. In this recapitulative event, unlike the biblical story, their "new Moses"—be it William Bradford of Plymouth Plantation or John Winthrop of the Massachusetts Bay Colony—had entered the Promised Land (a land described as a "howling wilderness") with the people.[35]

As Albert Raboteau has observed, the contrast between these two typological interpretations of the biblical exodus defines the contrast between black and white views of America: "The meaning of the Exodus story for America has remained fundamentally ambiguous." Echoing the question of W. E. B. DuBois, Raboteau asks, "Is America Israel, or is she Egypt?" For John Winthrop, governor of the Massachusetts Bay Colony, American was indeed Israel, and yet he recognized the conditions of taking possession of the land. Without upholding covenant obligations, he announced to his fellow voyagers on the deck of the flagship *Arabella* in 1630, "The Lord will surely break out in wrath against us . . . and make us know the price of the breach of such a covenant." The "only way to avoid this shipwreck and to provide for our posterity is to follow the counsel of Micah: to do justly, to love mercy, to walk humbly with our God."[36] Winthrop concluded his sermon by quoting Moses, who, at the end of his life and now within sight of the Promised Land, reaffirmed Yahweh's covenant with Israel (Deut. 30:15–17): if we follow the Lord and keep his commandments, we will be blessed; if our hearts turn away in disobedience, we will surely perish.

With Moses, Winthrop emphasized the "if . . . then," reciprocal relationship between God's blessing and America's future. If the Puritans fulfilled their obligations, God would bless America. If they did not, they would suffer the dire consequences. Indeed, the next century testified to the Puritan preoccupation with making sense of misfortune (both natural and man-made) in light of failed covenantal obligations. To seek God's favor during such disasters, the Puritans called for days of fasting and repentance and created a genre of sermonizing called the jeremiad (named after the weeping prophet, Jeremiah).

This typological mold, casting America as the new Israel, continued through the Revolutionary era and well into the early Republic, albeit with the events and actors in the exodus account rearranged to fit present-day circumstances. In their "Poem, On the Rising Glory of America" (1771), Philip Freneau and Hugh Henry Brackenridge, two of the so-called Connecticut Wits, described America as the site where "another Canaan shall excel the old." When war broke out between England and the colonies, Nicholas Street uplifted the parallels between the biblical exodus and America's condition in his sermon "The American States Acting over the Part of the Children of Israel in the Wilderness and Thereby Impeding Their Entrance into Canaan's Rest" (1777). Street identified the wilderness as a condition ("a state of trouble and difficulty") in which the British (Egyptians) and the British tyrant (Pharaoh) were "endeavouring to oppress, enslave and destroy these American States."[37]

These sentiments found expression in proposals for the nation's great seal. Benjamin Franklin suggested the scene of Moses with his upraised staff parting the Red Sea while Pharaoh and his army drowned as the collapsed wall of water engulfed them. The motto: "Rebellion to tyrants is obedience to God." Thomas Jefferson proposed the less violent episode of the Israelites being providentially guided out of Egypt by a cloud during the day and a pillar of fire at night (Exod. 13:21–22).[38] In the end, the eagle—the classical sign of ancient republics—was chosen for the seal, though it alluded as well to the biblical eagle of Exodus 19:4, where God informs Moses, "I bore you on eagles' wings and brought you to myself."

With independence achieved, a decided shift in American self-perceptions occurred. Past Puritan views of human depravity, God's sovereign designs, and the conditional nature of the covenant gave way to more optimistic appraisals of human ability and American destiny. As is clear from the very titles of contemporary sermons and poems, the rhetoric of the exodus remained, but now with a decidedly nationalist emphasis that expressed the myth of national chosenness and destiny. In "The United States Elevated to Glory and Honor" (1783), Yale's president Ezra Stiles hailed the new nation as "God's American Israel" and exuded with optimism over "the future prosperity and splendour of the United States." In his epic of the rising new nation, "Conquest of Canaan" (1785), Timothy Dwight, cleric, educator, and Stiles's successor at Yale, envisioned America "by heaven design'd, The last retreat for poor, oppress'd mankind."[39] God gave the land—a whole continent—to Americans as he did the Promised Land to the Israelites.

The Reverend Samuel Langdon, in "The Republic of the Israelites an Example to the American States" (1788), expressed the widely accepted view that George Washington was America's Moses. Finally, in his Thanksgiving Day sermon, "Traits of Resemblance in the People of the United States of America to Ancient Israel" (1799), the Reverend Abiel Abbot observed, "It has been often remarked that the people of the United States come nearer to a parallel with Ancient Israel, than any other nation upon the globe." Both peoples were the unique recipients of divine favor. When this notion of the new Republic as God's new Israel merged with the powerfully popular idea that America would become the inaugural site of the fast-approaching millennium, we are not far from a nationalist ideology of Anglo-Saxon expansionist Manifest Destiny having messianic, mercenary, and racist implications. As blacks knew only too well, there was a tragic irony to Americans' claim to be the new Israel—the reality of an enslaved old Israel in their midst.[40] America had become a New Canaan for whites, but at what cost to blacks?

Anticipating Exodus: The Christianization
of Africans in America

To grasp more fully the exodus theme in African American Christianity, we
must not only contrast its role in the white American imagination but also
place it within the larger context of the African American religious experience.
Although scholars continue to debate the extent to which traditional African
religious practices survived in North America, there is general agreement
that the actual form of evangelical Christianity eventually adopted by African
Americans represented the creative synthesis of African and Christian elements.[41] During the course of several centuries, blacks reinterpreted white
Euro-American Christianity to fit their own needs of survival and self-
preservation and their own experiences of suffering and struggle. The result
was a distinctive folk religion combining African ritual and communal consciousness with Christian theology, a Jewish and Christian faith fused to an
African base.

To be sure, the pace of Christianization is difficult to gauge. Despite justifications from western European nations that one of the primary reasons for
enslaving Africans was their conversion to Christianity (but not granting them
freedom), during the first 150 years of slavery in North America, little was done
to make this a reality. The Church of England made some inroads among the
slaves, but its formalism and emphasis on catechism—in short, its effort to
make good Anglicans—conspired against a major impact. Moreover, throughout much of the seventeenth century the church met resistance from slave
masters who feared that conversion to Christianity might entitle the slave to
equalities beyond their newfound standing before God and engender "saucy"
attitudes. But resistance to Christianizing slaves was not one-sided. Throughout the colonial period the vast majority of slaves retained their African tribal
beliefs or gave only a superficial assent to their master's religion.

Not until the southern phase of the First or Great Awakening in the 1760s
did an emotionally charged, experienced-based, and conversion-oriented faith
take hold among slaves who discovered a compatible religious orientation between their West and West Central African tribal faiths and evangelical Christianity. Baptists, with their emphasis on an instant conversion, and Methodists,
with their stress on the role of the Holy Spirit, tapped into a deep African
American religious reservoir. The spiritual explosion of the Great Revival, beginning in 1785, reverberated so completely throughout the African American
community that by 1815 evangelical Christianity defined the faith of African
American peoples. The egalitarian and affirmative nature of the conversion
experience became the single most important criterion for acceptance into the
evangelical communities.[42]

But blacks embraced and redefined Christianity on their own terms. In the reciprocal process of African tribal religion and evangelicalism, slave religion came to be defined by what Du Bois called "the Preacher, the Music, and the Frenzy." According to Sylvia Frey and Betty Wood, this evolution from traditional African religion to Christianity "was arguably the single most significant event in African American history." It "turned Africans into African Americans."[43] Integrally related to this process of Christianization was the African Americans' appropriation of Scripture. In particular, exodus-centered spirituals supplied the rudiments of a contextual theology that has informed African American Christianity to this day.

Exodus as Survival and Hope: Slave Spirituals

Spirituals, a genre of slave songs, represent African Americans' first effort to create a religious world of their own by making use of the cultural resources at hand—the teachings and stories from the Bible. They embody the "essence" or "foundation" of black religion. According to Vincent Wimbush, all subsequent interpretations of Scripture within the black community "would in some sense be built upon and judged against" the spirituals.[44]

Developed amid existential realities of sorrow, suffering, degradation, and oppression, spirituals delineate, in the words of Lawrence Levine, "the record of a people who found the status, the harmony, the values, and the order they needed to survive by internally creating an expanding universe, by literally willing themselves reborn."[45] Told incessantly to be obedient ("slaves, obey your masters"—Eph. 6:5) and to hope for future rewards in heaven, slaves distinguished between a counterfeit gospel of bondage and a genuine gospel of freedom. They perceived the plantation owners' interpretation of Scripture as a gross manipulation of the sacred text and little more than a hypocritical rationalization to justify their abhorrent treatment of fellow humans.

Lunsford Lane, an enslaved black who bought his freedom, heard all the stock biblical texts "prepared expressly for the colored people." He dismissed these attempts out of hand, even the efforts of a "very kind-hearted clergyman" who was much appreciated by the slaves until "he preached a sermon from the Bible that it was the will of Heaven from all eternity that we should be slaves, and our masters be our owners." In response, "many of us left him, considering, like the doubting disciple of old, 'This is a hard saying, who can hear it.'"[46]

Other slaves reacted to similar teachings by snoozing in church, expressing other forms of indifference, and concluding, in the words of an ex-slave, that she "didn't see the difference between the slaveholders who had religion and those who had not."[47] Denied opportunities to read the Bible and skeptical of their masters' interpretation of it, slaves created their own everyday faith in song, pleading to and praising a God who would sustain them daily and even lead them into freedom. Spirituals thus express a fundamental feature of what has been called the Invisible Institution—an indigenous "brush arbor theology" constructed in clandestine settings, often illegally, away from the oversight of the white master and his assistants.

The spiritual came into being in a spontaneous, piecemeal fashion, perhaps initiated by talented individuals who developed a finished version in the give-and-take of communal influence. Sung in every place—the cabin, the field, in individual or group settings—and ranging from joy to sorrow, spirituals disclose the influence of African religion in their performance and rhythm. As past and present scholars argue (with varying degrees of emphasis), spirituals must be placed within the African context of ceremonial dance and rhythm. Both imitating and reconceptualizing African religious rituals, the spirituals were typically sung (or "performed") in a circle and accompanied by a variety of physical expressions, including stamping, groaning, shouting, clapping, shrieking, and sobbing. In rhythmic quality, the spirituals "show a marked similarity to African songs in form and intervallic structure."[48]

In their general hermeneutic, spirituals focused not on the literal words of Scripture but on the social experiences that Scripture expressed. Because the Bible was heard more than read (it is estimated that not more than 5 percent of the slave population learned to read and write), spirituals allowed interpretive license, freeing the imagination to connect present realities with past events.[49] In spirituals (as well as in other media, such as preaching), the Bible became a living book, speaking directly to the oppressed conditions of slaves. Given the social-political-economic status of the slaves, it should come as no surprise that spirituals emphasized biblical narratives that addressed their own situation. The Old Testament, the slaves' "canon within the canon," included "wrestlin' Jacob," the exodus story, Joshua and the Promised Land, Daniel in the lion's den, and the prophets in their denunciation of social injustice. In the New Testament it included the teaching, suffering, and resurrection of Jesus. This creative and dynamic interplay between enslaved people and biblical texts meant simultaneously the re-creation of the text by the people and the re-creation of the people by the text.[50]

The primary biblical story told repeatedly in song was the exodus—"the primal hope act of God." God's deliverance of the Hebrews from Pharaoh's bondage became the paradigmatic expression of hope that God would also deliver African Americans from slavery. According to Newman White, southern whites drew from much of the same biblical material as blacks—such as the exodus account—but interpreted it in radically different ways. In a joint church service a planter might allegorize the public reading of the exodus and internalize Egyptian bondage as his own personal bondage to sin before Moses (a symbol for Jesus) delivered him.[51]

Some slaves might personalize the account in much the same way as the white planter, but more typically they would understand the exodus as one of actual liberation from physical bondage, believing that God would do the same for them. Recalled an ex-slave, "Aunt Jane used to tell us . . . that the children of Israel was in Egypt in bondage, and that God delivered them out of Egypt; and she said he would deliver us."[52] Like the oppressed Israelites, the slaves were chosen of God and destined for a special purpose. Hope, derived from the themes of deliverance and chosenness, counteracted the dehumanizing conditions of slavery in which African Americans were considered the lowliest of humans, if human at all. The identification of the God of the ancient Israelites as the God of the present-day African Americans is reiterated in "He's Jus' De Same Today":

> When Moses an' his soldiers, f'om Egypt's lan' did flee,
> His enemies were in behin' him,
> An' in front of him de sea.
> God raised de waters like a wall,
> An opened up de way,
> An' de god dat lived in Moses' time is jus the same today.[53]

The best known song, "Go Down Moses" (also known as "Let My People Go"), relates the story of Israel's oppression, deliverance, and eventual entry into "fair Canaan's land." In James Weldon Johnson's estimation, "there is not a nobler theme in the whole musical literature of the world." As in many spirituals, Moses is the human instrument of divine liberation, understood as functionally similar to the conjurer in West African religions.[54] The following are several verses and the chorus excerpted from one of the earliest published versions of "Let My People Go":

> When Israel was in Egypt's land,
>> O let my people go!
> Oppressed so hard they could not stand,
>> O let my people go!
>
> Chorus—O go down, Moses
> Away down to Egypt's land,
> And tell King Pharaoh
> To let my people go!
>
> Thus saith the Lord bold Moses said,
>> O let my people go!
> If not, I'll smite your first born dead,
>> O let my people go!
>
> No more shall they in bondage toil,
>> O let my people go!
> Let them come out with Egypt's spoil,
>> O let my people go!

An extended version published in the *National Anti-Slavery Standard* in 1861 concludes by drawing obvious parallels between ancient and present conditions:

> O let us all from bondage flee,
> > O let my people go!
> And let us all in Christ be free,
> > O let my people go!
>
> We need not always weep and mourn,
> > O let my people go!
> And wear these Slavery chains forlorn,
> > O let my people go!
>
> This world's a wilderness of woe,
> > O let my people go!
> O let us on to Canaan go,
> > O let my people go!
>
> What a beautiful morning that will be!
> > O let my people go,
> When time breaks up in eternity,
> > O let my people go.[55]

The mention of "Canaan" refers to heaven, though in other spirituals mention of the Promised Land had a decidedly this-worldly intent. Frederick Douglass, who as a young man escaped from slavery, described this ambiguous meaning: "A keen observer might have detected in our repeated singing of "O Canaan, sweet Canaan, / I am bound for the land of Canaan," something more than a hope of reaching heaven. We meant to reach the *North*, and the North was our Canaan." Or as another ex-slave put it, "All us had was church meetin's in arbors out in de woods. De preachers would exhort us dat us was de chillen o' Israel in de wilderness an' de Lord done sent us to take dis land o' milk and honey."[56] "Let God's Saints Come In" expressed this theme in song:

> Canaan land is the land for me,
> And let God's saints come in.
> Canaan land is the land for me,
> And let God's saints come in.[57]

The mention of Christ in "Go Down Moses" indicates the close association between two instruments of divine liberation. In the exodus account slaves found their own drama played out; in the suffering Jesus they found someone with whom they could identify. This conflation of Moses and Jesus is made explicit in other spirituals that link the two as contemporaries. Slaves sang

Gwine to write Massa Jesus,
To send some Valiant soldier,
To turn back Pharaoh's army, Hallelu!

Or

Jesus Christ, He died for me,
  Way down in Egyptland;
Jesus Christ, He set me free,
  Way down in Egyptland.[58]

Whether "the slaves were radically centered on Jesus," as Dwight Hopkins avers, or considered Moses their ideal and Jesus "as that of a second Moses," as a northern army chaplain in Decatur, Alabama, observed in 1864, it is clear that the two images often merged. This propensity to combine elements from the Old and New Testaments indicates both an oral tradition that seldom differentiated between the testaments and the mingling of parts of one song into another by a process of association. According to Eugene Genovese, Moses, the instrument of this-worldly freedom, and Jesus, the guarantor of an otherworldly redemption, "blended into a pervasive theme of deliverance."[59]

Inevitably Pharaoh and his minions got their due as the God of justice and power turned the tables on the oppressors. I noted earlier the black regiment that sang of the fate of the Confederate troops,

My army cross over,
My army cross over,
O Pharaoh's army drowned.

The moving spiritual "Didn't Old Pharaoh Get Los'?" rehearses the story of Moses from his infancy to the sojourn in the Sinai Desert. Throughout its many verses, the theme is one of confidence, not despondence, for

Didn't old Pharaoh get los,' get los,'
Didn't old Pharaoh get los.'
In de Red Sea
True Believer,
O didn't old Pharaoh get los'?[60]

And so the slave-owning pharaoh in the South would be vanquished:

When the children were in bondage,
They cried unto the Lord,
To turn back Pharaoh's army,
He turned back Pharaoh's army.

When Pharaoh crossed the water,
The waters came together,
And drowned old Pharaoh's army,
Hallelu![61]

Other antebellum spirituals that drew from the exodus story included "Oh Mary, Don't You Weep (Pharaoh's Army Got Drownded)" and "Sit Down."[62]

In summary, African American spirituals illustrate the way in which slaves, exiled in a foreign land, lacking reading and writing skills, and having no common language, eventually adopted the Bible as their own lingua franca, devising their own idiom of interpretation and communication.[63] In content, spirituals depicted an all-powerful, all-present God who continued to act in history on behalf of his chosen people to destroy the wicked and liberate the oppressed. As mask and symbol, spirituals carried multiple meanings, offering both the consolation of heaven and promise of worldly liberation. Certainly they may be viewed as a compensatory adaptation to the horrors of slavery, but they also offered more than a "pie in the sky" theology. Hope lies at the center of life's meaning, and slaves, seizing the exodus story as their own, affirmed their humanity, saying in essence, "We are the children of God, a chosen people."

Spirituals communicated a living reality having social, political, and theological implications. The exodus event functioned as an archetype, enabling slaves to live with the promise of a future when the captives would go free and the righteous would be rewarded. Spirituals may thus be seen as a portable survival kit whose words and music were carried in the hearts and minds of illiterate slaves from one plantation to another, from one generation to the next, all the while created and re-created by a communal process.

Exodus as Action: Slave Revolts, Nationalist Expressions, and Emancipation

Although the overwhelming majority of African Americans resigned themselves to their lot under slavery, and although some drew consolation and hope from the archetypal Hebrew experience, hoping and praying that God would act on their behalf, others concluded that God would avenge the oppressors and liberate the enslaved through human instrumentality. Exodus was a double-edged sword—its message adapted both to divine intervention and human initiative. On the one hand, Yahweh was a warrior; he alone defeated the Egyptians, and he alone would defeat the powers of slavery. This was the theme conveyed in the spirituals and one that worked its way into the consciousness of many slaves. Indeed, an elderly slave advised his people to do "as Moses commanded the children of Israel on the shore of the Red Sea, 'to stand and see the salvation of God' " [Ex.14:13].[64]

And yet Yahweh used human instruments such as Moses and Aaron (and later Caleb and Joshua) to crush his enemies. For a handful of African Americans, the line between Yahweh as a warrior and Moses and Aaron as instruments of his will was indistinguishable. They not only followed but also imitated Yahweh's actions, either in the extreme by taking up the sword to carry out God's designs or by protesting the oppressive conditions of slavery. As Vincent Harding, Gayraud Wilmore, and others have demonstrated, religion in general (including the incorporation of African beliefs) and the exodus theme in particular played a key role in several nineteenth-century slave insurrections led by black preachers and prophets.[65]

Gabriel Prosser and his brother Martin, who carefully planned the first explicit slave revolt on North American soil in Richmond, Virginia, in 1800, viewed their cause as similar to that of the Israelites under Egyptian bondage. In Charleston, South Carolina, the free black Denmark Vesey recruited insurrectionists within the African Methodist Episcopal Church—a church he helped to establish after blacks were denied participation in the affairs of the racially mixed Methodist Episcopal Church. When Vesey's sizable plot involving more than six thousand Christian and non-Christian blacks was uncovered, one of his conspirators confessed to the authorities that Vesey *"read to us from the Bible, how the children of Israel were delivered out of Egyptian bondage."*[66] The most famous of slave revolts, Nat Turner's Rebellion in Southampton County, Virginia, in 1831, though less reliant upon the exodus theme and more upon the exilic apocalyptic motif of a black avenging Messiah, reinforced the connection between religion and resistance. In these three slave insurrections, religion fueled rebellion rather than pacified it.

Antebellum blacks, then, did not merely wait for God to act but took it upon themselves to alter the course of history. Among the free black population in the North beginning in the late 1820s and extending through the 1840s, African Americans formulated new ways of thinking about the enslaved condition of their race. The biblical exodus narrative provided the model for a developing national consciousness and political resistance, for just as the Israelites had national ambitions, so did blacks. And yet blacks (and their white supporters) were by no means united in their solution to the problem of slavery. Many, such as Frederick Douglass and the followers of the Boston journalist and antislavery crusader William Lloyd Garrison, counseled moral reform or moral suasion as the appropriate course of action: convince a slaveholding society of the moral indefensibility of holding humans in bondage.

A few black radicals such as David Walker reluctantly embraced the possibility of armed resistance and in the case of Henry Highland Garnet, encouraged violent slave uprisings. To black theologians of the 1960s and 1970s,

Walker's "Appeal" (1829) and Garnet's "Address to the Slaves" (1843) "sounded like Black Power music in our ears." Both Walker and Garnet invoked the exodus narrative, comparing the conditions of slavery in the United States with Hebrew slavery in Egypt, but they reached different conclusions regarding its viability as a source of resistance. Walker, "one of the greatest ideologists of African liberation of the nineteenth century," held out exodus as a promise of hope, whereas Garnet discounted it, contending the exodus account did little more than induce passivity.[67]

In the second decade of the nineteenth century David Walker (1796–1830) journeyed by steamboat from his home in Wilmington, North Carolina, to Charleston, South Carolina. Attracted to the biracial revivals of the Second Great Awakening, as well as to the city's vibrant black community, Walker became involved in the newly formed African Methodist Episcopal (AME) Church. One of the first AME churches to be established after Richard Allen and his associates founded the denomination in Philadelphia in 1816, the Charleston AME church seethed with black discontent after whites tried to close it and, as noted, became the hub of Denmark Vesey's insurrection. There is good reason to believe that Walker participated in the plot and that upon its discovery, he disappeared from Charleston and eventually made his way to Boston in 1825. He soon became involved as a black activist, attacking slavery and advocating the intellectual and moral improvement of blacks in general.[68]

Walker's "Appeal to the Colored Citizens of the World" is now recognized as "one of the most neglected and yet most important political and social documents of the nineteenth century."[69] Gayraud Wilmore elevated the "Appeal" to the level of Luther's "Letter to the Christian Nobility of the German Nation" (1520), suggesting both were protest documents, pleading with people to alter radically their religious and political conditions. Peter Hinks, Walker's recent biographer, compared the psychological and social impact of the "Appeal" on African Americans to Thomas Paine's "Common Sense" on white patriots during the Revolutionary period. In this "black jeremiad" Walker excoriated whites for their brutal and unchristian treatment of blacks, especially slaves, noting how blacks had been deprived of education (even learning the Bible), civil liberties, and positions of responsibility.[70] Such barbaric treatment resulted in passivity among blacks themselves: they had come to accept their inferior status. Thus the "Appeal" was as much a wake-up call to blacks as an attack on white savagery.

Walker took up the familiar theme among antislavery supporters of comparing the conditions of modern slavery in the United States to ancient conditions.[71] He noted that the enslaved Hebrews were better off under the Egyptians than were blacks in America, and that slavery among the Romans was "no more than a *cypher*" when compared with slavery instituted by "an enlightened and Christian people" in America.[72] Nothing in the past compared to the degraded and dehumanized condition of blacks in America.

Moreover, in identifying his people with the Hebrews of old as a chosen *nation*, Walker appealed to a sense of national solidarity, consisting of a heightened consciousness of the black oppression and a hoped-for liberation. Walker proposed that America hold up a mirror to its ideals; he asked for nothing less than white Americans to extend to blacks the same opportunities that were open to them. If denied access, the God of judgment and the oppressed would vanquish the white slaveholders through the armed resistance of blacks.[73]

Whatever hesitation Walker expressed toward slave rebellion was countered by the Reverend Henry Highland Garnet's demand that slaves murder their masters. In his "Address to the Slaves of the United States of America," delivered at the Negro national convention in 1843 (published in 1848), Garnet called for the violent overthrow of southern slavery. A year earlier he had foresworn bloodshed, but recently published "scientific" views of race identifying blacks as inferior to whites, a Supreme Court decision that upheld the 1793 Fugitive Slave Law, and the expulsion from Congress of the antislavery crusader Joshua Giddings enraged Garnet.

This fugitive slave and pastor of an all-black Presbyterian church in Troy, New York, rejected the biblical exodus as a model for slave politics, claiming it encouraged passivity. He informed those held in bondage,

> If you must bleed, let it all come at once—rather *die as freemen, than live to be the slaves*. It is impossible, like the children of Israel, to make a grand exodus from the land of bondage. The Pharaohs are on both sides of the blood-red waters! You cannot move *en masse*, to the dominions of the British Queen—nor can you pass through Florida and overrun Texas, and at last find peace in Mexico.[74]

There was no place of refuge. Even Africa, with colonial powers dominating its continent, had its pharaohs. Slaves thus have a divine mandate to resist. Citing heroes of slave resistance such as Denmark Vesey, Nathaniel Turner, Joseph Cinque, and Madison Washington, Garnet urged slaves to take matters into their own hands: "Arise, arise! Strike for your lives and liberties. Now is the day and the hour. . . . Let your motto be resistance! *resistance!* RESISTANCE!"[75]

Although Garnet's inflammatory rhetoric supplied a historical basis for later black liberation theology, it further fractured the Northern antislavery movement, heightened Southern resistance, abetted a biblical defense of slavery—and never reached slave ears. In the end, not a slave rebellion led by a black Moses but another battle led by a white Moses ended 250 years of slavery. Abraham Lincoln's Emancipation Proclamation of January 1, 1863, followed by the adoption of the Thirteenth Amendment in 1865 in the wake of the Civil War, freed the slaves and prohibited slavery in the United States. Both Northern free blacks and recently freed slaves interpreted the final death knell of slavery in predictable ways, drawing from the exodus story.

Nearly fifty years earlier, in a thanksgiving sermon occasioned by Congress's abolition of the African slave trade (1808), the Reverend Absalom Jones, an ex-slave and founder and minister of the African Protestant Episcopal Church of St. Thomas in Philadelphia, drew a connection between the Exodus account of deliverance and subsequent events in world history. Indeed, the event they were celebrating was "a striking proof" that God *came down to deliver* our suffering countrymen."[76]

And so in the 1860s God "came down" to deliver African Americans from the institution of slavery itself, using Lincoln as the instrument of liberation. Initially, however, Lincoln was not embraced universally as the Moses to enslaved blacks. Because Lincoln postponed freeing the slaves and often overturned the emancipation pronouncements of his generals, Henry McNeal Turner, leader in the AME Church, called him a "mystic Pharaoh . . . [who] hardened his heart." But after his proclamation Lincoln was elevated to an undisputed Moses status. "The children of Israel was in bondage at one time," noted the ex-slave Mingo White, "and God sent Moses to 'liver them. Well, I s'pose that God sent Abe Lincoln to 'liver us." When news of Lincoln's proclamation reached an anticipating crowd at Boston's Tremont Temple, a black preacher led the joyous singing of "Sound the land timbrel o'er Egypt's dark sea, / Jehovah hath triumphed, his people are free."[77]

As Sherman's army marched through Georgia and finally reached Savannah, Union troops were greeted by slaves with shouts of "Glory to God, we are free!" and with the singing of the same jubilant hymn of thanksgiving sung at Tremont Temple. In 1864, a Union army chaplain from Iowa described the centrality of the exodus theme in the minds of recently freed slaves in Decatur, Alabama. "There is no part of the Bible with which they are so familiar as the story of deliverance of the children of Israel. Moses is their *ideal* of all that is high, and noble, and perfect, in man. I think they have been accustomed to regard Christ not so much in the light of a *spiritual* Deliverer, as that of a second Moses who would eventually lead *them* out of their prison-house of bondage."[78]

The God who came down to release the captives was also the God who came down in judgment. Unlike Lincoln, who puzzled over warring peoples praying to the same God for divine guidance and victory ("both can't be right"), slaves needed no special insight to conclude that the North's victory was God's judgment on slavery. An ex-slave from Missouri told of an episode in which a Baptist preacher kept a log chain around a slave's shoulder for so long that it cut to the bone. Seeing the slave in tortured agony, neighbors intervened and insisted he remove it. To the ex-slave the lesson was clear: "No wonder God sent war on this nation! It was the old story of the captivity in Egypt repeated. The slaveholders were warned time and again to let the black man go, but they hardened their hearts and would not, until finally the wrath of God was poured out upon them and the sword of the great North fell upon the first-born."[79]

God brought judgment upon slaveholders and liberation to this chosen people, and yet the Promised Land had not been reached. Despite the joy of freedom, an uncertain future lay ahead, one fraught with the same temptations and perils that the Israelites faced. As Brother Thorton, a contraband slave, told the refugees at Fort Monroe, Virginia, "Israel passed forty years in the wilderness, because of their unbelief. What if we cannot see right off the green fields of Canaan, Moses could not. He could not even see how to cross the Red Sea. If we would have greater freedom of body, we must free ourselves of the shackles of sin, and especially the sin of unbelief."[80] As blacks would soon find out, more than unbelief stood in the way of Canaan Land.

A Territorial Exodus: Exodusters, Back to Africa, and the Great Migration (1865–1930)

"The Lord will fight for you, and you have only to keep still." For the vast majority of evangelical blacks, these words of Exodus 14:14 encapsulated the momentous transition from slavery to freedom, and in fact, they guided the lives of most black Christians for a century—from the Civil War to the civil rights movement in the 1960s. An optimistic faith that God will make it right, if not in this world, then in the world to come, continued to supply psychological fortitude, but it also induced outward passivity in the face of continued oppression and injustice. Blacks continued to trust in a God that would "fight for them," but as the realities of the post-Reconstruction era set in, this warrior God seemed to disappear.

Freedom, citizenship, and the vote had come to four million blacks. However, after the Compromise of 1877, which gave the presidential election to Rutherford B. Hayes but left blacks in the South at the mercy of white supremacists, southerners invented numerous ways to disenfranchise blacks and maintain the levers of economic and political power. By 1880, 90 percent of all southern blacks continued the same jobs they had worked during slavery: personal and domestic service or farming. Those who farmed often found working conditions differed little from slavery. As tenant farmers beholden to propertied whites, they soon became tied to an invidious system that guaranteed lifelong indebtedness and poverty.

The vote was systematically denied through tactics such as the poll tax, the white-only primary, literacy tests, and unidentified ballot boxes. To ensure white rule, vigilante groups and terrorist organizations "policed" black communities through intimidation and violence, including the lynching of more than twenty-four hundred African Americans in the South from 1880 to 1918. Finally, a number of Supreme Court decisions, culminating in *Plessy v. Ferguson* (1896), opened the door to legalized segregation. By 1900 Jim Crow laws had become a permanent fixture throughout the South. "Whites Only" and "Colored" signage in public facilities proclaimed a world of separate existence between the races.

Southern blacks responded to these deteriorating conditions in a variety of ways. Most accepted their lot, remained in the South, and made the best of a bad situation. From 1870 to 1910, about 90 percent of all blacks in the United States lived in the South, a percentage only slightly less than that in 1790.[81] But some African Americans abandoned the South in search of cheap land and new opportunities elsewhere, especially in the midwestern states of Kansas and Oklahoma.

Others, both in the South and the North, dealt with dashed hopes by turning to black nationalism—the rejection of white American society and an emphasis on black unity—and looked to their African homeland as a way out. Still others, beginning in 1916, inaugurated what came to be known as the Great Migration to the North. Whatever the response, the exodus symbol, now infused with an emphasis on geographic deliverance (and, with it, civil and economic freedoms), retained a profound hold on the black community.

One of the earliest responses to newfound freedom was the establishment of all-black communities. From 1865 to 1915, some sixty communities were organized from Mississippi to Oklahoma. One of the more sensational relocation efforts occurred in the spring of 1879. Due in part to the advertisements circulated by Benjamin "Pap" Singleton, a Tennessee ex-slave, as well as fears among blacks that they would be reenslaved when Reconstruction ended, Kansas Fever Exodus struck about twenty thousand southern blacks from Kentucky, Louisiana, Mississippi, Tennessee, and Texas. Like Jesus, Singleton was a carpenter (cabinetmaker) who claimed a direct relationship to God. Yet he envisioned himself not as a messiah but as a self-styled "Father of the Exodus" or the "Moses of the Colored Exodus"—despite the fact that he provided no actual, hands-on leadership.[82]

Like the later Great Migration, the Kansas exodus was leaderless, a situation described by the comment of a New Orleans migrant: "Every black man is his own Moses now." Though without a Moses, the "Exodusters" envisioned themselves as a millenarian community of Israelites bound for the Promised Land, singing, "We are on our rapid march to Kansas, the land that gives birth to freedom." Indeed, one observer noted that blacks displayed "a sort of religious exaltation, during which they regarded Kansas as a modern Canaan and the God-appointed home of the negro race." An elderly Exoduster in St. Louis informed a reporter for the *Globe-Democrat* that "we's like de chilun ob Israel when dey was led from out o' bondage by Moses." St. Louis was the blacks' Red Sea, the place of deliverance between their former residences in the South and the Promised Land of Kansas.[83]

For other blacks, freedom lay not in Kansas or anywhere else in the United

States but in a return to Africa. In an age of immigration, when millions of eastern Europeans traversed the Atlantic Ocean in search of the Promised Land of America, blacks remained in an American Egypt—segregated, disenfranchised, threatened, beaten, and lynched. Since there was no future in a violent Jim Crow America, why not return to the precaptive homeland? Some sympathetic southern whites supported the move and urged the federal government to fund the repatriation of blacks to Africa. An anonymous white author (later identified) penned *An Appeal to Pharaoh,* recommending the repatriation of "pure blacks" (not mulattos) to Africa.[84]

To be sure, African Americans divided over the practicality of repatriation. Within the AME Church, Bishop Daniel A. Payne (1811–93) argued against what he considered a desperate and ill-conceived venture, whereas Bishop Henry McNeal Turner enthusiastically supported the "Liberian Exodus"—a title Payne rejected because "no *salvation of humanity*" was involved.[85] The project went forward, and the *Azor* departed in April 1878 with 206 emigrants bound for Liberia in what turned out to be an abortive endeavor. This single failed episode, however, neither quashed attempts to settle Liberia nor silenced what became increasingly strident calls for black nationalism and a return to Africa.

Repatriation rhetoric relied upon imagery in the Book of Exodus: African Americans imagined the return to Africa as a reversal of middle passage, indeed, as the crossing of the Red Sea—back to Egypt, the land not only of ancient Hebrew bondage but also of freedom. Exodus symbolism merged with what Albert Raboteau considers the most frequently quoted verse in African American religious history, Psalm 68:31: "Princes shall come out of Egypt; Ethiopia shall soon stretch her hands to God" (KJV). Although the precise meaning of this verse is obscure, late nineteenth-century blacks, according to Timothy Fulop, believed that Egypt and Ethiopia "referred to the African race and [they] looked to these ancient civilizations as proof of a glorious African past that rivaled European civilization."[86] American evangelical blacks, as the divinely chosen "princes out of Egypt," had a crucial missionary role to play in fulfilling the prophecy that Africa ("Ethiopia") would soon reach out her hands to the Christian God.

Considerably more significant for thousands of southern blacks and a harbinger of the massive shift in the African American population was the Great Migration of 1916 to 1918. Attracted by the demand for labor in war industries and only too ready to leave oppressive conditions in the South, approximately four hundred thousand southern blacks migrated to industrial cities of the North. The migration was more than a dual response to economic opportunity and existing injustices. It had deep religious meaning, rooted in the collective memory of resistance to slavery. As Milton Sernet observes, participants and commentators viewed the Great Migration "as a religious event—another chapter in the ongoing salvation history of African Americans, rich in symbolic and metaphoric content."[87]

Once again, blacks viewed the events of their history as the providential recapitulation of the exodus event. Trains heading to Chicago from the Mississippi delta bore the message, scratched in chalk, "Bound for the Promised Land." When a group of 147 migrants arrived at the Ohio River, the former border between slavery and freedom, they knelt and prayed, stopped their watches, and sang old spirituals, one bearing the words "I done come out of the Land of Egypt with the good news." At a railroad station, when asked where he was going, an elderly man replied, "I'm gwine to the promised land."[88]

Even natural disasters did not escape biblical comparisons. On the eve of the Great Migration, the God of the oppressed blacks visited "plagues" upon southern whites with the infestation of the boll weevil and flooding. Fifteen years later, in 1930, at the beginning of another "great" though less promising event (i.e., the Great Depression), a Chicago pastor, Harold Kingsley, recalled how the migrants "saw a parallel between [their] coming out of the South and the Hebrew children coming up out of the land of Egypt, out of the house of bondage." Their repertoire of songs included "Go Down, Moses, Tell Ole Pharaoh to Let My People Go" and "Pharaoh and His Army God Drowned."[89]

In two respects, this so-called Second Emancipation broke with the biblical exodus. First, it was a leaderless mass movement. Migrants to the North had no Moses to chart the way to the Promised Land. Second, the North was not a foreign land necessitating the removal of the inhabitants. Thousands of blacks already lived in the North, and many black churches participated in the recruitment and resettlement effort. The AME Council of Bishops voiced concern that the problem of resettlement presented a "new form of bondage" and so urged churches to provide assistance. Indeed, in 1917, W. G. Parks, pastor of Union Baptist Church in Philadelphia, informed new migrants that they had not arrived in the land of Canaan. "For there are those here in charge of the land and the government who are of another race," and with whom the city's blacks joined in discussing resettlement issues of housing and employment.[90]

Parks's analysis proved prophetic. With the onset of the Great Depression, the challenges facing northern urban blacks grew acute, and, for many, desperate. By the mid-1930s through the 1940s, the metaphor of the North as Canaan faded from consciousness. The realities of ghetto life, competition from the "new religions of the metropolis," and an exposure to a nationalist spirit (e.g., Garveyism) presented either alternative readings of the sacred text or, in the case of the Black Muslims, an altogether different sacred text (namely, the Quran). The territorial exodus from the rural South to the urban North resulted not in the fulfillment of Promised Land dreams but in the nightmare of a return to Egyptian-like bondage. There was no escape: the North was infected with its own brand of racism.

Exodus as Freedom: The Civil Rights Movement and Black Liberation Theology

The second half of the twentieth century witnessed the revival of the exodus motif applied primarily to the American political context. Beginning with the civil rights movement, followed by the emergence of black liberation theology in the 1960s and "womanist" theology in the 1980s, the ancient theme of liberation from oppressive conditions resounded throughout the black religious community. In speeches, sermons, books, and music, African Americans harked back to the paradigmatic exodus event with a heightened consciousness of the place of exodus imagery in their own history. Once again, blacks identified their condition with Israel's bondage under Pharaoh and centered their theology on God's desire to liberate all peoples from oppressive social and political conditions.

Beginning in the 1950s, a new exodus movement—the civil rights movement—challenged the continued practice of racial segregation and white supremacy. At once a grassroots movement led by people like Fannie Lou Hamer, whose educational background was limited to the fourth grade, and invigorated by the charismatic leadership of Martin Luther King, who had attained a Ph.D., the civil rights movement expressed exodus themes in song and sermon.

One of the most popular songs, "Go Tell It on the Mountain," conflated the traditional Christmas song by the same title with the spiritual "Go Down, Moses." Introduced by Hamer, a Christian civil rights activist from a sharecropper family and a direct descendant of slaves, the song was initially taught to local and national civil rights groups during a voting rights drive in Greenwood, Mississippi, in the fall of 1963.[91] The lyrics to Hamer's version of the chorus replaced the last line of the traditional "Go Tell It on the Mountain" ("That Jesus Christ is born") with "To let my people go." One of the verses reads:

> Who's that yonder dressed in red?
> Let my people go.
> Must be the children that Moses led,
> Let my people go.[92]

A clutch of Mississippi "pharaohs"—the police, the Ku Klux Klan, the Citizens' Councils, and the state Democratic Party—through intimidation, confusion, and violence, succeeded in keeping 95 percent of voting-age black Mississippians from voting. Now, through the voting rights drive, these pharaohs were challenged to "Let my people go!"[93] Other songs of the southern freedom movement expressed other exodus events of escape ("coming out of the wilderness") and reward ("marching to freedom land").[94]

The civil rights movement recognized its own Moses (and messiah figure as well) in the person of Martin Luther King Jr. Though more reticent than the press and his fellow civil rights leaders to apply the Moses persona to himself, King occasionally embraced the role to advance the cause of nonviolence, freedom, and equality. Early in his career, in a sermon delivered in January 1957 after the attempted bombing of his home in Montgomery, King cast himself in the role of Moses, looking out from Mount Pisgah on the Promised Land. "Tell Montgomery they can keep bombing and I'm going to stand up to them. If I die tomorrow morning I would die happy because I've been to the mountaintop and I've seen the promised land and it's going to be here in Montgomery."[95]

A decade later, on April 3, 1968, when the movement was flagging and on the eve of his assassination in Memphis, King again alluded to himself as a modern-day Moses. In his famous sermon "I See the Promised Land," King expressed confidence that, though he, like Moses, may not enter the Promised Land, his people would:

> Well, I don't know what will happen now. We've got some difficult days ahead. But it doesn't matter with me now. Because I've been to the mountaintop. . . . And I've looked over. And I've seen the promised land. I may not get there with you. But I want you to know tonight, that we, as a people will get to the promised land.[96]

More often than identifying himself as the Moses of his people, King invoked exodus imagery to describe the present-day conditions and possibilities for the deliverance of his people. In *Where Do We Go from Here?* (1967), King metaphorically linked the struggle for black freedom to the original account in Exodus: "The Bible tells the thrilling story of how Moses stood in Pharaoh's court centuries ago and cried, "Let my people go." This was the opening chapter in a continuing story. The present struggle in the United States is a later chapter in the same story."[97]

One of the earliest public instances of King's use of exodus language occurred in a sermon delivered in New York at the Church of St. John the Divine in May 1956. He employed the text of Exodus 14:30 ("And Israel saw the Egyptians dead upon the seashore") in response to the historic Supreme Court decision of 1954 *Brown v. Board of Education, Topeka, Kansas*. The decision reversed the policy of "separate but equal" facilities for the races and mandated desegregation of public schools. King likened the black struggle to the Israelites' struggle against and escape from Pharaoh. The drowning of Pharaoh's army symbolized the justice of God: "Today we are witnessing a massive change. A world-shaking decree by the nine Justices of the United States Supreme court opened the Red Sea, and the forces of justice are crossing to the other side . . . looking back we see the forces of segregation dying on the seashore."[98]

A year later, in front of the Lincoln Memorial in Washington, King appealed to the exodus theme of struggle and liberation. In "Give Us the Ballot—We Will Transform the South," he assured his audience "that as we struggle alone, God struggles with us. He is leading us out of a bewildering Egypt, through a bleak and desolate wilderness, toward a bright and glittering promised land." In 1965, before the historic voting rights march from Selma to Montgomery, he told an assembled gathering of two thousand participants: "Walk together, children; don't you get weary, and it will lead up to the Promised Land. And Alabama will be a new Alabama, and America will be a new America." Of course, white southern pharaohs would stand in the way, initially blocking the progress of freedom and then, when that tactic failed, counseling caution and a slow pace. But "what the pharaohs mean . . . is 'Never.' Pharaohs may try tokenism, but this is only a way to end pressure, not to begin the process of liberation."[99]

In the immediate aftermath of King's assassination, his memory more often evoked parallels to Jesus than to Moses. Still, as a letter on an op-ed page in the *Indianapolis Recorder* (May 8, 1968) revealed, King remained a popular Moses figure. "To his people," wrote Carol L. Johnson, "he was a leader, a veritable Moses, who practiced and preached non-violence, destined to lead his people out of the darkness of ignorance, despair, hate, inferior treatment into the light of hope, equality, and a sense of dignity and belonging." Nearly a decade later, in a 1977 sermon, Leonard Lovett observed striking parallels between Moses and Martin, including honorific titles (Moses, the servant of God; King, "the Peaceful Warrior"), a willingness to forsake prestigious careers (Moses, prince of Egypt; Martin, college presidencies), a willingness to suffer in order to liberate their people, courage in the face of death, and death in the prime of life and at the threshold of breakthrough to the Promised Land. More recently, James Cone has gone so far as to suggest that King "was the most important and influential Christian theologian in America's history," arguing that "no one has articulated the Christian message of freedom more effectively, prophetically, and creatively" than King.[100] This message of liberation was rooted in exodus theology and articulated in the teachings of Jesus.

In the wake of the assassinations of Malcolm X (February 1965) and King, amid deepening frustration, anger, despair, and increasing cries of "Black Power" in the African American community, black theology emerged as an alternative to traditional theological discourse. Radical black theologians accused the white church of failing to address the pressing needs of the African American community, due in part to its theological shortcomings. White theologians and the theological agenda they espoused ignored racial justice and white racism within mainstream Christianity and failed to challenge the existing oppressive structures that continued to bedevil the black community. "For the most part," wrote Cone, "theological talk in this country has been nothing but a participation in the structures of political oppression under the disguise of freedom and democracy."[101] As long as traditional white Christian theology prevailed, Martin King's vision of a "beloved community" would never be realized. To the oppressed black community's enduring question, "Why Lord?" white theologians had nothing to say.

Black Christians needed a voice, a theological voice, and black liberation theologians supplied that voice in an often strident, militant, angry, prophetic, in-your-face way. Working within the African American tradition of black resistance to slavery and institutional racism, black theologians looked to their own church history, to activists such as Gabriel Prosser, David Walker, and Henry McNeal Turner—not the classic sources of Protestant theology (Luther, Calvin, and Wesley)—as forerunners of a black theology of liberation.

They also reexamined the spirituals for insights into blacks' ability to resist the dehumanizing effects of slavery. If spirituals represented a survival mechanism in times of slavery, so now, according to Cone, the new black theology is "survival theology."[102] In appropriating these sources from their own tradition, black theologians discovered a motif running throughout African American religious history: the repeated invocation of the biblical exodus. To be sure, God's deliverance from bondage was not the only episode of liberation. The prophets excoriated the oppression of the weak and the outcasts, and Jesus, in his words and actions, completed the liberation of an oppressed people (thus, "Jesus Christ is Black, baby!"), but the exodus remained the founding event of liberation and hence critical for any discussion of black theology.

As Cone put it in his pioneering study, A Black Theology of Liberation (1970), "By delivering this people [the Israelites] from Egyptian bondage and inaugurating the covenant on the basis of that historical event, God reveals that he is the God of the oppressed, involved in their history, liberating them from human bondage. . . . God, because he is the God of the oppressed, takes sides with black people." And so "Christian theology must become Black Theology, a theology that is unreservedly identified with the goals of the oppressed community and seeking to interpret the divine character of their struggle for liberation."[103]

Cone's black theology, with its emphasis on God the liberator, was no passing fad. His subsequent writings as well as those of other black theologians, including a second generation now on the scene, continue to affirm that exodus is paradigmatic of God's action in history.[104] As well, the various liberation theologies now current—Third World (i.e., African, Asian, Latin American), feminist, "womanist," and so forth—appeal to the powerful symbolism in Exodus that points to God's opposition to whatever forces and ideologies obstruct freedom or a fullness of being.

At the same time, the Book of Exodus as an account of liberation presents its own challenges. As David Tracy has noted, "Even Exodus is not an innocent text." The people of Israel are liberated from bondage, but there are particulars in the story that give one pause: the extermination of murmuring Israelites in the wilderness and of indigenous Canaanites who occupied the Promised Land.

The black feminist ("womanist") theologian Delores Williams challenged Cone's fundamental contention that God is the God of liberation, who releases the captives and vindicates his cause. In identifying the black experience too closely with the elect people of Israel, Williams charged, Cone and other liberation theologians glossed over episodes where God's liberating activity involved the subjugation of others. Have liberation theologians, Williams wondered, "identified so completely with Israel's liberation that they have been blind to the awful reality of victims making victims in the Bible?"[105] God liberated some but not others.

For example, slavery was not outlawed among the Israelites, and God did not object to Hebrew men selling their daughters as slaves (Exod. 21:7–11). Williams lifted up the earlier biblical story of Hagar (Gen. 16, 21:8–21), Sarah's African slave, who was abandoned to the wilderness, as a poignant critique of liberation theology.[106] She pointed out that the exodus theme resonated during slavery, but that altered historical circumstances now required a more appropriate theme. A more compelling model, one that jibed with the experience of black women, was not liberation but wilderness, the inhospitable environment where women today, like Hagar of old, struggle for survival and well-being.

Exodus as Major Motif: Present Use, Future Prospects

Despite the womanist critique of liberation theology's reliance upon the exodus paradigm, exodus imagery persists within the black religious community, among liberationists and evangelicals alike. Warren Stewart proposes that black preachers adopt the exodus story and God's continuous activity throughout Scripture as their first hermeneutical principle: "He or she who interprets the Word *must know God to be actively involved in the continuous process of humankind's holistic liberation.*"[107] Indeed, African American preachers continue to find in the exodus narrative a ready resource for sermons.[108]

The background of all such sermonizing, of course, is the identification of the black American experience with the Hebrew experience in Egyptian bondage. Exodus-themed sermons typically begin with blunt observations that link the two experiences, such as Effie Clark's declaration in 1976 that blacks "are oppressed African people living in the captivity of America." Similarly, Alan Ragland observed in 1995, "The minorities in America and the Israelites in Egypt both were reduced to non-persons as racism institutionalized."[109]

A cursory content analysis of published sermons reveals a variety of applications drawn from the exodus event, though in each case there is a call for active engagement, whether by addressing spiritual matters or, more often, economic and political issues. Black passivity, whether rooted in spiritual convictions ("God will fight for you, only keep still"), spiritual indifference (neglecting to follow God's lead), or material well-being (some blacks have "made it" and ignore their people), is dismissed as irresponsible. Deotis Roberts declares that God will deliver the black community "only if we are able and willing to continue the fight for freedom, justice, and righteousness, doing what is in our hand [like the power of the staff Moses held in his hand] to do."[110] The Promised Land is at once near and far away, but it can be reached only by a community, not by individuals.

This sense of corporate responsibility harks back to the days of slavery, when a sense of communal consciousness found expression in the spirituals. It is also rooted in one of the main story lines in the exodus story itself, one that is often neglected in the current discussions among liberation theologians. To be sure, God is concerned about the plight of the oppressed, but as Exodus makes clear, an oppressed condition alone does not make a people the chosen of God. The goal of escape from Egypt was not only freedom *from* oppression but also freedom *to* serve Yahweh. It was the covenant—God's relationship with a nation—that liberated the Israelites, not solely their status of poverty or slavery. With this in mind, Alan Ragland declares, "It is essential for African-Americans to *remember who* we are and *whose* we are in our reestablishing of godly identity." For Ragland and others of a more conservative theological bent, liberation involves not only economic and political justice but also, more important, pressing on toward the "blessed homeland of the soul."[111]

Will the exodus paradigm remain one of the key motifs in the Afro-Christian religious experience? It continues to occupy a central place in discussions of African American biblical hermeneutics, primarily because it is so crucial to black history and self-understanding.[112] At the same time, the African American Christian community, though sharing a common history, is as diverse as American religion itself. Consider seminary training. Prospective black ministers may or may not attend predominantly black seminaries or other divinity schools where exodus themes inform biblical hermeneutics, theology, and ethics.

Moreover, black fundamentalists and, in some measure, black Pentecostals have been influenced by a (white) hermeneutic that ignores or gives less attention to exodus themes.[113] In addition, the exodus story does not resonate among blacks who do not feel oppressed or aggrieved—unless they retain a sense of solidarity with their race. And as I have noted, womanist theologians challenge the aptness of the exodus paradigm.

If, as I have suggested throughout this book, attention to selected biblical texts reflects responses to certain cultural or social conditions, then there is no assurance that the exodus paradigm will retain its primary significance in the black community. In fact, recent scholars analyzing current biblical themes within the African American Christian community observe the appropriation of assorted biblical motifs; the exodus theme is one among many.[114]

There are, however, two factors mitigating the likelihood of the exodus

disappearing from black consciousness. First, as long as suffering and oppression remain within a large segment of the black community, the exodus
paradigm will continue to resonate, offering the hope of God's liberating presence and challenging the forces of evil. Second, the exodus story is not just
any text of Scripture; it is the central plot in the divine story of redemption. It
occupies a place in Scripture that, for example, the story of the rich young ruler
or the Song of Songs does not. Because the exodus story is not just *a* story but
the story central to the Jewish and Christian metastory (the divine narrative),
the question is not whether it will remain within the drama. The question is
not *if* but *how* that drama will be interpreted and appropriated by its auditors.

How, then, shall the exodus story be construed? Although there is no single
definitive way of reading the text, the legacy of its understanding within the
African American community stands as a pointed challenge to the Euro-
American dominant paradigm of biblical interpretation. Who can hear the
story of the exodus, with its concern for the outcast, the oppressed, the suffering, and the powerless? Certainly those who are powerful and successful can
hear this story and find in it God's liberating grace. But throughout history
they are more the exception than the rule. The African American encounter
with the exodus, from slavery to emancipation, from the Kansas exodus to the
Great Migration, from Jim Crow to Fannie Lou Hamer, demonstrates that those
least skilled in the art of biblical interpretation are seemingly best equipped to
understand the heart of the biblical message.[115]

7

"Filled with the Holy Spirit"

The Roots of Pentecostalism

When the day of Pentecost had come, they were all together in one place. And suddenly from heaven there came a sound like the rush of a violent wind, and it filled the entire house where they were sitting. Divided tongues, as of fire, appeared among them, and a tongue rested on each of them. All of them were filled with the Holy Spirit and began to speak in other languages, as the Spirit gave them ability.

—Acts 2:1–4

I sometimes wonder how different my life would have been had I accepted my grandfather's offer. He made available free tuition to any grandchild who attended Evangel College, the liberal arts college of the Assemblies of God Church in Springfield, Missouri. As I recall, only one of his nine grandchildren took him up on his generous offer. Our family was deeply religious, but Pentecostal "holy rollers" we were not. My mother had grown up in Assemblies of God churches in Arkansas, first in Heber Springs and then in Hope— long before President Bill Clinton made this "Watermelon Capital of the World" famous. She even attended the Assemblies' Central Bible Institute (the predecessor of Evangel) in Springfield but then, in the early 1940s, traveled north to complete her education at Wheaton College, Illinois, at the same time as Wheaton's most famous alumnus, Billy Graham.

In those days, Wheaton was a bastion of Protestant fundamentalism known for its rigorous defense of the inerrancy of Scripture and its equally rigorous moral code of conduct. While open to students from Pentecostal backgrounds, Wheaton eschewed the Pentecostal distinctive of "speaking in tongues." Despite a close theological kinship between fundamentalism and Pentecostalism—both movements defended the "five fundamentals" of the Christian faith[1]—fundamentalists lambasted Pentecostals for their exaggerated stress on spiritual experience and deviation on some points of doctrine. At best, Pentecostals were deluded and deranged fanatics; at worst, they were diabolical and demonic cultists, "the last vomit of Satan," as G. Campbell Morgan, the popular expository preacher and writer in the English-speaking world, described them earlier in the century.[2]

Particularly unsettling to those like Morgan was the experiential dimension of Pentecostal worship. Fundamentalists were sober and generally restrained; Pentecostals were exuberant and often spontaneous. I know. During my childhood in the upper Midwest, many a family summer vacation was spent at my grandfather's lake house, and as a matter of habit (after all, my father was a minister) we attended Sunday church services at Grandpa Basye's Hope Gospel Tabernacle. For a child unaccustomed to shouting, bodily paroxysms, and a cacophony of spoken voices in group prayer, it was indeed an eerie experience. When we pietistic evangelicals were really serious about prayer, we knelt; when my Pentecostal grandfather was really serious about prayer, he stood with upraised arms. I was taught that God spoke in a hushed, "still small voice" (1 Kings 19:12, KJV), not in the hurricane-like "rush of a violent wind" of Pentecost (Acts 2:2). Such disparate approaches in worship epitomized the difference between the rationalistic, proposition-based fundamentalism of my youth (as I later came to understand it) and the spontaneous Holy Ghost outpouring of Pentecostalism.

I did not know what to make of Pentecostalism, something at once so foreign to me and yet so familiar to the Basye family. When in Hope, my father was often invited to preach at the Gospel Tabernacle. The folks there seemed to like his sermons—they accepted our brand of Christianity such as it was—but could we accept theirs? The world of Pentecostalism—a world that featured the likes of the motorcycle-riding evangelist "Sister Aimee" Semple McPherson, the evangelist and faith healer Oral Roberts, the snake handlers and poison drinkers in southern Appalachia—seemed far removed from my religious sensibilities.

Admittedly, back in the late 1950s and early 1960s there was a lot that I did not know about Pentecostalism. I was unaware, for example, that as early as 1943 fundamentalists and Pentecostals reached a rapprochement when "neo-evangelicals" moved away from their increasingly negative and defensive fundamentalist heirs and welcomed the Assemblies of God denomination into their newly created ecumenical organization, the National Association of Evangelicals. But I was not alone in my ignorance. Most Americans had never heard of Pentecostalism until an article written by Union Theological Seminary president Henry Pitney Van Dusen appeared in *Life* magazine in 1958. In his article, titled "The Third Force in Christendom," Van Dusen observed that Pentecostalism was taking its place alongside Catholicism and Protestantism as a viable movement in contemporary Christianity.[3]

Since Van Dusen's recognition of this "third force," Pentecostalism itself and attitudes toward the movement have changed drastically. What appeared to me as weird and what was disdained by fundamentalists and many of their evangelical heirs is presently one of the fastest growing religious movements in the world, at an incredible rate of about nineteen million new adherents annually. Not surprisingly, the world's largest church—the Yoido Full Gospel Church in Seoul, South Korea, with nearly a million members—is Pentecostal. This mother of all megachurches indicates not only Pentecostalism's magnitude but also its global reach and ethnic diversity. Indeed, within two years from its beginnings in the early twentieth century, Pentecostalism encircled the globe, attracted a cross section of the world's population, and spawned a dizzying array of movements, forms, denominations, and doctrinal variations.

Since the 1960s, the Pentecostal movement attained wider acceptance in major Protestant communions and the Catholic Church in North America and Europe as it incited an upsurge of spiritual renewal known as the Charismatic Movement. And by the 1980s, Pentecostal emphases upon "signs and wonders" and spiritual gifts (1 Cor. 12:7–11) extended to evangelical "third-wavers." More recently, Pentecostal effervescence made the headlines when the "fire" of Pentecostal revival fell upon the Toronto Airport Vineyard Church in the early 1990s with outbursts of holy laughter, miraculous healings, and spiritual renewal. And nine hundred miles to the south in Pensacola, Florida, at the Brownsville Assembly of God Church, a Pentecostal revival has attracted some two million people since its eruption in 1995.

Of course, one need not visit one of these churches to witness Pentecostal exuberance. Simply tune in to one of several major television networks that feature Pentecostal evangelists of varying stripes, some who sullied their reputations in 1990s by well-publicized financial and sexual scandals. But lest one dismiss Pentecostalism as a religious phenomenon isolated from the wider world, consider that John Ashcroft, former governor of and senator from Missouri and presently attorney general of the United States, is the son of an Assemblies of God minister and devout Pentecostal himself. Catholicism's Second Vatican Council may rank as the most important religious event of the twentieth century, but from an international perspective, Pentecostalism—with an estimated 550 million adherents worldwide in 2003—surely ranks as the century's most important Christian renewal movement.[4] Had I wanted to identify with a winner, I should have taken up my grandfather's offer.

Defining Pentecostalism

What is Pentecostalism, when did it arise, and where did it come from? If you have difficulty remembering dates, then the origins of traditional or classical Pentecostalism (as distinct from the more recent Charismatic Movement) should pose no problem. On New Year's Day, 1901, at Charles Parham's Bethel Bible School in Topeka, Kansas, Agnes Ozman was heard "speaking in tongues" just as the first Christians had done in Jerusalem when the Holy Spirit descended upon them. To be sure, the origins of Pentecostalism are far more complex than this single incident, but the new century conveniently signals the beginning of an extraordinary movement of spiritual renewal.

The "day of Pentecost," as noted earlier in the passage from Acts 2, traditionally marks the beginning of the Christian church. "Pentecost," which in Greek means "fifty," refers to the Old Testament Feast of Weeks, a spring harvest festival occurring on the fiftieth day (seven weeks) after Passover. The Jewish community subsequently endowed the festival with new religious meaning by making it a commemoration of the giving of the Law at Mount Sinai. On this annual holy day, following Jesus' postresurrection promise that his disciples would "receive power when the Holy Spirit has come upon you" (Acts 1:7), the Spirit descended afresh and supernaturally empowered the first Christians to speak in foreign languages unknown to them (2:4).

As students of comparative religion have observed, ecstatic utterance is not unique in Christianity. The Jewish tradition is filled with examples of Hebrew prophets—those who "forthtold" the message of God—engaging in Spirit-inspired speech. And throughout the ancient world, possession by a divine spirit (*pneuma*) was a common occurrence among the many sects and cults, mystery and Gnostic religions of the Roman Empire. Early Christians, however, described the phenomenon in their own terms and declared the preeminence of the Holy Spirit over its rivals. The Spirit-filled language in Acts 2 is technically known as *xenolalia* (or *xenoglossy*), the utterance of an actual foreign language unknown to the speaker. In this chapter, persons who spoke different languages heard those filled with the Spirit speak to them in intelligible speech in their own native tongue. Other New Testament passages, however, more often describe the practice of *glossolalia,* the uttering of unintelligible sounds as an angelic or heavenly language of praise, which require an interpreter for its meaning to be understood.

The general term used to describe both kinds of ecstatic utterance is "speaking in tongues" (or "tongues speech") or, with some imprecision, glossolalia. Although anthropologists refer to tongues speech as trance (the experience observed from the outside), spirit possession or ecstasy (the experience observed from the inside), and altered states of consciousness (unconscious or subconscious), this understanding is somewhat inaccurate. In each of these conditions there is typically a loss of awareness, but those who claim to have spoken in tongues report an ability to start and stop at will, and with full cognizance of what is taking place. Psychologists call it "disassociative speech," a form of involuntary speech indicative of an altered state of consciousness, and yet this condition more typifies biblical forms of prophecy than tongues speech.[5] Those who have observed tongues speech dispute whether there is any dissociation involved or, if so, consider it weak (analogous to thinking about jogging while driving home). Physiologically, speaking in tongues is a kind of spiritual default mechanism where the cortex of the brain—that which processes higher speech control—automatically defaults (by the infilling of the Spirit) to the medulla, the lower motor control in the brain.

Contrary to popular perceptions, speaking in tongues is not necessarily an irrational experience or aberrant behavior or a psychopathological condition; rather, it is a nonrational or an arational experience, the suspension of the ordinary rational process. Theologian Harvey Cox refers to this practice as "primal speech" and views it as a dimension of "primal spirituality"—"that largely unprocessed nucleus of the psyche in which the unending struggle for a sense of purpose and significance goes on." Similarly, Pentecostal theologian Frank Macchia suggests that speaking in tongues is the recognition that "language as rational communication cannot follow one into the depths of the encounter between the mystery of God and the mystery of the self before God." Tongues symbolize "a theophanic encounter with God that is spontaneous, free and wondrous." It is a revelation from God that results in a new personal relationship with God through the Spirit. Moreover, according to Macchia, glossolalia has a social and ethical dimension: "It is the lowest common denominator between people who might be very different from one another, revealing a deep sense of equality that cannot be denied and that challenges any discrimination based on gender, class, or race."[6]

Pentecostalism, then, is the encounter with God's Holy Spirit in an extraordinary way, expressed tangibly by speaking in tongues. Pentecostals distinguish between an initial reception of the Holy Spirit at conversion, often noting that the Spirit has baptized every believer into Christ, and a subsequent full reception or "infilling" of the Spirit, when Christ baptizes every believer into the Spirit. As John the Baptist proclaimed, "I have baptized you with water; but he [Jesus Christ] will baptize you with the Holy Spirit" (Mark 1:8). In addition to this twofold reception of the Spirit, Pentecostals distinguish between two types of speaking in tongues. Although the form is the same, the functions differ. The first, the *sign* or *initial evidence* of tongues, refers to what I have discussed earlier as the nonrepeatable postconversion experience that confirms the baptism in the Spirit. The second, the *spiritual gift* of tongues, discussed by Paul in 1 Corinthians 14, refers to other experiences of speaking in tongues whose purpose is to edify believers or convict unbelievers.[7] The gift is considered one among nine gifts (*charismata*) of the Spirit that include wisdom, knowledge, faith, healing, miracles, prophecy, discernment of spirits, various kinds of tongues, and the interpretation of tongues (see 1 Cor. 12:7–11).

As a distinct experience, baptism in the Spirit must be "earnestly" sought. It comes not to those who wait but to those who seek it through prayer, whether in a private or public setting. This is not to say that all who seek it will experience it. My mother never spoke in tongues, nor did more than half of the first-generation converts, nor have an estimated 35 percent of all current members in Pentecostal denominations.[8] In fact, from its beginnings and into the present, not all Pentecostals were (and are) convinced that tongues was the necessary or initial evidence of Spirit baptism. But a significant portion then and today insist that what was supernaturally given to the first Christians is available for and given to all Christians who seek it. The result of this initial evidence of tongues is a heightened intensification of the presence of Jesus in one's life, spiritual sensitivity and discernment, the illumination of Scripture in one's heart, praying in the Spirit, holy living, and above all, an empowerment for Christian witness.[9]

Clearly, Pentecostalism asserts a thoroughgoing restorationism: the primitive, wonder-working power of the first century is relevant, available, and even normative in the present day. As the first historian of Pentecostalism expressed it in 1916, "This movement has no history. It leaps the intervening years, crying 'back to Pentecost.'" Joseph Hutchinson, a former Presbyterian minister and first-generation Pentecostal, echoed a similar refrain: "There was not one gospel for the apostles and the early church and another for us." Rather, "the same gifts and powers [are] still in the church."[10]

Although speaking in tongues is the trademark of Pentecostalism, the phenomenon points to something beyond itself, to an "enduement with power," a power now available because God has poured out the Spirit in the "last times." According to Pentecostals, the outpouring of the Spirit in the first century and in the early twentieth century signaled the fulfillment of divine promises, especially Joel's prophecy concerning the "latter rain," a concept I will explore in greater detail later. Suffice it to say that in anticipation of the end of time, when Jesus will return and bring down the curtain of human history, God will do a new thing in pouring out his Spirit. Speaking in tongues was merely a confirmation, albeit a necessary one, that the last days were at hand.

As historians and theologians of Pentecostalism have pointed out, the driving force behind early Pentecostalism was not speaking in tongues (after all, it was not a unique phenomenon). Rather, it was the conviction (given tangible evidence by tongues and other miracles) that God was pouring out the Spirit on Christians and empowering them to share fully the life of the apostolic church, especially a life of witness to the world. "With one foot in creation and the other in the age to come," writes Steven Land in an important work on Pentecostal spirituality, "the Pentecostals hoped for the salvation of the lost and longed for Jesus to come."[11] Pentecostalism, then, was born in the fires of millennial expectation and fueled by missionary fervor.

Pentecostal Hermeneutics

Upon what biblical basis do Pentecostals lay claim for baptism in the Spirit? What Scriptures are formative to Pentecostal belief? What interpretive or hermeneutical principles support the Pentecostal perspective? These are critical questions, pursued with increasing self-awareness and sophistication among Pentecostal scholars since the 1970s. As French Arrington notes, "The real issue in Pentecostalism has become hermeneutics, that is, the distinctive nature and function of Scripture and the roles of the Holy Spirit, the Christian community, grammatical-historical research, and personal experience in the interpretive process."[12]

To place this discussion in the wider tradition of Christianity, it may be helpful to draw some comparisons between Catholics, traditional Protestants, and Pentecostals.[13] As we have seen in chapter 2, Catholics have traditionally viewed the church in terms of structure. Where one finds apostolic succession, there one finds the church, for it is through God-ordained authorities in the church that the grace of God is mediated through the sacraments and Christ's redeeming mission to the world is accomplished. The church existed prior to Scripture, and its authorities are preeminent. In this traditional Catholic view, the primary locus of the Holy Spirit is found in the church's ordained ministry. The Holy Spirit directs the church through the continuous line of apostolic succession, especially through the magisterium.

Protestants, in reaction against allegedly human traditions and unbiblical practices in Catholicism, placed the weight of authority on Scripture. Structure mattered less than the integrity of the message. For Protestants faith is a matter of belief, of right thinking or doctrinal assent. The source of belief is the Bible but with a particular focus. Classical Reformers such as Luther, Calvin, and Zwingli tended to read the New Testament through Pauline eyes (e.g., as we have seen in chapter 4, Romans 1:17 was a critical text for Luther), for it is through Paul's writings that the early church received its moral and theological instruction. In this traditional Protestant view, the primary locus of the Holy Spirit is found in the Bible. The Holy Spirit speaks to the believer through Scripture, especially through a learned minister's exposition of the Bible.

Both Catholic and Protestant perspectives preserve essential aspects of the church, yet both have been periodically troubled with formalism and lassitude. In Roman Catholicism, the church has taken on the appearance of a self-perpetuating corporation with wealth and a well-oiled bureaucracy. In Protestantism, the church has been guilty of an excessive creedal or doctrinal rigidity characterized by repeated schisms. In such cases, the Holy Spirit appears to have been domesticated, placed under human control.

David J. Du Plessis, the South African worldwide leader of Pentecostalism in the mid-twentieth century, poignantly expressed the difference between Pentecostal and non-Pentecostal approaches. Using an analogy of a frozen steak, Du Plessis noted that the steak was the "meat" or essential truths of Christianity. "You and I can sit around and analyze it," he told a group of Protestant ecumenical leaders. "We can discuss its lineage, its age, . . . its nutritive values. . . . But if my wife puts that steak on the fire, something different begins to happen. . . . Gentlemen," he concluded, "that is the difference between our ways of handling the same truth. You have yours on ice; we have ours on fire."[14]

Pentecostals agree with Catholics on the importance of the community of faith, and with Protestants they uphold the Bible as the all-sufficient guide for faith and practice, but they contend that the proper order of authority is Spirit, Scripture, and church. Without the Spirit there would be no Word (both incarnate and written), and without the Word, there would be no church. Where, then, does the Spirit reside? For Pentecostals, the locus of the Spirit is found in the human heart. The Christian life is a matter of the experienced power and presence of the Holy Spirit in the individual. The Spirit is understood not only in the traditional sense as "comforter," the "seal of redemption," the "anointer" with power, the "guide into all truth," and the "sanctifier" who enables believers to exhibit certain Christian characteristics (e.g., the "fruits of the Spirit": love, joy, peace, patience, gentleness, etc.). The Holy Spirit also "gifts" believers with tongues, healings, visions, dreams, prophecies, and their interpretations. For Pentecostals, there is a continuous, consistent activity of the Holy Spirit from creation to the present. "God is as much of an active causative agent today," writes Mark McLean, "as He is pictured in the biblical writings."[15]

Given the Pentecostal emphasis on experience, it should come as no surprise that, in the words of Gordon Fee, "hermeneutics has simply not been a Pentecostal thing. Scripture is the [literal] Word of God and is to be obeyed." This is not to suggest that Pentecostals have been indifferent to issues of biblical interpretation, for as we will see, Pentecostalism is built upon a distinctive hermeneutic. But until recently Pentecostals ignored historical-critical exegesis and a carefully constructed hermeneutic. "Filled with zeal, confident of the rightness of their cause," William Menzies and Robert Menzies observe that the first two generations of Pentecostals "connected successfully with common people around the world with a message of deliverance and hope. Serving in virtual isolation from the larger church world, they were not burdened by a need to argue fine points of theology." This was the case particularly during the movement's formative years (the first decades of the twentieth century) because Pentecostal hermeneutics developed after the fact. That is, the distinctive Pentecostal experience of the baptism in the Holy Spirit evidenced by speaking in tongues preceded a systematic Pentecostal hermeneutic. As Donald Gee, a first-generation Pentecostal leader in Britain, put it, "In the final analysis, the baptism in the Spirit is not a doctrine but an experience."[16] The experience was not so much extracted from a thorough exegesis of Scripture as the exegesis came after the experience. The supernatural endowment of the Holy Spirit came first, and then Pentecostals developed methods of biblical interpretation to support that experience.

The process by which Pentecostals concluded that tongues evidenced a baptism of the Holy Spirit, observes Frank Macchia, "is not so much a rationalistic inductive method of biblical interpretation as it is a creative interaction with the book of Acts in the context of Pentecostal worship."[17] For example, in the early stages of the movement, many of those who became Pentecostals agonized over their lack of spiritual power in ministry. Where was the dynamic, life-transforming power of Acts 2 in their own lives and ministries? When the experience of baptism in the Spirit ensued, they then sought scriptural support for that experience. Obviously, the particular experience of tongues would have never transpired without recourse to Scripture, and yet it is not clear that Scripture instructs all Christians to seek this experience.

On the one hand, there is at work what Donald Dayton calls a "subjectivizing hermeneutic," wherein the experience (speaking in tongues) is drawn from the recorded events in Scripture. On the other hand, the experience itself informs the interpretation of Scripture so that speaking in tongues confirms that the signs, wonders, and miracles of the New Testament are available in the present day. The rise of Pentecostalism, then, illustrates the intertextuality in the hermeneutic process, that is, the fusion of the social world of a believing community (the social context) with the Pentecost narrative of Acts 2.[18] In his firsthand description of the outpouring of the Spirit at the Azusa Street revival in 1906, Frank Bartleman captured the interplay of the social text with the first Pentecost in Jerusalem:

> Los Angeles seems to be the place and this the time in the mind of God, for the restoration of the church to her former place, favor, and power.... God has spoken to his servants in all parts of the world and has sent many of them to Los Angeles, representing every nation under Heaven. Once more, as of old, they are come up for "Pentecost," to go out again into all the world with the glad message of salvation. The base of operations has shifted, from old Jerusalem, for the latter "Pentecost," to Los Angeles. And there is a tremendous, God-given hunger for this experience everywhere.[19]

Bartleman's connection between an ancient and modern-day Pentecost points to the Pentecostal emphasis on passages of Scripture that describe the tangible work of the Spirit in the Christian community. And the most tangible expression of the Spirit's outpouring is that of speaking in tongues, as expressed in several passages in the Acts of the Apostles.

Sometimes called the "acts of the Holy Spirit" for its recurring references (forty-one times) to the work of the Spirit, the Book of Acts narrates the history of the first three decades of the Christian mission. The second volume in Luke's New Testament writings (the other being his Gospel), Acts offers an exciting, dramatic, whirlwind tour of Christianity's expansion as a worldwide inclusive community with a universal message. The Christian message begins in Jerusalem, extends throughout the eastern Mediterranean, and ends in Rome (thus the entire "world"), where Paul continues to preach while under house arrest. Luke's purpose is to authenticate the spread of this new faith through God's mighty acts by demonstrating the empowering work of the Holy Spirit in the lives of the first Christians, especially in two leaders, Peter (chapters 1–12) and Paul (chapters 13–28). The early Christians speak in tongues, work miracles, and are supernaturally delivered from danger and death. At the same time, they encounter resistance from Jewish and Roman authorities, resulting in arrests, imprisonment, beatings, and death. Yet they are not deterred. Through God's mighty acts in the Spirit the gospel spreads "throughout Judea, Galilee, and Samaria" (9:31), "as far as Phoenecia, Cyprus and Antioch" (11:19), "through the region of Phrygia and Galatia" (16:6), "over to Macedonia" (16:9), and finally "to Rome" (28:14).

With the rise of modern biblical studies, and increasingly since the nineteenth century, scholars' estimations of the historicity of Acts have ranged from the skeptical to the reliable, from the conviction that Acts is a pious fabrication of an idealized past to an accurate and most valuable source for the history of early Christianity.[20] Needless to say, early Pentecostals read Acts as generations of Christians read it, that is, as a straightforward narration of the history of the Christian mission in its first three decades as it "really happened." And yet they read it with a novel perspective that raises the crucial hermeneutical question of Luke's purpose. Was he writing history, theology, or a combination? Are his many references to the Holy Spirit in the life of the Christian (variously described as "baptized in the Spirit," "filled with the Spirit," and "receiving the Spirit") mere reportage, or is he intending (as Pentecostals affirm) to teach Christian believers that so-called Spirit baptism can and does recur in the experiences of successive generations? Is his Acts of the Apostles primarily descriptive, narrative history, or does he intend (again, as Pentecostals affirm) to teach something?

In the last half of the twentieth century, a number of influential biblical scholars downplayed Acts as reliable history but emphasized Luke's theological purpose. Working independent from Pentecostal concerns (and often indifferent, if not hostile, to them), redaction critics such as Hans Conzelmann (*The Theology of St. Luke*, 1954; *Acts of the Apostles*, 1987) emphasized that the Gospel writers were not merely compilers of stories and traditions but editors or redactors who reworked materials in light of their own theological concerns. Understood from this perspective, telling stories was a form of theological instruction—somewhat similar to Jesus' parables. Luke thus altered, omitted, or generalized what really happened in order to communicate an important theological message. "For Luke," writes Conzelmann, "history is identical with salvation history."[21]

In response to Conzelmann's doubts concerning the Acts' historicity, other scholars defended its historical veracity and argued that Luke's purposes were primarily historical. Martin Hengel, for example, admitted that for all of Luke's "tendentious distortions," he "is no less trustworthy than other historians of antiquity. . . . We have no reason to assume that . . . he made up his narrative largely out of his head." Indeed, "as a Christian 'historian,'" Luke "sets out to report the events of the past that provided the foundation for the faith and its extension. He does not set out primarily to present his own 'theology.'"[22]

Responding to this interpretive standoff, I. Howard Marshall, a non-Pentecostal evangelical scholar at the University of Aberdeen, affirmed both the historical integrity and the theological purposes of Luke in *Luke: Historian and Theologian* (1970).[23] Marshall offered students of Pentecostalism, coming of age in the 1970s and 1980s as the first generation of university-trained Pentecostal theologians and biblical scholars, a framework upon which to construct their own distinct biblical theology.[24] For example, working from the insights of Marshall, Roger Stronstad authored a pathbreaking work within the Pentecostal community in 1984, arguing that Luke narrated a "charismatic theology" that differed from the pneumatological emphasis in Paul's writings. Past efforts to reconcile the writings of Luke and Paul or to read Luke from the perspective of Paul not only were inappropriate, argued Stronstad, but also disregarded the distinct theological intentions of these writers. Whereas in his association of baptism in the Spirit with conversion-initiation and ethical behavior (e.g., the "fruits of the Spirit"), Paul presented a more complete understanding of the work of the Spirit than Luke, Luke emphasized what Pentecostals call "Spirit baptism" as the source of prophetic anointing subsequent to conversion. There is thus no need to reconcile Luke with Paul, for each has unique but complementary purposes in mind.[25]

Stronstad's approach shifted or at least broadened the traditional approach in Christian theology that focused primarily on Paul's emphasis upon the Spirit as a soteriological agent, that is, the source of salvation and sanctification (or moral renovation). This is not to say that Luke had no interest in the power of the Spirit to change human behavior, but he offered another model or theological pattern in the narrative portions in Acts that is the standard by which all Christians should judge a vital spiritual life. Luke's intent was to emphasize the Spirit's empowering work for missionary service, and the symbol or initial evidence of that empowerment was speaking in tongues.

Luke thus established a precedent of the initial evidence of speaking in tongues as a sign of Spirit baptism that should be regarded as normative.[26] This precedent or "pattern" is found in five passages where people are "filled" with the Holy Spirit, three in which tongues speaking is mentioned as an immediate result (2:4; 10:44–45; 19:6). In each pericope, argue Pentecostal scholars, the gift of the Spirit equips the disciples for service.[27]

1. In Jerusalem at Pentecost: "All of them were filled with the Holy Spirit and began to speak in other languages, as the Spirit gave them ability" (2:4).

2. In the village of Samaria: "Now when the apostles at Jerusalem heard that Samaria had accepted the word of God, they sent Peter and John to them. The two went down and prayed for them that they might receive the Holy Spirit (for as yet the Spirit had not come upon any of them; they had only been baptized in the name of the Lord Jesus). Then Peter and John laid their hands on them, and they received the Holy Spirit." (8:14–17).

3. Saul's (Paul's) reception of the Spirit, three days after his dramatic conversion on the road to Damascus: "So Ananias went and entered the house. He laid his hands on Saul and said, 'Brother Saul, the Lord Jesus, who appeared to you on your way here, has sent me so that you may regain your sight and be filled with the Holy Spirit.' And immediately something like scales fell from his eyes, and his sight was restored. Then he got up and was baptized" (9:17–18).

4. In the town of Caesarea, where the so-called Gentile Pentecost occurred at the house of Cornelius: "While Peter was still speaking, the Holy Spirit fell upon all who heard the word. The circumcised believers who had come with Peter were astounded that the gift of the Holy Spirit had been poured out even on the Gentiles, for they heard them speaking in tongues and extolling God" (10:44–46).

5. At Ephesus: "While Apollos was in Corinth, Paul passed through the interior regions and came to Ephesus, where he found some disciples. He said to them, 'Did you receive the Holy Spirit when you became believers?' They replied, 'No, we have not even heard that there is a Holy Spirit.' . . . When Paul had laid his hands on them, the Holy Spirit came upon them, and they spoke in tongues and prophesied" (19:1–2, 6).

A hermeneutic constructed around proof-texts is not unique to Pentecostals. Other Christian groups have engaged in a similar hermeneutic of exegeting certain practices from historical or descriptive passages. One could point out that various Christian practices such as baptizing infants, participating in the Lord's Supper every Sunday, selling one's possessions and having all things in common, and the handling of snakes are all derived more from historical precedent than from explicit teaching. But to derive prescriptive teaching from historical narrative is precisely where the criticism has been lodged against the Pentecostal conviction of initial evidence of baptism in the Spirit. There is no indication, argue critics of initial evidence (including even some Pentecostal scholars), that Luke intended to present these examples as models. To so conclude is an invalid inference, for how can one build a *doctrine* from a few *examples?*[28]

As Larry Hurtado, a New Testament scholar and former Pentecostal, understands the matter, Luke's association of tongues with Spirit baptism is normal but not the norm; it is *a* sign of the Spirit's work but not *the* sign. "The author's purpose," he continues, "was not to provide a basis for formulating how the Spirit is received, but rather it seems to have been to show that the Spirit prompted and accompanied the progress of the gospel at every significant juncture and was the power enabling the work of Christian leaders." In some cases the author describes specifically how the Spirit was manifested when people received the Holy Spirit (e.g., by speaking in tongues), but in other cases he does not (8:14–19; 9:17–19). The primary intent is to show "the validity of the gospel developments described," not "to teach a doctrine of the Spirit's reception." In short, the Pentecostal position results "from zealous but misguided handling of the biblical data."[29]

James Dunn, a prolific New Testament scholar who has carried on a lively running debate with the Pentecostal insistence upon a postconversion experience of the Spirit, expresses another major criticism. In his influential *Baptism in the Holy Spirit* (1970) and other writings, Dunn argues that for Luke (as for Paul), the real evidence and chief element of Christian experience is the presence of the Spirit in one's life, not some kind of distinctively postconversion experience of the Spirit. To be sure, the New Testament describes the action and work of the Holy Spirit in a variety of ways but none as a second experience that all Christians should seek. Rather, the gift of the Spirit is the essential aspect of the event or process of Christian conversion-initiation. "The Spirit itself," notes Dunn, "is the breath of divine life within the believer, the divine action within the human which links and bonds the human with the divine, the dynamic reality of spiritual sonship, without which no one can be said to belong to Christ." The same holds true of that phrase of initiation, "baptized in the Spirit." One must conclude perforce "that if a theology of 'baptism in the Spirit' is to be based on NT teaching on the subject, it must refer to the beginning of Christian experience, the action by which God draws the individual into the sphere of the Spirit, into the community of those 'being saved.' "[30]

Similarly, Max Turner, who argues from the standpoint of one within the charismatic community, stresses an underlying unity in the work of the Spirit taught throughout the New Testament. For Luke, Paul, and John, "the gift of the Spirit to believers affords the whole experiential dimension of the Christian life, which is essentially charismatic in nature. The gift is granted in the complex of conversion-initiation." Over against the classical Pentecostal view of the two-stage model of reception of the Spirit, Turner understands Luke's use of phrases such as "filled with the Spirit" and "full of the Spirit" to designate charismatic "moments" (e.g., Luke 1:41, 67; Acts 2:4; 4:8, 31; 7:55; 13:9) and to indicate sporadic longer term gifts for ministry (Luke 1:15; 4:1; Acts 9:17). Neither Paul nor Luke uses "to receive (the gift of) the Holy Spirit" in the sense of a second experience, apart from the conversion-initiation process. Writes Turner,

> There is simply no clear exegetical evidence to suggest that Luke, Paul, or John envisaged the possibility that there were in the post-Easter church two classes of Christians, distinguished by whether or not they had received the Pentecost gift of the Spirit. That there could be any "believers" who lacked the new Christian "Spirit of prophecy" was strictly an exceptional and anomalous possibility (as Acts 8 indicates), because this gift (with the charismata it afforded), was at the heart of the new life of salvation, service, and mission.

To be sure, there are different emphases in each writer, but they represent a unified whole when it is recognized that "Paul's concept of the gift of the Spirit is simply *broader* than Luke's, *while nevertheless containing everything that Luke implies.*" Luke thus does not add anything to Paul's more comprehensive understanding of the work of the Spirit. Turner remains open to the full expression of the gifts of the Spirit in our own day, but he rejects the Pentecostal two-stage model for a one-stage model of reception of the Spirit.[31]

Pentecostal scholars such as Robert Menzies respond to Dunn, Turner, and other critics by taking a broader view of Luke's understanding of the Spirit in Luke-Acts.[32] With Stronstad, Menzies affirms that Luke the theologian intended that the gift of the Spirit be experienced by everyone as a source of power for witness (Luke 12:12; Acts 1:8). Luke accented the Spirit's distinct work separate from the Spirit's work in conversion. For Menzies, the fundamental question is that of Luke's overall pneumatology, not the hermeneutics of historical precedent (proof-texting).

For example, one can see Luke's intentions at work in his editorial changes in Luke 11:13b, where he substitutes "Holy Spirit" for "good things" in Matthew 7:11b (which reflects the original wording).[33] Where Matthew 7:11 reads, "If you then, who are evil, know how to give good gifts to your children, how much more will your Father in heaven give *good things* [my emphasis] to those who ask him," Luke inserted "Holy Spirit." On three other occasions Luke edited the sources from which he drew by inserting "Holy Spirit" (Luke 4:1, 14; 10:21). This redactional activity "reflects Luke's intent to teach a Spirit-baptism for empowering, distinct from conversion."[34]

And what about speaking in tongues as the initial evidence of baptism in the Spirit? Menzies distinguishes between the prophetic character of the gift of the Holy Spirit (the source of power for effective witness) and tongues as initial evidence. Contrary to what many Pentecostals affirm, tongues speech is not the gift of the Spirit but rather a manifestation of that gift. Menzies agrees with those who argue that "tongues as initial evidence" is not explicitly or consistently taught in the New Testament. Nevertheless, the normative character of evidential tongues emerges not from Luke's primary intent but as an "appropriate inference drawn from the prophetic character of Luke's pneumatology (and more specifically, the Pentecostal gift) and from Paul's affirmation of the edifying and potentially universal character of the private manifestation of tongues." Where critics dismiss "implications" or "inferences" as invalid reasoning from which to construct a doctrine, Menzies concludes that the doctrine of initial evidence "is linked to a process of doctrinal development," not unlike that of the developed doctrine of the Trinity, "that extends back into the apostolic age."[35]

In one sense, Menzies's engagement with contemporary biblical scholarship to defend the classical Pentecostal doctrines is far removed from the inductive approach taken by Pentecostals in the early twentieth century. In another sense, however, though the first Pentecostals lacked the critical tools to express their convictions in a precise manner, they anticipated the use of such tools as redaction criticism. David Kerr, an early leader of the Assemblies of God, intuitively adopted a hermeneutic that is present in contemporary biblical scholarship when he observed that Luke selected "from a voluminous mass of material just such facts and just such manifestations of the power of God as served his purpose. What is his purpose? No doubt, his purpose is to show that what Jesus promised He hath so fulfilled. He says, 'they that believe shall speak in other tongues.' The 120 believed and, therefore, they spake in other tongues as the Spirit gave them utterance."[36] And the coming of the Spirit was accompanied not only by speaking in tongues but also by a new infusion of supernatural power and activity—by those charismata recited by Paul in 1 Corinthians.

By way of summary, Pentecostals extrapolate the "tongues of fire" that descended upon the Jerusalem Christians and make it the "initial evidence" teaching that forms the core theology of most classical Pentecostal churches around the world. This incident in Acts 2 and four other passages form the foundation of the two primary Pentecostal doctrines of the baptism in the Spirit accompanied by speaking in tongues as a distinct and simultaneous experience following conversion. According to conventional Pentecostal histories, when Agnes Ozman spoke in tongues on New Year's Day, 1901, the event marked the culmination of study of the Holy Spirit in the Book of Acts that pointed to a normative experience for all Christians. What happened?

Pentecostalism's Beginnings, Part 1: Topeka, Kansas

The Date: January 1, 1901
The Place: The "upper room" of the Bethel Bible School, Topeka,
Kansas
The Scene: Fire from heaven—a second Pentecost. Agnes Ozman, a
young student, speaks in tongues after asking the Reverend Charles
Fox Parham to lay his hands upon her.

Like many young, energetic, idealistic ministers, the Reverend Charles Fox
Parham (1873–1929) wanted results. And he wanted them his way. Licensed
by the Methodist Church, he served two small churches near Lawrence, Kansas, and had some success as an evangelist in the area. But Parham was a
restless soul with an independent, even rebellious, streak. Angered by
churches' reluctance to ordain him, frustrated by denominational constraints,
and critical of a creeping, cold formalism within Methodism, he resigned and
set out on his own. In the next few years he turned his attention to divine
healing and eventually opened the tuition-free Bethel Bible School in Topeka
in the fall of 1900. Parham taught about three dozen students, using the Bible
as the only text. Together teacher and students studied Scripture, prayed, fasted,
lived communally, and focused on the power of the Holy Spirit. In late December, before Parham left on a three-day speaking engagement, he instructed his
students "to carefully study the subject of the Baptism of the Holy Spirit." Was
there a common element, a unifying theme? he asked. Upon his return, his
band of students had found the answer. According to Parham, the students
reached the same conclusion: in those places in the Book of Acts where the
Spirit was initially received, it was accompanied (but not always, we might add)
by speaking in tongues (2:4; 10:44–46; 19:1–2, 6).[37]

According to Pentecostals, other passages in Scripture predicted these outpourings. Jesus himself was the model of one baptized in the Spirit. In Mark
1 at the beginning of Jesus' ministry, "John the baptizer appeared in the wilderness, proclaiming a baptism of repentance for the forgiveness of sins" (1:
4). Many confessed their sins and were baptized in water. John then declared
about the one who would come after him (identified in the Gospels as Jesus),
"I have baptized you with water; but he will baptize you with the Holy Spirit"
(1:8). Jesus was among those baptized by John, but only he is said to receive
the Spirit, for as Jesus "was coming up out of the water, he saw the heavens
torn apart and the Spirit descending like a dove upon him" (1:10). Three years
later, shortly before the day of Pentecost, Jesus instructed his disciples to remain in Jerusalem and "to wait there for the promise of the Father. 'This,' he
[Jesus] said, 'is what you have heard from me; for John baptized with water,
but you will be baptized with the Holy Spirit not many days from now'" (Acts

1:4–5). The gift the Father promised would be the Holy Spirit, it would come from Jesus, and the reception of that gift would be baptism in the Holy Spirit. On the day of Pentecost that promise was fulfilled.

And so it was at Parham's little Bible school, following study and fervent prayer, that Agnes Ozman, a young woman in search of palpable religious experiences, first spoke in tongues—Chinese to be exact. So struck was she by the Spirit that the following day she could not speak in English but communicated to others in written Chinese characters. Others followed, speaking in the tongues of other languages. The *Topeka Capital* announced in its headlines, "A Queer Faith, Strange Acts . . . Believers Speak in Strange Languages."[38] According to Parham, his students spoke in twenty-one known languages, none ever having studied the foreign tongues in which he or she spoke. A new missionary language training school had come into being.

In point of fact, the beginnings of modern Pentecostalism are a bit more complicated, for like the origins of all pivotal events, they have been subjected to mythmaking. Because the origins of a movement typically become a blueprint of "how things should really be," early historians of Pentecostalism, including Parham himself, related the events to fit their ideal biblical model of a second Pentecost. Thus the events and details of the early chapters of Acts were reenacted. Indeed, Parham claimed he had received a "God-given commission to deliver to this age the truths of a restored PENTECOST."[39] Parham conflated passages in Acts to suggest that speaking in tongues occurred after the Holy Spirit descended (2:4) upon 120 people (1:15) who were gathered in an "upper room" (1:13). So at Bethel Bible School, the Spirit descended upon some 120 persons (about 40 students and 75 visitors) in the second-story residence (the "upper room") of the Bible school after their study of Scripture made it clear that this was the norm. Parham himself received Holy Spirit baptism three days after Ozman's initial baptism.

But inconsistencies appear. According to a careful study by Robert Mapes Anderson, Ozman first spoke in tongues sometime before January 1, 1901, and rather than first consulting Acts 2 first and then speaking in tongues, the reverse occurred: Ozman spoke in tongues and then looked to the Bible for some confirmatory evidence. As she put it, "I did not know that I would talk with tongues when I received the Baptism."[40] The Acts 2 episode became normative after the fact of Ozman's experience. Furthermore, there is evidence that Parham was well aware of speaking in tongues and that he had formulated the doctrine before, not after, Ozman's experience. Finally, it should be noted that other groups laid claim to speaking in tongues in the decade prior to the outbreak at Parham's Bible school.[41]

Nevertheless, *something* had happened. What was unique in Ozman's experience and in Parham's theological self-understanding was that subsequent to conversion, Spirit baptism—an infilling for Christian witness and service— was linked to the accompanying sign of speaking in tongues.

Why Tongues Now? The "Latter Rain"

Exactly when and where modern Pentecostalism began remains uncertain, but this much is clear: the movement introduced something new and different and powerful to Christian experience—the unloosing of a tangible, spiritual power in tongues speaking. This very novelty, however, raises a vexing issue. If baptism in the Spirit accompanied by speaking in tongues is normative, then why do we not find consistent evidence of it throughout the history of Christianity? Why did tongues disappear after the first century only to reappear in the twentieth? What happened in the eighteen-hundred-year hiatus?

Before directly addressing these questions, I should note that although the idea of speaking in tongues is unusual, the post–New Testament understanding and practice of baptism in the Spirit is certainly not new. By the second century, this practice had assumed a sacramental character as a rite of initiation identified with water baptism, modeled on the baptism of Jesus. By the third century, the imparting of the Spirit and reception of various charismata became identified with rites of confirmation in the Western church and chrismation in the Eastern that included the imposition of hands and anointing.[42] From Augustine on through the sixteenth-century Reformers and into the early modern period, Western theologians emphasized the salvific work of the Spirit, that is, the work of the Spirit in applying the saving work of Christ to the believer. In theological terms, pneumatology was subsumed under soteriology. Luther and Calvin, for example, emphasized the Spirit's essential role in justification: the Spirit draws sinners to Christ and makes his benefits (atoning sacrifice and imputed righteousness) available to each believer and then enables the believer to grow in holiness (sanctification).

To be sure, there were exceptions and challenges to mainstream traditions. One could point to radical dualists such as Montanists, Gnostics, Messalians, and Cathars who rejected the institutional church and its flawed sacramental system in favor of their own pure rites by which one received the Spirit and even spoke in tongues. Or to mystics such as the Nicholas Cabasilas (d. ca. 1371) in the Orthodox East, who emphasized the impartation of the Spirit's gifts at chrismation and their realization of *theosis*, a godlikeness.[43] But the conclusions reached by Stanley Burgess, the author of a three-volume study of the Holy Spirit in Christian history, clarify the altogether unique convictions of Pentecostals.[44] According to Burgess,

> while the concept of Spirit baptism was very common throughout the Christian centuries, the modern Pentecostal identification of glossolalia as the "initial evidence" of such baptism is completely novel until the nineteenth-century Irvingites. Amazingly, in almost two millennia of Christian life and practice, no one from the apos-

FILLED WITH THE HOLY SPIRIT"   249

tolic period to the early nineteenth century—not even those who placed great emphasis upon the study of Scripture—associated tongues with the advent of the Spirit. Even tongues-speakers in earlier centuries did not make such a connection. Only Augustine addresses a possible linkage between glossolalia and Spirit entry, and he concludes that the connection ceased in the first-century church.[45]

Indeed, the traditional non-Pentecostal interpretation of speaking in tongues (and other charismata such as miraculous healings and prophetic speech) within Western Christianity is known as the "cessation of the charismata" teaching. Articulated first by Augustine and repeated in some version up to our own day, this view holds that the gifts of the Spirit had been divinely withdrawn from the church at the end of the apostolic age. The charismata were exceptional events in an extraordinary time and associated with the apostles for the specific purpose of *accrediting* the gospel—not *expressing* the gospel as Pentecostals contend.[46]

The coming of the Spirit was not so much a subsequent event sought after by the disciples as a sign of a new era of grace on earth. This sign extended first to the Jews and then into the Gentile world (note the different geographic locales and groups of people in the five Acts passages noted earlier). Non-Pentecostals contend that the Pentecost event is neither a recurring nor a required phenomenon in the life of the believer but a single event wherein the Holy Spirit was poured out at a specific time, in a specific place, upon a specific few, for the specific purpose of introducing a new era. At the close of the apostolic age, the miraculous gifts of the Holy Spirit ceased.

I have already noted the general Pentecostal understanding of Spirit baptism in the Book of Acts, but to answer more directly the question of Why now? Pentecostal apologists respond in two ways. First, they propose a "successionist theory," based upon the claim—though critics contend not without a stretch of historical credulity—that tongues never died out. There has been an unbroken succession of tongues in the "true" church since Pentecost. One need only look to individuals such as Montanus, the Phrygian prophet of the second century; Pachomius, the fourth-century monk; St. Vincent Ferrer and St. Francis Xavier, Catholic missionaries in the fourteenth and sixteenth centuries. Or to groups such as the twelfth-century Waldensians, the sixteenth-century Anabaptists in Appenzell, the seventeenth-century Jansenists, the eighteenth-century Camisards in France and Quakers, Shakers, and Methodists in Britain.

Increasing tongues activity is noticeable in the nineteenth century. This phenomenon was present in Britain among the Irvingites in the 1830s; in the United States in the frontier areas of the Second Great Awakening in the early 1800s; among the Mormons in the 1830s and 1890s; and in 1896 among a holiness group known as the Christian Union (later the Church of God [Cleveland, Tenn.]), the oldest Pentecostal church.⁴⁷ Speaking in tongues occurred throughout Christian history (admittedly at times in counterfeit forms), Pentecostals argue, but until the early twentieth century, it was considered an extraordinary event reserved for truly exceptional Christians and beyond the capacity of ordinary believers.

A second theory that explains the belated outbreak of twentieth-century tongues is what might be called the "fulfillment theory." Whereas the successionist theory appeals to historical precedent, the fulfillment theory appeals to biblical evidence, particularly to the "latter rain" mentioned by the prophet Joel:

> Be glad then, ye children of Zion, and rejoice in the Lord your God:
> for he hath given you the former rain moderately, and he will cause
> to come down for you the rain, the former rain, and the latter rain
> in the first month. . . . And it shall come to pass afterward, that I
> will pour out my spirit upon all flesh; and your sons and daughters
> shall prophesy, your old men shall dream dreams, your young men
> shall see visions. (Joel 2:23, 28, KJV)

In Acts 2:17–21, the apostle Peter quotes from Joel 2:28–32 to explain the descent of the Holy Spirit. What you are witnessing, said Peter to skeptics, was not drunken reveling but the fulfillment of the words spoken by the prophet Joel hundreds of years before. According to Pentecostal theologians, there was an *initial* fulfillment of Joel's prophecy at Pentecost, there is a *continuing* fulfillment during the present church age, and there will be an *ultimate* fulfillment at the Second Coming of Christ.⁴⁸ The present supernatural outpouring is to prepare God's people for the coming of Christ, to enable them to survive the Day of Judgment, and to empower them for witness. In this "latter rain" the restoration of the charismata was a sign of the imminent Second Coming of Christ.

Pentecostals also point to a supportive passage in James 5:7–8: "Be patient, therefore, beloved, until the coming of the Lord. The farmer waits for the precious crop from the earth, being patient with it until it receives the early and late rains. You also must be patient. Strengthen your hearts, for the coming of the Lord is near." The writer of James refers to the conditions in Palestine, where rainfall came in two seasons—an early rain in autumn (for initial planting) and a later rain in spring (for ripening at harvest). This rainfall pattern provides the image for Pentecostals in their understanding of their relationship to the early church. The original Pentecost was the "early rain" of the church, whereas the modern-day Pentecost was the "latter rain," with the outpouring of the Spirit in anticipation of the imminent return of Christ. Members of the first generation of modern Pentecostals were convinced that they were living in the last days before Christ would literally return to earth and establish his millennial (or thousand-year) kingdom. They were the key actors in this cosmic drama insofar as they were the recipients of this latter rain. Such a doctrine provided a rationale as to why signs and wonders and tongues should now reappear after such a long "drought."[49]

The latter rain theory fit into a larger myth of "fall" and "recovery," an ultra-supernaturalistic worldview that encompassed the successionist theory. The myth is expressed as follows: soon after the first century, the Christian church fell into apostasy. With the conversion of Constantine and the emergence of the Catholic Church, the primitive community of the Spirit degenerated into the worldly Roman Church, with its admixture of paganism and heresy. But a "saving remnant" survived the contempt and persecution of state and ecclesiastical authorities.

Beginning with the Protestant Reformation, several developments foreshadowed the latter rain. Luther asserted the doctrine of justification by faith alone, John Wesley recovered the doctrine of sanctification, and the holiness movement reinstituted the practice of healing. And now the baptism in the Spirit evidenced by the gift of tongues signaled that the final consummation was at hand.[50] The only sign remaining to be fulfilled was the worldwide propagation of the gospel. And xenoglossy would make possible the miraculous spread of Christianity. Agnes Ozman reportedly spoke in Chinese, Parham in Swedish, and others who followed in other foreign languages. Not until after 1907 did Pentecostals believe that tongues were anything but actual languages.[51] A supernaturally prepared missionary force would usher in the millennium.

Theological Antecedents

Other theological streams flowed into the making of modern Pentecostalism. The metaphor is apt, for Pentecostalism did not emerge de novo from its own wellspring but had its source in the headwaters of nineteenth-century radical evangelicalism. Among those who have ably navigated these waters are Edith Blumhofer and Grant Wacker, two of the more perceptive scholars of American Pentecostalism. Wacker describes Pentecostalism's origins as "above all, the product of clashing forces within the vast and amorphous holiness movement that had swept across evangelical Protestantism in the last third of the nineteenth century."[52]

Emerging out of this holiness milieu, Pentecostalism is traceable, observe Wacker and Blumhofer, to several closely related theological innovations whose institutional expressions were communicated in a vast array of publishing firms, tract societies, journals, camp meetings, annual conferences, independent churches, denominations, associations, and schools.[53] In particular, the National Holiness Association provided a loose interdenominational structure for the promotion of holiness. Despite the organic connection between the holiness and Pentecostal movements, most holiness groups vehemently re-jected the Pentecostal requisite of speaking in tongues, believing it to be un-scriptural.[54] Still, in the words of Wacker, "the momentum and direction" of this holiness environment "effectively predetermined that Holy Ghost ecstasy would emerge sooner or later."[55] At least four major theological developments contributed to the emergence of modern Pentecostalism.

1. The Wesleyan Influence: "Christian Perfection" or the "Second Blessing"

John Wesley, the founder of Methodist societies and a tireless preacher, teacher, and publisher of evangelical Christianity in Great Britain, exerted a profound influence on American spirituality. Although he was more of a practical re-former than an original thinker, Wesley's teaching of the sanctifying work of the Holy Spirit remains his theological legacy. In tracing the sources of Pen-tecostalism, Wesley's doctrine—albeit significantly altered in the American context—is fundamental. As scholars have affirmed repeatedly, without the Wesleyan holiness contribution there would have been no Pentecostalism.[56] For this reason, I give greater space to this theological innovation than to the others.

Methodism was a relative latecomer to America. Not until 1784 was the Methodist Episcopal Church formally organized in the infant nation. Whatever the movement lacked in longevity, however, it more than made up for in zeal, organizational structure, and populist appeal. As the American frontier ad-vanced, so did unlettered but disciplined, selfless Methodist circuit riders who, in the Second Great Awakening (1790s–1840s), barnstormed the country, led emotion-charged revivals, and established frontier camp meetings.

Like Pentecostals of the early twentieth century, Methodists of the early nineteenth century jumped, shouted, hollered, rocked, and rolled in religious ecstasy. They saw visions, dreamed dreams, believed in portents, prayed for healing, and held "love feasts." By 1850, the Methodists had overtaken the largest and most influential colonial denominations—the Congregationalists, Presbyterians, and Episcopalians—to become, with the Baptists not far behind, the largest Protestant denomination in the country.

Amid the wildfire spread of Methodism, Wesley's teaching on holiness, what he called "Christian perfection," faded somewhat into the background. By around midcentury, however, his views—or a variant thereof—gained heightened interest, transcended denominational boundaries, and eventually laid the foundation for the holiness movement. Wesley had argued that his views were not new but reflected teachings of Scripture that had been long neglected. Jesus, for example, instructed his followers to "be perfect as your Father who is in heaven is perfect" (Matt. 5:48) and throughout the writings of Paul, James, Peter, and John, a life of Christian perfection is urged.[57]

If perfection is commanded, reasoned Wesley, God would not leave Christians without the resources to become so. God who desires to implant the divine nature within humanity reciprocates a love for God. Wesley's reading of Scripture and his exposure to Christian writers, especially the fathers of Eastern Orthodox spirituality, led him to conclude that Christians can attain a perfect love. This perfection, or "entire sanctification" or "second blessing," Wesley taught, follows the "first blessing" of conversion. At conversion, a person's sins are forgiven (in theological terms, one is "justified") and the will is regenerated. Yet a sinful nature remains. Deliverance of "inbred sin" comes only with a second spiritual experience of entire sanctification, a cleansing act by which God makes one holy.

In his *Plain Account of Christian Perfection* (1766), a compendium of his views on the subject expressed over three decades, Wesley summarized what he called "the grand *depositum* of Methodism."[58] First, "Christian perfection is that love of God and our neighbour which implies a deliverance from *all sin*."[59] If a pure love fills the heart of a Christian, then there can be no room for sin. Wesley was not suggesting that no sins would be committed, for sins of ignorance or errors of judgment would occur by dint of the human condition; rather, sinful desires or intentions were eradicated to bring about perfection in love.

Second, Christian perfection is "received merely *by faith*" or a simple trust in God. Third, although "it is given *instantaneously*, in one moment," there is nevertheless "a gradual work both preceding and following that instant." The Christian continues to "grow in grace, in the knowledge of Christ, in the image of God."[60] Typically, that instant comes at death, though in some cases, it could be many years before.

Wesley's teaching on holiness crossed the Atlantic, but, in Wacker's words, "it underwent a partial sea change." In the context of pragmatic, optimistic, revivalistic mid-nineteenth-century America, Phoebe Palmer (1807–74) reduced his doctrine to a formula. Long neglected but recently rediscovered by religious historians, Palmer is variously hailed as the "Mother of the Holiness Movement" and "the most influential woman in the American Methodist Church in her century."[61] Beginning in 1835, Palmer and her sister Sarah Lankford led Tuesday Meetings for Promotion of Holiness, interdenominational prayer meetings held in homes in which entire sanctification was preached. This popular New York Methodist lay revivalist, holiness teacher, social reformer, feminist advocate, and prolific writer agreed with Wesley that the second blessing was instantaneous but disagreed that the process need be progressive. Devising what became known as "altar theology," Palmer drew upon Jesus' words that "the altar sanctifies the gift" (Matt. 23:19) and reasoned that if she "presented her body a living sacrifice" (Rom. 12:1) by "laying her all on the altar," then God would make her holy.

Palmer reduced the pursuit of entire sanctification to a simple three-step, nearly simultaneous process: entire *consecration* to God, a *faith* that God would make good on his promise to sanctify what he has consecrated, and a personal *testimony* to what God has done. Finally, Palmer popularized the phrase "Spirit baptism" or "baptism in the Spirit" as synonymous with the second blessing, and she instructed Christians to wait for, as she titled her book, "the promise of the Father." Although she never spoke in tongues, Palmer provided a theological rationale and vocabulary later appropriated by the Pentecostal movement.[62]

Near the end of the century, a Nebraska lawyer-turned-preacher named Benjamin Hardin Irwin revised and expanded Palmer's categories after encountering the writings of John Fletcher, Wesley's successor. In 1895, after experiencing a "baptism of fire" (Fletcher wrote of "baptism of the Holy Ghost and fire"), Irwin added a "third blessing," which he called "the fire," and organized the Fire-Baptized Holiness Association. He later encouraged followers to seek further experiences that he called the baptisms of dynamite, lyddite, and oxidite. As bizarre as these latter additions may seem, Irwin's distinctive third blessing of fire (called the "third blessing heresy" by holiness critics) met with popular approval and provided an important link in the emergence of Pentecostalism. Once speaking in tongues was added as the evidence of baptism in the Holy Ghost, the Pentecostal movement was born.

2. The Reformed Influence: The "Higher Life"

If according to the Gospel of John the Spirit "blows where it chooses" (3:8), then it must have chosen to blow with a gale force throughout America in the last quarter of the nineteenth century. As George Marsden has observed, "By 1870, holiness teachings of one sort or another seemed to be everywhere in American revivalist Protestantism."[63] Indeed, holiness teachings expanded beyond the Wesleyans to encompass those sympathetic to the Reformed perspective in what became known as the "higher life" movement. At first blush, reconciling the Calvinist conviction of human depravity and Methodist ideas of perfection seems improbable. In the Reformed understanding, a Christian's life was characterized by continual struggle and spiritual warfare, not a cheery confidence that perfection is attainable in this life. Despite God's act of regeneration, a sinful disposition (albeit now weakened) remained to thwart gains in holiness.

But if reconciliation between the Wesleyan and Reformed traditions was doubtful, a degree of synthesis was not. In the 1830s and 1840s a modified version of Methodist perfectionism, the "Oberlin Theology," was proposed by revivalist Charles Grandison Finney and his associate, Asa Mahan, though not until midcentury did various "higher life" teachings gain widespread popularity among Baptists, Congregationalists, and Presbyterians. With the publication of two best-sellers, William E. Boardman's *Higher Christian Life* (1859) and

Hannah Whithall Smith's *Christian's Secret to the Happy Life* (1875), the work of the Holy Spirit assumed center stage. At the same time, holiness teachings spread to England in the 1870s, when laity and clergy from America and England met for Bible study and the promotion of holiness in what would become an annual summer meeting at the scenic vacation village of Keswick. Though clearly a product of the American holiness movement, the Keswick Higher Life Movement soon developed its own indigenous tradition that refracted back to America.

What higher life advocates and Wesleyans shared was a two-stage view of the Christian life as one of initial conversion followed by a second work of sanctification or baptism in the Spirit. But higher life advocates rejected the notion that sin could ever by eradicated: the sinful nature could be subjugated or "counteracted" (a Keswick term) but not removed. Moreover, the second blessing of sanctification (viewed by Keswickians as repeated "fillings" with the Spirit) led not to a state of purity or sinless perfection but to an empowerment (or "endowment") by the Spirit for witness and service to Christ. As is apparent by the terminology invoked, theological nuances and complexities abounded within the higher life movement. What held it together and what it contributed to Pentecostalism's origins (though Pentecostals rejected the idea of repeated fillings) was a practical emphasis on an experience subsequent to conversion wherein the Spirit empowered one to witness.

3. Premillennialism

I return to a theme taken up in the discussion of latter rain doctrine—the imminent return of Christ. A preoccupation with God's judgment and Christ's return is as old as Christianity itself, but typically in movements whose focus is upon the Holy Spirit, a corresponding emphasis on eschatology is present. Just as the Spirit-led early church expected the imminent return of Christ, so in subsequent outpourings of the Spirit a similar expectancy abounded.

A key biblical text around which millennial thinking is derived is Revelation 20:1–10, where the author describes a period of peace and righteousness on earth when Satan is bound by an angel for a thousand years (a millennium). Historically, Christians have understood references to the millennium in roughly three ways, depending on where they place Christ's return in relation to the millennium and whether they expect a literal millennium. The Roman Catholic Church and the major Protestant traditions (e.g., Lutheran, Reformed, and Anglican) uphold the a-millennial position. According to this view, the thousand years is not a literal rule of Christ on earth but a figurative or symbolic reference to the period within the ministry of Christ and his Second Coming. Whereas what precedes and follows it is marked by struggle, the millennium is a time of respite.

Within the American revivalist tradition, two other millennial views successively prevailed. As early as the Great Awakening (1730s and 1740s), Jonathan Edwards proposed a postmillennial reading of the end times, convinced that Christ would return *after* (post-) the revivals of the mid-eighteenth-century Great Awakening inaugurated the beginning of the millennium. From this perspective, the new age would come through Christian teaching, preaching, and religious activity. Because the world was gradually getting better in anticipation of Christ's return, this view tended to be optimistic. Moreover, Christians who engaged in benevolent activities, social reform, and missionary outreach could actually play a role in ushering in the millennium. In the early nineteenth century, as Methodists rubbed shoulders with the indigenous revivalist tradition and experienced their own triumphs of holiness, they too embraced an optimistic postmillennial perspective.

However, as historical circumstances shifted, so too did the millennial paradigm. As evangelical Protestants witnessed the crumbling of their "righteous empire" during the latter decades of the nineteenth century, a new eschatological vision took hold. Beginning with the Civil War, the optimism inherent in the postmillennial view gave way to a more pessimistic reading of history, one that comported with a premillennial eschatology. According to this view, Christ would return *prior* to establishing his literal thousand-year reign. Various "signs of the times" heralded his imminent return: wars, apostasy, corruption, natural catastrophes, and the spread of the gospel to all nations.

In short, the world would get worse (in spite of the spreading gospel) before it would get better. One need only catalog the disruptions in American society to support this perspective: the devastation of the Civil War, the waves of threatening immigrants (Catholics, Jews, other non-Christians), the social strain created by industrialization and urbanization. Add to these the intellectual challenges posed by the rise of biblical higher criticism and the new sciences (geology, Darwinism) to conventional Christian views of Scripture and human origins, and the outlook was very gloomy indeed for traditional Protestants. The approaching end was identified not by progress but by degeneration. But even amid decline there was anticipation and hope, for Jesus' return at "any moment" energized the lives and ministries of hundreds of thousands of evangelicals.

Beginning in 1878, premillennial views were popularized at "prophecy conferences" by those such as Dwight L. Moody, the most popular revivalist of the day. Moody not only exposited Scripture's teaching regarding the end times but also, along with his associates such as R. A. Torrey, A. J. Gordon, and A. T. Pierson, emphasized that Christians should "walk in the Spirit" and experience the Spirit's "enduement with power for service." He even used the phrase "baptism in the Holy Spirit."[64] By the 1890s, premillennial views were firmly entrenched within the more radical wings of the holiness movement, and in the early twentieth century, these views would assume a dominant place in nearly all Pentecostal bodies. Convinced that the latter rain was itself a fulfillment of end-time prophecy, Pentecostals announced the "end of the age" and accentuated the role of the Holy Spirit in purifying believers for the coming of Christ and empowering them to evangelize the world.[65]

4. The "Faith Healing" Movement

Although Christians in all ages have believed in the miracle of physical healing, the most significant and direct theological influence upon Pentecostalism's embrace of faith healing came from the holiness movement.[66] The propagation of holiness teaching, with its emphasis upon "the baptism of the Holy Ghost," "the baptism of fire," and an "enduement of power," provided the theological milieu in which the supernatural gifts of God, including divine healing, could flourish. Once acknowledging that the Pentecostal power of Acts was still available for all believers, it was a logical step to affirm the accompanying spiritual gifts. Moreover, if sickness is ultimately the result of sin (with the fall came disease and sickness), and if the sanctified believer has power over sin, then that believer must have power over sickness as well (logic would seem to dictate that death could be overcome). Healing accompanied part of the purification of the nature from sin.

The single most important figure in the development of divine healing in America was the Episcopalian Charles Cullis, a medical doctor in Boston who convinced many holiness leaders that full salvation included the cure of body as well as soul. Among those he directly influenced were William Boardman; Hannah Whitall Smith; A. J. Gordon, pastor of the prestigious Clarendon Street Church in Boston; and A. B. Simpson, founder of the Christian and Missionary Alliance. In *The Ministry of Healing* (1882), a work considered a tour de force even by his critics, Gordon argued that Christ's earthly ministry was twofold: he healed the sick and forgave sinners; so the restoration of body and soul were in God's divine plan. Citing Matthew 8:17 ("Himself took our infirmities, and bare our sicknesses" [quoted from Isa. 53:4 and applied to Jesus]), Gordon suggested that in his atoning work on the cross Christ bore both the sin and the sickness of his people. A healing ministry was to be carried on by Christ's followers, for he instructed them "to lay hands on the sick and they shall recover" (Mark 16:18), and the promise was unconditionally given: "The prayer of faith shall save the sick and the Lord shall raise him up" (James 5:15). Simpson, healed of physical infirmities by Cullis in 1881, became one of the leading exponents of divine healing for nearly four decades. With Gordon, he located the source of healing in Christ's atonement which "reaches as far as the curse is found."

A discernible conversion experience, the baptism of the Spirit, the imminent return of Christ, the availability of divine healing—these theological themes (called in holiness-Pentecostal circles the "fourfold gospel" or "full gospel") converged in the life and teachings of Charles Fox Parham, a key figure within the first generation of Pentecostalism. Although permanently discredited when he was arrested on charges of committing "an unnatural offense" in 1907 (hence R. A. Torrey's blistering remark that Pentecostalism "was emphatically not of God, and founded by a Sodomite"), "to no one individual," writes Parham's biographer, "did the movement owe a greater debt."[67] When Parham added speaking in tongues as the initial evidence of baptism in the Holy Spirit to the "full gospel," Pentecostalism assumed its classic theological identity.

A brief sketch of Parham's early life reveals how the complex mingling of personal issues and theological convictions provided the context for the emergence of the Pentecostal movement.[68] His background and personality also typified the movement's earliest leaders: restless by nature, "come-outer" in ecclesiastical disposition, and marginal in social standing.

Born into a farming family in Iowa in 1873, Parham suffered from a variety of childhood ailments, including stunted growth (probably from encephalitis) and then, after the family moved to Kansas, rheumatic fever. As early as age nine he felt called to the ministry; at age twelve, following his devout mother's death, he converted and became involved in a local Congregational church. In 1890, he enrolled at Southwest Kansas College with the intention of preparing for the ministry. A year later, his call to the ministry was reaffirmed and his belief in divine healing confirmed after he survived a severe attack of rheumatic fever. He quit school in 1893 to become a supply pastor of several small Methodist churches. In the next two years Parham became increasingly attracted to holiness teaching and more firmly convinced of divine healing. He thus left the Methodist church in 1895 to embark on an independent ministry. A year later he married, and in 1898 the couple founded the Beth-el Healing Home in Topeka, and publicized holiness teachings in a bimonthly journal, the *Apostolic Faith*.

So captivated was Parham with holiness teaching that in the summer of 1900 he toured holiness religious centers around the country. A turning point in his understanding of the work of the Holy Spirit occurred during an extended stay at Frank W. Sandford's Holy Ghost and Us Bible School, a holiness commune in "Shiloh" (Durham), Maine. Sandford's emphasis on the latter rain encouraged Parham to seek a deeper spiritual experience. And when Sandford shared tales of xenoglossy among missionaries, Parham took these as a portent of the imminent return of Christ, for he was convinced that the supernatural creation of foreign-language-speaking missionaries would inaugurate a worldwide revival and hence usher in Christ's premillennial return.

In September, Parham returned to Topeka so charged with millennial fervor that he opened a Bible school to prepare prospective missionaries for the outpouring of the Holy Spirit. As noted, that outpouring came several months later. Of particular relevance here is the presentation of Parham as a paradigmatic figure of early Pentecostalism, for his life and thought clearly delineate the movement's theological and social roots. Parham uniquely defined Pentecostalism with his contention that baptism in the Holy Spirit was initially evidenced by speaking in tongues. Some five years later, the isolated sprinkling of the latter rain at Parham's Bible school gushed forth in a torrential outpouring in Los Angeles.

Pentecostalism's Beginnings, Part 2: The Azusa Street Revival

The Date: Monday evening, April 9, 1906
The Place: The home of Richard and Ruth Asberry, 214 N. Bonnie
Brae Street, Los Angeles
The Scene: Fire from heaven—a second Pentecost in Los Angeles,
"America's Jerusalem." Emboldened by news from William J. Seymour that Edward Lee has just spoken in tongues, a few members
of a Bible study and prayer group erupt into glossolalia. News of the
event spreads quickly and attracts growing numbers. Within a week
the group rents an old building at 312 Azusa Street. The Azusa
Street revival begins.

Charles Fox Parham may be the recognized founder of the Pentecostal movement, but William J. Seymour (1870–1922), the one-eyed black Baptist minister, is the single individual largely responsible for its spread. The Seymour-initiated Azusa Street revival is often viewed as the epicenter of the explosion of Pentecostalism, the "ground zero" that sent spiritual shock waves around the world. This contention, though not without some merit, is suggestive of the same kind of mythmaking observed with the "Topeka Pentecost." To attribute the early stages of Pentecostalism to these two events alone admittedly homogenizes a diverse and complex movement (e.g., a 1904 revival in Wales convinced many that this powerful awakening was the second Pentecost), but nevertheless they do provide a handle to grasp Pentecostalism's beginnings.[69]

Like Parham, Seymour's early career deserves attention not only because it illustrates the cluster of theological distinctives associated with Pentecostalism but also because it demonstrates the socioeconomic, interracial, interethnic, and ecumenical character of the early movement. Pentecostalism is one of the few religious movements, at least in its earliest stage, to transcend racial and ethnic barriers.[70]

The details of Seymour's early life are at best sketchy, owing no doubt to his family's impoverished background.[71] Born in Centreville, Louisiana, to parents who were former slaves, he was raised as a Baptist and, as with other shamanlike figures, given to dreams and visions in his youth. In 1895 he migrated to Indianapolis where he waited on tables at an upscale hotel and joined a local black congregation of the Methodist Episcopal Church. A nasty bout with the smallpox left him blind in his left eye. By age thirty he was living in Cincinnati, where he was introduced to the holiness movement. Soon he was "saved and sanctified" and joined up with the Church of God Reformation movement, also known as the Evening Light Saints, a revivalist group of radical Wesleyans whose distinctive teachings included healing and latter rain doctrine. Acting on a prior conviction to enter the ministry (prompted by his encounter with smallpox), Seymour was licensed and ordained as a Church of God minister.

In 1903 he moved to Houston and attended a black holiness church pastored by Lucy Farrow. When Farrow went to Kansas in 1905 to serve as a governess in the home of Charles Parham, Seymour took over as pastor. Farrow returned in October 1905 but not before her indoctrination in Pentecostal theology culminated in Holy Spirit baptism evidenced by speaking in tongues. As for Parham, during a four-year whirlwind tour he spread his message through Kansas, Missouri, and, in early 1905, Texas, where Farrow was initially exposed to his teachings.

Later in 1905, Parham opened another Bible school to train missionary evangelists. When Seymour heard of Parham's Houston Bible school, he sought him out and begged to be admitted. But Parham was a white man, a member of the Ku Klux Klan, and operated in a segregated Jim Crow South. How could Seymour be exposed to Parham's teachings? Something of a compromise—more indicative of Parham's paternalism than racism—was reached. Seymour was allowed to attend his lectures, but he would have to sit outside the classroom, where he could hear the lectures through either a partly opened window or classroom door. For five weeks Seymour listened intently to Parham's lectures, studied the Bible, and prayed fervently for the baptism in the Spirit as evidenced by tongues—but to no avail.

Meanwhile, at his Houston church, Seymour encountered a young woman from a recently established holiness church in Los Angeles. She invited him to visit her home church with the possibility of becoming its associate pastor. Seymour accepted an offer after the church's founder and pastor, Julia Hutchins, urged him to come. He arrived in this fastest growing city in the nation amid a holiness revival that by 1906 included more than one hundred churches preaching the "full gospel." A year earlier, F. B. Meyer brought first-hand reports of the great Welsh revival, and as early as 1903, Frank Bartleman, an independent holiness minister, arrived to conduct revival campaigns. Holiness people were abuzz in anticipation of the outpouring of the Spirit, though few expected it would come from an Azusa Street livery stable in the middle of an urban ghetto.

In Seymour's first sermon, much to the consternation of Hutchins, he preached from Acts 2:4 and urged the necessity of the Pentecostal experience.

Disowned by Hutchins and then locked out of the church, Seymour eventually found refuge at the wooden bungalow of the Asberrys on Bonnie Brae Street. There he continued to preach the doctrine of tongues to an assemblage of blacks and whites from a variety of holiness churches. After two weeks of Bible study and expectant prayer for revival, the much sought after experience came: Seymour and others spoke in tongues. News of this supernatural outpouring spread. Crowds filled the street to hear Seymour preach from the Asberrys' porch. More space was needed, and so a run-down African Methodist Episcopal Church, recently converted to a warehouse and livery, was rented.

On April 14 Seymour held his first meeting at 312 Azusa Street. By April 18, amid apocalyptic fever triggered by the fire and destruction of the San Francisco earthquake, a thousand people crowded into the forty-by-sixty foot makeshift chapel. Services began in the late mornings and continued until midnight. Though directed by Seymour, who usually sat behind the pulpit with his head bowed in prayer, the meetings often broke out into spontaneous eruptions of testimonies and prayers; altar calls for salvation, sanctification, and the baptism of the Spirit; extemporaneous sermons by "Elder" Seymour and visiting preachers; and visible signs of being "slain in the Spirit" or "fallen under the power." Jennie Evans Moore, an African American and the first woman at the Azusa Street revival to speak in tongues, recalled her experience:

> When the evening came, we attended the meeting [and] the power
> of God fell and I was baptized in the Holy Ghost fire. It seemed as
> if a vessel broke within me and water surged up through my being,
> which when it reached my mouth came out in a torrent of speech in
> the language which God had given me. . . . I sang under the power
> of the Spirit in many languages. . . . The Spirit led me to the piano,
> where I played and sang under inspiration, although I had not
> learned to play.[72]

At times silence reigned; more often a "Holy Ghost bedlam" prevailed. Every day of the week for nearly three years, the Azusa Street revival persisted, attracting inquisitors, seekers, skeptics, spiritualists, hecklers, and people of all races from every station in life. The Los Angeles Daily Times covered the revival and could conceal neither its scorn nor its sensationalist rhetoric: "Weird Babel of Tongues—New Sect of Fanatics Is Breaking Loose—Wild Scene Last Night on Azusa Street—Gurgle of Wordless Talk by a Sister," ran the headlines. Nor in a day of strict segregation did it overlook the mixed racial composition of those overcome by the Spirit, especially blacks. The Times recounted the "shouts of an old colored 'mammy'; in a frenzy of religious zeal" who, in "the strangest harangue ever uttered," cried out, " 'You-oo-oo gou-loo-loo come under the bloo-oo-oo boo-loo.' . . . Colored people and a sprinkling of whites compose the congregation, and night is hideous in the neighborhood by the howling of worshippers, who spend hours swaying forth and back in a nerve-wracking attitude of prayer and supplication. They claim to have the 'gift of tongues' and to be able to comprehend the babble."[73]

The contagion soon spread to the many other revivalist-holiness churches in the Los Angeles area and then raged along the Pacific Coast. Evangelists, missionaries, church executives, and publishers, many of them merely curious but others hoping for renewed spiritual power, passed through the Azusa Street Mission and carried the news elsewhere. The revival quickly spread across the country to Chicago and New York and to receptive regions in the South and Midwest. Almost as quickly the revival assumed an international dimension, spurred by the conviction among many that tongues had been given for missionary outreach. Pentecostal missionaries conducted revivals in Canada, England, Germany, Scandinavia, China, the Philippines, Hong Kong, Japan, India, South Africa, Egypt, Liberia, and South America. Within two years of the Azusa Street outpouring, the fervor of Pentecostalism had spread to fifty countries.[74]

At the same time, this outpouring of the Spirit became fraught with tension and soon fractured. An inclusive Pentecostal community, bound initially by the presence of the Spirit, mimicked the dizzying array of "come-outer" holiness groups from whence it had come. Seymour hoped for an ally when he asked Parham for ministerial credentials, but he was sorely disappointed when his "spiritual father" repudiated the work as of demonic "spiritualists" and attacked the revival as "Southern Darkey camp meetings" after a visit in October 1906.[75]

Frank Bartleman, an early participant at Seymour's mission and soon-to-become pioneer evangelist of Pentecostalism, offered a distinctly different perspective when he reported that at Azusa Street, "The color line has been washed away by the blood."[76] But by 1914 the color-blind character of the movement had disappeared, Azusa Street Mission became a local black church, and the movement reverted to the segregated pattern of American denominations. By 1908, Seymour's outreach ministry was effectively crippled when two female colleagues made off with the mailing list of the *Apostolic Faith*, the mission's widely circulated journal, with fifty thousand subscribers. Their theft was motivated largely by their opposition to Seymour's marriage to Jenny Moore, which, they believed, in light of the imminent return of Christ, distracted Seymour from carrying out the Great Commission.

Moreover, between 1906 and 1914, doctrinal disagreements surfaced over a range of issues, though most centered on the order, meaning, and even the necessity of tongues. Seymour himself eventually rejected speaking in tongues as the initial evidence of baptism in the Holy Spirit, calling it "an open door for witches and spiritualists and free loveism."[77] The "finished work" controversy polarized Pentecostals into two distinct theological camps. Those of Wesleyan-holiness persuasion viewed Christian development in three distinct stages (conversion, sanctification, baptism in the Spirit), whereas those with more Baptistic-Calvinist inclinations assigned sanctification to the act of conversion based on the "finished work of Christ on Calvary"—a distinct view of the Assemblies of God denomination. In addition, the Assemblies was racked by the "Jesus only" controversy, which resulted in a further splintering into several Pentecostal "Unitarian" denominations.[78]

Disagreements extended from abstract theology to practical behavior. Is wearing a necktie "worldly"? What about "mixed" bathing (swimming) of the sexes? (We had to confront this not so insignificant issue when members of my grandfather's church visited his lake house.) As scholars of Pentecostalism have observed, these many disagreements did not weaken but strengthened the movement. The more Pentecostals divided, the more they multiplied, so that by 1920, the movement in America had evolved into twenty-five separate denominations and hundreds of independent churches, though four main denominations encompassed the majority of Pentecostals: Church of God in Christ, Church of God (Cleveland, Tennessee), Pentecostal Holiness Church, and the Assemblies of God.

The Azusa Street revival remains the defining moment in the history of modern Pentecostalism. "Directly or indirectly," observes Vinson Synan, "practically all of the Pentecostal groups in existence can trace their lineage to the Azusa Mission."[79] Baptism in the Spirit—initiated by Seymour, embraced by the thousands who passed through the mission, and preached by the hundreds who carried the message around the nation and the world—meant above all a power for witness and service. "But you will receive power," Jesus told his followers, "when the Holy Spirit has come upon you; and you will be my witnesses in Jerusalem, in all Judea and Samaria, and to the ends of the earth" (Acts 1:8). With this fresh outpouring of the Spirit signaling the imminent return of Christ, a supernatural centrifugal force propelled men and women to the ends of the earth.

The Question of Social Factors

By and large I have focused on the theological and biblical background in the making of modern Pentecostalism and ignored social explanations. Can we explain the rise of Pentecostalism by looking at the kinds of people who were initially drawn to the movement? Generally speaking, we may view the rise of Pentecostalism as one more chapter in America's search for religious identity insofar as restlessness and innovation have characterized American religious life since the arrival of the first Puritans. Pentecostalism bears the indelible stamp "Made in the USA."

At the same time, scholars have long noted that early Pentecostalism drew many of its first adherents from the fringes of society in geographic areas of social ferment. The movement took root among poor whites, disenfranchised blacks, and powerless women in regions suffering disruption of a traditional way of life. This near-exclusive attraction among those on the periphery, some conclude, was related to efforts to compensate for social deprivation.

The movement is thus viewed as a lower-class religious protest against the social exclusiveness and religious coldness of middle-class mainstream Protestantism. The alienated, disadvantaged, and powerless were drawn to Pentecostalism as a way of gaining prestige and power. In a period of vast economic, social, and cultural changes, the material losers in this life compensated for their lack of status and thus became spiritual winners in the life to come. Their millenarian reading of current events proclaimed the existing world beyond human redemption and subject to imminent destruction, but out of this predicament would come the supernatural creation of a new heaven and a new earth. How could one compare the power of humans with the power of God? In short, as Robert Mapes Anderson argues, Pentecostalism originated as a lower-class, plain-folk religion responding in typical ways (in an ecstatic and millenarian fashion) to the cultural crises of the late nineteenth century.[80]

Undoubtedly this explanation has merit. In one form or another, this interpretation has been invoked by social scientists and other historians for whom popular religious movements mean little more than a flight from social reality to the comforts of social passivity and ecstatic escape. But as Albert Miller and Grant Wacker observe, the social deprivation theory explains only part of the story. Conditions where Pentecostalism flourished—more often in areas of social upheaval than social stability—existed in other parts of the country where Pentecostalism was absent. Put another way, if Pentecostalism attracted the disinherited, queries Miller, why did not all the disinherited become Pentecostals? In his recent book, Wacker challenges the compensatory theory by suggesting that Pentecostalism freed its adherents from old commitments and opened them to new opportunities to change their present situation. Moreover, after reviewing demographic data on early Pentecostals, Wacker questions whether in fact the movement attracted the socially disinherited: "Most Pentecostals, though hardly comfortable by modern standards, lived comfortably by the standards of their own day. . . . They lived pretty much like everybody else."[81]

In the end, the issues surrounding the social origins of Pentecostalism raise yet another question of whether the religious convictions of Pentecostals can be reduced to "nothing but" a set of social conditions. What sociologists refer to as a "functional" view of religion—the way that religion *does* something for an individual or group—is undoubtedly a useful but ultimately incomplete explanation for the rise of Pentecostalism. Suffice it to say that a wide range of complex factors encompassing novel theological convictions, dynamic social conditions, and peculiar psychological perspectives converged to generate the Pentecostal movement.

Conclusion: The Charismatic Movement and Beyond

In the mid-1960s, at about the same time that our summer vacations at Grandpa Basye's came to an end, the Charismatic Movement burst on the scene with full force. This "new Pentecost," occurring outside of traditional Pentecostal denominations as a renewing agency within older, established denominations, emphasized "Spirit-baptized" Christianity without demanding the initial evidence of speaking in tongues or, in most cases, the necessity of speaking in tongues. The movement's beginnings in North America are typically associated with Rector Dennis Bennett's announcement to his St. Mark's Episcopal Parish in Van Nuys, California, on Easter Sunday, 1960, that he had spoken in tongues.

To be sure, the roots of the Charismatic Movement (sometimes differentiated by reference to Protestant neo-Pentecostalism and Catholic Charismatic Renewal) are traceable to earlier developments, but Bennett's announcement at this upscale, liturgical church—an unlikely environment for "Holy Ghost" religion—was picked up by *Time* and *Newsweek* and given national prominence. Prior to Bennett's declaration, in the 1940s and 1950s, healing evangelists such as Oral Roberts and William Branham spread the Pentecostal message beyond traditional Pentecostal boundaries. And in 1951 Demos Shakarian, a California millionaire dairy farmer, founded the Full Gospel Business Men's Fellowship International (FGBMFI) as an organization of Spirit-filled businessmen to reach out to non-Pentecostals.

Then, in 1955, several pastors in the American Episcopal Church experienced speaking in tongues, related their baptism of the Spirit to parishioners, and encouraged anointing of the sick and prayer for healing. By the early 1960s, members of nearly every major Protestant denomination had experienced Spirit baptism, and in 1967, Charismatic Renewal surfaced among Catholics at Duquesne University in Pittsburgh and the Universities of Notre Dame and Michigan. By the 1970s, nearly every American denomination drew up an official church position statement regarding Spirit baptism, and a number of major communions (Catholic, Episcopal, Baptist, Lutheran, Reformed, Methodist) held their first national Charismatic Renewal conferences and publicized the movement through newsletters.[82]

Given the variety of denominational and theological traditions swept up into the movement, the nature of Spirit baptism was defined in several ways. Some Protestant neo-Pentecostals affirmed Spirit baptism as a second-stage development in the Christian life, that is, as a distinct experience following conversion. Catholic charismatics linked Spirit-baptism to the sacraments and rejected the classical Pentecostal view of a special group of those who are Spirit-baptized. As the 1974 Malines (Belgium) Document noted, "The decisive coming of the Spirit by virtue of which one becomes a Christian is related to the celebration of Christian initiation" (primarily baptism but also confirmation and the Eucharist). There is a "theological" sense in which every member of the Christian community is baptized in the fullness of the Spirit in the sacraments, and a subsequent "experiential" sense when that which is given in sacramental initiation comes into conscious experience of the Spirit.[83] This latter expression of the Spirit in the outward manifestation of charismata in service to the church and world (thus minimizing speaking in tongues) is what Catholics call Charismatic Renewal.

Unlike classical Pentecostalism, whose originating dynamic came from below as a popular religious movement, Charismatic Renewal originated predominantly from above, among leaders of established denominations and even the World Council of Churches (thanks to Du Plessis's influence), who then spread the message and experience of renewal to parishioners. At its core however, Charismatic Renewal includes the whole spectrum of Christians, lay and clerical. Kilian McDonnell observes that Catholic Charismatic Renewal "is a populist movement," because "everyone has some charism to exercise: a prayer to offer, a song to sing, a service to the sick to perform, a teaching ministry to carry out, a community to build. Everybody is a participant."[84]

According to Martin Marty, Charismatic Renewal was made possible by a mutual acceptance between Pentecostals and the larger religious culture.[85] Two things happened. First, Pentecostals such as Shakarian and his FGBMFI modified the Pentecostal distinctive of tongues as initial evidence in reaching out to a wider audience. For example, Catholics involved in renewal at Notre Dame received encouragement from the president of the South Bend chapter of the FGBMFI (as well as local Assemblies of God laypeople and ministers).[86] Second, those within the wider culture, such as Bennett and John Sherrill, became receptive to the Pentecostal message of Spirit baptism manifested by speaking in tongues and other charismata. Sherrill, the son of a famous Presbyterian educator, evolved from a curious outsider to a participant to an enthusiastic advocate of the Charismatic Movement in his popular book, *They Speak with Other Tongues* (1964).

Moreover, Pentecostals not only accommodated to the larger culture—initially pacifists opposed to World War I, they increasingly supported America's twentieth-century wars.[87] They also became concerned with status—once satisfied with unaccredited, storefront Bible schools, in 1964 they opened the fully accredited, professionally oriented, modern-designed Oral Roberts University in Tulsa, Oklahoma. Clearly, by the 1960s Pentecostals were well represented in the middle class, with a few attaining substantial wealth. Something happened. Over several generations, a movement evolved "from boundlessness to consolidation"—from Holy Ghost unstructured exuberance to organized denominations, to the expansion of denominational bureaucracies, seminaries, and systematic theologies. In classical sociological terms, a sect had become a church. Worldwide, Pentecostalism remains overwhelmingly a haven of the masses (nearly 90 percent of all Pentecostals are poor), but in the United States, Pentecostals have moved steadily into the middle and upper-middle income brackets.

I was an indirect beneficiary of Pentecostal social mobility. By the late 1950s my grandfather had the financial resources to purchase sizable acreage just outside of Hope, Arkansas. He grew watermelons for market, created an artificial lake, and built a comfortable lake house—our family vacation Shangri-la. Given his personal integrity and business acumen (he managed and then became partner in a wood handle factory), Grandpa Basye commanded respect in the Hope community. At the same time, he remained something of an outsider to the power structure of this small town, dominated as it was by those from more "respectable" denominations (namely, Southern Baptist and Methodist).

In revealing ways, the location and physical structure of my grandfather's church spoke volumes about the social status of Pentecostals. Hope Gospel Tabernacle was located in the northeast section of town, in a white, working-class neighborhood, several blocks away from the African Methodist Church and the all-black section of a then totally segregated community. Ironically, this Assemblies of God tabernacle was an old converted roller skating rink, now occupied by those dubbed "holy rollers." As for Grandpa Basye, he was the only white-collar professional in the church. His parents, first-generation Pentecostals with earlier ties to the Christian and Missionary Alliance (CMA Pentecostals eventually led the Assemblies of God), had passed on their spiritual legacy to their son. Despite a certain emotional reserve and southern propriety, Grandpa Basye gave initial evidence of Holy Spirit baptism by speaking in tongues and then subsequently exercised the spiritual gifts of prayer language and prophetic interpretation.

My grandfather had less success in bequeathing the Pentecostal legacy to his children. His oldest, a daughter, married a local Southern Baptist, and for nearly fifty years she served as organist for the First Baptist Church in Hope. His youngest child, a son, became involved in Independent Bible churches in Ohio. And his middle child, my mother, married a man with a Swedish Lutheran background. This family religious genealogy represents a microcosm of religion in America, where faith has rarely been a genetic given. Additionally, the parting of Pentecostal ways points beyond the United States to another, historic chapter in the Pentecostal movement. Although Pentecostal bodies in the United States continue to grow at a considerably faster rate than other denominations, stupendous gains have occurred in other parts of the world, including Latin America, Africa, Russia, and Korea. In a single century, "tongues of fire" have borne witness from the "American Jerusalem" of Los Angeles to the ends of the earth, making global Pentecostalism the most striking religious phenomenon of the twentieth century.

8

"One in Christ Jesus"

Women's Ministry and Ordination

There is no longer Jew or Greek, there is no longer slave or free, there is no longer male and female; for all of you are one in Christ Jesus.

—Galatians 3:28

On September 15, 1853, Luther Lee delivered the ordination sermon of the Reverend Antoinette Brown at the First Congregational Church of South Butler, New York. The occasion marked the first time that a woman was fully ordained in a major denomination in America and, more remarkably, perhaps the first ordination of a woman in the history of Christianity. Lee, a fiery leader of the re-formist and revivalist Wesleyan Methodist Connection in America, entitled his sermon "Woman's Right to Preach the Gospel." In his introductory remarks he observed that some Christian communions permitted women to preach, but none had gone so far as to grant them full equality in ministry. Although admitting reservations about the necessity of a formal ordination—he believed the "call" of God to preach was sufficient—Lee sensed the historic importance of this occasion. He would participate in the ordination service of the first woman minister in Christian history.[1]

At first glance, it seems unusual that a Methodist would preach at the ordination service of a Congregationalist, but the shared re-formist commitments of Lee and Brown, first to abolitionism and then to women's rights, transcended denominational differences. Not only did reformism promoted ecumenism, but religious convic-tion, deeply rooted in the evangelical revivalism of Charles Finney, also fueled social reform, including the first women's rights movement in the United States. In 1848 the Wesleyan Methodists of Seneca Falls, New York, opened their church for the first women's rights convention. Included among the convention's goals was the "overthrow of the monopoly of the pulpit, and for securing to woman an equal participation with men."[2] Brown, a "Finneyite" and a participant at the convention, was now formally challenging this monopoly five years later.

And so Lee, after initially turning down Brown's invitation to deliver the ordination sermon, preached what has become a classic defense for the full inclusion of women in Christian ministry. For his sermon text he chose Galatians 3:28: "There is neither male nor female; for ye are all one in Christ Jesus" (KJV). Lee confessed that the selection of this text was as unusual as the occasion itself and wondered aloud why his understanding of the text had "lain hid until this hour?"[3] From the ancient days of the church fathers to Lee's time, the traditional interpretation of Galatians 3:28 held that the text referred to a person's standing before God (*coram Deo*) and not, as Lee was arguing, to social relations that included women's equal participation in church ministry. In his letter to the Christians in Galatia, the apostle Paul declares unequivocally that through faith in Jesus Christ, all persons have equal access to and equal standing before God. One group is not privileged over another. Racial, ethnic, social, and sexual differences are meaningless in God's eyes. All are one in Christ Jesus.

True enough, admitted Lee, but the application of the text extended beyond the one-dimensional vertical divine-human relationship to the horizontal plane of relations among Christians. Moreover, the text had been "discovered and understood" but not "practically applied, as has been the case with a great many other truths." Lee (and almost every other nineteenth-century feminist) appealed to the well-known British Methodist scholar Adam Clarke, who in his 1837 New Testament commentary concluded that Galatians 3:28 meant that Christian men and women "have equal *rights*, equal *privileges*, and equal *blessings;* and let me add, they are equally *useful.*" Lee drew out the concrete application from Clarke's comment: "I cannot see how the text can be explained so as to exclude females from any right, office, work, privilege, or immunity which males enjoy, hold or perform. If the text means anything, its means that males and female are equal in rights, privileges and responsibilities upon the Christian platform."[4] And it means that properly qualified (i.e., "called") women such as Antoinette Brown can serve as equals with males in ministry.

In addition to invoking Galatians 3:28, Lee summoned three other biblical arguments to support women's full participation in Christian ministry. First, women exercised leadership and authority throughout Scripture, both in the days of Israel and in the early church. "All antiquity agrees that there were female officers and teachers in the Primitive Church, the only dispute being about what their functions were, and by what title they were known." Second, women shared in the outpouring of the Holy Spirit at Pentecost. In the Book of Acts (2:17), Peter quoted Joel 2:8: "And it shall come to pass afterward, that I will pour out my Spirit upon all flesh; and your sons and *your daughters* shall prophesy." Men and women spoke with prophetic authority in the early church, including Philip's daughters (Acts 21:9) and women in Paul's churches (1 Cor. 11:5). Third, women have an authoritative claim in the church inasmuch as they were the first witnesses to Christ's resurrection and were commissioned by him to announce it to the disciples. As we will see, Lee's main arguments in support of women's ministry continue to be cited in the contemporary debate. To be sure, the arguments are more extensive and sophisticated, grounded in more rigorous exegesis and methodology, yet nonetheless they mirror the four main biblical arguments sketched out by Lee.

Lee not only defended the propriety of women's call to ministry but also answered critics who appealed to two New Testament texts (1 Cor. 14:34–35; 1 Tim. 2:11–12) explicitly prohibiting women's public role in ministry. As characterizes contemporary solutions to these apparent counterarguments, Lee reconciled the contradictory texts by restricting their intent. He contended that we are to "regard these two texts as local and specific in their application, founded upon some peculiarity in the circumstances of the community at that time and in those places, and as having no general bearing on the question."[5] These texts, purportedly barring women from public ministry, applied to a particular time in a particular place and in a particular context and thus had no universal application.

Such were Lee's arguments in defense of women's ministry. What about the Reverend Antoinette Brown? Did her ordination open the floodgates of women's ordination into the Congregational ministry? Brown's ordination marked an inauspicious beginning for women clergy. Her ministry lasted but a few years. The Congregational Church of South Butler called and ordained her more out of desperation for a permanent pastor than from the conviction that Brown and the congregation were suitably matched. Disillusioned by her experience, Brown (Blackwell after her 1856 marriage) never again served a Congregational church and eventually joined the Unitarians. Moreover, her pioneering efforts drew few followers. Although the First Congregational Church was within its jurisdictional rights to ordain a woman, the Congregational General Conference opposed it. For more than a century, resistance within the denomination at both the leadership and lay level assured that few women were actually ordained. In 1889, only four women were listed as ministers in the Congregational yearbook, and as late as the 1950s, women constituted a mere 3 percent of the Congregational clergy.[6]

Not until the end of the 1970s did this trend change. By 1980, 9 percent of the clergy in what had now become the United Church of Christ (UCC; a merger of Congregationalists and several other bodies) were women, and by 1990 that percent had doubled. This trend is expected to continue in other

American Protestant denominations. Today more than one-third of seminary students are women, and in mainline Protestant denominations (e.g., UCC, United Methodist Church, American Baptist Church, Presbyterian Church in the U.S.A., Lutheran Church in America, U.S. Episcopal Church, Disciples of Christ, African Methodist Episcopal Church), nearly one-half are women.[7]

The slight gain in the number of women clergy from 1853 to 1970 raises the question of the actual impact of a text like Galatians 3:28. Did the Bible play a necessary but only tangential role in the movement to ordain women? Were there other pressures or forces at work—for example, the women's movement—that were more critical in bringing the issue to the fore? So thinks sociologist Mark Chaves, who argues that "a century of stalemate on the issue suggests that there is no compelling reason internal to the Bible to grant interpretive primacy either to the texts opposing gender equality or to the texts supporting gender equality."[8] Chaves locates the current support or opposition to women's ordination in a group's openness or resistance to the modern world. In turn, this cultural stance affects the way one approaches and interprets key biblical texts dealing with men and women.

No doubt such reasoning rankles many biblical scholars, who stake their professional reputations on their "correct" interpretation of texts. But Chaves's argument and Lee's self-awareness of an alternative reading of Scripture address the primary issue I have raised throughout this book, namely, how certain texts, discovered to have new and pregnant meaning, resonate with a certain individual or group and take on a life and history of their own. Once again, Lee and Chaves remind us that we are confronted with the serendipitous conjunction of a text—in this case the text that became the locus classicus in defense of women's ministry—and historical situations that provide the receptive environment for the text's appeal and particular interpretation.

The right of women to preach, first broached in the nineteenth century by Lee, Brown, and others during the "first wave" of the women's rights movement, resurfaced with renewed intensity during the "second wave" of the movement, beginning in the 1960s. Clearly, the rising number of women clergy not only in the UCC but also in other communions attests to the impact of the feminist movement upon Christian churches. At the same time, the decline of women clergy in some Protestant evangelical denominations, attributed in large part to the fundamentalist-modernist controversy in the early decades of the twentieth century, also attests to the impact, albeit negative, of the feminist movement. In the eyes of fundamentalists and other Protestant conservatives, women's ordination came to (and does) symbolize the capitulation of other Christian bodies to the "humanistic liberation theology of our age."[9]

Today those denominations that once authorized women's ordination or encouraged women's preaching, including the Church of the Nazarene (Holiness), the Assemblies of God (Pentecostal), and the Evangelical Free Church (Pietist), rarely or no longer do so. In recent denominational discussions, opponents of women's ordination invariably cite secular forces (e.g., the state or the women's movement), not a reasoned understanding of Scripture, as the driving force behind the plea to ordain women. At a 1984 national gathering of Southern Baptists, for instance, when "messengers" (representatives) broached the issue of women's ordination, the convention resolved not to "decide concerns of Christian doctrine and practice by modern cultural, sociological, and ecclesiastical trends or by emotional factors."[10]

To say the least, demands for and the entrance of women into the ordained ministry have sparked controversy—and a host of Web sites. No other issue in our time (homosexuality ranks a close second) has provoked such heated debate in ecclesiastical circles. Virtually every Christian denomination and organization has been forced to address the role of women in ministry. Most Protestant denominations have resolved the issue in favor of women's ordination; other major Christian traditions, however, such as Roman Catholicism, Orthodoxy, and a variety of bodies within American fundamentalism and evangelicalism, continue to resist granting women full priestly or pastoral authority.

As in the nineteenth-century debate, contemporary proponents of women's ordination uplift Galatians 3:28 as *the* crucial text.[11] The text is, it seems, as ubiquitous as the John 3:16 banners displayed at professional sporting events. Its appeal cuts across denominational boundaries and a wide spectrum of theological positions, although given the historical Protestant emphasis on *sola scriptura*, the text has greater authoritative weight than, say, in Orthodoxy, where tradition places certain boundaries around innovative interpretations of Scripture. In his programmatic essay *The Bible and the Role of Women* (1958; English translation, 1966), Krister Stendahl, the Swedish Lutheran New Testament scholar and professor at Harvard Divinity School, referred to Galatians 3:28 as Paul's "breakthrough."[12] Other proponents of women's ordination call it the "Magna Carta of Humanity," "the women's text," and "a cardinal statement in the Scriptures FOR the emancipation of men and women."[13] Opponents retort that Galatians 3:28 has been grossly "misused," "does not concern ministries," and is "wholly irrelevant" to the question of women holding office.[14]

Galatians 3:28 in the History of Interpretation

As is often the case in heated disputes, contending factions appeal to historical precedent to support their position. Opponents of women's ordination point to previous interpretations of Galatians 3:28 and observe that up until the nineteenth century, no orthodox Christian commentator ever took the verse to imply what modern interpreters suggest that it implies. There is simply no evidence that Galatians 3:28 was ever applied directly to the issue of what is called today the "ordained ministry."

Ancient Christian writers in the Greek East and Latin West construed the text in a variety of ways, but according to recent scholars, none supposed the text had anything to do with women in ministry.[15] For some, including the fourth-century Cappadocian Fathers (Gregory of Nazianzus and Gregory of Nyssa) and Augustine (d. 430), the text referred to the transcendence of ethnic, class, and gender differences among the saints. To be made in the "image" (or "prototype") of God (Gen. 1:26–27) or to be a "new creation" in Christ (2 Cor. 5:17)—identified as "intelligence" or the "rational element"—transcended sexual distinctions. Humankind in the image of God is not sexed; rather, sex is superimposed on the original image. Similarly, Galatians 3:28 had "now and not yet" eschatological implications. The now perfecting and the completed perfected soul in the eternal kingdom, according to Origen (d. ca. 254), John Chrysostom (d. 407), Paulinus of Nola (d. 431), Augustine, and Jerome (d. 420), surpassed masculine, feminine, and neuter categories.[16]

Other writers emphasized that those who are members of Christ, the "true wisdom," share a common spiritual bond of unity in which there are neither male nor female divisions. Offering an additional interpretation of Galatians 3:28, Chrysostom suggested that those "in Christ" represented an ideal of a past era when men and women practiced virtues transcending stereotypical character traits: "women practiced self-denial" and "manly courage," and men exhibited "gravity and chastity." For a number of other ancient commentators, including Athanasius (d. 373), Palladius (d. 425), the Syrian Aphraates (early fourth century), and Jerome, "neither male nor female" referred to a Christian's ideal state of liberation from the desires and impediments of the flesh. This celibate, chaste, and ascetic ideal anticipated the resurrected age to come, where the saints "neither marry nor are given in marriage, but are as the angels in heaven" (Matt. 22:30).[17]

Despite the recent upsurge in the ordination of women in Lutheran and Reformed Protestant denominations, neither Luther nor Calvin, the two theological giants from whom these traditions trace their roots, interpreted Galatians 3:28 as opening opportunities for women in ministry. To be sure, their overall attitudes departed sharply from the ascetic sexuality of the patristic tradition—as Steven Ozment has remarked, Luther "was a leading defender of the dignity of women and the goodness of marriage"—but they found no biblical support for women as equals to men in ministry. Luther did permit women to preach and even to administer the sacraments, but only under special circumstance where no man was present. In his *Lectures on Galatians* (1535), he declared that "in Christ Jesus all social stations, even those that were divinely ordained, are nothing." Yet in social relations, the "very great difference and inequality among persons . . . must be observed very carefully"; otherwise, "if a woman wanted to be a man . . . there would be a disturbance and confusion of all social stations and of everything." The "magnificent and very glorious words" of oneness in Christ Jesus refer to one's spiritual, not social, standing.[18]

Viewed from the perspective of Luther's two kingdom theology, Galatians 3:28 applies to the kingdom of God (gospel); the church, however, because it stands within the kingdom of the world (law), is governed by the same laws pertaining to civil society. Such laws, which take into account the result of the fall, subject women to men and deny them a public role in the affairs of the state. (Apparently, Luther could not conceive that should the civil laws change and grant opportunities to women, then ipso facto women could also serve as leaders in the church.)

So, too, in his commentaries, Calvin stressed that "Christ makes all one," and that Paul intended "to show that the grace of adoption and the hope of salvation do not depend on the law [for 'there is neither Jew nor Greek'] but are contained in Christ alone." Yet, according to Jane Dempsey Douglass, Calvin was not as strident as Luther and other Reformers in applying Paul's instructions for women to keep silent in the churches. Calvin is unique among the Reformers in placing the apostle's advice "among the indifferent things in which the Christian is free" and "not as eternal law which binds the conscience." No social revolutionary, Calvin accepted the subordination of women in church and society (just as Paul did in the first century) but viewed such arrangements as historically conditioned, not mandated by the Word of God.[19] He did, however, agree with Luther in upholding the traditional view prohibiting women from the office of teaching and administering the sacraments.[20] In sum, ancient Christian writers and major Protestant commentators never understood Galatians 3:28 to refer to anything other than a Christian's standing before God.

Proponents of women's ordination respond that the church fathers and Reformers did not grasp the full implications of Galatians 3:28 because their prejudices against women ruled out any understanding that this passage might grant women full involvement in Christian ministry. Paul expressed the ideal of gender equality in the Christian community in Galatians 3:28, and the earliest of Christians carried out this ideal. But by the fourth and fifth centuries, male leaders of the Christian church increasingly embraced the cultural values of Greco-Roman society, including a gender ideology that divided society into two spheres—a male public, political sphere and a female, private, domestic sphere.[21] With the adoption of such values that associated a woman in public with shame, women were excluded from positions of Christian leadership.

In addition, developments as early as the second century conspired against women as leaders of the church when fringe groups and heretical movements (e.g., the Montanists) allowed women high leadership roles, including sacramental ones. Ever since, with a guilt by association mentally, male leaders identified women's involvement in church leadership with suspicion, even as heretical. Writing against the Montanist movement in the fourth century, Epiphanius anticipated the two-millennia exegetical standoff between proponents and opponents of women's ordination:

> Women among them are bishops, presbyters, and the rest, as if
> there were no difference of nature. "For in Christ there is neither
> male nor female" [Gal. 3:28]. . . . Even if women among them are or-
> dained to the episcopacy and presbyterate because of Eve, they hear
> the Lord saying, "Your orientation will be toward your husband and
> he will rule over you" [Gen. 3:16]. The apostolic saying escaped their
> notice, namely that: "I do not allow a woman to speak or have au-
> thority over a man" [1 Tim. 2:12]. And again: "Man is not from
> woman but woman from man" [1 Cor. 11:8]; and "Adam was not de-
> ceived, but Eve was first deceived into transgression" [1 Tim. 2:14].[22]

Epiphanius reiterated the conventional view among the church fathers that
men and women have different natures: according to Scripture, women are
inferior to men.

A brief review of the ancient Christian writers cited earlier confirms a
rampant prejudice, even loathing, toward the female sex. According to Clement
of Alexandria, the male is naturally superior to the female; he represents the
complete *anthropos* (man, in the generic sense), whereas the female is derivative and incomplete. Women exist to receive the men's semen and to perform
domestic responsibilities. So, too, Jerome declared that a woman's reason for
being is to birth and raise children. If she wants to serve Christ, she must
"cease to be a woman and will be called 'man,' since we all desire to progress
'to the perfect man'" (Eph. 4:23). Augustine, whose views became enormously
influential in Roman Catholic theology, considered sex as suspect (quite literally, sin was a sexually transmitted disease) and women as naturally inferior to
men, subject to divine decrees of subordination and responsible for the original
sin.[23]

Taken together, the church fathers were, at best, ambivalent toward women
and, at worst, misogynist. As George Tavard incisively put it, "There is a thin
line between the idea of overcoming sex (thus arriving at male-female equality
by the denial of difference) and that of degrading sex as evil (and, in a masculine world, placing all the opprobrium on the woman)." In their approach
toward Scripture, the fathers either ignored interpretations that affirmed
women's role in ministry (e.g., Gal. 3:28) or cited biblical texts in support of
women's subjection to men.[24] For example, they often referred to the creation
account in Genesis 2 as an affirmation of woman's subordinate status and the
fall of Eve into sin in Genesis 3 as proof of her weakness (see later for further
discussion of these texts). Tertullian's bombastic remarks about women encapsulated the prevailing views of the fathers:

> And do you not know that you are (each) an Eve? The sentence of
> God on this sex of yours lives in this age: the guilt of necessity must
> live too. *You* are the devil's gateway; *you* are the unsealer of that (for-
> bidden) tree: *you* are the first deserted of the divine law: *you* are she

who persuaded him who the devil was not valiant enough to attack. *You* destroyed so easily God's image, man. On account of *your* desert—that is, death—even the Son of God had to die.[25]

According to proponents of women's ordination, prejudice against women holding public office in the church has been problematic since the second and third centuries. By the fourth and fifth centuries, women were effectively excluded from leadership. Although recent scholarship has uncovered instances of women as deacons, priests, presbyters, and even bishops in Catholic and Orthodox churches, such cases were exceptional and outside the bounds of accepted practice.[26] In the thirteenth century, theologian Thomas Aquinas augmented the prevailing view of women's unfit status for leadership (by virtue of their natural inferiority) by basing his arguments on the ancient authority of Aristotle. And as late as 1976, the Catholic Church appealed to the reasoning of Aquinas as the basis for the exclusion of women from the priesthood.

These restrictions on women, observe advocates of women's ordination, indicate that women's place in the church has been captive to prevailing cultural norms rather than guided by the practices of the earliest Christian community and Scripture itself. A brief historical excursus into nineteenth- and twentieth-century Protestant controversies in the United States over women's participation in ministry illustrates the promises and perils of challenging these norms.

The Emergence of and Controversy over Women in Ministry

As we have seen in the case of Antoinette Brown's ordination, not until the nineteenth century, when the first women's movement followed in the wake of religious revival, were these cultural norms—including the "monopoly of the pulpit"—successfully challenged. Women questioned traditional ways of thinking by appealing to secular democratic ideals ("all men and *women* are created equal"), to the anointing of the Holy Spirit to preach ("your sons and your *daughters* shall prophesy"), and to the Bible itself, which was subjected to fresh reinterpretation. By the end of the nineteenth century, these lines of questioning moved in different directions—one in the direction of the secular feminist movement's platform of equal rights, particularly the vote, the other in the direction of the evangelical feminist movement's platform of women in the pulpit.

Initially, however, they were integrally tied together. For example, in the 1830s, Sarah Grimké (1792–1873), a pioneering figure in the abolitionist and women's rights movements, centered her arguments for women's equality, including the right to preach, on the Bible alone. In her "Letters on the Equality of the Sexes, and the Condition of Women," a groundbreaking study in feminist biblical exegesis, she noted her reliance "solely on the Bible to designate the spheres of women." Nearly everything written on women had "been the result of a misconception of the simple truths revealed in Scripture, in consequence of the false translation of many passages of Holy Writ." She would set the record straight, dispense with the biased King James English translation, consult the original languages, challenge the anti-Christian "traditions of men," and prove that the Bible supported the equality of women.[27]

Many who defended a woman's right to preach did not go so far as Grimké in championing full equality between the sexes, but they agreed with her that Paul's liberating declaration in Galatians 3:28 confirmed that a woman "is designed to be a fellow laborer with her brother" in ministry.[28] Grimké, along with many others in her day, recognized what has now become a received axiom: a person's historical setting, religious commitments, church tradition, sex, race, morals, politics, and social and economic standing influence (to a lesser or greater extent) the interpretation of the Bible.

The primary impetus behind the reconsideration of biblical prohibitions against women preachers occurred prior to the rise of the first feminist movement in the outpouring of revivals in the eighteenth and nineteenth centuries. As in the first century, amid the heightened religious fervor of the Great Awakening (1730s–1740s) and the Second Great Awakening (1790s–1840s), women sensed the call of God to preach and minister. The Spirit unloosed social conventions and broke down traditional gender expectations. In addition, a post-Revolutionary cultural environment that deemed women as more virtuous than men opened up spiritual opportunities for women. Pastors coveted women's prayers, exulted in their conversions, and encouraged their participation in lay religious activities.

As Catherine Brekus has shown, in the first four decades of the nineteenth century, more than one hundred women preachers gave voice to the beckoning of the Spirit. Challenging the New England Calvinist orthodoxy of the day, these women from newly established dissenting sects such as the Christian Connection, Free Will Baptists, Methodists, African Methodists, and Millerites portrayed themselves as "women" called to preach as "Sisters in Christ" and "Mothers of Israel." Uneducated, they relied upon divine inspiration and envisioned themselves as prophets to whom God communicated through dreams, visions, and voices. With the exception of one female evangelist, none sought ordination in a formal sense because they felt it was either unnecessary or inappropriate—inappropriate because they accepted the prevailing view of the sexes. That is, these women preachers were biblical, not secular, feminists who based their right to preach not on the equality of the sexes but on a spiritual right of all Christians, male and female, to witness to their faith.[29] This was the meaning of Galatians 3:28. Unlike Sarah Grimké, these women continued to assume that the male was the divinely ordained head of the wife and home, and seldom did they challenge women's economic and political subordination to men.

Despite this cautious feminism, a backlash against women preachers occurred in the 1830s and 1840s. As Charles Finney, the Presbyterian revivalist, social reformer, and president of Oberlin College, promoted opportunities for women (though he did not go so far as to advocate women's ordination), his own denomination formally pronounced against women praying, preaching, and lecturing in public. And as those very sects that permitted women to preach grew larger, more efficient, and into a middle-class status—in short, as institutionalization occurred and respectability mattered—they increasingly closed opportunities for women preachers. A similar phenomenon occurred in the early church and would be repeated in the latter part of the nineteenth and early twentieth centuries. In sociological terms, leadership shifted from prophetic to priestly authority as the group moved from a sect to a denomination. Female prophetic authority, based upon direct divine revelation, gave way to male priestly authority, based upon conferred status.

At the same time that opportunities for women closed in one setting, they opened in another. In the 1840s the holiness movement, beginning within Methodism and then splintering into numerous sects, affirmed the right of women to preach, and in some cases (as we have seen with Luther Lee) defended their right to ordination. Biblical support for women's ministry revolved around three hermeneutical approaches, the first two often employed in tandem. First, as we have seen in Sarah Grimké and Luther Lee, some proponents of women in ministry embraced Galatians 3:28 as a clarion call for equal rights. The statement "There is neither slave nor free" was invoked first within the antislavery movement; soon, as women abolitionists realized they were in a similar state of subjection, they added "There is neither male nor female" as a declaration of their own right to preach. In 1891, nearly forty years after Lee's ordination sermon, B. T. Roberts, a convert through Phoebe Palmer's ministry and founder of the Wesleyan Methodist Church, defended the right of women's ordination from Galatians 3:28. "Make this the KEY TEXT upon this subject," he announced, "and give to other passages such a construction as will make them agree with it, and all is harmony."[30]

Implicit within this hermeneutic was a recognition of a cultural distance between the first century and the present, that a correct interpretation of Scripture required sensitivity to historical development, and that the interpreter can separate what is human, relative, and culture bound from what is divine, universal, and transcultural. Roberts drew a parallel between ancient views of women and slavery and advances in his own day. Though the apostle Paul enjoined slaves to obey their masters, his instruction was an accommodation to conditions of the ancient world. And just as slavery had been recently abolished, the conventions that divided males from females must also be eliminated. From this perspective, the women's rights movement, including women's ordination, was the culmination of New Testament teaching. As Roberts noted, "We must either go back or we must go ahead. We must either give her equal rights with men or we must reduce her to the servitude of by-gone ages. Either we must be governed by the Christian law of love and equity, or we must take a step back into barbarism and be governed by the law of brute force."[31]

A second hermeneutic, one that reflected continuity with earlier nineteenth-century arguments, relied on the Pentecost event. Just as the special outpouring of the Spirit opened up opportunities for women in the first century, so in these later times of outpouring the opportunities once again became available. Some defenders of this line of interpretation, including Phoebe Palmer, the "mother of the holiness movement," retained traditional views of gender. In her 429-page defense of the right of women to preach (*Promise of the Father*), Palmer wrote nothing about ordination. At the outset, she remarked that she did "not intend to discuss the question of 'Women's Rights' or of 'Women's Preaching,' [i.e., ordination], technically so called." For "woman has her legitimate sphere of action, which differs in most cases materially from that of man; and in this legitimate sphere she is both happy and useful." Palmer's cautious biblical feminism (i.e., the right to preach but not be ordained) and acceptance of the conventional views of men and women became the standard approach by other holiness writers in the nineteenth and well into the twentieth centuries.[32]

Proposed later in the century, a third hermeneutic revealed the influence of the emerging fundamentalist-modernist controversy. Against critics who dismissed some portions of Scripture as myth, fable, or contradictory, inerrantists (i.e., those who believe that in its original autographs, the Bible, rightly interpreted, is without error) such as Katharine Bushnell (1856–1946) argued otherwise. In *God's Word to Women* (1919), Bushnell, a Methodist medical doctor and reformer, applied her impressive historical, philological, and exegetical skills to defend the right of women to preach. To the increasing number of biblical critics who suggested that Paul's instruction "to keep silent" reflected the influence of his rabbinic teaching or that his reasoning was flawed, Bushnell responded with fundamentalist indignation: "We are accustomed to believe that the Holy Spirit prompted Paul's writing; and we do not believe the Spirit needed to study rabbinical rubbish to suggest a reason for silencing and subordinating women." No, Paul "only recommended a temporary 'quietness' [a more accurate translation than 'silence'] on the part of women in the Church because there was a special peril to the Church."[33]

One might conclude that the enthusiasm generated for women's preaching within the Methodist-holiness movement and the consequent endorsement of women's ordination by holiness denominations (e.g., Church of the Nazarene, Church of God, Free Methodist Church) would point to an upward trajectory of increased numbers of women in ministerial leadership throughout the twentieth century. But such was not the case. As in the 1830s and 1840s, a backlash occurred. With the exception of the Salvation Army (which to this day maintains a high percentage of women clergy), nearly all holiness denominations silenced women. To cite but one example: in 1908, women constituted 20 percent of the clergy in the Church of the Nazarene; by 1973, they constituted 6 percent; and in 1989, less than 1 percent served within the denomination's more than five thousand churches.[34]

Similar trends occurred in other evangelical venues. As we have seen in the previous chapter, Pentecostalism burst on the scene in the early twentieth century. Partly founded by women, the movement uplifted their preaching, healing, and prophetic experiences. In its early phase, during the white heat of revival and overwhelming displays of the Spirit, the religious playing field was leveled as women participated as equals with men. The urgency of the millennial task—for Christ could return at any moment—called for religious energies expended irrespective of gender. The gifting of the Spirit crossed all barriers, whether ethnic, racial, class, or sexual. Eventually, however, fewer and fewer women entered full-time ministry. Whereas in 1918, 21 percent of the ministers in the Assemblies of God were women, by the 1990s that figure had fallen to 18 percent. More revealing of the true state of affairs in the late twentieth century was that 38 percent of credentialed women were sixty-five years or older and only 7 percent held senior pastor positions.[35]

Outside holiness-Pentecostal circles, other evangelical institutions and denominations that once welcomed women also closed the door of opportunity. At Moody Bible Institute, a bastion of fundamentalism, women enrolled in the three-year "Pastor's Course," the first female graduating in 1929. Many others followed and went on to become preachers, pastors, evangelists, teachers, and even ordained ministers in a variety of denominations. A half century later, however, Moody's administration announced that "we do not endorse or encourage the ordination of women nor do we admit women to our Pastoral Training Major" and claimed in a fog of historical amnesia that its position was consistent with past practices. A similar development occurred in the Evangelical Free Church, an immigrant denomination of Scandinavian Pietist heritage. Early records (ca. 1880–1930) indicate that the church sent out more than fifty ordained female evangelists and pastors, but by the 1980s the denomination restricted ordination of pastors and teachers to males.[36]

Why this shift from women's public role in ministry to quiescence and even silence? Four reasons may be cited.[37] First, a similar development occurred within holiness, Pentecostal, and other evangelical groups as occurred within the evangelical sects earlier in the nineteenth century. As these groups underwent the process of institutionalization, in some cases moving from cultural outsiders to insiders, or from traveling evangelists to settled ministers, or from a charismatic lay ministry to a professional, seminary-trained clergy, they adopted the male leadership patterns of major denominations and the prevailing culture.

Second, as many of these denominations moved into the orbit of the separatist fundamentalist movement during the first half of the twentieth century, they adopted its reactionary ideology of separate domains and gender-based hierarchy. The highest calling for a Christian woman, previously regarded as the divine call to preach, now became that of wife, mother, and homemaker under the benevolent authority of her husband. As Nazarene historian Rebecca Laird expressed it, "The Spirit that blew at Pentecost still was calling God's daughters to prophesy, but the church of the mid–twentieth century encouraged women to put family first and then declared the way to do so was to stay at home."[38]

Third, as noted earlier, as less conservative, mainline denominations granted ordination to women (which they had resisted until the mid–twentieth century), fundamentalists viewed the move as one more concession to the modern liberal spirit of individual rights that culminated in the secular radical feminist movement of the 1960s and 1970s. Finally, these last two developments turned fundamentalist biblical exegesis in the direction of a literalistic hermeneutic. Where texts limiting female participation in worship (e.g., 1 Cor. 14; 1 Tim. 2) were previously understood as Paul's response to specific problems in the churches at Corinth and Ephesus, they were now given universal and timeless application. In the eyes of many fundamentalists, views on women in ministry became a litmus test for biblical inerrancy.

Hermeneutics and Culture

I have departed somewhat from Galatians 3:28 in the history of interpretation, but my purpose has been to highlight the emergence and reception of this key text within periods of heightened religious expectation and cultural transformation. My review of the checkered receptivity of female preaching points out that the critical issue raised by opponents and proponents of women clergy revolves around the inextricable relationship between biblical hermeneutics and culture. Several questions come to mind. To what extent are hermeneutics influenced by cultural factors? Can one extract from Scripture a principle that supports women's full participation in ministry, or is support for a female clergy derived from a desire to conform to the spirit of the age? How does one determine what biblical examples, commands, principles, and teachings are culture bound or transcultural?

Those who favor women's ordination often point to recent historical developments and raise questions regarding the tardy and reactionary response from Christian churches. Over the past century, as women have made legal, political, and economic gains, and as they have assumed positions of leadership in corporations and educational institutions, are they now not entitled to the same opportunities for leadership within religious institutions? Why is it that nearly every religious group endorses the right of a woman to become president of the United States, but these very groups prohibit a woman from becoming a pastor?

Those who oppose women's ordination raise questions regarding the tendency of denominations to mimic the agenda of modernity. What do women's rights and sexual equality—modern ideas rooted largely in secularist Enlightenment thought—have to do with God's revelation in Scripture? The real question is, Does God call women to the priesthood or the ministry? Orthodox, Catholic, and Protestant opponents of women's ordination categorically argue that "no woman is ever called to this vocation," for "a vocation cannot be reduced to a mere personal attraction, which can remain purely subjective." A woman convinced she is called is mistaken.[39]

The diametrically opposed and often highly charged conclusions regarding the application of Galatians 3:28 (and other related texts) to that of women's ordination remind us that no other contemporary issue has so challenged scholars' exegetical acumen, exposed their ideological biases, and forced them to clarify their hermeneutical principles. As we have seen throughout this book, no interpretation of the Bible (or any piece of writing) takes place in a vacuum. Clearly, the debate over women (and men) is not a dispassionate search for the truth. Participants enter the debate with preconceived ideas and their own convictions about the truth.

Given such strong dispositions, one wonders if the interpreter concludes from a text like Galatians 3:28 what he or she wants it to mean. As one commentator observes, the text "has become a hermeneutical skeleton key by which we may go through any door we choose."[40] Would more insight into the text change a person's view? Does the attitude "Don't confuse me with the facts; I've already made up my mind" prevail? Can biblical interpretation challenge the ideology of the interpreter, or is biblical interpretation largely (and unavoidably) shaped by the interpreter's ideology? These questions have been raised throughout this book, but perhaps not as explicitly as in the issue at hand.

To address these questions in light of Galatians 3:28 as the primary text in support of women's ordination, we must consider the wider biblical record. No single verse or passage of Scripture provides definitive support either for or against women's ordination. One must approach relevant passages throughout all of Scripture, giving attention to the historical context of each passage and the broader theological principles expressed. I thus offer a summary, albeit far too brief and at the risk of oversimplification, of those key texts and interpretations that define the current ordination debate. We then take up three recent interpretations of Galatians 3:28 in support of ordaining women (or the full equality of men and women in ministry) from the perspective of a mainline Protestant, a Catholic feminist, and a Protestant evangelical.

The Ordination Debate Today

Although women assumed a variety of roles in the early church—teachers, preachers, prophets, patrons, hosts, and so forth—the New Testament neither discusses women's specific ministerial functions nor defines ordination per se. Jesus himself "called" disciples and apostles, but he did not ordain them to any kind of office. We simply do not know what ordination meant in the early Christian community. Given this uncertainty, some critics question the practice of ordination and propose that the church be structured around tasks of ministry (e.g., teaching, preaching, hospitality), not particular offices (e.g., pastor, priest, elder, deacon).

Still, the New Testament does discuss various tasks, which in some cases are accompanied by commissioning practices, most commonly prayer and the "laying on of hands." Paul and Barnabas were set apart for a special spiritual mission (Acts 13:1–3), as was Timothy in recognition that the Spirit had gifted him to preach and teach (1 Tim. 4:13–14). Yet being commissioned for special service or appointed to a particular ministry is different from an office wherein authority resides by virtue of the position itself. Just as the New Testament prescribes no specific form of church government, so in matters pertaining to church office and ordination, no clear-cut instructions are given.[41] Fluidity of practice, not structured rites, characterized the early church. Eventually, Catholics and Orthodox conferred a technical and sacramental meaning to ordination but not until the third and fourth centuries. Given these developments in leadership in the early centuries of the church, the question still remains— are females entitled to preach and teach or to exercise leadership and oversight?

As it has evolved, the practice of ordination means different things to different church bodies. Some Protestant denominations do not use the term or accept the concept, reasoning (as did Luther Lee) that people do not ordain, only God calls. In this sense, ordination merely validates what has already taken place. Other Protestants revere ordination and view it as a legitimate aspect of a divine call to preach the gospel and minister in Christ's name. Catholic and Orthodox adherents view ordination as a sacrament conferring special spiritual power upon the priest to grant absolution and celebrate the Mass.

Additionally, standards of ordination vary. In some denominations, ordination is a permanent state; in others, it is temporary, identified with a period of active service or for a particular task. Many denominations ordain at different ranks (e.g., deacon, elder, priest, and bishop) and with different rights and responsibilities. Despite these variations, ordination is the typical way of induction into the office of ministry in the major ecclesiastical traditions. We may view ordained clergy as those who have "full ministry" or hold an office "having the most complete and unrestricted set of functions relating to the ministry of the Gospel, administering Word and Sacrament or carrying out the office of pastor or priest in the church."[42] Proponents of women's ordination argue that all grades and functions of ministry should be open equally to men and women. God is an equal opportunity employer; the divine call to ministry is not restricted by gender.

The issue of ordination, then, is not over ministry per se but over certain functions of ministry. "The priesthood of all believers," a concept first proposed by Luther and identified with Protestantism, is embraced by all Christian traditions and denominations if understood in the sense that all Christians are enjoined to serve others in various capacities. As scholars have amply documented, women have served in numerous leadership roles throughout Christian history—deaconesses, educators, missionaries, evangelists, abbesses, sisters, theologians, and exhorters—without being ordained.[43]

During the nineteenth and early twentieth centuries, female Protestant missionaries performed the functional work of clergy as evangelists, ministers, and teachers without formal ordination. The same is true of Catholic women today who fulfill the role of deacon and priest as teachers of religion, chaplains, parish associates, spiritual directors at retreat centers, campus ministers, catechists, missionaries, social justice workers, directors of religious education, youth leaders—all serving without ordination. Ironically, "religious organizations with restrictive gender rules may be the only organizations in our society that are more sexist in theory than in practice."[44] The debate, then, is not over women's involvement in ministry but over "full ministry"—what we call today ordination.

What, then, are the current arguments for and against women's ordination? I offer a general summary of the current biblical debate, acknowledging that the literature is vast—indeed, whole books have been written on a single passage cited for or against women's ordination.[45] Moreover, within each position, whether pro and con, a variety of interpretations and positions are advanced by individuals and organizations that are not wholly consistent with each other, either in interpretation or in the weight of argument.

Arguments against Ordination: The Traditionalist View

Biblical Perspectives

The debate over women in the church is not just about ordination, which is an ecclesiological issue; as I have intimated, it encompasses broader, more fundamental anthropological questions about the nature of men and women. One's position on women's ordination depends on one's understanding of the biblical view of human nature. What is God's design for women and men? What is the biblical view of gender?

"Traditionalists" or "hierarchicalists" (or the preferred self-designation, "complementarians") assert that God has so ordered human relationships that woman is subordinate to man. By intention and design before the fall of Adam and Eve into sin, God providentially created men and women with complementary functions and hence different gifts by nature. In this understanding of God's "order of creation" or "ordinance of creation" (found in the creation accounts in Genesis 1–3), the relationship of woman to man is not one of inequality or inferiority but of distinctive *ontological* difference. By their very natures, men and women have distinct identities and functions. The fall did not change an original God-intentioned situation of equality or egalitarian relationships into one of subordination as proponents of women's ordination argue. Rather, the relationship belongs to the very structure of created existence.

Such remains the case even in the "order of redemption"—the relationship of the redeemed to God and to each other in the new creation or new world established by Jesus Christ. Indeed, Galatians 3:28 speaks of a new life in Christ through baptism (3:27), a new relationship to him both now and at the final consummation in the age to come. But this new life has not altered male and female identities. "Now it would be rather strange," writes the Catholic Manfred Hauke, "if these deep-seated and God-willing differences between men and women were to be restricted to the order of creation. Rather, they must also, in some way or other, enter into the realization of the order of redemption."[46]

According to the traditionalist reading of the second creation account (Gen. 2:18–23), Eve was created second in the divine order after Adam and was intended to be his "helper." By virtue of his temporal precedence, Adam has primacy of place. This perspective is amplified in the account of the fall (3:1–6), where Eve is viewed as the weaker partner and temptress of Adam. As a consequence, her punishment includes bearing children in pain and being ruled over by her husband (3:16).

This hierarchical, dominate-subordinate view was cited frequently (and practiced) in the Israelite tradition and taken over by the primitive church. The apostle Paul explicitly recognized the order of creation in three passages concerned with women in the church. The second account of creation (the first is found in Genesis 1) in Genesis 2:18–25 reads as follows:

> Then the LORD God said, "It is not good that the man should be
> alone; I will make him a helper as his partner." So out of the ground
> the LORD God formed every animal of the field and every bird of the
> air, and brought them to the man to see what he would call them;
> and whatever the man called every living creature, that was its

name. The man gave names to all the cattle, and to the birds of the air, and to every animal of the field; but for the man there was not found a helper as his partner. So the LORD God caused a deep sleep to fall upon the man, and he slept; then he took one of his ribs and closed up its place with flesh. And the rib that the LORD God had taken from the man he made into a woman and brought her to the man. Then the man said, "This at last is bone of my bones and flesh of my flesh; this one shall be called Woman, for out of Man this one was taken." Therefore a man leaves his father and his mother and clings to his wife, and they become one flesh. And the man and his wife were both naked, and were not ashamed.

In 1 Corinthians 11:3–16, Paul argues for the "headship" of man (understood as having authority over or prior and determinative) on the basis of this Genesis passage:

But I want you to understand that Christ is the head of every man, and the husband is the head of his wife, and God is the head of Christ. Any man who prays or prophesies with something on his head disgraces his head, but any woman who prays or prophesies with her head unveiled disgraces her head—it is one and the same thing as having her head shaved. For if a woman will not veil herself, then she should cut off her hair; but if it is disgraceful for a woman to have her hair cut off or to be shaved, she should wear a veil. For a man ought not to have his head veiled, since he is the image and reflection of God; but woman is the reflection of man. Indeed, man was not made from woman, but woman from man. Neither was man created for the sake of woman, but woman for the sake of man. For this reason a woman ought to have a symbol of authority on her head, because of the angels. Nevertheless, in the Lord woman is not independent of man or man independent of woman. For just as woman came from man, so man comes through woman; but all things come from God. Judge for yourselves: is it proper for a woman to pray to God with her head unveiled? Does not nature itself teach you that if a man wears long hair, it is degrading to him, but if a woman has long hair, it is her glory? For her hair is given to her for a covering. But if anyone is disposed to be contentious—we have no such custom, nor do the churches of God.

Several chapters later (1 Cor. 14:33b–36), Paul appeals to the "law" (perhaps a reference to Genesis 2) as the basis for the subordination of women:

As in all the churches of the saints, women should be silent in the churches. For they are not permitted to speak, but should be subordinate, as the law also says. If there is anything they desire to

know, let them ask their husbands at home. For it is shameful for a
woman to speak in church. Or did the word of God originate with
you? Or are you the only ones it has reached?

In his letter to Timothy (1 Tim. 2:8–15), Paul (or a later anonymous author
or authors, as many scholars believe) cites two specific passages from Genesis
to demonstrate that women should not teach or exercise leadership over men
in the church. Paul assigns headship to man because Adam was created first
(Gen. 2:20–22) and Eve was deceived in the fall (Gen. 3:6).

> I desire, then, that in every place the men should pray, lifting up
> holy hands without anger or argument; also that the women should
> dress themselves modestly and decently in suitable clothing, not
> with their hair braided, or with gold, pearls, or expensive clothes,
> but with good works, as is proper for women who profess reverence
> for God. Let a woman learn in silence with full submission. I permit
> no woman to teach or to have authority over a man; she is to keep
> silent. For Adam was formed first, then Eve; and Adam was not de-
> ceived, but the woman was deceived and became a transgressor. Yet
> she will be saved through childbearing, provided they continue in
> faith and love and holiness, with modesty.

Admittedly, concede opponents of women's ordination, some of Paul's
language is difficult to understand (e.g., what does it mean that the women
"will be saved through childbearing"?), and it addresses certain cultural conventions (e.g., women wearing veils) that do not apply today. But the general
scriptural principle is clear. Paul, the former rabbi, steeped in Hebrew Scripture, appeals to the anthropological model in Genesis as his guide for women's
role in the church. Woman is permanently subordinate to the spiritual leadership of man: she is man's "helper" (Gen. 2:18); she is to defer to man's
leadership in the home (Eph. 5:22–23; cf. 1 Pet. 3:1–7) and in the congregation;
therefore, she is not to exercise leadership and authority in the church.

At the same time, traditionalists are quick to affirm the important role of
women throughout Scripture. In the patriarchal society of the Old Testament,
women served as a judge (Deborah) and prophets (Miriam, Deborah, Huldah)
and participated in private and public worship. In the New Testament, women's
involvement in and opportunities for ministry expanded. Jesus departed radically from the prevailing attitudes of disdain and condescension toward
women, affirmed their personhood, and included them in his ministry. Jesus
counted women among his closest companions and most faithful followers.
In the apostolic church, women were present at the initial outpouring of the
Holy Spirit, endured persecution and suffering, witnessed to their faith in
Christ, and played an integral role in building up the body of Christ. They also
participated in various activities in the apostolic church, including prophesying,

engaging in charitable services, and serving as missionary workers and deacons. In sum, the Bible does not demean women, as some feminists suggest; rather, both the Old and New Testaments affirm the service of women.

However, the New Testament offers no unequivocal statements regarding women in office as it does for men holding the office of elder and bishop. As noted, the three prominent texts from 1 Corinthians 11, 14 and 1 Timothy 2 offer the most explicit directives restricting women's role in the church. Yes, women prophesied, served as missionaries, and so forth, but these activities were distinct from authoritative preaching, teaching, and ruling. There may be some flexibility regarding the precise ministries in which women may be involved (e.g., whether they can pray or lead in formal worship, be deaconesses, teach adults), but opponents of ordination agree that the ordination of women to the divinely instituted ministry of Word and sacraments is prohibited.

Sacramental Perspectives

A final argument against women's ordination, one embraced more consistently by sacramentarian traditions (Roman Catholics, Orthodox, and Anglicans) than nonsacramentarian (though certainly not exclusive to those traditions, as the following quotation indicates), centers on Jesus' choice of disciples. As a French Calvinist theologian observes, "The New Testament . . . never testifies that a woman could be in a public and authorized way, representative of Christ. To no woman does Jesus say, 'He who hears you, hears me.' To no woman does he make the promise to ratify in heaven what she has bound or loosed on earth. To no woman does he entrust the ministry of public preaching . . . [or] the command to baptize or to preside at the communion of his Body and Blood. To no woman does he commit his flock."[47]

We should observe that among many sacramentarians, this argument bears no necessary connection to previous arguments rooted in the order of creation and women's inherent subordinate status. Indeed, sacramentarians and egalitarians agree on the interpretation of many passages of Scripture relating to gender relations. As early as 1963, Pope John XXIII, in the encyclical *Pacem in Terris*, affirmed the equality of persons, noting that women "are demanding both in domestic and in public life the rights and duties which belong to them as human persons." Moreover, the Pontifical Biblical Commission concluded its study, "Can Women Be Priests?" with the admission that "it does not seem that the New Testament by itself alone will permit us to settle in a clear way and once and for all the problem of the possible accession of women to the presbyterate."[48] The issue is less one of subordination or complementary status and more directly centered on the fact that women cannot represent Christ in the Eucharist because Christ was male.

The "Declaration on the Question of the Admission of Women to the Ministerial Priesthood" (also known as *Inter Insigniores*) (1976), the first major statement by the Roman Catholic Church on the ordination of women and also endorsed by major Orthodox leaders, observed that the twelve (and, later, the seventy) were male not by happenstance or by social convention but by divine intention. Jesus did not entrust the apostolic office to women because Jesus himself is male, and those who minister in his place must in the most basic way resemble him. In exercising ministry, the bishop or priest does not act in his own name but represents Christ to the congregation.

This representation is most fully present in the Eucharist, "the sacrificial meal in which the People of God are associated in the sacrifice of Christ." The priest, who alone has the power to perform the Eucharist, "acts not only through the effective power conferred on him by Christ, but *in persona Christi*, taking the very role of Christ, to the point of being his very image, when he pronounces the words of consecration."[49] The priest is a sign, and that sign must be discernible to others. That is, there must be a natural resemblance between the sign (priest) and the thing signified (Christ). If the priest were not a male, it would be difficult to see the image of Christ in the minister. Similar thinking is expressed among Protestants who reject the theology of the mass yet retain the notion that the pastor, like Jesus, presides over the "Last Supper" in its reenactment.

Traditionalists contend that an all-male priesthood is supported in the Old Testament. First, only males constituted the ancient priestly office of the Hebrews. To be sure, Hebrew society was patriarchal, but a male priesthood pointed beyond social structures to deeper religious reasons. Many of the surrounding Canaanite Baal cults involved male and female fertility deities. As a way of worship and enticing the gods to procreative acts (so as to "reproduce" crops), priests and priestesses (prostitutes) imitated the activities of these deities through sexual intercourse in the temple precincts.

For the Hebrews, however, God was not a male God who needed a female consort to ensure that crops would grow. Yahweh, neither a male nor female God, transcended the sexual activities of creatures. God required no reminders from his creatures to make the crops grow. Rather, as part of the order of creation, God established the processes by which fertility would occur. To preserve this conception of God over against the deities of fertility religions, women were totally excluded from the office of priest.[50]

Moreover, that the Hebrew God is most commonly referred to in masculine terms (King, Father, Judge, Husband, Master, Lord, etc.) not only speaks of a personal god (not an "it") but also assures that this God would not be identified with creation. In goddess worship, the distinction between the Creator and creation is often lost insofar as the creature and creation share in the deity's substance. The masculine language used for God has implications regarding those who represented God to the people and the people to God. A male priest under the Old Covenant, as a representative of the people to God and God to the people, assured there would be no confusion between the

Creator and the creature by implying that the deity took part in human creation, particularly human sexuality. This same thinking continued under the New Covenant, where the church offices of elder and bishop consistently followed the Old Testament office of a male priesthood.[51]

Biblical support for a male priesthood is also found in the nuptial imagery of the bride and bridegroom as an expression of the union between God and his people. In the Song of Songs and the prophetic Book of Hosea, God (or Jesus, in Christian allegorical or typological interpretation) is the wooing, faithful bridegroom to his bride, the Israelites (the church). In the New Testament, this imagery continues: Christ is the bridegroom, and the church is his bride. The deep symbolism of the mystery of Christ in relation to his people cannot ignore the fact that Christ is male. The authors of *Inter Insigniores* argue that "it must be admitted that, in actions which demand the character of ordination and in which Christ himself, . . . the Bridegroom and Head of the Church, is represented, exercising his ministry of salvation—which is in the highest degree the case of the Eucharist—his role (this is the original sense of the word *persona*) must be taken by a man."[52]

Pope John Paul II's letter "On the Dignity and Vocation of Women," (1988) confirmed the perspective of *Inter Insigniores*:

> Since Christ, in instituting the Eucharist, linked it in such an explicit way to the priestly service of the Apostles, it is legitimate to conclude that he thereby wished to express the relationship between man and woman, between what is "feminine" and what is "masculine." It is a relationship willed by God both in the mystery of creation and in the mystery of Redemption. It is the Eucharist above all that expresses the redemptive act of Christ the Bridegroom towards the Church the Bride. This is clear and unambiguous when the sacramental ministry of the Eucharist, in which the priest acts "in persona Christi," is performed by a man.[53]

In sum, traditionalists either base their arguments against women's ordination on interrelated views of human nature and ministry or else separate the one from the other and stress the sacramentarian view of ministry. Thomas Hopko, an Orthodox theologian, encapsulates the interrelated view by reasoning, "As Jesus, the personal image of God the Father, is the head and husband of the Church which is his body and bride, so the Christian man is to be the head and husband of his wife, and the presbyter/bishop the head and husband of the church." To tamper with what is in essence the order of creation is to tamper with the very essence of Christianity. What Peter Moore fears about the ordination of women in the Anglican Church is no less true for other Christian denominations: it is "more fundamentally subversive . . . than anything that has happened since the Reformation."[54]

Arguments for Ordination: The Egalitarian View

Proponents of women's ordination are convinced that each of the arguments cited by their opponents can be reasonably refuted. The totality of Scripture, not a few select texts, points to an egalitarian relationship between men and women and hence to the ordination of women. The trajectory of Scripture, especially in the New Testament, increasingly affirms women and signals their enhancement and equality. Beginning with the order of creation, God structured relationships between woman and man not as one subordinate to the other but as free, equal, and interdependent partners within a harmonious world. Indeed, they complement each other, each having its distinct place, capacity, and function (largely due to biological differences) but without priority. The real disagreement between egalitarians and traditionalists is not over role differentiation per se but over what constitutes male-female differentiation.

According to egalitarians, there is no reference in the creation accounts of Genesis 1–2 to a divine mandate for man to exercise authority over woman. The first creation narrative in Genesis 1:26–28 affirms that man and woman are created in God's image and both are given stewardship responsibilities over creation.

> Then God said, "Let us make humankind in our image, according to
> our likeness; and let them have dominion over the fish of the sea,
> and over the birds of the air, and over the cattle, and over all the
> wild animals of the earth, and over every creeping thing that creeps
> upon the earth." So God created humankind in his image, in the
> image of God he created them; male and female he created them.
> God blessed them, and God said to them, "Be fruitful and multiply,
> and fill the earth and subdue it; and have dominion over the fish of
> the sea and over the birds of the air and over every living thing that
> moves upon the earth."

Man and woman are equal in origin and destiny, created in God's image (i.e., having the capacity of reasoning and morality) and given stewardship of the creation. The second account of creation, describing Eve's creation after Adam as his helper, implies no subordinate status. If one followed the logic of the order of creation, that is, from an uncreated state to more complex forms of existence, then one would have to conclude that Eve, since she is created *after* Adam, is the supreme expression of creation.

Moreover, if prior existence entailed some kind of authority, then the animals, since they were created before Adam, should rule over him. The ascription to Eve as "helper" to Adam means not one who is subordinate but in Hebrew is the same word used in many biblical references to God as the one who rescues or aids (see Ps. 46:1). The subordination and subjugation of the woman becomes a reality, not as part of God's order of creation but as consequence of the curse. Because of the fall, God informs the woman that "he shall rule over you" (Gen. 3:16). Adam and Eve are held equally responsible for the fall; Eve is neither the weaker one nor the temptress. Nothing in the first three chapters of Genesis affirms an order of creation in which the female is ontologically or spiritually subordinate to the male.

The order of redemption not only repaired the broken relationship between humanity and God but also transformed all human relationships, including that between men and women. In Christ there is a new created order. Men and women are "subject to one another" in Christ (Eph. 5:21), interdependent in Christ (1 Cor. 11:11–12), "heirs of the gracious gift of life" (1 Pet. 3: 7), and equal in Christ (Gal. 3:28). The religious realm is transformed, and social relations are redeemed. Jesus embodies this view in his treatment of women.[55] As noted earlier, not only did Jesus elevate women beyond the conventions of the day but women were the first witnesses to his resurrection and were instructed to "go and tell" the others (Matt. 28:7). That Jesus did not include women among his twelve disciples is no indication of his intention for all male leaders; Jesus did not include Gentiles as his disciples either, yet soon they were counted among his followers.

What about the three passages in the apostle Paul's writings that enjoin women to keep silent in the churches and be in subjection to their husbands? Proponents of women's ordination have ignited a lexical and exegetical battle with traditionalists, arguing that critical words have been misinterpreted, that the exact purposes of these passages are unclear, and that the cultural context being addressed is not transparent. For example, egalitarians observe that the meaning of "head" (kephale) in 1 Corinthians 11:3 ("Christ is the head of every man, and the husband is the head of his wife, and God is the head of Christ") is more accurately rendered "source" or "origin" rather than "authority." In this sense, Paul was speaking of a chronological order of origin: man originated from Christ by whom all things are created (John 1:3; Col. 1:16), the woman originated from man (Gen. 2:21–22), and the source of Christ is God (John 1:1).

Or the key word "authority" (authentein) in 1 Timothy 2:12 ("I permit no woman to teach or to have authority over a man") has a negative connotation, referring to a specific situation of abuse or violence in the church rather than having a universal application.[56] The context indicates that Paul is prohibiting not the exercise of any authority but an abusive use of authority. Or one might concede that indeed Paul is unequivocally forbidding women to teach in this particular situation, but he is not making a universal rule. This passage is exceptional, addressed to a specific cultural context, and thus is not applicable to our own situation.

Whatever the final meaning of the 1 Corinthians 11:3–16 passage (commentators agree this is a most difficult passage to exegete), it is clear that women were prophesying and praying in the church (v. 5) and that men and women were viewed as being interdependent (vv. 11–12). For Paul, the issue for women was one of public decorum; better that women conform to the custom of the day and wear veils than go without. The arguments he cites to support his views are no less culturally embedded than the practice of veiling itself.[57] In short, those who argue for a wife's subjection to her husband but believe that veiling is no longer necessary beg the question. One argues either for veils and wifely submission or for no veils and husband-and-wife equality.

In 1 Corinthians 14:33b–36, Paul requests that "women should be silent in the churches," and yet, as we have just seen, women were praying and prophesying. In all probability, Paul was responding to disruptions in public worship at Corinth from uneducated women who were interrupting the expositions of Scripture with questions. If one is to take Paul's instructions literally, then of course women are not allowed to sing and speak liturgical responses or pray aloud. A more critical perspective, and one embraced by a majority of modern scholars, contends that these verses were a later addition or interpolation. According to Gordon Fee, a well-respected Pentecostal-evangelical scholar, these verses "were first written as a gloss in the margin by someone who, probably in light of 1 Tim. 2:9–15, felt the need to qualify Paul's instructions even further." Fee concludes that it is not authentic and hence "certainly not binding for Christians."[58]

This latter criticism is made even more strongly for 1 Timothy 2. In the eyes of most biblical scholars, 1 Timothy reflects post-Pauline thinking of Christians who departed from the radical implications of Galatians 3:28 and began to conform to the patriarchal structures of their surrounding culture. Assuming, however, that Paul or someone in Paul's circle did write 1 Timothy or that because of its placement in the New Testament canon, 1 Timothy should be granted an authoritative status, we confront the only explicit statement in the Bible prohibiting women from teaching. And yet one must ask, when Paul wrote, "I permit no woman to teach or to have authority over a man," did he mean for all time or within the specific circumstances he was addressing? Proponents of women's ordination raise again the issue of cultural circumstances, noting that this passage conflicts with other passages in which Paul encourages the ministry of women. In all probability, Paul encountered the same problem in Ephesus (the letter is addressed to Timothy in Ephesus) as he did in Corinth. That is, Paul enjoins the same quiet, "learners' attitude" on novices who were not yet well grounded in the faith, though in Ephesus the situation was all the more serious because false teachers (men) were exploiting less educated women to spread their teachings.

Confounding these three culturally situated passages limiting women's role in the Corinthian and Ephesian churches is Paul's own support for women acting as deacons, prophets, and other leaders in the early Christian community. He was accompanied on his missionary travels by the wife-and-husband team of Priscilla and Aquila, who instructed Apollos in the deeper things of the faith (Acts 18:18–26). As we have seen, he affirmed women praying and prophesying in public worship (1 Cor. 11:5). In Romans 16:1–16 he mentions eight female coworkers, including Phoebe, a deacon (traditionally mistranslated as "servant"), and Junia, "prominent among the apostles." And in Philippians he describes Euodia and Syntyche as two women who "have struggled beside me in the work of the gospel" (4:3).

Then, too, the apostle mentions spiritual gifts ("charismata") regardless of sexual distinctions (see Rom. 12:4–5; 1 Cor. 12:4–11; Eph. 4:11). Given Paul's openness toward women in ministry, Ben Witherington III concludes his study of women in the earliest churches with this observation: "The question of women's ordination is not discussed or dismissed in the New Testament, but there is nothing in the material that rules out such a possibility. If the possibilities for women in the earliest churches, as evidenced in the NT, should be seen as models for church practice in subsequent generations, then it should be seen that women in the NT era already performed the tasks normally associated with ordained clergy in later eras."[59]

What, then, is one to make of the important role of women in Paul's ministry over against his instructions that women keep silent in the church? Proponents of women's ordination offer several observations of these apparently contradictory positions. Some point to the inconsistency in Paul's own thought (Paul the chauvinist Jewish rabbi versus Paul the Christian apostle) and his inability at times to live up to his own ideals, especially as expressed in Galatians 3:28.[60] Some point out that Paul changed his mind: in Galatians he affirmed women's equality with men, but in his later writings to the Ephesians and Corinthians he retreated to a more conservative view (e.g., he omits the "male/female" phrase in 1 Cor. 12:13). Others deny Pauline authorship of 1 Timothy, Ephesians, and parts of 1 Corinthians and so distinguish between the anonymous critics of women and the authentic Paul of Galatians 3:28.[61] Still others seek to harmonize the various positions in Paul, distinguishing between culture-specific instructions that limit women's roles and universal principles that support women's full participation in ministry.[62]

In response to the sacramentarian position that the priest must be male to represent Christ, advocates of women's ordination query whether maleness is really the essential thing to represent Jesus. Jesus was male, and he called male disciples, but must these facts be elevated to a normative principle that all priests must be male? Is not the true representation of Christ by a priest or pastor a vocal or oral representation, not an actual or bodily representation? That is, in the Eucharist the priest *speaks* the words of Christ rather than *embodies* Christ. Moreover, is not the priest a representative, not a representation, of Christ? A representative does not impersonate or embody but speaks for or acts on behalf of someone else. The idea that a priest as representative must be male rests on a faulty understanding of analogy and religious symbolism.

Viewed from recent Catholic and traditional Orthodox perspectives, it is more accurate to say that the priest represents the church that is the body of Christ. The priest represents the people to Christ, not Christ to the people. At the Eucharist, "the most important of all priestly acts," observes the Orthodox Bishop Kallistos, "the celebrant does not serve as an icon of Christ."[63] The iconic argument, he adds, is not as conclusive as those within his tradition think. Since the church is composed of both males and females, then the representative role of the priest would seem to require both a male and a female priesthood. And, yes, Christ is depicted in nuptial imagery as the bridegroom who loves his bride the church, but the church is made up of both males and females who together are depicted in feminine imagery.

Symbols are complex and polyvalent. How can one logically deduce from this symbolism that those who represent Christ must be male? Hans Küng and others have pointed out that one can follow this line of reasoning in another direction: "Are we to think that only married and gainfully employed Jews [as were the original disciples] . . . will now be considered for the office of priest or bishop?"[64] How is it that we can ignore Jesus' Jewishness but not his maleness? The real significance of Jesus is not his maleness, but his humanness, and therefore a man or woman can represent Christ.

What about the argument that priests must be male because they represent a God who is described primarily and intentionally in masculine terms so as to combat goddess worship and the temptation to identify the Creator with the creature? Paul K. Jewett responds by making the following observations. First, there is no evidence that worship of female deities was any more offensive to the prophets than the worship of other deities. "It is the worship of false gods, not female gods as such, that is the ultimate abomination to the Lord. The gulf is just as deep between the worship of Baal [the male deity] and Jahweh as it is between the worship of Asherah [the female deity] and Jahweh."[65]

Second, although God is described predominantly in male terms, the Old Testament uses female imagery as well. The prophet Isaiah likens God to a woman giving birth (42:14; 46:3), a woman nursing her child (49:15), and a mother comforting her child (66:13). Clearly, this language—whether male or female (and all language about God)—is analogical, for God transcends sexual distinctions. "The long and short of it is," writes Jewett, "that if God transcends human sexual distinctions in his essential being, then one cannot predicate of him either masculinity or femininity in the human sense of the terms."[66] God's representatives need not be defined by their sex but by their calling to divine service.

The Decisive Text: Galatians 3:28

To resolve the exegetical and hermeneutical standoff between opponents and proponents of women's ordination, egalitarians play the "trump card" of Galatians 3:28. For hundreds of years this text lay dormant as applicable to social relations in the Christian community; only recently has it emerged as an ideal expressed by the apostle Paul whose time has now come. To appreciate the full significance of this radical statement purportedly endorsing the full participation of women in church ministry, I will set the text in the wider context of Paul's letter to the Galatia.[67] We will then engage the work of scholars from a variety of contemporary interpretive communities that favor women's ordination.

Paul's short letter to the Galatians offers a window through which to peer into an era of flux. We are presented with one of the earliest and most contentious issues in these newly formed Christian communities, namely, the relationship between the emerging faith and Jewish law. During one of Paul's missionary journeys, he evangelized a part of Asia Minor known as Galatia, where he established a number of Christian communities among the pagan Hellenized Gentiles. After his departure, an evangelistic team of Christian Jews came to the area and challenged Paul's converts by announcing that they must observe key provisions of the Mosaic law, in particular, the rite of circumcision (5:2–4; 6:12–13).

In response to this proposed revision, Paul wrote an emotional and highly personal letter in which he bitterly denounced these teachers (1:8), arguing that they preached "a different gospel" (1:6) and perverted the gospel that he originally proclaimed to the Galatians (1:7). Justification was not dependent upon Christ *plus* works of the law but on Christ alone. By his atoning death, Christ repaired the broken relationship between humankind and God. Christ alone "gave himself for our sins to set us free from the present evil age" (1:4); he "was publicly exhibited as crucified!" (3:1); and he "redeemed us from the curse of the law by becoming a curse for us" (3:13). Though a Jew himself, Paul knows "that a person is justified not by the works of the law but through faith in Jesus Christ" (2:16), who lives within each believer through the Spirit (5:5). Those who live by the Spirit are not to use their "freedom as an opportunity for self-indulgence, but through love" (5:13) they are to serve others by practicing the virtues of "love, joy, peace, patience, kindness, generosity, faithfulness, gentleness, and self-control" (5:22).

Galatians 3:28 fits into Paul's general discussion (2:15–5:1) that justification comes not through obedience to the law but through faith in Jesus Christ. Now that faith has come, Paul writes, "we are no longer subject to a disciplinarian [the law], for in Christ Jesus you are all children of God through faith" (3:25–26). All are children because of the promise to Abraham that "all the Gentiles shall be blessed in you." Some 430 years before the law was given to Moses (3:17), Abraham adumbrated the gospel in living by faith, for he "believed God, and it was reckoned to him as righteousness" (3:6). The law, then, was an extended parenthesis, effective from Moses until the coming of Christ, but the promise to Abraham continued uninterrupted and found its fulfillment in Christ. All who express faith in Christ are not only children of Abraham, heirs of the covenant made to the ancient patriarch (3:7–9, 14) but, more supremely, children of God (3:26; 4:7), having this status because they are in Christ Jesus (3:26) by virtue of having been "baptized into Christ" and "clothed . . . with Christ" (3:27). There is then "no longer Jew or Greek" and, Paul adds, "there is no longer slave or free, there is no longer male and female; for all of you are one in Christ Jesus" (v. 28). All human distinctions are removed; all are the adopted children of God and thus heirs of the privileges and freedom in the Spirit (4:1–7).

Two other observations about verses 27 and 28 are pertinent. First, there is a popular hypothesis among scholars that this text—viewed as an early Christian baptismal liturgy—predates Paul (see also structural similarities in 1 Cor. 12:13 and Col. 3:9–11) and that he invokes this liturgy but applies it for his own uses.[68] In the actual rite, initiates removed their clothing as they entered the water and donned a new white garment as they emerged, signaling that the believer put off the "old man" of sin and was now a "new creation" in Christ (6:15). Second, of the three polarities in verse 28—Jew/Greek, slave/free, male/female—only the first is directly relevant to Paul's discussion—again suggestive that Paul was drawing from a baptismal confession and reminding his readers of what they themselves affirmed in their own baptism.

Although Paul makes no further comment on the last two couplets, their inclusion reveals three of the most crucial social tensions within Greco-Roman society, as well as in the Christian community. Several commentators observe the structural similarity between the baptismal liturgy and other formulaic devices that appear in Jewish and Greek writings. In Judaism, three "blessings" were said at the beginning of Jewish morning prayers: "Blessed is he [God] that he did not make me a Gentile; blessed is he that did not make me a woman; blessed is he that did not make me a boor [peasant or slave]." Similar sayings appear in ancient Greek writings attributed to Thales and Socrates, whose expressions of "gratitude" included "that I was born a human being, not a beast; a man and not a woman; thirdly, a Greek and not a barbarian."[69] In contrast to these "blessings" and expression of "gratitude," the Christian baptismal confession announced that racial, ethnic, class, and sexual divisions—those very divisions that defined Greek and Jewish society—were healed. No longer was one's spiritual relationship to God defined on these terms; all were incorporated into a new community that did away with these barriers to oneness in Christ Jesus.

Clearly, the primary meaning of this proclamation refers to the universal

standing of all people before God, but according to egalitarians, the early
church and Paul pointed to and even practiced the kind of revolutionary social
ethic implied in this confession. Members of the new community of Christ,
as a new creation, transcend the deepest cultural divisions in society. There is
nothing to exclude women from full participation in church ministry; in fact,
they must be included in order to embody the corporate character of the new
creation. In the last half century, not one but several interpretive approaches
uplift Galatians 3:28 as a preeminent statement in support of women's ministry.

A Mainline Protestant Perspective: Krister Stendahl

One of the earliest essays, and perhaps the most influential, in the movement
for women's ordination since the 1950s was written by Krister Stendahl, an
internationally renowned New Testament scholar and dean of Harvard Divinity
School. *The Bible and the Role of Women* appeared in 1958 during the heated
and bitter debate over the ordination of women in the Church of Sweden.
Unlike in the United States, where other external pressures were brought to
bear on the issue (e.g., the women's movement), the case in Sweden grew out
of pressure applied by the government on the state-supported Church of Sweden (Lutheran).

Under this church-state arrangement, matters pertaining to church law
had to be passed by Parliament with the consenting vote of the General Synod
of the Church. Inasmuch as the government had passed equal opportunity
legislation in 1945 and the church was supported by the state, questions arose
over the Church of Sweden limiting the priesthood to males. In the late 1940s
the government appointed a study commission, which in 1950 recommended
women's ordination, but the General Synod of the Church rejected the suggestion. Stendahl wrote his essay in preparation for the synod's special called
session to vote on ordination. His position prevailed: the synod approved
women's ordination in 1958 and two years later ordained the first women in
the Church of Sweden.

Subtitled *A Case Study in Hermeneutics,* Stendahl's study brought to light
the questions that have preoccupied modern biblical scholars. How does one
apply the Bible to contemporary life? How does one separate the timeless from
the contingent? Stendahl dismissed what he labeled the "biblical view" as "naïve" and "a nostalgic attempt to play 'First Century.'" This view attempts
through historical and descriptive methods to systematize the events, assumptions, and views expressed in the Bible. From this perspective, "the actual stage
of implementation in the first century becomes the standard for what is authoritative."[70]

For example, because Jesus called only male apostles, only males may be
priests. But the question is raised, "By what right is this act made binding and

interpreted to mean that only males may serve in ministry?" Is that the point of Jesus appointing male apostles? Given the cultural context and the identification of the Twelve Apostles with the male leaders of the twelve tribes of Israel, what other alternative was there? Jesus ordered his disciples to walk with staff in hand. Should today's ministers follow Jesus' command? "The authority of biblical sayings," observed Stendahl, "indeed even the words of Jesus, is not blind. They must be applied and interpreted according to certain principles, and when we do so, there is naturally the risk of arbitrariness. This risk cannot be eliminated through any simple claim of faithfulness to the Bible."[71]

As we have seen, there are concrete examples in the New Testament supportive of women's subordination. According to Stendahl, each reflects a Jewish patriarchal milieu, and each is grounded in the prior order of creation. At the same time, this "fundamental view determined by the order of creation . . . is broken through in . . . Galatians 3:26–28."[72] Stendahl observes that there is a slight difference in phrasing in the third pair of couplets. Translated from Greek, the first two, Jew/Greek and slave/free, are rendered "neither . . . nor," whereas the third, male/female is most accurately expressed as "no male and female"—and is a direct citation from the Septuagint version of Genesis 1:27 ("male and female created he them"). Paul is suggesting that the most basic division of God's creation—male and female—is overcome in Christ Jesus.

Paul's intent is to show that the "order of creation is wrong."[73] He is not repudiating biological differences between the sexes and advocating some androgynous ideal, but he is making a statement "directly against" the order of creation and in tension with Pauline and non-Pauline statements found elsewhere in Scripture upholding the subordination of women. "Just as Jews and Greeks remain what they were, so man and woman remain what they are; but in Christ, by baptism and hence in the church—not only in faith—something has happened which transcends the Law itself and thereby even the order of creation."[74] All three pairs have the potential for implementation in the life of the church, and now with the implementation of the third pair they all are actualized. The division between Jew and Greek was resolved in the first century, between slave and free in the nineteenth, and now, suggests Stendahl, reconciliation between the sexes must be addressed in the twentieth.

For Stendahl, the New Testament contains "elements, glimpses which point beyond and even 'against' the prevailing view and practice of the New Testament church." One cannot harmonize Galatians 3:28 with the orders of creation. "Our problem is not to harmonize the two tendencies into a perfect system. It is—as always in truly Christian theology—to discern where the accent should lie now, the accent in the eschatological drama which we call the history of the church and the world."[75]

Where does all this lead in terms of women's ordination? In the New Testament wherever women's role is discussed, it is always in terms of subordinate status—whether in the home, society, or church. Even Priscilla, Phoebe, and other Christian women carried out their various ministries under the aegis of the order of creation and restrictive "household codes" (e.g., Eph. 5:22–23). Thus emancipation in one area cannot be separated from the other. It makes no sense to say that women can be emancipated in legal, political, and economic matters but not in religious. If one concluded that emancipation in secular affairs was permitted but not in religious, then one would be driven to conclude that the emancipation of slaves is acceptable in the world but not in the church. In short, "ordination cannot be treated as a 'special' problem, since there is no indication that the New Testament sees it as such." The basic question about the ordination of women is not a question about what office they may fill but a question about "the right relationship between man and woman in Christ, whether it applies to political office, civil service, career, home life, the ministry, or to the episcopate."[76]

A Feminist Perspective: Elizabeth Schüssler Fiorenza

That we place feminist scholarship after the mainline Protestant view of Krister Stendahl is ostensibly unusual insofar as feminists (predominantly but not exclusively females) have been the strongest advocates for the ordination of women and repeatedly invoked Galatians 3:28 as "their" text.[77] Chronologically, however, Stendahl's essay appeared before the second wave of feminism in the 1960s made inroads into divinity schools, before there was such a thing as feminist theology. To be sure, protofeminist voices emerged among Protestants as early as 1948 within the World Council of Churches, and among Catholics as early as 1962, when, on the eve of the Second Vatican Council, a petition advocating the discussion of women priests was submitted to the council's preparatory commission.[78] But not until the late 1960s and especially the 1970s were these voices heard in a significant way.

Although there is no single monolithic feminist theology or feminist approach in biblical studies, mainstream Christian feminists share several general convictions.[79] First, they believe in the full equality of men and women, whether at home, in the workplace, or in the church. Second, their scholarship is informed by gender as a primary analytical category, whether applied to biblical, theological, ethical, or historical studies. Third, feminists are acutely aware that language, especially biblical language of God as male, shapes perceptions of reality and goes hand in hand with male-dominated societies. Hence they insist that worship practices and publications, especially the Bible, must be revised into gender-inclusive (or gender-neutral) language. Fourth, feminists contend in varying degrees that the Bible is the product of an ancient patriarchal culture and expresses (consciously or unconsciously) male-centered (androcentic) biases and patriarchal values.

Summarized by Catherine Mowry LaCugna, "Christian feminism is a far-

reaching critique of the fundamental sexism of the Christian tradition inasmuch as it has valued men over women, has seen masculine experience as
normative for women's experience, has imaged God in predominantly masculine metaphors, or has used the Christian message to support violence
against women."[80] In some form, Christian feminists are found in every Christian tradition, save in Protestant fundamentalist circles. Some feminists (e.g.,
Mary Daly) have concluded that the Christian faith is so irredeemably patriarchal and repressive toward women that it cannot be salvaged and hence have
abandoned the church for alternative religions such as Wicca. Often, the apostle Paul is singled out as the main perpetrator of women's subjugation, for his
writings (and pseudonymous writings ascribed to him) are responsible for the
continued oppression of women throughout history.[81] Ironically, in their estimation of Paul, radical feminists reach the same conclusion as traditionalists:
Paul advocated women's subordinate status as a part of the divinely created
order. The difference, of course, is that traditionalists embrace this teaching,
whereas radical feminists categorically reject it. Most Christian feminists, however, while critical of Paul and of the Christian tradition in general, remain
committed to furthering their reformist cause within the faith.

One such feminist is Elisabeth Schüssler Fiorenza, a Roman Catholic, the
first occupant of the Krister Stendahl Professor of Divinity chair at Harvard
Divinity School, and one of the most prominent scholars in the field of New
Testament studies. Like most feminists, she is no mere theoretician. Feminism
is not simply "a world view or a perspective but a woman's liberation movement for social and ecclesiastical change." In her groundbreaking book, *In
Memory of Her* (1983), she offered a historical reconstruction of the early Jesus
movement, arguing that women were "prominent leaders and missionaries . . .
both before Paul and independently of Paul. Without question, they were equal
and sometimes even superior to Paul in their work for the gospel."[82]

Schüssler Fiorenza approaches the biblical text with a *"hermeneutics of suspicion* rather than with a hermeneutics of consent and affirmation." According
to her feminist theory, "all texts are products of an androcentric patriarchal
culture and history." Males not only wrote them but also have dominated their
interpretation. Consequently, one must engage in a two-tier demythologization
and "reclaim the Bible and early Christian history as women's beginnings and
power." Because the text is the word of *men*, it is not authoritative and "cannot
claim to be the revelatory Word of God." The Bible itself must be liberated
from its "perpetuation and legitimization of such patriarchal oppression and
forgetfulness of, silence about, or eradication of the memory of women's suffering."[83]

Rather than appeal to a "canon within the canon"—a tack typifying many
of the hermeneutical stances discussed throughout this book and one that
some feminists take in accentuating the prophetic-liberating theme of the Bible—Schüssler Fiorenza calls for a "canon outside the canon."[84] She proposes

"that the revelatory canon for theological evaluation of biblical androcentric traditions and their subsequent interpretations cannot be derived from the Bible itself but can only be formulated in and through women's struggle for liberation from all patriarchal oppression." The New Testament is not the archetype—an ideal, unchanging, timeless pattern—but a prototype, an original, to be sure, but "critically open to the possibility of its own transformation."[85] The text itself is no longer the interpretive authority; rather, the "personally and politically reflected experience of oppression and liberation must become the criterion of appropriateness for biblical interpretation and evaluation of biblical authority claims." The Bible "no longer functions as authoritative source but as a *resource* for women's struggle for liberation."[86]

In sum, "a feminist paradigm of critical interpretation is not based on a faithful adherence to biblical texts or obedient submission to biblical authority but on solidarity with women of the past and present whose life and struggles are touched by the role of the Bible in Western culture." Women's experience in their contemporary struggle against racism, sexism, and other forms of oppression is the standard by which to approach and interpret Scripture. Thus only those portions of Scripture "that transcend critically their patriarchal frameworks and allow for a vision of Christian women as historical and theological subjects and actors" are worthy to be considered divine revelation and truth.[87]

Employing this hermeneutic, Schüssler Fiorenza reconstructs the early Christian movement. She argues that two main traditions characterized early Christianity—an earlier tradition of Jesus (found authentically in the Gospels of Mark and John and in Paul's genuine writings) and a later tradition introduced by followers of Paul and subsequent interpreters. In the earlier radical Spirit-inspired tradition of Jesus, women functioned as apostles, missionaries, prophets, and deaconesses. They played an important role in founding and promoting house churches and were viewed as equals to men in leadership. Beginning in the last third of the first century and depicted by post-Pauline New Testament literature, however, the latter tradition suppressed the first, and the early Christian movement adapted itself to the patriarchal structures of the surrounding Greco-Roman culture.

Galatians 3:28 embodies the ideals and the reality of the early Christian movement. Rejecting both Stendahl's contention that this text represents a theological breakthrough and the traditionalists' perspective that it is an isolated text overshadowed by passages of subordination, Schüssler Fiorenza declares that this early baptismal formula is "a key expression, not of Pauline theology but of the theological self-understanding of the Christian missionary movement which had far-reaching historical impact." The text is pre-Pauline, indicative of the missionary movement's theology of the Spirit. "Neither male and female" refers not to some androgynous ideal (i.e., the rejection of one's sexual nature) but to marriage and gender relationships. It affirms that "women and men in the Christian community are not defined by their sexual procreative capacities or by their religious, cultural or social gender roles, but by their discipleship and empowering with the Spirit."[88]

In Paul's instructions to the Corinthians he somewhat modified his unequivocal affirmation of Christian equality and freedom. In order to shield the Christian movement from accusations that it differed little from orgiastic, esoteric, oriental cults, he enjoined Christian women to exhibit decorous behavior in worship (1 Cor. 11:2–16) and limited the active participation of married women in Christian assemblies (1 Cor. 14:33–36). In both cases, Paul's "major concern . . . is not the behavior of women but the protection of the Christian community." These modifications and qualifications were developed later in the last decades of the first century in the "deutero-Pauline" New Testament texts (i.e., texts written not by Paul but by his disciples or those who claim his authority) of Colossians, Ephesians, and the three Pastorals (1 and 2 Timothy; Titus). The "love patriarchalism" in the household codes (Col. 3:18–4:1; Eph. 5:21–33; 1 Pet. 2:11–3:12) and other injunctions against women "lead in the future to the gradual exclusion of all women from ecclesial office and to the gradual patriarchalization of the whole church."[89] Such developments represent a departure from the house churches of the early Christian movement and led in turn to a spiritualized reinterpretation of Galatians 3:28.

In sum, Schüssler Fiorenza attempts to demonstrate that the earliest form of Christianity, beginning with the teachings and actions of Jesus, supported Spirit-led equal opportunity missionary outreach by men and women. Only later was this radical, prophetic, counterculture message distorted into a male-dominated, institutionalized movement culminating in a monarchical episcopacy. The result was, as Schüssler Fiorenza noted in an earlier article, "the sad demise of the original Christian vision of oneness in Christ." The later-developing "sociological and theological stress on submission and patriarchal superordination has won out over its sociological and theological stress on altruistic love and ministerial service. Yet this 'success' can not be justified theologically, since it cannot claim the authority of Jesus for its own Christian praxis."[90]

In the same way, the present office of priesthood cannot be justified, for it is not based on the earliest New Testament leadership model of Spirit-gifting. Schüssler Fiorenza questions the feminist agenda of ordaining women to the priesthood, for it is little more than conforming to patriarchal-authoritarian structures—a concern shared by others.[91] Since the gifts of the Spirit are not restricted to a cultic priesthood, "everyone is able and authorized in the power of the Spirit to preach, to prophesy, to forgive sins, and to participate actively in the celebration of the Lord's Supper." The feminist issue is not women's ordination; rather, it is a reconceptualization and transformation of church structures and ministry into the "ekklēsia of women."[92]

An Evangelical Perspective: Richard Longenecker

During the 1970s, increasing numbers of evangelicals reread the Bible from the perspective of women. Though influenced by the steady stream of feminist literature churning out of the women's movement, as well as by decisions among more liberal Protestant groups to ordain women, evangelicals nevertheless appealed to the final authority of Scripture in their judgments about women in ministry. Although they endorsed some aspects of the women's movement, "biblical feminists" distanced themselves from their secular counterparts. Gretchen Gaebelein Hull stressed this divergence by observing that the secular feminist says, "I want my rights. I want to be able to compete on an equal basis with men," whereas the biblical feminist says, "I want to be free to be the person God created me to be and to have the privilege of following Christ as He calls me to do."[93]

Upholding Scripture's infallibility, divine inspiration, and ultimate authority in matters of faith and conduct, evangelical egalitarians reconsidered biblical texts and mined the historical record to support their case. Evangelical traditionalists responded in kind, resulting in a flurry of publications focused on exegeting the problematic passages I have discussed.[94] The result has fractured evangelicalism, with no repair in sight; if anything, the positions have hardened into a hermeneutical standoff.[95]

Since the 1970s, biblical feminists have repeatedly cited Galatians 3:28 as the locus classicus in support of women in ministry. In their landmark study, *All We're Meant to Be* (1974), Nancy Hardesty and Letha Scanzoni opined that Galatians 3:28 "holds the key to bringing harmony and removing the dissonant clash that is bound to exist as long as one sex is looked upon as superior and the other as being inferior and the source of evil."[96] F. F. Bruce, the "dean" of evangelical New Testament scholarship at the University of Manchester, claimed that in this liberating verse Paul "voices a revolutionary sentiment." Richard Longenecker called the text "the boldest statement in all the New Testament on the equality of women with men before God," having "both spiritual and social dimensions, both vertical and horizontal implications." Similarly, Klyne Snodgrass wrote that "Galatians 3:28 *is* the most socially explosive text in the New Testament, and if given its due, it will confront and change our lives and our communities. The only question is *how* socially explosive it is." As recently as 1998, David Scholer considered Galatians 3:28 "to be the fundamental Pauline theological basis for the inclusion of women and men as equal and mutual partners in all of the ministries of the Church."[97]

What hermeneutic do these evangelicals employ to support the controlling feature of this text? Several New Testament scholars illustrate the hermeneutical tack taken by evangelicals. Richard Longenecker, who has taught at Trinity Evangelical Divinity School and the University of Toronto (Wycliffe College), takes what he calls a "developmental approach" toward the Bible and issues of women. He claims this hermeneutic "compels us as Christians to stress the redemptive notes of freedom, equality, and mutuality that are sounded in the New Testament."[98]

Longenecker supports his assertion with four observations.[99] First, he acknowledges that "the data in the New Testament on the status of women appear to be diverse, even contradictory," and so dismisses attempts by fundamentalist "inerrantists" to reconcile egalitarian texts with subordinationist texts. These different texts are rooted in two categories of thought—the order of creation, with its emphasis on hierarchical order and subordination, and the order of redemption, with its emphasis on freedom, mutuality, and equality. Of the two, "redemptive categories of thought are crucial to a Christian understanding of the status of women" because they characterize a trajectory in Scripture that increasingly affirms women.[100]

Second, the developmental approach emphasizes the New and not the Old Testament as the point of departure in understanding women's role in ministry. Hence Jesus' attitude toward women and principles of the gospel declared in the New Testament become fundamental. "That is why Galatians 3:28 is so important for our discussions, for there the gospel is clearly stated as having revolutionary significance for the cultural, social, and sexual areas of life."[101]

Third, a developmental approach emphasizes *what* is proclaimed over *how* the gospel is practiced in the New Testament. Within the New Testament, the implementation of full equality falls short of the expressed ideal; it is left to successive generations of Christians to work out the full implications of that ideal. Longenecker reiterates the argument made by the neo-evangelical Paul Jewett, who was indebted to the insights of Krister Stendahl. In *Man as Male and Female* (1975), Jewett observes, "In its implementation, the New Testament church reflects, to a considerable extent, the prevailing attitudes and practices of the times. Because of this, we should look to the passages which point beyond these first-century attitudes toward women to the ideal of the new humanity in Christ."[102]

To illustrate his point, Jewett (and others since, including Longenecker) made the same argument as nineteenth-century evangelical feminists did regarding slavery, though, as we have seen, the latter began as antislavery advocates and then shifted to women's rights. Slavery was not abolished in the New Testament church—in fact, as Kevin Giles has recently argued, the Bible endorsed the practice and institution of slavery. Indeed, during the antebellum era, most American theologians in the South and many in the North concluded that the Bible sanctioned slavery.[103]

Thus Holy Writ and its interpreters supported a practice viewed today as abhorrent. In the case of slavery, does not the Bible reflect the culture of its authors? And so, too, does not the Bible reflect the culture of its authors in the case of women? Do we not have, Gretchen Gaebelein Hull suggests, "the paradox of the true record [Scripture] of the false idea" [patriarchy]? Concludes Jewett: "The church today should not strive to maintain the status quo of church life in the first century, as though it were normative for all time. Rather, the church should seek to implement fully the principle that in Christ women are truly free."[104] In short, the slave/women issue presents a significant exception to the old goal of reforming/restoring the church, for on these crucial points, it did not implement the ideals/ideas that it transmitted to later times.

Finally, Longenecker's developmental approach recognizes that the varied circumstances Christians faced called for varied responses, some of which emphasized equality of men and women, others the subordination of women to men. Though Paul was acutely aware that newfound freedom in Christ restructured social relations, he was "also alert to the dangers of alienating Jews and confusing Gentiles by appearing to be too radical."[105] In his effort to be "all things to all people," Paul made concessions to prevailing chauvinist attitudes of his day.

Evangelical scholars such as Longenecker are guided by a hermeneutic that admits the necessary inclusion of other related biblical texts in constructing a biblical theology of women, and hence they deal with texts on both sides of the issue of women's equality. They distinguish, however, between principles proclaimed (e.g., the new creation in Galatians with its attendant freedom) and specific circumstances addressed (e.g., the silencing of women in 1 Tim. 2) and conclude that the principle takes precedence over the circumstantial. In addition, they recognize a developmental aspect in Scripture that points to an ideal to be realized even now, for the new creation is a present reality, though to be sure, a fully realized reality in the eschaton. Although the implementation of this ideal falls short even in the New Testament, it remains for Christians to work out the implications of a newly created and redeemed order within subsequent history.

In summary, the history of the interpretation of Galatians 3:28 illustrates that interpretations are not presuppositionless—that there is a pre-understanding in the interpretive endeavor. At the same time, it is important to recognize that not all presuppositions are equally valid. Although my task has been more descriptive than evaluative, to reach a personally satisfying and logically consistent resolution to the issue of women in the church we would need to scrutinize further the hermeneutical foundations of the scholars just discussed. We might ask, for example, is Stendahl justified in concluding that Paul is saying the order of creation is wrong? In Schüssler Fiorenza's hermeneutic, what exactly is women's experience, and how can it serve as a reliable standard of interpretation? Or, for Longenecker, why, in his developmental approach, are redemptive categories given priority over creation categories? We are back to questions raised earlier of how a hermeneutic relates to one's understanding of the overall teachings and purposes of Scripture.

Conclusion

During my sophomore year in college in 1969, a professor in my world literature class returned from the annual meeting of the Modern Language Association and announced to the class that a new movement was transforming
social relations, higher education, and traditional views of ministry. I had no
idea what she was talking about. Within a generation, however, what was foreign has become familiar. The world of academics, particularly in the human-
ities and social sciences, now considers the study of women (both as agents
and as a perspective) an integral part of the academic enterprise.

The academic study of religion reflects this momentous change.[106] For
example, when I enrolled for doctoral studies at the University of Chicago in
1977, the Divinity School had two women faculty and a cohort of twenty-five
female Ph.D. students. Nearly twenty-five years later (2001), the school's female faculty had grown to eleven and the number of women enrolled in Ph.D.
programs to ninety-eight.[107] In part by trickle-down effect, what is found in
institutions that investigate the phenomenon of religion is also found in seminaries that promote its practice (some, like Chicago, do both). Recall that
nearly half of seminary students in mainline Protestant seminaries are women.

During the last half century, as broad social changes expanded equal opportunity for women and culminated in the momentous pressures exerted by
the women's movement, the text of Galatians 3:28 has been retrieved (from its
nineteenth-century invocation), reexamined, and reinterpreted in a new light.
As influential as these recent developments may be, however, they are the
occasion and not the cause of the discussion of women in ministry, for as we
have seen, the roots of the issue extend into the fertile soil of the New Testament itself. The Bible, an ancient document with a living message, continues
to nourish and challenge its readers to restudy and reapply its teachings in
fresh ways in response to a changing world. The pre-understanding readers
bring to the Bible, how they sift and interpret the biblical data, differentiate
the transient from the timeless, the cultural from the normative, the limited
from the general, all these shape their position on women in ministry. "Texts
trigger readings," writes Mieke Bal; "that is what they are: the occasion of a
reaction."[108] And so it has been for Galatians 3:28.

Conclusion

Concluding chapters are intended to wrap things up, reiterate basic arguments, summarize themes, and point to future developments. These I intend to offer but with a frank admission that this closure is tentative rather than definitive, for this study has raised as many questions as answers.

We are left to ask, given the varied approaches and interpretations of biblical texts, a passel of questions. Is there an inexhaustible number of meanings in texts? Does one interpreter or hermeneutical approach preclude others? Is there only one primary meaning (namely, the author's intention) to a text, but other legitimate secondary meanings? If we agree that the primary meaning is the author's intention, can we ever know or reasonably expect to approximate the author's original meaning or intention? Because we are creatures of history, limited by historical circumstances (social, economic, political, psychological, geographic), can we transcend those circumstances to achieve a sound understanding of the text? Will all interpretations be approximations or probabilities? Is subjective, individual interpretation checked by the voice of an interpretive Christian community, including the living and the dead? Does the theological conviction that the text is ultimately of divine origin guarantee a true meaning? If so, can we know the mind of God?

These questions take us into the complex and contentious area of contemporary hermeneutics, but the point I want to make is that these are not merely contemporary questions but historical questions, that is, questions of long standing, raised in studying the history of texts and their effects. Undoubtedly, the challenges are more formidable today because of the shift in interpretive perspective from author and text to the reader and the consequent so-called deconstructive agenda of uncovering embedded power relations in all texts. In this latter hermeneutical turn, the ultimate meaning of the text is as much the reader's contribution to the text as the author's. Yet historically, the deconstructive challenge has always been present, though authorities called it by a different name—heresy.

I have raised questions—some of whose answers are more appropriately left to the constructive work of biblical scholars and theologians—but what I have pursued in these eight chapters invites broader and deeper inquiry into the relationship between biblical texts and history. To restate the point made in the introduction: this study has been selective and episodic rather than comprehensive, tilted toward events and figures in Western Christianity and more specifically (as seen in the last three chapters) in the America context. Future endeavors (a second volume?) beg for shifting the history of the effects of Scripture to non-Western environments such as the continents of Asia and Africa. In the sixteenth century and accelerating since the nineteenth, the globalization of Christianity—really, a phenomenon that began in the first century—has preceded or simultaneously proceeded along with other forms of globalization. The center of gravity of the Christian faith has moved from the West to the "global South," from Euro–North America to Latin America, sub-Saharan Africa, the South Pacific, and parts of Asia.[1]

Given the opening (in some cases reopening) of these non-Western lands to Christianity, we need to ask of these varied regions the same set of questions regarding the history of the effects of Scripture that have been asked throughout the book. What biblical texts have informed or been particularly compelling in these contexts? What historical and cultural circumstances brought otherwise neglected texts to the fore, transforming individuals and peoples? From its origins, Christianity has been a portable faith—a faith of "infinite translatability," as Andrew Walls puts it—and not only because its portable Scriptures are open to translation. More decisively, "The great Act on which Christian faith rests, the Word becoming flesh and pitching tent among us, is itself an act of translation."[2] That is, the incarnation was the original act of Christian inculturation, the initial and fundamental expression of Christian contextualization.

What, then, does the highly translatable biblical message look like in a global Third World context?[3] How might it be received and interpreted in a place such as Ghana, Africa? Kwame Bediako suggests that the New Testament Book of Hebrews is particularly applicable to the people of Ghana because its presentation of Christ as high priest, sacrifice, and ancestor touch salient themes in their traditional Akan religion.[4] Just as Bernard of Clairvaux found a receptive audience to the Song of Songs among mature monks in the Cistercian order, so the Book of Hebrews as a highly translatable text among the Akan finds acceptance. How critical has this text been to the development of

Christianity among the Akan? In what specific ways has it been appropriated? What is the history of this text in different non-Western linguistic and cultural settings? These questions and others regarding the interplay of history and Scripture merit further examination.

So much for potential vistas of new inquiry. What can be said about the texts we have pursued through Western space and time? We have seen that Scripture has functioned in a reflexive, push-pull, dialectical interplay of influences; texts have shaped history, and history has shaped the interpretation of texts. The focus has been on episodes or critical junctures when the serendipitous conjunction of a text and a historical situation provided a receptive environment for the text's appeal and particular interpretation. In this context of reciprocal circularity, the texts functioned in at least five ways.

First, *texts as transforming agents*. Through Christian history, the Bible has functioned not merely as a book of story, instruction, and inspiration but as the vehicle of divine communication and supernatural transformation. Texts were recognized to contain something valuable and true because they originated in God. When Anthony heard the text of Matthew 19:21 and gave away all his possessions to follow Christ, or when Bernard pored over the Song of Songs and experienced a mystical encounter with divine reality, or when Luther "sweated over" Romans 1:17 and came to a new realization of God's grace, or when Agnes Ozman personalized the utterance of glossolalia in the Book of Acts—in each episode, an individual was transformed existentially by the divine Word. The "Good Book" it is but also more: it has been a life-changing word of conversion to another way of thinking and acting, believing and behaving.

Second, *texts as re-created meaning*. Texts of Scripture are not merely agents of transformation but are re-created and resuscitated in the interpretive and historical process. Texts re-create people, and people re-create texts. New ways of understanding are elicited by contexts. As a particular text works its way through history, it undergoes multiple interpretations and applications. So Anthony, Bernard, and Luther were not only re-created by texts; they invested texts with new meaning. African Americans made the exodus story their story— first a story of deliverance from slavery, then one of God's deliverance from all forms of oppression. In some cases a text lies dormant, becomes active, and may or may not return to dormancy. The Petrine text (Matt. 16:18–19), for example, lay dormant for several centuries before it was invoked as a proof-text for the primacy of the bishop of Rome. The Song of Songs, once the most frequently read and expounded book in the medieval monastery, is largely ignored today.

Third, *select texts as comprehending sources*. A particular text of Scripture has functioned as a key text around which other texts of Scripture are illuminated, and these in turn refract back to the original text. Or to change the metaphor: a particular text functions as a centripetal force, drawing other biblical texts into its thematic orbit. So Bernard focused on the Song of Songs and used it as the centerpiece by which to comprehend other passages of Scripture alluding to the love of God in Christ Jesus.

Fourth, *texts as hermeneutical keys*. A text functions not only as a comprehending source but also as an interpretive key to unlock the essential meaning of Scripture or resolve tensions within Scripture. African Americans discovered in the exodus motif the hermeneutical key to Scripture. The exodus theme of deliverance and liberation became "the most significant myth for American black identity, whether slave or free." Christians favoring the equality of men and women uplift Galatians 3:28 as the locus classicus in defense of the full participation of women in ministry, superseding other texts that restrict women's role. It is the "Magna Carta of Humanity," Paul's "breakthrough," a "socially explosive text," the "key to bringing harmony and removing the dissonant clash" between the sexes.

Fifth, *texts as secondary justifications*. A particular text of Scripture functions to legitimize what has already occurred or to support the current climate of opinion. In a sense, many texts function in this way, for they confirm already existing notions, ideas, or convictions in the mind of the reader. Practice typically precedes theory. In some cases, however, texts are explicitly cited to support an existing historical reality. The Petrine text (Matthew 16:18–19), for example, represents a "retreat from exegesis to later history," for it was cited after the fact as *the* biblical justification for the primacy of the bishop of Rome. Critics of Christian feminists contend that egalitarians have done the same in their forced reading of Galatians 3:28. That is, egalitarians found in this text support for what they wanted to conform to the secular women's movement.

A somewhat different development occurred among Anabaptists, whose pacifist convictions emerged from the whipsaw of events and ideas. Their pacifism was not derived from a preexisting blueprint but evolved within the vicissitudes of history. In the context of oppression and persecution, a specific way of reading the Bible emerged. By some historical accounts, Anabaptist pacifism grew primarily from historical expediency and secondarily from a biblical vision. But the vision is no less normative because it occurred amid historical circumstances, argue Anabaptist theologians, for the Anabaptist position defines not so much historical movement as a hermeneutic that correctly understands Scripture.

The Bible in history—for two millennia Christians have engaged the sacred text by hearing, reading, studying, memorizing, applying, and meditating upon its words in countless settings. Scripture has been pondered in caves, cabins, cloisters, castles, and cathedrals. Its message has been proclaimed from pulpits, street corners, brush arbors, and jails. Its content has been studied in private, small groups, academies, schools, monasteries, and universities. Its meaning has been explained by prophets and popes, monks and missionaries, laypeople and clergy, scholars and the unlettered. Its teaching has been expressed in homilies, sermons, music, and art and formalized in councils, commentaries, creeds, and confessions. It has been used to support the status quo and motivate revolutionary behavior. It has been translated into more languages than any other book, and it remains the best-selling nonfiction book of all time. It is a guide and an authoritative source. It inspires and challenges, comforts and mystifies, transforms and instructs.

Above all, for Christians, the Bible ultimately centers on Jesus—as the gospel hymn expresses it—on "the old, old story of Jesus and his love." The Bible has been a point of departure but never the final destination; it is a sign, pointing beyond itself to another Word.

Notes

HTR	*Harvard Theological Review*
IB	*Interpreter's Bible.* Edited by G. A. Buttrick et al. 12 vols. New York: Abingdon, 1951–57.
ICC	International Critical Commentary
ITC	International Theological Commentary
JAAR	*Journal of the American Academy of Religion*
JAH	*Journal of American History*
JBC	*Jerome Biblical Commentary.* Edited by Raymond E. Brown et al. Englewood Cliffs, N.J.: Prentice Hall, 1968.
JBL	*Journal of Biblical Literature*
JES	*Journal of Ecumenical Studies*
JETS	*Journal of the Evangelical Theological Society*
JPT	*Journal of Pentecostal Theology*
JPTSS	Journal of Pentecostal Theology Supplement Series
JR	*Journal of Religion*
JRS	*Journal of Roman Studies*
JSNT	*Journal for the Study of the New Testament*
JSNTSS	Journal for the Study of the New Testament Supplement Series
JTS	*Journal of Theological Studies*
LCC	The Library of Christian Classics. Edited by J. Baillie et al. 26 vols. Philadelphia: Westminster, 1953–66.
LCL	Loeb Classical Library
LQ	*Lutheran Quarterly*
LW	*Luther's Works, American Edition.* Edited by Jaroslav Pelikan, vols. 1–30; Helmut T. Lehman, vols. 31–55. St. Louis: Concordia, and Philadelphia: Fortress (formerly Muhlenberg Press), 1955–86.
MFC	Message of the Fathers of the Church
MQR	*Mennonite Quarterly Review*
MS	*Monastic Studies*
NCB	New Century Bible (Commentary)
NICNT	New International Commentary on the New Testament
NICOT	New International Commentary on the Old Testament
NIGTC	New International Greek Testament Commentary
NPNF	*A Select Library of the Nicene and Post-Nicene Fathers of the Christian Church.* Edited by Philip Schaff et al. 2 series (14 vols. each). 1887–94. Reprint, Grand Rapids, Mich.: Eerdmans, 1952–56.
NTM	New Testament Message
OTG	Old Testament Guides
OTL	Old Testament Library
Pneuma	*Pneuma: Journal for the Society of Pentecostal Studies*
PSB	*Princeton Seminary Bulletin*
SAC	Studies in Antiquity and Christianity
SP	Sacra Pagina

SEC   *Studies in Early Christianity: A Collection of Scholarly Essays.* Edited by Everret Ferguson. 18 vols. New York: Garland, 1993.
StPatr   *Studia Patristica*
ThTo   *Theology Today*
TLS   Theology and Life Series
TNTC   Tyndale New Testament Commentaries
TOTC   Tyndale Old Testament Commentaries
TPINTC   TPI New Testament Commentaries
TS   *Theological Studies*
WBC   Word Biblical Commentary
WC   Westminster Commentaries

INTRODUCTION

1. For two accessible histories of biblical interpretation, see Robert M. Grant, with David Tracy, *A Short History of the Interpretation of the Bible,* 2nd ed. (Philadelphia: Fortress, 1984); George T. Montague, *Understanding the Bible: A Basic Introduction to Biblical Interpretation* (New York: Paulist Press, 1997).

2. Paul Ricoeur, "Preface to Bultmann," in *Essays on Biblical Interpretation,"* ed. Lewis Mudge (Philadelphia: Fortress, 1980), 53.

3. For an extended discussion of these questions, see David Tracy, *Plurality and Ambiguity: Hermeneutics, Religion, Hope* (San Francisco: Harper and Row, 1987), chap. 1.

4. The term is Lionel Thornton's, cited in Martin E. Marty, *The Modern Schism: Three Paths to the Secular* (New York: Harper and Row, 1969), 14.

5. Gerhard Ebeling, *The Word of God and Tradition* (Philadelphia: Fortress, 1968); Karlfried Froelich, "Church History and the Bible," in *Biblical Hermeneutics in Historical Perspective: Studies in Honor of Karlfried Froelich on His Sixtieth Birthday,* ed. Mark S. Burrows and Paul Rorem (Grand Rapids, Mich.: Eerdmans, 1991), 1–15; Ulrich Luz, *Matthew in History: Interpretation, Influence, and Effects* (Minneapolis, Minn.: Fortress, 1994); Roland Murphy, "Reflections on the History of the Exposition of Scripture," in *Studies in Catholic History in Honor of John Tracy Ellis,* ed. Robert Frederick Trisco, Nelson H. Minnich, Robert B. Eno, John Tracy Ellis (Wilmington, Del.: Michael Glazier, 1985), 489–99; Murphy, "Scripture and Church History," in *Exodus: A Lasting Paradigm,* ed. Bas van Iersel and Anton Weiler (Edinburgh: T. & T. Clark, 1987), 3–10. Recent authors include John A. Sawyer, *The Fifth Gospel: Isaiah in the History of Christianity* (Cambridge: Cambridge University Press, 1996); John R. Levison and Priscilla Pope-Levison, eds., *Return to Babel: Global Perspectives on the Bible* (Louisville, Ky.: Westminster John Knox, 1999); and Walter Dietrich and Ulrich Luz, eds., *The Bible in a World Context: An Experiment in Cultural Hermeneutics* (Grand Rapids, Mich.: Eerdmans, 2002).

6. Froelich, "Church History and the Bible," 11.

7. Edmund Sears Morgan, ed., *Puritan Political Ideas: 1558–1794* (Indianapolis: Bobbs-Merrill, 1965), xiii.

8. For example, earlier tentative chapters included the 2 Peter 1:4 in the Ortho-

dox tradition; John 6:53–55 and controversies over sacramental theology; and the Epistle to the Hebrews in the contemporary cross-cultural setting of Ghana, Africa.

9. Though see, for example, David C. Steinmetz, "The Superiority of Pre-critical Exegesis," *ThTo* 27 (1980): 27–38.

10. In addition to the works cited in note 1, the following articles offer helpful summaries of the history of biblical interpretation: John F. A. Sawyer, "Interpretation, History of," in *A Dictionary of Biblical Interpretation*, ed. R. J. Coggins and J. L. Houlden (Philadelphia: Trinity Press, 1990), 316–20; Ben C. Ollenburger, "Interpretation, Biblical," in *Eerdmans Dictionary of the Bible*, ed. David Noel Freedman (Grand Rapids, Mich.: Eerdmans, 2000), 641–45; Philip Alexander et al., "Interpretation, History of," in *The Oxford Guide to Ideas and Issues of the Bible*, ed. Bruce M. Metzger and Michael D. Coogan (New York: Oxford University Press, 2001), 219–46.

11. Hans W. Frei, *The Eclipse of Biblical Narrative: A Study of Eighteenth and Nineteenth Century Hermeneutics* (New Haven, Conn.: Yale University Press, 1974), 1.

12. Ibid., 2–3.

13. John Goldingay, *Models for Interpretation of Scripture* (Grand Rapids, Mich.: Eerdmans, 1995), 18.

14. For an awareness of these hermeneutical concerns in contemporary Christian ethics, see Richard B. Hays, *The Moral Vision of the New Testament: Community, Cross, New Creation* (San Francisco: HarperCollins, 1996). The literature on contemporary hermeneutics is immense, but for a useful sampling, see Donald K. McKim, ed., *A Guide to Contemporary Hermeneutics: Major Trends in Biblical Interpretation* (Grand Rapids, Mich.: Eerdmans, 1986); John Reumann, "After Historical Criticism, What? Trends in Biblical Interpretation and Ecumenical, Interfaith Dialogues," *JES* 29 (winter 1992): 55–86; Steven L. McKenzie and Stephen R. Haynes, eds., *To Each Its Own Meaning: An Introduction to Biblical Criticisms and Their Application* (Louisville, Ky.: Westminster John Knox, 1993); Fernando F. Segovia and Mary Ann Tolbert, eds., *Reading from This Place*, vol. 1, *Social Location and Biblical Interpretation in the United States* (Minneapolis, Minn.: Fortress, 1995).

15. Wesley A. Kort, *"Take, Read": Scripture, Textuality, and Cultural Practice* (University Park: Pennsylvania State University Press, 1996), 8.

16. Northrop Frye, *The Great Code: The Bible and Literature* (New York: Harcourt Brace Jovanovich, 1982).

CHAPTER I

1. Fulton Oursler, *The Greatest Story Ever Told: A Tale of the Greatest Life Ever Lived* (Garden City, N.Y.: Doubleday [ca. 1949]).

2. For example, Matthew has the man "coming" to Jesus, whereas Mark has him "running to" Jesus; Matthew avoids Mark's "Good Teacher" for "Teacher, what good deed"; Matthew adds the requirement of love toward neighbor to the laws and also injects the idea of perfection; Mark notes that Jesus looked on the man and loved him. On Matthew's sources and variations in the synoptic accounts, see W. D. Davies and Dale Allison Jr., *A Critical and Exegetical Commentary on the Gospel according to Saint Matthew*, 3 vols., ICC (Edinburgh: T. & T. Clark, 1988–97), 3:39–50.

3. Ulrich Luz, *Matthew 8–20: A Commentary*, trans. Wilhelm C. Linss, Hermenia (Minneapolis, Minn.: Augsburg Fortress, 2001), 513–14.

4. Boniface Ramsey, "Desert," in *The New Dictionary of Catholic Spirituality*, ed. Michael Downey (Collegeville, Minn.: Liturgical Press, 1993), 264; *JBC*, 2:96–97; David Knowles, *Christian Monasticism* (New York: McGraw Hill, 1969), 227–30.

5. Ambrose, "Concerning Widows," *NPNF*, 2nd ser., 10:403; *Letters of St. Paulinus of Nola*, 2 vols., trans. and annot. P. G. Walsh, ACW 36 (New York: Newman Press, 1967), 2:69–70; John Cassian, *The Conferences*, trans. and annot. Boniface Ramsey, ACW 57 (New York: Paulist Press, 1997), 723; Augustine, "Sermons on New Testament Lessons," *NPNF*, 1st ser., 6:366.

6. Richard Webb Haskin, "The Call to Sell All: The History of the Interpretation of Mark 10:17–33 and Parallels" (Ph.D. diss., Columbia University, 1968), 103–8, 179–81, 204–5.

7. Martin Hengel, *Property and Riches in the Early Church*, trans. John Bowden (Philadelphia: Fortress, 1974), 84; Davies and Allison, *Commentary on Matthew*, 3:47. For Luz, Matthew's "demand to give up one's possessions is a fundamental demand that applies to everyone" (*Matthew 8–20*, 514).

8. Luke T. Johnson, *The Literary Function of Possessions in Luke-Acts*, Society of Biblical Literature Dissertation Series 39 (Missoula, Mont.: Scholars Press, 1977), 158–59.

9. Luz, *Matthew 8–20*, 514.

10. Craig L. Blomberg, *Neither Poverty nor Riches: A Biblical Theology of Material Possessions* (Grand Rapids, Mich.: Eerdmans, 1999), 212.

11. L. William Countryman, "Asceticism in the Johannine Letters?" in *Asceticism and the New Testament*, ed. Leif E. Vaage and Vincent L. Wimbush (New York: Routledge, 1999), 383; Marilyn Dunn, *The Emergence of Monasticism: From the Desert Fathers to the Early Middle Ages* (Malden, Mass.: Blackwell, 2000), 6; Vincent Wimbush, "The Ascetic Impulse in Early Christianity: Some Methodological Challenges," *StPatr* 25 (1993): 464–67.

12. See Vaage and Wimbush, *Asceticism and the New Testament*; J. Duncan M. Derrett, *Ascetic Discourse: An Explanation of the Sermon on the Mount* (Eilsbrunn: Ko'amar, 1989).

13. Hans von Campenhausen, "Early Christian Asceticism," in *Acts of Piety in the Early Church*, ed. Everett Ferguson, vol. 17 of *SEC*, 209, 210; Anthony J. Saldarini, "Asceticism and the Gospel of Matthew," in *Asceticism and the New Testament*, 24. My earlier comments on asceticism in Matthew are drawn from this article, 20–23.

14. Haskin, "Call to Sell All," 396–418, 6–7, 430–38, 390 (quote). For a brief history of interpretation of Matthew 19:21, see Luz, *Matthew 8–20*, 518–23.

15. Haskin, "Call to Sell All," 52–55, 66–73.

16. Campenhausen, "Early Christian Asceticism," 179; Clement of Alexandria, "Salvation of the Rich Man," *ANF*, 2:594.

17. Quoted in Haskin, "Call to Sell All," 75.

18. Peter Walpot, "True Yieldedness and the Christian Community of Goods" (1577), in *Early Anabaptist Spirituality*, trans. and ed. Daniel Liechty, CWS (New York: Paulist Press, 1994), 150, 191.

19. Wesley quoted in Haskin, "Call to Sell All," 316; and in Henry D. Rack, *Rea-*

sonable Enthusiast: John Wesley and the Rise of Methodism, 2nd ed. (Nashville, Tenn.: Abingdon, 1993), 366; Beecher quoted in Paul F. Boller Jr., *American Thought in Transition: The Impact of Evolutionary Naturalism, 1865–1900* (Chicago: Rand McNally, 1969), 118.

20. R. V. G. Tasker, *The Gospel According to St. Matthew*, TNTC (1961; reprint, Grand Rapids, Mich.: Eerdmans, 1981), 187.

21. *IB*, 7:484; Davies and Allison, *Commentary on Matthew*, 3:47–48; David Hill, *The Gospel of Matthew*, NCB (1972; reprint, Grand Rapids, Mich.: Eerdmans, 1972), 283; Daniel J. Harrington, *The Gospel of Matthew*, SP (Collegeville, Minn.: Liturgical Press, 1991), 278; John P. Meier, *The Vision of Matthew: Christ, Church and Morality in the First Gospel* (New York: Paulist Press, 1979), 140; Eduard Schweizer, *The Good News according to Matthew*, trans. David E. Green (Atlanta: John Knox, 1975), 388; Tasker, *Matthew*, 186; Simon Légasse, "The Call of the Rich Man," in *Gospel Poverty: Essays in Biblical Theology*, ed. Augustin George, trans. Michael D. Guinan (Chicago: Franciscan Herald Press, 1977), 55, 72–76.

22. Calvin quoted in Davies and Allison, *Commentary on Matthew*, 47; John Calvin, *Institutes of the Christian Religion*, 2 vols., ed. John T. McNeill, LCC (1962), 2:1268; Dietrich Bonhoeffer, *The Cost of Discipleship*, rev. ed. (New York: Macmillan, 1963), 82, 84.

23. William L. Lane, *The Gospel according to Mark*, NICNT (Grand Rapids, Mich.: Eerdmans, 1974), 367–68; Blomberg, *Neither Poverty nor Riches*, 145–46; Richard Batey, *Jesus and the Poor* (New York: Harper and Row, 1972), 18–22.

24. Larry Hurtado, *Mark*, GNC (San Francisco: Harper and Row, 1983), 15.

25. Luz, *Matthew 8–20*, 522.

26. Schweizer, *Good News according to Matthew*, 388.

27. James E. Goehring, *Ascetics, Society, and the Desert: Studies in Early Egyptian Monasticism*, SAC (Harrisburg, Pa.: Trinity Press, 1999), chaps. 1, 10; Harnack quoted in Samuel Rubenson, *The Letters of St. Antony: Monasticism and the Making of a Saint*, SAC (Minneapolis, Minn.: Fortress, 1995), 126.

28. The most accessible and scholarly edition of *Life of Anthony* and the one to which I refer is Robert C. Gregg, trans., introd. *Athanasius: The Life of St. Antony and the Letter to Marcellinus*, CWS (New York: Paulist Press, 1980).

29. David Brakke, *Athanasius and the Politics of Asceticism*, Oxford Early Christian Studies (Oxford: Clarendon Press, 1995), 242–65; Douglas Burton-Christie, *The Word in the Desert: Scripture and the Quest for Holiness in Early Christian Monasticism* (New York: Oxford University Press, 1993), 47.

30. In his careful analysis of *The Life of Anthony* and other sources, Rubenson disputes the notion that Anthony was unlettered and contends that Anthony wrote at least seven letters in Coptic (*Letters of St. Antony*, 141–42, 185).

31. *Life of Antony*, 32, 36.

32. On contact between monks (especially monastic communities) and nearby communities, see Goehring, *Ascetics, Society, and the Desert*, chap. 2.

33. The classic discussion of the monk as holy man is Peter Brown, "The Rise and Function of the Holy Man in Late Antiquity," *JRS* 61 (1971): 80–101.

34. *Life of Antony*, 98.

35. Ibid., 42–43; Graham Gould, *The Desert Fathers on Monastic Community* (Oxford: Clarendon Press, 1993).

36. Anthony Meredith, "Asceticism—Christian and Greek," in *Acts of Piety in the Early Church*, vol. 17 of *SEC*, 175; Campenhausen, "Early Christian Asceticism," 205; Hengel, *Property and Riches in the Early Church*, 51.

37. Quoted in Peter Brown, *The World of Late Antiquity, AD 150–750* (1971; reprint, New York: Harcourt Brace Jovanovich, 1976), 96.

38. Eusebius, *The History of the Christian Church from Christ to Constantine*, trans., introd. G. A. Williamson, Penguin Classics Series (New York: Penguin Books, 1965), 243–44, 247.

39. Meredith, "Asceticism," 166–67.

40. "I Clement," in *The Apostolic Fathers*, 2 vols., trans. Kirsopp Lake, LCL (Cambridge, Mass.: Harvard University Press, 1970, 1977), 1:9; "Epistle to Diognetus," in *Apostolic Fathers*, 2:359, 361.

41. Quoted in Herbert B. Workman, *Persecution in the Early Church* (1906; reprint, Oxford: Oxford University Press, 1980), 50.

42. Quoted in Ernst Benz, *The Eastern Orthodox Church: Its Thought and Practice* (Garden City, N.Y.: Doubleday, 1963), 165.

43. Roland Bainton, *Christianity* (1964; reprint, Boston: Houghton Mifflin, 1987), 101; senator quotation in William J. La Due, *The Chair of St. Peter: A History of the Papacy* (Maryknoll, N.Y.: Orbis, 1999), 47.

44. C. Wilfred Griggs, *Early Egyptian Christianity: From Its Origins to 451 C.E.*, 2nd ed., (Leiden: Brill, 1991), 106.

45. Quoted in E. R. Dodds, *Pagan and Christian in an Age of Anxiety: Some Aspects of Religious Experience from Marcus Aurelius to Constantine* (1965; reprint, New York: Norton, 1970), 57.

46. Brown, *World of Late Antiquity*, 101; Graham Gould, "Lay Christians, Bishops, and Clergy in the *Apophthegmata Patrum*," *StPatr* 25 (1993): 396–404.

47. Hugh T. Kerr and John M. Mulder, eds., *Conversions: The Christian Experience* (Grand Rapids, Mich.: Eerdmans, 1983), 13.

48. Barnabas Lindars, "The Bible and the Call: The Biblical Roots of the Monastic Life in History and Today," *BJRL* 66 (1983–84): 228–45 (and references in endnotes); Meredith, "Asceticism," 160.

49. Rubenson, *Letters of St. Antony*, 185, 72. For a critique of Rubenson's conclusions, see Graham Gould, "Recent Work on Monastic Origins: A Consideration of the Questions Raised by Samuel Rubenson's *The Letters of St. Antony*," *StPatr* 25 (1993): 405–16; Douglas Burton-Christie, "Oral Culture, Biblical Interpretation, and Spirituality in Early Christian Monasticism," in *The Bible in Greek Christian Antiquity*, ed. and trans. Paul M. Blowers (Notre Dame, Ind.: University of Notre Dame Press, 1997), 417–18.

50. Burton-Christie, *Word in the Desert*, 297–98, 4.

51. Andrew Louth, *The Wilderness of God* (Nashville, Tenn.: Abingdon, 1991), 11.

52. *Life of Antony*, 37; Claude Peifer, "The Biblical Foundations of Monasticism," *CS* 1 (1966): 23; Belden C. Lane, *The Solace of Fierce Landscapes: Exploring Desert and Mountain Spirituality* (New York: Oxford University Press, 1998), 162.

53. Richard Valantasis, "Constructions of Power in Asceticism," *JAAR* 63 (winter 1995): 808. Valantasis discusses "the combative subject" as one of five types of ascetic models.

54. Louth, *Wilderness of God*, 61; *Life of Antony*, 61.

55. Lecky quoted in Burton-Christie, *Word in the Desert*, 12; Dodds, *Pagan and Christian*, 35.

56. Brown, "Rise and Function of the Holy Man," 84; Kallistos Ware, "The Way of the Ascetics: Negative or Affirmative?" in *Asceticism*, ed. Vincent L. Wimbush and Richard Valantasis (New York: Oxford University Press, 1995), 10.

57. Teresa M. Shaw, *The Burden of the Flesh: Fasting and Sexuality in Early Christianity* (Minneapolis, Minn.: Fortress, 1998), 79–128, esp. 124–28; Dunn, *Emergence of Monasticism*, 16–17.

58. Elizabeth A. Clark, *Women in the Early Church*, MFC, vol. 13 (Collegeville, Minn.: Liturgical Press, 1983), chap. 3; Peter Brown, *The Body and Society: Men, Women, and Sexual Renunciation in Early Christianity* (New York: Columbia University Press, 1988), 223; Brakke, *Athanasius and the Politics of Asceticism*, 240–42; *Life of Antony*, 42, 98.

59. Brown, *Body and Society*, 226; Ware, "Way of the Ascetics," 5–6.

60. The following discussion is indebted to Sandra M. Schneiders, "Scripture and Spirituality," in *Christian Spirituality: Origins to the Twelfth Century*, ed. Bernard McGinn and John Meyendorff, vol. 16 of *World Spirituality: An Encyclopedic History of the Religious Quest* (New York: Crossroad, 1992), 5–7.

61. Scholars are convinced that the spread of early Christianity was aided by the displacement of the unwieldy scroll by the compact codex (Brown, *World of Late Antiquity*, 94; Burton-Christie, *Word in the Desert*, 43).

62. Among the modern, accessible editions of the *Sayings* are Benedicta Ward, trans., *The Sayings of the Desert Fathers: The Alphabetical Collection* (Kalamazoo, Mich.: Cistercian Publications, 1975); and Owen Chadwick, trans., *Western Asceticism*, LCC (1958).

63. Burton-Christie, *Word in the Desert*, 97.

64. Burton-Christie, "Oral Culture," 423; Burton-Christie, *Word in the Desert*, 115; *Life of Antony*, 32.

65. Besides the exemplary approach, monks used other interpretive methods, including the allegorical and the ethical. These hermeneutical approaches were no different than those used by the Christian church in general, except that the life situation of the monks shaped a particular application of method. For example, monks took the Matthew 19:21 text literally, whereas a Clement of Alexandria understood it allegorically or "spiritually"; that is, the heart must be cleansed of its desire for riches. See Burton-Christie, *Word in the Desert*.

66. Haskins, "Call to Sell All," 92–94, 112–18; Luz *Matthew 8–20*, 518 (Basil quotation); John Chrysostom, "Homilies on the Gospel of St. Matthew," *NPNF*, 1st ser., 10:533–34; "Homilies on First Corinthians," *NPNF*, 1st ser., 12:189, 207; Cyprian, "On Works of Alms," *ANF*, 5:478; Maximus of Turin, *Sermons*, trans. and annot. Boniface Ramsey, ACW 50 (New York: Newman Press, 1989), 113; *Letters of Paulinus of Nola*, 216; Augustine, "Sermons on New Testament Lessons," *NPNF*, 1st ser., 6:292, 366–67, 373; *On Faith and Works*, trans. Gregory J. Lombardo, ACW 48 (New York: Newman Press, 1988), 35.

67. Augustine, "The Work of Monks," *NPNF*, 1st ser., 3:518; Jerome, *The Letters of St. Jerome*, vol. 1, *Letters 1–22*, introd. and notes, Thomas Comerford Lawler; trans. Charles Christopher Mierow, ACW 33 (New York: Newman Press, 1963), 64; Cassian,

Conferences, 121, 127, 293, 721–23, 744; John Cassian, *The Institutes*, trans. and annot. Boniface Ramsey, ACW 58 (New York: Paulist Press, 2000), 177, 182, 268.

68. Burton-Christie, *Word in the Desert*, 299, 261.

69. Lane, *Solace*, 175.

70. Armand Veillux, "Holy Scripture in the Pachomian Koinonia," *MS* 10 (1974): 153, 152.

71. *The Rule of St. Benedict*, trans. and introd. Anthony C. Meisel and M. L. de Mastro (Garden City, N.Y.: Doubleday, 1975), 43, 106; Peifer, "Biblical Foundations," 17, 19; Kathryn Sullivan, "A Scripture Scholar Looks at the Rule of St. Benedict," in *Rule and Life*, ed. M. Basil Pennington, CSS 12 (Spencer, Mass.: Cistercian Publications, 1971), 73.

72. Jean Leclercq, *The Love of Learning and the Desire for God*, 2nd ed., trans. Catharine Misrahi (New York: Fordham University Press, 1977), 125.

73. Quoted in Roland Bainton, *Here I Stand: A Life of Martin Luther* (1950; reprint, New York: New American Library, n.d.), 156.

74. *LW*, 41:259, 315; 44:253.

75. Quoted in Haskin, "Call to Sell All," 244–45.

76. Ibid., 279.

77. François Biot, *The Rise of Protestant Monasticism* (Baltimore: Helicon, 1963), 65–105, 144–51.

78. Henri Nouwen, *The Way of the Heart: Desert Spirituality and Contemporary Ministry* (1981; San Francisco: HarperCollins, 1991), 92.

79. Kathleen Norris, *Dakota: A Spiritual Geography* (New York: Ticknor and Fields, 1993), 23.

80. Kathleen Norris, *The Cloister Walk* (New York: Riverhead Books, 1996), 121, 117.

CHAPTER 2

1. Quoted in Joseph A. Burgess, "Lutherans and the Papacy," in *A Pope for All Christians? An Inquiry into the Role of Peter in the Modern Church*, ed. Peter J. McCord (New York: Paulist Press, 1976), 21.

2. Quoted in J. Michael Miller, *What Are They Saying about Papal Primacy?* (New York: Paulist Press, 1982), 20; *Catechism of the Catholic Church* (New York: Catholic Book, 1994), 141–42.

3. Frederick C. Grant, *Rome and Reunion* (New York: Oxford University Press, 1965), 21; Ulrich Luz, "The Primacy Text (Mt. 16:18)," *PSB* 12 (1991), 41; Hans Küng, "Editorial," in *Papal Ministry in the Church*, Concilium, vol. 64, ed. Hans Küng (New York: Herder and Herder, 1971), 9.

4. Patrick Granfield, *The Limits of the Papacy: Authority and Autonomy in the Church* (New York: Crossroad, 1987), 39–41; Richard P. McBrien, *Catholicism: Study Edition* (Minneapolis, Minn.: Winston Press, 1981), 830; James F. McCue, "Roman Primacy in the First Three Centuries," in *Papal Ministry in the Church*, 36.

5. Henry Denzinger, *The Sources of Catholic Dogma*, trans. Roy J. Deferrari (St. Louis: B. Herder, 1957), 452 (no. 1822) (my emphasis).

6. Luz, "Primacy Text," 44; Robert B. Eno, *The Rise of the Papacy*, TLS 32 (Wil-

mington, Del.: Michael Glazier, 1990), 15–16; Oscar Cullmann, *Peter: Disciple, Apostle, Martyr. A Historical and Theological Essay*, 2nd ed. (Philadelphia: Westminster, 1962), 175; Avery Dulles, "Papal Authority in Roman Catholicism," in *A Pope for All Christians?* 53.

7. Andrew M. Greeley, "Advantages and Drawbacks of a Centre of Communications in the Church: Sociological Point of View," in *Papal Ministry in the Church*, 101.

8. Daniel Patte, *The Gospel according to Matthew: A Structural Commentary on Matthew's Faith* (Philadelphia: Fortress, 1987; reprint, Valley Forge, Pa.: Trinity Press, 1996), 231.

9. On Wilke, see Joseph A. Burgess, *A History of the Exegesis of Matthew 16:17–19 from 1781 to 1965* (Ann Arbor, Mich.: Edward Brothers, 1976), 69; on Holtzmann, see Cullmann, *Peter*, 170.

10. Cullmann, *Peter*, 174; Raymond E. Brown, Karl P. Donfried, and John Reumann, eds., *Peter in the New Testament* (Minneapolis, Minn.: Augsburg; 1973), 85 n. 192 (quotation).

11. Ben F. Meyer, *The Aims of Jesus* (London: SCM, 1979), 186. For a survey of the disputed words of Jesus, see W. D. Davies and Dale C. Allison Jr., *A Critical and Exegetical Commentary on the Gospel according to Saint Matthew*, 3 vols., ICC (Edinburgh: T. & T. Clark, 1988–97), 2:604–15; Bernard P. Robinson, "Peter and His Successors: Tradition and Redaction in Matthew 16:17–19," *JSNT* 21 (1984): 85–104.

12. Eduard Schweizer, *The Good News according to Matthew*, trans. David E. Green (Atlanta: John Knox, 1975), 337–38; Günther Bornkamm, "End-Expectation and Church in Matthew," in Günther Bornkamm, Gerhard Barth, and Heinz Joachim Held, *Tradition and Interpretation in Matthew* (London: SCM, 1982), 44–46; Luz, "Primacy Text," 46, quotation on 47; Ulrich Luz, *Matthew 8–20: A Commentary*, trans. Wilhelm C. Linss, Hermeneia (Minneapolis, Minn.: Fortress, 2001), 358–59.

13. Denzinger, *Sources*, 452–53 (no. 1823), 453 (no. 1825).

14. Meyer, *Aims of Jesus*, 185–97; Robert H. Gundry, *Matthew: A Commentary on His Literary and Theological Art* (Grand Rapids, Mich.: Eerdmans, 1982), 330–37; Davies and Allison, *Commentary on Matthew*, 2:609–15, quotation on 615.

15. In the exegesis that follows, I have relied upon the following commentaries that represent a wide range of scholarship and confessional traditions: William F. Albright and C. S. Mann, *Matthew*, AB 26 (Garden City, N.Y.: Doubleday, 1971), 193–98; Davies and Allison, *Commentary on Matthew*, 2:623–43; J. C. Fenton, *Saint Matthew*, WC (Philadelphia: Westminster, 1963), 264–70; R. T. France, *Matthew: Evangelist and Teacher* (Grand Rapids, Mich.: Zondervan, 1989), 244–51; Gundry, *Matthew*, 330–37; Donald A. Hagner, *Matthew 14–28*, WBC 33b (Dallas: Word Books, 1995), 469–75; Daniel J. Harrington, *The Gospel of Matthew*, SP 1 (Collegeville, Minn.: Liturgical Press, 1991), 246–52; John P. Meier, *The Vision of Matthew: Christ, Church, and Morality in the First Gospel* (New York: Paulist Press, 1979), 106–21; Meyer, *Aims of Jesus*, 186–97; Patte, *Matthew*, 232–33; Schweizer, *Good News*, 341–44.

16. Davies and Allison, *Commentary on Matthew*, 2:627. But Gundry (*Matthew*) is convinced that *petra* = Christ or the law of Christ. Chrys C. Caragounis, *Peter and the Rock* (New York: Walter de Gruyter, 1990), and Everett Ferguson, *The Church of Christ: A Biblical Ecclesiology for Today* (Grand Rapids, Mich.: Eerdmans, 1996), 47–52, make a strong case that *petra* = Peter's confession of faith in Jesus' messiahship. For

extensive documentation of the consensus view, see Scott Butler, Norman Dahlgren, and David Hess, *Jesus, Peter and the Keys: A Scriptural Handbook on the Papacy* (Santa Barbara, Calif.: Queenship, 1996), 14–37.

17. Burgess, *History of the Exegesis of Matthew 16:17–19*, 168; Hagner, *Matthew 14–28*, 470. Others, however, argue for a Greek origin. Luz believes that *kēpa* refers to "stones," not rock, and thus a Greek origin is more probable ("Primacy Text," 46). Gundry asserts, "No Semitic tradition stands behind these verses" (*Matthew*, 335).

18. Davies and Allison list twelve different interpretations (*Commentary on Matthew*, 2:630–32); Patte, *Matthew*, 233; see also Ferguson, *Church of Christ*, 52–53.

19. Albright and Mann, *Matthew*, 196; Brown, Donfried, and Reumann, *Peter in the New Testament*, 100, 107; Walter B. Abbott, ed., *The Documents of Vatican II* (London: Geoffrey Chapman, 1966), 3.22 (p. 42); Harrington, *Gospel*, 21.

20. Wayne A. Meeks, ed., *The HarperCollins Study Bible, NRSV* (New York: HarperCollins, 1993), 2053 n; Meier, *Vision of Matthew*, 114; Hagner, *Matthew 14–28*, 473; Ferguson, *Church of Christ*, 54–55.

21. Meier, *Vision of Matthew*, 114; Albright and Mann, *Matthew*, 195; Davies and Allison, *Commentary on Matthew*, 2:643.

22. In the portrait that follows, I have relied upon Luz, "Primacy Text," 47–49; Luz, *Matthew 8–20*, 366–67; Davies and Allison, *Commentary on Matthew*, 2:647–52; Pheme Perkins, *Peter: Apostle for the Whole Church*, Studies on Personalities of the New Testament (Columbia: University of South Carolina Press, 1994); Veselin Kesich, "Peter's Primacy in the New Testament and the Early Tradition," in *The Primacy of Peter: Essays in Ecclesiology and the Early Church*, ed. John Meyendorff (Crestwood, N.Y.: St. Vladimir's Seminary Press, 1992), 35–44; and esp. Brown, Donfried, and Reumann, *Peter in the New Testament*, 158–68.

23. Klaus Schatz, *Papal Primacy: From Its Origins to the Present*, trans. John A. Otto and Linda M. Maloney (Collegeville, Minn.: Liturgical Press, 1996), 1–2.

24. Thomas P. Rausch, *The Roots of the Catholic Tradition*, TLS 16 (Collegeville, Minn.: Liturgical Press, 1991), 163.

25. The following discussion of the rise of the papacy relies upon Paul C. Empie and T. Austin Murphy, eds., *Papal Primacy and the Universal Church*, Lutherans and Catholics in Dialogue V (Minneapolis: Augsburg, 1974); Eno, *Rise of the Papacy*; McCue, "Roman Primacy in the First Three Centuries"; Rausch, *Roots of the Catholic Tradition*; Schatz, *Papal Primacy*; Jean-M.R. Tillard, *The Bishop of Rome*, trans. John de Satge, TLS 5 (Wilmington, Del.: Michael Glazier, 1983); William J. La Due, *The Chair of Saint Peter: A History of the Papacy* (Maryknoll, N.Y.: Orbis, 1999).

26. Roman Catholic exegetes, but not all, traditionally identified Peter's going to "another place" (Acts 12:17) as Rome. 1 Peter 5:13 indirectly alludes to Peter's presence in Rome if one construes, as does most scholars, that "your sister church in Babylon" is a code name for Rome (the "new "Babylon").

27. Cyril C. Richardson, ed., *Early Christian Fathers*, LCC 1 (1953), 46. References and quotations from the writings of Clement, Ignatius, Justin, and Irenaeus are taken from this edition.

28. Raymond E. Brown and John P. Meier, *Antioch and Rome: New Testament Cradles of Catholic Christianity* (New York: Paulist Press, 1983), 100–102; Henry Bettenson, ed., *Documents of the Christian Church*, 2nd ed. (New York: Oxford University Press, 1963), 2.

29. On New Testament patterns of ministry, see James G. D. Dunn, *Unity and Diversity in the New Testament: An Inquiry into the Character of Earliest Christianity* (Philadelphia: Westminster Press, 1977) 103–23, who adopts an evolutionary model of institutionalization.

30. J. Fuellenbach, *Ecclesiastical Office and the Primacy of Rome: An Evaluation of Recent Theological Discussion of First Clement* (Washington, D.C.: Catholic University Press of America, 1980); Brown and Meier, *Antioch and Rome*, 159–83.

31. Richardson, *Early Church Fathers*, 36.

32. Robert M. Grant, *Augustus to Constantine: The Thrust of the Christian Movement into the Roman World* (New York: Harper and Row, 1970), 184.

33. On apostolic succession, see Arnold Ehrhardt, *Apostolic Succession in the First Two Centuries of the Church* (London: Lutterworth, 1953); Hans von Campenhausen, *Ecclesiastical Authority and Spiritual Power in the Church of the First Three Centuries*, trans. J. A. Baker (Stanford, Calif.: Stanford University Press, 1969).

34. Hans Küng, *The Church* (New York: Doubleday, 1976), 587; Tertullian, *Treatises on Penance: On Penitence and On Purity*, trans. and annot. William P. Le Saint, ACW 28 (New York: Newman Press, 1959), 120–22; see also Tertullian, *On Prescription against Heretics* 22, ANF, 3:253.

35. Henry Chadwick, *Early Christian Thought and the Classical Tradition* (1966; New York: Oxford University Press, 1984), 71–82; Robert M. Grant with David A. Tracy, *A Short History of the Interpretation of the Bible*, 2nd ed. (Philadelphia: Fortress, 1984), 56–62; Joseph Wilson Trigg, *Origen: The Bible and Philosophy in the Third-Century Church* (Atlanta: John Knox, 1983), 120–28.

36. *ANF*, 10:456, 457.

37. *The Letters of St. Cyprian*, 4 vols., trans. and annot. G. W. Clarke, ACW 43 (New York: Newman Press, 1984–89), 2:40, 64.

38. "Introduction," in *The Lapsed: The Unity of the Christian Church*, trans. and annot. Maurice Bévenot, ACW 25 (New York: Newman Press, 1956), 6, 46–47 (on two editions).

39. *Letters of St. Cyprian*, 4:79; 88–89.

40. *NPNF*, 2nd ser., 14:15; Geoffrey Barraclough, *The Medieval Papacy* (New York: Norton, 1968), 10.

41. *NPNF*, 2nd ser., 14:178, 176–77; quoted in Eno, *Rise of the Papacy*, 88–89.

42. Eno, *Rise of the Papacy*, 98 (quotation), 100.

43. Walter Ullmann, "Leo I and the Theme of Papal Primacy," *JTS* 11 (April 1960): 25; Donald Joseph Grimes, "The Papacy and the Petrine Texts: A Study in the History of Biblical Exegesis (A.D. 800–1300)" (Ph.D. diss., Fordham University, 1981), 32.

44. *NPNF*, 2nd ser., 12:8, 117; see also *Letters* 33.1 (p. 47), 156.2 (p. 100); and *Sermon* 62.2 (p. 174).

45. *NPNF*, 2nd ser., 14:259, 287; Francis Dvornik, *Byzantium and the Roman Primacy* (New York: Fordham University Press, 1966), 54.

46. Quotations in Eno, *Rise of the Papacy*, 124, 128.

47. La Due, *Chair of Saint Peter*, 60.

48. Harmann J. Pottmeyer, *Towards a Papacy in Communion: Perspectives from Vatican Councils I and II*, trans. Matthew J. O'Connell (New York: Crossroad, 1998), 26, 27.

49. Theodore Tahaney, *The History of the Exegesis of Matthew 16:18–19 in Commentaries of the Early Middle Ages* (Woodstock, Md.: Woodstock College Press, 1961), 8; Karlfried Froehlich, "Saint Peter, Papal Primacy, and the Exegetical Tradition, 1150–1300," in *The Religious Roles of the Papacy: Ideals and Realities, 1150–1300,* ed. Christopher Ryan (Toronto: Pontifical Institute of Mediaeval Studies, 1989), 9–10.

50. Pottmeyer, *Papacy in Communion,* 30.

51. Froehlich, "Saint Peter," 3, 17, 40 (Kantorowicz quotation); Grimes, "Papacy," 185.

52. Grimes, "Papacy," 123–24, 128, 155; Christopher Ocker, "The Fusion of Papal Ideology and Biblical Exegesis in the Fourteenth Century," in *Biblical Hermeneutics in Historical Perspective: Studies in Honor of Karlfried Froelich on His Sixtieth Birthday,* ed. Mark S. Burrows and Paul Rorem (Grand Rapids, Mich.: Eerdmans, 1991), 131–32.

53. John E. Bigane, *Faith, Christ or Peter: Matthew 16:18 in Sixteenth Century Roman Catholic Exegesis* (Rockville, Md.: University Press of America, 1971), 19; Ocker, "Fusion," 133–34.

54. Ocker, "Fusion," 141–42.

55. Ibid., 145–46, 150.

56. John Meyendorff, "St. Peter in Byzantine Theology," in *Primacy of Peter,* 68, 69.

57. Ibid., 70.

58. Ibid., 72, 73–74.

59. Ibid., 75–83.

60. Ibid., 83–90.

61. Quoted in Bigane, *Faith, Christ or Peter,* 16.

62. St. Augustine, *Sermons on Selected Lessons of the New Testament,* 2 vols. (London: Walter Smith, 1883–85), 1: 215–16 (Sermon 26.2–3); Bigane, *Faith, Christ or Peter,* 81.

63. Grimes, "Papacy," 141, 203; Bigane, *Faith, Christ or Peter,* 106.

64. Bigane, *Faith, Christ or Peter,* 123–24.

65. Ibid., 199.

66. *LW,* 41:303, 333, 329, 335, 306.

67. Scott H. Hendrix, *Luther and the Papacy: Stages in a Reformation Conflict* (Philadelphia: Fortress, 1981), xi, 21.

68. Quoted in Jon Whitman, "A Retrospective Forward: Interpretation, Allegory, and Historical Change," in *Interpretation and Allegory: Antiquity to the Modern Period,* Brill's Studies in Intellectual History, vol. 101 (Leiden: Brill, 2000), 3.

69. *LW, Companion Volume: Luther the Expositor,* 113–19, quotation on 114; Hendrix, *Luther and the Papacy,* 83.

70. *Three Treatises,* rev. ed. (Philadelphia: Fortress, 1970), 20 (for an extended exegesis, see *LW,* 40:321–77); *LW,* 39:87.

71. *LW,* 41:312, 309, 310.

72. Cullmann argues that the apostolic foundation is unique, that the foundation (of the apostles) and the building (of the elders and bishops) are not interchangeable (*Peter,* 65–66, 218–42).

73. Denzinger, *Sources of Catholic Dogma,* 454 (no. 1826).

74. John Borelli and John H. Erickson, eds., *The Quest for Unity: Orthodox and Catholics in Dialogue* (Crestwood, N.Y.: St. Vladimir's Seminary Press, 1996), 154;

Robert McAfee Brown, *The Spirit of Protestantism* (New York: Oxford University Press, 1961), 163; Miller, *What Are They Saying about Papal Primacy?* 86–92; Robert W. Jensen, *Unbaptized God: The Basic Flaw in Ecumenical Theology* (Minneapolis, Minn.: Fortress, 1992).

75. John R. Quinn, *The Reform of the Papacy: The Costly Call to Christian Unity* (New York: Crossroad, 1999), 14, 178–80, quotation on 9.

CHAPTER 3

1. Origen, *The Song of Songs: Commentary and Homilies*, trans. R. P. Lawson, ACW 26 (New York: Newman Press, 1956), 23 (hereafter cited as Origen, *Song of Songs*); Gregory of Nyssa, *Commentary on the Song of Songs*, trans. and introd. Casimir McCambley (Brookline, Mass.: Hellenic College Press, 1987), 43; Kilian Walsh and Irene M. Edmonds, trans., *The Works of Bernard of Clairvaux: On the Song of Songs*, 4 vols., CFS 4, 7, 31, 40 (Spencer, Mass.: Cistercian Publications, 1971–80), 1:2, 7 (hereafter cited as Bernard, *Song of Songs*).

2. Athalya Brenner, *The Song of Songs*, OTG 18 (Sheffield, Eng.: Sheffield Academic Press, 1989), 13.

3. Michael V. Fox, *The Song of Songs and Ancient Egyptian Love Songs* (Madison: University of Wisconsin Press, 1985); Dianne Bergant, *Song of Songs: The Love Poetry of Scripture*, Spiritual Commentaries (Hyde Park, N.Y.: New City Press, 1998), 163.

4. Jean Leclercq, *The Love of Learning and the Desire for God: A Study of Monastic Culture*, rev. ed., trans. Catharine Misrahi (New York: Fordham University Press, 1974), 106; E. Ann Matter, *The Voice of My Beloved: The Song of Songs in Western Medieval Christianity* (Philadelphia: University of Pennsylvania Press, 1990), 3; George L. Scheper, "The Spiritual Marriage: The Exegetic History and Literary Impact of the Song of Songs in the Middle Ages" (Ph.D. diss., Princeton University, 1971), 8; George L. Scheper, "Reformation Attitudes toward Allegory and the Song of Songs," *Publications of the Modern Language Association of America* 89 (1974): 556.

5. Marvin H. Pope, *Song of Songs: A New Translation with Introduction and Commentary*, AB 7C (Garden City, N.Y.: Doubleday, 1977), 17; Roland E. Murphy, *The Song of Songs: A Commentary on the Book of Canticles or The Song of Songs*, Hermeneia (Minneapolis, Minn.: Fortress, 1990), 12. Other surveys of the history of interpretation include Christian D. Ginsburg, *The Song of Songs and Coheleth* (New York: Ktav, 1970), 20–124; Pope, *Song of Songs*, 34–37, 89–229; H. H. Rowley, *The Servant of the Lord and Other Essays on the Old Testament*, 2nd ed., rev. (Oxford: Basil Blackwell, 1965), 197–245; Tremper Longman III, *Song of Songs*, NICOT (Grand Rapids, Mich.: Eerdmans, 2001), 20–47.

6. Murphy, *Song of Songs*, 136; Othmar Keel, *The Song of Songs: A Continental Commentary*, trans. Frederick J. Gaiser (Minneapolis, Minn.: Fortress, 1994), who argues that a better translation for "lily" is "water lily" or, better yet, "lotus" (78); G. Lloyd Carr, *The Song of Solomon: An Introduction and Commentary*, TOTC 17 (Leicester, Eng.: Inter–Varsity Press, 1984), 87–88.

7. "The Lily of the Valley," in *Evangelistic Songs and Hymns*, ed. Claude P. Ganus (Winona Lake, Ind.: Rodeheaver, Hall-Mack, 1962), 104.

8. Joseph C. Dillow, *Solomon on Sex: A Biblical Guide to Married Love* (Nashville, Tenn.: Thomas Nelson, 1977).

9. On authorship, date, and canonicity, see Pope, *Song of Songs*, 18, 22–33 (Akiba quotation, 19); Murphy, *Song of Songs*, 3–7, Longman, *Song of Songs*, 2–9.

10. Bernard, *Song of Songs*, 1:6; Matter, *Voice of My Beloved*, 10.

11. For an exhaustive treatment (1,028 pages) of the history of interpretation of the Song in the patristic, medieval, and Renaissance periods, see Scheper, "Spiritual Marriage."

12. Jon Whitman, ed. and intro., *Interpretation and Allegory: Antiquity to the Modern Period*, Brill's Studies in Intellectual History 101 (Leiden: Brill, 2000), 58.

13. Matter, *Voice of My Beloved*, 39.

14. Pope, *Song of Songs*, 114.

15. Stephen D. Moore, "The Song of Songs in the History of Sexuality," *CH* 69 (June 2000): 331, 332, 339.

16. Denys Turner, *Eros and Allegory: Medieval Exegesis of the Song of Songs*, CSS 156 (Kalamazoo, Mich.: Cistercian Publications, 1995), 18; Tod Linafelt, "Biblical Love Poetry (. . . and God)," *JAAR* 70 (June 2002): 337–39; Carey Ellen Walsh, *Exquisite Desire: Religion, the Erotic, and the Song of Songs* (Minneapolis, Minn.: Fortress, 2000), 50. See also Jean Leclercq, *Monks on Marriage: A Twelfth–Century View* (New York: Seabury, 1982), chap. 7; Jean Leclercq, *A Second Look at Bernard of Clairvaux*, trans. Marie Bernard Saïd, CSS 105 (Kalamazoo, Mich.: Cistercian Publications, 1990), chap. 6.

17. Murphy, *Song of Songs*, 16; Augustine quotation in Henri de Lubac, *Medieval Exegesis*, vol. 1, *The Four Senses of Scripture*, trans. Mark Sebanc (1959; Grand Rapids, Mich.: Eerdmans, 1998), 245.

18. Origen, *Song of Songs*, 6.

19. Ibid., 220.

20. "Introduction," in Rowan A. Greer, trans. and introd., *Origen: Selected Writings*, CWS (New York: Paulist Press, 1979), 32; Lawson, *Origen*, 24–28, 44.

21. Greer, *Origen*, "On First Principles, Book IV," 187.

22. Karen Jo Torjesen, *Hermeneutical Procedure and Theological Method in Origen's Exegesis* (Berlin: Walter de Gruyter, 1985); Murphy, *Song of Songs*, 19; Ronald Heine, "Reading the Bible with Origen," in *The Bible in Greek Christian Antiquity*, The Bible through the Ages, vol. 1, ed. Paul M. Blowers (Notre Dame, Ind.: University of Notre Dame Press, 1997), 135–39.

23. Torjesen, *Origen's Exegesis*, 23; Origen, *Song of Songs* 21.

24. Torjesen, *Origen's Exegesis*, 55–56.

25. Origen, *Song of Songs*, 59, 60, 61.

26. Torjesen, *Origen's Exegesis*, 61; Elizabeth A. Clark, "The Uses of the Song of Songs: Origen and the Later Latin Fathers," in Clark, *Ascetic Piety and Women's Faith: Essays on Late Ancient Christianity*, Studies in Women and Religion 20 (Lewiston, N.Y.: Edwin Mellon Press, 1986), 392–98.

27. Bernard McGinn, *The Foundations of Mysticism*, vol. 1 of *The Presence of God: A History of Western Christian Mysticism* (New York: Crossroad, 1991), 204.

28. To Clark's three ("Uses of the Song of Songs," 401–9), I have added the liturgical use as discussed in Jean Danielou, *The Bible and the Liturgy* (Notre Dame, Ind.: University of Notre Dame Press, 1956), 191–207.

29. McGinn, *Foundations of Mysticism*, 213. Ambrose's *On Isaac or the Soul*, "arguably the first great masterpiece of Western mysticism" (McGinn, *Foundations of*

Mysticism, 203), contains one hundred direct references or allusions to the Song of Songs. See Saint Ambrose, "Isaac, or the Soul," in *Seven Exegetical Works*, trans. Michael P. McHugh, FC 65 (Washington, D.C.: Catholic University Press of America, 1972), 10–65.

30. Clark, "Uses of the Song of Songs," 403.

31. For examples, see Charles Christopher Mierow and Thomas Comerford Lawler, eds., *The Letters of St. Jerome*, vol. 1, ACW 33 (New York: Newman Press, 1963), 135, 149, 158, 159, 179.

32. Danielou, *The Bible and the Liturgy*, 191–207; Ambrose quotation on 196.

33. Murphy, *Song of Songs*, 141. "Foxes" may refer to lusty young men, "vineyards" to nubile young women. See Wayne A. Meeks, ed., *The HarperCollins Study Bible: New Revised Standard Version* (New York: HarperCollins, 1993), 1004n.

34. Matter, *Voice of My Beloved*, 87–90.

35. Clark, "Uses of the Song of Songs," 407–09; Peter Brown, *Augustine of Hippo: A Biography* (Berkeley: University of California Press, 1967), 212–13.

36. John G. Snaith, *The Song of Songs: Based on the Revised Standard Version*, NCB (Grand Rapids, Mich.: Eerdmans, 1993), 3.

37. Ann W. Astell, *The Song of Songs in the Middle Ages* (Ithaca, N.Y.: Cornell University Press, 1990), 42–60; quotation on 43.

38. John H. Van Engen, *Rupert of Deutz*, Publications of the UCLA Center for Medieval and Renaissance Studies 18 (Berkeley: University of California Press, 1983), 3; quotation on 294.

39. Matter, *Voice of My Beloved*, 151.

40. Rachel Fulton, "Mimetic Devotion, Marian Exegesis, and the Historical Sense of the Song of Songs," *Viator: Medieval and Renaissance Studies* 27 (1996): 85–116, 108; quotation on 89.

41. Van Engen, *Rupert*, 294.

42. Matter, *Voice of My Beloved*, 159; Fulton, "Mimetic Devotion," 114.

43. Hans Ur Von Balthasar, "Preface," in Greer, *Origen*, xiv.

44. Turner, *Eros and Allegory*, 111; Matter, *Voice of My Beloved*, 94.

45. Gregory the Great, "Exposition of the Song of Songs," in Turner, *Eros and Allegory*, 219, 218, 222, 223.

46. Gregory, "Exposition," 225–30; Matter, *Voice of My Beloved*, 95; Leclercq, *Love of Learning and the Desire for God*, 37–38.

47. Matter, *Voice of My Beloved*, 103, 104, 106.

48. Bernard McGinn, *The Growth of Mysticism*, vol. 2 of *The Presence of God: A History of Western Christian Mysticism* (New York: Crossroad, 1994), 164; Jean Leclercq, "Introduction," in Bernard, *Song of Songs*, 4:ix.

49. Jean Leclercq, *Bernard of Clairvaux and the Cistercian Spirit*, trans. Claire Lavoie, CSS 16 (Kalamazoo, Mich.: Cistercian Publications, 1976), 9.

50. Ibid., 105–115; "Editor's Note" and "Introduction," in Bernard of Clairvaux, *The Love of God and Spiritual Friendship*, ed. and introd. James M. Houston, Classics of Faith and Devotion (Portland, Ore.: Multnomah Press, 1983), xviii–xxii, xxvii.

51. Leclercq, *Second Look*, 38–39; Adrian H. Bredero, *Bernard of Clairvaux: Between Cult and History* (Grand Rapids, Mich.: Eerdmans, 1996), 280–81.

52. Brian P. McGuire, *The Difficult Saint: Bernard of Clairvaux and His Tradition*, CSS 126 (Kalamazoo, Mich.: Cistercian Publications, 1991), 18–20.

53. Jean Leclercq, *Monks and Love in Twelfth-Century France: Psycho-Historical Essays* (New York: Oxford University Press, 1979), 105.

54. McGuire, *Difficult Saint*, 20.

55. Pope, *Song of Songs*, 123.

56. McGuire, *Difficult Saint*, 21–22; Leclercq, *Monks and Love*, 100; see also Walsh, *Exquisite Desire*, 50.

57. Leclercq, *Bernard and the Cistercian Spirit*, 95.

58. Leclercq, *Monks and Love*, 9–16.

59. Matter, *Voice of My Beloved*, 111.

60. Bernard, *Song of Songs*, 2:208.

61. Ibid., 4:98; 3:109; 4:38; 1:7; 3:72, 142; 3:60.

62. Colin Morris, *The Discovery of the Individual: 1050–1200* (New York: Harper and Row, 1972); Bernard, *Song of Songs*, 2:182.

63. Pope, *Song of Songs*, 123; Bernard, *Song of Songs*, 2:129.

64. Beryl Smalley, *The Study of the Bible in the Middle Ages* (Notre Dame, Ind.: University of Notre Dame Press, 1964); Peter Norber, "Lectio Vere Divina: St. Bernard and the Bible," *MS* 3 (1965): 165–81.

65. G. R. Evans, *The Mind of St. Bernard of Clairvaux* (New York: Oxford University Press, 1983), 74.

66. Leclercq, *Bernard and the Cistercian Spirit*, 21–25; Denis Farkasfalvy, "The Role of the Bible in St. Bernard's Spirituality," *Analecta Cisterciensia* 25 (January–June 1969): 4–6

67. Farkasfalvy, "Bible in Bernard's Spirituality," 3.

68. Michael Casey, *Sacred Reading: The Ancient Art of* Lectio Divina (Liguori, Mo.: Triumph Books, 1995), vi; see also Leclercq, *Love of Learning;* Claude J. Peifer, *Monastic Spirituality* (New York: Sheed and Ward, 1966).

69. Casey, *Sacred Reading*, 57.

70. Smalley, *Study of the Bible*, 281.

71. Bernard, *Song of Songs*, 1:114–15; 2:216.

72. M. B. Pranger, *Bernard of Clairvaux and the Shape of Monastic Thought: Broken Dreams*, Brill's Studies in Intellectual History 56 (Leiden: Brill, 1994), 10.

73. Bernard, *Song of Songs*, 4:152–56; 3:175–77, 179–206; 1:99; 1:41; 1:120–21; 2:105.

74. Ibid., 2:58–63.

75. Ibid., 1:4; McGinn, *Foundations of Mysticism*, xvii.

76. Bernard, *Song of Songs*, 1:16.

77. Bernard, *Song of Songs*, 3:141; Bernard McGinn, "The Language of Love in Christian and Jewish Mysticism," in *Mysticism and Language*, ed. Steven T. Katz (New York: Oxford University Press, 1992), 210; Bernard, *Song of Songs*, 1:39.

78. Bernard, *Song of Songs*, 1:6. On Bernard's use of the term "experience," see Kilian McDonnell, "Spirit and Experience in Bernard of Clairvaux," *TS* 58 (1997): 3–18.

79. Bernard, *Song of Songs*, 4:137–38.

80. Ibid., 1:54.

81. Ibid., 2:178.

82. Ibid., 2:178; 4:180–81, 184.

83. On "image and likeness" in Bernard's thought, see Etienne Gilson, *The Mys-*

tical Theology of Saint Bernard, trans. A. H. C. Downes (London: Sheed and Ward, 1940), 33–59; Robert P. Stepsis, "Fulfillment of Self and Union with God in the Writings of Bernard of Clairvaux," *ABR* 24 (1973): 348–64; Gerald S. Towmey, "St. Bernard's Doctrine of the Human Person as the Image and Likeness of God in Sermons 80–83 on the Song of Songs," *CS* 17 (1982): 141–49; Leclercq, *Bernard and the Cistercian Spirit*, 76–77.

84. Bernard, *Song of Songs*, 4:146, 149.

85. Ibid., 4:163, 164.

86. Ibid., 4:177, 172–73, 176, 177–78, 179.

87. Ibid., 2:229, 4–5.

88. Ibid., 4:182; 1:33.

89. Ibid., 1:152.

90. Ibid., 1:2.

91. Ibid., 1:21, 16.

92. McGinn, *Growth of Mysticism*, 183.

93. Bernard, *Song of Songs*, 1:22, 23.

94. Ibid., 1:21, 19, 17, 36–37.

95. Ibid., 1:19.

96. Ibid., 1:20, 21, 52, 49.

97. Ibid., 1:46; see also 4:151–52.

98. Ibid., 1:63; Caroline Walker Bynum, "The Cistercian Conception of Community: An Aspect of Twelfth-Century Spirituality," *HTR* 68 (1977): 282.

99. Bernard, *Song of Songs*, 2:28.

100. Ibid., 2:30, 31, 32.

101. Ibid., 2:33, 35, 38, 37, 40.

102. Ibid., 3:53, 54, 22, 52; 4:209, 6–7.

103. Ibid., 4:56; 2:135.

104. Matter, *Voice of My Beloved*, chap. 7; Astell, *Song of Songs*, chaps. 4, 6, 7; Turner, *Eros and Allegory*; Scheper, "Spiritual Marriage"; James I. Wimsatt, "St. Bernard, the Canticle of Canticles, and Mystical Poetry," in *An Introduction to the Medieval Mystics of Europe*, ed. Paul E. Szarmach (Albany: State University of New York Press, 1984), 77–95.

105. Scheper, "Reformation Attitudes," 551–62.

106. *LW*, 54:46, 47.

107. Ibid., 15:191, 196, 194.

108. Endel Kallas, "Martin Luther as Expositor of the Song of Songs," *LQ* 2 (1988): 323–42.

109. *LW*, 15:191, 192.

110. Kallas, "Luther as Expositor," 334.

111. *LW*, 15:192, 196, 264.

112. Scheper, "Reformation Attitudes," 558–59. For a survey of references to the Song of Songs in literature, see *The Song of Solomon: Love Poetry of the Spirit*, ed., Lawrence Boadt (New York: St. Martin's Griffin, 1999).

113. Christopher Hill, *The English Bible and the Seventeenth-Century Revolution* (New York: Penguin, 1994), 362, 365–66; Pope, *Song of Songs*, 128; Douglas S. O'Donnell, "Walking on 'The Ashes of God's Saints': John Donne's Interpretation of

the Song of Songs and the Origenist Exegetical Tradition" (M.A. thesis, Trinity International University, 2001), esp. chap. 5.

114. Murphy, *Song of Songs*, 38–39; Pope, *Song of Songs*, 131–32.

115. Pope, *Song of Songs*, 132–34, 136–41.

116. Ibid., 145–53, 210–29; Murphy, *Song of Songs*, 39–40.

117. Raymond Jacques Tournay, *Word of God, Song of Love: A Commentary on the Song of Songs*, trans. J. Edward Crowley (New York: Paulist Press, 1988), 166; Pope, *Song of Songs*, 179; Luis Stadelmann, *Love and Politics: A New Commentary on the Song of Songs* (New York: Paulist Press, 1992), 2, 26–29.

118. Dietrich Bonhoeffer, *Letters and Papers from Prison* (New York: Macmillan, 1953), 175.

119. Athalya Brenner, ed., *A Feminist Companion to the Song of Songs*, FCB 1 (Sheffield, Eng.: Sheffield Press, 1993), 65, 79, 85, 97.

120. Phyllis Trible, *God and the Rhetoric of Sexuality* (Philadelphia: Fortress, 1978), 144, 160, 161.

121. Roland Murphy, "History of Exegesis as a Hermeneutical Tool: The Song of Songs," *BTB* 16 (1986): 89.

122. Walsh, *Exquisite Desire*, 201.

123. Murphy, "History of Exegesis," 90; Francis Landy, *Paradoxes of Paradise: Identity and Difference in the Song of Songs* (Sheffield, Eng.: Almond Press, 1983), 32.

CHAPTER 4

1. Mark U. Edwards Jr., *Printing, Propaganda, and Martin Luther* (Berkeley: University of California Press, 1994), xii; Gordon Rupp, *Luther's Progress to the Diet of Worms* (1951; New York: Harper Torchbook, 1964), 1. On the Weimar corpus, see Gerhard Ebeling, *Luther: An Introduction to His Thought*, trans. R. A. Wilson (Philadelphia: Fortress, 1972), 43–55; and Mark U. Edwards Jr., "Luther," in *Reformation Europe: A Guide to Research*, ed. Stephen Ozment (St. Louis: Center for Reformation Research, 1982), 60–61.

2. At the onset it is important to note the semantic difficulties created by the English language. The words "justice" (and its related words "just," "justify," "justification," etc.) and "righteousness" (and its related words "righteous," etc.) are all cognates, derived from the Hebrew *sedeq* and the Greek verb *dikaioō* (*dikaiosynē* = n., "righteousness"). English Bibles more often use "righteousness" terms than "justification" terms. In Paul's usage, they are simply semantic equivalents: both embrace a single biblical concept—the state of being in the right or the exculpation of guilt. In translating the verb *dikaioō*, the Latin "justify" is used (the Greek equivalent would be "rightify"). "To justify" refers to the idea "to make right," though in English usage it often means to provide reasons (or even excuses) for. Given these semantic confusions, Leander Keck prefers "rectify" for "justify"—to make right, not just to make just in the sense of fair or equitable (*Paul and His Letters*, 2nd ed., Proclamation Commentaries [Philadelphia: Fortress, 1988], 111–12).

3. Anders Nygren, *Agape and Eros*, trans. Philip S. Watson (Philadelphia: Westminster, 1953), 681–91; Eric W. Gritsch, *Martin—God's Court Jester: Luther in Retrospect* (Philadelphia: Fortress, 1983), 170.

4. H. George Anderson, T. Austin Murphy, and Joseph A. Burgess, eds., *Justification by Faith: Lutherans and Catholics in Dialogue VII* (Minneapolis, Minn.: Augsburg, 1985), 25, 320 n. 51.

5. Heiko A. Oberman, *The Reformation: Roots and Ramifications*, trans. Andrew Colin Gow (Grand Rapids, Mich.: Eerdmans, 1994), 53–54. On Luther interpretations, see Bernard Lohse, *Martin Luther: An Introduction to His Life and Work*, trans. Robert C. Schultz (Philadelphia: Fortress 1986), 199–237.

6. Oberman, *Reformation*, 57–58.

7. The sale of indulgences became the catalyst for Luther going public with his views and posting his Ninety-five Theses. An indulgence was a remission of all ("plenary") or part of the temporal (not eternal) punishment due to sin. A priest (acting in the name of God through the church) granted it at the sacrament of penance upon the condition of true contrition and in consideration of some pious deed (e.g., prayers or good works). Indulgences became popular and profitable in the eleventh century with the beginning of the Crusades. Christians unable to participate personally in the Crusades were granted indulgences upon the donation of alms. In the thirteenth and fourteenth centuries theologians devised the idea of a "treasury of merits"—an excess amount of merits (a "treasury of grace") accumulated by Christ and the saints, whereby the pope could dispense these merits through indulgences. In the fifteenth century, popes claimed to be able to release the dead from purgatory by granting indulgences. In the fifteenth and sixteenth centuries, indulgences became a lucrative trade and a major source of papal revenue. The immediate circumstance triggering Luther's ire was the sale of indulgences by the well-known vendor Johann Tetzel, a Dominican friar, who "closed the deal" with anxiety-ridden parishioners with the jingle: "As soon as the coin in the coffer rings, a soul from purgatory springs." Luther's protest against indulgences was neither original nor unprecedented, but clearly his protest, abetted by the printing press, struck a raw nerve among Christians concerned with deplorable conditions in the church.

8. Lohse, *Martin Luther*, 145.

9. For biographical details and many of the insights into Luther's life, I have relied upon Roland H. Bainton, *Here I Stand: A Life of Martin Luther* (1950; New York: New American Library, n.d.); Martin Brecht, *Martin Luther: His Road to Reformation, 1483–1521*, trans. James L. Schaaf (Philadelphia: Fortress, 1985); James M. Kittelson, *Luther the Reformer: The Story of the Man and His Career* (Minneapolis: Augsburg, 1986); Richard Marius, *Martin Luther: The Christian between God and Death* (Cambridge, Mass.: Harvard University Press, 1999); Heiko A. Oberman, *Luther: Man between God and the Devil*, trans. Eileen Walliser-Schwarzbart (New York: Doubleday, 1992).

10. Marilyn J. Harran, *Martin Luther: Learning for Life* (St. Louis: Concordia, 1997), discusses the uncertainty regarding exactly when, where, and under whom Luther received his early education (chap. 1); Ian Siggins, *Luther and His Mother* (Philadelphia: Fortress, 1981).

11. Oberman, *Luther*, 127.

12. On Luther's indebtedness to Staupitz, see David C. Steinmetz, *Luther and Staupitz: An Essay on the Intellectual Origins of the Protestant Reformation*, Duke Monographs in Medieval and Reformation Studies, no. 4 (Durham, N.C.: Duke University Press, 1980); quotation on 144.

13. Brecht, *Martin Luther*, 74.

14. Alister E. McGrath, *Luther's Theology of the Cross: Martin Luther's Theological Breakthrough* (Oxford: Basil Blackwell, 1985), 10; Brecht, *Martin Luther*, 69.

15. Quoted in Oberman, *Luther*, 128; quoted in David C. Steinmetz, *Luther in Context* (Bloomington: Indiana University Press, 1986), 7.

16. Thomas N. Tentler, *Sin and Confession on the Eve of the Reformation* (Princeton, N.J.: Princeton University Press, 1977), 65.

17. Steinmetz, *Luther in Context*, 2–7, notes that two general penitential traditions prevailed in the later Middle Ages. One tradition emphasized the disposition of the penitent in the confessional, the other emphasized the authority of the church through the priest to effect absolution. Possibly during his formative years in Eisenach, Luther was exposed to and came to favor the tradition of disposition.

18. *LW*, 27:13.

19. Bainton, *Here I Stand*, 42; quoted in Steinmetz, *Luther in Context*, 8; Steinmetz, *Luther and Staupitz*, 33–34.

20. On Luther's relationship to mysticism, see Steinmetz, *Luther and Staupitz*, 126–40, who notes that Luther's mystical theology is an outgrowth of his insight into justification by faith through grace (140); and Heiko A. Oberman, *The Dawn of the Reformation* (1986; Grand Rapids, Mich.: Eerdmans, 1992), 126–54.

21. For a helpful discussion of the *via moderna*, see Alister McGrath, *The Intellectual Origins of the European Reformation* (Cambridge, Mass.: Blackwell, 1987), 70–85, 108–120. According to McGrath, the designation *via moderna* is presently accepted as the best way of referring to the movement once known as "nominalism." Nominalism refers to a philosophy of knowledge (not a specific theology) that dominated the later part of Scholastic period (ca. 1350–ca. 1500). Nominalism denied the reality of universals outside the mind (e.g., there is no "blackness" or a universal concept of blackness; rather, there are only particular black things).

22. In an effort to counter moral laxity among Christians, Pelagius (ca. 350–ca. 425), Augustine's contemporary and theological nemesis, de-emphasized humankind's fallen state and emphasized freedom of the will and the necessity of good works for the Christian. To hold people morally responsible, they must be free to choose good or evil. This ability to choose rather than to act by natural necessity is unique to humans and is a gracious gift of God. Thus the desire for the good and its realization lies within human nature, which, at birth, has no sinful proclivity. Augustine argued that humans are so anchored in sin that they cannot free themselves from its influence without God's grace. Sinners have a (limited) free will; they can choose, but they will not choose the good. This incapacitated will can only be healed by grace, and grace itself is a gift of God. To a greater or lesser extent, observes Alister E. McGrath, "*all* medieval theology is 'Augustinian'" (*Iustitia Dei: A History of the Christian Doctrine of Justification*, 2 vols. [Cambridge: Cambridge University Press, 1986], 1: 24). Pelagius's views were condemned at several fifth-century councils, the most important being the Council of Orange (418). Its fifth canon taught the bondage of the human will unless aided by divine grace, and the necessity of grace in order for humans to obey the commandments of the law. The decisive anti-Pelagian pronouncement came at the second Council of Orange (529), where the idea that humans can take the initiative in their own salvation was condemned. Curiously, the

decisions of this council appear to have been unknown from the tenth through the mid–sixteenth century (see McGrath, *Iustitia Dei*, 1: 73–75).

23. McGrath, *Luther's Theology*, 60.

24. Ebeling, *Luther*, 71.

25. Quoted in Oberman, *Luther*, 160.

26. *LW*, 54:50.

27. Willem Jan Kooiman, *Luther and the Bible*, trans. John Schmidt (Philadelphia: Muhlenberg Press, 1961), 1–19; quoted in A. Skevington Wood, *Captive to the Word; Martin Luther: Doctor of Sacred Scripture* (Grand Rapids, Mich.: Eerdmans, 1969), 13.

28. Ebeling, *Luther*, 17.

29. McGrath, *Iustitia Dei*, 1:11; Martin Luther, "Preface to the Psalms," in John Dillenberger, ed. and introd. *Martin Luther: Selections from His Writings* (Garden City, N.Y.: Anchor Doubleday, 1961), 38.

30. Quoted in Wilhelm Pauck, trans. and ed., *Luther: Lectures on Romans*, LCC 15 (1961), xxvii; McGrath, *Luther's Theology*, 77–78.

31. *LW*, 10:4; quoted in James Samuel Preus, *From Shadow to Promise: Old Testament Interpretation from Augustine to the Young Luther* (Cambridge, Mass.: Harvard University Press, Belknap Press, 1969), 137. Luther's christocentric approach also bore the influence of neo-Platonist mystics, including Dionysius Arepagitica, the Victorines, Nicholas of Cusa, and Marsilio Ficino.

32. Preus, *From Shadow to Promise*, 143; McGrath, *Luther's Theology*, 78; *LW*, 10:7.

33. Gerald L. Bruns, *Hermeneutics Ancient and Modern* (New Haven, Conn.: Yale University Press, 1992), 140.

34. *LW*, 10:402; Steinmetz, *Luther and Staupitz*, 78–92.

35. *LW*, 10:99, 197.

36. Steinmetz, *Luther and Staupitz*, 88; Heiko A. Oberman, " 'Iustia Christi' and 'Iustia Dei': Luther and the Scholastic Doctrines of Justification," *HTR* 59 (January 1966): 20.

37. *LW*, 10:402.

38. *LW*, 10:406, 408.

39. Gordon Rupp, *The Righteousness of God* (London: Hodder and Stoughton, 1953), 136; McGrath, *Luther's Theology*, 128, 131; *LW*, 11:419; Steinmetz, *Luther and Staupitz*, 36.

40. Ebeling considers these antitheses the clue to understanding Luther's thought (*Luther*, 25).

41. For a summary of the debate and various positions taken, see Steinmetz, *Luther and Staupitz*, 68–71; McGrath, *Luther's Theology*, 142–44; Marius, *Martin Luther*, 190–218.

42. Oberman, *Reformation*, 94; quoted in Brecht, *Martin Luther*, 86.

43. *LW*, 34:336–37.

44. Kittelson, *Luther the Reformer*, 91; Oberman, *Luther*, 165; McGrath, *Luther's Theology*, 145–46; Steinmetz, *Luther and Staupitz*, 142.

45. Joseph A. Fitzmyer, *Romans*, AB 33 (New York: Doubleday, 1993), xiii; Karl Barth, *The Epistle to the Romans*, trans. Edwyn C. Hoskyns, 6th ed. (London: Oxford University Press, 1933), 2.

46. *LW*, 25:361.

47. Rupp, *Righteousness of God*, 129; James M. Kittelson, "The Accidental Revolutionary," *Christian History* 11 (1992): 12.

48. The discovery of the manuscript and its subsequent impact on Luther studies is discussed in *LW*, 25:xii–xiii; and Pauck, *Lectures on Romans*, xviii–xxiv.

49. *LW*, 54:193–94 (1532), 308–9 (1538), 442–43 (1542–43). Luther's sparse comment on this passage gives credence to scholars who late-date his breakthrough.

50. *LW*, 25:151, 152.

51. Ibid., 25:497.

52. Ibid., 25:135–37 (quotation on 135).

53. Ibid., 25:263, 261 (see also 338–39), 344. The reference is to Aristotle's *Nicomachean Ethics*. Luther's opposition to Aristotelian philosophy (scholasticism) was formalized before the academic community in his *Disputation against Scholastic Theology* (1517). Luther was not opposed to philosophy per se, for as he affirms in *Disputation concerning Man* (1536), properly understood, reason is actually something divine. His main point is that the intrusion of scholastic philosophy into theology made for bad theology (see Ebeling, *Luther*, 76–92).

54. *LW*, 25:299.

55. Ibid., 25:313, 258, 257, 260 (see also 262–63).

56. Ibid., 25:236.

57. Ibid., 25:188–89.

58. Quoted in Bainton, *Here I Stand*, 90; Lohse, *Martin Luther*, 154.

59. On Luther's view of tradition, see Jaraslov Pelikan, *Luther the Expositor: Introduction to the Reformer's Exegetical Writings*, *LW*, *Companion Volume* (St. Louis: Concordia, 1959), 71–88.

60. Quoted in Rupp, *Luther's Progress*, 94, 96.

61. McGrath, *Intellectual Origins*, 32–68.

62. Quoted in Ebeling, *Luther*, 45–46.

63. Quoted in Philip S. Watson, *Let God Be God! An Interpretation of the Theology of Martin Luther* (1947; Philadelphia: Fortress, 1970), 149.

64. Quoted in Ebeling, *Luther*, 131.

65. Martin Luther, "Preface to the New Testament," in Dillenberger, *Luther*, 18.

66. Quoted in Anderson, Murphy, and Burgess, *Justification*, 29.

67. Martin Luther, "Commentary on Galatians," in Dillenberger, *Luther*, 145, 140, 141.

68. *LW*, 27:235, 224; Watson, *Let God Be God!* 159.

69. Gerald Bray, *Biblical Interpretation: Past and Present* (Downers Grove, Ill.: InterVarsity Press, 1996), 212.

70. Fitzmyer, *Romans*, 181–86; T. H. L. Parker, *Commentaries on the Epistle to the Romans, 1532–1542* (Edinburgh: T. & T. Clark, 1986), viii.

71. See Steven Ozment, *Protestants: The Birth of a Revolution* (1991; New York: Doubleday, 1993).

72. Quoted in Rupp, *Righteousness of God*, 123. For a summary of the history of Western exegesis of the Epistle to the Romans, see C. E. B. Cranfield, *A Critical and Exegetical Commentary on the Epistle to the Romans*, 2 vols., ICC (Edinburgh: T. & T. Clark, 1975), 1:30–44.

73. McGrath, *Luther's Theology*, 103–4; Rupp, *Righteousness of God*, 124–26.

74. McGrath, *Iustitia Dei*, 1: 181.

75. Fitzmyer, *Romans*, 259–60.

76. Rupp, *Luther's Progress*, 104; John Reumann, *"Righteousness" in the New Testament: "Justification" in the United States Lutheran-Roman Catholic Dialogue* (Philadelphia: Fortress, 1982), 191.

77. McGrath, *Iustitia Dei*, 1:182–84.

78. But note: Greek verbs that end in -oō (such as *dikaioō*) usually mean "to make someone X" or "to cause X to happen"; hence "to make righteous" is indeed accurate. See Joseph A. Fitzmyer, *Pauline Theology: A Brief Sketch* (Englewood Cliffs, N.J.: Prentice-Hall, 1967), 52.

79. The real problem is not lexical, for as observed in note 78, "to make righteous" is an accurate rendering in Greek. But that translation conflicts with reality: the justified are not righteous but still sinful. Hence, human experience causes one to look for an alternative rendering that can be both lexically justified and congruent with the human condition. Thus, "to declare righteous" and Luther's doctrine of "simultaneously just and a sinner." One can indeed identify non-Pauline texts where a declarative sense of *dikaioō* is likely (esp. in the Septuagint), but the key issue remains what Paul meant, and that cannot be decided by lexicography alone.

80. McGrath, *Iustitia Dei*, 1:186.

81. Alister McGrath, "Do We Still Need the Reformation? A Review of the New Catholic Catechism," *Christianity Today*, December 12, 1994, p. 30; "Canons and Decrees of the Council of Trent," in *Creeds of the Churches: A Reader in Christian Doctrine from the Bible to the Present*, rev. ed., ed. John N. Leith (Atlanta: John Knox, 1973), 411, 412 (my emphasis), 417.

82. McGrath, "Do We Still Need the Reformation?" p. 31.

83. Anderson Murhpy, and Burgess, *Justification*, 38, 49.

84. Though Carl E. Braaten and Robert W. Jensen, eds., *Union with Christ: The New Finnish Interpretation* (Grand Rapids, Mich.: Eerdmans, 1998) challenge this view.

85. This is the term used in the 1997 Joint Declaration (see John Reumann, "Justification by Faith: The Lutheran-Catholic Convergence," *Christian Century*, October. 22, 1997, p. 946).

86. Anderson, Murphy, and Burgess, *Justification*, 58, 16; quoted in David Van Biema, "A Half-Millennium Rift," *Time*, July 6, 1998, p. 80; http:www.justification .org/Doc 1 (11/09/99).

87. Anderson, *Justification*, 50–51; Carl E. Braaten, *Justification: The Article by Which the Church Stands or Falls* (Minneapolis, Minn.: Fortress, 1990), 7.

88. For a helpful summary of recent perspectives on Roman 1:16–17, see Reumann, *"Righteousness,"* 64–67.

89. James D. G. Dunn, *Romans 1–8*, vol. 38a, *Romans 9–16*, vol. 38b, WBC (Dallas: Word Books, 1988); James D. G. Dunn and Alan M. Suggate, *The Justice of God: A Fresh Look at the Old Doctrine of Justification by Faith* (Grand Rapids, Mich.: Eerdmans, 1994).

90. This insight, traced primarily to the work of H. Cremer, is noted in Anderson, Murphy, and Burgess, *Justification*, 59; Fitzmyer, *Romans*, 262; Cranfield, *Romans*, 1:94; Dunn, *Romans 1–8*, 40–41; Matthew Black, *Romans*, NCB, 2nd ed. (Grand Rapids, Mich.: Eerdmans, 1989), 31–33; J. A. Ziesler, *Pauline Christianity*, rev. ed. (New York: Oxford University Press, 1990), 88.

91. Dunn, *Romans 1–8*, 41 (see also Anderson, *Justification*, 59; Fitzmyer, *Romans*, 257).

92. Dunn, *Romans 1–8*, 41; Douglas J. Moo, *The Epistle to the Romans*, NICNT (Grand Rapids, Mich.: Eerdmans, 1996), 74. Moo agrees with Luther: "What is meant is a status *before* God and not internal moral transformation—God's activity of 'making right' is a purely forensic activity, an acquitting, and not an 'infusing' of righteousness or a 'making right' in a moral sense" (74–75).

93. Ernest Käsemann, " 'The Righteousness of God' in Paul," in *New Testament Questions of Today* (Philadelphia: Fortress, 1969), 168–82; Dunn, *Romans 1–8*, 42. Or as expressed as a "material convergence" in the Catholic-Lutheran dialogue: "By justification we are both declared and made righteous. Justification, therefore, is not a legal fiction. God, in justifying, effects what he promises; he forgives sin and makes us truly righteous" (Anderson, Murphy, and Burgess, *Justification*, 71).

94. Black cites five alternative understandings of the phrase (*Romans*, 35). For those supporting an emphasis on "faith through and through," see Leon Morris, *The Epistle to the Romans* (Grand Rapids, Mich.: Eerdmans, 1988), 70; Cranfield, *Romans*, 100; Anders Nygren, *Commentary on Romans*, trans. Carl C. Rasmussen (1949; Philadelphia: Fortress, 1949), 78–81; John Ziesler, *Paul's Letter to the Romans*, TPINTC (London: SCM, 1989), 71.

95. *LW*, 25:153.

96. On the history of the decisive role of this text in other settings, see Nygren, *Romans*, 81–83, 90.

97. Dunn, *Romans 1–8*, 48–49; Ziesler: "Faith is the way to righteousness, *and* it is how the righteous live" (*Paul's Letter to the Romans*, 72).

98. A small cottage industry of biblical scholarship has grown up over Luther's (mis)understanding of Paul and of Paul's relationship to Judaism. The key issue revolves around the Protestant tendency to view Luther's experiences as analogous to Paul's—as if Paul shared Luther's troubled conscience, and as if Luther's protest against the "works theology" of his own day paralleled Paul's protest against an ostensible works-driven Judaism in the first century. Scholars such as Dunn who embrace the "new perspective" (first articulated by E. P. Sanders in *Paul and Palestinian Judaism* [1977]) on Paul challenge what they consider to be a caricature of Paul (primarily from Protestants and especially German Lutherans) and argue that when Paul objected to "works of the law," he had something specific in mind. Throughout Hebrew Scripture God's grace preceded the law; God's covenant—the calling and choosing of a people—presupposed God's gracious initiative. From Paul's perspective, God's covenant promise and law had become too closely allied with "boundary markers" or "identity badges": circumcision, kosher food, and Sabbath observance to the point of creating a misplaced nationalistic zeal. In short, Luther's concerns were not the same as Paul's. See Dunn, *Romans 1–8*, lxiv–lxxii; Dunn and Sugate, *Justice of God*, 13–16. For a recent volume focused specifically on the new perspective, see D. A. Carson, Peter T. O'Brien, and Mark A. Seifrid, eds., *Justification and Variegated Nomism*, vol. 1, *The Complexities of Second Temple Judaism* (Grand Rapids, Mich.: Baker, 2001).

99. McGrath, *Iustia Dei*, 1:1.

100. Gerhard Ebeling, "The New Hermeneutics and the Early Luther," *ThTo* 21 (1964): 34–35.

CHAPTER 5

1. Quoted in Roland H. Bainton, *Christian Attitudes toward War and Peace: A Historical Survey and Critical Evaluation* (Nashville, Tenn.: Abingdon, 1960), 97.

2. "Ten Years," *Sojourners* 10 (September 1981): 4. The discussion on *Sojourners* is taken from David W. Kling, "*Sojourners*," in *Religious Periodicals of the United States: Academic and Scholarly Journals*, ed. Charles H. Lippy (Westport, Conn.: Greenwood Press, 1986), 479–80.

3. "What Is the People's Christian Coalition?" *Post-American* 1 (winter 1972): 7; "Ten Years," 4.

4. Leonard Verduin, *The Reformers and Their Stepchildren* (Grand Rapids, Mich.: Eerdmans, 1964); Roland Bainton, "The Left Wing of the Reformation," *JR* 21 (April 1941): 125–34; George H. Williams, *The Radical Reformation* (Philadelphia: Westminster, 1962); Donald F. Durnbaugh, *The Believers' Church: The History and Character of Radical Protestantism* (New York: Macmillan, 1968).

5. Both books trace their respective histories of persecution from the earliest Christian accounts. Two-thirds of the 1,140 pages of the *Martyrs Mirror* details Anabaptist persecutions. See Thieleman J. van Braght, comp., *The Bloody Theater, or, Martyrs Mirror of the Defenseless Christians Who Baptized Only upon Confession of Faith*, trans. Joseph F. Sohm (Scottdale, Pa.: Mennonite Publishing House, 1950).

6. *Martyrs Mirror*, 417.

7. Franklin H. Littell, *The Origins of Sectarian Protestantism: A Study of the Anabaptist View of the Church*, rev. ed. (New York: Macmillan, 1964), 109; *Martyrs Mirror*, 425.

8. *Martyrs Mirror*, 541–42.

9. Ibid., 775.

10. Stuart Murray, *Biblical Interpretation in the Anabaptist Tradition* (Kitchener, Ont.: Pandora Press, 2000), chap. 4.

11. Hans Hillerbrand, "Anabaptism and History," *MQR* 45 (April 1971): 119.

12. Ben C. Ollenburger, "The Hermeneutics of Obedience: Reflections on Anabaptist Hermeneutics," in *Essays on Biblical Interpretation: Anabaptist-Mennonite Perspectives*, ed. Willard Swartley (Elkhart, Ind.: Institute of Mennonite Studies, 1984), 49.

13. Williams, *Radical Reformation*, xxiv. The first edition of more than nine hundred pages has been superseded by a third edition of more than fifteen hundred pages (Kirksville, Mo.: Sixteenth Century Publishers, 1992). Subsequent citations are from the first edition.

14. Hillerbrand, "Anabaptism and History," 108.

15. G. R. Elton, *Reformation Europe, 1517–1559*, Fontana History of Europe (London: Collins, 1963), 103.

16. Harold S. Bender, "The Anabaptist Vision." Presidential address, December 28, 1943, published in *CH* 13 (March 1944): 3–24; reprinted in Guy F. Hershberger, ed., *The Recovery of the Anabaptist Vision* (Scottdale, Pa.: Herald Press, 1957), 29–54.

17. Ibid., 35–36.

18. Ibid., 42, 51.

19. Ibid., 41.

20. Walter Klaassen, *Anabaptism: Neither Catholic nor Protestant* (Waterloo, Ont.:

Conrad Press, 1973), 77; Robert Friedman, *The Theology of Anabaptism*, Studies in Anabaptist and Mennonite History, no. 15 (Scottdale, Pa.: Herald Press, 1973), 27. See also Friedman, "The Essence of Anabaptist Faith: An Essay in Interpretation," *MQR* 41 (January 1967): 5–24.

21. James M. Stayer, *Anabaptists and the Sword*, 2nd ed. (Lawrence, Kans.: Coronado Press, 1976), 9, 20. His introduction (1–23) contains a helpful, though scathing, historiographical overview of works on Anabaptist origins. In his "Reflections and Retractions" to the second edition, Stayer notes that his introduction "reflected, rather than caused," a shift in historical paradigms, and that "the time for the sort of polemic with which I began my book is past" (xii). For more recent historiographical analysis, see James M. Stayer, "The Anabaptists," in *Reformation Europe: A Guide to Research*, ed. Steven Ozment (St. Louis: Center for Reformation Research, 1982), 135–59; Werner O. Packull, "Between Paradigms: Anabaptist Studies at the Crossroads," *CGR* 8 (winter 1990): 1–22; Abraham Friesen, *Erasmus, the Anabaptists, and the Great Commission* (Grand Rapids, Mich.: Eerdmans, 1998), 6–19.

22. James M. Stayer, Werner Packull, and Klaus Depperman, "From Monogenesis to Polygenesis: The Historical Discussion of Anabaptist Origins," *MQR* 49 (April 1975): 83–121, quotation on 85; James Stayer, "The Easy Demise of a Normative Vision of Anabaptism," in *Mennonite Identity: Historical and Contemporary Perspectives*, ed. Calvin Wall Redekop (Lanham, Md.: University Press of America, 1988), 109–16.

23. Rodney J. Sawatsky, "The Quest for a Mennonite Hermeneutic," *CGR* 11 (winter 1993): 1–20; Redekop, *Mennonite Identity*.

24. James M. Stayer, "Anabaptists and the Sword," *MQR* 44 (October 1970): 375; Hans-Jürgen Goertz, "History and Theology: A Major Problem of Anabaptist Research Today," *MQR* 53 (July 1979): 187.

25. J. Denny Weaver, *Becoming Anabaptist: The Origin and Significance of Sixteenth-Century Anabaptism* (Scottdale, Pa.: Herald Press, 1987), 23, 121.

26. Arnold Snyder, "Beyond Polygenesis: Recovering the Unity and Diversity of Anabaptist Theology," in *Essays in Anabaptist Theology*, Text and Reader Series no. 5, ed. H. Wayne Pipkin (Elkhart, Ind.: Institute of Mennonite Studies, 1994), 9; C. Arnold Snyder, *Anabaptist History and Theology* (Kitchener, Ont.: Pandora Press, 1995), 83–99.

27. J. Denny Weaver, "Reading Sixteenth-Century Anabaptism Theologically: Implications for Modern Mennonites as a Peace Church," *CGR* 16 (winter 1998): 42–43; C. Arnold Synder "Anabaptist History and Theology: History or Heresy? A Reply to J. Denny Weaver," *CGR* 16 (winter 1998): 57; J. Denny Weaver, *Anabaptist Theology in Face of Postmodernity: A Proposal for the Third Millennium*, C. Henry Smith Ser., vol. 2 (Telford, Pa.: Pandora Press, 2000), chap. 4; Gerald J. Biesecker-Mast, "Anabaptist Separation and Arguments against the Sword in the Schleitheim *Brotherly Union*," *MQR* 73 (July 2000): 381–402.

28. Stayer, *Anabaptists and the Sword*, 6; Weaver, *Becoming Anabaptist*, 121; Yoder quoted in Sawatsky, "Quest for a Mennonite Hermeneutic," 13. For a critique of Stayer's assumptions, see Thomas Heilke, "Theological and Secular Meta-narratives of Politics: Anabaptist Origins Revisited (Again)," *Modern Theology* 13 (April 1997): 227–52. The most up-to-date analysis of Anabaptist historiography is John D. Roth, "Recent Currents in the Historiography of the Radical Reformation," *CH* 71 (September 2002): 523–35.

29. Friesen, *Erasmus, the Anabaptists*, 19, 96; see also 170 n. 71.

30. Ibid., 68, 98.

31. My discussion of the Swiss Brethren relies upon Cornelius J. Dyck, *An Introduction to Mennonite History: A Popular History of the Anabaptists and Mennonites*, 3rd ed. (Scottdale, Pa.: Herald Press, 1993); William R. Estep, *The Anabaptist Story: An Introduction to Sixteenth-Century Anabaptism*, 3rd ed. (Grand Rapids, Mich.: Eerdmans, 1996); Hans-Jürgen Goertz, *The Anabaptists*, 2nd ed., trans. Trevor Johnson (London: Routledge, 1996); Snyder, *Anabaptist History and Theology*; Weaver, *Becoming Anabaptist*.

32. Quoted in Goertz, *The Anabaptists*, 10.

33. William R. Estep Jr., ed., *Anabaptist Beginnings (1523–1533): A Sourcebook* (Nieuwkoop: B. De Graff, 1976), 18; Abraham Friesen, "The Radical Reformation Revisited," *Journal of Mennonite Studies* 2 (1984): 151.

34. Friesen, *Erasmsus, the Anabaptists*, 77–82.

35. Estep, *Anabaptist Beginnings*, 32, 33, 35–36, 38.

36. Quoted in Friesen, *Erasmus, the Anabaptists*, 54.

37. Walter Klaassen, "The Rise of Baptism of Adult Believers in Swiss Anabaptism," in *Anabaptism Revisited*, ed. Walter Klaassen (Scottdale, Pa.: Herald Press, 1992), 94.

38. John C. Wenger, "The Biblicism of the Anabaptists," in *Recovery of the Anabaptist Vision*, 167–79; Perry Yoder, "The Role of the Bible in Mennonite Self-Understanding," in *Mennonite Identity*, 69–82.

39. John H. Yoder, ed. and trans., *The Schleitheim Confession* (Scottdale, Pa.: Herald Press, 1977), 7–19.

40. Willard M. Swartley, *Slavery, Sabbath, War, and Women: Case Issues in Biblical Interpretation* (Scottdale, Pa.: Herald Press, 1983), chap. 3; Albert Curry Winn, *Ain't Gonna Study War No More: Biblical Ambiguity and the Abolition of War* (Louisville, Ky.: Westminster/John Knox, 1993); John A. Wood, *Perspectives on War in the Bible* (Macon, Ga.: Mercer University Press, 1998).

41. It is not entirely clear that the earliest followers of Jesus advocated pacifism. In Luke 3:14, John the Baptist does not insist that soldiers leave the military but to refrain from abusing their position for monetary gain. Similarly, Cornelius does not cease to be a centurion once he is baptized (Acts 10). See also Jesus' statement about the centurion in Luke 7:8 and the story in Matthew 8:5–13. At no point is there a hint that these men are to cease from their duties as soldiers. At the same time, this argument from silence (because Jesus did not say anything about military service, he evidently did not condemn it) does not prove that Jesus was indifferent to bloodshed and military service.

42. Stayer, *Anabaptists and the Sword*. Much of the following discussion on "the sword" is indebted to Stayer.

43. Williams, *Radical Reformation*, 226; quoted in Stayer, *Anabaptists and the Sword*, 54.

44. Quoted in Stayer, *Anabaptists and the Sword*, 58.

45. Bernd Moeller, *Imperial Cities and the Reformation*, ed. and trans. by H. C. Erik Midelfort and Mark U. Edwards Jr. (Philadelphia: Fortress, 1972), 75–90.

46. Estep, *Anabaptist Beginnings*, 35; Stayer, *Anabaptists and the Sword*, 104–7 (Waldshut), 112 (Blaurock).

47. Biesecker-Mast, "Anabaptist Separation," 391, 396.

48. Ibid.; *Schleitheim Confession*, 13, 14; Leo Driedger and Donald B. Kraybill, *Mennonite Peacemaking: From Quietism to Activism* (Scottdale, Pa.: Herald Press, 1994), 36.

49. *Schleitheim Confession*, 14–16.

50. Stayer, *Anabaptists and the Sword*, 123.

51. Walter Klaassen, "The Bern Debate of 1538: Christ the Center of Scripture," in *Essays on Biblical Interpretation*, 106–14, quotation on 110; Williams, *Radical Reformation*, 830.

52. Klaassen, "Bern Debate," 110.

53. Ibid., 111.

54. Quoted in ibid.

55. Williams, *Radical Reformation*, 485–99.

56. William Klassen, "The Relation of the Old and New Covenants in Pilgram Marpeck's Theology," *MQR* 40 (April 1966): 97–111.

57. William Klassen, *Covenant and Community: The Life, Writings and Hermeneutic of Pilgram Marpeck* (Grand Rapids, Mich.: Eerdmans, 1968), 123–24.

58. John Howard Yoder, "The Hermeneutics of the Anabaptists," in *Essays on Biblical Interpretation*, 26–27.

59. Klassen, *Covenant and Community*, 181.

60. Quoted in Stephen B. Boyd, *Pilgram Marpeck: His Life and Social Theology*, Duke Monographs in Medieval and Renaissance Studies 12 (Durham, N.C.: Duke University Press, 1992), 111. See also "Concerning the Love of God in Christ," in *The Writings of Pilgram Marpeck*, ed. and trans. William Klassen and Walter Klaassen (Scottdale, Pa.: Herald Press), 528–48. This letter "is as powerful a statement on the power of love and nonviolence as one can find in Anabaptist literature" (528).

61. Driedger and Kraybill, *Mennonite Peacemaking*, 30. But see Arnold Snyder, "Orality, Literacy, and the Study of Anabaptism," *MQR* 65 (October 1991): 371–92, who downplays the central role of the Sermon on the Mount in the early Swiss documents.

62. Driedger and Kraybill, *Mennonite Peacemaking*, 39–59; Perry Bush, *Two Kingdoms, Two Loyalties: Mennonite Pacifism in Modern America* (Baltimore: Johns Hopkins University Press, 1998), chaps. 6–9; Fred Kniss, *Disquiet in the Land: Cultural Conflict in American Mennonite Communities* (New Brunswick, N.J.: Rutgers University Press, 1997).

63. Driedger and Kraybill, *Mennonite Peacemaking*, 122.

64. Ibid., 121–22.

65. Keith Graber Miller, *Wise as Serpents, Innocent as Doves: American Mennonites Engage Washington* (Knoxville: University of Tennessee Press, 1996); Driedger and Kraybill, *Mennonite Peacemaking*, 124–131, 133–58 (quotation on 154). This uncertainty or hint of compromise is expressed in Driedger and Kraybill, *Mennonite Peacemaking*, 265–73. These questions are confronted directly and compellingly in Rodney J. Sawatsky and Scott Holland, eds., *The Limits of Perfection: Conversations with J. Lawrence Burkholder* (Waterloo, Ont.: Institute of Anabaptist-Mennonite Studies, 1993).

66. For a biographical profile, see Mark Thiessen Nation, "John H. Yoder, Ecumenical Neo-Anabaptist: A Biographical Sketch," in *The Wisdom of the Cross: Essays in*

Honor of John Howard Yoder, ed. Stanley Hauerwas Chris K. Huebner, Harry J. Hueb-ner, Mark Thiessen Nation (Grand Rapids, Mich.: Eerdmans, 1999), 1–23.

67. Quoted in Nation, "John H. Yoder," 20, 21.

68. John Howard Yoder, *The Christian Witness to the State,* Institute of Mennon-ite Studies Series, no. 3 (Newton, Kans.: Faith and Life Press, 1964).

69. John Howard Yoder, *The Politics of Jesus* (Grand Rapids, Mich.: Eerdmans, 1972), 14, 12. For Yoder's interpretation of the one episode of "violence" committed by Jesus (the "cleansing of the temple"), see 47–53.

70. Ibid., 132, 243.

71. Guy Franklin Hershberger, *War, Peace, and Nonresistance,* 3rd ed. (Scottdale, Pa.: Herald Press, 1969), viii, 53, 233. For a discussion of Hershberger, see Driedger and Kraybill, *Mennonite Peacemaking,* 71–107.

72. Ronald J. Sider, *Christ and Violence* (Scottdale, Pa.: Herald Press, 1979).

73. John Howard Yoder, *The Original Revolution: Essays on Christian Pacifism* (Scottdale, Pa.: Herald Press, 1971), 91–111; Hershberger, *War, Peace, and Nonresis-tance,* vii, 34.

74. Yoder, *Original Revolution,* 98–100.

75. Ibid., 101–3, Yoder, *Politics,* 80, 80 n. 3 (quotation).

76. Yoder referred to unpublished material that Lind has since published. See Millard C. Lind, *Yahweh Is a Warrior: The Theology of Warfare in Ancient Israel* (Scott-dale, Pa.: Herald Press, 1980); and Lind, *Monotheism, Power, Justice: Collected Old Tes-tament Essays,* Text Reader Series no. 3 (Elkhart, Ind.: Institute of Mennonite Studies, 1990), quotation on 171.

77. Yoder, *Politics,* 81–82.

78. Yoder, *Original Revolution,* 104–5.

79. Yoder, *Politics,* 88; Yoder, *Original Revolution,* 13–33. A number of scholars at-tacked Yoder's contention that Jesus considered the Zealot option. For a rebuttal, see *Politics,* 2nd ed. (Grand Rapids, Mich.: Eerdmans, 1994), 56–59; and William Klassen, "Jesus and the Zealot Option," in *The Wisdom of the Cross,* 131–49.

80. Yoder, *Politics,* 62–63.

81. Ibid., 115–62.

82. Ibid., 147–48.

83. Ibid., 193–214 (quotations on 207, 214).

84. John D. Roth, "Community as Conversation: A New Model of Anabaptist Hermeneutics," in *Anabaptist Currents,* 51–64; Murray, *Biblical Interpretation in the Anabaptist Tradition,* chap. 10.

85. Driedger and Kraybill, *Mennonite Peacemaking,* 19–37, 61–158; Snyder, *Ana-baptist History and Theology,* 388–90; John Howard Yoder, *Nevertheless: The Varieties of Religious Pacifism* (Scottdale, Pa.: Herald Press, 1971), 105–13.

86. John Howard Yoder, *The Priestly Kingdom: Social Ethics as Gospel* (Notre Dame, Ind.: University of Notre Dame Press, 1984), 135–47; Littell, *Origins of Sectar-ian Protestantism,* 46–78. For a contrary interpretation, see Daniel H. Williams, "Con-stantine, Nicaea and the 'Fall' of the Church," in *Christian Origins: Theology, Rhetoric and Community,* ed. Lewis Ayres and Gareth Jones (New York: Routledge, 1998), 117–36.

87. Warren S. Kissinger, *The Sermon on the Mount: A History of Interpretation*

and Bibliography, ATLA Bibliography Series, no. 3 (Metuchen, N.J.: Scarecrow Press, 1975), 6, 16–125.

88. Richard A. Horsley, "Ethics and Exegesis: 'Love Your Enemies' and the Doctrine of Non-Violence," *JAAR* 54 (spring 1986): 3–31, is critical of Yoder's exegesis (see 26–27) but reaches similar conclusions.

89. The literature is extensive, but see Marlin E. Miller and Barbara Nelson Gingerich, eds., *The Church's Peace Witness* (Grand Rapids, Mich.: Eerdmans, 1994; Paul Peachey, *Peace, Politics, and the People of God* (Philadelphia: Fortress, 1986); Glen H. Stassen, *Just Peacemaking: Transforming Initiatives for Justice and Peace* (Louisville, Ky.: Westminster/John Knox, 1992); Glen Stassen, ed., *Just Peacemaking: Ten Practices for Abolishing War* (Cleveland: Pilgrim Press, 1998).

CHAPTER 6

1. Maya Angelou, *I Know Why the Caged Bird Sings* (1969; New York: Bantam Books, 1970), 40, 20.

2. Ibid., 160.

3. James Cone, *Risks of Faith: The Emergence of a Black Theology of Liberation, 1968–1998* (Boston: Beacon Press, 1999), ix.

4. Cone, *Risks of Faith*, xi; Angelou, *I Know*, 15.

5. Thomas Hoyt Jr., "Interpreting Biblical Scholarship for the Black Church Tradition," in *Stony the Road We Trod: African American Biblical Interpretation*, ed. Cain Hope Felder (Minneapolis, Minn.: Fortress, 1991), 29, 30.

6. Michael Walzer, *Exodus and Revolution* (New York: Basic Books, 1985), 7; Donald Harman Akenson, *God's Peoples: Covenant and Land in South Africa, Israel, and Ulster* (Ithaca, N.Y.: Cornell University Press, 1992), 5.

7. Albert J. Raboteau, "The Black Experience in American Evangelicalism: The Meaning of Slavery," in *African-American Religion: Interpretive Essays in History and Culture*, ed. Timothy E. Fulop and Albert J. Raboteau (New York: Routledge, 1997), 101.

8. See Sarah H. Bradford, *Harriet Tubman: The Moses of Her People* (1886; Bedford, Mass.: Applewood Books, 1993).

9. Robert S. Starobin, ed., *Denmark Vesey: The Slave Conspiracy of 1822* (Englewood Cliffs, N.J.: Prentice-Hall, 1970), 21.

10. Thomas Wentworth Higginson, *Army Life in a Black Regiment, and Other Writings*, introd. R. D. Madison (New York: Penguin, 1997), 191.

11. Timothy E. Fulop, " 'The Future Golden Day of the Race': Millennialism and Black Americans in the Nadir, 1877–1901," in *African-American Religion*, 235.

12. Katherine L. Dvorak, *An African-American Exodus: The Segregation of Southern Churches* (Brooklyn, N.Y.: Carlson, 1991), 178–86.

13. Herbert G. Gutman, *The Black Family in Slavery and Freedom, 1750–1925* (New York: Pantheon, 1976), 186–87.

14. See Edwin S. Redkey, *Black Exodus: Black Nationalist and Back-to-Africa Movements, 1890–1910* (New Haven, Conn.: Yale University Press, 1969).

15. Dickson D. Bruce Jr., "On Dunbar's 'Jingles in a Broken Tongue': Dunbar's Dialect Poetry and the Afro-American Folk Tradition," in *A Singer in the Dawn: Rein-*

terpretations of Paul Laurence Dunbar, ed. Jay Martin (New York: Dodd, Mead, 1975), 94–113; David T. Shannon, "'An Antebellum Sermon': A Resource for an African American Hermeneutic," in *Stony the Road We Trod*, 98–123.

16. W. E. Burghardt Du Bois, *The Souls of Black Folk* (1903; New York: Fawcett, 1961), 87.

17. James Weldon Johnson, *God's Trombones: Seven Negro Sermons in Verse* (New York: Viking, 1927), 45–52.

18. Quoted in James H. Cone, *For My People: Black Theology and the Black Church* (Maryknoll, N.Y.: Orbis Books, 1984), 207. Cone substitutes the gender-inclusive "God" for "His," but I have retained Tindley's original words. The hymn is reproduced in Ralph H. Jones, *Charles Albert Tindley: Prince of Preachers* (Nashville, Tenn.: Abingdon, 1982), 167–68, and can also be found in many Protestant hymnals.

19. Ralph Ellison, *Invisible Man* (1947; New York: New American Library, 1952), 109.

20. Claude Brown, *Manchild in the Promised Land* (New York: Signet Books, 1965); Al Sharpton and Anthony Walton, *Go and Tell Pharaoh: The Autobiography of the Reverend Al Sharpton* (New York: Doubleday, 1996).

21. Dvorak, *African-American Exodus*; Nicholas Lemann, *The Promised Land: The Great Black Migration and How It Changed America* (New York: Random House, 1991); Garth Baker-Fletcher, *Xodus: An African American Male Journey* (Minneapolis, Minn.: Fortress, 1996); Milton C. Sernett, *Bound for the Promised Land: African American Religion and the Great Migration* (Durham, N.C.: Duke University Press, 1997); Eddie S. Glaude, *Exodus! Religion, Race, and Nation in Early Nineteenth-Century Black America* (Chicago: University of Chicago Press, 2000); Albert J. Raboteau, *Canaan Land: A Religious History of African Americans* (New York: Oxford University Press, 2001).

22. Quoted in Keith Gilyard, "The Bible and African American Poetry," in *African Americans and the Bible: Sacred Texts and Social Textures*, ed. Vincent L. Wimbush (New York: Continuum), 208–9.

23. Godfrey Ashby, *Go Out and Meet God: A Commentary on the Book of Exodus*, ITC (Grand Rapids, Mich.: Eerdmans, 1998), 62.

24. David W. Wills, "The Central Themes of American Religious History: Pluralism, Puritanism, and the Encounter of Black and White," in *African-American Religion*, 9–20.

25. Pinchas Lapide, "Exodus in the Jewish Tradition," in *Exodus—A Lasting Paradigm*, ed. Bas van Iersel and Anton Weiler, Concilium, vol. 187 (Edinburgh: T. & T. Clark, 1987), 48.

26. James B. Pritchard, ed., *Ancient Near Eastern Texts Relating to the Old Testament*, 3rd ed. (Princeton, N.J.: Princeton University Press, 1969), 378. According to the traditional view, the Pharaoh was probably Thutmose III of the Eighteenth Dynasty (ca. 1490–1436 B.C.E.), although more recent scholarship favors Sethos (ca. 1305–1290 B.C.E.) or Ramesses II (ca. 1290–1224 B.C.E.) of the Nineteenth Dynasty.

27. John Bright, *A History of Israel*, 3rd ed. (Philadelphia: Westminster, 1981), 120–29.

28. Ibid., 120; James K. Hoffmeier, *Israel in Egypt: The Evidence for the Authenticity of the Exodus Tradition* (New York: Oxford University Press, 1997); Rita Burns, "The Book of Exodus," in *Exodus—A Lasting Paradigm*, 13.

29. John I. Durham, *Exodus*, WBC, vol. 3 (Waco, Tex.: Word Books, 1987), xxv.

30. Brevard S. Childs, *The Book of Exodus: A Critical, Theological Commentary*, OTL (Philadelphia: Westminster, 1974); Nahum M. Sarna, *Exploring Exodus: The Heritage of Biblical Israel* (New York: Schocken Books, 1986); Donald E. Gowan, *Theology in Exodus: Biblical Theology in the Form of a Commentary* (Louisville, Ky.: Westminster John Knox, 1994); Durham, *Exodus*; Ashby, *Go Out and Meet God*.

31. J. Philip Hyatt, *Exodus*, NCB (Grand Rapids, Mich.: Eerdmans, 1971), 66.

32. Durham, *Exodus*, 210.

33. Werner Sollors, *Beyond Ethnicity: Consent and Descent in American Culture* (New York: Oxford University Press, 1986), 43.

34. The typological interpretation reads the Old Testament from the perspective of the New; Old Testament persons, places, events, and symbols (types) prefigured New Testament realities (antitypes). The basic assumption was that by itself the Old Testament was an incomplete document containing providentially inspired prophetic adumbrations of Christ. In the Old Testament, Christ was veiled in images, types, and shadows; in the New he was revealed. For example, the episode of Jonah's "three days and three nights in the whale's belly" prefigured Jesus' "three days and three nights in the heart of the earth" (Matt. 12:40). At the same time, Puritans expanded the type-antitype structure beyond Scripture and viewed the redemptive aspects of Puritan New England fulfilling Old Testament prefigurations.

35. Cotton Mather, "Magnalia Christi Americana" (1702), quoted in Sollors, *Beyond Ethnicity*, 43.

36. Albert Raboteau, "African-Americans, Exodus, and the American Israel," in *African-American Christianity*, ed. Paul E. Johnson (Berkeley: University of California Press, 1994), 15; John Winthrop, "A Model of Christian Charity," in *The American Puritans: Their Prose and Poetry*, ed. Perry Miller (Garden City, N.Y.: Anchor Books, 1956), 83.

37. Quoted in Sollors, *Beyond Ethnicity*, 43; Nicholas Street, "The American States Acting over the Part of the Children of Israel in the Wilderness and Thereby Impeding Their Entrance into Canaan's Rest," in *God's New Israel: Religious Interpretations of America's Destiny*, ed. Conrad Cherry (Englewood Cliffs, N.J.: Prentice-Hall, 1971), 69–70.

38. Walzer, *Exodus and Revolution*, 6; Sollors, *Beyond Ethnicity*, 43–44.

39. Quoted in Raboteau, "African-Americans, Exodus, and the American Israel," 11; quoted in Sollors, *Beyond Ethnicity*, 43.

40. Samuel Langdon, "The Republic of the Israelites an Example to the American States," in *God's New Israel*, 98–99; Abiel Abbot, "Traits of Resemblance in the People of the United States of America to Ancient Israel," in *The American Republic and Ancient Israel* (New York: Arno Press, 1977), 6. On expansionism, see Ernest Lee Tuveson, *Redeemer Nation: The Idea of America's Millennial Role* (Chicago: University of Chicago Press, 1968), chaps. 4, 5; on tragic irony, see Raboteau, "African Americans, Exodus, and the American Israel," 9 (citing Vincent Harding).

41. There is extensive scholarly literature on (and debate over) the extent of African religious influences on the African American slave. Some scholars have argued for complete obliteration, others for enduring influence. More recent scholarship generally affirms continued African influence. For a sampling of these interpretations, see Eugene D. Genovese, *Roll Jordan Roll: The World the Slaves Made* (1972; New York: Viking, 1976), 209–12; Albert J. Raboteau, *Slave Religion: The "Invisible Institution" in*

the Antebellum South (New York: Oxford University Press, 1978), chap. 2; John W. Blassingame, *The Slave Community: Plantation Life in the Antebellum South*, rev. ed. (New York: Oxford University Press, 1979), chaps. 1, 2; Sterling Stuckey, *Slave Culture: Nationalist Theory and the Foundations of Black America* (New York: Oxford University Press, 1987), introd., chap. 1; Dwight N. Hopkins, "Slave Theology in the 'Invisible Institution,'" in Dwight N. Hopkins and George C. L. Cummings, *Cut Loose Your Stammering Tongue: Black Theology in Slave Narratives* (Maryknoll, N.Y.: Orbis, 1991), 1–45; Charles H. Long, "Perspectives for a Study of African-American Religion in the United States," in *African-American Religion*, 21–35; Sidney W. Mintz and Richard Price, "The Birth of African-American Culture," in *African-American Religion*, 36–53; Will Coleman, *Tribal Talk: Black Theology, Hermeneutics, and African/American Ways of "Telling the Story"* (University Park: Pennsylvania State University Press, 2000), chap. 3.

42. Although evangelical Christianity became the faith of African Americans, most blacks had no formal affiliation with religion. In 1830, about 140,000 Southern blacks in a population of more than 2 million held membership in evangelical churches; by 1859, there were 468,000 black church members in a population of more than 4 million. The greatest gain in the nineteenth century came in the decades following emancipation. By 1900, there were 2.7 million black church members in a population of 8.3 million Southern blacks. See Donald G. Mathews, *Religion in the Old South* (Chicago: University of Chicago Press, 1977), 137; Raboteau, *Slave Religion*, 209.

43. Du Bois, *Souls of Black Folk*, 141; Sylvia R. Frey and Betty Wood, *Come Shouting to Zion: African American Protestantism in the American South and British Caribbean to 1830* (Chapel Hill: University of North Carolina Press, 1998), 1.

44. James H. Cone, *The Spirituals and the Blues: An Interpretation* (New York: Seabury Press, 1972), 30; Donald H. Matthews, *Honoring the Ancestors: An African Cultural Interpretation of Black Religion and Literature* (New York: Oxford University Press, 1998), 11; Vincent L. Wimbush, "The Bible and African Americans: An Outline of an Interpretive History," in *Stony the Road We Trod*, 89.

45. Lawrence W. Levine, *Black Culture and Black Consciousness: Afro-American Folk Thought from Slavery to Freedom* (New York: Oxford University Press, 1977), 33.

46. Quoted in Margaret Washington, "The Meanings of Scripture in Gullah Concepts of Liberation and Group Identity," in *African Americans and the Bible*, 333.

47. "Susan Boggs," in *Slave Testimony: Two Centuries of Letters, Speeches, Interviews, and Autobiographies*, ed. John W. Blassingame (Baton Rouge: Louisiana State University Press, 1977), 420. See also Frederick Douglass, *Narrative of the Life of Frederick Douglass*, ed. Benjamin Quarles (Cambridge, Mass.: Belknap Press of Harvard University Press, 1980), 84, 87–88; 110 ("For of all slaveholders with whom I have ever met, religious slaveholders are the worst"); 157 ("Revivals of religion and revivals in the slave-trade go hand in hand together"); 155–63.

48. Raboteau, *Slave Religion*, 55–75, 243–46; Stuckey, *Slave Culture*, 17–21; James Weldon Johnson, ed., *The Book of American Negro Spirituals* (New York: Viking, 1925), 17–21 (quotation on 19).

49. William E. Montgomery, *Under Their Own Fig Tree: The African-American Church in the South, 1865–1900* (Baton Rouge: Louisiana State University Press, 1993),

143; Janet Duitsman Cornelius, *"When I Can Read My Title Clear": Literacy, Slavery, and Religious in the Antebellum South* (Columbia: University of South Carolina Press, 1991).

50. Vincent L. Wimbush, "Introduction: Reading Darkness, Reading Scriptures," in *African Americans and the Bible*, 15.

51. Dwight N. Hopkins, *Down, Up, and Over: Slave Religion and Black Theology* (Minneapolis, Minn.: Fortress, 2000), 158; Newman I. White, *American Negro Folk-Songs* (Hatboro, Pa.: Folklore Associates, [1928], 1965), 45, cited in Dvorak, *African-American Exodus*, 25–26.

52. Octavia V. Rogers Albert, *The House of Bondage; or Charlotte Brooks and Other Slaves* (1890; New York: Oxford University Press, 1988), 31 (see also 130).

53. Johnson, *Book of American Negro Spirituals*, 80–81.

54. Ibid., 13. A conjurer, also known as a root doctor, hoodoo doctor, and two-facer, had supernatural powers, including the ability to heal, tell fortunes, and ward off evil (or good, depending on whether the conjurer's source of power was God or the devil). See Raboteau, *Slave Religion*, 275–88; Theophus H. Smith, *Conjuring Culture: Biblical Formation of Black America* (New York: Oxford University Press, 1994), chap. 2.

55. Both versions are found in Dena J. Epstein, *Sinful Tunes and Spirituals: Black Folk Music to the Civil War* (Urbana: University of Illinois Press, 1977), appendix III (363, 365).

56. Frederick Douglass, *Life and Times of Frederick Douglass, Written by Himself*, introd. Rayford W. Logan (1892; New York: Bonanza Books, 1962), 159; quoted in Hopkins, "Slave Theology," 13.

57. William Francis Allen et al., comps.; introd. W. K. McNeil, *Slave Songs of the United States* (1867; Baltimore: Clearfield, 1992), 76.

58. Eddie S. Glaude Jr., *Exodus! Religion, Race, and Nation in Early Nineteenth-Century Black America* (Chicago: University of Chicago Press, 2000), 4; John Lovell Jr., *Black Song: The Forge and the Flame* (New York: Macmillan, 1972), 234.

59. Dwight N. Hopkins, *Shoes That Fit Our Feet: Sources for a Constructive Black Theology* (Maryknoll, N.Y.: Orbis, 1993), 29; Levine, *Black Culture and Black Consciousness*, 50; Genovese, *Roll Jordan Roll*, 252.

60. Johnson, *Book of American Negro Spirituals*, 60–61.

61. Lovell, *Black Song*, 235.

62. Langston Hughes and Arna Bontemps, eds., *The Book of Negro Folklore* (New York: Dodd, Mead, 1958), 299–300, 303–4.

63. Wimbush, "The Bible and African Americans," 82–83.

64. "Narrative of James Curry," in *Slave Testimony*, 136.

65. Vincent Harding, "Religion and Resistance among Antebellum Negroes, 1800–1860," in *Religion in American History: Interpretive Essays*, ed. John M. Mulder and John F. Wilson (Englewood Cliffs, N.J.: Prentice-Hall, 1978), 270–87; Gayraud S. Wilmore, *Black Religion and Black Radicalism: An Interpretation of the Religious History of Afro-American People*, 2nd ed. (Maryknoll, N.Y.: Orbis, 1983), 53–73; Mechal Sobel, *Trabelin' On: The Slave Journey to an Afro-Baptist Faith* (Westport, Conn.: Greenwood Press, 1979), 159–68.

66. Harding, "Religion and Resistance," 272; Starobin, *Denmark Vesey*, 21.

67. James H. Cone, "Black Theology as Liberation Theology," in *African-American Religious Studies: An Interdisciplinary Anthology*, ed. Gayraud Wilmore (Durham, N.C.: Duke University Press, 1989), 183; Stuckey, *Slave Culture*, 137.

68. On biographical details of Walker's life, see Peter P. Hinks, *To Awaken My Afflicted Brethren: David Walker and the Problem of Antebellum Slave Resistance* (University Park: Pennsylvania State University Press, 1997); Peter Hinks, ed. and introd., *David Walker's "Appeal to the Colored Citizens of the World"* (University Park: Pennsylvania State University Press, 2000).

69. Hinks, *Walker's "Appeal,"* xxv.

70. Wilmore, *Black Religion and Black Radicalism*, 38; Hinks, *To Awaken My Afflicted Brethren*, xiv; Glaude, *Exodus!*, 34.

71. For other contemporary examples, see "The Sons of Africans: An Essay on Freedom with Observations on the Origin of Slavery. By a Member of the African Society in Boston," in *Early Negro Writing, 1760–1837*, ed. Dorothy Porter (Boston: Beacon, 1971), 13–22; Ottobah Cugoano, "Thoughts and Sentiments on the Evil and Wicked Traffic of the Slavery and Commerce of the Human Species," in *Pioneers of the Black Atlantic: Five Slave Narratives from the Enlightenment, 1772–1815*, ed. Henry Louis Gates Jr. and William L. Andrews (Washington, D.C.: Civitas Counterpoint, 1998), chap. 3.

72. Hinks, *Walker's "Appeal,"* 16, 9.

73. Hinks, *To Awaken My Afflicted Brethren*, 198.

74. Henry Highland Garnet, "An Address to the Slaves of the United States of America" (1843), in *Black Nationalism in America*, ed. John H. Bracey Jr., August Meier, and Elliot Rudwick (Indianapolis: Bobbs-Merrill [1970]), 73. Informed discussions of "Address to the Slaves" are found in Glaude, *Exodus!*; Stuckey, *Slave Culture*, chap. 3.

75. Garnet, "Address to the Slaves," 75, 76.

76. Absalom Jones, "A Thanksgiving Sermon, Preached January 1, 1808, . . . On Account of the Abolition of the African Slave Trade," in *Early Negro Writing*, 338, 337.

77. Turner quoted in Stephen Ward Angell, *Bishop Henry Ward Turner and African-American Religion in the South* (Knoxville: University of Tennessee Press, 1992), 41; White quoted in Levine, *Black Culture and Black Consciousness*, 137; quoted in John Hope Franklin, *The Emancipation Proclamation* (Garden City, N.Y.: Anchor Books, 1965), 106.

78. Levine, *Black Culture and Black Consciousness*, 137; quoted in Raboteau, *Slave Religion*, 311–12.

79. Blassingame, *Slave Testimony*, 504.

80. Quoted in Raboteau, *Slave Religion*, 320.

81. Sernet, *Bound for the Promised Land*, 17.

82. Nell Irvin Painter, *Exodusters: Black Migration to Kansas after Reconstruction* (New York: Knopf, 1977), 206–8.

83. Quoted in Painter, *Exodusters*, 188; quoted in Timothy E. Fulop, " 'The Future Golden Day of the Race': Millennialism and Black Americans in the Nadir, 1877–1901," in *African-American Religion*, 236; quoted in David W. Wills, "Exodus Piety: African American Religion in an Age of Immigration," in *Minority Faiths and the American Protestant Mainstream*, ed. Jonathan D. Sarna (Urbana: University of Illinois Press, 1998), 148, 147.

84. Redkey, *Black Exodus*, 53–54.

85. Quoted in Angell, *Bishop Henry Ward Turner*, 136.

86. Albert J. Raboteau, *A Fire in the Bones: Reflections on African-American History* (Boston: Beacon, 1995), 42; Fulop, "Future Golden Day," 237.

87. Sernet, *Bound for the Promised Land*, 58.

88. Ibid., 59, quotations on 61, 62.

89. Ibid., 64, quotations on 85–86.

90. Ibid., 79–83, 124, quotation on 84.

91. Cheryl A. Kirk-Duggan, *Exorcising Evil: A Womanist Perspective on the Spirituals* (Maryknoll, N.Y.: Orbis, 1997), 251.

92. Quoted in ibid., 253.

93. Ibid., 251, 254.

94. See "How Did You Feel?", "Ain't Gonna Let Nobody Turn Me Round," "Come and Go with Me to That Land," and "I'm on My Way to the Freedom Land," in *We Shall Overcome: Songs of the Southern Freedom Movement*, comp. Guy and Candie Carawan (New York: Oak Publications, 1963), 18, 60–61, 66–67, 68–69; Keith Miller, "City Called Freedom: Biblical Metaphor in Spirituals, Gospel Lyrics, and the Civil Rights Movement," in *African Americans and the Bible*, 546–57.

95. Quoted in Scott W. Hoffman, "Holy Martin: The Overlooked Canonization of Dr. Martin Luther King, Jr.," *Religion and American Culture* 10 (summer 2000): 128.

96. James M. Washington, ed., *A Testament of Hope: The Essential Writings and Speeches of Martin Luther King, Jr.* (New York: HarperCollins, 1986), 286.

97. Ibid., 619.

98. Quoted in John Newton, "Analysis of Programmatic Texts of Exodus Movements," in *Exodus—A Lasting Paradigm*, 57.

99. *Testament of Hope*, 200; quoted in James Wm. McClendon Jr., *Biography as Theology: How Life Stories Can Remake Today's Theology* (Nashville, Tenn.: Abingdon, 1974), 84.

100. Quoted in Hoffman, "Holy Martin," 133; Leonard Lovett, "How Far Is the Promised Land?" in *Outstanding Black Sermons*, vol. 3, ed. Milton E. Owens (Valley Forge, Pa.: Judson Press, 1982), 38; Cone, *Risks of Faith*, xvi, 72.

101. James H. Cone, *A Black Theology of Liberation* (Philadelphia: Lippincott, 1970), 90.

102. Ibid., 34–45.

103. Ibid., 18–19, 26, 11.

104. For examples, see Cone, *For My People*, 80; *God of the Oppressed*, rev. ed. (Maryknoll, N.Y.: Orbis, 1997), 57–66; Cone, *Risks of Faith*, 32. On second-generation scholarship, see Dwight N. Hopkins, "Black Theology and a Second Generation: New Scholarship and New Challenges," in *Black Theology: A Documentary History*, vol. 2, *1980–1992* (Maryknoll, N.Y.: Orbis, 1993), 61–70.

105. David Tracy, "Theological Reflection," in *Exodus—A Lasting Paradigm*, 120; Delores S. Williams, *Sisters in the Wilderness: The Challenge of Womanist God-Talk* (Maryknoll, N.Y.: Orbis, 1993), 149.

106. Williams, *Sisters*, 6, 144–48.

107. Warren H. Steward Jr., *Interpreting God's Word in Black Preaching* (Valley Forge, Pa.: Judson Press, 1984), 21.

108. For examples, see Charles B. Copher, "Transforming the Land of Oppres-

sion into the Promised Land," 25–30; and J. Deotis Roberts Sr., "Afflicted, but Not Defeated," 64–67, in *Preaching the Gospel*, ed. Henry J. Young (Philadelphia: Fortress, 1976); Effie M. Clark, "How a People Make History," in *Outstanding Black Sermons*, ed. J. Alfred Smith (Valley Forge, Pa.: Judson Press, 1976), 25–32; Dwight Clinton Jones, "The Lord Is on Our Side," in *Outstanding Black Sermons*, vol. 2, ed. Walter B. Hoard (Valley Forge, Pa.: Judson Press, 1979), 57–63; Lovett, "How Far Is the Promised Land," 37–45; and the following articles in *Living in Hell: The Dilemma of African-American Survival*, ed. Mose Pleasure Jr. and Fred C. Lofton (Grand Rapids, Mich.: Zondervan, 1995): Alan V. Ragland, "From Heaven to Hell: What Went Wrong in Egypt?" 36–43; Edward L. Wheeler, "Going Beyond News from the Brickyard," 46–52; Charles Williams Butler, "The Conquest of Hell: An Essay," 210–16.

109. Clark, "How a People Make History," 25; Ragland, "From Heaven to Hell," 39.

110. Roberts, "Afflicted, but Not Defeated," 66.

111. Judd Kruger Levintston, "Liberation Theology and Judaism," in *Judaism, Christianity, and Liberation: An Agenda for Dialogue*, ed. Otto Maduro (Maryknoll, N.Y.: Orbis, 1991), 9; Ragland, "From Heaven to Hell," 42, 43.

112. See Latta R. Thomas, *Biblical Faith and the Black American* (Valley Forge, Pa.: Judson Press, 1976), 69–71; Felder, *Stony the Road We Trod*, Parts I and II; Robert A. Bennet, "Black Experience and the Bible," in *African American Religious Studies: An Interdisciplinary Anthology*, ed. Gayraud Wilmore (Durham, N.C.: Duke University Press, 1989), 129–39; Cain H. Felder, "The Bible, Re-contextualization and the Black Religious Experience, in *African American Religious Studies*, 155–76.

113. Wimbush, "The Bible and African Americans," 95–97.

114. For example, see the following articles in *African Americans and the Bible*: Velma Love, "The Bible and Contemporary African American Culture I," 49–65; James M. Shopshire, Ida Rousseau Mukenge, Victoria Erickson, and Hans A. Baer, "The Bible and Contemporary African American Culture II," 66–80; James M. Shopshire, "The Bible as Informant and Reflector in Social-Structural Relationships of African Americans," 123–37.

115. This point is made by Mark A. Noll, "The United States as a Biblical Nation," in *The Bible in America: Essays in Cultural History*, ed. Nathan O. Hatch and Mark A. Noll (New York: Oxford University Press, 1982), 51.

CHAPTER 7

1. These include the divine inspiration and infallibility of Scripture; the deity of Jesus Christ; the veracity of biblical miracles (including the virgin birth); the physical death of Christ for humanity's sins and his physical resurrection; and the personal return of Christ at his Second Coming. By and large Pentecostals were untouched by the Fundamentalist Controversy and consequently never became part of the organized fundamentalist movement, though to be sure, they embraced fundamentalist teachings.

2. Quoted in Harvey Cox, *Fire from Heaven: The Rise of Pentecostal Spirituality and the Reshaping of Religion in the Twenty-first Century* (Reading, Mass.: Addison-Wesley, 1995), 75.

3. Henry Pitney Van Dusen, "The Third Force in Christendom," *Life*, 9 June 1958, pp. 113–24.

4. David B. Barrett and Todd M. Johnson, "Annual Statistical Table on Global Mission: 2003," *International Bulletin of Missionary Research* 27 (January 2003): 25. See also D. B. Barrett, "Statistics, Global," in *Dictionary of Pentecostal and Charismatic Movements*, ed. Stanley M. Burgess and Gary McGee (Grand Rapids, Mich.: Zondervan, 1988), 810–30 (hereafter *DPCM*). This figure includes people associated with classical Pentecostalism, the Charismatic Movement, and so-called third-wavers (nonpentecostal, noncharismatic, church renewal adherents).

5. Ann Taves, *Fits, Trances, and Visions: Experiencing Religion and Explaining Experience from Wesley to James* (Princeton, N.J.: Princeton University Press, 1999), 7–9; H. Newton Malony and A. Adams Lovekin, *Glossolalia: Behavioral Science Perspectives on Speaking in Tongues* (New York: Oxford University Press, 1985), 98–100.

6. Cox, *Fire from Heaven*, 81; Frank Macchia, "Sighs Too Deep for Words: Toward a Theology of Glossolalia," *JPT* 1 (1992): 61, 49, 66. Macchia's interpretation of glossolalia somewhat shifts the classical Pentecostal understanding of the phenomenon as empowerment to that of revelation as the basic category of understanding Spirit baptism. The power to witness is a consequence of this revelatory experience.

7. Frederick Dale Bruner, *A Theology of the Holy Spirit: The Pentecostal Experience and the New Testament Witness* (Grand Rapids, Mich.: Eerdmans, 1970), 143–44. This is an evenhanded yet critical work.

8. Grant Wacker, *Heaven Below: Early Pentecostals and American Culture* (Cambridge, Mass.: Harvard University Press, 2001), 41; Barrett, "Statistics, Global," 820.

9. William G. McDonald, "Pentecostal Theology: A Classical Viewpoint," in *Perspectives on the New Pentecostalism*, ed. Russell P. Spittler (Grand Rapids, Mich.: Baker, 1976), 66.

10. Quoted in Edith L. Blumhofer, *Restoring the Faith: The Assemblies of God, Pentecostalism, and American Culture* (Urbana: University of Illinois Press, 1993), 13; quoted in Wacker, *Heaven Below*, 71.

11. Steven J. Land, *Pentecostal Spirituality: A Passion for the Kingdom*, JPTSS 1 (Sheffield, Eng.: Sheffield Academic Press, 1993), 65.

12. French L. Arrington, "The Use of the Bible by Pentecostals," *Pneuma* 16 (spring 1994): 101. For examples of the increasing importance and variety of hermeneutics among Pentecostal scholars, see the articles in issues of *Pneuma* 15 (fall 1993) and 16 (spring 1994).

13. These comparisons are made by Land, *Pentecostal Spirituality*, 32–47; and R. P. Spittler, "Spirituality, Pentecostal and Charismatic," *DPCM*, 804, who refer to Lesslie Newbigen categories in *The Household of God* (New York: Friendship Press, 1954), 94–95, 102–8. I have also included the insights of Eduard Schweizer, *The Holy Spirit*, trans. Reginald H. Fuller and Ilse Fuller (Philadelphia: Fortress, 1980), 2–5.

14. Quoted in John L. Sherrill, *They Speak with Other Tongues* (1964; Old Tappan, N.J.: Fleming H. Revell, 1975), 58–59.

15. Mark D. McClean, "Toward a Pentecostal Hermeneutic," *Pneuma* 6 (fall 1984): 38.

16. Gordon D. Fee, "Hermeneutics and Historical Precedent—A Major Problem in Pentecostal Hermeneutics," in *Perspectives on the New Pentecostalism*, 121; William

W. Menzies and Robert P. Menzies, *Spirit and Power: Foundations of Pentecostal Experience* (Grand Rapids, Mich.: Zondervan, 2000), 209; quoted in Gary B. McGee, "Early Pentecostal Hermeneutics: Tongues as Evidence in the Book of Acts," in *Initial Evidence: Historical and Biblical Perspectives on the Pentecostal Doctrine of Spirit Baptism*, ed. Gary B. McGee (Peabody, Mass.: Hendrickson, 1991), 106.

17. Frank D. Macchia, "Tongues as a Sign: Towards a Sacramental Understanding of Pentecostal Experience," *Pneuma* 15 (spring 1993): 65.

18. Donald W. Dayton, *Theological Roots of Pentecostalism* (Grand Rapids, Mich.: Zondervan, 1987), 23; F. L. Arrington, "Hermeneutics, Historical Perspectives on Pentecostal and Charismatic," *DPCM*, 383; Murray W. Dempster, "Paradigm Shifts and Hermeneutics: Confronting Issues Old and New," *Pneuma* 15 (fall 1993): 129–30.

19. Quoted in Dempster, "Paradigm Shifts and Hermeneutics," 130.

20. For a review of modern scholarship on Acts, see W. Ward Gasque, *A History of the Interpretation of the Acts of the Apostles* (Peabody, Mass.: Hendrickson, 1989); Ernst Haenchen, *The Acts of the Apostles: A Commentary* (Philadelphia: Westminster, 1971), 14–50; and C. K. Barrett, *A Critical and Exegetical Commentary on The Acts of the Apostles*, 2 vols., ICC (Edinburgh: T. & T. Clark, 1998), 2:lxxii–lxxxi. For a sampling of recent perspectives on Acts, see Colin J. Hemer, *The Book of Acts in the Setting of Hellenistic History*, ed. Conrad H. Gempf (Winona Lake, Ind.: Eisenbraus, 1990); Richard I. Pervo, *Profit with Delight: The Literary Genre of the Acts of the Apostles* (Philadelphia: Fortress, 1987); and Ben Witherington III, *The Acts of the Apostles: A Socio-Rhetorical Commentary* (Grand Rapids, Mich.: Eerdmans, 1998).

21. Hans Conzelmann, *Acts of the Apostles: A Commentary on the Acts of the Apostles*, trans. James Limburg, A. Thomas Kraabel, and Donald H. Juel, Hermenia Series (Philadelphia: Fortress Press, 1987), xliii.

22. Martin Hengel, *Acts and the History of Earliest Christianity*, trans. John Bowden (Philadelphia: Fortress, 1980), 38, 60, 61, 67–68.

23. I. Howard Marshall, *Luke: Historian and Theologian* (Grand Rapids, Mich.: Zondervan, 1970).

24. Menzies and Menzies, *Spirit and Power*, 40–41.

25. Roger Stronstad, *The Charismatic Theology of St. Luke* (Peabody, Mass.: Hendrickson, 1984); Roger Stronstad, "The Prophethood of All Believers: A Study in Luke's Charismatic Theology," in *Pentecostalism in Context: Essays in Honor of William W. Menzies*, ed. Wonsuk Ma and Robert Menzies, JPTSS 11 (Sheffield, Eng.: Sheffield Academic Press, 1997), 60–77.

26. For a brief discussion of general hermeneutical principles in the context of Pentecostalism, see Fee, "Hermeneutics and Historical Precedent," 118–32. Fee is convinced that because speaking in tongues gave evidence of the coming of the Spirit, so contemporary Christians may expect the same. But against the traditional Pentecostal view, he concludes that the experience is not normative. "If the Pentecostal may not say one *must* speak in tongues, he may surely say, why *not* speak in tongues?" (132).

27. For a summary treatment of these passages, see Stronstad, *Charismatic Theology of St. Luke*, 49–73. For critiques of the Pentecostal approach, see James D. G. Dunn, *Baptism in the Holy Spirit: A Re-examination of the New Testament Teaching on the Gift of the Spirit in Relation to Pentecostalism Today* (Philadelphia: Westminster, 1970), 38–102; Bruner, *Theology of the Holy Spirit*. For a direct response to Dunn's *Baptism in the Holy Spirit*, see Howard M. Ervin, *Conversion-Initiation and the Baptism*

in the Holy Spirit: A Critique of James D. G. Dunn, Baptism in the Holy Spirit (Peabody, Mass.: Hendrickson, 1984).

28. Fee, "Hermeneutics and Historical Precedent," 122–23; J. Ramsey Michaels, "Evidences of the Spirit, or the Spirit as Evidence? Some Non-Pentecostal Reflections," in *Initial Evidence,* 203.

29. Larry W. Hurtado, "Normal, but Not a Norm: 'Initial Evidence' and the New Testament," in *Initial Evidence,* 194, 192.

30. James D. G. Dunn, "Baptism in the Spirit: A Response to Pentecostal Scholarship on Luke-Acts," *JPT* 3 (1993): 5, 6.

31. Max Turner, *The Holy Spirit and Spiritual Gifts: Then and Now* (Carlisle, Eng.: Paternoster, 1996), 158–59, 154.

32. See Menzies and Menzies, *Spirit and Power;* Robert P. Menzies, *The Development of Early Christian Pneumatology: With Special Reference to Luke-Acts,* JSNTSS 54 (Sheffield, Eng.: JSOT Press, 1991).

33. Menzies and Menzies, *Spirit and Power,* 116.

34. Ibid., 117.

35. Ibid., 130.

36. Quoted in McGee, "Early Pentecostal Hermeneutics," 104.

37. Charles F. Parham, *A Voice Crying in the Wilderness,* in *The Sermons of Charles F. Parham* (1944; reprint, New York: Garland, 1985), 33, 36.

38. Quoted in Vinson Synan, *The Holiness-Pentecostal Movement in the United States* (Grand Rapids, Mich.: Eerdmans, 1971), 102.

39. Quoted in Wacker, *Heaven Below,* 97.

40. Agnes N. O. [Ozman] LaBerge, *What God Hath Wrought: Life and Work of Mrs. Agnes N. O. LaBerge* (1921; reprint, New York: Garland, 1985), 29.

41. Robert Mapes Anderson, *Vision of the Disinherited: The Making of American Pentecostalism* (New York: Oxford University Press, 1979), 52–57; see also Synan, *Holiness-Pentecostal Movement,* 80–81, 120–21.

42. Kilian McDonnell and George T. Montague, *Christian Initiation and Baptism in the Holy Spirit: Evidence from the First Eight Centuries* (Collegeville, Minn.: Liturgical Press, 1991), Part II.

43. These observations are taken from Stanley M. Burgess, "Evidence of the Spirit: The Ancient and Eastern Churches" and "Evidence of the Spirit: The Medieval and Modern Western Churches," in *Initial Evidence,* 3–40.

44. See Stanley M. Burgess, *The Spirit and the Church: Antiquity* (Peabody, Mass.: Hendrickson 1984); Burgess, *The Holy Spirit: Eastern Church Traditions* (Peabody, Mass.: Hendrickson, 1989); Burgess, *The Holy Spirit: Medieval Roman Catholic and Reformation Traditions (Sixth–Sixteenth Centuries)* (Peabody, Mass.: Hendrickson, 1997).

45. Burgess, "Evidence of the Spirit," 37.

46. Jon Ruthven, *On the Cessation of the Charismata: The Protestant Polemic on Postbiblical Miracles,* JPTSS 3 (Sheffield, Eng.: Sheffield Academic Press, 1993), 23.

47. S. M. Burgess, "Medieval Examples of Charismatic Piety in the Roman Catholic Church," in *Perspectives on the New Pentecostalism,* 14–26; Burgess, "Evidence of the Spirit," 28–36; George H. Williams and Edith Waldvogel (Blumhofer), "A History of Speaking in Tongues and Related Gifts," in *The Charismatic Movement,* ed. Michael P. Hamilton (Grand Rapids, Mich.: Eerdmans, 1975), 61–113.

48. J. Rea, "Joel, Book of," *DCPM*, 495.

49. Dayton, *Theological Roots of Pentecostalism*, 26–28.

50. Anderson, *Vision of the Disinherited*, 81–88; Land, *Pentecostal Spirituality*, 18.

51. For an explanation of this xenoglossic phenomenon, see James R. Goff Jr., "Initial Tongues in the Theology of Charles Fox Parham," in *Initial Evidence*, 58, 66.

52. Grant Wacker, "Pentecostalism," *Encyclopedia of American Religious Experience*, 3 vols., ed. Charles H. Lippy and Peter W. Williams (New York: Scribner, 1988), 2:935.

53. Ibid., 936; Blumhofer, *Restoring the Faith*, chap. 1.

54. For example, holiness groups such as the Church of God (Cleveland, Tenn.), the Pentecostal Holiness Church, and the Church of God in Christ embraced the Pentecostal distinctive. Other groups or movements associated with the holiness movement (e.g., the Keswick Movement and A. B. Simpson and the Christian and Missionary Alliance denomination noted later) opposed Pentecostal evidence. See K. Kendrick, "Initial Evidence: A Historical Perspective," *DPCM*, 459–60.

55. Wacker, *Heaven Below*, 54.

56. There is a historical debate regarding the roots of American Pentecostalism. Some scholars, such as Vinson Synan (*Holiness-Pentecostal Movement*) stress its near-exclusive Wesleyan roots. Others, such as Anderson (*Vision of the Disinherited*), Wacker ("Pentecostalism"), and Edith L. Walvogel (Blumhofer), ("The 'Overcoming Life': A Study in the Reformed Evangelical Origins of Pentecostalism" [Ph.D. diss., Harvard University, 1977]), recognize (with varying degrees of emphasis) the Reformed contribution. For a discussion of Pentecostal historiography, see G. Wacker, "Bibliography and Historiography of Pentecostalism (U.S.)," *DPCM*, 65–76; and Augustus Cerillo, "The Beginnings of American Pentecostalism: A Historiographical Overview," in *Pentecostal Current in American Protestantism*, ed. Edith L. Blumhofer, Russell P. Spittler, and Grant Wacker (Urbana: University of Illinois Press, 1999), 229–59.

57. John Wesley, *A Plain Account of Christian Perfection* (1952; reprint, London: Epworth Press, 1976), 108–9.

58. Quoted in Synan, *Holiness-Pentecostal Movement*, 18 (n. 11).

59. Wesley, *Plain Account*, 41.

60. Ibid., 112, 53 (referring to 2 Pet. 3:18).

61. Wacker, "Pentecostalism," 935; quoted in Charles White and Nancy Hardesty, "Introduction," *Phoebe Palmer: Selected Writings*, ed. Thomas C. Oden, CWS (New York: Paulist Press, 1988), 5, 3.

62. C. E. White, "Palmer, Phoebe Worrall," in *Dictionary of Christianity in America*, ed. Daniel G. Reid. (Downers Grove, Ill.: InterVarsity Press, 1990), 861.

63. George M. Marsden, *Fundamentalism and American Culture: The Shaping of Twentieth-Century Evangelicalism: 1870–1925* (New York: Oxford University Press, 1980), 75. See also Grant Wacker, "The Holy Spirit and the Spirit of the Age in American Protestantism, 1880–1910," *JAH* 72 (June 1985): 45–62.

64. Edith L. Blumhofer, "Purity and Preparation: A Study in the Pentecostal Perfectionist Heritage," in *Reaching Beyond: Chapters in the History of Perfectionism*, ed. Stanley M. Burgess (Peabody, Mass.: Hendrickson, 1986), 268; Blumhofer, *Restoring the Faith*, 30.

65. Blumhofer, "Purity and Preparation," 269; D. William Faupel, *The Everlasting Gospel: The Significance of Eschatology in the Development of Pentecostal Thought,* JPTSS 10 (Sheffield, Eng.: Sheffield Academic Press, 1996), 114.

66. My discussion of faith healing closely follows P. G. Chappell, "Healing Movements," *DPCM,* 356–63.

67. Quoted in Anderson, *Vision of the Disinherited,* 142; J. R. Goff, "Parham, Charles Fox," *DPCM,* 661.

68. The best and most recent biography of Parham is James R. Goff Jr., *Fields White unto Harvest: Charles Fox Parham and the Missionary Origins of Pentecostalism* (Fayetteville: University of Arkansas Press, 1988). My discussion of Parham is largely taken from Goff, "Parham," 660; and Synan, *Holiness-Pentecostal Movement,* 99–103.

69. For a critical assessment of the Azusa Street revival as *the* event of Pentecostal origins, see Joe Creech, "Visions of Glory: The Place of the Azusa Street Revival in Pentecostal History," *CH* 65 (September 1996): 405–24.

70. Dale T. Irvin, " 'Drawing All Together in One Bond of Love': The Ecumenical Vision of William J. Seymour and the Azusa Street Revival," *JPT* 6 (1995): 25–53.

71. The sketch of Seymour and the Azusa Street revival are drawn from Cox, *Fire from Heaven,* chap. 1; C. M. Robeck Jr., "Azusa Street Revival," *DPCM,* 31–36; H. V. Synan, "Seymour, William Joseph," *DPCM,* 778–81.

72. Quoted in Wacker, "Pentecostalism," 938.

73. *Los Angeles Times,* 18 April 1906, quoted in Philip Jenkins, *Mystics and Messiahs: Cults and New Religions in American History* (New York: Oxford University Press, 2000), 65, 66, and quoted in Faupel, *The Everlasting Gospel,* 190–91.

74. For the global expansion of early Pentecostalism, see Walter J. Hollenweger, *The Pentecostals* (Minneapolis, Minn.: Augsburg, 1977).

75. Quoted in Jenkins, *Mystics and Messiahs,* 66.

76. Quoted in Synan, "Seymour," 781.

77. Quoted in Robeck, "Azusa Street Revival," 36.

78. Synan, *Holiness-Pentecostal Movement,* 147–63; Anderson, *Vision of the Disinherited,* chap. 9.

79. Synan, *Holiness-Pentecostal Movement,* 114.

80. Anderson, *Vision of the Disinherited.*

81. Albert G. Miller, "Pentecostalism as a Social Movement: Beyond the Theory of Deprivation," *JPT* 9 (1996): 111; Wacker, *Heaven Below,* 210, 211.

82. On denominational statements, see Kilian McDonnell, ed., *Presence, Power, Praise: Documents on the Charismatic Renewal,* 3 vols. (Collegeville, Minn.: Liturgical Press, 1980).

83. "Malines Document 1, Roman Catholic Church International," in *Presence, Power, Praise,* 3:27, 39, 40. For a historical defense of this position, see McDonnell and Montague, *Christian Initiation and Baptism in the Holy Spirit.*

84. Kilian McDonnell, "The Charismatic Renewal and Ecumenism," in *Presence, Power, Praise,* 3:182.

85. Martin E. Marty, *A Nation of Behavers* (Chicago: University of Chicago Press, 1976), 107.

86. F. A. Sullivan, "Catholic Charismatic Renewal," *DPCM,* 114.

87. Wacker, *Heaven Below,* 240–50. For early Pentecostals' otherworldly perspec-

tive in civil matters, see Grant Wacker, "Early Pentecostals and the Almost Chosen People," *Pneuma* 19 (fall 1997): 141–66.

CHAPTER 8

1. Luther Lee, "Woman's Right to Preach the Gospel. A Sermon, Preached at the Ordination of the Rev. Miss Antoinette Brown, at South Butler, Wayne County, N.Y., Sept. 15, 1853," in Luther Lee, *Five Sermons and a Tract*, ed. Donald W. Dayton (Chicago: Holrad House, 1975), 79.

2. "Seneca Falls Convention," in *The Feminist Papers: From Adams to de Beauvoir*, ed. Alice S. Rossi (New York: Columbia University Press, 1973), 420. On the close relationship between nineteenth-century women's rights and evangelicalism, see Nancy A. Hardesty, *Women Called to Witness: Evangelical Feminism in the Nineteenth Century*, 2nd ed. (Knoxville: University of Tennessee Press, 1999).

3. Lee, "Woman's Right," 81.

4. Ibid., 81–82, 80; Adam Clarke, *The New Testament of Our Lord and Saviour Jesus Christ . . . with a Commentary and Critical Notes*, 2 vols. (1837; New York: Abingdon-Cokesbury, n.d.), 2:402.

5. Lee, "Woman's Right," 95.

6. Barbara Brown Zikmund, "Women's Ministries within the United Church of Christ," in *Religious Institutions and Women's Leadership: New Roles Inside the Mainstream*, ed. Catherine Wessinger (Columbia: University of South Carolina Press, 1996), 68–69.

7. Ibid., 74; Barbara G. Wheeler, "Fit for Ministry?" *Christian Century*, April 11, 2001, p. 16

8. Mark Chaves, *Ordaining Women: Culture and Conflict in Religious Organizations* (Cambridge, Mass.: Harvard University Press, 1997), 101.

9. Quoted in Frank J. Smith, "Petticoat Presbyterianism: A Century of Debate in American Presbyterianism on the Issue of the Ordination of Women," *Westminster Theological Journal* 51 (1989): 69.

10. Southern Baptist Convention, "Statement on Women's Ordination" (1984), in *The Churches Speak On: Women's Ordination. Official Statements from Religious Bodies and Ecumenical Organizations*, ed. J. Gordon Melton (Detroit: Gale Research, 1991), 236. In its 2000 revision of "The Baptist Faith and Message," the convention affirmed that "the office of pastor is limited to men as qualified by Scripture" (see www .sbc.net/bfm/bfm2000.asp, "Article VI. The Church").

11. More recently, Gal. 3:28 is no longer as frequently cited or as central as it was to the discussion ten years ago. As will be apparent in what follows, both sides of the women's debate recognize that a holistic approach toward Scripture is necessary.

12. Krister Stendahl, *The Bible and the Role of Women: A Case Study in Hermeneutics*, trans. Emilie T. Sander (Philadelphia: Fortress, 1966), 32.

13. Paul K. Jewett, *Man as Male and Female: A Study in Sexual Relationships from a Theological Point of View* (Grand Rapids, Mich.: Eerdmans, 1975), 142–47; Anne E. Carr, *Transforming Grace: Christian Tradition and Women's Experience* (1988; New York: Continuum, 1996), 31; Evangelical Lutheran Church in America, "Report on the Ordination of Women" (1970), in *Churches Speak*, 115.

For a sampling of other appeals to Gal. 3:28 in support of women's ordination from a cross section of Christian traditions, see Georgia Harkness, *Women in Church and Society* (Nashville, Tenn.: Abingdon, 1972), 227; John L. McKenzie, "St. Paul's Attitude toward Women," in *Women Priests: A Catholic Commentary on the Vatican Declaration*, ed. Leonard Swidler and Arlene Swidler (New York: Paulist Press, 1977), 212–15; Aphrodite Clamar, "American Athena: A Modern Woman and the Traditional Greek Orthodox Church," in *A Time to Weep, a Time to Sing: Faith Journeys of Women Scholars of Religion*, ed. Mary Jo Meadow and Carole A. Rayburn (Minneapolis, Minn.: Winston Press, 1985), 190; Jon Nilson, "'Let Bishops Give Proof of the Church's Motherly Concern': The Prospect of Women Bishops in Light of Vatican II," *JES* 25 (fall 1988): 522; Denise Lardner Carmody, *Biblical Woman: Contemporary Reflections on Scriptural Texts* (New York: Crossroad, 1989), 132–36; Rebecca Merrill Groothuis, *Good News for Women: A Biblical Picture of Gender Equality* (Grand Rapids, Mich.: Baker, 1997), 25–26; John E. Alsup, "Imagining the New: Feminism, Galatians 3:28 and the Current Interpretive Discussion," *Austin Seminary Bulletin* 105 (spring 1990): 91–108; Clarence Boomsma, *Male and Female, One in Christ: New Testament Teaching on Women in Office* (Grand Rapids, Mich.: Baker, 1993), chap. 2.

14. Michael Harper, *Equal and Different: Male and Female in Church and Family* (London: Hodder and Stoughton, 1994), 50; Roman Catholic Church, "Declaration on the Question of the Admission of Women to the Ministerial Priesthood" (1976), in *Churches Speak*, 8; Reformed Church in America, Minority Report, "Report to the Committee on the Ordination of Women" (1957), in *Churches Speak*, 193.

15. S. Lewis Johnson Jr., "Role Distinctions in the Church: Galatians 3:28," in *Recovering Biblical Manhood and Womanhood: A Response to Evangelical Feminism*, ed. John Piper and Wayne Grudem (Wheaton, Ill.: Crossway, 1991), 154–64; Thomas Hopko, "Galatians 3:28: An Orthodox Interpretation," *St. Vladimir's Theological Quarterly* 35 (1991): 169–86; Nonna Verna Harrison, "Orthodox Arguments against the Ordination of Women as Priests," in *Women and the Priesthood*, ed. Thomas Hopko, new ed. (Crestwood, N.Y.: St. Vladimir's Press, 1999), 175–77.

16. Gregory of Nanzianzus, *Funeral Orations*, trans. Leo P. McCauley, FC 22 (Washington, D.C.: Catholic University of America Press, 1953), 24; Gregory of Nyssa, "On the Making of Man," *NPNF*, 2nd ser., 5:104; Augustine, "Confessions," *NPNF*, 1st ser., 1:201; Augustine, "On the Holy Trinity," *NPNF*, 1st ser., 3:159–60; Augustine, *The Literal Meaning of Genesis*, vol. 2 (bks. 7–12), trans. John Hammond Taylor, ACW 42 (New York: Newman Press, 1982), 175; Augustine, *On the Psalms*, 2 vols., trans. Scholastica Hebgin and Felicitas Corrigan, ACW 29 (New York: Newman Press, 1960), 1:283; Origen, *The Song of Songs: Commentary and Homilies*, trans. R. P. Lawson, ACW 26 (New York: Newman Press, 1956), 201; John Chrysostom, "Homilies on S. Ignatius and S. Babylas, *NPNF*, 1st ser., 9:135; Paulinus, *The Poems of St. Paulinus of Nola*, trans. P. G. Walsh, ACW 40 (New York: Newman Press, 1975), 251; Augustine, *The Lord's Sermon on the Mount*, trans. John J. Jepson, ACW 5 (New York: Newman Press, 1948), 50; Jerome, "Letters," *NPNF*, 2nd ser., 6:155.

17. Clement of Alexandria, "Exhortation to the Heathen," *ANF*, 2:203; Clement of Alexandria, "The Instructor," *ANF*, 2:217; Gregory of Nyssa, *Ascetical Works*, trans. Virginia Woods Callahan, FC 58 (Washington, D.C.: Catholic University of America Press, 1967), 64; Saint Hilary of Poitiers, *The Trinity*, trans. Stephen McKenna, FC 25 (New York: Fathers of the Church, 1954), 281; Augustine, "On the Gospel of St. John," *NPNF*, 1st ser., 7:408; Augustine, "Epistle to the Galatians," in *Ancient Chris-*

tian Commentary on Scripture, vol. 8, ed. Mark J. Edwards (Downers Grove, Ill.: InterVarsity Press, 1999), 51; John Chrysostom, "Homilies on the Gospel of Matthew," *NPNF*, 1st ser., 10:443; Athanasius, "Four Discourses against the Arians," *NPNF*, 2nd ser., 4:386; Palladius, *The Lausiac History*, trans. Robert T. Meyer, ACW 34 (New York: Newman Press, 1964), 132; Aphrahat (Aphraates), "Select Demonstrations," *NPNF*, 2nd ser., 13:367–68; Jerome, *Dogmatic and Polemical Works*, trans. John N. Hritzu, FC 53 (Washington, D.C.: Catholic University Press of America, 1965), 98; Augustine, *Sermon on the Mount*, 50–51.

18. Steven Ozment, *Protestants: The Birth of a Revolution* (New York: Doubleday, 1991), 152; *LW*, 36:152 (see also Evangelical Lutheran Church in America, "Can Women Serve in the Ordained Ministry?" [1973], in *Churches Speak*, 120); *LW*, 26:354 (see also *LW*, 30:55); *LW*, 26:356.

19. *Calvin's Commentaries: The Epistle of Paul the Apostle to the Galatians, Ephesians, Philippians and Colossians*, trans. T. H. L. Parker, ed. David W. Torrance and Thomas F. Torrance (Grand Rapids, Mich.: Eerdmans, 1965), 69; John Calvin, *Commentary on the Epistles of Paul to the Corinthians*, trans. John Pringle, 2 vols. (Grand Rapids, Mich: Eerdmans, 1948), 1:468; Jane Dempsey Douglass, "Christian Freedom: What Calvin Learned at the School of Women," *CH* 53 (June 1984): 155, 165, 166

20. *LW*, 30:55; 36:152; 41:154–55; 28:276–77; John Calvin, *Commentary on the Epistles to Timothy, Titus, and Philemon*, trans. William Pringle (Grand Rapids, Mich.: Eerdmans, 1948), 67. For an exception to prevalent sixteenth-century views toward women, see Henricus Cornelius Agrippa, *Declamation on the Nobility and Preeminence of the Female Sex*, trans. and ed. Albert Rabil Jr. (Chicago: University of Chicago Press, 1996). Agrippa's work, first published in 1529, argued from the Bible (including Gal. 3:28) that women were superior to men. Despite what appeared to be a satirical look at women (better yet, men), the influence of the *Declamation* in the sixteenth century was "enormous" (3) and piqued Calvin's ire (29), though as Douglass suggests, it may have influenced the Genevan reformer ("Christian Freedom," 167–69).

21. See Karen Jo Torjesen, *When Women Were Priests* (New York: HarperCollins, 1993).

22. Quoted in ibid., 44.

23. J. Kevin Coyle, "The Fathers on Women and Women's Ordination," in *Women in Early Christianity*, ed. David M. Scholer, vol. 14 of *SEC*, 120, 125, 127.

24. George H. Tavard, *Woman in Christian Tradition* (Notre Dame, Ind.: University of Notre Dame Press, 1973), 56–57; Elizabeth A. Clark, "Introduction," in *Women in the Early Church*, ed. Elizabeth A. Clark, MFC 13 (Collegeville, Minn.: Liturgical Press, 1983), 15

25. Tertullian, "On the Apparel of Women," *ANF*, 4:14.

26. For example, see Joan Morris, *The Lady Was a Bishop: The History of Women with Clerical Ordination and the Jurisdiction of Bishops* (New York: Macmillan, 1973); Lynda L. Coon, Katherine J. Haldane, and Elisabeth W. Sommer, eds., *That Gentle Strength: Historical Perspectives on Women in Christianity* (Charlottesville: University Press of Virginia, 1990); Beverly Mayne Kienzle and Pamela J. Walker, eds., *Women Preachers and Prophets through Two Millennia of Christianity* (Berkeley: University of California Press, 1998); Kyriaki Karidoyanes FitzGerald, "The Nature and Characteristics of the Order of Deaconesses," in *Women and Priesthood*, 93–137.

27. Sarah Grimké, *Letters on the Equality of the Sexes and Other Essays*, ed. and

introd. Elizabeth Ann Bartlett (New Haven, Conn.: Yale University Press, 1988), 31, 31–32, 38.

28. Ibid., 96; for other references to Gal. 3:28, see 42, 90.

29. Catherine A. Brekus, *Strangers and Pilgrims: Female Preaching in America, 1740–1845* (Chapel Hill: University of North Carolina Press, 1998), 119–24.

30. Nancy Hardesty, Lucille Sider Dayton, and Donald W. Dayton, "Women in the Holiness Movement: Feminism in the Evangelical Tradition," in *Women of Spirit: Female Leadership in the Jewish and Christian Traditions*, ed. Rosemary Ruether and Eleanor McLaughlin (New York: Simon and Schuster, 1979), 244–46; B. T. Roberts, *Ordaining Women* (1891; Indianapolis: Light and Life Press, 1992), 38.

31. Roberts, *Ordaining Women*, 45.

32. Phoebe Palmer, *Promise of the Father; or, A Neglected Specialty of the Last Days* (Boston: Henry V. Degen, 1859; reprint facsimile, New York: Garland, 1985), 1; L. E. Maxwell, *Women in Ministry* (Wheaton, Ill.: Victor Books, 1987). Maxwell, founder and president of Prairie Bible Institute, defended women's spiritual right to ministry but affirmed that in social relations, the woman was "the weaker vessel" (44) and, by divine ordering, was to be "subordinate to man in the activities of the church and the home" (83).

33. Katharine C. Bushnell, *God's Word to Women: One Hundred Bible Studies on Woman's Place in the Divine Economy*, 4th ed. (Corona, Calif.: Scripture Studies Concern, 1930), Lesson 46, no. 348 (no page numbers).

34. Susie C. Stanley, "The Promise Fulfilled: Women's Ministries in the Wesleyan/Holiness Movement," in *Religious Institutions and Women's Leadership*, 148.

35. Deborah Gill, "The Contemporary State of Women in Ministry in the Assemblies of God," *Pneuma* 17 (fall 1995): 242–45.

36. Janette Hassey, *No Time for Silence: Evangelical Women in Public Ministry around the Turn of the Century* (Grand Rapids, Mich.: Zondervan, 1986), 31, 88, 81.

37. See Hassey, *No Time for Silence*, 137–43; Stanley, "Promise Fulfilled," 148–50; Margaret M. Poloma, "Charisma, Institutionalization and Social Change," *Pneuma* 17 (fall 1995): 245–52.

38. Rebecca Laird, *Ordained Women in the Church of the Nazarene* (Kansas City, Mo.: Nazarene Publishing House, 1993), 146. On women and the fundamentalist movement, see Betty A. DeBerg, *Ungodly Women: Gender and the First Wave of American Fundamentalism* (Minneapolis, Minn.: Fortress, 1990); Margaret Lamberts Bendroth, *Fundamentalism and Gender, 1875 to the Present* (New Haven, Conn.: Yale University Press, 1993).

39. Thomas Hopko, "Women and the Priesthood: Reflections on the Debate—1983," in *Women and the Priesthood*, 243; Sacred Congregation for the Doctrine of the Faith, *Inter Insigniores*, in *Women Priests*, 46; John Piper and Wayne Grudem, "An Overview of Central Concerns," in *Recovering Biblical Manhood and Womanhood*, 76.

40. Klyne Snodgrass, "Galatians 3:28: Conundrum or Solution," in *Women, Authority and the Bible*, ed. Alvera Michelson (Downers Grove, Ill.: InterVarsity Press, 1986), 161.

41. Ruth A. Tucker and Walter Liefeld, *Daughters of the Church: Women and Ministry from New Testament Times to the Present* (Grand Rapids, Mich.: Zondervan, 1987), 465–71; "Ordination," in *Encyclopedia of Early Christianity*, ed. Everett Ferguson. (New York: Garland, 1990), 646–66.

42. Quoted in Barbara Brown Zikmund, Adair T. Lummis, and Patricia M. Y. Chang, *Clergy Women: An Uphill Calling* (Louisville, Ky.: Westminster John Knox, 1998), 3–4.

43. See Barbara J. MacHaffie, *Her Story: Women in Christian Tradition* (Philadelphia: Fortress, 1986); Tucker and Liefeld, *Daughters of the Church.*

44. Quoted in Chaves, *Ordaining Women,* 26.

45. Helpful discussions that I have incorporated into my summary are found in Madeleine Boucher, "Some Unexplored Parallels to 1 Cor. 11, 11–12 and Gal. 3, 28: The NT on the Role of Women," *Catholic Biblical Quarterly* 31 (1969): 50–51; Robert K. Johnston, *Evangelicals at an Impasse: Biblical Authority in Practice* (Atlanta: John Knox, 1979), chap. 3; Constance F. Parvey, "Exploring the Context," in *Ordination of Women in Ecumenical Perspective,* ed. Constance F. Parvey (Geneva: World Council of Churches, 1980), 29–34; Willard M. Swartley, *Slavery, Sabbath, War, and Women: Case Issues in Biblical Interpretation* (Scottdale, Pa.: Herald Press, 1983), chap. 4; Gary L. Ward, "Introductory Essay: A Survey of the Women's Ordination Issue," in *Churches Speak,* xvii–xxii; Evangelical Lutheran Church in America, "Can Women Serve in the Ordained Ministry?" 117–24; Lutheran Church–Missouri Synod, "Women in the Church: Scriptural Principles and Ecclesial Practice" (1985), in *Churches Speak,* 125–43; Reformed Church in America, "Report of the Committee on the Ordination of Women" (1957), in *Churches Speak,* 195–211.

46. Manfred Hauke, *Women in the Priesthood? A Systematic Analysis in the Light of the Order of Creation and Redemption,* trans. David Kipp (San Francisco: Ignatius Press, 1988), 204. See also Barbara Albrecht, "On Women Priests," in *The Church and Women: A Compendium,* ed. Helmut Moll (San Francisco: Ignatius Press, 1988), 201–4; Lutheran Church–Missouri Synod, "Women in the Church," 134–37.

47. Quoted in Bishop Kallistos, "Man, Woman and the Priesthood of Christ," in *Women and the Priesthood,* 25.

48. Pope John XXIII, *Pacem en Terris,* www.vatican.va/holy_father/john_xxiii, no.41; Biblical Commission Report, "Can Women Be Priests?" in *Women Priests,* 346.

49. "Declaration," in *Women Priests,* 43.

50. Stephen Sapp, *Sexuality, the Bible, and Science* (Philadelphia: Fortress, 1977), 2–3; Mary Hayter, *The New Eve in Christ: The Use and Abuse of the Bible in the Debate about Women in the Church* (Grand Rapids, Mich.: Eerdmans, 1987), 14–18.

51. E. L. Mascall, *Women Priests?* 2nd ed. (London: Church Literature Association, 1977), 13–17.

52. "Declaration," 44–45.

53. "On the Dignity and Vocation of Women (*Mulieris Dignitatem*)," in *Churches Speak,* 29.

54. Thomas Hopko, "Presbyter/Bishop: A Masculine Ministry," in *Women and the Priesthood,* 158; Peter Moore, "Introduction," in *Man, Woman, Priesthood,* ed. Peter Moore (London: SPCK, 1978), 1.

55. See conclusions in Ben Witherington III, *Women in the Ministry of Jesus* (Cambridge: Cambridge University Press, 1984), 125–31.

56. For a helpful summary of this explosive and often tedious debate within the evangelical community, see David M. Scholer, "The Evangelical Debate over Biblical 'Headship,'" in *Women, Abuse, and the Bible: How Scripture Can Be Used to Hurt or to*

Heal, ed. Catherine Clark Kroeger and James R. Beck (Grand Rapids, Mich.: Baker, 1996), 28–57.

57. For a sampling of responses to other problematic phrases in this text ("the head of a woman is her husband" [v. 3], "woman is the glory of man" [v. 7], and that a woman should veil herself "because of the angels" [v. 10]), see Gail Peterson Corrington, "The 'Headless Woman': Paul and the Language of the Body in 1 Cor. 11:2–16," *Perspectives in Religious Studies* 18 (Fall 1991): 223–31; Craig S. Keener, *Paul, Women, and Wives: Marriage and Women's Ministry in the Letters of Paul* (Peabody, Mass.: Hendrickson, 1992), chap. 1; Groothuis, *Good News for Women*, chap. 6.

58. Gordon D. Fee, *The First Epistle to the Corinthians*, NICNT (Grand Rapids, Mich.: Eerdmans, 1987), 705, 708. For arguments against the text's authenticity, see 699–708.

59. Ben Witherington III, *Women in the Earliest Churches* (Cambridge: Cambridge University Press, 1988), 219–20.

60. Jewett, *Man as Male and Female*.

61. Elisabeth Schüssler Fiorenza, *In Memory of Her: A Feminist Theological Reconstruction of Christian Origins* (New York: Crossroad, 1983).

62. Snodgrass, "Galatians 3:28."

63. Kallistos, "Man, Woman and the Priesthood of Christ," 47.

64. Quoted in *Women Priests*, 8.

65. Paul K. Jewett, *The Ordination of Women: An Essay on the Office of Christian Ministry* (Grand Rapids, Mich.: Eerdmans, 1980), 37.

66. Ibid., 43.

67. Commentaries that I have found particularly helpful are Hans Dieter Betz, *Galatians*, Hermenia Series (Philadelphia: Fortress, 1979); Carolyn Osiek, *Galatians*, NTM 12 (Wilmington, Del.: Michael Glazier, 1980); F. F. Bruce, *The Epistle to the Galatians*, NIGTC (Grand Rapids, Mich.: Eerdmans, 1982); Richard N. Longenecker, *Galatians*, WBC 41 (Dallas: Word Books, 1990); James D. G. Dunn, *A Commentary on the Epistle to the Galatians*, BNTC (London: A & C Black, 1993); J. Louis Martyn, *Galatians*, AB 33A (New York: Doubleday, 1997).

68. According to Wayne Meeks, Paul appealed to the androgynous ideal that defined the creation of man in the divine image (Gen. 1:27), though that state would not be attained until the eschaton. Contra Meeks, Dennis McDonald argues that "no male and female" is an appeal to a present, not a future, ideal. See Wayne A. Meeks, "The Image of the Androgyne: Some Uses of a Symbol in Earliest Christianity," *History of Religions* 13 (1974): 165–208; and Dennis R. McDonald, *There Is No Male and Female: The Fate of a Dominical Saying in Paul and Gnosticism*, Harvard Dissertations in Religion 20 (Philadelphia: Fortress, 1987). For Sam K. Williams, *Galatians*, ANTC (Nashville, Tenn.: Abingdon, 1997), Paul borrowed his metaphor from neither Gnostics nor mystery religions but from Scripture itself (105).

69. Quoted in Boucher, "Some Unexplored Parallels," 53; quoted in Ben Witherington, "Rite and Rites for Women—Galatians 3.28," *New Testament Studies* 27 (October 1981): 594. Boucher points out the possibility of Paul quoting other parallel, positive sayings within rabbinic Judaism. She notes, however, that uncertainty remains because rabbinic materials were not put into writing until the end of the second century. One can only hypothesize that Paul drew from these sources in their prewritten, oral form (54).

70. Stendahl, *The Bible and the Role of Women*, 20, 35–36.

71. Ibid., 21–22.

72. Ibid., 31–32.

73. Ibid., 34. For a supporting view, see Wayne Litke, "Beyond Creation: Galatians 3:28, Genesis and the Hermaphrodite Myth," *Studies in Religion/Sciences Religieuses* 24 (1995): 173–78. For a critique of Stendahl's view, see Boucher, "Some Unexplored Parallels," esp. 57–58.

74. Stendahl, *The Bible and the Role of Women*, 34.

75. Ibid., 34, 37.

76. Ibid., 41, 43.

77. For an exception, see Lone Fatum, "Image of God and Glory of Man: Women in the Pauline Congregations," in *The Image of God: Gender Models in Judaeo-Christian Tradition*, ed. Kari Elisabeth Børresen (Minneapolis, Minn.: Fortress, 1991), 50–133. According to Fatum, Gal. 3:28 deals with liberation in Christ, "but there is no indication whatsoever either positively or negatively, of its liberating consequence for Christian women as women" (76). Thus, "there is no longer any excuse for investing Paul with the legitimization of an apologist of feminist theology" (81).

78. Carr, *Transforming Grace*, 45; Mary Jo Weaver, *New Catholic Women: A Contemporary Challenge to Traditional Religious Authority* (San Francisco: Harper and Row, 1985), 111.

79. See Mary Ann Tolbert, "Defining the Problem: The Bible and Feminist Hermeneutics," in *The Bible and Feminist Hermeneutics*, Semeia, vol. 28, ed. Mary Ann Tolbert (Chico, Calif.: Scholars Press, 1983), 113–26; Katherine Doob Sakenfield, "Feminist Uses of Biblical Materials," in *Feminist Interpretation of the Bible*, ed. Letty M. Russell (Philadelphia: Westminster, 1985), 57–63; Sharon H. Ringe, "When Women Interpret the Bible," in *Women's Bible Commentary Expanded Edition*, ed. Carol A. Newsom and Sharon H. Ringe (Louisville, Ky.: Westminster John Knox, 1998), 1–9

80. Catherine Mowry LaCugna, "Introduction," in *Freeing Theology: The Essentials of Theology in Feminist Perspective*, ed. Catherine Mowry LaCugna (New York: HarperCollins, 1993), 2.

81. Susanne Heine addresses this issue in *Women and Early Christianity: A Reappraisal*, trans. John Bowden (Minneapolis, Minn.: Augsburg, 1988), chap. 5.

82. Elisabeth Schüssler Fiorenza, *Bread Not Stone: The Challenge of Feminist Biblical Interpretation* (Boston: Beacon, 1984), 5; Schüssler Fiorenza, *In Memory of Her*, 161.

83. Schüssler Fiorenza, *Bread Not Stone*, 15 (the full implications of this hermeneutic are discussed in *In Memory of Her*, 3–95); Schüssler Fiorenza, *In Memory of Her*, xv, 26, 32.

84. Aptly observed by Kevin J. Vanhoozer, *Is There a Meaning in This Text? The Bible, the Reader, and the Morality of Literary Knowledge* (Grand Rapids, Mich.: Zondervan, 1998), 181.

85. Schüssler Fiorenza, *In Memory of Her*, 32, 33.

86. Ibid., 32; Schüssler Fiorenza, *Bread Not Stone*, 14.

87. Schüssler Fiorenza, *Bread Not Stone*, 14–15; Schüssler Fiorenza, *In Memory of Her*, 30.

88. Schüssler Fiorenza, *In Memory of Her*, 199, 212–13.

89. Ibid., 232, 233.

90. Elisabeth Schüssler Fiorenza, "Word, Spirit and Power: Women in Early Christian Communities," in *Women of Spirit*, 57; Schüssler Fiorenza, *In Memory of Her*, 334.

91. Elisabeth Schüssler Fiorenza, *Discipleship of Equals: A Critical Feminist Ekklēsia-logy of Liberation* (New York: Crossroad, 1993), 31. See Mary Stewart Van Leeuwen, ed., *After Eden: Facing the Challenge of Gender Reconciliation* (Grand Rapids, Mich.: Eerdmans, 1993), 585; Paula D. Nesbitt, *Feminization of the Clergy in America: Occupational and Organizational Perspectives* (New York: Oxford University Press, 1997), 167.

92. Schüssler Fiorenza, *Discipleship of Equals*, 34; Schüssler Fiorenza, *In Memory of Her*, 343–51 (see also *Discipleship of Equals*, chaps. 2, 6, 10, 17).

93. Gretchen Gaebelein Hull, *Equal to Serve: Women and Men in the Church and Home* (Old Tappan, N.J.: Fleming H. Revell, 1987), 56.

94. For a recent overview of the current debate with extensive bibliography, see James R. Beck and Craig L. Blomberg, eds., *Two Views on Women in Ministry* (Grand Rapids, Mich.: Zondervan, 2001).

95. For efforts to clarify this standoff from a traditionalist perspective, see Terrence Tiessen, "Toward a Hermeneutic for Discerning Universal Moral Absolutes," *JETS* 36 (June 1993): 189–207; Andreas J. Köstenberger, "Gender Passages in the NT: Hermeneutical Fallacies Critiqued," *Westminister Theological Journal* 56 (1994): 259–83. From the egalitarian perspective, see Johnston, *Evangelicals at an Impasse*, chap. 3; and David M. Scholer, "Feminist Hermeneutics and Evangelical Biblical Interpretation," *JETS* 30 (December 1987): 407–20.

96. Letha Scanzoni and Nancy Hardesty, *All We're Meant to Be: A Biblical Approach to Women's Liberation* (Waco, Tex.: Word, 1974), 15. In their third revised edition, *All We're Meant to Be: Biblical Feminism for Today* (Grand Rapids, Mich.: Eerdmans, 1992), the authors retreat from uplifting this key text.

97. F. F. Bruce, *A Mind for What Matters* (Grand Rapids, Mich.: Eerdmans, 1990), 262. See also Bruce, *Galatians*, 190; Richard N. Longenecker, *New Testament Social Ethics for Today* (Grand Rapids, Mich.: Eerdmans, 1984), 74, 75; Snodgrass, "Galatians 3:28," 168–69; David M. Scholer, "Galatians 3:28 and the Ministry of Women in the Church," *Covenant Quarterly* 56 (August 1998): 8.

98. Richard N. Longenecker, "Authority, Hierarchy and Leadership Patterns in the Bible," in *Women, Authority and the Bible*, 84. A similar stress on this redemptive, developmental approach, albeit from a very self-conscious hermeneutical perspective, is William J. Webb, *Slaves, Women and Homosexuals: Exploring the Hermeneutics of Cultural Analysis* (Downers Grove, Ill.: InterVarsity, 2001).

99. These are noted (with a slight change in order) in Longenecker, *New Testament Social Ethics for Today*, 84–85, and Longenecker, "Authority, Hierarchy and Leadership Patterns," 81–84.

100. Longenecker, "Authority, Hierarchy and Leadership Patterns," 71, 81.

101. Ibid., 82–83.

102. Jewett, *Man as Male and Female*, 148.

103. Kevin Giles, "The Biblical Argument for Slavery: Can the Bible Mislead? A Case Study in Hermeneutics," *Evangelical Quarterly* 66 (1994): 3–17; Mark A. Noll, *America's God: From Jonathan Edwards to Abraham Lincoln* (New York: Oxford University Press, 2002), 388–89. Traditionalists argue that the slavery parallel breaks down

because slavery is not a creation ordinance, whereas the subordination of women is God's intention for the created order.

104. Hull, *Equal to Serve*, 84; Jewett, *Man as Male and Female*, 148.

105. Longenecker, *New Testament Social Ethics*, 85.

106. For a recent evaluation of these developments, see Elizabeth A. Clark, "Women, Gender, and the Study of Christian History," *CH* 70 (September 2001): 395–426.

107. E-mail correspondence: Richard Rosengarten, academic dean of the Divinity School, The University of Chicago to author, September 13, 2001.

108. Quoted in Cullen Murphy, *The Word According to Eve: Women and the Bible in Ancient Times and Our Own* (Boston: Houghton Mifflin, 1998), 109.

CONCLUSION

1. See Philip Jenkins, *The Next Christendom: The Coming of Global Christianity* (New York: Oxford University Press, 2002).

2. Andrew F. Walls, *The Missionary Movement in Christian History: Studies in the Transmission of Faith* (Maryknoll, N.Y.: Orbis, 1996), 22, 23.

3. There is a growing literature on the Bible's place in the Third World. For a recent work, see R. S. Sugirtharajah, *The Bible and the Third World: Precolonial, Colonial, and Postcolonial Encounters* (Cambridge: Cambridge University Press, 2001).

4. Kwame Bediako, "Jesus in African Culture: A Ghanaian Perspective," in *Emerging Voices in Global Christian Theology*, ed. William A. Dyrness (Grand Rapids, Mich.: Zondervan, 1994), 93–121. See also Bediako, *Theology and Identity: The Impact of Culture upon Christian Thought in the Second Century and in Modern Africa* (Oxford: Regnum, 1992).

General Index

Index of Scripture